Colin Lindsay

The Evidence for the Papacy

As Derived from the Holy Scriptures and from Primitive Antiquity

Colin Lindsay

The Evidence for the Papacy
As Derived from the Holy Scriptures and from Primitive Antiquity

ISBN/EAN: 9783337279455

Printed in Europe, USA, Canada, Australia, Japan

Cover: Foto ©Lupo / pixelio.de

More available books at **www.hansebooks.com**

THE EVIDENCE FOR
THE PAPACY.

THE EVIDENCE FOR
THE PAPACY,

AS DERIVED FROM THE HOLY SCRIPTURES
AND FROM PRIMITIVE ANTIQUITY.

WITH AN INTRODUCTORY EPISTLE.

BY

THE HON. COLIN LINDSAY.

"Thou art Peter, and upon this Rock I will build My Church, and the gates of hell shall not prevail against it ; and I will give to thee the keys of the King-dom of Heaven ; and whatsoever thou shalt bind upon earth, it shall be bound in heaven ; and whatsoever thou shalt loose on earth, it shall be loosed also in heaven."—*S. Matt.* xvi. 18, 19.

LONDON:
LONGMANS, GREEN, & CO. PATERNOSTER ROW.
MDCCCLXX.

LONDON
STRANGEWAYS AND WALDEN, PRINTERS,
Castle St. Leicester Sq.

✠

𝔗o the Memory

OF

ONE LATELY DECEASED

WHO

WHEN IN LIFE

EXPRESSED A DESIRE THAT THE AUTHOR OF THIS WORK

WOULD STATE IN WRITING

THE GROUNDS WHICH LED TO HIS CONVERSION

TO

THE CATHOLIC CHURCH.

———

Requiescat in pace.

PREFACE.

THIS Work does not claim to be in any sense original: the only difference between it and others on the same subject, is its arrangement, and perhaps its treatment. In investigating the Roman Claim, it appeared to me that it would be more satisfactory to treat it as a strictly legal question, to be decided after perusing the evidence. The Church is a corporation, governed and administered according to the terms of its Charter, and in order that we may ascertain what these terms are, we must examine carefully the Patent of incorporation, and all the numerous documents that serve to throw light on the subject in question.

Instead, therefore, of writing a Treatise, I have preferred to adopt this method—that is, to prepare a case for consideration, and then to form a judgment upon the evidence adduced.

I admit that this method is not so interesting as a treatise might be, but it appeared to me that to those who desire to study the question of the Papacy it would be more satisfactory; especially as it would enable them to examine the Evidence apart from the argument based thereon.

The Introductory Epistle prefixed to this Work was originally prepared for those in whom I have an immediate interest, and this circumstance will account for some expressions which would not have appeared had the Letter been addressed to a mere friend.

Many of the translations of passages from the Fathers and Councils have been taken from the "Faith of Catholics," "The Library of the Fathers," the "Ante-Nicene Library," and other valuable works, chiefly Anglican and Protestant. I have preferred, whenever possible, the adoption of Anglican and Protestant translations of the Fathers, &c., believing that they would be more acceptable to those for whom this work was mainly undertaken. I have not, however, accepted these without examination, for every passage that has been made use of has been carefully compared with the originals and verified; and whenever the rendering was not as accurate as I considered it ought to be, I have not scrupled to amend it.

Quotations from the Holy Scriptures have, for the same reason, been mostly taken from the English Authorized Version.

The translations from the Fathers have been proved from the following editions : S. Clement and S. Ignatius, Patrum Apost. Antw. 1688. S. Irenæus, ed. Ben. Paris, 1710. Tertullian, ed. Venet. 1744. Origen, Ben. ed. Paris, 1733. S. Cyprian, ed. Baluz., Paris, 1716. Eusebius, Hist. Eccles. Vales. Camb. 1720. Eusebius, Præparatio Evan. Colon. 1688. S. Hilary of Poitiers, Paris, 1693. S. Cyril of Jerusalem, Venet. 1763. S. Ephraem Syrus, Rom. 1732. S. Gregory of Nyssa, Paris, 1638. S. Gregory of Nazianzum, Paris, 1630. S. Basil, Paris, 1721. S. Epiphanius, Colon. 1682. S. Ambrose, Paris, 1686. S. Jerome, Paris, 1693. S. Chrysostom, Paris, 1724. S. Augustine, Ant. 1700, and Paris, 1833. S. Cyril of Alexandria, Paris, 1638. Theodoret, Opera, Halle, 1796. S. Peter Chrysologus, Colon. 1627. S. Leo, Venet. 1753. Other authors in Gallandius, Bib. Vet. Pat. Venet. 1765, &c.

Labbé, S. Concil. Venet. 1728. Hardouin, Concil. Act. Collect. Paris, 1715. Fleury, Eccl. Hist. Paris, 1722.

The reader will find much repetition of passages from Scripture and the Fathers, as well as of argument, but in order to carry out effectually the legal treatment of the subject of this Work, I found it impossible to avoid this defect. It seemed to me of the first importance that each Part and Section of the Work should be complete in itself. I have, therefore, not scrupled to repeat my arguments and proofs as often as I thought necessary.

I cannot conclude without expressing my deep obligations and thanks to my friend and connection, the Rev. Father Eyre, S. J., who has most kindly revised the proof-sheets of this Work.

Rome, Dec. 1869.

CONTENTS.

FIRST INQUIRY.

S. PETER'S SUPREMACY.

PART I. HOLY SCRIPTURE.

1. PROPHECY.

PART II.

I. CONSENSUS PATRUM.

PART III. AUDI ALTERAM PARTEM.

SECOND INQUIRY.

THE PAPAL SUPREMACY.

PART I. S. PETER'S SUCCESSORS IN THE APOSTOLIC SEE.

S. PETER AT ROME.

I. HOLY SCRIPTURE.

2. Testimony of Councils.

PART III. PAPAL ACTA, EPISTLES, &c.

PART IV. AUDI ALTERAM PARTEM.

AN INTRODUCTORY EPISTLE.

My dear ———

I HAVE been asked, by several persons, to state the reasons that induced me to quit the communion of the Church of England, in which I was born and bred, and to become a member of the Roman Catholic Church. Considering my near relationship to you, the active part I have taken for many years in " Church work," and my having occupied positions of some responsibility, this request is, I admit, reasonable, and I think I should be doing wrong if I did not accede to it.

In complying with this request, I cannot do better than address myself to you, who have the first right to be informed on a matter of such grave moment to you and myself, and which could not fail, I grieve to say, to have given you much pain.

I.

REASONS FOR SECESSION.

The immediate cause that led me to study the Roman question, was my engagement in a work I intended publishing, and which had partly been printed, on the doctrine and discipline of Christ as the " Church of England had received the same, according to the commandments of God." In a work of that sort, it was impossible to avoid a complete investigation of those principles of Church government which Christ had instituted for the benefit of His people. Upon this point alone I devoted more than six months to incessant study, and at last I arrived, at that time reluctantly indeed, but not so now, at the following conclusions : (1), That our Lord designed the formation of one Kingdom and Church on earth, which

He solemnly promised should remain indefectible and infallible till the end of the world; precluding, thereby, the possibility of any *real* disunion or failure within the one royal Fold He established; so much so, that the necessary inference must be drawn, that among the many religious communities or sects now existing, one, and one only, could be regarded as that one Church and Kingdom which He founded. (2), That in constituting His Kingdom and Church, Christ did appoint one of the Apostles—even S. Peter—to be the Rock and Foundation, upon whom He built His Church, to whom He gave the Supreme Jurisdiction, as signified under the Symbol of the Keys, which were delivered to him alone; whom He commissioned to strengthen or confirm the Brethren in their Faith, and to be the Shepherd of the Universal Flock : and (3), That these High Prerogatives passed to the Bishops of Rome, as Successors to the Chair or Cathedra of S. Peter which he erected in the Imperial city. Having arrived at these conclusions, a further truth became apparent, viz., that the Catholic Church, strictly so called, is limited to those Pastors and people who are in visible communion with S. Peter and his Successors in the See of Rome. A still further result, also, was inevitable, viz., that all communions and religious communities not in visible communion with the Apostolic See, were necessarily in a state of rebellion and schism, and that every one, Priest and people, under such circumstances, was really guilty, though without doubt unintentionally, of a sacrilegious crime every time he ministered or received the Sacraments. Having, then, come to these conclusions, there was but one step for me to take, as a loyal subject of my Lord and God, and as one entrusted with the charge of a family, and further, as one, who had for many years taken a somewhat prominent part in Church matters, viz., to submit to that Body, which I had become persuaded was the only one true Catholic Church, which Church alone was in possession of the road to eternal life, which alone inherited the promises made to the Fathers, and which alone enjoyed the right to represent Jesus Christ, and to exercise His Jurisdiction upon earth—in a word, I considered it my duty to become a member of the Holy Roman Catholic and Apostolic Church, the Mother and Mistress of all Churches.

It is due to myself to say, that up to the time I commenced the study of this question of Church Government, I had no suspicion whatever that the Primacy of Rome rested upon any other foundation than that of ecclesiastical ordinance or custom. In common with other Anglicans I believed that this Primacy was one of honour and dignity only, in no way essential to the existence of the Church as a Divine polity,—a dignity which had been, as I believed, granted to the Roman Bishop, because of his See being situated in the Imperial city.

I cannot, however, affect to deny that I had long been dissatisfied with the state of things in the Church of England, for I could never conscientiously admit, that it was right and proper that her oral teaching, and her practice, should be, in some important particulars, directly opposed to her written law, or that it was honest that contrariety of opinion on some of the most vital points of faith should be permitted, with the approval of her Bishops, to be openly held and taught by her ministers. The knowledge of these blemishes,—and they are most fearful blemishes,—never aroused any suspicion in my mind of the Catholicity of the Anglican Church, or of the validity of her orders; the only effect it had was to incite me, in concert with others, to labour for her emancipation from State thraldom, and for her restoration to true unity and peace.

After this statement, it is a natural question on your part to ask me to submit to you the nature and extent of those authorities upon which I have based my present convictions, and which of course *alone* justify my conduct. It is my purpose both in this letter, and in the Work to which it is an Introduction, to lay before you the arguments as well as the evidence, which have brought me into the True Church of Christ.

The evidence which I have collected with as much care as I could, I have arranged under the form of Two Inquiries; the First having reference to the Divine commission to S. Peter alone, and to S. Peter and the Apostles. The Second refers to the fact of S. Peter having visited Rome, erecting there his Cathedra or Chair, to the occupancy of which his Successors, Bishops of Rome, have succeeded, inclusive of all the exalted Prerogatives inherent in that Cathedra. The evidence itself, you will find, consists of Holy Scripture, and the Traditions of the Church for the first five centuries of the Christian era. I have fixed upon this period, because it is that which the Church and State of England have accepted as one remarkable for the perfect purity of doctrine and discipline, taught and enforced by the Catholic Church. In one of her Homilies, the Church of England says, "Now although our Saviour Christ taketh not or needeth not any testimony of men . . . yet for our further contentation, it shall . . . be declared . . . that this truth and doctrine concerning the forbidding of images, and the worshipping of them, taken out of the Holy Scripture, as well of the Old Testament as the New, was believed and taught by the old Holy Fathers, and most ancient doctors, and received in the old Primitive Church, which was most uncorrupt and pure." (*Hom. Idol. Part II.*)

The Order of Council, issued under Queen Elizabeth, against the Papists, and which was agreed to by the Church of England, clearly shows the principle of interpretation adopted by the Church of England, and her opinion respecting the condition of the Primitive Church till just before the commencement of the Pontificate of S. Gregory I. ". . . . If they [the Papists] shall show any ground of Scripture, and wrest it to their own sense, let it be showed by the interpretation of the old doctors; such as were before Gregory I. . . . . If they can show no doctor to agree with them . . . . then to conclude that they have no succession in that doctrine from the time of the Apostles, and above four hundred years after (when doctrine and religion were most pure). For that they can show no predecessor whom they might succeed in the same." (*Strype, Life of Archbp. Whitgift, vol. I. p.* 197. *Ed. of* 1822.) Again, the acts of Parliament fully endorse these principles. The Statute 2 & 3 Edw. VI. c. 1, for enforcing uniformity to the new Book of Common Prayer, declares it to have been drawn up by those who had "as well eye and respect to the most sincere and pure Christian Religion, taught by the Scripture, as to the usages in the Primitive Church." In the Act of Elizabeth "for restoring to the Crown the ancient jurisdiction over the Estate Ecclesiastical," the decrees of the first four General Councils, and of every other General Council, respecting heresy, are, provided they are in accordance with Holy Scripture, formally incorporated into the civil and ecclesiastical law of England. With regard to the area of the Primitive age of the Church, the Order in Council above quoted adopts the period of 400 years after the Apostolic age, that is, the first 500 years of the Christian Dispensation, "when religion and doctrine were most pure." The statute, too, of 1 Edw. VI. c. 1, pronounces the Primitive age to be a "space of 500 years and more after Christ's Ascension."

The following principles of evidence which the Church of England admits as binding upon herself consist, then, as follows : (1), Succession of doctrine from the Apostolic times and for above 400 years after, that is, to the close of the fifth century : and (2), The decrees of General Councils being agreeable to Holy Scripture. This period of the first 500 years she has adopted, on the ground that it was "most pure and uncorrupt," "when doctrine and religion were most pure."

As a loyal son of the Church of England, I restricted my investigation to the documents of the first five centuries, by which means I was persuaded I should, with God's help, arrive at the truth, whatever it might be.

The evidence, then, which I have collected, of the first 500 years, I have arranged under the "Two Inquiries" mentioned above; to which I have added Comments, critical and argumentative, with the view of bringing out into relief the real doctrine, which the Fathers, as it appeared to me, taught on the subject of this Work. I have not omitted to insert a chapter under each "Inquiry," entitled, "*Audi alteram Partem*" (or, "Hear the other side"), in which I have considered, to the best of my ability, the arguments advanced by Anglicans against the Supremacy of S. Peter and of the Holy See: whether or not with success, I must leave it with you to decide for yourselves.

Such is the general outline of my Work, which, if you will study carefully in connexion with this epistle, you will, I think, agree with me that I could come to no other conclusion than I have done. Would that you, too, could see the Truth, and enter that one true Ark of God, which alone can resist the billows of that terrible flood of scepticism and lawlessness now ascending from the depths of the lowest hell.

Before dismissing this portion of my letter I wish to inform you, that in this investigation I did not wholly trust to my own guidance: I consulted several learned theologians; to them I explained my difficulties, submitting to them some of the most startling evidence I had collected: but from them I received no real assistance; one suggested that there was a variety of interpretations put by the Fathers upon the words, "Thou art Peter," and "Feed My Sheep;" that the Popes were fallible men, and that they had erred in faith, as for instance Honorius; and another informed me that the opinions of the Fathers were not binding upon us; and that no dogma whatever was of faith unless formally decreed by a Free Œcumenical Council. After ruminating upon this, I concluded that there was something fundamentally wrong in the arguments of my friends. In the first place, I could not conceive how the Fathers could *really* vary in their teaching on any essential or fundamental point of Faith. No doubt they did apparently differ from each other in their interpretation of passages of Scripture; but when we carefully scrutinize their interpretations, they are not diverse from each other, as some assume: they turn out to be but variations, in which true harmony of teaching is throughout maintained.

Then with respect to Pope Honorius, it is evident, after reading his extant letters, that he was no heretic, though he was blameworthy in not detecting the deceit of Sergius, Patriarch of Constantinople. And as regards the opinion that no dogma or doctrine is binding unless formally decreed by an Œcumenical Council, if this was true, much of the Catholic Faith would even now be reduced to a nullity.

If this opinion be sound, then it was permissible, without censure, for one of the Faithful, before the Council of Nicæa, to deny the Divinity of our Lord, simply because, though believed as *de fide*, it had not been formally and dogmatically affirmed by a General Council.

Towards the close of my career as an Anglican, I forwarded to one whom I have ever loved and respected, and whom I shall always love and respect, the evidence I had collected upon the question of the Papacy, and after waiting a considerable time without receiving any acknowledgment, I concluded that no answer was forthcoming. It is but fair to add, that after my secession, my friend informed me that he had been preparing an answer to the paper I had sent him. Had I known this, I would unquestionably have waited for it, as in duty bound; but day after day passed away without receiving any reply to my letter, and as conviction was growing stronger and stronger every hour, gathering force from frequent thought and re-peated investigation, I felt I should be trifling with God and my own conscience, if I deferred any longer to submit myself to the Chair of S. Peter at Rome, to which is subjected, as I firmly believe, by God Himself, every Episcopal Chair of the Universal Church.

You will perhaps assert, and so will probably my friend, of whom I have just spoken, that I was too far gone to be saved, that it would be a useless waste of time to make any serious attempt to prevent the inevitable step being taken. To this I would reply, Not so. There were two circumstances that rendered change distasteful: the first was, that I was not, and never had been, what is called a "Romanizer;" although I held what are called extreme High Church opinions, I had no sympathy with what was held to be distinctively "Romish"; the second was, that my own reputation required me to remain where I was. If it could have been shown to me that the evidence I had collected for the Papacy was false, and that it was capable of a totally different interpretation from that which I had, conscientiously I trust, put upon it, I should then have been better pleased, for it would have enabled me with a good conscience to have continued in the vocation to which I then believed God to have called me, and in which my heart was engaged.

Having explained my reasons for "changing my religion," I propose now to invite your attention to two very important subjects: the first is the duty of inquiry into the grounds of the Faith that is in us, not, indeed, in the spirit of scepticism, but with a view of estimating the foundation on which we stand: the second, of acquiring a correct knowledge of the characteristics of that identical Church which Christ Himself founded on earth, previous to His departure to the Right

Hand of God His Father. It seems to me that a correct knowledge of the character of the Church is essential to a right comprehension of the whole question of Church Government, whether it should turn out to be Papal, Episcopal, or Presbyterian. When once we grasp the form, the nature, and the marks of the original Church, as she issued from Christ, when He breathed into her nostrils the breath of a never-dying life, we shall be in a position of great advantage in the study of the great question arising in this investigation.

II.

THE DUTY OF INQUIRY.

It is not an uncommon practice for clergymen of the Church of England to assert, if not the unlawfulness, at least the impropriety, of any of her members investigating some of the foundations on which she rests her claim to their exclusive allegiance. If there existed on earth only one Christian community, then their objection might be tenable, because such an examination might imply a doubt of Christ and the Religion He taught. But when we know that Christians are divided to a very great extent, that there are many Christian communities and sects, all professing to worship Christ as God and Man, it is impossible for us to avoid, if we have any regard to our ultimate salvation, the necessity of making a careful examination of the grounds on which the communion to which we, each of us, belong, claims our respect and adhesion. While Christendom is in the condition it now is, is it not wrong (it cannot be otherwise) to prevent any one from inquiring into the truth of the religious system in which he was brought up? For if there be one only Church on earth, which Christ recognises as His Church, it must be of prime importance to us to be in its communion, else we run the risk of condemnation at the last day. Our Lord's parting address to the Apostles contained these fearful words, " He that believeth and is baptized shall be saved; but he that believeth not shall be damned." (*S. Mark*, xvi. 16.) It cannot be doubted that when our Saviour said, " He that believeth," He meant, he that believeth in Me, and in My doctrine, and in the ordinances I have instituted, shall be saved ; and contrariwise, he that refuses to believe in what I have ordained, and in what I have taught, shall be damned. It was also taught, he that breaketh one commandment, breaketh the whole law of God; so he that declines to accept any one article of faith is an unbeliever, and in danger of condemnation. Now, if Christ really

did establish a particular religious community, and if He did institute
one only system of ecclesiastical authority, it follows that he who
declines to accept it is an unbeliever in the scriptural sense, and
entails upon himself condemnation.   This is, I think, a fair and
legitimate application of this passage to the subject under discussion.
Again, S. Peter, in his Catholic Epistle, says, "Wherefore the rather,
brethren, give diligence to make your calling and election sure."
(2 *Peter*, i. 10.)   The Apostle in the context alludes to certain
"exceeding great and precious promises," by which we "might be
partakers of the divine nature, having escaped the corruption that is in
the world through lust," and he then proceeds to counsel us to add to
our "faith, virtue; and to virtue knowledge; and to knowledge temperance; and to temperance patience; and to patience godliness; and
to godliness brotherly kindness; and to brotherly kindness charity."
He then says, "If these things be in (us) and abound," we shall be
neither "barren nor unfruitful in the knowledge of our Lord Jesus
Christ;" but if we lack these things, *i. e.* faith, virtue, knowledge, &c.,
then are we "blind and cannot see afar off, and (have) forgotten that
(we were) purged from (our) old sins."   "Wherefore," he adds, "the
rather, brethren, give diligence to make your calling and election sure;
for if (we) do these things, (we) shall never fail; for so an entrance
shall be ministered unto (us) abundantly into the everlasting kingdom
of our Lord and Saviour Jesus Christ."   To "make our calling and
election sure," it is necessary that we should examine whether we
possess "faith," and "knowledge," no less than "virtue," "patience,"
&c.   This necessarily involves inquiry whether we really hold the
true "Faith," and whether we are in possession of sound "knowledge," for if our "Faith" and "Knowledge" be defective, how can
our "calling and election" be reckoned by ourselves as "sure?"—nay,
on the contrary, our "calling and election," in this case, must be
without any solid foundation, and consequently we run the risk of
having "no entrance . . . . into the everlasting Kingdom of our
Lord and Saviour Jesus Christ."   The injunction, then, to "make
our calling and election sure," involves the necessity of a diligent
inquiry into the foundation of the Faith we have been taught, and
the religious system in which we have been brought up; for if that
system be not of God, then we have no true Faith, we are not in
Jesus Christ, and we have the benefit of none of the Sacraments
He ordained.

   S. Paul in different words declares the same counsel: "If a man
also strive for mastery, yet is he not crowned, except he strive
lawfully." (2 *Tim.* ii. 5.)   The Apostle compares our pilgrimage to
a soldier's warfare, in which we are admonished to endure hardness,

and not to entangle ourselves with the affairs of this life: that is to say, we must war as Jesus Christ wills, and in accordance with those laws and principles He ordained. The army of Jesus Christ is one, it has over it one Captain-general, that is Himself, and, as we shall see, one Lieutenant-general, to whom He has committed all His authorities, until He returns to resume His command in Person.

Every soldier, then, if he desires to be crowned, must fight in that army, even that particular army, subject to that officer Christ has appointed to the command, and to no other. Now, as it is notorious that there are many separate armies, claiming Jesus Christ as their Captain,—(1), the Roman Church; (2), the Greek Church; (3), the Anglican Church; and (4), the Presbyterian, Lutheran, Calvinistic, Wesleyan, and Baptist communities,—it is necessary that we should investigate which of these is the army of Jesus Christ. They cannot all be His army, for the very essence of an army is perfect unity and absolute obedience to martial law, and to its commanders: whereas all these armies disagree with each other on fundamental points, and every one of them, except the Roman Catholic Church, is externally and internally divided into sectarian parties, warring against each other, instead of against the foes of Christ. To strive then lawfully, that is, in obedience to the faith of Christ, in the one army He has established, is essential to obtain the crown; it therefore follows that a careful inquiry is needful, that we may ascertain whether we really are striving lawfully in that great war against the world, the flesh, and the devil.

And this duty of inquiry is enforced by our blessed Lord Himself: "Search the Scriptures; for in them ye think ye have eternal life: and they are they which testify of Me." (S. John, v. 39.) You see that Jesus Christ, notwithstanding He was very God, to whom every creature is subject, whether they will or no, invited, nay commanded, His hearers to inquire whether He was not really and truly their true Messiah. To inquire, in this case, was absolutely necessary, for if He was the Messiah, God manifest in the flesh, to reject Him was to subject themselves to certain condemnation; and to have accepted Him as God, if he had not really been what He claimed to be, would have been equally hazardous. Therefore Christ said, "Search the Scriptures," examine the Word of God, and ascertain whether I am or am not your long-predicted Messiah. This principle, too, S. Luke witnesses approvingly in the Acts with respect to the Bereans. The Thessalonians evidently at first rejected the doctrine taught by S. Paul, apparently without any inquiry, but the Bereans "received the word with all readiness of mind, and searched the Scriptures daily, whether these things were so." (Acts, xvii. 11.)

It cannot, therefore, be an act of disloyalty to the religious community in which one happens to have been brought up, to inquire into the foundations on which it rests its claims to our allegiance. But, contrariwise, it is a duty to search and see whether these things are so. For as there cannot be many Christs, so there cannot be many Churches. In the midst, then, of conflicting claims, it would be an act of disobedience to Christ to refuse to inquire, with a view of ascertaining which of these multitudes of religious communities, or sects, is that which He instituted; and it would be an act of sheer folly to imitate the uninquiring spirit of the Thessalonians, and reject the claims of any particular church, without "searching daily," to see "whether these things were so."

For any clergyman of the Church of England, for a minister of any denomination, to forbid us to follow the admonition of Christ and His Apostles, to "search the Scriptures," and to ascertain with as much certainty as possible the ground on which our faith is based, in order that we may "make our calling and election sure," and be in a position of striving lawfully in the army of the Lord, and thus obtain the crown, is an act of gross injustice and cruelty; for no man can part with his responsibility. He is responsible to God for the soul God has given him, and he is bound to act according to the ability God has blessed him with. In the midst of rival communities he is bound to ascertain, as best he may, which of all these is "the Church of the Living God, the Pillar and Ground of the Truth." To refuse to do so, is to run a most fearful risk, for should his "calling and election" be baseless, and should he, consequently, be striving unlawfully, rejecting the ordinances of God, then how can he fail to forfeit the crown he longs one day to receive on his brow as a faithful soldier of Jesus Christ?

Let me, then, as one who feels a deeper interest in you than any one else can possibly do, implore you not to permit any fanciful notions of loyalty to prevent you from examining the foundations of that communion you were brought up in, for, be assured, that if it be of God, it will have a Rock for its foundation; but if it be not of God, then you will discover, before it is too late, that it is founded upon the ever-shifting sands. What I ask of you is this, viz. to look to your foundation, and see if it is on the solid Rock; for if it is not, how can you hope to escape ultimate ruin if you elect to remain in such a house? What will it avail you, if after this life, when you are standing before the bar of the last dread Tribunal, you should discover, to your dismay, that during the seventy or eighty years of your sojourn on earth, you have not been worshipping God according to His will, that you have adhered to ecclesiastical systems which He never instituted, and that you have partaken of sacramental ministrations He never authorized ? What will be your plea when standing before that final Court of Appeal, if you should discover that you were not in the Ark of God's Church ? Will it be " Invincible Ignorance?" " Invincible Ignorance" will, doubtless, avail to arrest the hand of the Executioner; but then, before relying upon this, let us understand what we mean by this term. A person cannot, I apprehend, put in this plea, unless he has taken every pains to learn the truth. If he has refused during life, especially when invited, to investigate the foundation of his faith, how can he say that he is invincibly ignorant, seeing that he has never made an attempt even to inform himself on the vital question which has been raised ? The term " Invincible Ignorance," I conceive, implies ignorance after an honest and conscientious endeavour to learn the Truth of God, which however, owing to some mental or moral defect, is unattainable. Such an one may escape condemnation if not in the true Church : but he who has wilfully and obstinately refused to inquire, how can he say before the bar of the Eternal Judge and His assessors, " I was invincibly ignorant ?"

If, then, we desire to be on the safe side, we must inquire into the character and foundation of that system of which we are members ; else, if we find ourselves in the wrong one, our chance of ultimate salvation, if God's words be true, will be, to say the least, extremely doubtful. You may depend upon it that if any minister of religion, or any other person, should take upon himself to forbid you to inquire, it is because he knows that the foundations are not faultless. One thing is certain, that the true Church of God, whichever it is, has nothing to fear from the most searching examination.

III.

DISCERNMENT OF CHURCHES.

The Apostle S. Paul informs us that one of the gifts of the Spirit is " discernment of spirits," that is, the power of judging in spiritual matters, to determine whether they are genuine. S. John supports this principle, when he counsels his disciples to "believe not every spirit, but (to) try the spirits whether they are of God : because many false prophets are gone out into the world." (1 *John*, iv. 1.) S. Paul again confirms this, when he directs the Thessalonians to " despise not prophesyings," but to "prove all things." (1 *Thess.* v. 20, 21.) From these Apostolical admonitions we may draw legitimately three inferences, viz. the duty of trying of what Spirit the ecclesiastical system to which we are attached is composed; whether it rests upon that Rock which Christ Himself created and planted on this earth, as the firm foundation of His Church. And, surely, there is good reason for our endeavouring to exercise such powers as God has given us, intellectual and moral, or both, for the discernment of the many spirits which are abroad, exercising their prophetic office for the propagation of damnable heresies. You know that this Apostle foretold, that " in the latter times some shall depart from the faith, giving heed to seducing spirits, and doctrines of devils : speaking lies in hypocrisy; having their conscience seared with a hot iron ;" " who shall bring in damnable heresies, even denying the Lord that bought them, and bring upon themselves swift destruction : and many shall follow their pernicious ways; by reason of whom the way of truth shall be evil spoken of." (1 *Tim.* iv. 1, 2. 2 *Pet.* ii. 1, 2.) You are also aware that our Lord foreshewed, that in the latter days there should be both false apostles and false prophets, who would deceive the people. You cannot then doubt, that if ever there was a time when the spiritual faculty of " discerning the spirits,"—distinguishing the good from the bad, the true from the false—be necessary, that time is pre-eminently the present. You will not forget how the Spirit commended the Ephesian Church for exercising this discernment. " I know thy works, and thy labour, and thy patience, and how thou canst not bear them which are evil : and thou hast tried them which say they are apostles, and are not, and hast found them liars." (*Rev.* ii. 2.)

You will, however, ask me the very natural question, How am I, an ignorant Layman, to discern out of the many churches and religious communities now existing, which of them is the Church of God ? To this I would reply, provided you are earnestly endeavouring to serve God, and are not obstinately prejudiced, you will not find it so difficult to acquire a knowledge of the truth in a matter of this kind. You will, perhaps, answer me by asserting your inability to read and understand the writings of the Holy Fathers ? But it is not necessary for you to study the Fathers; they are most valuable auxiliaries to those who have the means and time to study them ; there is one Book which is sufficient of itself for this purpose, viz. the Holy Bible, the written Word of God. This Holy Book, if read with an honest and believing mind, will unfold to us how we may discern the many theological spirits which are abroad, and discover which of them is of God.

Before, however, you can make use of this gift of discernment, you must first inform your minds thoroughly of the character and

attributes of that Church which Christ founded, and which He designed should continue till the end of time; and then by comparing
the communion in which you have been brought up, with the description of that Church, you will thus be enabled to discern the True
Church of God.

Let us now proceed with all reverence to discuss the character
and attributes of that Church which Christ Himself instituted. In pur-
suing this inquiry we cannot do better than follow the counsel given
as to this matter by the Church of England. In her Homily (2d part)
for Whitsunday, she says, " The true Church is an universal congregation or fellowship of God's faithful and elect people, built upon the
foundation of the Apostles and Prophets, Jesus Christ Himself being
the Head Corner Stone. And it hath always three notes or marks
whereby it is known: pure and sound doctrine, the sacraments
ministered according to Christ's institution, and the right use of
ecclesiastical discipline;" and she adds, "The description of the
Church is agreeable both to the Scriptures of God, and also to the
doctrine of the ancient Fathers, so that none may justly find fault
therewith." (*Hom. Whitsunday,* 2nd pt.)

The first note or mark which the Church of England admits as
essential for discerning the true Church is " pure and sound doctrine." Now a principal article of the Creed as received by her is, " I
believe in One Holy, Catholic, and Apostolic Church." It is a
part of " pure and sound doctrine" to hold this dogma thoroughly and
without equivocation. I will now, in the words of Holy Scripture,
delineate, to the best of my ability, the character and attributes of
that Church which Christ Himself founded.

I. Unity and Indefectibility.—" Upon this Rock I will
build My Church, and the gates of hell shall not prevail against
it." In these few words are enunciated two important points, viz.
unity and indefectibility. The solid Rock is itself a symbol of
perfect unity, of massive strength, of irresistible power, and un-
decaying durability. Our Lord Himself comments, by anticipa-
tion, on the nature of this symbol: " Whosoever heareth these
sayings of Mine, and doeth them, I will liken him unto a wise
man, which built his house upon a rock; and the rain descended,
and the floods came, and the winds blew, and beat upon that house;
and it fell not; for it was founded upon a Rock." (*S. Matt.* vii. 24,
25.) And He contrasts this with the foolish man, who built his
house on the sands. "And the rain descended, and the floods came,
and the winds blew, and beat upon that house; and it fell; and
great was the fall of it." (*Ib.* 26, 27.) The Rock, then, was the

indefectible foundation of the House of the wise man, and consequently it was able to resist all the violence of the elements; while
the House which was erected by the foolish man fell, because, being
built upon the sand, it had no real foundation whatever. Christ, the
great Master-Builder, erected His House upon the solid Rock, and
notwithstanding the rains, the floods, and the hurricane, it stood,
because it was founded upon the Rock.

But, perhaps, you will say that a Rock may be rent by the
violence of nature, and that which was once one rock might become
two or more rocks. In answer to this objection, I would point to the
words, "And the gates of hell shall not prevail against it;" that is,
against the Church so built on the Rock. Whether or no this might
be possible through the violence of nature concerns us not, because
we have a solemn guarantee given us, on the most sacred word of
Christ, that against the House or Church which He founded upon the
Rock of His appointment "the gates of hell shall not prevail;"
therefore that Rock which He selected as the basis of His Church
cannot be divided or broken; and the Church built thereon, par-
taking as it does of the unity, power, and strength of that Rock,
can neither be divided nor broken.

Again. The Rock is not merely an inert or lifeless foundation;
it is, as S. Peter and S. John imply, a living Stone. It is a Stone
which grows. Daniel, in his prophecy of the Church, declares that
the Stone which smote the Image, and cast it down, "became a great
mountain, and filled the whole earth:" and it is added, that this
Mountain-Kingdom "shall never be destroyed;" nor be "left to
other people, but it shall break in pieces, and consume all these
kingdoms, and it shall stand for ever." (*Dan.* ii. 35, 44.) I
cannot imagine a more perfect symbol than this universal mountain, or a trope more expressive of an indivisible unity, and an
incorruptible indefectibility. For how can such a mountain as this,
which fills the whole earth, be ever divided into separate parts; and
what chance or possibility exists of the hand of man destroying this
impenetrable unity? The Rock-Mountain, then, is a symbol of the
perfect unity and indefectibility of the Church and Kingdom of
Christ. When, then, our Lord said, "Upon this Rock I will build My
Church, and the gates of hell shall not prevail against it," we are to
understand that that Church—not every Church, but that Church only
which was built on the Rock of His selection—is one, indivisible,
and indefectible, for its unity cannot be divided, nor can it be
broken in twain, for "the gates of hell shall not prevail against it."

But the Lord has, in His mercy and goodness, left on record, for
our solace and assurance, that magnificent Prayer which He addressed

to the Father for the perpetual unity of His Church and Kingdom. He thus prayed: "I have given unto them (the Apostles) the words which Thou gavest Me . . . . I pray for them ; I pray not for the world, but for them which Thou hast given Me ; for they are Thine. . . . . Holy Father, keep through Thine own Name those whom Thou hast given Me, that they may be one, as We are. . . . . Neither pray I for these alone, but for them also which shall believe on Me through their word ; that they all may be one ; as Thou, Father, art in Me, and I in them, that they also may be one in Us : that the world may believe that Thou hast sent Me. And the glory which Thou gavest Me I have given them ; that they may be one, even as We are one : I in them, and Thou in Me, that they may be made perfect in one; and that the world may know that Thou hast sent Me, and hast loved them as Thou hast loved Me." (S. John, xvii.) I, for my part, cannot see, after reading the words of our Lord, " Upon this Rock I will build my Church, and the gates of hell shall not prevail against it," and this most beautiful and affecting Prayer, how it is possible that that Church and Kingdom which He instituted could ever really be divided or broken ; for not only has He given us His most solemn word that it never should be, but He has addressed to His Father this intercessory Prayer for the perpetual unity of His Church, first as represented by His Apostles, and secondly by those who should succeed them. But what was the nature of that unity for which Christ prayed ? Let us examine carefully the words He employed. " That they all may be one, as Thou, Father, art in Me, and I in Thee, that they also may be one in Us. . . . . I in them, and Thou in Me, that they may be made perfect in one." The Unity, then, which Christ desired for His Church was a unity resembling that of the Three Persons in the Most Holy Trinity. " As Thou, Father, art in Me, and I in Thee," so I beseech Thee, "they also may be one in Us :" such is the prayer. The Unity in the Holy Trinity is that of Substance, consequently the Holy Trinity is said to be undivided, for it is impossible to divide that Substance. As they were one, one with each other, and in each other, being all Three of one Substance, so is the Church, which Christ established on the Rock, against which "the gates of hell shall not prevail," for she is one in Christ—being Bone of His Bone, and Flesh of His Flesh, by the union of Water and Blood, which flowed from His wounded side—even as Christ is one with the Father ; so it must follow that as the Holy and Blessed Trinity is one and indivisible,— i. e. the Substance cannot be divided—so also the Church, which is the Body of Christ, is one and indivisible.

It is impossible, then, not to perceive that the Church which Christ designed was one which was perfect in all respects — perfect as to her foundation—a Rock ; perfect in her superstructure ; perfectly impregnable against all the forces of the infernal powers, and perfectly united in her organic constitution, for it is as thoroughly one in God, and in herself, as " the Trinity in Unity," and " the Unity in Trinity."

But, further, in order that you may see how this indivisible and uncorrupt indefectibility is a characteristic of the true Church, let me set before you some passages which still further enforce this great truth.

I have already pointed out the great mountain which covered the whole earth as being the most perfect symbol of this unity and indefectibility. There are other tropes which, in their degree, equally represent this truth. " The kingdom of God is like to a grain of mustard-seed, which a man took, and sowed in his field : which indeed is the least of all seeds ; but when it is grown, it is the greatest among herbs, and becometh a tree, so that the birds of the air come and lodge in the branches thereof." (*S. Matt.* xiii. 31, 32.) This type of Unity is analogous to that of the Stone—the small Stone—which struck the colossal Image (*i. e.* the fourth Universal Empire) on its extremities, and, destroying it, occupied its place, and thence grew into a great mountain, filling the whole earth. Now a tree is a perfect Unity ; for it consists of three organic parts—the root, the trunk, and the branches. These cannot be divided without producing the dissolution of the part severed. The branch cannot live separate from the trunk, nor can the trunk apart from the root. A tree is an indivisible unity ; it cannot be divided without causing the destruction of the tree ; but, on the other hand, the root and the trunk possess an inherent life independent of the branches, so much so that, if many were cut off, the tree would still remain whole, and also would still retain its inborn vigour. The Church is likewise compared to a human body, which, like the tree, consists of three main divisions—the head, the torso, and the members. The members cannot exist apart from the body, nor the body from the head ; but so long as the head and the body are united, a man may live his allotted time, in health and vigour, even if several of his members had been amputated.

Now the Church which Christ constituted is His Body, and that can no more be really divided than a tree or a human body. Her unity is not broken, though many of her members have been severed from her body. As the tree and the human body both retain their perfect unity and indefectibility, though divested of some of their respective branches and members, so also the Church : the loss of the Greeks on the one side and the Anglicans on the other may, indeed, have terribly shaken her, but her unity and indivisibility, notwithstanding, remain intact.

The Church can be no more divided than Christ Himself. S. Paul asserts that in his Epistle to the Ephesians: "There is one Body, and one Spirit, even as ye are called in one hope of your calling; one Lord, one Faith, one Baptism, one God and Father of all, who is above all, and through all, and in you all." (*Eph.* iv. 3–6.) As, then, God is one, Christ one, and the Holy Ghost one; so also is the Body of Christ, that is, the Church. As, then, God the Father, God the Son, and God the Holy Ghost, are each an indivisible Unity, and together form one undivided Unity, so also is the Kingdom and Church one, and organically indivisible, and absolutely indefectible; for as the Three Blessed Persons cannot be severed from each other, or be injured by the armies of hell, no more can this Kingdom and Church be severed in twain or broken by the hand of man or devil.

I might continue the Scriptural evidence for this absolute oneness and indefectibility by referring to an enclosed city, a house, or building, or family, each of which fully sustains the idea of this perfect unity.

I think I have now proved from Holy Scripture one point in the character and attributes of that Church which Christ established, viz. her perfect indivisible Unity and absolute indefectibility. I have shown that Christ erected His Kingdom and Church on the Rock, which Rock grew into a great mountain filling the whole earth; and also that this Kingdom and Church, in accordance with the prophecy of Daniel, would never be destroyed, but would stand for ever. Our gracious Lord promised most solemnly, " The gates of hell shall not prevail against it," that is, it shall never be overcome with heresies, it shall never be divided, but shall stand in its perfect unity and strength for ever; it shall never decay by lapse of time, nor shall it ever be broken by the hand of man or by the shafts of the Arch-enemy of mankind: and in order to sanctify this unity and indefectibility, our Lord offered on the eve of His Passion that sublime and most affecting prayer to His Father, by which He consecrated His new Kingdom and Church, sanctifying it by the word of truth, and cementing its unity in His own Blood, which He had just before offered to His Father, and which He was about on the morrow to shed in dread reality for His Church. This prayer alone is a guarantee of the indivisible Unity and perfect indefectibility of His Church, to say nothing of His sacred promise, " The gates of hell shall not prevail against it," even that Church which was founded on the Rock ·of His selection—even Peter—*i. e.* the Rock, Peter.

II. SANCTITY.—The Church is holy, because her code of doctrine and morality is derived from God; because Christ our Lord is present by means of the Sacraments; because the Holy Ghost dwells in the Church; and, lastly, because the whole Body is holy through the washing of·regeneration. The point, however, I desire particularly to draw your attention to, is the indwelling of the Holy Ghost in the Church, by which, in accordance with the promise of our Lord, she is not only one and indefectible, but also infallible in all matters relating to faith and morality. Indeed, this is the necessary corollary, if the Unity of the Church be indivisible and her inde-fectibility unimpeachable.

Let us now see what Holy Scripture teaches us on this point. During our Lord's visible residence with the Church which He had constituted, He was her infallible Paraclete, *i. e.* her Teacher, Guide, and Counsellor, in all that appertained to truth and practice. For three years S. Peter and the Apostles were under His personal training; and after His resurrection, S. Luke informs us of all that occurred during those forty days He sojourned on earth, " Until the day in which He was taken up, after that He, through the Holy Ghost, had given com-mandments unto the Apostles whom He had chosen: to whom also He showed Himself alive after His passion by many infallible proofs, being seen of them forty days, and speaking of the things pertaining to the kingdom of God." (*Acts*, i. 2, 3.)   And just before His Ascen-sion He addressed His Apostles, saying, " Go ye, therefore, and teach all nations . . . . teaching them to observe all things whatsoever I have commanded you : and lo, I am with you alway, even unto the end of the world." (*S. Matt.* xxviii. 19, 20.)   From the time, then, Christ commenced His ministry till the last moment of His visible residence on earth, the Church and Kingdom He had instituted pos-sessed an infallible Teacher, Guide, and Counsellor.

The question which immediately occurs to one's mind now is, Did our Lord make no provision for continuing this infallibility after His Ascension? Was the infant Church, which was under a personal, infallible Teacher and Guide, intended, as soon as Christ and His Apostles had departed from this world, to be left entirely to her own resources, to be the prey and sport of speculators and infidels, without any such supernatural assistance as would be sufficient to preserve her from error and apostasy? Was she, who had been under the personal supervision of her Divine Founder, to be left without a substitute of equal authority and equal infallibility? Reason would,

I think, assure us this would be impossible ; but, thank the Lord
of All, Holy Scripture determines this for us, as fully and as
satisfactorily as possible.

Towards the close of our Blessed Lord's ministry, He startled
His hearers and the Apostles by saying : "Little children, yet a
little while I am with you. Ye shall seek Me : and as I said
unto the Jews, Whither I go, ye cannot come ; so now I say to
you." Simon Peter immediately replies, " Lord, whither goest Thou ? "
Jesus answered him, Whither I go, thou canst not follow Me now ;
but thou shalt follow Me afterwards." (*S. John*, xiii. 33-36.) This
departure of Christ, which He announced, probably referred only to
His temporary absence in Hades ; but He soon after began to prepare His Apostles for His final departure from this earth.   He
commenced by saying, " Let not your heart be troubled : ye believe
in God, believe also in Me.   In My Father's house are many mansions : if it were not so, I would have told you."   He here raises
the hearts of His Apostles, strengthening their faith in Himself, and
unfolds to their gaze the glorious mansions in heaven.   Having thus
prepared them, He says abruptly, " I go to prepare a place for you.
And if I go and prepare a place for you, I will come again, and
receive you unto Myself : that where I am, there ye may be also ; and
whither I go ye know, and the way ye know."   One may well imagine
the alarm the Apostles felt when they heard these startling words,
" I go."   S. Peter was probably aware what was about to happen, for
Jesus had announced his intention not long before to him ; and it is
not unlikely that he, to whom was revealed the Divinity of Christ,
might have known more than his brother Apostles.   At any rate he
was silent.   After this, and after enforcing the duty of faith in Himself, Christ announces His gracious intention of supplying a Substitute,
equal in all respects to Himself—in dignity, in knowledge, and in
power—who should be for the future the Teacher, the Guide, and
the Counsellor of the Church, for ever.   " And I will pray the Father,
and He shall give you another Comforter (or, Paraclete), that He may
abide with you for ever ; even the Spirit of Truth ; whom the world
cannot receive, because it seeth Him not, neither knoweth Him : but
ye know Him ; for He dwelleth with you, and shall be in you.   I will
not leave you comfortless" (or rather, orphans) ; " I will come to you."
(*S. John*, xiv. 16-18.)   Again He repeats the afflicting words, " Yet a
little while, and the world seeth Me no more," with a view, apparently,
of impressing on the minds of His Apostles the reality of what was
about to happen, and yet to comfort them by adding, " But ye see
me : because I live, ye shall live also.   At that day ye shall know
that I am in My Father, and ye in Me, and I in you." (*Ib.* 19, 20.)

Then He recurs to His promise : " But the Comforter " (or, Paraclete), " which is the Holy Ghost, whom the Father will send in My name, He shall teach you all things, and bring all things to your remembrance whatsoever I have said unto you." Again He affectingly reverts to His approaching departure ; but now He braces up the souls of His Apostles : " If ye loved Me, ye would rejoice, because I said, I go unto the Father : for My Father is greater than I." And further He encourages them, saying, " And now I have told you before it come to pass, that, when it is come to pass, ye might believe." (*Ib.* 26–30.) Still the Apostles sorrowed, as well they might, notwithstanding the tender consolations of their Lord and Master. He then affectionately addressed them the third time on this subject : " But because I have said these things unto you, sorrow hath filled your heart. Nevertheless I tell you the truth ; it is expedient for you that I go away : for if I go not away, the Comforter " (*i.e.* the Paraclete) " will not come unto you ; but if I depart, I will send Him unto you. And when He is come, He will reprove the world of sin, and of righteousness, and of judgment : of sin, because they believe not on Me ; of righteousness, because I go to My Father, and ye see Me no more ; of judgment, because the prince of this world is judged. I have yet many things to say unto you, but ye cannot bear them now. Howbeit when He, the Spirit of truth, is come, He will guide you into all truth : for He shall not speak of Himself ; but whatsoever He shall hear, that shall He speak : and He will show you things to come. He shall glorify Me : for He shall receive of Mine, and shall show it unto you." (*Ib.* xvi. 6–13.) Christ again reminds His Apostles of His approaching departure, evidently knowing that they could not realise to themselves that He would really leave them. There are no incidents in Holy Scripture so ·pathetic as this. Our Lord and the Apostles loved each other with a love past comprehension—with love so intense that there are no words to give it adequate description ; He loved them with all the power of spirit, soul, and body, but, more than that, He loved them with a Divine love, for He was very God. Their love was, if I may say so with reverence, equal to His — *i. e.* in their degree they loved with as much fervour ; they loved Him fervently and passionately. Great, indeed, must have been their affliction and heartrending sorrow when they heard He was about to leave them. Oh, it must have been a most terrible sorrow : so great that their minds were, so to say, stunned, for they could not understand what He meant, and they would not believe what He said—nay, they could not, so great was the depth of their affliction. But we are indebted to this sorrow of the Apostles, for it drew out from our dear Lord His most gracious and sacred intentions respecting His Church; for through this grief we learn all about that Divine Substitute He was about to send immediately on His departure to the right-hand of the Father.

Let us now carefully realize Who this Substitute was, and the nature of the mission He was to execute during the absence of the Lord Jesus Christ. It is plainly stated that He who should come would be the Holy Ghost, the third Person of the Holy and Undivided Trinity. He was to come, not as an influence, but as a Person, to dwell with the Church as personally as Christ did before His Ascension, the only difference consisting in His not being visible to us, inasmuch as He has never assumed a body, though at the baptism of Christ He was manifested under the form or shape of a "dove," and on his descent on the Apostles and disciples under the sign of " cloven tongues like as of fire." That His presence was Personal is evident from His mode of operation ; for He spoke, on different occasions, audibly to Apostles and Prophets : for example, " As they ministered to the Lord, and fasted, the Holy 'Ghost said, Separate Me Barnabas and Saul for the work whereunto I have called them." (*Acts*, xiii. 2.) " And were forbidden of the Holy Ghost to preach the word in Asia." (*Ib.* xvi. 6.) And again, after the Council of Jerusalem had decided the circumcision case, the Apostles and Elders, in their Synodical Epistle, say, " For it seemed good to the Holy Ghost, and to us," &c. (*Ib.* xv. 28.) These expressions clearly indicate that the Holy Ghost was present in very Person, teaching, guiding, and counselling, as Christ had been before His departure. This point is of greater importance than it seems at first sight; for, were He present merely influentially by grace, it would by no means fulfil the Lord's promise of sending some one to take His place in the Church, as His Divine Substitute, by whose personal supervision His Church would 'be taught all that she ought to know, and be guided in all things she was to do, even to the reproving "the world of sin, of righteousness, and of judgment." For what is the exact meaning of the word Paraclete, translated in the English Authorized Version as Comforter ? It signifies literally a legal assistant, an advocate, or intercessor. This is what our Lord was to His Church : He was her Advocate—*i. e.* He represented her, pleading her cause—and her Intercessor, inasmuch as He prayed for her and obtained benefits for her; among them, the gift of the Holy Ghost But He was more: He was her instructor, her teacher, and her guide ; so also is the Holy Ghost, whom He sent, after His Ascension, to occupy His place on earth, in the Church He had established.

It may be, however, remarked, that He no longer governs the Church personally, His voice is no longer heard, and He does not take, as it were, any active part in the government and administration of the Church. But visible or audible manifestations are not essential as proofs of His personal Presence. We each of us know we have a Soul, a substance separate and distinct from the Body it inhabits; we have never seen it, or heard it speak; our acquaintance with our own Soul is the innate consciousness that it is within us, and our knowledge of its existence is by its manifestation through the mind and the intellect, and the organism of the body. The real existence, then, within us, is not dependent upon any visible or audible manifestations. So also in the Church. The Holy Ghost dwells within the Church as a Divine Person. It is true that at first He manifested Himself by descending, as it were, visibly under the form of " cloven tongues like as of fire," and by giving directions to the Apostles audibly, and by guiding them by means of a strong and overpowering impulse. But this was to assure the infant Church of His real and true Presence, in very Person, so that we might perceive that the fulfilment of the Lord's promise had been really accomplished; and having once come in very Person, He could not depart, because of the engagement Christ — so to speak — entered into as the condition of His departure, that He would send the Holy Ghost in His place, who would abide with the Church for ever, so that having once come as a Divine Person, and as the Substitute of the Lord, He would ever continue, personally governing and administering the Church in which He dwells. The Presence of the Holy Ghost is now ordinarily known by His manifestations through the Body of Christ. He speaks through her constituted authorities; and He directs the Church by those appliances which God has provided, and He governs her by means of those customs and laws which He has caused to prevail. He promulgates decrees, too, by Councils, which are drawn up in the name of the Holy Ghost. His actual Presence is also discerned by the condition of the Church or community He is said to reside in; where He is present, there is necessarily unity and concord in all matters appertaining to the doctrine of Faith and morality; where disunion and discord prevail, we may be quite certain that He cannot be in that community. But one thing is certain, that the Church into which He descended, must have retained all the characteristics which were the result of His coming; and further, that having come, He must be in the Church at this present time; and therefore it may be safely concluded that the Church must be even now remarkable for its unity, its interior peace, and its restless earnestness in the performance of its functions. But I am anticipating my subject.

Let us now examine carefully the mission the Holy Ghost was

sent to execute. He was (1) to abide or dwell with the Church for ever. During the whole Christian Dispensation He was to dwell personally with the Church of Christ. (2) He "shall teach you all things," *i.e.*, He shall be the Teacher of the Church, instructing her in everything she ought to know. (3) He "shall guide you into all Truth;" the whole doctrine of Christ shall be brought to the mind of the Church. (4) He "shall bring all things to your remembrance whatsoever I have said," *i.e.*, every truth which Christ had revealed to the Apostles, in the secret chamber, and after His resurrection, during those forty days before the Ascension, should be brought to the recollection of the Church. (5) He shall also "show unto you," what "He shall receive of Mine;" that is, He will inform the Church of the whole mystery of the Incarnation and the Atonement of our Lord. (6) He "shall show you things to come," that is, He will prophesy in the Church, by those whom He shall from time to time move so to do. And (7) He "shall glorify Me," that is, He shall so inspire the Church, that she shall glorify Him by her witness of Him, by her devotion to Him, and by her works.

The Holy Ghost is therefore to the Church what Christ was when on earth, her Paraclete, *i.e.*, her Teacher, her Guide, her Remembrancer, and her Inspirer. He was to fulfil this great mission, not for a time merely, not by the Apostles only, but "for ever," *i.e.*, until the close of the Age or Dispensation. It is impossible to doubt that the Church which possesses the Holy Ghost as her Teacher, her Guide, her Counsellor, her Remembrancer, and her Inspirer, must be infallible in her teaching, in respect both to doctrine and morality, and also in all her decrees when pronounced in accordance with those ecclesiastical principles which have always been in force. It is impossible that the Church can be fallible in the performance of its functions, if the Holy Ghost be really and truly present in the manner and for the purpose our Lord intimated to His afflicted Apostles. It is impossible that the Holy Ghost is not in her, dwelling in and with her, as her personal Teacher and Guide; because if it were not so the words of Christ would be falsified, and His promises would be of none effect. It follows, then, that the Holy Ghost is in the Church at this moment personally; and therefore the Church is not only indivisibly one, and incorruptibly indefectible, but she is absolutely infallible in the performance of every function she has been commanded by God to perform for the promotion of His glory and the benefit of mankind.

III. CATHOLICITY.—The Church of Christ is portrayed in Scripture as not insular or national, but as universal. The Stone by which the Lord struck the old empires of the Pagan world was not intended to be located merely in the place where it fell, but to grow into a great mountain, and to fill the whole earth. Such was the prediction of the prophet, and the terms of the commission signify nothing less. "Go ye therefore and teach all nations." (*S. Matt.* xxviii. 19.) "Go ye into all the world, and preach the Gospel." (*S. Mark,* xvi. 15.) S. Paul describes the Catholic Church as " the whole Family in heaven and earth " (*Eph.* iii. 15); and S. Peter, as "a chosen generation, a royal priesthood, an holy nation, a peculiar people." (1 *S. Pet.* ii. 9.) These expressions are borrowed from the Old Testament, which are descriptive of the holy people God then called, of their nation, and their Church. But that Kingdom, when Christ came, after its renewal, was intended to burst its boundaries, and to envelop in its dominion the whole world. " Enlarge the place of thy tent, and let them stretch forth the curtains of thine habitations : spare not, lengthen thy cords, and strengthen thy stakes ; for thou shalt break forth on the right hand and on the left ; and thy seed shall inherit the Gentiles, and make the desolate cities to be inhabited." (*Isaiah,* liv. 2, 3.)

It is, then, an essential characteristic of the Church, that she should not only be one and indefectible and infallible, but also universal, for the Church was not designed to be composed of a number of countless denominations and of independent branches, but one compact Empire, consisting of all nations and languages, together forming one " peculiar people," one " holy nation," under the government of one Lord, and one Hierarchy.

IV. APOSTOLICITY.—This is another feature by which the true Church is characterized in Holy Scripture. The Church instituted by Christ must have for its base the ordinances and commandments of the Holy Apostles. During the sojourn of Christ on earth, He called together His Twelve Apostles, and instructed them in all matters which were of Faith ; He taught them the divine law of the New Dispensation in fulness, which they were commanded to teach to all nations, giving them the Holy Ghost to guide them into all truth, and their Successors also, by virtue of the promise that the Spirit would abide in His Church for ever, bringing to their recollection all that He had said at the beginning. These institutes of the Lord the Apostles handed down, commanding their Successors to adhere to them under pain of anathema. " But God be thanked that . . . . ye have obeyed from the heart that Form of Doctrine which was delivered to you." (*Rom.* vi. 17.) " Now I praise you, brethren,

that ye remember me in all things, and keep the ordinances, as I
delivered them to you." (1 *Cor.* xi. 2.) "Stand fast, and hold the
traditions which you have been taught, whether by Word, or our
Epistle." (2 *Thess.* ii. 15.) "O Timothy, keep that which is committed to thy trust." (1 *Tim.* vi. 20.) "Hold fast the form of sound
words, which thou hast heard of me . . . . That good thing which
was committed unto thee keep by the Holy Ghost, which dwelleth
in us." (2 *Tim.* i. 13, 14.)

And S. Peter adds, "This second Epistle, beloved, I now write
unto you; in both which I stir up your pure minds by way of
remembrance: that ye may be mindful of the words which were
spoken before by the holy prophets, and of the commandment of us
the apostles of the Lord and Saviour." (2 *S. Pet.* iii. 1, 2.) These
passages prove clearly that the doctrine of the Church which the
faithful were commanded to obey, was Apostolical. And not only
the doctrine, but the whole framework of the Kingdom and
Church was Apostolical: "Now therefore ye are no more strangers
and foreigners, but fellow-citizens with the saints, and of the household of God; and are built upon the foundation of the apostles and
prophets, Jesus Christ himself being the chief corner-stone." (*Ephes.*
ii. 19, 20.)

The essential character of the Church of Christ, as set forth in
the Holy Scriptures, consists of an organization indivisibly one,
incorruptibly indefectible, absolutely infallible in its teaching and
conduct, universal in its territorial extent, and apostolical in its
foundation. Such is the "pure and sound doctrine" enforced by
the Church of England in the Homily alluded to above, which
insists on the one Church, so indivisibly one that she cannot be
divided; so perfectly indefectible as to be impregnable against all
the assaults of hell; so truly infallible that she cannot teach falsely,
for her dogmas are founded upon the sacred Traditions of the
Apostles—partly written and partly unwritten—which are made
known to the Church by God the Holy Ghost, who dwelleth in her
as her Divine Paraclete; and so universal in her empire that there is
no room for any other religious community of Christians, except as
in the character of rebels against the authority of Christ and His
own Body the Church.

V. PERPETUITY OF THE CHURCH.—But there is a further question to be considered, viz. Was it God's intention that this Scriptura
Church should continue in its perfect unity and indefectibility,
together with the gift of infallibility, to the end of time? This perpetuity of her perfect integrity has, indeed, been anticipated in the

foregoing pages, but in order that you may see the truth in its fulness, I will set before you, in a concentrated form, the authorities which guarantee this perpetuity.

1. You will recollect the prophecy before referred to, that the great Universal Spiritual Kingdom of God, which was to break up and destroy the pagan Empire of Rome, and take possession of its capital, was intended to be everlasting in its duration. "And in the days of these kings shall the God of heaven set up a Kingdom which shall never be destroyed; and the Kingdom shall not be left to other people, but it shall break in pieces and consume all these kingdoms, and it shall stand for ever." (*Dan.* ii. 44.) No language can be more precise than this, viz. that the Kingdom of Christ was to be an institution of perpetual duration.

2. "The gates of hell shall not prevail against it," *i. e.* the Church founded upon the Rock of Christ's selection. The " gates of hell," signify the powers of hell, which from the commencement of the world have been in malignant array against God and man. Now this is a promise that the Devil shall not prevail to overthrow the Church. If heresy should ever obtain possession of that Church, then her end has come, for a divided house cannot stand. If the institution ceased to exist as soon as the last surviving Apostle had breathed his last, then Satan would have succeeded in defeating the prophecy, and the words, "the gates of hell shall not prevail," would have been found to be nothing more than empty sounds, having no real meaning. The Rock is the symbol not only of indivisible unity and indefectibility, it is also the symbol of perpetual durability; so that here we have as strong an assurance as possible that the identical Church which Christ established should never be destroyed, but shall last for ever, and that all the powers of hell shall not avail to injure it.

3. "Lo, I am with you alway, even unto the end of the world;" or, more literally, "Lo, I am with you all the days until the consummation of the dispensation." (*S. Matt.* xxviii. 20.) This was addressed to the Apostles, and had reference not to them personally, but to the office to which they had been appointed by Christ. The office of the Apostleship was, then, one of a perpetual ordinance; it was to last till the end of the dispensation, *i. e.* till the Second Advent.

4. The promise of the Holy Ghost, as the Divine Substitute of our Lord during His absence, consisted not merely in this, that He should guide the Church into all truth, but that He should abide with her for ever. "And I will pray the Father, and He shall give you another Paraclete, that He may abide with you for ever." (*S. John,* xiv. 16.)

You cannot, then, resist the truth, that the identical Church which Christ our Lord founded before His Passion must be existing at this moment somewhere in the world : and not only so, but it must be in that state of supernatural perfection in which she was first created. Her unity and indefectibility at this day must be as undivided and as uncorrupted as in the day when Christ said, " The gates of hell shall not prevail." Her infallibility in all that concerns the Faith, Morality, and the Worship of the Church, must be as certain now as in the time of the Holy Apostles, because of the promise that the Holy Ghost " shall abide with you for ever," and because of the further guarantee delivered immediately before the Ascension, " Lo, I am with you all the days till the consummation of the dispensation."

Where, then, in this wide world is that Church which is one and indefectible, infallible, universal, and Apostolic? This is the problem we have now to solve.

IV. THE TEST.

Such are the Scriptural characteristics of that Church which Jesus Christ instituted before His departure to the Right Hand of the Father, — one, indivisible, indefectible, infallible, universal, and Apostolic,—and which was intended by Christ to continue in her integrity till the end of time.

If this description of the Church of Christ is correct, it necessarily follows that this Church is existing somewhere, or rather everywhere, at this present time ; and it behoves us, therefore, to look around us, and endeavour, with God's help, and by the exercise of our own reason, to discern it.

Now there are in this world three great Churches, claiming to be Divine and Apostolical in their foundation, and known as the Roman, the Greek, and the Anglican communions, each of which, in its degree, challenges the obedience of the Faithful.

Upon this there are maintained two hypotheses which must be carefully investigated, viz. (1) That these three Churches in their divided state, together form the one Body of Christ ; and (2) That one only of these communions is the true Church. We will discuss these separately.

I. Anglicans maintain that the whole Church consists of an innumerable company of Bishops, clergy, and people, of every nation, who confess the Faith as once delivered to the Saints, and which has been handed down by the Catholic Creeds. The two great Fathers of the Primitive age upon whom they rely as their authority for their hypothesis, are S. Ignatius and S. Cyprian, who, they allege, regard each individual Bishop as the sole centre of unity to his flock, to whom they are to look up as their guide and counsellor, as absolutely and unreservedly as a flock of sheep regard their particular shepherd.

The Anglican idea, then, as founded upon the alleged opinion of these two Fathers, is, that the ecclesiastical system consists of an innumerable number of fixed centres, round which revolve obediently their respective satellites, which, according to their measure, illuminate the darkness of that particular sphere within their domain.

In the course of my work it will be shown that while this theory, as far as it goes, has the support of S. Ignatius and S. Cyprian, and, I might add, of every Catholic; yet it by no means exhausts the whole of their teaching on this point. When S. Ignatius described one particular Church, in contrast to all others, as emphatically the Presiding Church, " presiding over the Love with the Name of Christ, with the Name of the Father," he taught, implicitly at least, that however independent a Bishop might be within his diocese (to use modern nomenclature), he was yet subject to an authority higher than himself; for if one particular See possesses the Presidency, it follows as a consequence self evident, that all other kindred bodies must be under its jurisdiction. And so with respect to S. Cyprian, that while he held extremely high views respecting the dignity and supreme authority of the Bishop within his diocese, he nevertheless, with S. Ignatius, regarded one particular " Place " as pre-eminent, wherein was established what he described as the "Principal or Chief Church, whence the unity of the Priesthood took its rise."

It is here where the Anglican theory fails; it conceives that every orthodox Bishop, no matter how isolated he may be, is one of many episcopal centres, which, together with all his brethren, whether visibly united in inter-communion or not, form, in the aggregate, the one Body of Christ. But this, as will be demonstrated, is not the doctrine of the Fathers generally, or of these two in particular.

What they one and all held was, that while there were indeed many separate centres in the firmament of the Church, yet were these themselves under the control of centres of greater magnitude, and all under the authority of a common Centre. The Episcopal systems, as it seems to me, as taught by the Bible and Antiquity, may be described as composed of circles within circles, the whole under the supreme authority of one cardinal centre, which by its own centripetal force maintains the cohesion and the equilibrium of the whole ecclesiastical system. The Hierarchical system of the Church, as old certainly as the Ante-Nicene age, fully supports this opinion, for we have episcopal systems within systems, till they reach the highest authority. The first are the Priests, under whose care are the deacons, and those in minor orders, and also the people : the second is the Bishop, to whom all these are subject : the third is the Metropolitan, who governs canonically the Bishops, the Clergy, and the people of his province; then fourthly, in some parts of the world, the Patriarch, who possesses canonical authority over the Metropolitans and Bishops constituting his Patriarchate ; and lastly, that Prelate, who occupies the " Place," which S. Cyprian asserted was " the Place of Peter;" and who is the Bishop of that Church, which S. Ignatius described as the Presiding Church, S. Irenæus as the "more powerful Principality," and S. Cyprian as " the Chief or Principal Church."

The Anglican theory, then, that each individual Bishop, no matter how orthodox he may be in Faith, is an independent centre ; and that it is not of so vital a consequence as to affect life, whether he is or is not united in communion with the Church generally; utterly breaks down : for such a theory is in direct opposition to the hierarchical system, which has been in full operation from the very earliest period of ecclesiastical history.

1. But it is impossible that the three antagonistic Churches, the Roman, the Greek, and the Anglican, can together form the one Body—the Church—which Christ instituted, for such a notion is contrary to the description of that Church as given in Holy Writ. For the first essential mark or characteristic is unity—unity in organism, unity in faith and doctrine, unity in communion. Can it be truthfully asserted that the three Churches agree in matters of faith? In answer to this it will be sufficient to refer you to the Article xix of the Church of England, in which she says, " As the Church of Jerusalem, Alexandria, and Antioch, have erred ; so also the Church of Rome hath erred, not only in their living and manner of ceremonies, but also in matters of Faith ;" and in her xxiind, " The Romish doctrine concerning Purgatory, Pardons, Worshipping and Adoration, as well of Images as of Reliques, and also invocation of Saints, is a fond thing vainly invented, and grounded upon no warranty of Scripture, but rather repugnant to the Word of God ;" and again in the Article xxxi. she adds, " Wherefore the sacrifices of Masses, in the which it was commonly said, that the Priest did offer Christ for the quick and the dead, to have remission of pain òr guilt, were blasphemous fables, and dangerous deceits." By these three Articles the Church of England solemnly rejects both the Roman and the Oriental Churches as guilty of error, and she accuses the Roman Communion especially of inno-

d

vating in doctrine and practice, and of performing certain solemn functions, which she asserts to be "blasphemous fables and dangerous deceits." Where, then, is the essential unity which Anglicans say exists between the separated communions of the one Body the Church? But what do we understand by essential unity? Is it outward communion? This has been long suspended. Is it in holding the same Faith and Doctrine? No such unity exists between the Church of England and the Roman and Greek Churches. Is it in sacraments, and especially in the Blessed Sacrament of the Altar, all eating the same Bread, and drinking of the same Cup? To this I answer that the Church of England accuses the Roman Communion of heresy in doctrine, in innovation as regards the Cup, and of blasphemy in that she pretends to offer the Blessed Sacrifice of the Altar for "the quick and the dead," "for the remission of pain or guilt." There is no essential unity whatever, either external or internal, either in Faith or Sacraments, subsisting between the Anglican and the Roman, and, I will add, the Greek Church. It follows, then, that the three Churches cannot together form that Body which Holy Scripture describes as one.

2. Not only is the Church one, but she is so one, that she is indivisible and indefectible; that is, she cannot possibly be divided, or overcome by heresies. Now the three Churches are notoriously divided; and not only divided, but each one is antagonistic to the other; each declaring the other to be in error and schism. This state of things alone disposes of this triple unity.

3. How about infallibility? Do the three Churches form that infallible Body which Christ created? Does the Holy Ghost, which Christ promised should abide personally as His Substitute, for ever with His Church, dwell in all three communions, teaching one dogma at Rome, another at Constantinople, and yet another at Canterbury; denouncing from the Chair of S. Augustine the heresies that proceed by His inspiration from the Chair of S. Peter, and proclaiming from the ecclesiastical throne of Byzantium that the dogma of the Double Procession which He had taught in the West is contrary to the Truth? And yet if the three Churches, the Roman, Greek, and Anglican, be together the one Church of Christ, the Holy Ghost must abide equally in every part, so governing the minds of their several hierarchies, that all should speak the same thing, and all be joined together in the same judgment. This contrariety of utterance at once disposes of this theory, for it is impossible, if the blessed Paraclete be God, that He can be dwelling in antagonistic Churches, and be the author of all their solemn diverse decrees regarding Faith and Doctrine. We may now, I think, dismiss as utterly

untenable the notion that the Roman, Greek, and Anglican Churches, together, notwithstanding their separation, can form that one Church which Christ established.

II. The other hypothesis is much more reasonable and more probably true, viz., that one only of these three communions, — the Roman, the Greek, or the Anglican — is that one, indivisible, and indefectible Body which Christ instituted, and which is infallible in its judgments, universal in its dominion, and Apostolic in its doctrine. Let us bring each of these to the test.

1. We will begin with the Anglican Church, because she has so far spoken with solemn authority, decreeing *ex cathedrâ*, as far as she could, that both the Oriental and Western Churches are in error, the Catholic especially, "not only in their living and manner of ceremonies, but also in matters of Faith." By rejecting the whole Church, except her own body, she has thus constituted herself as that "One, Holy, Catholic, and Apostolic Church," which she confesses as often as she recites the Creeds contained in her Book of Common Prayer. Let us then prove her claim by the Scriptural characteristics of the true Church.

Is she one, indivisible, and indefectible in her doctrine and discipline? Here let me premise that it is far from being my desire to say anything painful to your feelings, or to give expression to any sentiments that would be considered as wounding charity, but in a discourse of this kind it would be wrong in me to keep back any portion of what I believe to be the truth, and necessary for the elucidation of the subject now under treatment. ·

With respect then to this point, can it be said with any seriousness that the Church of England enjoys any unity of opinion concerning vital points of Faith and Doctrine? What does she teach, for instance, about the Sacraments, especially of Baptism and the Holy Eucharist? It is well known that ever since the Reformation there have been two or more antagonistic schools of opinion on the doctrine of Baptismal Regeneration, the Real Presence in the Eucharist, and the Sacrifice of the Altar: the one school being founded mainly upon the doctrine of the Prayer Book, the other upon the Articles. In the Book of Common Prayer, Baptismal Regeneration is unquestionably taught; but after examining "Articles of Religion," xxv and xxvii., we see that if they do not directly contradict the Prayer Book, they, at least, so dilute it, that it is impossible to say what is the dogmatic doctrine on this point.

The difficulty of determining what the Church of England really holds respecting Baptism, was, without doubt, felt by the Judicial Committee of the Privy Council in the famous Gorham case. Had the doctrine of Baptismal Regeneration been as dogmatically defined as the dogma respecting the Holy Trinity, the Incarnation of Christ, and the Procession of the Holy Ghost from the Father and the Son, it is impossible not to believe that the Judgment of the Court of Final Appeal would have been very different from what it was. That this doctrine was evidently felt to be, more or less, an open question, is evident from the fact, that notwithstanding that the Convocation of Canterbury has been revived for more than twenty years, the English Bishops and Clergy have never deemed it necessary either to protest synodically against the Gorham judgments, or to pronounce judicially the true doctrine of this part of the Catholic Faith. Upon the question, then, of Baptismal Regeneration, it is evident that the Church of England is, at least, not in earnest in maintaining it, in that she allows a difference of opinion to be taught her children, not certainly to their souls' health. And this indifference, which has always existed, has led to a depreciation of the other Sacraments, and to the expurgation from her sacramental system of the Unction of the Sick, which was enjoined by Apostolic ordinance no less than Confirmation, &c.

Indeed her pronouncement with respect to what some describe as the minor sacraments, shows this very strongly. " Those five commonly called Sacraments, that is to say, Confirmation, Penance, Orders, Matrimony, and Extreme Unction, are not to be counted for Sacraments of the Gospel, being such as have grown partly of the corrupt following of the Apostles, partly are states of life allowed in the Scriptures."—*Art.* xxv. From this then we learn that the Sacraments of Confirmation, Penance, and Extreme Unction (for these are not states of life) are not Sacraments of the Gospel, but a " corrupt following of the Apostles," the other two being of course " states of life allowed in the Scriptures." Hence for many years Confirmation, though prescribed, notwithstanding its being "a corrupt following of the Apostles," in the Prayer Book, was very seldom if ever administered; and Penance, for the administration of which a very beautiful form of Absolution is provided, far stronger in terms than is customarily used in the Roman Church, fell into universal desuetude till very recently ; and, as I observed above, Unction of the Sick has been entirely abolished as utterly useless, notwithstanding that S. James the Apostle in his inspired Epistle commands its observance.

Here we have a contrariety of opinion respecting the value of three Sacraments, which, if not of the Gospel, are at least of the Apostles ; and this, after all, is much the same thing. The Article condemns them as a " corrupt following of the Apostles," and the Prayer Book provides for the ministration of two of them. Respecting, then, Holy Baptism,

Confirmation, and Penance, the Church of England has no very decided opinion, and she consequently allows her ministers and people to hold and teach what they please.

But by far the most serious defection of unity is the Anglican teaching respecting the Blessed Sacrament of the Eucharist. Since the days of Queen Elizabeth there have existed three streams of tradition, wholly diverse, concerning the Presence of our Lord and the Sacrifice. One party asserting the Real Presence absolutely under the form of Bread and Wine, and the oblation to the Father of the Body and Blood of Christ, under these signs, for the remission of sins : another party, that the Presence is not real and objective, but only spiritual and subjective, manifested alone to the worthy receiver; and that the sacrifice is merely commemorative of what occurred more than eighteen centuries ago on Calvary. A third party denies any Real Presence at all — objective or subjective — the opinion being that we merely eat and drink the sacramental elements in remembrance of Christ; at most they only admit a Presence by virtue and effect, which, in point of fact, is no Presence at all.

Now these three sets of opinions respecting one of the most vital doctrines of Christianity, are allowed *advisedly* to be held and taught by the clergy of the Anglican Church; that is to say, it is allowable to teach that Christ—God and Man—is present under the form of Bread and Wine, in the Eucharist, and, at the same time, and even in the same church, that He is not present at all : and that He is offered by the priest to the Father for the remission of sins; and again, that no sacrifice at all is offered in the Blessed Sacrament. In plain words, it is advisedly allowable for the ministry of the Anglican Church to teach the doctrines both of the Real Presence and of the Real Absence ; of the Sacrifice of the Altar, and of no such Sacrifice.

Surely it must be of tremendous importance to any Christian to know whether Christ is or is not really, truly, and substantially, present in the Sacrament; and for this reason, if for no other, that if He be really present, to decline to bend the knee in adoring worship is an act of rebellion and contempt of His Majesty ; and if He be not present, to adore the elements is idolatry. Conceive and realise the spectacle which is common in every English church in this land, of one portion of the congregation adoring a present God, as they believe ; and another, equally devout in their way, refusing adoration on the ground of His not being really present. In all sincerity, I ask you, Can you imagine a more horrible state of things? For many years I have contemplated in my own mind this hideous spiritual phenomenon with horror and amazement, wondering how any Church could possibly permit such an insult to our Lord (as it always appeared to me, and does so still) to continue.

But is this diversity and contrariety of doctrine accidental or of purpose? Had it been accidental, the late Pan-Anglican Council would not have lost the opportunity of denouncing it, and of defining, with some precision, what the faithful ought to believe. It is, however, not accidental, but of set purpose. It is the boast of Anglicans that their faith is comprehensive, that it includes within the pale of the Church of God (what are called) all shades of orthodox opinion, to the admittance even of diverse and contrary views on some of the fundamental verities of our holy religion.

The present Bishop of Ely elaborately explained this, in a speech he delivered in Convocation in 1868, which met with the evident approval of all the assembled prelates, of whom not less than sixteen were present.

" . . . . To come to the question concerning doctrine, I most certainly agree with the words of the Bishop of Oxford yesterday, that it is most undesirable to limit the comprehensive character of the Church of England,—that in all times since the Reformation people have been allowed to hold extreme doctrines on the one side and on the other, and I hope most earnestly that the time will never come when members of the Church of England will not be allowed to hold extreme doctrines on the one side and on the other. I think I may venture to explain that. If a clergyman in my diocese were to write to me and say, 'There is a layman in my parish who holds the doctrine of Transubstantiation, the doctrine of the Immaculate Conception, and has even a tendency to worship the Blessed Virgin; can I admit him to Communion?' my answer would be, 'You certainly can. He has not rejected the doctrines of the Creeds. He is a Christian; though he may be a mistaken Christian. He has not renounced the communion of the Church, and it is not in your power to excommunicate him.'"

Thus is the Roman "extreme" permitted to lay-communicants of the Church of England; but what is the other "extreme?" It is the rejection, *in toto*, as damnable heresies, of these doctrines which may be held without censure by the supposed Romanising Churchman in the diocese of Ely. This is what is called "comprehensive" doctrine, which consists in members of the same body being permitted to hold, as *De Fide*, directly contrary opinions on most vital points of faith. But further. The Bishop of Ely later on in his speech, says, " . . . . It has been said that the Immaculate Conception is an open doctrine in the Church of England. Now, as a

Bishop of the Church of England, I am prepared to say that the Immaculate Conception is a distinct heresy against the Incarnation and Mediation of our blessed Lord." (*Chron. Convocat. Sess. Feb.* 19, 1868, *pp.* 1128, 1131. Rivingtons). So that it is permissible for a lay-communicant to believe, as very truth, a doctrine which the Bishop, and the other Bishops who heard him and did not object, solemnly averred to be a "distinct heresy against the Incarnation and Mediation of Christ."* This is, indeed, "comprehensiveness" run mad; and yet, if we are to interpret the Bishop's language literally, he would wish that the time should never arrive "when members of the Church of England should not be allowed to hold extreme doctrines on the one side and the other," inclusive of one which he solemnly, "as a Bishop of the Church of England," pronounces to be "a distinct heresy against the Incarnation and Mediation of Christ." Now this "comprehensiveness" is fatal to any Church accepting such a principle as the foundation for the truth which she teaches. Christ sent the Church into the world to *teach*, not to speculate ; to enforce obedience, not to allow men to hold what opinions they please. The Church then which is "comprehensive" in her doctrine, permitting "extreme opinions" to be held "on the one side," and "on the other side," can be no real Church of Christ, in any sense of the term ; for the instant she admits this principle as fundamental, she, *ipso facto*, ceases to be a Church. "I would that thou wert cold or hot. So then, because thou art lukewarm, and neither cold nor hot, I will spue thee out of My mouth." (*Rev.* iii. 15, 16.)

The Church of England, then,—from the foregoing remarks, and notably from what has fallen from the Bishop of Ely, that speech bearing the character of a quasi-synodical utterance,—is a house divided against itself : it admits advisedly of contrary opinions, touching the most vital points of faith,—Baptismal Regeneration and no Baptismal Regeneration ; the Real Presence and the Real Absence ; the Sacrifice of the Altar and no Sacrifice ; the necessity of Confirmation, and the opinion that it "is a corrupt following of the Apostles ;" Transubstantiation, Invocation of Saints, and the Immaculate Con-

---

* It is only fair to say that the Bishop draws a distinction between an ordinary lay-communicant, and one who holds or may hold an ecclesiastical office. But I confess I do not perceive the distinction.—If it is lawful for a lay-communicant to hold "extreme opinions" on the one side or the other, I do not see why even the Dean of the Arches should not enjoy this belief. If extremes on both sides are lawful, all lay-communicants, be they judges, commissaries, or private individuals, have an equal right to entertain them. If unlawful, then they are unlawful to all classes.

ception ("a distinct heresy," according to the Bishop of Ely, "against the Incarnation and Mediation of Christ"), and, of course, the reverse of these doctrines. These are what are called the "extremes of the one side and of the other;" but between these two extremes there may be held many "shades of opinion," so that it is simply impossible for any one to say with certainty, what are the distinctive doctrines of the Church of England, inasmuch as Orthodoxy and Heterodoxy, Truth and Heresy, have a legitimate home in the Anglican communion. How, then, can the Anglican Church meet the Scriptural Test of the true Church of Christ? Is she one? No, she is diverse and contrary. Is she undivided? Yes, for the present, but at the compromise of Truth; but when the foundation on which she now stands shall be removed, then she will be split up into divers sects, or, what is more probable, her catholic-minded children will go elsewhere for shelter. Is she indefectible? Heresy and Latitudinarianism have possession of most of her high places, her formularies are contradictory, and her oral teaching is double and multiform. Is she infallible? It is simply impossible that the Holy Ghost can be the author of " extreme doctrines on the one side" and extreme doctrines "on the other." He is the Spirit of Truth, and can teach only the Truth. He cannot teach both Truth and Falsehood. Is she universal? Certainly not, for her aspirations are purely national; and she is not Apostolic in her doctrine, inasmuch as one half of her teaching never came from the Holy Apostles. You cannot then honestly say that the Church of England represents the Church of the Bible : for remember that Church possesses, by solemn promise, the Holy Ghost as her perpetual Paraclete, whose commission is to guide her into all Truth, bringing to her recollection all that Christ ever said to the Apostles : and a Church which advisedly admits " comprehensiveness " of doctrine, which is another word for misbelief if not total unbelief, cannot be, in any sense of the term, representative of that Church. It is, I contend, impossible, if the words of Christ are to be believed. The conclusion, then, with respect to the Anglican Communion, at which you cannot fail to arrive, after careful and unprejudiced consideration, is, that she fails under the searching tests supplied by Holy Scripture for the discernment of Churches.

2. The Greek Church fares but little better than the English communion.— She possesses no real unity, for she is split up into a variety of communions, known as Orthodox, Copt, Nestorian, &c., which have distinct and separate Hierarchies. She has long ceased, as just shown, to be *indivisible;* and she cannot claim indefectibility, seeing that almost all her sacred Thrones have been at divers

times defiled by fearful heresies, even to the denial of the Lord Jesus Christ. Even now she is heretical respecting the doctrine of the holy and undivided Trinity, in that she refuses to confess that the Eternal Spirit proceeds from the Father and the Son. Infallibility she, in consequence of these heresies, cannot claim; universality she has not, for she has never merged beyond her ancient dominion; and as for Apostolicity, though many of her great sees were founded by the Apostles, they have frequently departed from Apostolic teaching. The Eastern communion no less than the Church of England fails under the Scriptural Tests.

3. We have now to consider the claim of that great Church known as the Holy Roman, Catholic, and Apostolic Church; even that Communion which both Anglican and Greek have rejected on the ground of heresy.

Among all the Churches there is none so remarkable for her Unity as the Roman Catholic communion. So perfect is her Unity, that it is the marvel as well as the envy of the world. Her unity in organization is perfect: the whole of her vast Hierarchy is consistent in all and every part; and each rank and grade is thoroughly subordinate to that which is superior in the order of its constitution. Every Priest regards his Bishop as his spiritual Lord; every Bishop recognises his Metropolitan as his Chief; every Metropolitan his Patriarch (where there is such); and every Patriarch, together with all Archbishops, Metropolitans, Bishops, Pastors, Deacons, Subdeacons, and other ministers, and the whole body of the Faithful, is subject to the Pope, as the Successor of S. Peter in the See of Rome. Her unity, too, in Faith is faultless. In every part of the world, where she has subjects, she teaches the same faith, the same doctrine; she worships after the same form, and she enforces everywhere an uniformity of discipline. Transubstantiation, the Immaculate Conception, Purgatory, &c. &c., no less than the doctrines of the Holy and undivided Trinity, the Incarnation, the Atonement, &c., are taught with precision in every Cathedral, Minster, Church, and Chapel, in every part of the world; in the North and in the South, in the East and in the West; in the Old World and in the New; in the land we inhabit, and its antipodes. In all that concerns the Faith, there is no faltering in the utterances of her Bishops and Priests; her trumpet blows no uncertain sound; her blast is loud, full, and sonorous, and is heard in every region under the sun. The citadel of Truth, planted on the tops of the mountains, even upon the seven-hilled city, is as "a city set upon an hill," which is visible to all, and is by all the Faithful regarded as their sacred metropolis, from which truth and holiness derive their source. This marvellous unity is not a

mere accident, the result of favourable circumstances ; it is not an
unity of the day only, it is one which has been a most remarkable
feature in the Roman Catholic Church, (and by this term I mean the
whole Church in union with Rome), from the very beginning of
Christianity. During the primitive ages of bloody persecution under
the heathen Emperors, and subsequently under their Christian successors, both in the East and in the West ; during the dominancy
of Arianism and its kindred heresies ; during the glorious middle
ages, when Faith was in the ascendant ; during the time subsequent
to the ecclesiastical revolution in the sixteenth century ; in the present half-infidel age, this Holy Church has ever preserved her Divine Unity unsullied, teaching, through good report and evil report,
amid the crash of empires and the fall of particular Churches, " the
same thing," ever being " joined together in the same mind and in
the same judgment." Truly her Unity is marvellous, and well may
Churches and communions envy the Holy Roman Church her
glorious unity.   And she is as indefectible as she is one.   No
heresy has ever obtained possession of the Chair of S. Peter at
Rome.   Every one of the Apostolic Thrones of the Church, except
S. Peter's at Rome, has been defiled with deadly heresy.   The
Apostolic thrones of Alexandria, Antioch, Jerusalem, and the episcopal throne of Constantinople, have all, in their day, denied the
saving truths of the Gospel, at one time denying the Divinity of the
Lord Jesus Christ, and at another the integrity of His human
nature, and even to this day, as above said, refusing to confess
the Procession of the Holy Ghost from the eternal Son ; thus
showing how the influence of Arianism still has possession of these
ancient Apostolic Thrones.   And in like manner in the extreme West
of Europe, the venerable throne of S. Augustine of Canterbury has
long yielded to the alluring pleasure of profane speculation ; for her
Prelates (let us admit for the sake of argument that they are Bishops)
have by turns held every heretical opinion, short of denying the Lord
Jesus Christ.   But no heresy has ever obtained possession, even for a
moment, of the Throne of S. Peter at Rome.   Not a single Pope has
ever been a heretic.   Several Popes may have erred through fear, as
Liberius, or may have for the moment been deceived by the subtle lucu-
brations of heretics (for in craft and subtlety heretics are peculiarly
fertile) ; and some may have delivered erroneous judgments on matters
of discipline ; but not a single Pope, from S. Peter till the present day,
has ever, when pronouncing *ex cathedrâ*, and in the full enjoyment
of his individual liberty, and when fully informed of all the circumstances of any particular case or cause submitted to his judgment,
erred in any matters involving the doctrine of Faith.   The Church

of Rome has never faltered in her Faith, as the Oriental and
Anglican Churches have done, on any one point of the Catholic
Faith. The whole doctrine of the Holy Trinity, the Incarnation, the
Divine and Human Natures of our Lord in one Person, and the
Atonement, have ever been fully taught and enforced in that Church.
S. Athanasius the Great, in the midst of his persecutions, found a
home in the Roman Church; S. Celestine, by S. Cyril, whom he
appointed as his Vicar for the purpose, deposed Nestorius, and
affirmed the doctrine of the hypostatic union, and S. Leo the Great
condemned the Eutychian heresy. And equally, in modern times,
we find the Roman Church true and orthodox respecting the Faith
of Christ. As in ancient times the Oriental communions erred respecting the doctrine of the Incarnation; so in modern times, in the
Western parts, we observe how grievous error has arisen concerning
the Sacramental System, which is the extension of the Incarnation.
As the East formerly denied Christ as God and man, so in these
latter days certain Western Churches repudiate Him in His Sacraments. The Roman Church, instead of yielding to misbelief and error,
loudly proclaimed the reality of our Lord's Presence in the Eucharist;
and as she, with the Fathers of old, pronounced that the Son of
God was consubstantial with the Father, when men denied His
Godhead, so has she, in these latter days, affirmed the dogma of
Transubstantiation, to exclude from her communion all who should
presume to assert that the words " This is My Body," " This is My
Blood," are not to be taken according to their literal signification.
And in the same manner as regards the Immaculate Conception; in
the early ages the East denied, implicitly at least, and by consequence, that Blessed Mary was the Mother of God, and in these
modern times, in the West, men have endeavoured to depreciate her
character, to lower her dignity in the scale of creation, reducing her
to a mere instrument for bringing forth the Lord of Glory, and even
to deny her Virginity before and after the Incarnation: hence it
was that the Holy Roman Church, with the vast majority of her
Bishops, with the Pope at their head, with characteristic instinct, proclaimed the dogma of the Immaculate Conception. Well, but you
will say, these are new dogmas. Doubtless the dogmas may be new,
but the doctrines they teach are as old as the Apostles. They are
not newer in principle than the dogma of Consubstantiality which has
been received by all Christians. If it is unlawful to promulge any
new dogma now, it was equally wrong for the Church of the fourth
century to pronounce the decree of the Consubstantiality of the
Eternal Son. You will probably add that the Consubstantiality of
the Son was at least a Scriptural doctrine; I would reply, that

Transubstantiation possesses an equal Scriptural basis. The words,
"This is My Body," "This is My Blood," involve this dogma, just
as much, if not more so, as "the Word was God," justified the term
Consubstantial in respect to our Lord's Divine Nature. So also in
the dogma of the Immaculate Conception, there are direct and
indirect Scriptural proofs for it. The Angelic salutation involves it;
and it is manifest that there are only two persons mentioned in Holy
Writ as "Full of Grace," the one was our Lord Jesus Christ
(*S. John*, i. 14), and the other was His own Divine Mother, the
Blessed Virgin Mary. No other persons are described as being
"Full of Grace," and this expression involves absolute perfection
from the very beginning of existence. Indeed Dr. Pusey, in his
recent work, almost admits this doctrine, for he says, "For no óne
who thinks can well doubt that as much (if not more) was vouchsafed
to the Mother of his Redeemer, as was granted to Jeremiah or
S. John the Baptist. Since, then, they were, according to Holy
Scripture, sanctified in their mother's womb, it is intrinsically probable that so was the Blessed Virgin, because she had a nearness to
our Lord, such as no other created being could have. Although this
(as some of the older of these [Fathers] who maintain it say) is not
stated in Holy Scripture, it seems almost involved in the belief as to
Jeremiah and S. John the Baptist, which is so contained." (*Eirenicon*,
Pt. ii. *p.* 392.)

So you see how earnest and energetic the Roman Church has
ever been in defence of the Faith,—of the Incarnation, of the
Consubstantiality of the Eternal Son, of Transubstantiation in the
Eucharist, and of the Divine Motherhood of Blessed Mary. It is
impossible to show that, in any one point touching the Faith, the
Church of Rome has ever admitted heresy to be taught. Her
indefectibility, then, is as invulnerable as her Unity.

She is also indivisible : to this hour her communion has never been
divided into hostile sects. All who have held the Catholic Faith in
its fulness and integrity, have ever remained in visible communion
with the Holy See. The Orientals fell away through their heresies,
and notably through that heresy which to this time terribly sullies their
orthodoxy ; and, latterly, certain Westerns in England and Germany,
who have erred in many particulars: but the fall of Churches
does not divide Unity. S. Irenæus says, "that the Church, which is the
salt of the earth, has been left on the earth's confines, suffering what
is human ; and while entire members are often rent from it, still it
continues a statue of salt (in allusion to Lot's wife), that is, the ground
of faith, confirming and forwarding the sons to their Father."
(*Adv. Hæres. l.* iv. *c.* xxxi. *n.* 3. *p.* 269.) S. Cyprian says, "that the

Church is not *without*, nor can it be separate nor divided against itself, but that it preserves the unity of an inseparable and undivided house, the testimony of divine Scripture manifests." (*Ep.* lxxvi. *Ad Magnum*, *p.* 151.) And again, "The Spouse of Christ cannot become adulterous, she is undefiled and chaste. She owns but one home ; with spotless purity she guards the sanctity of one chamber ; she keeps us for God ; she appoints unto a Kingdom the sons that she has born. Whosoever, having separated from the Church is joined to an adulteress, is cut off from the promises of Christ. Neither shall he come unto the rewards of Christ, who leaves the Church of Christ. He is an alien, he is profane, he is an enemy. He can no longer have God for a Father who has not the Church for his mother. . . . . And does any one believe that this Unity, thus proceeding from the divine immutability and cohering in heavenly sacraments, can be rent asunder in the Church, and be split by the divorce of antagonist wills ? . . . Because Christ's people cannot be rent, His tunic, woven and conjoined throughout, was not divided by those to whom it fits." (*De Unitate, p.* 196.) Many testimonies can be added to show that the Church cannot be divided and rent asunder. Indeed one great Father affirms that heretics do not rend the Church, but they rend themselves. Now the Church of Rome, notwithstanding the loss of the Oriental and Anglican Communions, is not divided nor rent : they separated themselves from her, and so ceased to be in her communion, but she herself remains whole and entire as she was before. She is as indivisible as a tree which has lost some of its branches, and as a body which has suffered the amputation of a leg or an arm. This Church then possesses, to its full perfection, the characteristic of indivisibility.

She is, too, as infallible as she is one, indivisible, and indefectible : indeed the acquisition of these three characteristics necessarily proves that she is infallible ; for if she is, and always has been, one, indivisible, and indefectible, how can she be otherwise than infallible in her teaching ? A Church which has never faltered in her faith, which from the days of S. Peter has always taught the same truth respecting Christ and His Sacraments, and has never contradicted herself in any matter whatever of Faith, how can it be said that she is not infallible ? Her consistency in all ages in defence of Truth, the perfect unanimity which has always prevailed concerning any Article of the Catholic Creed, and the wonderful submission of the whole body of the Faithful to her decrees as soon as pronounced by the highest authority, show clearly enough that infallibility of teaching is a very strong characteristic of the Holy Roman Catholic Church. Certainly no other Church ever exhibited in such marked perfection these characteristics. The Oriental Churches and the Anglican Communions, as has been already shown, have not preserved their unity and indefectibility unsullied, and consequently the gift of infallibility cannot be with them. Indeed they do not claim it for themselves, which they certainly would if they were conscious they possessed it; but the Roman Church does claim it for herself, because she holds that the Catholic Church is composed of the Apostolic See, together with all the Bishops, Priests, and Faithful in communion with her. And this innate consciousness goes a long way to prove, coupled with the fact that she has ever preserved her unity and her indefectibility, that she verily and indeed does possess the gift of infallibility in all that concerns the Catholic Faith.

The universality of the Roman Church is, as all must admit, indisputable. Neither the Greek nor the Anglican Churches claim to exercise jurisdiction over the whole world. The Church of Rome claims universal jurisdiction in every country where there are baptized members of Christ, and she exhibits her universality by establishing everywhere her Hierarchy. Not only in Italy, but in all Western Europe, in the East, in Asia, in Africa, in America, in Australia, and in the Islands of the Sea, her Hierarchy and her Priesthood are to be found. She is the only one of the Churches which can say that she has for her dominion "all peoples, nations, and languages."

The Apostolicity of the Church of Rome has been virtually proved by the fact that she possesses all the former characteristics which Scripture supplies us for discerning the true Church. It is in vain for persons to deny that her constitution as a Church, her form of doctrine, her manner of worship, and her code of discipline, are not Apostolic. Her essential doctrine and worship, and her principles of discipline, have never undergone any change. The symbol of Faith may vary from time to time as the exigencies of the Church demand: when heresies arise, definitions drawn up with precision may become necessary in order to preserve that Faith whole and undefiled: canons of discipline may, from time to time, be altered to suit the requirements of different ages, and even the ceremonials of Churches may not always be the same; but the Truth is ever the same in all its full integrity. Dogmas may develop the Faith as once delivered to the Saints, but it continues what it ever has been, Apostolic. The Church of Rome has, as I have already said, never changed her faith; her doctrine at this day is identical in essence with that which was held in the age of the Apostles; so likewise of the Immaculate Conception of the Blessed Virgin, Transubstantiation, and the Consubstantiality of the Second Person of the Holy Trinity. Those who deny that the Church of Rome is Apostolical in her foundation and doctrine, endeavour to explain away the statements contained in Holy Writ, which contain the full germ of every Dogma the Church of Rome has ever promulged. If they can establish the non-existence of these germs of doctrine, then, of course, the super-structure must fall to the ground. They must get rid by fair argument of the words, "Thou art Peter," &c., "Hail, thou that art full of grace," "This is My Body," "This is My Blood," &c., &c., before they can prove that the Dogmas of Rome are not Apostolic in their foundation.

I think I have now demonstrated that of the three Churches,— the Anglican, the Greek, and the Roman,—the last named is the only one that can meet the Scripture tests of the true Church of Christ, with any success. The Anglican Church breaks down utterly when we apply the test of unity, indivisibility, and indefectibility; and hence she is neither infallible in her teaching, nor Apostolic in her foundation. Nor does she lay claim to be the Universal Church, which she is bound to do, if she persists in her rejection of the Roman and Greek Church on the ground of error. The Greek Church fails, too; for she has, over and over again, been guilty of most fearful heresies concerning the true nature of our Lord; and even now, as observed above, she is heretical touching the doctrine of the Holy and Undivided Trinity. The Roman Church alone, to the exclusion of all Churches out of her communion, is properly one, indivisible, and indefectible, for she has never for an instant admitted any heresy to defile her glorious Apostolic Throne; she has never failed in-fallibly to proclaim the whole Truth without reserve; she has ever aspired to be universal, claiming all the earth for her dominion; and she has never forfeited her title to be Apostolic in her Faith, her Doctrines, her Worship, and her Discipline.

What, then, is the conclusion which we are forced, by logical necessity, to accept? If all other Churches have failed to endure the Scripture tests of a true Church, and if the Roman Church can fearlessly submit with success to this tremendous ordeal, what other conclusion can we arrive at, than that she alone is the Church of Christ; that she alone is the Catholic Church; that she alone is the Tabernacle and Ark of the Holy Ghost, who rules and governs her, speaking through her constituted authorities, bringing to her recollection all that Christ ever revealed to His Apostles; Christ who is the centre of her marvellous unity, the fountain of her wonderful indivisibility, the maintainer of her extraordinary indefectibility, the true source of her ineffable infallibility, the Divine cause of her glorious universality of dominion, and the power by which she ever remains fixed upon her Apostolic foundation?

I repeat, then, that if we apply to all the Churches those characteristics of the true Church which Holy Scripture describes, the Holy
Roman Catholic communion is the only one that can with any
success submit to the ordeal; and, therefore, I conclude that, according to the doctrine of Scripture, she alone, to the exclusion of
all others out of her pale, is that true Church of Christ, even that
One, Holy, Catholic and Apostolic Church, which was founded upon
S. Peter alone, and afterwards upon S. Peter and all the Apostles.

V.

ROME IS THE NORMAL CHURCH.

But why is it that the Holy Roman Church is the only Church that
is really one, indivisible, indefectible, infallible, universal, and Apostolic? It is because, as will be demonstrated more particularly in
the body of my Work, she is the Normal Church; and that by Divine
appointment.

This, I believe, was the subject of Prophecy; it was foretold that
a Stone, cut without hands from the mountain of Sion, would descend
upon Pagan Rome, and would destroy that Power, take possession of it, and from thence would grow into a Universal Spiritual
Empire, which should "never be destroyed," but which should
"stand for ever." That Stone was Christ, and, in a secondary sense,
His Vicar S. Peter, whom He surnamed Cephas, and created a
Rock, upon whom He founded His Church, delivering to him the keys
of jurisdiction and authority, commending to his care the Faith of
the Apostles, and entrusting to his guardianship the nourishment of
His sheep and lambs. This great Apostle came to the capital of the
world, and there, in conjunction with S. Paul, founded and constituted the Roman Church, wherein he erected his Cathedra, or
Chair, and thus made her the Presiding and Ruling Church. Thus
she became the Normal Church; the "Mother," "the Root," and
"the Matrix" of the Universal Church, as S. Cyprian said; the
source of Unity, as the same Father witnessed; the fountain of all
the rights of venerable communion, as S. Ambrose and the Council
of Aquileia declared; in which, as S. Augustine wrote, the Princedom of the Apostolical Chair has ever been in force. It is in consequence of this fact,— for, let people say what they will, it is a fact
as certainly ascertained as any other fact in history—that the Church
of Rome is pre-eminently the Catholic Church, and hence is she
the legitimate heir of all the royalties of Christ; the inheritor of all

the sacred promises of perpetual Unity, Indivisibility, and Indefectibility, and of the divine gift of her ever indwelling Paraclete. To this Church the dominion of the world has been conceded, for in the heart of her Empire is located the Presiding Chair of S. Peter, to which all Chairs are subject.

It is the object of the Work, to which this Epistle is introductory to prove what I have asserted. Whether I have made out my case, it is for you, so far as you are yourself concerned, to determine. What I ask of you is this,—that you will read what I have written with care and attention, and without prejudice ; for, remember, it is an article of faith in the Church to which you are attached, as well as in that to which I have now the happiness to belong, that out of the Catholic Church there is no salvation. It is for you, after having read the evidence which I have collected, to say, whether the Catholic Church consists of the three divided Churches (the gates of hell having so far prevailed to destroy the building Christ instituted), or of that one Church which Christ has founded upon the Rock Peter, against which He promised, upon His most sacred word, that " the gates of hell shall not prevail."

Your most affectionate ——,

COLIN LINDSAY.

e

ERRATA.

PAGE

25. Under "S. Firmilian," *for* 231 *read* 257.
30. In the "Comment," line 10, col. 1, *for* for *read* from.
38. Line 15, col. 1, *for* Choir *read* Chair.
107. Line 38, *before* be *insert* to.
126. In "Comment" on S. Chrysostom, line 1, col. 2, *for* the *read* that.
137. In "S. Cyprian," line 18, col. 2, and p. 141, in "Comment," lines 33, 36, 42, col. 2, *for* Apostolic *read* sacerdotal.
160. Line 29, col. 2, *for* Church *read* Rock.
172. Line 45, *for* Revelations *read* Revelation.
183. Line 8, col. 1, *for* canon *read* canons.
187. Line 16, col. 2, *after* required *insert* a semicolon.
Line 17, col. 2, *omit* the parentheses.
195. Line 14, col. 1, *for* Bishop *read* Bishops.
196. Line 43, col. 2, *between* the *and* blessed *insert* voice of the.
276. Line 1, *for* every Catholic is *read* all Catholics are.

FIRST INQUIRY.

I. WHETHER S. PETER WAS APPOINTED BY CHRIST TO BE HIS VICAR AND THE SUPREME GOVERNOR OF THE CHURCH.

PART I. HOLY SCRIPTURE.

I. THE PROPHECY.

(1.) Vision of Nebuchadnezzar.

"Thou, O king, sawest, and behold a great image. This great image, whose brightness was excellent, stood before thee ; and the form thereof was terrible.

"This image's head was of fine gold,

his breast and arms of silver,

his belly and his thighs of brass,

his legs of iron, his feet part of iron and part of clay.

(2.) Vision of Daniel.

"I saw in my vision by night, and, behold, the four winds of the heaven strove upon the great sea. And four great beasts came up from the sea, diverse one from another.

"The first was like a lion, and had eagle's wings : I beheld till the wings thereof were plucked, and it was lifted up from the earth, and made stand upon the feet as a man, and a man's heart was given to it.

"And behold another beast, a second, like to a bear, and it raised up itself on one side, and it had three ribs in the mouth of it between the teeth of it : and they said thus unto it, Arise, devour much flesh.

"After this I beheld, and lo another, like a leopard, which had upon the back of it four wings of a fowl ; the beast had also four heads ; and dominion was given to it.

"After this I saw in the night visions, and behold a fourth beast, dreadful and terrible, and strong exceedingly ; and it had great iron teeth : it devoured and brake in pieces, and stamped the residue with the feet of it : and it was diverse from all the beasts that were before it ; and it had ten horns . . . .

B

"Thou sawest till that a Stone was cut out without hands, which smote the image upon his feet that were of iron and clay, and brake them to pieces. Then was the iron, the clay, the brass, the silver, and the gold, broken to pieces together, and became like the chaff of the summer threshingfloors; and the wind carried them away, that no place was found for them : and the Stone that smote the image became a great mountain, and filled the whole earth." (*Dan.* ii. 31–35.)

* "I saw in the night visions, and, behold, one like the Son of Man came with the clouds of heaven, and came to the Ancient of days, and they brought Him near before Him. And there was given Him dominion, and glory, and a kingdom, that all people, nations, and languages, should serve Him : His dominion is an everlasting dominion, which shall not pass away, and His kingdom that which shall not be destroyed." (*Dan.* vii. 2–14.)

THE INTERPRETATION OF THE FIFTH EMPIRE, *i.e.*, THE CHURCH.

"And in the days of these kings shall the God of heaven set up a kingdom, which shall never be destroyed : and the kingdom shall not be left to other people, but it shall break in pieces and consume all these kingdoms, and it shall stand for ever. Forasmuch as thou sawest that the Stone was cut out of the mountain without hands, and that it brake in pieces the iron, the brass, the clay, the silver, and the gold; the great God hath made known to the king what shall come to pass hereafter : and the dream is certain, and the interpretation thereof sure." (*Ib.* 44, 45.)

"I saw in the night visions," as above.

OBSERVATIONS.

Historical facts prove demonstratively, that this prophecy has long ago begun to be fulfilled, (1.) From Nebuchadnezzar till the coming of Christ there have been, no more and no less, than four universal Empires, viz., Babylon; Medo-Persia, which conquered Babylon; Macedonia, under

---

* I have omitted verses 8–12, as the prophecy therein contained refers to the last age of the world, and to the Second Advent. Compare this with Rev. i. 13–15, and with verse 7, which states the period when the Apocalyptic prophecy will begin to be fulfilled. The fact of the erection of the kingdom of God, by our Lord (see S. Luke, xxii. 29), proves that Daniel's prophecy of the "Stone," and of the everlasting Empire of Christ, has been fulfilled, and is still fulfilling.

Alexander the Great; and the Roman Empire.* (2.) At the time of Christ's appearance on earth, the Empire of Rome consisted of the dominions of the above-mentioned kingdoms, and, in addition, of Western Europe, *i.e.* the image in its full stature and development of power, glory, and excellence. (3.) When the Stone, *i.e.*, the Son of Man, smote the capital of Rome (the legs and feet of the image) this colossal Empire first tottered, declined, and then was absolutely annihilated ; the four kingdoms as comprised under the Empire, "the wind carried away, that no place was found for them." (4.) It is a fact that the Roman Empire, as a polity, no longer exists in any form, and its metropolis has for ages ceased to be the capital of any civil state. The Stone, which smote the great Roman Head, remained where it fell, and it has grown into a great Mountain, and filled the whole earth ; *i.e.*, it has become a great universal spiritual Empire, the centre of which is ecclesiastical Rome. S. Cyprian, in allusion to certain persons taking letters to Rome, says, they dared to carry them "to the chair of Peter, and to the principal Church, whence the unity of the priesthood took its rise." (*Ep.* lix. *ad Cornel.* Libr. Fathers, *pp.* 164, 165.)

The prophecy, however, points to further events connected with the last phase of this world's history which it is necessary to notice. The Apocalypse informs us that the beast, out of whose head will arise the ten horns, and among them the little horn (*i.e.*, the Man of Sin and Antichrist), will be an empire composed of the symbolic leopard, the bear, and the lion ; *i.e.*, as I apprehend, the Macedonian Empire, with its former Asiatic conquests of Babylon and Medo-Persia. Rome and the West are apparently excluded from this prophecy; and the reason of this seems to be, that Rome is consecrated to be the capital of Christendom, for it is *there* where the Stone smote the Fourth Empire and reduced it to ruin, and from *thence* it grew into a great Mountain, filling the whole earth. And it was further predicted that the dominion of Christ, as symbolized by this Stone, would be "an everlasting dominion, which shall not pass away," and a kingdom "which shall not be destroyed." Rome, then, the seat of the Empire of Christ, will remain, notwithstanding, possibly, many temporary vicissitudes, the property of the Church, until "the times of the Gentiles be fulfilled."

2. THE STONE CUT WITHOUT HANDS.

(I.) THE STONE IS CHRIST.

"Jesus saith unto them, Did ye never read in the Scriptures, The Stone which the builders rejected, the same is become the Head of the corner : this is the Lord's doing, and it is marvellous in our eyes? Therefore say I unto you, The kingdom of God shall be taken from you, and given to a nation bringing forth the fruits thereof. And whosoever shall fall on this

* See S. Jerome *in Dan. T.* iii. *pp.* 1081-1082 ; also S. Chrysost. *in Dan. T.* vi. *p.* 212, &c.; also Dr. Pusey's *Daniel, pp.* 60-67.

Stone shall be broken : but on whomsoever It shall fall, It will grind him to powder." (*S. Matt.* xxi. 42–44 ; see *Acts*, iv. 11 ; 1 *Pet.* ii. 4–8.)

"And are built upon the foundation of the Apostles and Prophets, Jesus Christ Himself being the Chief Corner Stone." (*Eph.* ii. 20.)

(2.) THE ROCK IS CHRIST.

"And that Rock was Christ." (1 *Cor.* x. 4 ; see also *Deut.* xxxii. 15, 18, 30, 31 ; 2 *Sam.* xxii. 47 ; *Ps.* xviii. 2 ; xlii. 9, &c.)

(3.) THE STONE IS S. PETER.

"And He brought him (Peter) to Jesus. And when Jesus beheld him, He said, Thou art Simon the son of Jona : thou shalt be called Cephas, which is by interpretation, A stone" (Πέτρος). (*S. John*, i. 42.)

(4.) THE ROCK IS S. PETER.

" And I say also unto thee, That thou art Peter (a rock), and upon this (the) rock I will build My church ; and the gates of hell shall not prevail against it. And I will give unto thee the keys of the kingdom of heaven : and whatsoever thou shalt bind on earth shall be bound in heaven : and whatsoever thou shalt loose on earth shall be loosed in heaven." (*S. Matt.* xvi. 18, 19.)

(5.) THE JASPER STONE.

"And he carried me away in the spirit to a great and high mountain, and shewed me that great city, the holy Jerusalem, descending out of heaven from God, having the glory of God : and her light was like unto a Stone most precious, even like a jasper stone,* clear as crystal . . . And the wall of the city had Twelve Foundations, and in them the names of the Twelve Apostles of the Lamb . . . . And the building of the wall of it was of jasper : and the city was pure gold, like unto clear glass. And the foundations of the wall of the city were garnished with all manner of precious stones. The First Foundation was jasper; the Second, sapphire ; the Third, a chalcedony ; the Fourth, an emerald ; the Fifth, sardonyx ; the Sixth, sardius ; the Seventh, chrysolyte ; the Eighth, beryl ; the Ninth, a topaz ; the Tenth, a chrysoprasus ; the Eleventh, a jacinth ; the Twelfth, an amethyst." (*Rev.* xxi. 10–20.)

OBSERVATIONS.

1. The typical Stone that smote the head of the Roman Empire has evidently a double signification ; first, it represents the Son of Man, Jesus Christ—the Stone rejected by the builders ; and secondarily,

---

* "I was in the spirit : and, behold, a throne was set in heaven, and One sat on the throne. And He that sat was to look upon like a jasper and a sardine stone." (Rev. iv. 2, 3).

Simon Bar-Jona, who was called a Stone by Christ, and afterwards surnamed Peter, a rock. Thus did Christ name him after Himself the true Rock and the true Stone, pointing him out thereby as His Representative and Vicar ; the foundation of the Church, and the source of Unity.

2. The Stone which struck the image " became a great Mountain and filled the whole earth." S. John saw in a vision the great walled city which crowned the summit of this " great Mountain," doubtless in its ultimate glory and beauty, subsequent to the period of Antichrist. This he describes under the metaphor of precious stones. Of the Twelve Stones, one is pre-eminent and *predominant*, viz. the Jasper. This Stone is the symbol (1) of Christ The Stone ; (2) of S. Peter, also the Stone ; and (3) of the city wall, of which material it is *exclusively* built, none of the precious Stones, emblematic of the other Apostles, having any share whatever in its composition.

The Stone, then, that was cut out of the Mountain of Sion, without hands, was primarily our Lord, who sent His chief Apostle,—also called the Stone (who, like Himself, was symbolised by the Jasper), even S. Peter— to Rome, who there established the kingdom of God, which has since grown into a great Mountain, filling the whole earth.*

The Stone which the builders rejected fell on the legs of the image of Nebuchadnezzar, even Rome, and ground it to powder.

II. The Divine Commission.

1. Of the Apostles.

(1.) *As Priests.* " This do in remembrance of me." (S. Luke, xxii. 19.) (2.) *As Kings.* " I appoint unto you a Kingdom, as My Father hath appointed unto Me." (Ib. 29). (3.) *As Judges.* " Whosesoever sins ye remit, they are remitted unto them ; and whosesoever sins ye retain, they are retained." (S. John, xx. 23.) And (4.) *As Evangelists.* " Go ye into all the world, and preach the gospel to every creature," " teaching them to observe all things whatsoever I have commanded you : and lo ! I am with you alway, even to the end of the world. Amen." (*S. Mark*, xvi. 15 ; *S. Matt.* xxviii. 20.)

2. Of S. Peter.

" And I say unto thee, That thou art Peter, and upon this rock I will build my church : and the gates of hell shall not prevail against it. And

---

* The story of S. Peter meeting our Lord at the gate when leaving Rome to escape the persecution, throws some light on this mystery. S. Peter said to Christ, on His entering the gate, " Whither art Thou going?" To which He replied, " I am coming hither to be crucified again." He was crucified again at Rome in the person of his servant, S. Peter. The Stone that was rejected at Jerusalem was again to be rejected at Rome, in the person of him whom he had surnamed " the Stone." There is a great mystery in this Stone. See Milner's *Church History*, who credits this story. Vol. i. pp. 99, 100.

I will give unto thee the Keys of the kingdom of heaven : and whatsoever thou shalt bind on earth shall be bound in heaven : and whatsoever thou shalt loose on earth shall be loosed in heaven." (*S. Matt.* xvi. 18, 19.)

" And I appoint unto you a Kingdom, as My Father hath appointed unto Me : that ye may eat and drink at My table in My Kingdom, and sit on thrones judging the twelve tribes of Israel. And the Lord said, Simon, Simon, behold, Satan hath desired to have you, that he may sift you as wheat : but I have prayed for thee, that thy faith fail not : and when thou art converted, Strengthen* thy brethren." (*S. Luke,* xxii. 29-32.)

" Jesus saith to Simon Peter, Simon, son of Jonas, lovest thou Me more than these ? He saith to Him, Yea, Lord ; Thou knowest that I love Thee. He saith unto him, Feed my lambs. He saith unto him again the second time, Simon, son of Jonas, lovest thou Me ? He saith unto Him, Yea, Lord ; Thou knowest that I love Thee. He saith unto him, Feed my sheep. He saith unto him the third time, Simon, son of Jonas, lovest thou Me ? Peter was grieved because He said unto him the third time, Lovest thou Me ? And he said unto Him, Lord, Thou knowest all things ; Thou knowest that I love Thee. Jesus saith unto him, Feed my sheep."† (*S. John,* xxi. 15-17.)

---

* It is important to notice the real force of this word " Strengthen." The verb στηρίζω is almost always used in the New Testament in connection with the gifts of grace. " For I long to see you, that I may impart unto you some spiritual gift, to the end ye may be established," στηριχθῆναι (Rom. i. 11) : in the same manner as regards S. Timothy, who was sent to the Thessalonians to establish or confirm (στηρίξαι) their faith. (1 Thess. iii. 2.) It is used also for grace received direct from Christ, as in Rom. xvi. 25 ; 2 Thess. ii. 17 ; and iii. 3. The verb στηρίζω signifies to prop, to support, to make fixed or firm. The commission then given to S. Peter, as the Head of the viceroys of God's kingdom, was to perform the function of confirming, or fixing immovably the faith of his brethren, the Apostles ; imparting to them that gift or grace of Strength, which he (S. Peter), as the Rock appointed by God, received from Him (the true Rock) for that end. For which purpose Christ said to S. Peter, " I have prayed for thee, that thy faith fail not." By S. Peter's immovable faith he was to be the prop, support, and the sustainer of his brethren, the Apostles.

† Much stress is laid upon the circumstance that several of the Fathers say, that our Lord was merely testing S. Peter's fidelity ; for, as he had three times denied Him, so he was three times to confess his love and attachment to Him. But this does not in the least degree touch the question at issue. It has always been the custom of God to try His servants before calling them to any great work. Abraham was tried, and found faithful. Blessed Mary's faith was tried, and she believed. The Apostles were tried, when Christ said to them, " Whom say ye that I am ?" S. Peter alone answered, whom He had predestined to become the Rock, and to receive the Keys. And now our Lord, just before His departure, intending to complete His work of organizing the Church, and of appointing one in His place as Chief Shepherd, tried S. Peter's love ; and after each confession of his love, delivered to his special care the lambs and sheep of the Church.

3. THE STATER AND THE TWO SHIPS.

" And when they (Christ and His Apostles) were come to Capernaum, they that received tribute money came to Peter, and said, Doth not your Master pay tribute? He saith, Yes. And when he was come into the house, Jesus prevented him, saying, What thinkest thou, Simon? of whom do the kings of the earth take custom or tribute? of their own children, or of strangers? Peter saith unto Him, Of strangers. Jesus saith unto him, Then are the children free. Notwithstanding, lest We should offend them, go thou to the sea, and cast an hook, and take up the fish that first cometh up; and when thou hast opened his mouth, thou shalt find a piece of money (stater): that take, and give unto them for Me and thee."* (S. Matt. xvii. 24–27.)

"And it came to pass, that as the people pressed upon Him to hear the word of God, He stood by the lake of Gennesaret, and saw two ships standing by the lake : but the fishermen were gone out of them, and were washing their nets. And He entered into one of the ships, which was Simon's, and prayed him that he would thrust out a little from the land. And He sat down, and taught the people out of the ship. Now when He had left speaking, He said unto Simon, Launch out into the deep, and let down your nets for a draught. And Simon answering said unto Him, Master, we have toiled all the night, and have taken nothing: nevertheless at Thy word I will let down the net. And when they had this done, they inclosed a great multitude of fishes : and their net brake. And they beckoned unto their partners, which were in the other ship, that they'

---

* There are three points to be noticed here. (1) The tax-gatherers recognised S. Peter as our Lord's steward or agent, and they accost him, saying, " Doth not your Master pay tribute ?" (2) Our Lord directed S. Peter to extract a stater out of the fish's mouth ; and added (3) " That take and give unto them for Me and thee." Why "Me and thee," and not also the other Apostles, who were with Him? or if they did not lodge with Him, then the position of S. Peter is stronger in relation to our Lord, still more intimate, inasmuch as he of all the rest was selected to be nearest His Person. " Me and thee," then, identifies the two, the Master and the Chief Servant; the Householder and the Steward ; the Principal and His Delegate. Origen has some remarkable observations on this passage. "Jesus having assigned a reason for paying the tribute-money, sends Peter to draw out with the hook a fish, in the mouth of which He declares a stater would be found, to be given for Himself and Peter. It seems, therefore, to me, that they, considering this to be the greatest honour to Peter on the part of Jesus, as judging him greater than the rest of the disciples (κρίναντες αὐτὸν μείζονα τῶν λοιπῶν γνωρίμων), wished to ascertain clearly that which they fancied ; and they accordingly inquired, in order to learn from Jesus whether, as they suspected, He had separated Peter as greater than they ; and they at the same time, hoped to know the cause of Peter's having been preferred before the rest." (T. iii. Comment. in Matt. Tom. xiii. n. 14, pp. 588, 589.) Whether Origen's reasoning is sound may be a question, but the point in his comment, so far as our subject is concerned, appears to be this, viz., that it was believed that our Lord intended by this incident to show, how exalted was to be S. Peter' position in the household of God. Doubtless the " We," and " Me and thee" express relationship of the very closest and most intimate nature, implying that S. Peter held a position next to the very Person of his Lord.

should come and help them. And they came, and filled both the ships, so that they began to sink. When Simon Peter saw it, he fell down at Jesus' knees, saying, Depart from me; for I am a sinful man, O Lord. For he was astonished, and all that were with him, at the draught of the fishes which they had taken : and so was also James and John, the sons of Zebedee, which were partners with Simon. And Jesus said unto Simon, Fear not; from henceforth thou shalt catch men."* (S. Luke, v. 1–10).

III. S. Peter recognised as the Head of the Apostles.

1. On the Appointment of a New Apostle.

"And in those days Peter stood up in the midst of the disciples, and said, . . . Men and brethren, this scripture must needs have been fulfilled, which the Holy Ghost by the mouth of David spake before concerning Judas, which was guide to them that took Jesus. [Describing Judas' death, he continues] : Wherefore of these men which have companied with us all the time that the Lord Jesus went in and out among us, . . . must one be ordained to be a witness with us of His Resurrection. And they appointed two, Joseph called Barsabas, who was surnamed Justus, and Matthias. And they prayed and said, &c. . . . And they gave forth their lots; and the lot fell upon Matthias; and he was numbered with the eleven Apostles."† (Acts, i. 15–26.)

---

* Nothing could be more pointed or more marked than our Lord's preference for S. Peter. Let us consider each point in order :— (1) Christ entered "one of the ships, which was Simon's." (2) "He sat down and taught the people out of (this) ship." (3) When he had finished, he said, "Launch out into the deep, and let down your nets for a draught." (4) On a great multitude of fishes being taken, Simon summoned his partners to his help, and they came and filled both the ships, *i. e.* the second ship received of the overflow of S. Peter's. (5) S. Peter's astonishment was so great that he fell down and adored Christ ; and (6) our Lord said, "Fear not, from henceforth *thou* shalt catch men." It seems impossible to avoid the inevitable conclusion that our Lord, by this incident, was pointing out S. Peter as the Head and Chief of His Church, for He teaches out of his ship, *i.e.* the Church; and, without reference to the others, directs him to let down his net for a draught of fishes (*i. e.* of men), the others, S. James and S. John, assisting as his partners ; and He then informs S. Peter, in their presence, "Henceforth thou" (not ye, but thou, Peter,) "shalt catch men." S. Ambrose thus observes on this incident, " The ship is not agitated wherein prudence sails, where perfidy is not, where faith breathes. For how could that be agitated, over which he (Peter) presided, in whom is the foundation of the Church ? . . . Though the rest are ordered to let down their nets, yet to Peter alone it is said, *Launch out into the deep;* that is, into the depth of disputations. . . . Into this deep of disputation the Church is led by Peter, so as to see thence rising again the Son of God, thence flowing the Holy Spirit. . . . They of the synagogue came to Peter's ship, that is, unto the Church." (T. 1, *Expos. in Luc.* l. iv. n. 70, 71, 77, p. 1353, 4.)

† S. Peter here assumes, as a matter of right, the function of Chief Governor, and Chief Pastor of the Church. A vacancy occurs in the apostolic body, through

"Then after three years I went up to Jerusalem to see Peter,[*] and abode with him fifteen days. But other of the Apostles saw I none, save James the Lord's Brother." (Gal. i. 18, 19.)

2. ON THE DAY OF PENTECOST.

[After the outpouring of the Holy Ghost on the day of Pentecost, and the wonders occasioned by it, so much so as to induce the unbelieving Jews to say, "These men are full of new wine," S. Peter arose, and] "standing up with the eleven, lifted up his voice, and said unto them, Ye men of Judæa, and all ye that dwell at Jerusalem, be this known unto you, and hearken to my words," &c.[†] (See Acts, ii. 13, 40.)

3. THE APOSTLES BEFORE THE SANHEDRIM.

[On account of the many signs and wonders which were wrought by the Apostles, the high-priest and council were incensed, and having had them arraigned before them, said], "Did not we straitly command you that ye should not teach in this Name? and, behold, ye have filled Jerusalem with your doctrine, and intend to bring this Man's Blood upon us. Then Peter and the other Apostles answered and said, We ought to obey God rather than men," &c.[‡] &c. (See Acts, v. 28-32.)

the treason and death of Judas. He then, apparently without previous concert with his co-apostles, directs, not *suggests*, as some say, but directs, or rather *commands*, another to be ordained in his place; and he further states authoritatively, from what class of men a successor must be chosen, limiting thereby their choice; "wherefore of these men which have companied with us all the time that the Lord Jesus went in and out among us . . . must one be ordained," &c. From the above nothing can be clearer than the nature of that office S. Peter assumed on this occasion, namely, that of the Ruler, the Governor, and Chief Pastor of the Church. (See *S. Chrys. Comment. Extract*, No. 75. Part II.)

[*] Why does S. Paul mention this event, if there was no important reason for so doing? Did he recognise by this visit S. Peter's office as the Chief Shepherd, to whom he was under the necessity of showing respect, if nothing more? Else why did he see none of the other Apostles save S. James? And why did he see S. James? Surely because he was the Bishop of Jerusalem and "the Lord's Brother," to whom honour was due. S. Chrysostom believes that S. Paul's visit to S. Peter was in order to recognise his Headship. (See *Extract*, No. 73, Pt. II.)

[†] Here, again, S. Peter assumes the position of the Leader and the Mouthpiece of the Church. He speaks in behalf of the Church as her Representative, which he was, as S. Augustine says (see *Extract*, No. 86, Pt. II.), by reason of the *Principatus Apostolatus* (*i. e.* the Principate or Sovereignty of the Apostleship.) The other Apostles, standing up with him, recognise him as their Chief.

[‡] Here, again, S. Peter's pre-eminence is apparent, as at least the Leader of the Apostles; the First in order, having the right of first speech.

4. THE OPENING OF THE KINGDOM OF GOD TO THE GENTILES.

" Peter went up upon the housetop to pray about the sixth hour: and
he became very hungry, and would have eaten: but while they made
ready, he fell into a trance, [here follows the vision of the great sheet
let down from heaven] and there came a voice to him, Rise, Peter;
kill and eat.   But Peter said, Not so, Lord; for I have never eaten
any thing that is common or unclean.   And the voice spake unto him
again the second time, What God hath cleansed, that call not thou
common.   This was done thrice : and the vessel was received up again
into heaven. [The deputation arrived from Cornelius, S. Peter accompany-
ing them back to Cæsarea, and there received the account of the visit of
the angel to Cornelius, who said to him, " Send therefore to Joppa, and call
hither Simon, whose surname is Peter; . . . who, when he cometh, will
speak unto thee."]   " Then Peter opened his mouth, and said, Of a truth
I perceive that God is no respecter of persons : but in every nation he
that feareth Him, and worketh righteousness, is accepted with Him. . . .
While Peter yet spake these words the Holy Ghost fell on all them which
heard the word . . .   Then answered Peter, Can any man forbid water,
that these should not be baptized, which have received the Holy Ghost as
well as we?   And he commanded them to be baptized in the name of the
Lord." * (Acts, x.)

5. THE FIRST COUNCIL OF JERUSALEM.

[This council was assembled to determine whether the Gentiles should
be subject to the Jewish rite of circumcision.]   " And the Apostles and
elders came together for to consider of this matter.   And when there had
been much disputing, Peter rose up, and said unto them, Men and
brethren, ye know how that a good while ago God made choice among
us, that the Gentiles by my mouth should hear the word of the gospel,
and believe. . . .   Now therefore why tempt ye God, to put a yoke upon
the neck of the disciples, which neither our fathers nor we were able to
bear?   But we believe that through the grace of the Lord Jesus Christ we
shall be saved, even as they." [After this SS. Barnabas and Paul addressed the synod, " declaring what miracles and wonders God had
wrought among the Gentiles by them."]   " And after they had held their

* S. Peter had received the Keys of the kingdom of heaven, and, consequently, he alone could open heaven to the Gentiles.   Accordingly, Cornelius was
directed to send men to Joppa to invite S. Peter to visit him.   While they were
on their way, the Lord made known to S. Peter His will respecting the Gentiles,
and directed him to go down to Cæsarea, " doubting nothing."   S. Peter obeyed,
heard what Cornelius had to say, and after witnessing the miraculous descent of
the Holy Ghost upon the Gentiles, " commanded them to be baptized in the
name of the Lord."   This was the exercise of the Supreme use of the Keys, of
which he was the Custodian, and this too without any previous consultation with
his brother Apostles.   S. Peter acted here in his capacity as our Lord's Vicegerent, on whom He built His Church, and to whom He had intrusted the Keys of
the kingdom of heaven.   There is no passage in the New Testament which exhibits
S. Peter's supremacy in the Church more fully than this.

peace, James answered, saying, Men and brethren, hearken unto me : Simeon hath declared how God at the first did visit the Gentiles, to take out of them a people for His Name. And to this agree the words of the prophets. . . . Wherefore my sentence is, that we trouble not them, which from among the Gentiles are turned to God : but that we write unto them, that they abstain from pollutions of idols, and from fornication, and from things strangled, and from blood," &c.* (Acts, xv.)

* The proceedings of this Council have been held by some to prove the superior position of S. James as the President of the Council ; but it is very questionable whether the acts of this synod will support this view. In the first place, it is not said that S. James presided, nor does the text imply it ; then, secondly, S. James did not take the lead in the discussion. Let this point be carefully considered. First, there was much disputing, by whom is not stated ; but after awhile S. Peter arose, and in the language of authority addressed the assembled Apostles and elders. He, first of all, informs them of the revelation he had received from God on the subject ; and he then rebukes the party of the circumcision, saying, " Why tempt ye God to put a yoke upon the neck of the disciples ?" S. Paul and S. Barnabas do not seem to have spoken on the subject in dispute, contenting themselves with recounting the great miracles and wonders which had been wrought among the Gentiles. S. James closes the debate, and delivers his judgment; but how ? His judgment is based professedly upon that of S. Peter, "Simeon hath declared how God at the first did visit the Gentiles," and then he adduces the testimony of prophecy in support of what S. Peter had said, concluding, "Wherefore my sentence, or decree," &c· There is nothing in this account which witnesses against S. Peter ; on the contrary, what little is said confirms the position he is alleged to have held, for he *first* delivered judgment, and the cause was virtually concluded ; for all accepted his judgment as final. S. James did but echo what S. Peter said, and supported it by reference to the prophecies. (See *S. Chrys. Extract*, No. 77, Pt. II.) It is, however, maintained that the "Simeon," referred to by S. James, was not S. Peter, but the " Simeon " who circumcised our Lord, because, in his canticle, he prophesied saying, " Which thou hast prepared before the face of all the people ; a light to lighten the Gentiles, and the glory of thy people Israel " (S. Luke, ii. 31, 32). If it was not for the similarity of the name of "Simeon," it would never have occurred to any one to suppose, that S. James meant the aged priest under the law. It is alleged that S. Chrysostom fell into this mistake, but after carefully reading his Homily on this chapter, I venture to think that this is very doubtful. There are two considerations which will, it is submitted, dispose of this objection. First, S. James evidently refers to a person who had been speaking. Secondly, he recites "how God at the first did visit the Gentiles," *i.e.*, by Peter, whom He sent for the purpose of preaching the Gospel to them, and, as S. James adds, "to take out of them a people for His name." When our Lord was taken to be circumcised the Gentiles were not then visited, and this visitation, as a matter of fact, did not take place before the conversion of Cornelius and his house. These two considerations alone determine this point. But there is a third consideration which should not be overlooked, and that is, that S. Peter was sometimes called " Simeon." In his Second Epistle he thus commences, " Simeon (Συμεων) Peter, a servant and Apostle of Jesus Christ" (2 Pet. i. 1). Fair inference, as well as common sense, requires us to suppose that S. James alluded to S. Peter when he commenced his judgment.

IV. OBJECTIONS.

Several passages are adduced to prove the contrary position, that S.
Peter was not only not Supreme Head of the Apostles, but that he and
the eleven were of one order and dignity, co-equal and co-ordinate ; and
that consequently he had no greater authority than any other Apostle.

1. "Upon this rock I will build my Church."—It is held that all
the Apostles were rocks : this is true ; but one rock was pre-eminent and
predominant. The Church is built upon Twelve Foundations, but the
emblematic Stone of the First Foundation is identically the same as that
which symbolised our Lord,—the true Stone,—and also the wall of the city,
of which it is *exclusively* composed. Therefore, though all the rocks and
all the stones were equal, yet One was supreme; and besides S. Peter was
expressly called the Rock by Christ, when He gave Him this name (even
His own Name), which He did not bestow upon any other Apostle.

Again, it is said, The Church is built upon S. Peter's confession,—
not upon the *man* Peter,—very probably, and so some of the Fathers
teach ; but who made the confession ? Not the other Apostles,—for
when Christ asked *them,* "Whom say *ye* that I am ?" all were silent
save one, and that one, S. Peter, merited to be the chosen Foundation of
the Church. But it is alleged that Christ addressed all in S. Peter, and
that S. Peter answered for all. No doubt this is true ; but it is not the
less true that the other Apostles, who had eagerly answered the first question, "Whom do men say that I the Son of Man am ?" because they
knew what to answer, were silent when Christ said, "But whom say ye
that I am ?" Why were they thus silent ? If they had known what to
reply, they would have done so as eagerly as they had done before to the
previous question. But S. Peter alone answered. Why ? Because the great
doctrine he confessed was revealed to him *alone,*—not to the others : hence
he *alone* confesses, "Thou art the Christ the Son of the Living God." He
indeed confessed on behalf of the Church, which was *then* in him singly
and alone, for he was the type, the representative, the figure, and the person
of the Church, and this because, as S. Augustine says, he held the "Principate of the Apostleship." (See Extract, Part II. Nos. 83, 86.)

Once more. The Rock is Christ, say others ; true, for Christ is the
true Rock, and the true Foundation, nevertheless He created, in the
person of S. Peter, another Rock, which He Himself laid as the Foundation
on which to build his Church. These objections do not really touch the
point, for in the office of the Rock, our Lord and S. Peter are one, the
latter assuming a position of peculiar relationship to Christ, as His
especial Representative.

2. "I will give thee the keys."—These keys, it is alleged, were delivered
to all the apostles. No doubt they were, but there was much difference.
To S. Peter our Lord delivered the keys absolutely, without reserve, and
without any reference to the other Apostles. Afterwards he gave them
to the eleven, but not independently of S. Peter; so that while S. Peter
could use them without being under the necessity of consulting his brother-
Apostles, they, on the other hand, could not do so, except in concert with
him. This truth seems evident from the circumstance that after our Lord

had promised the keys to all, S. Peter came to Him and said, "Lord, how oft shall my brother sin against me, and I forgive him? till seven times? Jesus saith unto him, I say not unto thee, Until seven times : but, Until seventy times seven." (S. Matt. xviii. 21, 22.) S. Peter here, speaking in the first person, indicates that in the sentence to be pronounced upon erring brethren, he has a voice, not as a member merely of the Sacred College, but as the Head and Chief. Origen evidently thought that S. Peter held a superior jurisdiction. (See Extract, Pt. II. No. 9.)

3. The strife among the Apostles for pre-eminence, and our Lord's re-buke, is said to witness (1) against any pre-eminence whatever, and (2) from the very fact of such a dispute having arisen amongst them, it is evident that the Apostles were ignorant of our Lord's intention of constituting S. Peter as their Head. Now as regards the first point, our Lord's objection was against the notion of a *temporal* or *secular* empire : * this is plain from what follows ; for He immediately after formally constituted His spiritual Kingdom. Another object He had was to reprove them for their ambition and lust of power, which was wicked in such of them as had received no commission to be chief; and He concluded by enjoining humility, pointing to Himself as their model, who served them as a servant. It is next alleged that these disputes showed that the Apostles did not understand, that S. Peter was their elected Head, and therefore, it is concluded, there was no such Head appointed. But this argument is fallacious, for, first, our Lord had not yet fully commissioned S. Peter; He had indeed pointed him out as the Rock, and had promised him the Keys, but He did not commission him to "Strengthen the brethren," or to "Feed the sheep," until after this incident. Certainly after our Lord had finally constituted him Chief Pastor, we read no more of any disputes, who should be the greatest. S. Peter assumed the position Christ gave him, and the Apostles, as a matter of course, accepted it.

4. "Now when the Apostles which were at Jerusalem heard that Samaria had received the word of God, they sent unto them Peter and John." (Acts, viii. 14.) This, it is held, shows that S. Peter was subject to the College of the Apostles ; but this proves too much : for then the circumstance that the Church of Antioch "determined that Paul and Barnabas . . . . . . should go up to Jerusalem unto the Apostles and elders about" the question of circumcision, would prove the infe-riority of the great Apostle of the Gentiles to the local Church of Antioch (Acts, xv. 2.)

5. "Have we not power to lead about a sister, a wife, as well as other Apostles, and as the brethren of the Lord, and Cephas?" (1 Cor. ix. 5.) This, it is asserted, demonstrates the exact equality of all the Apostles; if so, why did S. Paul distinguish S. Peter from the "other Apostles?" No doubt in such trifling matters, having no concern with the faith, or government of the Church, S. Paul claimed to be equal to the Chief Apostle;

---

* That the Apostles believed that they were to be the rulers of *earthly* do-minion is evident from their asking our Lord after His resurrection, "Wilt thou at this time restore again the kingdom to Israel?" (Acts, i. 6.)

and he advances his claim by a regular ascending scale. He says he is equal in this respect, (1) to the "other Apostles," (2) to "the brethren of the Lord," and (3) highest of all, even to "Cephas," *i.e.* S. Peter. If any thing, this proves S. Peter's high position in the apostolic hierarchy. S. Chrysostom on this passage says, "Observe his (S. Paul's) skilfulness. The leader of the choir stands last in his arrangement : since that is the time for laying down the strongest of all one's topics. Nor was it so wonderful for one to be able to point out examples of this conduct in the rest, as in the foremost champion, and in him who was entrusted with the keys of heaven. But neither does he mention Peter alone, but all of them : as if he had said, Whether you seek the inferior sort, or the more eminent, in all you find patterns of this sort drawn out for you. For the brethren too of the Lord being freed from their first unbelief, had come to be among those who were approved, although they attained not to the Apostles. And accordingly the middle place is that which he hath assigned to them, setting down those who were in the extremes (*i.e.* the eleven,—the brethren,—S. Peter), before and after. (*Hom.* xxi. *in* 1 *Cor.* ix. 5, *see Lib. Fath.* pp. 280, 1.) It is evident, then, that, in S. Chrysostom's opinion, S. Paul regarded S. Peter as higher than the eleven, and in order to give full force to his claim to certain privileges, he maintains his equal rights (1) to the Apostles and (2), to the great Apostle S. Peter.

6. "But when Peter was come to Antioch, I withstood him to the face, because he was to be blamed." (Gal. ii. 11.) How dare S. Paul thus publicly rebuke his Chief and Head, say Protestants? But why not? The twelve Apostles, as we have remarked, were all of the same order and dignity, though one was recognised as their Chief; and there is nothing extraordinary, in one of the Apostles expostulating with him if he erred in conduct. Even in a State, it has been no uncommon thing for a minister to remonstrate with his Sovereign, and sometimes even publicly oppose him, if he despise the law, or trample upon the liberties of his subjects ; and such an act on a part of a subject towards his King does not by any means impair his imperial dignity and authority. S. Peter in this instance acted a timid part ; which S. Paul saw would be injurious to the Church, and he consequently "withstood him to the face." But this does not in the least disprove that S. Peter was the Chief of the Apostles. Indeed, in the previous chapter, S. Paul had pointed him out as *the* Apostle he went up to Jerusalem *purposely* to visit, and in this very chapter he acknowledged that the gospel of the circumcision irrespective, as it would seem, of the eleven had been committed to him.

The objections against S. Peter are, it is submitted, pointless. The great stress laid by Protestants is, that all the Apostles were equal in dignity and authority, but it does not seem to have occurred to them that equals have a Head over them. In all republics there is a Head, who performs the duties of the Executive ; in the United States, equals elect one of their own co-equal body, to be their Sovereign President for a term of years; the Swiss Confederation do the same ; Republican France, and England under the Commonwealth, acknowledged Napoleon and Cromwell as their respective Chiefs. In the case of the Church, Christ from among equals selected one to be the source of unity and jurisdiction, to be in His Stead the Rock of the Church, the Support of the Brethren, and the Chief Pastor of the Flock.

V. SUMMARY OF THE EVIDENCE.

Holy Scripture then seems to attest the following facts :—First, that four great empires were to arise one after the other, viz., the Babylonian, the Medo-Persian, the Macedonian, and the Roman. Secondly, that when the Empire arrived at the fulness of its power and glory, a Stone, cut out of the mountain of Sion, would smite it, and gradually destroy it ; and that this Stone would supplant it, take possession of the Kingdom, and itself grow into one great universal Empire, to which would be subject "all peoples, nations, and languages." Thirdly, that Christ and the Church are described under the metaphor of Stones : (1) Christ and the Apostles as precious stones, and the faithful as stones which form the "living stones" of the building. Fourthly, among the precious stones, symbolical of Christ and the Twelve, it has been shown that one was pre-eminent and *predominant*, viz., the jasper. This stone was emblematic (1) of Christ our Lord, (2) of S. Peter, and (3) of the material of the city wall. The other precious stones were foundations, nothing more; the Jasper Stone, *i. e.*, our Lord and His vicar S. Peter, typified the first Foundation and the very substance of the walls of the holy city. The prophecy, then, of Daniel, together with that of S. John, demonstrated the great fact that the Foundation and Source of that great Empire God intended to establish on the ruins of Rome were (1) the Lord Jesus Christ, and (2) His chief Apostle, S. Peter. Fifthly, that the various events and incidents recorded in the Gospel explain what was our Lord's will respecting S. Peter. It was shown that, when He first saw him, He said, " Thou art Simon the son of Jona : thou shalt be called Cephas, which is by interpretation, a Stone " (John, i. 42). Sixthly, that on this Apostle confessing His divinity, Christ did then solemnly change his name, saying, " Thou art Peter," a rock ; giving him His own name, by which He had been known from the very beginning of the Mosaic dispensation. By thus naming him the Rock He pointed out S. Peter as his Vicegerent, as the Foundation of the Church, and Source of all jurisdiction. " Thou art Peter, and upon this Rock I will build my Church ; and the gates of hell shall not prevail against it. And I will give unto thee the keys of the kingdom of heaven : and whatsoever thou shalt bind on earth shall be bound in heaven : and whatsoever thou shalt loose on earth shall be loosed in heaven" (S. Matt. xvi. 18, 19). Seventhly, no sooner had our Lord constituted His kingdom than He immediately pointed out S. Peter as its firm Supporter. " When thou are converted, strengthen [or confirm, or fix immoveably] thy brethren " (S. Luke, xxii. 29–32). This was the application of the office of the Rock—Peter, viz. to uphold, support, and sustain the faith of the Church. Eighthly, after our Lord's resurrection, and immediately before His ascension, it was proved that He delivered to S. Peter a most solemn charge, viz., to Feed the lambs and sheep of His Church. Here, again, is another application of the office of the Rock—Peter,—viz. that he was to be the all-powerful Protector of the flock, and the invincible Guardian of the Fold. The commission then granted to S. Peter *alone*, was to be a Rock to the Church, that is to say, the Chief Foundation of the Church, the Main Source of jurisdiction and unity, and the Universal Shepherd of the Lord's people ; in a word, to be the Chief Pastor of the Catholic Church,—an office which contains within itself every prerogative of government, jurisdiction, and priestly power.   Ninthly, after the Ascension S. Peter immediately assumed the exalted position to which Christ had appointed him ; He (1) directed the election of a new Apostle in the room of Judas Iscariot, settling the conditions of election ; (2) upon the day of Pentecost, standing up with the eleven, as the Mouthpiece of the Church and the Head of the Apostles, he addressed the multitude ; (3) as the Leader of the Apostles he addressed the high-priest, saying, "We ought to obey God rather than men" (Acts, v. 19) ; (4) S. Peter, as holding the keys of the kingdom of heaven, is commanded to open the kingdom to the Gentiles, and he admits them by his sole authority into the Church : and (5) at the Council of Jerusalem it was S. Peter who delivered the oracle of God respecting the obligation of circumcision on Gentile converts, the other Apostles with S. James accepting his judgment, the latter basing his own upon that of S. Peter.   Scripture, then, represents S. Peter as fulfilling a double office ; (1) as the Deputy of our Lord, with a commission to rule in His Stead, and (2) as the Representative of the Church, which he was, because he was first named an Apostle ; because the Church was first formed singly and alone in him ; and, thirdly, because he held the Principate of the Apostleship.   In this double capacity he performed the office of Head, Governor, Ruler, and Chief Pastor of the universal Empire-Church of Christ.   Tenthly, with regard to the arguments adduced against S. Peter's supremacy, it has been seen how groundless they are. It was proved that, notwithstanding that the Apostles were co-equal and co-ordinate, yet that that did not prevent them from having an executive Head.   Every nation, as it was observed, has a ruling Head ; every republic—a nation composed of equals—possesses a Sovereign Head. Why not the Apostolic Church ?   The constitution of the present universal episcopate explains how this may be.   The Church is divided into Patriachates, Provinces, and Dioceses ; all the bishops, without any exception, are co-equal and co-ordinate in the rule of the provincial Church, yet the Bishop of the diocese is subject to the supremacy of the Metropolitan ; and the Metropolitan to the Patriarch ; and the Patriarch,—is he subject to any one, and if so, to whom ?   The principle of this arrangement corresponds to the constitution of the Apostleship, *i.e.*, consisting of co-equal and co-ordinate Governors, subject to the one Head— S. Peter.   It is unquestionable that our Saviour marked out S. Peter as the Chief of the Apostles ; there is nothing in Scripture contradictory or inconsistent with this appointment, and it is certain that, whenever present, he was invariably the Leader and Governor ; and it is also certain that Christ made him the Rock, the Sustainer, and the Shepherd of His flock.

PART II.

I. CONSENSUS PATRUM.

[IN the study of the writings of the holy Fathers, it is important to remember that they assume a *previous* knowledge of the doctrine and discipline of the Church on the part of Christians to whom they were addressed. Without this previous knowledge much of the language of the Fathers would have been unintelligible. The procem to S. Ignatius' Epistle to the Romans would have sorely puzzled their Bishop and priests, if they had never heard till then, that the great Roman Church was the *presiding* Church, and that it was in some way distinct from other churches, being named " with the Name of Christ (and) with the Name of the Father."]

S. IGNATIUS.

A.D. 107.

1. "Ignatius . . . . to the Church . . . . which presides in the place of the Romans (ἥτις καὶ προκάθηται ἐν τόπῳ χωρίου 'Ρωμαίων), all-godly, all-gracious, all-blessed, all-praised, all-prospering, all-hallowed, and presiding over love, with the Name of Christ, with the Name of the Father (καὶ προκαθημένη τῆς ἀγάπης χριστωνύμος, πατρωνύμος), which (Church) I greet in the Name of Jesus Christ," &c. *Ep. ad Rom. Procem.*

2. " Entreat Christ for me, that by these instruments I may be found a sacrifice (to God). I do not, as Peter and Paul, issue commandments unto you. They were Apos-

tles of Jesus Christ, but I am the very least : they were free as the servants of God, while I am, even until now, a servant." *Ib. c.* iv.

3. "Let us therefore prove ourselves worthy of that Name which we have received. For whosoever is called by any other name besides this, he is not of God ; for he has not received the prophecy which speaks thus concerning us : *The people shall be called by a new name*, &c. (*Isa.*lxii. 2.) This was first fulfilled in Syria (Antioch), for *the disciples were called Christians at Antioch*, when Paul and Peter were laying the foundations of the Church." *Ep. ad Mag. c.* x.

COMMENT.

S. Ignatius was a disciple of S. John, and Bishop of Antioch. He was martyred in A.D. 108, *seven* years after the death of S. John the Apostle. The procem to the epistle to the Romans differs *essentially* from the procems to his other

C

epistles ; and the difference consists in this, that while S. Ignatius describes the Churches of the Ephesians, the Magnesians, the Trallians, the Philadelphians, the Smyrnæans, as "predestinated before the beginning of time ; " as "elected through the true Passion of Christ ; "—as "blessed in the grace of God ; "—as " possessing peace ; "— as "rejoicing exceedingly in the Passion of our Lord," and as "filled with all-mercy . . . . which (Church) I salute in the Blood of Jesus Christ . . . especially to those who are in unity with the Bishop," &c., "who have been appointed by the will of God the Father, through the Lord Jesus Christ, who . . has firmly established his Church upon a rock, by a spiritual building, not made with hands, against which the winds and the floods have beaten, yet have not been able to overthrow it ; "—as having "obtained every kind of gift ; "— as "filled with faith and love, and is deficient in no gift ; "—as " most worthy of God, and adorned with holiness ; "—he describes the Roman Church in terms fundamentally distinct ; viz. as " all-godly, all-gracious, all-blessed, all-praised, &c. ;" as "presiding over love, with the Name of Christ, with the Name of the Father." Now, whence is this distinction ? Why did S. Ignatius regard the Roman Church, as so different from other churches, so much so as to address it as " presiding over love," as having the " Name of Christ," and the " Name

of the Father?" The answer is *implicitly* given in the body of the epistle (*see Ext.* No. 2) because of its having been evidently constituted by those great Apostles S. Peter and S. Paul. When S. Ignatius says, "I do not, as Peter and Paul, issue commandments *unto you,*" he evidently alludes to both Apostles, as having had a *local* connexion with the See of Rome ; as having bestowed upon that Church a dignity and an authority superior to other Churches. But did S. Ignatius regard S. Peter and S. Paul as superior to other Apostles ? it would seem so ; because he said, in his epistle to the Magnesians, that "*the disciples were called Christians at Antioch,* when Paul and Peter were laying the foundations of the Church." (*See Extract*, No. 3.) If all the Apostles were upon an *exact* equality, why not have said, "when the *Apostles* were laying the foundations of the Church ? " It is evident, then, that from the very form of the expression, from the fact that the Roman Church was the presiding Church, and endowed "with the Name of Christ (and) with the Name of the Father " (which Name S. Peter alone bore, and which consequently could have been derived from no other source), that S. Ignatius regarded these two Apostles,—S. Peter and S. Paul—as the two great Chiefs of the universal Church. The other points especially connected with the See of Rome will be considered in the next " inquiry."

S. IRENÆUS.

A.D. 178.

4. " But as it would be a very long task, to enumerate in such a volume as this, the successions of all the Churches, we do put to confusion all those who . . . assemble in unauthorised meetings, (we do this, I say), by indicating that tradition, derived from the Apostles, of the very great, the very

ancient, and universally known Church, founded and constituted at Rome, by the two most glorious Apostles, Peter and Paul ; as also (by pointing out) the faith preached to men, which comes down to our time by means of the successions of the Bishops. For it is a matter of necessity that every Church should agree with this (the Roman) Church, on account of its pre-eminent authority (or, its more powerful principality ; *Ad hanc enim ecclesiam propter potentiorem* (or, *potiorem*) *principalitatem necesse est* *omnem convenire ecclesiam*), that is, the faithful everywhere, inasmuch as the apostolical tradition has been preserved continuously by those who exist everywhere." *Adv. Hæres. l.* iii. *c.* 3, *n.* 2, *pp.* 175, 6.

COMMENT.

S. Irenæus was Bishop of Lyons, and flourished about seventy years after the death of the last surviving Apostle. He was a disciple of S. Polycarp, who was himself a disciple of S. John. S. Irenæus, in the above extract, supplies the information S. Ignatius omits *explicitly* to give, namely, that S. Peter and S. Paul constituted the Roman Church. Now we may understand why that Church was "all-godly, all-gracious, all-blessed, all-hallowed," why it had the presidency over love, and why it was endowed "with the Name of Christ, (and) with the Name of the Father." It is because these two Apostles founded and constituted this Church, and made it, as S. Irenæus asserts, a *more powerful principality.* S. Irenæus, then, evidently held that S. Peter and S. Paul were the two great Chiefs of the Apostolic Church, possessing certain prerogatives, distinct from other Apostles, which they communicated to the Roman Church. Indeed this is in keeping with what S. Paul says, that to S. Peter was given "the gospel of the circumcision," and to himself (S. Paul) "the gospel of the uncircumcision." (Gal. ii. 7.) Taking then these two Fathers, S. Ignatius and S. Irenæus, together, we obtain a glimpse of the truth in this matter, within a century after the decease of the beloved Apostle. And we may also discern this by the aid of Scripture, by which we at once perceive why the former addressed the Roman Church in terms essentially different from other Churches ; and why the latter regarded this Church as a "more powerful principality." It was, because of the Supremacy, which Christ first gave to S. Peter, and subsequently in a measure to S. Paul the Apostle of the Gentiles.

TERTULLIAN.

A.D. 195.

5. . . . "Was anything hidden from Peter, who was called the *Rock* whereon the Church was to be built ; who obtained *the keys of the kingdom of heaven,* and the power of loosing and of binding in heaven and on earth?" *De Præscript. Hæret. n.* 22, *p.* 209.

6. "For if thou thinkest heaven is still closed, remember that the Lord left here the keys thereof to Peter, and through him to the Church (*memento claves ejus hic Dominum Petro, et per eum, ecclesiæ reliquisse*) ; which keys every one that is here questioned and confesses, shall carry with him." *Scorpiace, n.* x. *p.* 496.

COMMENT.

Tertullian was a contemporary of S. Irenæus, and a native of Carthage. He evidently held that S. Peter possessed, singly and alone, in the *first instance, at least,* "the keys of the kingdom of heaven," and that through him they passed to the Church. S. Peter was then, according to this Father, the Source or Origin of all such jurisdiction as were symbolised by the keys. He was, too, the *Rock*,—even the Rock on which Christ built His Church. The Rock is the symbol of unity and power, for by its massive and immovable strength, it supports with power the whole fabric built upon it, preserving it in compact unity and order. S. Peter was this Rock (hewn out of the True Rock), whose commission it was to "confirm the brethren," and to shelter the sheep and lambs of the flock from the winds and tempests of hell.

ORIGEN.

A.D. 216.

7. "See what is said by the Lord to that great Foundation of the Church, and to the most solid Rock, upon which Christ founded the Church (*ecclesiæ fundamento, et petræ solidissimæ, super quam Christus fundavit ecclesiam*)." *T.* ii. *Hom.* v. *in Exod. n.* 4, *p.* 145.

8. "*At the same time came the disciples unto Jesus, saying, Who is the greatest in the kingdom of heaven?* (S. Matt. xviii. 1.) . . . We must not suffer the design of the Evangelist, in the words *at the same time,* to pass by unexamined. . . . Jesus, therefore, had *come,* together with His disciples, *to Capernaum;* then *they that received tribute-money came to Peter, and said, Doth not your Master pay tribute?* Then when Peter had answered them, and said, *Yes;* Jesus having assigned a reason for paying the tribute-money, sends Peter to draw out with the hook a fish, in the mouth of which he declares a stater would be found, to be given for Himself and Peter. It seems, therefore, to me, that they,—considering this to be the greatest honour to Peter on the part of Jesus, as judging him greater than the rest of the disciples, (μεγίστην νομίσαντες ταύτην εἶναι ὑπὸ τοῦ Ἰησοῦ πρὸς τὸν Πέτρον τιμήν, κρίναντες αὐτὸν

μείζονα τῶν λοιπῶν γνωρίμων)—wished to ascertain clearly that which they supposed; and they accordingly inquired in order to learn from Jesus, whether, as they suspected, He had separated Peter as greater than they; and they, at the same time, hoped to know the cause of Peter having been preferred before the rest." *T.* iii. *Comment. in Matt. Tom.* xiii. *n.* 14, *pp.* 588–9.

9. "What in a previous passage (S. Matt. xvi. 19) was granted to Peter alone, seems here (xviii. 18) to be shown to be granted to all who have addressed three admonitions to all sinners, in order that, if they be not listened to, they may *bind on earth* the person condemned to be *as an heathen man and a publican,* since such an one is *bound in heaven.* But, as it was fit,—even though something in common was spoken of Peter, and of those who should thrice admonish the brethren,—that Peter should have something peculiar above those who should thrice admonish (Ἔχειν, εἰ καὶ κοινόν τι ἐπὶ τοῦ Πέτρου καὶ τῶν νουθετησάντων . . . λέλεκται ἐξαίρετον ἔχειν τὸν Πέτρον παρὰ τοὺς τρεῖς νουθετήσαντας); this was previously ordained separately respecting Peter; thus, *I will give unto thee the keys of the kingdom*

of heaven, before (it was said) *and whatsoever thou shalt bind on earth*, and what follows ; and truly, if we sedulously attend to the evangelical writings, even in them we may discover,—with regard even to those things which seem to be common to Peter and to those who have thrice admonished the brethren,—much difference and preeminence in the words spoken to Peter, beyond those spoken to in the second place" (παρὰ τοὺς δευτέρους). *T.* iii. *in Matt. Tom.* xiii. *n.* 31, *p.* 613-4.

10. "Peter upon whom is built Christ's Church (Πίτρος δὲ ἐφ' ῷ

οἰκοδομεῖται ἡ Χριστοῦ ἐκκλησία), against which *the gates of hell shall not prevail,*" &c. *T.* iv. *In Joan. Tom.* v. *p.* 95 (*Ex Euseb. H. E. l.* vi. *c.* 25).

11. "When the Chief Authority as regards the feeding of the sheep was delivered to Peter ; and on him, as on the earth, the Church was founded (*Petro cum summa rerum de pascendis ovibus traderetur, et super ipsum, velut super terram, fundaretur ecclesia*) ; of no other virtue was the confession required, than that of love." *T.* iv. *l.* 5, *in Ep. ad Rom. n.* 10, *p.* 568.

COMMENT.

Origen was born in Egypt, and was celebrated for his great learning. He regards S. Peter (1) as "The Foundation of the Church," and the "most solid Rock upon which Christ built His Church ;" (2) as possessing the keys in greater fullness than the other Apostles ; and (3) as having "the Chief authority" in the feeding of the sheep.

1. The Foundation. The word *Fundamentum* has a definite meaning ; viz., the basis of any superstructure ; here, this word is used metaphorically to signify the Chief Stone of the fabric it supports. When, then, S. Peter is described as the Foundation, we are to understand that he was not only the Foundation on which the Church was originally built, but that he was the main Stone of the Church, its main Pillar and Supporter. He is, too, the "most solid Rock," signifying that his strength, as the Foundation and Stone of the Church, is that of a solid and impregnable rock,—against which the gates of hell shall not prevail.

2. That Origen regarded S. Peter as superior to the rest, is evident from

his comment on S. Matt. xviii. (See *Extract*, No. 8.) It seems, according to his interpretation of the incident of the stater, that the Apostles did not understand why our Lord directed S. Peter to pay the tax for himself and his Lord, *exclusive*, as it would seem, of themselves, who were also associated with him in the apostolate : in order to ascertain our Lord's will on this point, they immediately asked Him, "Who is the greatest in the kingdom of heaven ?" By this they hoped to discover, whether our Lord had indeed separated S. Peter, as greater than themselves, and why He did so. The doctrine then involved in this comment of Origen is obvious, viz. that he regarded S. Peter as separated from the other Apostles in dignity, and even in person : for if the incident of the stater is to be interpreted as showing our Lord's intention of separating S. Peter as greater than the rest, it can signify nothing less than that He meant to teach them that he was to be His *special* Representative.

3. The Keys. Origen believes that all the Apostles received the power of

binding and loosing, but that S. Peter obtained the same in larger measure. Comparing the two occasions (first to S. Peter and then to the Twelve), when our Lord promised the keys, Origen says, there was "much difference and pre-eminence in the words spoken to Peter, *beyond* (παρά) those spoken" on the second occasion. Origen must have believed that S. Peter had a superior jurisdiction.

4. Furthermore, Origen evidently con-sidered that S. Peter had "the Chief authority" in the feeding of the sheep.

There can be little doubt that Origen held that S. Peter was the Head and Chief of the Apostles; that he was the Foundation and main-stay of the Church: that, although all the Apostles had the keys, yet, he had them pre-eminently and in larger measure: that he was exhibited to the Apostles as their Superior, and, lastly, that in the pastoral charge he had the chief share.

S. CYPRIAN.

A.D. 246.

12. "Peter on whom the Church had been built by the Lord Him-self (*Petrus super quem ædificata ab eodem Domino fuerat ecclesia*), one speaking for all, and reply-ing with the voice of the Church (*unus pro omnibus loquens, et ec-clesiæ voce respondens*), says, *Lord, to whom shall we go?*" *Ep.* lv. *Ad Cornel. p.* 83.

13. "There (S. John, vi. 68–70) speaks Peter, upon whom the Church was to be built (*super quem ædificanda fuerat ecclesia*), teach-ing and showing, in the name of the Church, that, although a contuma-cious and proud multitude of such as will not obey may depart, yet the Church departeth not from Christ; and the people united to the priest, and the flock adhering to its shep-herd, they are the Church." *Ep.* lxix. *ad Pupian. p.* 123.

14. "There is one baptism, and one Holy Ghost, and one Church, founded by Christ our Lord upon Peter for (or, from) an original and principle of unity (*una ecclesia a Christo Domino super Petrum origine unitatis et ratione fun-data*)."

Ep. lxx. *ad Januar. et Ep. Numid. p.* 125.

15. . . . "For not even did Peter, whom the Lord chose the first (*nam nec Petrus, quem primum Domi-nus elegit*), and upon whom He built His Church, when Paul after-wards disputed with him respecting circumcision, claim anything to himself insolently, or assume any thing arrogantly, so as to say, that he held the Primacy (*prima-tum*), and that obedience ought rather to be paid to him by those who were novices and had come after him. Nor did he despise Paul because he had been originally a persecutor of the Church, but he admitted the counsel of truth, and readily assented, to the legitimate reasons (or, method) which Paul vindicated, giving, to wit, to us an example of unanimity and patience, that we may not with pertinacity love what is our own, but rather the things that are at times use-fully and beneficially suggested by our brethren and colleagues, to account them, if they be true and lawful, as our own." *Ep.* lxxi. *ad Quintum, p.* 127.

16. "For first to Peter, upon whom He built the Church, and from whom He appointed and showed that unity should spring (*Nam Petro primum Dominus, super quem ædificavit ecclesiam, et unde unitatis originem instituit et ostendit*), the Lord gave this power that that should be loosed in heaven which he should have loosed on earth. And, after the resurrection also, He speaks to the Apostles, saying, *As My Father hath sent me, even so send I you*," &c., quoting S. John, xx. 21-23. *Ep.* lxxiii. *ad Jubaian.* p. 131.

17. "Whither shall he come that thirsteth ? To heretics where the fountain and river of water is no way life-giving, or to the Church which is one, and was by the voice of the Lord founded upon one (Peter), who also received the keys thereof (*Quæ una est, et super unum, qui et claves ejus accepit, Domini voce fundata est*). She it is that alone holds and possesses the whole power of her Spouse and Lord." *Ib. p.* 132.

18. "Peter also to whom the Lord commends His sheep to be fed and guarded (*Petrus etiam cui oves suas Dominus pascendas tuendasque commendat*), on whom He laid and founded the Church, says," &c. *De Habitu Virg. p.* 176.

19. "To the seven children there is evidently conjoined their mother, the origin and root (*origo et radix*) which afterwards bare seven Churches, herself having been founded first and alone, by the voice of the Lord, upon Peter (*Ipsa prima ut una super Petrum Domini voce*

fundata)." *De Exhort. Martyr. p.* 270.

20. "The Lord says to Peter, *I say unto thee*, saith He, *that thou art Peter, and upon this rock I will build My Church*, &c. Upon that one (Peter) He builds His Church, and to him He assigns His sheep to be fed. And although to all the Apostles, after His resurrection, He gives an equal power, and says, *As My Father hath sent me, even so send I you*, &c.; yet, in order to manifest unity, He has, by His own authority, so placed the origin of that same unity, as that it begins from one. Certainly, the other Apostles also were what Peter was, endowed with an equal fellowship both of honour and power, but the commencement proceeds from unity, and the Primacy is given to Peter (*Exordium ab unitate proficiscitur, et primatus Petro datur*), that the Church may be set forth as one, and the Chair as one. . . . He who holds not this unity of the Church, does he think that he holds the faith ? He who strives against and resists the Church, he who abandons the Chair of Peter, upon whom the Church was founded, does he feel confident that he is in the Church ? " *De Unitate, p.* 195.

21. "God is one, and Christ is one, and the Church is one, and the Chair one, founded, by the Lord's word, upon a rock (*et una ecclesia, et cathedra una super petram Domini voce fundata*), another altar and a new priesthood, besides the one altar and the one priesthood, cannot be set up." *Ep.* xl. *ad Pleb. p.* 53.

COMMENT.

S. Cyprian, the most illustrious Father of the Ante-Nicene period of the Church, was Bishop of Carthage and Primate of Africa. He flourished within 150 years after the death of S. John. His doctrine respecting the Primacy of S. Peter is very apparent. He held that S. Peter was the first chosen by our Lord ; that He founded and built the Church upon him ; that He gave him the keys and commended to his care His sheep, to be fed and guarded. S. Cyprian, indeed, believed that all the Apostles were "equal" to S. Peter in "power," and that they had "an equal fellowship" with him, "both of honour and power ; " yet, he adds, "in order to manifest unity, He has, by His own authority, so placed the origin of that same unity, as that it begins from one. . . . and the Primacy is given to Peter, that the Church may be set forth as one, and the Chair as one." This last clause is held to be spurious, but the Benedictine editors, who were careful, after a strict critical investigation, to expurgate all interpolations from the text of S. Cyprian as well as of other Fathers, have deliberately retained it as genuine. But this is not worth contention here, for there are other passages, *undisputed*, which equally serve our purpose. S. Cyprian says in one of his epistles (see *Extract*, No. 15), that, when S. Paul remonstrated with S. Peter in reference to his conduct at Antioch, he (Peter) did not "assume anything arrogantly, so as to say that he held the Primacy, and that obedience ought rather to be paid to him" by novices. Now, there are two points to be noted, the Primacy of Peter on the one part, and obedience on the other part, by novices, to S. Peter. Now the question immediately arises, if the Primacy on the one hand, and obedience on the other, were novelties unheard of in the primitive age, how comes it that S. Cyprian mentions them? His argument is very simple ; he is commending S. Peter for his humility, in that, notwithstanding that he held the Primacy, and that obedience on the part of novices was due to him, yet, for all that, he received S. Paul's rebukes with meekness ; not silencing him, by claiming "anything to himself insolent-

ly," or by assuming "anything arrogantly," that is, his Primacy.

This allusion, then, to an office evidently existing, indicates that in the opinion of S. Cyprian, S. Peter possessed the Primacy. Then, again, with regard to the unity of the "Chair;" if the clause in the passage quoted above be spurious, then the following *undisputed* one will supply its place. "God is one, Christ one, and the Church one, and the Chair one, founded by the Lord's word upon a Rock." (See *Extract*, No. 21.) Therefore, the meaning of S. Cyprian is clear, viz., that while all the Apostles were equal in power and honour, yet to manifest unity the Lord "so placed the origin of that same unity," as it should proceed from one, "and the Primacy is given to Peter, that the Church may be set forth as one, and the Chair one." But what is the exact meaning of the word Primacy? Here we arrive at the main point under discussion. *Primatus* signifies the chief place, the highest estate,—pre-eminence ; that is, one who fills the chief place. This word is used to express the office of an Archbishop or Metropolitan, which is one not of mere honour or rank, but of *rule and authority*. The 34th canon apostolical provides that nothing of importance shall be done by the Bishops of any country without the consent of him who is the First amongst them, *i.e.* the Primate ; and *vice versa*. The Primate or Metropolitan, or he who was the First, had a co-ordinate authority with the Bishops subject to him. The Œcumenical canon provides that no Bishop shall be chosen or consecrated without his consent ; so that the Metropolitan is the source of order, mission, and jurisdiction, *within* his province. So that S. Cyprian, when alluding to the Primacy of S. Peter in the apostleship, and to the obedience due to him on the part of novices, evidently believed that the Prince of the Apostles held an office in the apostolic college somewhat analogous to that of a Primate, Archbishop, or Metropolitan of a province. It is by reason of this Primacy or Chieftain-ship which S. Peter held, that he was commissioned to "speak for all," and to reply "with the voice of the Church." "There is," as S. Cyprian forcibly informs us, "one Baptism, and one Holy Ghost, and one Church founded by

Christ our Lord upon Peter, for an Original and Principle of unity;" (*see* *Ext.* No. 14), to whom the Lord delivered the keys, and to whom He commended His sheep to be fed and guarded.

S. FIRMILIAN.

A.D. 231.

22. "But how great his (Stephen's) error, how exceeding his blindness, who says remission of sins can be given in the synagogues of heretics, not abiding on the foundation of the one Church, which was once first established by Christ on a Rock, may hence be understood that to Peter alone Christ said, *Whatsoever thou shalt bind*, &c. ; and again, in the Gospel, when Christ breathed on the Apostles alone, saying, *Receive ye the Holy Ghost*, &c. The power, therefore, of forgiving sins, was given to the Apostles, and to the Churches which they, sent forth by Christ, founded, and to the bishops who, by vicarious ordination, have succeeded to them. . . And here, in this matter, I am justly indignant at this so open and

manifest folly of Stephen, that he, who so prides himself on the place of his episcopate, and contends that he holds the succession of Peter, upon whom the foundations of the Church were laid, introduces many other *rocks* (*Qui sic de episcopatus sui loco gloriatur, et se successionem Petri tenere contendit, super quem fundamenta ecclesiæ collocata sunt, multas alias petras inducat*), and sets up the new buildings of many Churches, while by his authority he maintains that there is baptism amongst them. . . Stephen, who proclaims that he occupies by succession the Chair of Peter, is moved with no kind of zeal against heretics." *Inter Ep. S. Cyp. Ep.* lxxv. *p.* 148.

COMMENT.

Firmilian was Bishop of Cæsarea in Cappadocia, and was a friend of Origen and S. Cyprian. The point in the above extract is this, that he, in accordance with the belief of the whole Church believed that to S. Peter *alone*, in the

first instance, Christ said, "*Whatsoever thou shalt bind,*" &c. ; and that "upon (S. Peter) the foundation of the one Church was laid ;" and, further, that afterwards the keys were given to the Apostles of the Church.

S. PETER OF ALEXANDRIA.

A.D. 306.

23. " Peter, who was the pre-   κρίτος τῶν ἀποστόλων Πέτρος.)
ferred one to the Apostles" ('Ο προ-   Canon. ix. Galland. T. iv. p. 98.

COMMENT.

S. Peter was Bishop of Alexandria.
He says that S. Peter was ὁ προκρίτος
τῶν ἀπόστολων, that is, the preferred one

of the Apostles ; the one judged superior to the rest.

EUSEBIUS.

A.D. 325.

24. "His Apostle and Disciple
Peter, who had been chosen before
the rest ('Ο πάντων αὐτῶν προεκ-
κριμένος), without torment or threat
from a ruler, denied Him thrice."
Demons. Evang. l. iii. n. 7, p. 123.

25. "The providence of the Universal Ruler led, as it were, by the
hand to Rome, that most powerful
and great one of the Apostles, and,
on account of his virtue, the Mouthpiece (or, Leader) of the rest, Peter,
against that sad destroyer of the
human race (Simon Magus). He, as
a noble general (appointed) of God
(τὸν καρτερὸν καὶ μέγαν τῶν ἀποστόλων

. . . τῶν λοιπῶν ἀπάντων προήγορον.
Πέτρον . . . ὅς οἷα τις γενναῖος τοῦ Θεοῦ
στρατηγὸς), armed with heavenly
weapons, brought the precious mer-
chandize of intellectual light from
the East to the dwellers in the
West. *H. E.* l. ii. c. 14, p. 63, 4.

26. "He became a stranger to
these His brethren (Ps. lxviii. 9), at
the time of His Passion, when all
His disciples leaving Him fled, and
he, the very Head of the Apostles
(αὐτὸς τὶ ὁ κορυφαῖος τῶν ἀποστόλων),
Peter, denied Him thrice." *Comm.
in Ps.* lxix. *t.* i. *p.* 373, *Nov. Collect.*

COMMENT.

Eusebius, the first great historian
of the Church, says, that S. Peter was
chosen before the rest of the Apostles.
The verb προκρίνω means to choose before all others, to pick out, to select.
Eusebius, then, intended to state that S.
Peter had been chosen in preference to
the other Apostles, *evidently* as their
Chief. *Evidently*, because, in his commentary on the Psalms, he styles him
"the very Chief of the Apostles."
The word κορυφαῖος signifies, one standing at the highest point or head, *i.e.*

the Head man or Chief. (*See* Extract,
No. 26.) That Eusebius considered S.
Peter as holding a position distinct
from the other Apostles, is clear from
his styling him "that most powerful
and great one," who as "a noble General, armed with heavenly powers,
brought," &c. (Extract, No. 25). The
word στρατηγὸς signifies a general or
leader of an army. In the estimation,
then, of Eusebius, S. Peter was the
Head, the Leader, and the Ruler or
Governor of the Church.

S. JAMES OF NISIBIS.

A.D. 340.

27. " And Simon, the Head of the Apostles (*Simon, caput discipulorum*), he who denied Christ, saying, *I saw Him not*, and cursed and swore that *he knew Him not*, as soon as he offered to God contrition and penitence, and washed his sins in the tears of his grief, our Lord received him, and made him the Foundation, and called him the Rock of the edifice of the Church (*et vocavit eum petram ædificii ecclesiæ*)." *Orat.* vii. *De Pænit.* n. 6, p. lvii. *Galland.* t. v. *p.* lxxxiv.

COMMENT.

S. James, Bishop of Nisibis, in Mesopotamia, describes S. Peter as "the Head of the Disciples," whom our Lord made "the Foundation, and called him the Rock of the edifice of the Church." The word *caput* represents that member which exercises the functions of government of the whole body.

When, then, S. Peter is called the Head, it is signified that in him is the seat of authority and government. He, too, is the Foundation of the spiritual building, which rests upon him, and is by him, — the Rock, doubtless, hewn from the Rock Christ, — sustained in unity and strength.

S. HILARY OF POICTIERS.

A.D. 356.

28. " On an occasion that the Only-Begotten spoke to His disciples certain things concerning His Passion, and Peter expressed his abhorrence, as if it were unworthy of the Son of God, He took up Peter, — to whom He had just before given *the keys of the kingdom of heaven*, upon whom He was about to build the Church (*super quem ecclesiam ædificaturus erat*), against which *the gates of hell should not* in any way *prevail*, who, *whatsoever* he should *bind or loose on earth*, that should abide *bound or loosed in heaven*, — this same Peter then, when expressing his abhorrence in such reproachful terms, He took up with, *Get behind me, Satan, thou art an offence to Me.* For it was with Him

so sacred a thing to suffer for the salvation of the human race, as thus to designate with the reproachful name Satan, Peter, the first Confessor of the Son of God, the Foundation of the Church (*ecclesiæ fundamentum*), the Door-keeper (*janitorem*) of the heavenly kingdom, and in his judgment on earth a Judge of heaven (*et in terreno judicis judicem cæli*)." *Tract. in Ps.* cxxxi. n. 4, p. 447.

29. " Peter believeth the first, and is the Prince of the Apostolate (*Apostolatus est princeps*)." *Comm. in Matt. c.* 7, n. 6, p. 642.

30. " And in sooth Peter's confession obtained a worthy recompense. Blessed is he that is praised as having both remarked and seen

beyond the ken of human eyes, not regarding what was of flesh and blood, but by the revelation of the heavenly Father, beholding the Son of God, and judged (*judicatus*) worthy to be the first to acknowledge what was in the Christ of God. Oh! in thy designation by a new name, happy Foundation of the Church, and a Rock worthy of the building up of that which was to scatter the infernal laws, and the gates of hell, and all the bars of death! O blessed Keeper of the gate of heaven, to whose disposal are delivered the keys of the entrance into eternity; whose judgment on earth is an authority prejudged in heaven, so that the things that are either loosed or bound on earth, acquire in heaven too a like state of settlement. (*O in nuncupatione novi nominis felix ecclesiæ fundamentum, dignaque ædificatione illius petra, quæ infernas leges, et tartari portas, et omnia mortis claustra dissolveret! O beatus cæli janitor, cujus arbitrio claves æterni aditus traduntur, cujus terrestre judicium præjudicata auctoritas sit in cælo; ut quæ in terris aut ligata sint aut soluta, statuti ejusdem conditionem obtineant et in cælo.*) Comm. in Matt. c. xvi. n. 7, p. 690, 691.

31. ". . . And from blessed Simon, who after his confession of the mystery, was placed under the building of the Church, and received the keys of the kingdom of heaven. (*Beatus Simon ædificationi ecclesiæ subjacens et claves regni cælestis accipiens*)." *De Trinit. l.* vi. *n.* 20, *p.* 891, 892.

COMMENT.

S. Hilary was Bishop of Poictiers, and was in his day a great star in the firmament of the Church. He testifies that our Lord gave the keys to S. Peter, "upon whom He was about to build His Church." He calls him "the first Confessor of the Son of God, the Foundation of the Church, the Doorkeeper of the heavenly kingdom;" and he adds that in his judgment on earth "he is a Judge of heaven;" and he moreover styles him "The Prince of the Apostolate." It is impossible to doubt what S. Hilary means by the title of "Prince," certainly not a mere *Primus inter pares*. S. Hilary, no doubt, with S. Cyprian, believed in the co-equality of the Apostles in power and honour; but he, notwithstanding, held with Origen that there was "*a something peculiar to Peter*"—a prerogative superior to the others—otherwise he could not have thus apostrophized with any truth, "O blessed Keeper of the gate of heaven, to whose disposal are delivered the keys of entrance into eternity, whose judgment on earth is an authority prejudged in heaven, so that the things that are either loosed or bound on earth acquire in heaven too a like state of settlement." (*Extract,* No. 30.) If S. Peter was nothing more than a *Primus inter pares*, such language could not with any truth have been admissible. S. Hilary then believed that S. Peter was the Prince of the Apostles, the supreme Head of the Church, the supreme Door-keeper, and the supreme Judge; in a word, that he was the Centre of unity, and the Foundation and Origin of unity and jurisdiction.

S. CYRIL OF JERUSALEM.

A.D. 363.

32. " Peter the Chiefest and Fore-most (leader) of the Apostles (Πέτρος ὁ κορυφαιότατος καὶ πρωτοστάτης τῶν ἀποστόλων), before a little maid," &c. *Catech.* ii. *n.* 19, *p.* 31.

33. [In reference to the over-throw of Simon Magus by the united prayers of SS. Peter and Paul, this Father says] : " And though the thing be wonderful, it is no wonder : for it was Peter, he who bears with him the keys of heaven, (ὁ τὰς κλεῖς τῶν οὐρανῶν περιφέρων). It is not worth our wonder ; for it was Paul, he who was caught up into the third heaven." *Catech.* vi. *n.* 15, *p.* 96.

34. " Our Lord Jesus Christ then became man, but by the many He was not known. But wishing to teach that which was not known, having assembled the disciples, He asked, *Whom do men say that I the Son of Man am ?* . . . .

And all being silent (for it was be-yond man to learn) Peter, the Fore-most of the Apostles, and Chief Herald of the Church (Πέτρος ὁ πρωτοστάτης τῶν ἀποστόλων καὶ τῆς ἐκκλησίας κορυφαῖος κῆρυξ), not using language of his own finding, nor persuaded by human reasoning, but having his mind enlightened from the Father, says to Him, *Thou art the Christ*, not simply that, but, *the Son of the living God.* And a blessing follows the speech . . . . *Blessed art thou*," &c. *Catech.* xi. *n.* 3, *p.* 150.

35. " In the power of the same Holy Spirit, Peter, also the Fore-most of the Apostles, and the Key-bearer of the kingdom of heaven (τῆς βασιλείας τῶν οὐρανῶν κλειδοῦ-χος), healed Eneas the paralytic in the Name of Christ." *Catech.* xvii. *n.* 27, *p.* 227.

COMMENT.

S. Cyril describes S. Peter as the Chiefest and Foremost of the Apostles. The words, κορυφαιότατος and πρωτο-στάτης are exceedingly strong terms, the former signifying standing at the head or foremost place ; the latter, standing in the first rank. S. Cyril in his de-scription of the exploits of S. Peter and S. Paul, in their conflict with Si-mon Magus, draws a distinction be-tween the two, which is noteworthy. He says, alluding to the overthrow of Simon, "It is no wonder : for it was Peter, *he who bears with him the keys*

of heaven ; . . . for it was Paul, he who was caught up into the third heaven." Although S. Paul no doubt shared with S. Peter in the use of the keys, yet, according to S. Cyril, the latter was the Key-bearer (*See Extract,* No. 35) ; or, as S. Hilary says, "the Door-keeper of the heavenly kingdom." (*Ext.* No. 28.) S. Cyril styles S. Peter as the *Chief Herald* of the Church. It is clear, then, that S. Cyril held that S. Peter was the Chief Ruler of the Church.

S. OPTATUS, OF MILEVIS.

A.D. 368.

36. "Blessed Peter, to whom after his denial, it were enough if he obtained pardon, merited both to be preferred (*preferri*) before all the Apostles, and he alone received of the kingdom of heaven the keys to be communicated to the others (*et claves . . . . communicandas cæteris, solus accepit*) . . . The Head of the Apostles (*caput apostolorum*) could so have governed himself as not to incur a crime of which he would have to repent." *De Schism. Don. l.* vii. *n.* 3, *Galland. t.* v. *p.* 501.

COMMENT.

S. Optatus was bishop of a city in Numidia. He asserts that S. Peter "merited to be preferred before all the Apostles," and that "he alone received of the kingdom the keys to be communicated to the others." This explains the meaning of S. Cyprian, when he said, that the Lord founded His Church "first and alone" "upon Peter, for an original and principle of unity" (*See Extract*, 14), "for whom he appointed and showed that unity should spring" (*Ext.* 16), as we shall see further on, from S. Augustine, who says that the Church was founded singly upon Peter, to be afterwards enlarged so as to include all the Apostles. It is evident that S. Peter, *for a time*, was the sole Apostle, whom the Lord established as the Rock and Foundation of the Church ; the one Source of jurisdiction and authority to the Church. *Afterwards* our Lord addressed the eleven who were *to share* with S. Peter in the government of the Church. S. Optatus, then, well expresses the truth that he (Peter) *alone* received the kingdom the keys, to be communicated to the others." See above what Tertullian and Origen said (*Extracts*, 6 and 9). This reminds me of a somewhat parallel case under the Law : "And the Lord said unto Moses, Gather unto me seventy men of the elders of Israel, whom thou knowest to be the elders of the people, and officers over them ; and bring them unto the tabernacle of the congregation, that they may stand there with thee. And I will come down, and talk with thee there : and I will take of the Spirit which is upon thee, and will put it upon them ; and they shall bear the burden of the people with thee, that thou bear it not thyself alone." (Numb. xi. 16, 17.) The parallel of course must not be pressed too far, but nevertheless, it explains much. God had chosen Moses as His sole Representative, and as the sole Ruler of the people. As the duties of government increased, they were found to be over-burdensome to Moses,—God provided a remedy by instituting colleagues to share with him in the administration of the government. This is what our Lord provided in the case of S. Peter. For a short while he was the sole Apostle, who alone and singly possessed the keys. Our Lord, foreknowing the necessity of making a similar provision, as in the case of Moses, appointed eleven other Apostles, who were to share with S. Peter in the government of the Church. As God took of Moses' Spirit and put it upon the seventy elders, so did our Lord extend the power of the keys from S. Peter to the rest, that all might be equal in power to him, yet subject to him, whom alone He appointed to be the Foundation and Rock, and to whom alone He said, "Feed my sheep." S. Optatus, in affirming that S. Peter alone received of "the kingdom the keys to be communicated to the others," inferred two great truths : (1) that S. Peter received in the first place the keys alone ; and (2) that the other Apostles received the keys from our Lord ; but, as Tertullian says (*Ext.* 6), *through* S. Peter. These are in perfect accord with the doctrine of S. Cyprian and other Fathers. S.

Optatus describes S. Peter as the Head (*caput*) of the Apostles, and this further explains his meaning. For it is from the Head all government and authority proceed ; and so it was with S. Peter, for he was the Head, the Foundation and Source from whence unity did spring.

S. EPHRAEM, OF SYRUS.

A.D. 370.

37. " Mount Sinai falls in the tenth year ; it sings hymns of praise to the Lord that is born. Of old, Sion melted at His Presence, and fell away. But it will soon perceive Him aimed at with stones thrown by impious hands : he that was to build His Church upon Cephas, receives on Him stones. Admire the workmanship of the divine Artificer." *T.* ii. *Syr. Serm.* xiii. *in Nat. Dom. p.* 433-34.

38. . . . " Have they (Bardesanes and Manes) not even respected the sentence of the Apostle, who condemns such as say, *I am of Cephas?* Now if it was the duty of the sheep to refuse even the name of Cephas, although he was the Prince of the Apostles, and had received the keys, and was accounted the Shepherd of the flock, what execration is to be deemed too dreadful for him, who fears not to designate sheep that are not his, by his own name." *T.* ii. *Syr. Serm.* lvi. *Adv. Hæres. p.* 559.

39. " To whom, O Lord, didst Thou entrust that most precious pledge of the heavenly keys ? To Bar Jonas, the Prince of the Apostles, with whom, I implore thee, may I share thy bridal chamber ;

and thee, most holy assembly of Apostles . . . . to you also, ye Prophets, &c. *T.* iii. *Syr. Paræn.* 33, *p.* 486.

40. " Peter, who was called Cephas, he who was captured on the sea-shore, and who received a testimony from the great Pastor, that *Upon this rock I will build my church,* by means of the priesthood received also the keys of heaven, as worthy (of them ")." *T.* iii. *Gr. De Sacerd. p.* 3.

41. Thee, O Simon Peter, will I proclaim the blessed, who holdest the keys, which the Spirit made. A great and ineffable word, that he binds and looses those in heaven, and those under the earth . . . O thou blessed one, that obtainedst the Place of the Head and of the Tongue, in the body of thy brethren, which (body) was enlarged out of the disciples and sons of thy Lord." *Asseman. Bibl. Orient. t.* i. *p.* 95.

42. We hail thee, .Peter, the Tongue of the disciples ; the Voice of the heralds ; the Eye of the Apostles ; the Keeper of heaven ; the First-born of those that bear the keys." *T.* iii. *Gr. in SS. Apost. p.* 464.

COMMENT.

The opinions of S. Ephræm are in accord with that of other Fathers.

There is a remarkable passage, well worthy of notice (*See Extract,* No. 38.)

Writing against the sect of Manes, he says, "Have they not even respected the sentence of the Apostle, who condemns such as say, *I am of Cephas?* Now if it was the duty of the sheep to refuse even the name of Cephas, although he was the Prince of the Apostles, and had received the keys, and was accounted the Shepherd of the flock, what execration," &c. His argument brings out in relief the exalted position of S. Peter. This Father condemns all sects, pointing out their iniquity, he condemns too, Manes, (and in him all other schismatics), "who fear not to designate sheep that are not his, by his own name," for if it was unlawful even for the Chief of the Church, the Prince of the Apostles, and the Shepherd of the flock, to designate his own sheep by his own name, much less was it lawful for Manes or any such to so designate

his own sect. This is his argument. It is impossible to suppose that any author would make use of such an argument to condemn schism, if he did not believe that S. Peter was the Head and Chief of the apostolic college, and Chief Shepherd of the Church. The following language is very strong, "O thou (Peter) blessed one that obtainest the Place of the Head, and of the Tongue, in the body of thy brethren." The Head, properly speaking, is Christ; when, then, it is said S. Peter obtained the *Place* of the Head, is meant (it is submitted) the position of Christ in the Church during His absence. So the fathers believed that S. Peter was the Vicar of Christ. He was also the "Tongue in the body of the brethren;" *i.e.* he delivered to them the oracles of God. This he did in the matter of circumcision among the Gentiles at the Council of Jerusalem.

S. GREGORY, OF NYSSA.

A.D. 370.

43. "Peter, with his whole soul, associates himself with the Lamb; and, by means of the change of his name, he is changed by the Lord into something more divine; instead of Simon being both called and having become a Rock (Peter) . . . . The great Peter did not by advancing by little and little attain unto this grace, but at once he listened to his brother, believed in the Lamb, and was through faith perfected, and, having cleaved to the Rock, became Peter (a Rock — προσφυεὶς τῇ πέτρα Πέτρος ἐγένετο"). *T.* i. *Hom.* xv. *in C. Cantic. p.* 691.

44. "Through Peter He gave to the Bishops the key (διὰ Πέτρου

ἔδωκε τοῖς ἐπισκόποις τὴν κλεῖδα) of the heavenly honours." *T.* iii. *De Castig. p.* 314.

45. "The memory of Peter, the Head of the Apostles (ἡ κεφάλη τῶν ἀποστόλων), is celebrated; and magnified indeed with him are the other members of the Church; but (upon him) is the Church of God firmly established. For he is, agreeably to the gift conferred upon him by the Lord, that unbroken and most firm Rock upon which the Lord built His Church. (Οὗτος γὰρ ἐστι κατὰ τὴν δοθεῖσαν αὐτῷ παρὰ τοῦ Κυρίου δωρίαν ἡ ἀῤῥαγὴς, καὶ ὀχυρωτάτη πέτρα, ἐφ' ἧν τὴν ἐκκλησίαν ὁ Σώτηρ ᾠκοδόμησι)." *Alt. Or. De S. Steph. Galland. t.* vi. *p.* 600.

COMMENT.

S. Gregory was Bishop of Nyssa. He states his opinion of St. Peter's

position very explicitly. He says that he first listened to his brethren, then believed in the Lamb, and was perfected through faith : secondly, that cleaving to the Rock, that is Christ, "he became Peter," that is, that he himself became a Rock. S. Gregory maintains that in changing his name, he was changed "into something more divine ; " for by virtue of the gift conferred upon him, he became " that unbroken and most firm Rock upon which the Lord built His Church " (*See Extract*, No. 45). Two of the results, following this change of name, are mentioned by S. Gregory, (1) that the " key of heavenly honours " was given to the Bishops "*through* Peter." Here the harmony between this Father, S. Optatus, S. Cyprian, Origen, and Tertullian, is apparent, namely, that S. Peter was the Origin and Principal, whence the unity of the priesthood welled forth. He was the one Foundation of Apostolic power which Christ

established, and Bishops who were equally endowed with Apostolic power, received it *through* S. Peter. (2) The second result, mentioned by this Father, is, that S. Peter was regarded as "*the Head* of the Apostles." Indeed, κιφαλη signifies the Head, and, like *caput*, is the name of that principal member, which is charged with the function of ruling and governing the whole body subject to it. Such, then, is the expressed doctrine of S. Gregory, viz. that S. Peter was the Rock of the Rock, on which the Church was built and firmly established ; and by the changing of his name to Peter, Christ made him " something more divine," pointing him out as the Rock of the Church, and as THE HEAD (the definite article is prefixed) of the Apostles, through whom (Peter) the "key of heavenly honours " were conferred upon the Bishops.

S. GREGORY OF NAZIANZUM.

A.D. 370.

46. "Seest thou that of the disciples of Christ, all of whom were great and deserving of the choice, one is called a Rock (ὁ μὲν πέτρα καλεῖται) and is entrusted with the Foundations of the Church; whilst another is the best beloved, and reposes on the breast of Jesus ; and the rest bear with the Prior Honour (thus bestowed (φέρουσιν οἱ λοιποὶ τὴν προ-τίμησιν)." T. i. *or.* xxxii. *n.* 18, *p.* 591.

47. "Neither does a man know,

though he be the parent of an evil like unto Judas, whether his offspring shall be called the god-like Paul, or be like unto Peter,—Peter who became the unbroken Rock, and who had the keys delivered unto him (πέτρης ἀῤῥαγέος γενίτης κληῖδα λαχοντος)." T. ii. *Carm.* 2, *p.* 51.

48. " Peter, the Chief of the disciples, but he was a Rock (Πέτρος μαθήτων ἄκρος, ἀλλὰ Πέτρος ἦν), not as a fisherman, but because full of zeal." T. ii. *p.* 790.

COMMENT.

S. Gregory was first Bishop of Nazianzum and afterwards Patriarch of Constantinople, and esteemed one of the great doctors of the Eastern Church.

He affirms that S. Peter was named the Rock, and was entrusted with the foundations of the Church ; that he not only was *called* the Rock, but that he *be*-

D

came the unbroken Rock, and that to him were delivered the keys. S. Gregory declares him to be the "Chief of the disciples."

The word ἄκρος literally means either highest, topmost, or outermost. But concerning *degree*, it signifies the highest of its kind. S. Peter was, therefore, regarded as the highest in the Apostolic Office, and having also the strength of the Rock, he was able to succour and support his brethren.

S. MACARIUS OF EGYPT.

A.D. 371.

49. "For of old Moses and Aaron, when this priesthood was theirs, suffered much ; and Caiaphas, when he had their Chair, persecuted and condemned the Lord... Afterwards Moses was succeeded by Peter, who had committed to his hands the new Church of Christ, and the true priesthood." *Hom.* xxvi. *n.* 23, *Galland. T.* vii. *p.* 101.

50. "Jannes and Mambre opposed Moses, and as Simon (Magus) set himself against that Chief, Peter. ('Ως Σίμων τῷ κορυφαίῳ Πέτρῳ ἀντιφερόμενος)." *Ib. Ascet. de Patient. n.* 3, *p.* 180.

COMMENT.

S. Macarius was a contemporary of S. Athanasius, and a friend of S. Anthony. He regards S. Peter as the successor of Moses ; and that, as Moses was directed to build up the polity of Israel and to govern the people in his day, so, in like manner, was S. Peter commissioned to perform similar functions for the foundation, establishment, and government of the new Israel,—the Kingdom of Christ. In another place he contrasts Jannes and Mambre, who opposed Moses, with Simon Magus, setting "himself up against that Chief, Peter."

S. BASIL.

A.D. 371.

51. "When we hear the name of Peter, that name does not cause our minds to dwell on his substance, but to figure to our minds the properties that are connected with him. For we at once, on hearing that name, think of the son of him that came from Bethsaida, Andrew's brother ; him that was called from amongst fishermen unto the Ministry of the Apostleship; him who, on account of the Pre-eminence of his faith, received upon himself the building of the Church (τὸν διὰ πιστίως ὑπεροχὴν ἐφ' ἑαυτὸν τὴν οἰκοδομὴν τῆς ἐκκλησίας δεξάμενον)." *T.* i. *l.* ii. *Adv. Eunom. n.* 4, *p.* 240.

52. The house of God, which is the Church of the living God, the foundations of which are on the holy mountains, for it is built upon the foundation of Apostles and Prophets. One also of these mountains was Peter, upon which Rock the Lord promised to build His Church (ἐφ' ἧς καὶ πέτρας ἐπηγγείλατο ὁ Κύριος

οἰκοδομήσειν αὐτοῦ τὴν ἐκκλησίαν.)"
T. i. *Comment. in Esai. c.* ii. *n.* 66, *p.* 427.

53. "And when he, the instrument of such and so great a judgment ; he the minister of the so great wrath of God upon a sinner ; that blessed Peter, who was pre-ferred (προκριθεὶς) before all the disciples ; who alone received a greater testimony and blessing than the rest ; he to whom were entrusted the keys of the kingdom of heaven, &c." T. ii. p. 1. *Procem. de Judic. Dei, n.* 7, *p.* 221.

COMMENT.

S. Basil, one of the great doctors of the Church, was Bishop of Cæsarea, in Cappadocia. He says we ought not to dwell on Peter's substance, that is, his flesh, or his mere person, but on the properties connected with him. When we hear his name (Peter), we, he says, think of him who was called from a humble fisherman unto the Ministry of the Apostleship ; who, "on account of the Pre-eminence of his faith, received upon himself the building of the Church," *i.e.* that S. Peter being found worthy was appointed the Master builder of the kingdom of our Lord. S. Basil considers the Church, built upon the Apostles and Prophets, to be founded upon the holy mountains, *i.e.* upon many mountains, one of which was the Mountain of S. Peter; upon which Rock,—*i.e. upon S. Peter's Mountain* (for remember that the "Stone became a great Mountain," see Daniel, ii. 35)—"the Lord promised to build His Church." There can be no doubt of S. Basil's meaning, that the Mountain of S. Peter, *i.e.* the Church of S. Peter, was the governing Church, the principal Church, that "more powerful principality," which S. Irenæus described it to be, to which it is necessary that the other mountains, *i.e.* the other churches, should "resort" as to the centre of unity. This, too, is in harmony with what S. Cyprian said, "To the seven children there is evidently conjoined their Mother, their Origin and Root, which afterwards bare seven Churches, herself having been founded *first and alone*, by the voice of the Lord, upon Peter," (see *Extract*, No. 19). S. Peter's Church, and S. Peter's Mountain, on which it is built, is that great mother-Church, from which all other Churches proceed, and by which they are sustained. S. Basil affirms that S. Peter was preferred to all the disciples, and that he *alone* received a greater testimony and blessing than the rest ;—even him who "was intrusted with the keys of the kingdom of heaven."

S. EPIPHANIUS.

A.D. 385.

54. "... And the blessed Peter, who for awhile denied the Lord, Peter who was the Chiefest of the Apostles, he who became unto us truly a firm Rock upon which is based the Lord's faith, upon which (Rock) the Church is in every way built (ἰφ' ἡ ᾠκοδόμητο ἡ ἐκκλησία κατὰ πάντα τρόπον) ; first, in that he confessed that Christ was the Son of the living God, and heard that upon this Rock of firm faith I will build my Church. ... Further, he then also became a firm Rock of the building, and Foundation of the house of God (ἐνταῦθα στερεία πίτρα

οἰκοδομῆς, καὶ θιμίλιος οἶκου Θεοῦ), in that having denied Christ, and being again converted, being both found of the Lord and found worthy to hear, *Feed my sheep and feed my lambs.*" *Adv. Hæres. p.* 500.

55. "Holy men are therefore called the temple of God, because the Holy Spirit dwells in them ; as that Chief (κορυφαῖος) of the Apostles testifies, he that was found worthy to be blessed by the Lord, because the *Father had revealed unto him.* To him then did the Father reveal His true Son, and he is *blessed;* and the same (Peter) furthermore reveals the Holy Ghost. This was befitting in that First of the Apostles, that firm Rock upon which *the Church* of God *is built* (ἴδι τὸν πρῶτον τῶν ἀποστόλων τὴν πέτραν τὴν στερεὰν, ἐφ'

ἦν ἡ ἐκκλησία τοῦ Θεοῦ ᾠκοδόμηται), and *the gates of hell shall not prevail against it.* The *gates of hell* are heretics and heresiarchs. For in every way was the faith confirmed in him who received *the keys of heaven ;* who *looses on earth and binds in heaven.* For in him are found all the subtle questions of faith. . . . He was aided by the Father, so as to be (or, lay) the Foundation of the security (firmness) of the faith (τὴν ἀσφάλειαν τῆς πιστίως θεμιλιῶν) . . . He heard from that same God, Peter, *feed My lambs;* to him was entrusted the flock ; he leads the way admirably in the power of his own Master (ὁ πιπιστευμένος τὴν ποίμνην· ὁ καλῶς ὁδηγῶν ἐν τῇ δυνάμει τοῦ ἰδίου δισπότου)." T. ii. *in Anchor. n.* 9, *p.* 14, 15.)

COMMENT.

S. Epiphanius was Bishop of Salamis in Cyprus. He affirms that S. Peter was "the Chiefest of the Apostles," that he became unto the Church "a firm Rock, upon which is based the Lord's faith," upon which "the Church is in every way built :" against which the gates of hell, that is, heretics and heresiarchs, shall not prevail. This Father also says that S. Peter, though he denied the Lord, yet, on his conversion, was found worthy to hear the words, "Feed My sheep ;" so that, according to S. Epiphanius, S. Peter received the commission to be the Chief Pastor of the flock. To S. Peter the Father revealed the Son and also the Holy Ghost, and he adds,

"This was befitting," as S. Peter was "the First of the Apostles, and that firm Rock upon which the Church of God is built," who received the keys, and in whom was found the solution of "all the subtle questions of faith." It is impossible not to see that this Father regarded S. Peter as far above his co-apostles in pre-eminence and authority; for "to him," he says, "was entrusted the flock," and "he leads the way admirably in the power of his own Master." When S. Epiphanius penned this last clause, the ruling idea in his mind must have been that S. Peter, like Moses of old, was acting in behalf of our Lord as his special representative.

S. AMBROSE.

A.D. 385.

56. "It is that same Peter to whom He said, *Thou art Peter, and upon this rock I will build my Church.* Therefore where Peter is, there is the Church; where the Church is, there death is not, but life eternal; and therefore it was added, and *the gates of hell shall not prevail against it,* and, *I will give to thee the keys of the kingdom of heaven.* Blessed Peter, against whom the gates of hell prevailed not, nor were the gates of heaven closed against him; but who, on the contrary, destroyed the porches of hell and opened the heavenly places." T. i. *In Ps.* xl. *n.* 30, *p.* 879, 880.

57. "In fine, Peter, after having been tempted by the devil, is set over the Church (*Petrus ecclesiæ præponitur*). The Lord, therefore, foreshowed (referring to S. Luke, xxii. 31, 32) what that was, that he afterwards chose him as the Pastor of the Lord's flock (*quod postea eum pastorem eligit Dominici gregis*). For to him He said, *But when thou art converted strengthen thy brethren.*" *Ib. in Ps.* xliii. *n.* 40, *p.* 904.

58. "Therefore did Christ also commit to Peter *to feed His flock,* and to do the will of the Lord, because He knew his love." *Ib. in Ps.* cxviii. (*Mem.*) *n.* 3, *p.* 1131.

59. "The ship is not agitated wherein prudence sails, where perfidy is not, where faith breathes. For how could that be agitated, over which he (Peter) presided, in whom is the Foundation (*firmamentum*) of the Church?... Though the rest are ordered to let down their nets, yet to Peter alone is it said, *Launch*

out *into the deep;* that is, into the depths of disputations... Into this deep of disputation the Church is led by Peter (*ecclesia a Petro ducitur*), so as to see thence rising again the Son of God, thence flowing the Holy Spirit.... They of the synagogue came to Peter's ship; that is, unto the Church." T. i. *Expos. in Luc. l.* iv. *n.* 70, 71, 77, *pp.* 1353–4.

60. "... Christ is the *Rock, For they drank of that spiritual Rock that followed them, and that Rock was Christ,* and He did not refuse to bestow the favour of this title even upon His disciple, so that he, too, might be Peter (or Rock), in that he has from the Rock a solid constancy, a firm faith (*ut et ipse sit Petrus, quod de petra habeat soliditatem constantiæ*)." *Ib. l.* vi. *n.* 97, *pp.* 1406–7.

61. "Peter was grieved because he is asked the third time, *Lovest thou Me?* For he is questioned who is doubted; but the Lord does not doubt; and He inquires not to learn, but to teach, now that He is about to be raised to heaven, whom He was leaving unto us, as it were, the Vicar of His own love (*amoris sui nobis velut vicarium relinquebat*). For thus have you it, *Simon, son of John, lovest thou me? Yea, Lord, Thou knowest that I love Thee. Jesus saith to him, Feed my sheep.* ... Who else could readily make this profession for himself? And, therefore, because he alone amongst all makes this profession, he is preferred before all (*omnibus antefertur*), for love is greater than all. ... And now he is not ordered, as at first, to *feed His lambs,* nor

His younger sheep, as in the second instance, but *His sheep*, that the more perfect might govern the more perfect (*perfectiores ut perfectior gubernaret*)." *Ib. l.* x. *n.* 175–6, *p.* 1542.

62. "... What fellowship, then, can these men (Novatians) have with thee ; men who receive not the keys of the kingdom, and who deny that they ought to forgive sins ? Which, indeed, is rightly acknowledged on their parts ; for they have not Peter's inheritance who have not Peter's Choir (*non habent Petri hæreditatem, qui Petri sedem non habent*), which with impious disunion they rend asunder : but they act wickedly in that they deny that even in the Church sins can be pardoned; whereas to Peter was it said, *I will give thee the keys,* &c. ; whereas also that vessel of the Lord's election says, *To whom ye forgive,* &c. (2 Cor. ii, 10). Why then do they read Paul if they think that he erred so impiously as to claim unto himself his Lord's rights ? But he claimed what he had received : he usurped not what belonged not to him." *T.* ii. *De Pæn. l.* i. *c.* vii. *n.* 32, 33, *p.* 399.

63. " Further, that thou mayest know that, as man, He prays ; as God, He commands ; thou hast in the Gospel that He said to Peter, *I have prayed for thee that thy faith fail not.* But to that same Peter when He said on an earlier occasion, *Thou art the Christ, the Son of the living God,* He answered, *Thou art Peter, and upon this Rock I will build my Church, and I will give unto thee the keys of the king-*

dom *of heaven.* How could he not confirm his faith, unto whom of His own authority He gave the kingdom, and whom when He styles a Rock, He pointed (*indicavit*) out the Foundation (*firmamentum*) of the Church ?" T. ii. *l.* iv. *De Fide, c.* v. *n.* 56, *p.* 531.

64. " Thou art silent, O Simon Peter, whilst the rest reply, though thou art the First (*cum ipse sis primus*), and though thou dost, even not asked, put thy questions. . . . He, therefore, who had been silent . . . when he heard, *But whom say ye that I am ?* at once, not unmindful of his position, exercised the Primacy ; the Primacy, to wit, of confession, not of honour, the Primacy of faith, not of rank ; that is to say, Now let none surpass me, now is my part. . . . This, then, is that Peter who answers for the rest, yea, as above the rest (*pro ceteris apostolis, immo præ ceteris*), and therefore is he called the Foundation, because he knows how not only to keep his own, but also that in common (to all). . . . Faith, therefore, is the foundation of the Church, for not of Peter's flesh, but of his faith, was it said that *The gates of hell shall not prevail against it;* but that confession vanquished hell. And this confession has shut out more than one heresy ; for whereas the Church, like a good ship, is often buffeted by many a wave, the Foundation of the Church ought to have strength to withstand every heresy." *Ib. De Incarn. c.* iv. *n.* 30, 32, 33; *et c.* v. *n.* 1, *p.* 710–11.

COMMENT.

S. Ambrose, some time Bishop of Milan, and one of the most illustrious Doctors of the Church, teaches that S.

Peter was the Chief Pastor of the flock, and Vicar of Jesus Christ.

1. With respect to the inquiry of our

Lord, "*Whom say ye that I am?*" S. Ambrose says that S. Peter, "at once not unmindful of his position, exercised the Primacy; the Primacy, to wit, of confession, not of honour, the Primacy of faith, not of rank;" that is, that in answering this question, as the Representative of the rest, he receives the Primacy of faith, so that he First confessed whom he First believed. This "confession vanquished hell." The Foundation of the Church is based, not upon the *flesh* of Peter, but upon his faith, against which *the gates of hell shall not prevail.*

2. In his exposition of the incident connected with the two ships at the Lake Gennessaret, recorded in S. Luke, S. Ambrose points out that when our Lord directed S. Peter to *launch out into the deep*, he signified by the *deep* "the depths of disputation," into which "the Church is led by Peter." From this we learn that it is one of the prerogatives of S. Peter to expound the truth to the Church; *i.e.* as S. Chrysostom says, as "the Teacher of the whole universe." This office he exercised at the Council of Jerusalem, for he taught the whole Church the truth as he had received it from Heaven (for the revelation that the Gentiles were to be fellow-heirs, was revealed to him *alone*, even as the Divinity of our Lord had been on a former occasion) and they accepted his teaching and confirmed his dogma. Even S. James' judgment was founded upon that of S. Peter. This opinion of S. Ambrose is supported by S. Hilary (See *Ext.* 28).

3. But S. Ambrose asserts that S. Peter was the Vicar of Christ. There is no mistaking the meaning of the word *vicarius*, that is, one occupying the place of another. He says that our Lord, when about to be raised to heaven, left unto the Church S. Peter, as the "Vicar of His own love," that is, he was to stand in Christ's Stead in the performance of the functions of Chief Pastor. S. Ambrose is not the only one who has taught that S. Peter was appointed Vicar of Christ; S. Ephraem Syrus had expressed that same sentiment when he said, "O thou blessed one, that obtainedst the Place of the Head" (See *Ext.* 41); and also subsequently S. Peter Chrysologus, who says, He commended His sheep to be fed by Peter "in His Stead;" and S. Epiphanius meant the same when he said, that he (Peter) "leads the way admirably in the power of his own Master." (See *Ext.* No. 55). It seems, then, the belief of both East and West that S. Peter filled the office of our Lord, viz. that of the Head of the universal Church; and certainly this is abundantly implied, for how could he, who was the co-Rock, the co-Foundation, the Key-bearer with Him, the Confirmer of the brethren, and the Chief Pastor of the flock, by express delegation,—how could he who had been commanded, by his own single authority, to open heaven to the Gentiles,—how could he who in all things assumed the functions of the Head, be otherwise than the Vicar of Him from whom he has received all these exalted offices?

4. Holding this doctrine S. Ambrose is perfectly consistent when he affirms that S. Peter was "set over the Church;" *præponitur* signifies set over in the sense of giving one the charge or command of any place or business, *i.e.* to make one Ruler or Chief. S. Ambrose means, then, that S. Peter was set over the Church as its Governor and Ruler. Hence, then, we understand the further statement of S. Ambrose that "where Peter is there is the Church," that is, all who are in communion with S. Peter as the Vicar of Christ, and Head of the Church, form together with him the Church. Hence, again, the contrary position, "They have not Peter's inheritance who have not Peter's chair," *i.e.* they who are without, *i.e.* out of the communion of S. Peter, are not in the Church, for the Church is in Peter, and the brethren who are in union with him.

The doctrine, then, of S. Ambrose is perfectly clear, viz. that S. Peter was the Vicar of Jesus Christ, the Foundation and the Rock of the Church, the Chief and Head of the Church, the Chief Judge in controversies of faith, and the Chief Pastor of the flock; that wherever he is, there is the Church, and wherever he is

not, there is not the Church; and those who are not in union with the chair of S. Peter, have no share in his inherit- ance. Such is S. Ambrose's testimony in regard to the position of this great Apostle.

S. JEROME.

A. D. 385.

64*. " If, then, the Apostle Peter, upon whom the Lord built the Church (*Petrus, super quem Do- minus fundavit ecclesiam*), has re- corded that the prophecy and pro- mise of the Lord was at that time fulfilled, how can we fix on another time, as on fancy?" *T.* iv. *Ep.* xxvii. *Pt.* ii. *col.* 64.

65. " But you say that the Church is built upon Peter, though in an- other place the same thing is done upon all the Apostles, and all re- ceive *the keys of the kingdom of heaven,* and the strength of the Church is settled equally upon them ; yet for this reason One is chosen out of the Twelve, that a Head being appointed, the occasion of schism might be removed. (*Ta- men propterea inter duodecim unus eligitur, ut capite constituto, schis- matis tollatur occasio.*) But why was not John, the virgin, chosen? Deference was paid to age, seeing that Peter was older; lest one yet a

youth, and almost a boy, would be set above (*præferretur*) men of ad- vanced age." *Ib. adv. Jovin. Pl.* ii. *col.* 170.

66. " As Plato was the prince of philosophers, so was Peter the Prince of the Apostles, on whom the Church of the Lord in enduring massive- ness was built ; a Church which neither by the assaulting wave, nor by any tempest, is shaken." *Ib. contr. Pelag. Pl.* ii. *col.* 491.

67. " *Thou art Peter, and upon this rock I will build my Church.* As He bestowed light on His Apostles, so that they were to be called *the light of the world,* and as they ob- tained other titles from the Lord, so also to Simon, who believed on the Rock Christ, was given the name Peter (Rock). And in accordance with the metaphor of a rock, it is justly said to him, *I will build my Church upon thee* (*Ædificabo ec- clesiam meam super te*)." *Ib. l.* iii. *Comm. in Matt. Pl.* i. *col.* 74.

COMMENT.

S. Jerome, a Priest and Doctor of the Church, affirms that " the Lord built his Church upon S. Peter," and although it is true that the keys were given to all the Apostles, and that the strength of the Church was settled equally upon all, yet " One is chosen out of the Twelve, that a Head being appointed the occasion of schism might be removed." The word *caput* is here used, showing that this Headship was to be a *governing power;* and indeed S.

Jerome's reasoning involves it, for how could schism be prevented, and unity maintained by the One Chosen Head, unless he was armed with the necessary authority and power to act when need- ful ? Much stress is laid upon S. Jerome comparing the *principatus* of S. Peter with that of Plato over philosophers, showing thereby that S. Jerome held only a primacy of honour ; but there is a wide distinction between the primacy of Plato and that of S. Peter, for of the latter it is said that "the Church of the Lord in enduring massiveness was built." No doubt schools of philosophy were founded on Plato's doctrines, but who ever said to him, "I will give thee the keys," or "Feed My sheep?" A certain resemblance doubtless there is be-

tween the two Primacies; but one thing is clear, that what S. Jerome meant with regard to S. Peter, was, that he should have and exercise the Primacy of authority, and as a Head rule the brethren that schism may be prevented.

S. CHRYSOSTOM.

A. D. 387.

68. " Peter himself the Head or Crown of the Apostles, the First in the Church (ἡ κορυφή τῶν ἀποστόλων, ὁ πρῶτος ἐν τῇ ἐκκλησίᾳ).the Friend of Christ, who received a revelation, not from man, but from the Father, as the Lord bears witness to him, saying, *Blessed art thou, &c.* This very Peter—and when I name Peter I name that unbroken Rock, that firm Foundation, the Great Apostle, the First of the disciples (τὴν πέτραν λέγω τὴν ἀρραγῆ, τὴν κρηπίδα τὴν ἀσάλευτον .... τὸν πρῶτον τῶν μαθητῶν), the First called, and the First who obeyed—he was guilty of a deed not slight, but exceeding great, even the denying of the Lord." *T.* ii. *Hom.* iii. *de Pœnit. n.* 4, *p.* 300.

69. " And yet after so great an evil (his denial), he again raised him to his former honour, and entrusted to his hand the Government of the universal Church (τὴν ἐπιστασίαν τῆς οἰκουμενικῆς ἐκκλησίας ἐνεχείρισε.)" *T.* ii. *Hom.* v. *de Pœnit. n.* 2, *p.* 309.

70. " Great was God's consideration towards this city (Antioch), as He manifested by deeds, inasmuch as Peter, who was set over the whole habitable world ; he, in whose hands He placed the keys of heaven; him, to whom He intrusted the doing and supporting all things (Τὸν γοῦν τῆς οἰκουμένης ἐπιστάτον ἁπάσης

Πέτρον, ᾧ τὰς κλεῖς ἐνεχείρισε τῶν οὐρανῶν, ᾧ πάντα ἄγειν καὶ φέρειν ἐπέτρεψι) ; him He ordered to tarry here for a long time ; thus this one city (Antioch) was to him equivalent to the whole world." *Ib. In.* S. Sq. M. *n.* 4, *p.* 579.

71. " Peter, the Leader of the choir of the Apostles, the Mouth of the disciples, the Pillar of the Church, the Buttress (foundation) of the faith, the Foundation of the confession, the Fisherman of the universe." *T.* iii. *Hom. de Dec. Mill. Talent. n.* 3, *p.* 4, 5.

72. Peter, that Leader of the choir, that Mouth of the rest of the Apostles, that Head of the brotherhood, that One set over the entire universe, that Foundation of the Church (ἡ κεφαλὴ τῆς φατρίας ἐκείνης, ὁ τῆς οἰκουμένης ἁπάσης προστάτης, ὁ θεμέλιος τῆς ἐκκλησίας.)" *T.* vi. *In illud, hoc Scitote, n.* 4, *p.* 282.

73. " Jesus saith to Simon Peter, *Simon, son of John, lovest thou Me more than these?* And why, then, passing by the rest, does He discourse with Peter concerning these things? He was the Chosen One of the Apostles, and the Mouth of the disciples, and the Head of the choir (ἔκκριτος ἦν τῶν ἀποστόλων, καὶ στόμα τῶν μαθητῶν, καὶ κορυφὴ τοῦ χοροῦ). For this cause

also did Paul come upon an occasion to see him before the rest. And withal showing him, that thenceforward he must be confident, as, having done away with his denial, He (Christ) places in his hands the Government over the brethren (ἐγχειρί-ζεται τὴν προστασίαν τῶν ἀδελφῶν), and He brings not forward that denial, neither does He reproach him with the past, but says to him, If thou love me, preside (προίστασο) over the brethren." *T.* viii. *Hom.* lxxxviii. *in Joan. n.* i. *p.* 525.

74. "And should any one say, 'Why then did James receive the throne of Jerusalem?' This is my answer : That He appointed this man (Peter) not teacher of that throne, but of the habitable globe. (Ὅτι τοῦτον οὐ τοῦ θρόνου, ἀλλὰ τῆς οἰκουμένης ἐχειροτόνησι διδάσκαλον.)" *Ib. n.* 6, *p.* 527.

75. "*And in those days Peter stood up in the midst of the disciples, and said* (Acts, i. 15.) Both as being ardent, and as having had intrusted to him by Christ the flock ; as the First of the choir, he always is the First to begin the discourse. Lo, there were *a hundred and twenty;* and he asks for one out of the whole multitude. Justly, he has the First authority in the matter, as having had all intrusted to him (πρῶτος τοῦ πράγματος αὐθεντεῖ ἅτε αὐτὸς πάντας ἐγχειρισθεὶς). For to him Christ said, *When thou art converted, strengthen thy brethren.*" *T.* ix. *Hom.* iii. *in Act App. n.* 3. *p.* 26.

76. "For if on account of the two brethren they were filled with indignation, much more here ; for they had not yet had the Spirit vouchsafed to them. But afterwards they were not such men. For everywhere they yielded the First honours to Peter (πανταχοῦ τῶν πρωτείων παραχωροῦσι), and put him forward in the addresses to the people, although more roughly disposed than any of them." *T.* vii. *Hom.* l. *in Matt. n.* 2, *p.* 515.

77. "See how Paul speaks after Peter, and no one restrains ; James waits and starts not up, for'he it was to whom had been intrusted the Government* (τὴν ἀρχὴν ἐγκεχειρισάμενος)." *T.* ix. *Hom.* xxxiii. in *Act. App. n.* 2, *p.* 255.

78. "For this cause not even in the kingdom is the honour equal; nor amongst the disciples were all equal ; but the three were pre-eminent amongst the rest, and amongst these three again there was much difference. For with God there is a very exact method even to the lowest. Yea, *for one star differeth from another star in glory,* is said. And though all were Apostles, and all were to sit on twelve thrones, and all had left their goods, and all companioned with Him, still it was the three He took. And again, even of these three He said that some were under, and some superior (καὶ τούτων αὐτῶν ἔφησε τινας ἐγχωρεῖν καὶ ὑπερέχειν.) *To sit on my right hand and on my left is not,* he says, *mine to give,* but to *them for whom it is prepared.* And He sets Peter before them (καὶ τὸν Πέτρον

---

* The editor of " Faith of Catholics " says, in a note on the word ἀρχὴν, which he translates *government,* that in the same vol. *Hom.* ii. in *Ep. Rom.* p. 474 (Paris, 1837), ἀρχὴν is used for the sovereign *empire* of Rome, " having recently acquired the *empire* of the world " (τῆς οἰκουμένης τὴν ἀρχὴν). (See *Faith of Cath.,* note, vol. ii. p. 35.)

δὲ αὐτῶν προτιθήσι), saying, *Lovest thou Me more than these?* And John was loved above the rest." *Ib.*

Hom. xxxi. *in Ep. ad Rom. n.* 4, *p.* 750.

COMMENT.

S. John Chrysostom, Patriarch of Constantinople, and one of the great Doctors of the Church, is very explicit in the statement of his opinion concerning S. Peter's position in the Apostolic Hierarchy. He says that S. Peter is the "Head or Crown of the Apostles," "The First in the Church," "The Leader of the Choir," "The Mouth of the Disciples," "The Pillar of the Church," "The Buttress of the Faith," "The Foundation of the Confession," "The Teacher of the habitable Globe," "The Fisherman of the Universe," "The Head of the Brotherhood," &c. Titles, it must be confessed, indicating the prerogative of ruling, teaching, leading, and of representing the Church by himself alone. The two Greek words, translated Head, are κορυφὴ or κιφαλὴ, signifying, the one the Crown of the head, and the other the head itself; so that S. Chrysostom believed that in S. Peter was the royalty of our Lord, and that he was the Head of the brotherhood. S. Peter was then the Supreme Pastor, the Supreme Governor or Ruler of the Church, invested with all the prerogatives of royal authority. And this is plain from this Father's further asseverations, for he avers that the Lord "entrusted to his hands the government over the universal Church," that he was "set over the whole habitable world," "in whose hands He placed the keys of heaven," to " whom He entrusted the doing and supporting of all things," to whom " was entrusted by Christ the flock." This is language which cannot by any possibility be ignored or explained away. It is plain that this Father held the Supremacy of S. Peter to the fullest extent, consistent with the rights of the rest of the Apostles. But let us examine the above extract

more closely, "Government over the universal Church." The word τὴν ἐπιστασίαν, signifies command, government, direction, it includes the office of general, inspector, or overseer. S. Peter then had the Government and Direction of the universal Church. "Set over the whole habitable world," and "set over the entire universe;" the words used here are ἐπιστάτον and προστάτης, the former signifying chief, commander, or general in command, an inspector, or superintendent, Chief President ;* the latter a chief, or leader, superintendent, an overseer or director, a president, a guardian, a patron, a protector. There can be little doubt, then, that S. Chrysostom meant to say, that to S. Peter was committed the Government of the whole world. To " whom He entrusted the doing and supporting all things." The verb ἐπιτρέπω signifies to transfer or bequeath, to entrust as to a trustee, a guardian or vicegerent, so that this great doctor held that the Lord committed all things, connected with His Church, to the care of S. Peter.

(1) But perhaps the most valuable testimony of S. Chrysostom is to be found in those Homilies which treat upon S. Peter's *administration* of the Government within a few years after the ascension. (1.) In the election of a new Apostle in the room of Judas Iscariot: a vacancy having occurred, it was S. Peter's duty to provide for the election of a new Apostle : why ? S. Chrysostom answers, Because (1) "as having had entrusted to him by Christ the flock," *i.e.* as Chief Pastor, his business was to cause pastors to be chosen for the well-being of the flock ; (2) because "as the First of the choir, he always is the First to begin the discourse," *i. e.* as holding the

---

* Chief President of the Church. (See *Liddell Lex.*)

Primacy of honour; and (3) because, "as having had all entrusted to him," "justly, he was the First authority in the matter," i. e. as "having had placed in his hands the Government over the brethren." The word προστασίαν signifies one standing in front, at the head, as having authority and power to command others; the kindred word προστάσις has a similar meaning. He then who had the First authority in this matter, exercised it by directing the election of an Apostle to be made on certain conditions to the vacant chair. It is manifest, then, that in this proceeding S. Peter acted the part of the Chief Pastor, and the Chief Governor or Ruler of the universal Church.

(2) The visit of S. Paul to S. Peter. "For this cause also did Paul come upon an occasion to see him (Peter) before the rest?" What was "that cause?" because S. Peter was "the Chosen One of the Apostles," "the Mouth of the disciples," and "the Head of the choir." In a word, because of his Supremacy. By this visit S. Paul recognised S. Peter as the Head and Chief Pastor of the Church.

(3.) The Council of Jerusalem. S. Chrysostom says, "See how Paul speaks after Peter...James waits and starts not up, for he it was to whom had been intrusted the government." There seems to be some difference of opinion whether "he" in the last clause of this passage refers to S. Peter or S. James. The translator of S. Chrysostom's Homilies on the Acts of the Apostles, in the Library of the Fathers, has, without note or comment, without even the use of brackets, substituted "James" in the place of the pronoun "he." The following is his version: "There was no arrogance in the Church. After Peter Paul speaks, and none silences him: James waits patiently, not starts up (for the next word). Great the orderliness (of the proceedings). No word speaks John here, no word the other Apostles, but held their peace, for James was invested with the chief rule,

and thinks it no hardship." (Hom. xxxiii. in Act. App. p. 455; Lib. Fath. Oxf.) The following is the text: οὕτως οὐδεὶς τύφος ἦν ἐν τῇ ἐκκλησίᾳ, ἀλλὰ πολλὴ ἡ εὐταξία· καὶ ὅρα, μετὰ Πέτρον Παῦλος φθέγγεται, καὶ οὐδεὶς ἐπιστομίζει· Ἰάκωβος ἀναχίναι, καὶ οὐκ ἀποπηδᾷ, ἐκεῖνος γὰρ ἦν τὴν ἀρχὴν ἐγκεχειρισμένος. οὐδὲν Ἰωάννης ἐνταῦθα· οὐδὲν οἱ ἄλλοι ἀπόστολοι φθέγγονται· ἀλλὰ σιγῶσι, &c., Hom. xxxiii. in Act. App. T. ix. n. 2, p. 255. Bened. 1731. It is, however, of very little consequence to whom the ἐκεῖνος ("he") refers. It is quite possible, and not improbable, that S. James occupied the chair of the Moderator, in virtue of his position as Bishop of the then holy city, and, especially so, because of his near relationship to Christ, as "The Lord's Brother." It is not, however, essential that the Chief Ruler on all occasions, either personally or by deputy, should preside. At the Council of Chalcedon the officials of the Emperor presided, notwithstanding the presence of the Legates, who do not seem to have recorded any protest against their so doing. The real question at issue is this, not who presided, but who determined the controversy, which was the occasion for convoking the Synod? If we read the account, as given in the Acts of the Apostles, two facts are apparent, (1) that S. Peter informed the council of the truth he had received, and (2) that his definition or decree was accepted and confirmed by the whole Church, S. James himself basing his own judgment upon that of S. Peter. But whatever S. Chrysostom meant, it must be clear that he could not have intended to assert that to S. James had been committed the government of the Church, for this would have been a direct contradiction to his oft-repeated testimony in favour of S. Peter's Supremacy. The above extract plainly shows this. Nor could he have meant to say, that S. James was "the Teacher of the World," for he had already committed himself to a different opinion in the following words: "Why did James receive the throne of Jerusalem? This is my answer: that He appointed this man (Peter), not teacher of that throne (Jerusalem), *but of the habitable world."* (See *Ext.* 74.) It must be concluded that S. Chrysostom, if he believed S. James presided (which, to say the least, is doubtful), did not ignore S. Peter's office, even in this council, as "the Teacher of the World."

S. Chrysostom's doctrine concerning S. Peter is very manifest, viz. that he was the Chief Pastor, Chief Ruler, and Chief Judge, to whom the Lord intrusted the Government and sustainment of His Church.

PRUDENTIUS. (A.D. 405.)

79. " And already have most assured pledges of this hope ; for here already reign two Princes of the Apostles—one the Apostle of the Gentiles, the other holding the First chair, flings open the portals of eternity, that have been entrusted to him."

(Heic nempe jam regnant duo
Apostolorum principes,
Alter vocator gentium,
Alter cathedram possidens
Primam, recludit creditas
Æternitatis januas.)
Hymn ii. *in Honor. S. Laurent.* v. 459–64.
Galland, T. viii. *p.* 440.

COMMENT.

Prudentius was a Spanish poet. The point in this *extract* is that he regards S. Peter and S. Paul as the two reigning Princes of the Apostles—one of the Gentiles ; the other, as the occupant of the First chair, "flings open the gates of eternity," which had been placed under his charge as, according to S. Hilary, "the Gate-keeper," and S. Cyril, "the Key-bearer."

POPE S. INNOCENT. (A.D. 410.)

80. " Let us therefore, begin, with the help of the holy Apostle Peter, through whom both the Apostolate and the Episcopate took their rise in Christ (*per quem et apostolatus et episcopatus in Christo cœpit exordium.*") *Ep.* ii. *Galland. t.* viii. *n.* 2, *p.* 547.

S. AUGUSTINE. (A.D. 400.)

81. " If the order of bishops succeeding to each other is to be considered, how much more securely, and really beneficially, do we reckon from Peter himself, to whom, bearing a Figure of the Church, the Lord says, *Upon this rock I will build my Church.*" *T.* ii. *E.* liii. *Generos. col.* 91.

82. " . . . He began to wash the feet of His disciples . . . . and then it is added, He went therefore to Simon Peter, as if He had already washed the others, and after them He came to the First, for who can be ignorant that the most blessed Peter is the First of the Apostles (*primum apostolorum*)?" *T.* iii. *Tract.* lvi. *in Joan. n.* 1, *col.* 476.

83. " Of this Church, Peter, the Apostle, on account of the Primacy of his Apostleship (*propter apostolatus sui primatum*), bore a character which represented the whole Church. For as to what personally regards him, he was by nature but one man, by grace one Christian, by a more abundant grace, one, and that the First Apostle ; but when there was said to him, *I will give unto him the keys,* &c., He signified the whole

Church, which, in this world, is, by divers trials, as it were, by rains, rivers, and tempests, agitated, but falls not, because it was built upon a Rock, whence Peter derived his name. For a rock (*petra*) is not derived from Peter (*Petro*), but Peter from a Rock, as Christ is not derived from Christian, but Christian from Christ. For therefore does the Lord say, *Upon this rock I will build my Church,* because Peter had said, *Thou art the Christ, the Son of the living God.* Upon this Rock, therefore, which thou hast confessed, I will build My Church. For Christ was the Rock; upon which Foundation, even Peter himself was built. *For other foundation can no man lay but that which is laid, which is Christ Jesus.* The Church therefore which is founded on Christ, received in Peter the keys of the kingdom of heaven from Him, that is, the power of binding and of loosing sins." *T.* iii. *Tract.* cxxiv. *in Joan. n.* 5, *col.* 599.

84. "We know that Peter was a fisherman: what then could he give up, to follow our Lord? Or his brother Andrew, or John and James, the sons of Zebedee, themselves also fishermen; and yet what did they say? *Behold, we have forsaken all, and followed Thee.* Our Lord said not to him, Thou hast forgotten thy poverty; what hast thou resigned, that thou shouldest receive the whole world? He, my brethren, who resigned not only what he had, but also what he longed to have, resigned much. . . . . Peter did indeed resign the whole world: and Peter did indeed receive the whole world." *T.* iv. *in Psal.* ciii. *Serm.* iii. *n.* 16, *col.* 871.

85. "For as some things are said which seem peculiarly to apply to

the Apostle Peter, and yet are not clear in their meaning, unless when referred to the Church, whom he is acknowledged to have figuratively represented, on account of the Primacy which he bore among the disciples (*propter primatum quem in discipulis habuit*) ; and it is written, *I will give unto thee the keys of the kingdom of heaven,* and other passages of the like purport ; so Judas does represent those Jews who were enemies of Christ." *Ib. in Psal.* cviii. *n.* 1, *col.* 911, 12.

86. "The Gospel (S. Matt. xiv.), which has just been read, touching the Lord Christ, who walked on the waters of the sea; and the Apostle Peter, who as he was walking, tottered through fear, and sinking in distrust, rose again by confession, gives us to understand that the sea is the present world, and the Apostle Peter the Type of the one Church. For Peter is in the order of Apostles First (*primus*), and in the love of Christ most forward, answers oftentimes alone for all the rest. Again, when the Lord Jesus Christ asked, Whom men said that He was, and when the disciples gave the various opinions of men, and the Lord asked again and said, *But whom say ye that I am?* Peter answered, *Thou art the Christ, the Son of the living God.* One for many gave the answer, Unity in many (*unus pro multis dedit responsum, unitas in multis*). Then said the Lord to him, *Blessed art thou, Simon Barjonas; for flesh and blood hath not revealed it unto thee, but my Father which is in heaven.* Then He added, *And I say unto thee.* As if He had said, " Because thou hast said unto Me, Thou *art the Christ, &c.;* I say unto thee, *Thou art Peter.* For before he was called Simon. Now this

name Peter was given him by the Lord, and that too a Figure, that he should signify the Church. For seeing that Christ is the Rock (*petra*), Peter is the Christian people. For the Rock (*petra*) is the original name. Therefore Peter is so called from the Rock, not the Rock from Peter ; as Christ is not called Christ from the Christian, but the Christian from Christ. *Therefore*, he saith, *Thou art Peter ;* and *upon this Rock,* which thou hast confessed, upon this Rock which thou hast acknowledged, saying, *Thou art the Christ, the Son of the living God, will I build my Church ;* that is, upon Myself, the Son of the living God, *will I build My Church.* I will build thee upon Myself, not Myself upon thee. For Men who wished to be built upon Men, said, *I am of Paul; and I of Apollos; and I of Cephas,* who is Peter. But others who did not wish to be built upon Peter, but upon the Rock, said, *But I am of Christ.* And when the Apostle Paul ascertained that he was chosen, and Christ despised, he said, *Is Christ divided? was Paul crucified for you? or were you baptized in the name of Paul?* And, as not in the name of Paul, so neither in the name of Peter; but in the Name of Christ: that Peter might be built upon the Rock, not the Rock upon Peter. This same Peter therefore, who had been by the Rock pronounced *blessed*, bearing the Figure of the Church, holding the Principate of the Apostleship (*apostolatus principatum*), a very little while after that he had heard that he was *blessed*, a very little while after that he had heard that he was *Peter*, a very little while after that he had heard that he was to be *built upon the Rock*, displeased the Lord when He had heard of

His future Passion, for He had foretold His disciples that it was soon to be. . . . Yet see this Peter, who was then our Figure ; now he trusts, and now he totters ; now he confesses the Undying, and now he fears that he should die. Wherefore? because the Church of Christ hath both strong and weak ones ; and cannot be without either strong or weak; whence the Apostle Paul says, *Now we that are strong, &c.* (Rom. xv. 1.) In that Peter said, *Thou art the Christ, &c.* he represents the strong; but in that he totters, and would not that Christ should suffer, in fearing death for him, and not acknowledging the Life, he represents the weak ones of the Church. In that one Apostle then, that is, Peter, in the order of the Apostles First and Chiefest, in whom the Church was Figured, both sorts were to be represented, that is, both the strong and the weak ; because the Church doth not exist without them both." *T. v. Serm. lxxvi. in Matt. n. 1–4, col.* 290–1.

87. "When our Lord then was speaking on this occasion, He said, that He is *the Shepherd,* He said also that He *is the Door.* You find them both in that place, both *I am the Door,* and *I am the Shepherd.* In the Head He is the Door, the Shepherd in the Body. For He saith to Peter, in whom singly He formeth the Church (*in quo uno format ecclesiam*); *Peter, lovest thou Me?* he answered, *Lord, I do love Thee. Feed My sheep.* And, a third time, *Peter, lovest thou Me? Peter was grieved because He asked him the third time;* as though He who saw the conscience of the denier, saw not the confession faith. [Drawing a comparison between S. Peter and an invalid who knew not his strength, S.

Augustine continues] : Peter then was at that time the invalid, and the Lord the Physician. The former declared that he had strength, when he had not ; but the Lord touching the pulse of his heart, declared that he should deny Him thrice. And so it came to pass, as the Physician foretold, not as the sick presumed. Therefore, after His resurrection, the Lord questioned him, not as being ignorant with what a heart he would confess the love of Christ, but that he might by a threefold confession of love, efface the threefold denial of fear." *Ib. Serm.* cxxxvii. *n.* 3, *col.* 463.

88. "But what now ? The Lord asketh him, as ye heard when the Gospel was being read, and saith to him, *Simon, son of John, lovest thou me more than these ?* He answered, and said, *Yea, Lord, Thou knowest that I love Thee.* And again the Lord asked this question, and a third time He asked it. And when he asserted in reply his love, He commended to him the flock (*et respondenti dilectionem, commendavit gregem*). For each several time the Lord Jesus said to Peter, as he said, *I love Thee; Feed my lambs,* feed My *little sheep.* In this one Peter was figured the unity of all pastors, of good pastors, that is, who know that they feed Christ's

sheep for Christ, not for themselves." (*In uno Petro figurabatur unitas omnium pastorum,* &c.) *Ib. Serm.* cxlvii. *n.* 2, *col.* 489.

89. "For Peter in many places of the Scriptures appears to personate the Church; especially in that place where it was said, *I give unto thee the keys, &c.,* what I did Peter receive these *keys,* and Paul not receive them? Did Peter receive them, and John, and James, and the rest of the Apostles, not receive them? Or are not these *keys,* in the Church, where sins are daily remitted ? But since in Figure Peter represented the Church, what was given to him alone (*quod illi uni datum est*), was given to the Church? Peter then represented the Church, the Church is the Body of Christ." *Ib. Serm.* cxlix. *n.* 7, *col.* 492.

90. "For not without cause among all the Apostles doth Peter sustain the Person of this Church Catholic (*non enim sine causa inter omnes Apostolos hujus ecclesiæ catholicæ personam sustinet Petrus*) ; for unto this Church were the keys of the kingdom of heaven given, when they were given unto Peter : and when it is said unto him, it is said unto all, *Lovest thou Me ? Feed My sheep.*" *T.* vii. *De Agone Christiano, n.* 32, *col.* 190.

COMMENT.

S. Augustine was Bishop of Hippo, and one of the most illustrious Doctors of the Church. He considers S. Peter as the "Type," the Figure, the Representative of the Church. The Rock, he interprets to be Christ, on whom S. Peter was himself built. He says that the Church was formed "singly" in S. Peter, that the keys were given "alone" to him, so that until our Lord extended the commission to the

other Apostles, S. Peter was "singly" the Church. He therefore represented the Church, yea, he alone "sustained the Person of the Church." And not only was he in a general sense to represent the Church, but also specially the strong and the weak ; this was typified, when he confessed the Divinity of Christ, and became a Rock from the Rock Christ ; and when he denied His Lord, thereby representing the weakness of some in the Church. S. Peter then was truly a perfect Figure and Representative of the Church, including both the weak and the strong: but he was more, for he "singly" was made the Church, and he "singly" received the keys, the emblem of supreme jurisdiction. This is evidently a replication of Tertullian's and S. Cyprian's doctrine. The former taught that the keys were *through* him (Peter) granted to the other Apostles; and the latter, that he was the Origin and Principle of unity, from whence the unity of the priesthood did rise. So that S. Augustine's doctrine is in perfect harmony with the Fathers before him. But we now arrive at the main point, Why was S. Peter the Figure of the Church? Why did he personate the Church? S. Augustine replies without hesitation, in one place, "On account of

the Primacy (*primatus*) of his Apostleship;" and in another, because he held the "Principate (*principatus*) of the Apostolate." The words *primatus* and *principatus* denote much more than a mere Primacy of honour, or of order; the former word has been explained above (see comment, p. 24), the latter signifies sovereignty, dominion, the chief power or government, so that there cannot be any doubt that this eminent Father and Doctor believed, with his cotemporaries and predecessors, that S. Peter was the Head and Prince of the Apostles, and the Centre of unity, from whom, as from a fountain, the Church of Christ arose, having her foundations laid upon the Rock of Ages, which he (Peter), as a Rock (hewn from the true Rock), was commissioned to Sustain, Govern, and Feed.

S. MAXIMUS.

A.D. 424.

91. "On account of this confession, the blessed Apostle merited to hear from the mouth of the Lord, *Thou art Peter, and upon this rock, &c.* That is, thou art the First to confess Me on earth, and I will make thee to have a perpetual Primacy in heaven, and in My Kingdom. And what more just than that the Church should be built on him, who gives so mighty a Foundation to the Church. (*Id est tu me confessus es primus in terris; ego te in cælo regnoque meo*

perpetuum faciam habere primatum. Et quid justius . . . . quam ut supra eum fundaretur ecclesia, qui tantum dedit ecclesiæ fundamentum.) What could be more religiously done, than that he should receive the *keys of heaven*, he who revealed the Lord of the heavenly kingdom; inasmuch as he who opened to believers the gates of faith, the same should also open for them the gates of heaven." *Serm.* lxxii. *De Dict. Ev.* "*Vos estis sal terræ.*" *Galland. t.* ix. p. 393.

COMMENT.

S. Maximus was Bishop of Turin: he asserted that to S. Peter was given a perpetual Primacy in heaven and in (Christ's) Kingdom, that is, the Church. This Father seems to hold that S. Peter held the Primacy of the Church above, as well as the Primacy of the Church below; and in both cases in

perpetuity. Holding the keys of heaven, he opens to believers on earth the gates of faith, and above the gates of heaven. There is no doubt Maximus believed that S. Peter held the Primacy, *i.e.*, not of order, but of Authority; for he who possesses the Key, is the Master of the house.

E

POPE S. BONIFACE.

A.D. 419.

92. "The blessed Apostle Peter, to whom by the Lord's voice was granted the highest place of the priesthood (*arx sacerdotii*), is beyond measure gratified," &c. *Ep.* iv. *Rufo, n.* 1, *Galland. t.* ix. *p.* 49.

93. "The institution of the universal Church took its beginning from the honour bestowed on blessed Peter, in whom its Gov-

ernment and Headship reside. (*Institutio universalis ecclesiæ de beati Petri sumsit honore principium, in quo regimen ejus et summa consistit*). For from him as its Source did ecclesiastical discipline flow over all the churches, when the culture of religion had begun to make progress." *Ep.* xiv. *Epis. Thess. Galland. t.* ix. *p.* 57

COMMENT.

S. Boniface maintains that S. Peter occupied "the highest place in the priesthood." The expression *arx sacerdotii*, is very strong, indicating that S. Peter was the Crown of the priesthood : S. Boniface, also affirms that "the universal Church took its beginning from the honour bestowed on the blessed Peter,"

"in whom the (Church's) Government and Headship reside, for from him as its Source did ecclesiastical discipline flow over all the churches ;" this agrees with what S. Cyprian affirmed of "the Chair of Peter, from whence the unity of the priesthood took its rise."

S. CYRIL, OF ALEXANDRIA.

A.D. 424.

94. Commenting on *Thou art Simon, the son of Jonas, &c.*, (S. John, i. 42) "He suffers him no longer to be called Simon, exercising authority and rule over him already as having become His own. But by a title suitable to the thing, He changed his name into Peter, from the word *petra* (rock) ; for on him He was afterwards to found His Church." *T.* iv. *Comm. in Joan. p.* 131.

95. "And even the blessed Peter, though set over the holy disciples (καίτοι τῶν ἁγίων προεκκείμενος μαθητῶν), says, *Lord, be it far from me*," &c. *Ib. l.* xi. *p.* 924.

96. "If Peter himself, that Prince of the holy disciples (αὐτὸς ὁ τῶν ἁγίων μαθητῶν προκρίτος Πέτρος), was upon an occasion," &c. *Ib. l.* xii. *p.* 1064.

97. "Besides all these, let there come forward that Leader of the holy disciples (ὁ τῶν μαθητῶν ἡγούμενος Πέτρος), Peter, who, when the Lord, on a certain occasion, asked him, *Whom do men say that the Son of Man is?* instantly cried out, *Thou art the Christ, the Son of the living God.*" *T.* v. *Pt.* 2. *Hom.* viii. *De Fest. Pasch. p.* 105.

98. "When, therefore, the Lord

intimated the denial of His disciple (Peter), He said these words : *I have prayed for thee, that thy faith fail not;* He straightway infers and utters the language of consolation : *And after thou art converted con-* *firm thy brethren;* that is, Be thou the Foundation and the Teacher of those who by Faith come unto me." *S. Luke*, c. xxii. *Apud Cord. Mai. Nov. Bibliot. Pat. T.* ii. *p.* 419, 420.

COMMENT.

S. Cyril, Patriarch of Alexandria, believed that in the changing of S. Peter's name, the Lord signified, that " on him He was afterwards to found His Church." He styles him " the Prince " and " Leader of the holy disciples." He further affirms that when our Lord said, *When thou art converted, &c.*, He made S. Peter " the Foundation and the Teacher" of all the Faithful. This is very strong testimony to S. Peter's Supremacy.

THEODORET.

A.D. 424.

99. Quoting S. Luke, xxii. 31-2, he says, " For as I, Christ said, despised not thee when thou wast shaken, so do thou also be a Support to thy brethren when troubled, and grant them that help of which thou hast partaken, and do not cast down the falling, but raise up those who are in danger. For, for this cause do I suffer thee to stumble first, but permit thee not to fall, providing stability, through thee, for the wavering. Thus did this great Pillar support the tottering world, and suffered it not in any wise to fall, but placed it upright, and made it firm, and received a command to *feed the Lord's sheep*." *T.* iii. *Orat. de Carit. p.* 1309.

COMMENT.

Theodoret, Bishop of Cyrus, seems to regard S. Peter much as S. Augustine did, as a Type of the Church, especially of its weak members. He considers that he was permitted to stumble, but not to fall, *i.e.*, from the faith, in order that Stability through him might be provided for the wavering. Hence is he that " great Pillar of a tottering world," which he has placed upright and made firm ; and hence, he received the command " to Feed the Lord's sheep."

S. PETER CHRYSOLOGUS.

A.D. 440.

100. " Hence it is that the Master Himself seeks for helpers, for associates to take charge of the whole world, saying, *Sing joyfully* to God, all the earth (Ps. xcix). Hence it it is that, when about to return to heaven, He commends His sheep to be fed by Peter, in his Stead.

(*vice sua ut pasceret* . . . . .
commendat). Peter, says He,
*lovest thou Me ? Feed My sheep."
Serm.* vi. *In Ps.* xcix. *p.* 10.

101. " As Peter obtained his
name from *a Rock*, because he was
the First, that merited to found the
Church by the firmness of his
faith, so Stephen was so called
from a *crown*, because he was the
first who merited to engage in conflict for the name of Christ. . . .
Let Peter hold his long-established
Princedom (*principatum*) over the
Apostolic Choir; let him open the
Kingdom of heaven for those who
enter in ; let him with power bind
the guilty ; with clemency absolve
the penitent." *Serm.* cliv. *p.* 217.

COMMENT.

S. Peter Chrysologus, Bishop of Ra-
venna, believed that our Lord, who
was about to return to heaven, did appoint S. Peter in His Place, as the feeder
of the sheep, and to have the charge of
the whole world. This Father then supposed that Peter was, in a special sense,
appointed the Vicar or Representative of
Jesus Christ ; and in this he agrees with
S. Ambrose and S. Ephraem Syrus, who
expressly assert this doctrine, and with
others, as S. Epiphanius, who imply the
same in their writings. He apostro-
phizes S. Peter to hold his long-established Primacy or Government over the
Apostolic Choir, using the word *principatum*, which, as has been seen, signifies the principality or sovereignty of
the Apostleship. He holds that the keys
are in the possession of S. Peter as the
Custodian.

POPE S. LEO.

A.D. 440.

102. " Though Peter alone received many things, nothing passed
unto any one else without his participation in it. . . . Out of the
whole world the one Peter is
chosen, to be set over the vocation
of all the nations, and over all the
Apostles, and all the Fathers of the
Church ; that so, though there be
in the people of God, many priests
and many pastors, Peter especially
(or, of his own right) may rule all,
whom Christ also rules primarily
(or, as the Head) (*omnes tamen pro-
prie regat Petrus, quos principaliter
regit et Christus*) . . . He is the First
in the apostolic dignity. When he
said, *Thou art the Christ, the Son
of the living God;* Jesus answers
him, *Blessed art thou, Simon; My
Father which is in heaven. . . and
I say to thee*, that is, as My Father
has manifested to thee My Divinity,
so do I make known to thee thy excellence. For *thou art Peter;* that is,
whereas I am the inviolable *Rock;*
I that *Chief Corner - stone ;* I *who
make both one* (Eph.ii.6), *I the Foundation besides which no one can lay
other*, nevertheless thou also art a
Rock, because thou art consolidated
by My power, that what things are
mine by My power, may be common
to thee by being made partaker of
them with Me. Upon this strength,
he says, I will raise an everlasting
temple, and the lofty building of
My Church, reaching unto heaven,

shall arise on the firmness of this faith. The *gates of hell* shall not hold, the bonds of death shall not bind, this confession ; for this word (voice), is the word (voice) of life. . . . For which cause it is said to the most blessed Peter, *To thee I will give the keys*, &c. The right of this power passed also indeed to the other Apostles, and what was ordained by this decree, has passed unto all the Princes of the Church, but not in vain is that intrusted to One which may be intimated to all. For, therefore, is this intrusted to Peter individually (or, especially), for as much as the pattern of Peter is set before all the Rulers of the Church. . . . [Referring to the words, *Confirm thy brethren*, S. Luke, xxii. 32, he says] The danger from the trial of fear was common to all the Apostles, and they stood equally in need of the aid of the divine protection. . . . And yet of Peter special care is taken by the Lord, and for the faith of Peter in particular does He pray, as though the condition of the rest would be more secure, provided the mind of Peter was not subdued. In Peter, therefore, is the strength of all defended, and the aid of divine grace is so disposed as that the firmness which is bestowed on Peter by Christ, may be conferred by Peter on the Apostles (*per Petrum apostolis conferatur*). Wherefore, my beloved, since we see that so great a safeguard has been divinely instituted for us, reasonably and justly do we rejoice in the merits and dignity of our Leader, giving thanks to our everlasting King and Redeemer, the Lord Jesus Christ, for that He gave so great power to him whom He made the Prince of the whole ‘ Church (*quem totius ecclesiæ principem*

fecit) ; that if it so be that any thing is rightly done by us in these our days, arid rightly ordered, it be referred to his doing, to his governing, unto whom it was said, *And when thou art converted, strengthen thy brethren;* and to whom, after the resurrection, the Lord, for a triple confession of everlasting love, with a mystic meaning thrice said, *Feed my sheep.*" T. i. *Serm. iv. in Anniver. Assumpt. c.* i.-iv. *col.* 16-19.

103. Alluding to S. Peter's confession, S. Leo says, "And by this his loftiness of faith, he gave so much pleasure, as to receive the sacred Firmness of an inviolable Rock, upon which the Church being founded, it should prevail over *the gates of hell* and the laws of death." T. i. *Serm.* li. *Homil. Sabbat. ante Secund. Dom. Quadr. c.* i. *col.* 193.

104. " But the Lord willed the sacrament of this office (of the apostolic trumpet) to pertain to all the Apostles in such manner, as that He placed it principally in the blessed Peter, the Chief of all the Apostles, and wishes His gifts to flow unto the whole body, from him (Peter) as from a Head ; that whoso should dare withdraw from the solidity of Peter, might know himself to be an alien from the divine mystery. For it was His will that this man whom He had taken into the fellowship of an indivisible unity (or, taken for the connexion of an indivisible unity) should be named that which Himself was (*i.e.* the Rock), by saying, *Thou art Peter, and upon this rock I will build My Church*, that the building of an everlasting temple might, by the marvellous gift of the grace of God, be compacted together in the Solidity of Peter, by this Firmness strengthening His Church, so as that neither human temerity should

be able to injure (assault) it, nor the *gates of hell prevail against it.*" T. i. *Ep.* x. *ad Episcopos per* *Provinc. Viennens. constitutos, in caussa Hilarii Arelat. Epis. c.* 1, 2, *col.* 633-35.

COMMENT.

S. Leo affirms (1) that though S. Peter received many things, yet nothing passed unto any one else "without his participation." This is confirmed in the Gospel, wherein it is very clear, that while S. Peter received the fulness of every prerogative without other Apostles sharing at first, at least, in them, yet none of them received any thing apart from S. Peter. This is an echo of the doctrine of S. Augustine, who said that S. Peter received the Church "singly," *i.e.* without the participation of others, because in him alone was *there* the Church. Hence S. Leo says, that S. Peter who *alone* received all things, had a right to rule all.

2. Christ, he declares, "is the inviolable Rock," and the " First Corner-stone," yet S. Peter is nevertheless a Rock,—an "inviolable Rock,"—because he is consolidated by the power of Christ, and, what things belong to Christ, by His power, he (Peter) is made partaker of them. Upon this strength, then, that is, upon Christ the inviolable Rock, and upon S. Peter the consolidated Rock, is raised the everlasting Temple of God, against which the gates of hell shall not prevail.

3. The keys were delivered to S. Peter, but the "right of this power, passed to all the other Apostles, and unto all the Princes of the Church ;" but, S. Leo adds, " Not in vain is that intrusted to One, which may be intimated to all." From this it would appear that S. Peter is the sole custodian of the keys, but the use of them is in the power of all other Apostles and Bishops, in union with him. S. Peter may use them without reference to his co-Apostles, while they on the other hand could not do so except in concord with him. This seems to be S. Leo's doctrine.

4. Alluding to the trials that would visit the Apostle, S. Leo says, "that

special care was taken that the faith of S. Peter should not fail, as though the condition of the others would be more secure, if he did not succumb." In this Apostle, then, is the strength of all defended, and that by the Firmness bestowed upon him, it may be conferred by S. Peter upon the other Apostles. The commission, *Strengthen, or confirm, thy brethren,* according to S. Leo, meant, that a Prerogative of power might be in Peter, which would enable him to uphold the faith of the Church.

5. S. Peter, then, being endowed with the Prerogatives of Christ, on whom with Christ his Master the Temple of the Lord has been raised, and having received so much power, is made the Prince of the whole Church, its Ruler and Governor, the Confirmer of the brethren and the Chief Pastor of the flock.

6. But S. Leo says that our Lord willed that sacrament of his office should pertain to all the Apostles, but in such manner, as it is placed principally in S. Peter, the Chief of the Apostles, and that from him, as from a Head, all His gifts should flow to the whole body. This is in harmony with many preceding Fathers, who taught that S. Peter was the Origin and Source of the priesthood.

7. S. Leo considers that communion consists in being in union with S. Peter, for he says that if any one should " dare to withdraw from the Solidity of Peter, might know himself to be an alien from the divine mystery." For as our Lord had taken S. Peter into the fellowship of an indivisible unity, having named him from himself, the Rock, on which He built the Church, which is compacted together in the Solidity of Peter, so all who are not in union with S. Peter are aliens. In a word, S. Leo regards S. Peter as the sole Centre

of unity. And he agrees with S. Augustine, who holds that S. Peter was the Figure of the Church, on whom singly the Church was founded, and hence everything that proceeds from S. Peter is of the truth, and such as does not proceed from him, is of error.

S. Leo, then, believes as follows: (1) That S. Peter received all things alone, the others not without his participation; (2) That he is with Christ, the inviolable Rock, upon whom the Temple of God is raised. (3) That he received the keys, but the other Apostles shared with him in their use; (4) That he was the Confirmer of the brethren; (5) That he was Prince of the whole world, the Ruler of the Church, and the Feeder of the people; (6) That while all shared in his prerogatives, yet he possessed them principally, and that from him, as an Original, all gifts flow to the whole body: and lastly, that all are aliens who are not joined to S. Peter.

POPE S. FELIX.

A.D. 490.

105. "I am also cheered by the purport of your letter, wherein you have not omitted to state that blessed Peter is the Chief of the Apostles and the Rock of faith (*summum apostolorum beatum Petrum, et petram fidei esse*), and have judiciously proved that to him were intrusted the keys of the heavenly mysteries." *Ep.* iv. *Imper. Zenoni, Galland, t.* x. *p.* 671–72.

COMMENT.

S. Felix expresses S. Peter's position by *summum*. This may signify any sort of extreme exaltation. It may mean he was the highest in rank and dignity, or in authority and power. But as he asserts that S. Peter was the Rock of faith, then he must be understood as declaring that S. Peter was the Chief authority in all that concerned the faith.

POPE S. GELASIUS.

A.D. 492.

106. Referring to the adjudication of the Primacy to Rome, he says, " as being men who bore in mind the Lord's sentence, *Thou art Peter, and upon this rock I will build My Church,* &c. And again to the same Peter, *Lo ! I have prayed for thee that thy faith fail not, and converted, confirm the brethren,*" and that sentence, *If thou lovest Me, feed my sheep.* Wherefore, then, is the Lord's discourse so frequently directed to Peter? Was it that the rest of the holy and blessed Apostles were not clothed with his virtue? Who dare assert this? No, but that, by a Head being constituted, the occasion of schism might be removed; and that the compact bond

of the body of Christ, thus uniformly tending, by the fellowship of a most glorious love, to one Head, might be shown to be one; and that there might be one Church faithfully believed in, and one house of the one God and of the one Redeemer, wherein we might be nourished with one bread and one chalice.

. . . . There were assuredly twelve Apostles, endowed with equal merits and equal dignity; and whereas they all shone equally with spiritual light, yet was it Christ's will that One amongst them should be the Ruler (prince) (*principem*), &c." *Galland, t.* x. *p.* 677.

COMMENT.

S. Gelasius, referring to the several commissions to S. Peter, asks, whether the other Apostles did not participate in them? Thus he affirms and maintains the equality of all the Apostles in merit and dignity, yet, evidently quoting S. Jerome, says, " was it Christ's will that One amongst them should be the Ruler," that the occasion of schism might be avoided. S. Peter then according to this Pope was the Head and Ruler, the other Apostles sharing with him equally in merit and dignity, yet, nevertheless, subject to him.

S. AVITUS.

A.D. 494.

107. " Peter, the Head of the Apostles, that is, the Prince of the Princes." *Fragm.* i. *Galland. t.* x. *p.* 746.

II.—ANALYSIS OF PATRISTIC DOCTRINE RELATIVE TO S. PETER.

The evidence adduced in the preceding chapter respecting the Primacy of S. Peter, is now arranged analytically, in order that the teaching of the primitive age on this subject may be fully understood and comprehended.

I. THE PRIMACY GENERALLY.

S. Peter, "Chosen The First." *S. Cyprian, Extract*, No. 15.

S. Peter, "The First Confessor of the Son of God." *S. Hilary, Extract*, No. 28.

S. Peter "merited to be Preferred before all the Apostles." *S. Optatus, Extract*, No. 36.

S. Peter, "The First-born of those who bear the keys." *S. Ephraem, Extract*, No. 42.

S. Peter had "The Prior honour." *S. Gregory Naz. Extract*, No. 46.

The "blessed Peter who was Preferred." *S. Basil, Extract*, No. 53.

"Who (Peter) Alone received a Greater testimony and blessing than the rest." *Ib.*

S. Peter, "First of the Apostles." *S. Epiphanius, Extract*, No. 55.

"He (Peter) is Preferred before all." *S. Ambrose, Extract*, No. 61.

"Thou (Peter) art The First." *Ib. Extract*, No. 64.

S. Peter had "The Primacy of confession" and "of faith." *Ib.*

S. Peter, "The First in the Church." *S. Chrysostom, Extract*, No. 68.

S. Peter, "The Chosen One of the Apostles." *Ib. Extract*, No. 73.

S. Peter, "The First of the Choir." *Ib. Extract*, No. 75.

"Who can be ignorant that the most blessed Peter is The First of the Apostles?" *S. Augustine, Extract*, No. 82.

"Peter in the order of the Apostles First." *Ib. Extract*, No. 86.

II. THE ROCK.

1. *The Rock is Christ.* "The Rock Christ." *S. Jerome, Extract*, No. 67.

"For Christ was The Rock, upon which Foundation even Peter himself was built." *S. Augustine, Extract*, No. 83.

"Peter is so called from The Rock, not The Rock from Peter; as Christ is not called Christ from the Christian, but the Christian from Christ." *Ib. Extract*, No. 86.

"Christ The Inviolable Rock." *S. Leo, Extract*, No. 102.

2. *The Rock is S. Peter.* S. Peter, "called The *Rock*, whereon the Church was to be built." *Tertullian, Extract*, No. 5.

S. Peter "The most Solid Rock, upon which Christ founded the Church." *Origen, Extract*, No. 7.

Christ "called him (Peter) The Rock of the edifice of the Church." *S. James of Nisibis, Extract*, No. 27.

S. Peter, "happy Foundation of the Church, and a Rock worthy of the building." *S. Hilary, Extract*, No. 30.

S. Peter, "That Unbroken and most Firm Rock upon which the Lord built His Church." *S. Gregory of Nyssa, Extract*, No. 45.

"Peter who became The Unbroken Rock." *S. Gregory of Nazianzum, Extract*, No. 47.

"Upon which Rock (Peter) the Lord promised to build His Church." *S. Basil, Extract*, No. 52.

S. Peter "became unto us truly a Firm Rock ; on which is based the Lord's faith; upon which the Church is in every way built." *S. Epiphanius, Extract*, No. 54.

S. Peter "became a Firm Rock of the building." *Ib.*

S. Peter, "That Unbroken Rock." *S. Chrysostom, Extract*, No. 68.

S. Peter received "the sacred firmness of an Inviolable Rock, upon which the Church being founded," &c. *S. Leo, Extract*, No. 103.

III. THE FOUNDATION OF THE CHURCH.

"The Church was to be built," *i.e.* on Peter. *Tertullian, Extract*, No. 5.

S. Peter, "That great Foundation of the Church." *Origen, Extract*, No. 7.

"Peter upon whom is built Christ's Church." *Ib. Extract*, No. 10.

"On him (Peter), as on the earth, the Church was founded." *Ib. Extract*, No. 11.

"Peter on whom the Church had been built." *S. Cyprian, Extract*, No. 12.

"Peter, upon whom the Church was to be built." *Ib. Extract*, No. 13.

"One Church founded by Christ our Lord upon Peter." *Ib. Extract*, No. 14.

"Upon whom (Peter) He built His Church." *Ib. Extract*, No. 15.

"On whom (Peter) He laid and founded the Church." *Ib. Extract*, No. 18.

"Upon that one (Peter) He builds His Church." *Ib. Extract*, No. 20.

"Peter upon whom The Foundations of the Church were laid." *S. Firmilian. Extract*, No. 22.

"Upon whom (Peter) He was about to build the Church." *S. Hilary, Extract*, No. 28.

S. Peter "happy Foundation." *Ib. Extract*, No. 30.

"He that was to build His Church upon Cephas." *S. Ephraem, Extract*, No. 37.

"(On Peter) is the Church of God firmly established." *S. Gregory of Nyssa, Extract,* No. 45.

S. Peter "intrusted with The Foundations of the Church." *S. Gregory of Nazianzum, Extract,* No. 46.

" He (Peter) a Firm Rock ; upon which is based the Lord's faith ; upon which the Church is everyway built." *S. Epiphanius, Extract,* No. 54.

" In whom is The Foundation of the Church." *S. Ambrose, Extract,* No. 59.

Faith of Peter " The Foundation of the Church." *Ib. Extract,* No. 64.

" Upon whom (Peter) the Lord built the Church." *S. Jerome, Extract,* No. 64.

" The Church is built upon Peter." *Ib. Extract,* No. 65.

" On whom (Peter) the Church of the Lord in enduring Massiveness was built." *Ib. Extract,* No. 66.

S. Peter "The Firm Foundation." *S. Chrysostom, Extract,* No. 68.

S. Peter " The Foundation of the confession." *Ib. Extract,* No. 71.

" S. Peter That Foundation of the Church." *Ib. Extract,* No. 72.

"In whom (Peter) Singly He formeth the Church." *S. Augustine, Extract,* No. 87.

" For on him (Peter) He was afterwards to found His Church." *S. Cyril of Alexandria, Extract,* No. 94.

" Be thou (Peter) The Foundation and The Teacher of those who by Faith come unto Me." *Ib. Extract,* No. 98.

IV. S. PETER THE VICAR, OR REPRESENTATIVE OF CHRIST.

The Church "having been founded First and Alone, by the voice of the Lord, upon Peter." *S. Cyprian, Extract,* No. 19.

" . . . To Peter Alone Christ said, *Whatsoever thou shalt bind,*" &c., and afterwards to the other Apostles. *S. Firmilian, Extract,* No. 22.

" O thou blessed one (Peter) that obtainedst the Place of the Head." *S. Ephraim, Extract,* No. 41.

" To Peter Alone is it said, *Launch out unto the deep* . . . . into the depths of disputation the Church is led by Peter." *S. Ambrose, Extract,* No. 59.

"Whom (Peter) He was leaving with us, as it were, the Vicar of His own love." *Ib. Extract,* No. 61.

" How could He not confirm His faith, unto whom, of His own authority, He gave the Kingdom, and whom, when He styled a Rock, He pointed out The Foundation of the Church." *Ib. Extract,* No. 63.

" He (Peter) who was Set Over the whole habitable world . . . . to whom He intrusted the Doing and Supporting all things." *S. Chrysostom, Extract,* No. 70.

" Peter . . . . The Pillar of The Church, The Buttress of the faith, The Foundation of the confession, The Fisherman of The universe." *Ib. Extract,* No. 71.

" He places in his hands The Government over the brethren." *Ib. Extract,* No. 73.

" Peter did, indeed, receive the whole world." *S. Augustine, Extract,* No. 84.

' " Hence it is that the Master Himself seeks for helpers, for associates to take charge of the whole world. . . . Hence it is that when about to return to heaven He commends His sheep to be fed by Peter in His Stead." *S. Peter Chrysologus, Extract,* No. 100.

" Peter is chosen to be Set Over the vocation of all the nations," &c. *S. Leo, Extract,* No. 102.

" That what things are Mine by My power, may be Common to thee being made Partaker of them with Me." *Ib.*

V. S. PETER THE REPRESENTATIVE OF THE CHURCH.

" One speaking for all, and replying with The Voice of the Church." *S. Cyprian, Extract,* No. 12.

" O thou blessed one (Peter), that obtainedst The Place of The Head, and of The Tongue, in the body of thy brethren, which was enlarged out of the disciples and sons of thy Lord." *S. Ephraem, Extract,* No. 41.

" We hail thee, Peter, The Tongue of The disciples, The Voice of The heralds, The Eye of the Apostles, The Keeper of heaven, The First-born of those that bear the keys." *Ib. Extract,* No. 42.

" Where Peter is there is the Church." *S. Ambrose, Extract,* No. 56.

" This, then, is that Peter who Answers for the rest, yea, as Above the rest." *Ib. Extract,* No. 64.

" Peter . . . The Mouth of The disciples, The Pillar of The Church, The Buttress of the faith, The Foundation of the confession, The Fisherman of the Universe." *S. Chrysostom, Extract,* No. 71.

S. Peter, " to whom bearing a Figure of the Church." *S. Augustine, Extract,* No. 81.

S. Peter " bore a Character which Represented the whole Church." *Ib. Extract,* No. 83.

" The Apostle Peter The Type of the one Church." *Ib. Extract,* No. 86.

" Now this name Peter was given him by the Lord, and that too a Figure that he should Signify the Church." *Ib.*

" Peter is the Christian people." *Ib.*

" This same Peter, therefore, who had been by the Rock pronounced ' blessed,' bearing The Figure of the Church, holding The Principate (or The Sovereignty) of the Apostolate." *Ib.*

" In this one Peter was Figured the unity of all pastors." *Ib. Extract,* No. 88.

" In Figure Peter Represented the Church." *Ib. Extract,* No. 89.

S. Peter " sustains the Person of this Church Catholic." *Ib. Extract,* No. 90.

VI. THE CHURCH FOUNDED IN S. PETER SINGLY AND ALONE.

" What in a previous passage was granted to Peter Alone (the keys)' seems here to be shown to be granted" to other Apostles. *Origen, Extract,* No. 9.

The Church "having been founded First and Alone, by the voice of the Lord upon Peter." *S. Cyprian, Extract,* No. 19.

" To Peter Alone Christ said, *Whatsoever thou shalt bind, &c.*," and afterwards, &c. *Firmilian, Extract,* No. 22.

" He (Peter) Alone received . . . the keys, to be communicated, &c." *S. Optatus, Extract,* No. 36.

" S. Peter, The First-born of those who bear the keys." *S. Ephraem, Extract,* No. 42.

" Who (Peter) Alone received a greater testimony of and blessing than the rest." *S. Basil, Extract,* No. 53.

" To Peter Alone is it said, *Launch out into the deep.*" *S. Ambrose, Extract,* No. 59.

" In whom (Peter) Singly He formeth the Church." *S. Augustine, Extract,* No. 87.

" What was given to him (Peter) Singly was given to the Church." *Ib. Extract,* No. 89.

VII. S. Peter the Origin and Source of Unity and Jurisdiction.

" Remember that the Lord left here the Keys (of heaven) to Peter, and Through him to the Church." *Tertullian, Extract,* No. 6.

The " Church founded by Christ our Lord upon Peter, for an Original and Principle of unity." *S. Cyprian, Extract,* No. 14.

" From whom (Peter) He appointed and showed that Unity should Spring." *Ib. Extract,* No. 16.

" He has, by His own authority, so placed the Origin of that same Unity, as that it Begins from One (Peter). *Ib. Extract,* No. 20.

" He (Peter) Alone received of the Kingdom of heaven the Keys to be Communicated to the others." *S. Optatus, Extract,* No. 36.

" Through Peter He gave to the Bishops the Key of the heavenly honours." *S. Gregory of Nyssa, Extract,* No. 44.

" Through whom (Peter) both the Apostolate and the Episcopate took their Rise in Christ." *S. Innocent, Extract,* No. 80.

" The Church, therefore, which is founded on Christ, Received in Peter the Keys of the Kingdom of heaven." *S. Augustine, Extract,* No. 83.

" What was to him (Peter) Singly given, (*i. e.* the Keys) was Given to the Church." *Ib. Extract,* No. 89.

" The institution of the universal Church took its Beginning from the honour bestowed on blessed Peter." *S. Boniface, Extract,* No. 93.

" For from him (Peter) as its Source did ecclesiastical discipline Flow over all the Churches." *Ib.*

" And wishes His gifts to Flow unto the whole body, from him (Peter) as from a Head." *S. Leo, Extract,* No. 104.

VIII. The Divine Commission to Peter.

1. *Supreme Jurisdiction.*—" Who (Peter) obtained ' the Keys of the Kingdom of heaven,' and the Power of loosing and of binding in heaven and in earth." *Tertullian, Extract,* No. 5.

" That Peter should have Something Peculiar Above" the other Apostles respecting the use of the Keys. *Origen, Extract,* No. 9.

" With regard even to those things which seem to be common to Peter" and the other Apostles, "much Difference and Pre-eminence in the words spoken to Peter (*i. e.* about the Keys) Beyond those spoken" to the other Apostles. *Ib.*

" The Lord Gave this Power that that should be loosed in heaven which he (Peter) should have loosed on earth." *S. Cyprian, Extract,* No. 16.

Peter, " who also Received the Keys thereof." *Ib. Extract,* No. 17.

" To whom (Peter) He had just before Given *the Keys of the Kingdom of Heaven* .... who, *whatsoever* he should *bind* or *loose* on earth, that should abide *bound* or *loosed* in heaven." *S. Hilary, Extract,* No. 28.

" Peter ... the Door-keeper of the heavenly Kingdom, and in his Judgment on earth, a Judge in heaven." *Ib.*

" O blessed Keeper of the gate of heaven, to whose Disposal are delivered the Keys of the entrance into eternity; whose Judgment on earth is an Authority prejudged in heaven, so that the things that are either loosed or bound on earth, acquire in heaven too a Like State of settlement." *Ib. Extract,* No. 30.

" He who Bears with him the Keys of heaven." *S. Cyril of Jerusalem, Extract,* No. 33.

" Peter, the Key-bearer of the Kingdom of heaven." *Ib. Extract,* No. 35.

" And he Alone Received of the Kingdom of heaven the Keys to be communicated to the others." *S. Optatus, Extract,* No. 36.

" To whom (Peter), O Lord, didst thou Intrust the most precious pledge of the heavenly Keys." *S. Ephraem, Extract,* No. 39.

" Thee, O Simon Peter, will I proclaim the blessed, who Holdest the Keys, which the Spirit made. A great and ineffable word, that he binds and loosens those in heaven, and those under the earth." *Ib. Extract,* No. 41.

Peter ... " who had the Keys Delivered unto him." *S. Gregory of Nazianzum, Extract,* No. 47.

" To whom (Alone) were Intrusted the Keys of the Kingdom of heaven." *S. Basil, Extract,* No. 53.

" Who (Peter) Received the *Keys of heaven;* who *looses on earth and binds in heaven.* For in him (Peter) was Found all the Subtle Questions of faith." *S. Epiphanius, Extract,* No. 55.

" He (Peter) in whose hands He Placed the Keys of heaven." *S. Chrysostom, Extract,* No. 70.

" Let Peter Hold his long-established Principate over the Apostolic choir ; let him open the Kingdom of heaven for those who enter in ; let him with Power bind the guilty; with Clemency absolve the penitent." *S. Peter Chrysologus, Extract,* No. 101.

2. *S. Peter the Supreme Pastor.* "When the Chief Authority as regards the feeding of the sheep was Delivered to Peter." *Origen, Extract,* No. 11.

"Peter also to whom the Lord Commends His sheep to be Fed and Guarded." *S. Cyprian, Extract,* No. 18.

"To him (Peter) He Assigns His sheep to be Fed." *Ib. Extract,* No. 20.

S. Peter "was Accounted the Shepherd of the flock." *S. Ephraem, Extract,* No. 38.

"He afterwards Chose him (Peter) as the Pastor of the Lord's flock." *S. Ambrose, Extract,* No. 57.

"Having had Intrusted to him (Peter) by Christ the flock." *S. Chrysostom, Extract,* No. 75.

"But when He asserted in reply His love, He Commended to him (Peter) His flock." *S. Augustine, Extract,* No. 88.

"Thus did this great Pillar (Peter) support the tottering world . . . and Received a command to *Feed the Lord's sheep." Theodoret, Extract,* No. 98.

"Hence it is that, when about to return to heaven, He Commends His sheep to be Fed by Peter in His Stead." *S. Peter Chrysologus, Extract,* No. 100.

IX. Co-EQUALITY IN THE APOSTOLATE.

"What in a previous passage, was granted to Peter alone, seems (here) to be shown to be granted to all who have addressed three admonitions to all sinners . . . . . But, as it was fit . . . . . that Peter should have something peculiar above those who should thrice admonish . . . . and truly, if we sedulously attend to the evangelical writings, even in them we may discover, with regard even to those things which seem to be common to Peter and to those (*i.e.* the other Apostles) who have thrice admonished the brethren, much difference and pre-eminence in the words spoken to Peter, beyond those spoken in the second place." *Origen, Extract,* No. 9.

"And although to all the Apostles after His resurrection He gives an equal power . . . . yet, in order to manifest unity, He has by His own authority so placed the Origin of the same unity, as that it begins from one. Certainly, the other Apostles also were, what Peter was, endowed with an equal fellowship both of honour and power, but the commencement proceeds from unity." *S. Cyprian, Extract,* No. 20.

"The strength of the Church is settled equally upon them (*i.e.* the Apostles); yet for this reason one is chosen out of the Twelve, that a Head being appointed, the occasion of schism might be removed." *S. Jerome, Extract,* No. 65.

"But though all were Apostles, and all were to sit on twelve thrones, ... still it was the three He took. And again, even of these three, He said that some were under, and some superior. And He sets Peter before them." *S. Chrysostom, Extract,* No. 78.

"What! did Peter receive these keys, and Paul not receive them? Did Peter receive them, and John, and James, and the rest of the Apostles not receive them? . . . . But since in figure Peter represented the Church, what was given to him singly was given to the Church." *S. Augustine, Extract,* No. 89.

" The right of this power (the keys) passed also indeed to the other Apostles, and what was ordained by this decree, has passed unto all the Princes of the Church, but not in vain is that entrusted to one, which may be intimated to all." *S. Leo, Extract,* No. 102.

" But the Lord willed the sacrament of this office to pertain to all the Apostles in such manner as that He placed it principally in the blessed Peter." *Ib. Extract,* No. 104.

" There were assuredly twelve Apostles, endowed with equal merits and equal dignity ; and whereas they all shone equally with spiritual light, yet was it Christ's will that one amongst them should be the Ruler." *S. Gelasius, Extract,* No. 106.

X. S. PETER THE SUPREME HEAD AND RULER.

" When The Chief Authority as regards the feeding of the flock was delivered to Peter." *Origen, Extract,* No. 11.

" So as to say that he (Peter) held The Primacy." *S. Cyprian, Extract,* No. 15.

" Peter, who was The Preferred One to the Apostles." *S. Peter of Alexandria, Extract,* No. 23.

" He The Very Head of the Apostles, Peter, denied Him thrice." *Eusebius, Extract,* No. 26.

" Simon, The Head of the Apostles." *S. James of Nisibis, Extract,* No. 27.

" Peter, The Prince of the Apostolate." *S. Hilary, Extract,* No. 29.

" Peter, The Chiefest and Foremost of the Apostles." *S. Cyril of Jerusalem, Extract,* No. 32.

" Peter The Foremost of the Apostles and Chief Herald of the Church." *Ib., Extract,* No. 34.

" Peter, who was The Foremost of the Apostles, and The Key-bearer of the kingdom of heaven." *Ib. Extract,* No. 35.

Peter, " The Prince of the Apostles." *S. Ephraem, Extract,* No. 39.

Peter " that obtained The Place of the Head." *Ib. Extract,* No. 41.

" Peter, The Head of the Apostles." *S. Gregory of Nyssa, Extract,* No. 45.

" Peter, The Chief of the disciples." *S. Gregory of Nazianzun, Extract,* No. 48.

" Peter, who was The Chiefest of the Apostles." *S. Epiphanius, Extract,* No. 54.

" Peter . . . . is Set Over the Church." *S. Ambrose, Extract,* No. 57.

" One is chosen out of the Twelve, that a Head being appointed, the occasion of schism might be removed." *S. Jerome, Extract,* No. 65.

" As Plato was the prince of the philosophers, so was Peter The Prince of the Apostles, on whom the Church of the Lord in enduring massiveness was built." *Ib. Extract,* No. 66.

" Peter himself The Head of the Apostles." *S. Chrysostom, Extract,* No. 68.

" And intrusted to his (Peter's) hand The Government of the universal Church." *Ib. Extract,* No. 69.

"Inasmuch as he Peter, who was Set Over the whole habitable world." *Ib. Extract*, No. 70.

"Peter. . . . That Head of the Brotherhood That one Set over the entire universe." *Ib. Extract*, No. 72.

Peter "The Head of the Choir." *Ib. Extract*, No. 73.

"If thou (Peter) love Me, Preside over the brethren." *Ib.*

"Peter, The Apostle, on account of the Primacy of his Apostleship." *S. Augustine, Extract*, No. 83.

"Peter did indeed Receive the whole world." *Ib. Extract*, No. 84.

"Peter holding The Principate of the Apostolate." *Ib. Extract*, No. 86.

"Peter, in the order of the Apostles, First and Chiefest." *Ib.*

"To whom (Peter) by the Lord's voice was Granted the Highest Place of the priesthood." *S. Boniface, Extract*, No. 92.

"In whom (Peter) its Government and Headship reside." *Ib. Extract*, No. 93.

"Peter though Set Over the holy disciples." *S. Cyril of Alex. Extract*, No. 95.

"If Peter himself, That Prince of the holy disciples." *Ib. Extract*, No. 96.

"Be thou (Peter) . . . The Teacher of those who by faith come unto Me." *Ib. Extract*, No. 98.

"Let Peter hold his long-established Princedom over the Apostolic Choir." *S. Peter Chrysol. Extract*, No. 101.

"Out of the whole world the one Peter is chosen to be Set Over the vocation of all the nations." *S. Leo, Extract*, No. 102.

"That so, though there be in the people of God many priests and pastors, Peter especially may Rule all." *Ib.*

"Whom he (Peter) made The Prince of the whole Church." *Ib.*

"Peter The Chief of all the Apostles." *Ib. Extract*, No. 104.

"And wishes His gifts to flow unto the whole body from him (Peter), as from a Head." *Ib.*

"Blessed Peter is The Chief of the Apostles." *S. Felix, Extract*, No. 105.

"Yet was it Christ's will that One (Peter) amongst them should be The Ruler." *S. Gelasius, Extract*, No. 106.

"Peter The Head of the Apostles, that is The Prince of the Princes." *S. Avitus, Extract*, No. 107.

According to the testimony of the Holy Fathers of the primitive age, it is clear that S. Peter was regarded as the Vicegerent of Jesus Christ, and the Representative of the Catholic Church; and hence he became the Rock and Foundation of the Church; its Source of Jurisdiction; and, moreover, its Head, its Governor, and its Supreme Pastor.

PART III.

AUDI ALTERAM PARTEM.

It is time now to inquire what can be advanced against the Scriptural and Patristic argument on the subject of S. Peter's Supremacy in the hierarchy of the holy Apostles and Disciples of the Lord. As Dr. Barrow's "Treatise on the Pope's Supremacy" seems to be the most exhaustive work on the Anglican side of this great question, we cannot do better than adopt it as our text-book, feeling sure that every argument that can be adduced against the position claimed for S. Peter will be found therein.

Dr. Barrow admits that S. Peter may have had a "Primacy of worth or merit," "of repute," and "of order or bare dignity." We will pass over his observations on these points, and confine ourselves to the main question of the "Primacy," of "power, command, or jurisdiction," which he denies S. Peter ever received from our Lord.

I.

NECESSITY OF A "CLEAR REVELATION."

Dr. Barrow thus commences his argument :—" For such a power (being of so great importance) it was needful that a commission from God, its founder, should be granted in downright and perspicuous terms ; that no man concerned in duty grounded thereon, might have any doubt of it, or excuse for boggling at it ; it was necessary not only for the apostles, to bind and warrant their obedience, but also for us, because it is made the sole foundation of a like duty incumbent on us ; which we cannot honestly discharge without being assured of our obligation thereto, by clear revelation or promulgation of God's will in the Holy Scripture." (*Supremacy, p.* 49 ; see also *p.* 85, *Oxf. Edit.* 1836.)

Now, surely, there is something fundamentally erroneous in the above statement of the learned Doctor. From the premiss which he here lays down, it would follow that no dogma of the Church would be binding on the consciences of men, unless there could be found a "clear revelation or promulgation of God's will on the subject in the Holy Scripture." Let us test this. No member of the Church of England will deny that the great doctrine of the "Unity in Trinity and Trinity in Unity" is a fundamental one, involving the penalty of damnation, if not accepted and believed. But it may be questioned very much whether this tremendous dogma could be apprehended, even by the most learned scholar, without the authoritative exposition of the Catholic Church.

There is only one passage which expressly asserts the *unity* of the

Three Persons, but the nature of that unity is not, either in this or any other part of the Bible, very clearly defined, certainly not in such "downright and perspicuous terms" as would satisfy Dr. Barrow. "There are Three that bear record in heaven, the Father, the Word, and the Holy Ghost, and these Three are One." (1 *S. John*, v. 7.)

Let us consider three points—the co-eternity, the co-equality, and the con-substantiality of the Three Persons, which are essential parts of the doctrine of the Holy Trinity. Can this be so clearly proved from the Bible (without the aid of the Church) as to exclude all possibility of dispute, even from good and intelligent Christians? The passage above states that the Three Persons are One, but what is meant, generally, by "One?" There are various sorts of unity; as, for instance, the "unity" between a father and a son, and between a husband and his wife. It is known that the father and son are of one substance, *i. e.* that the flesh of the son is derived from his parents, but it cannot be said that he is either co-eternal,—at least from the beginning of life,—or co-equal with them. Then, again, a husband and wife are one, but they are neither consubstantial, nor of similar age, nor co-equal. Therefore the mere assertion that the Three Persons are One does not *necessarily* prove "the Trinity in Unity," nor "the Unity in Trinity;" inclusive of the fundamental verities of consubstantiality, co-equality, and co-eternity. But let us suppose that the authenticity of the passage in 1 John, v. 7, above quoted, to be at least doubtful, as Horne, Dr. Clark, Bishop Marsh, and others maintain.* In that case we should be under the necessity of concluding that there existed in Scripture no *direct* proof for the establishment of the great doctrine respecting the Holy Trinity (for this is the only passage which declares *explicitly* that the Three Persons "are one"), and consequently we should be compelled, if we adopted Dr. Barrow's rule of Scripture interpretation, to reject as utterly untenable this mysterious and awful dogma, disbelief in which entails eternal punishment. Dr. Barrow, indeed, admits the principle of implicit Revelation, but only on the condition that it is so "pregnantly implied"† as would "serve to satisfy any reasonable man, and to convince any froward gainsayer." (See *sup.* p. 85.) But is the doctrine of the Holy Trinity so "pregnantly implied," that any intellectually gifted man, who had never before heard of the dogma, could by the mere force of his reasoning powers discover it, even on the surface of Holy Scripture? It is very true that Christ said, "I and My Father are one" (*S. John*, x. 30) ; but it is equally true that on another occasion He said, "Why callest thou Me good? none is good, save one, that is God." (*S. Luke*, xviii. 19.) And again, "I go to My Father ; for My Father is greater than I." (*S. John*, xiv. 28.) And when alluding to the final judgment, He informs His disciples that "of that day and that hour knoweth no man, no, not the angels which are in heaven, neither the Son, but the Father." (*S. Mark*, xiii. 32.) Now these passages *seem* to strike at the belief that Christ was

---

* See *Horne, Introd. Holy Scrip.* vol. ii. pt. i. c. iii. s. iv. pp. 141-3, and vol. iv. pt. ii. c. iv. s. vi. pp. 448, 449. Lond. : 1839.

† The original is "imply."

God, and, by consequence, to disprove the notion that He was co-eternal, co-equal, and consubstantial with the Father. Then, further, under similar conditions, it would be impossible for any man, by his mere reasoning faculties, to discover the doctrine of the Consubstantiality of the Holy Ghost with the Father and the Son, and His Procession from both ; so it cannot be asserted with any truth that these doctrines are so clearly expressed, or so " pregnantly implied," that a person who had never been instructed on those points could, without the Tradition of the Church, have discovered them for himself. Of course every Catholic believes that the doctrine of the Holy Trinity is contained in Holy Scripture, and understands how to interpret *seemingly* contradictory passages, but without the infallible guiding voice of the Church it is impossible for any man, no matter what may be the depth of his erudition, to discern these and other tremendous truths of the Gospel.

Then, again, it is very doubtful whether there is any " clear revelation or promulgation of God's will in the Holy Scripture " respecting the Apostolical Succession, which is held to be essential to the very being of the Church. Holy Scripture tells us that S. Paul ordained S. Timothy, Titus, &c., and that he directed them to ordain "elders in every city ; " but, where in the New Testament is the *necessity* of Holy Orders asserted in such " downright and perspicuous terms" or, so " pregnantly implied " as would satisfy controversialists of Dr. Barrow's stamp?

I venture, then, to assert that the position Dr. Barrow has assumed is fundamentally unsound, and if applied for the proof of some of our holy doctrines (without the light of God's Church) would necessarily result in the undermining of that Faith which the Apostles received from our Lord, and which they handed down to their successors. We have all seen how the protestant principle (*i. e.* " the Bible alone") has worked in England, Scotland, and other countries ; how every system, not excluding the Church of England, has fallen into serious heresies respecting some of the fundamental dogmas of Religion. For it should be borne in mind that the Holy Ghost in Scripture does not profess invariably to teach every verity with precision ; the inspired writers, as a matter of fact, assume on the part of Christians a *previous* knowledge of the elements of Divine truth, and there cannot be a doubt that when the Evangelists and the Apostles wrote the Gospels and the Epistles, they intended them for the instruction, not of heathens, but of Christians.

The position, then, of Dr. Barrow is untenable. But in the case of S. Peter's Supremacy, I venture to deny that there is no "clear revelation and promulgation of God's will in the Holy Scripture." Indeed there is more said about S. Peter, and the Office he was to fill, than upon any doctrine of Christianity. It appears to me that the terms by which our Lord delivered to S. Peter his commission are clear and precise. " Thou art Peter (a Rock), and upon this Rock I will build my Church ;" " I will give unto thee the Keys of the kingdom of heaven ;" " When thou art converted, Strengthen, confirm, or fix immovably, thy brethren ;" " Feed My sheep," and " Feed My lambs." These words were never addressed to any other Apostle, and I submit that, *apart from all glosses*, his commission was " granted" in such " downright and perspicuous terms, that no man concerned in duty grounded thereon, might have any doubt of it, or excuse for boggling at it." I say, apart from all glosses, because the difficulty of understanding the true meaning arises not from any obscurity in the sacred text itself, or from the want of "a clear revelation and promulgation of God's will in the Holy Scripture," but from the variety of interpretations that have been put upon it, not by the Primitive Fathers so much as by modern Anglican Divines, whose main object is to get rid, by fair means or otherwise, of the Papal authority, and to substitute in its stead the Royal Supremacy, which, as *now* enforced by the Crown, is the most impious and blasphemous assumption of ecclesiastical jurisdiction ever attempted by secular rulers.

II.

S. PETER'S COMMISSION.

Dr. Barrow asserts that " if St. Peter had been instituted sovereign of the apostolical senate, his office and state had been in nature and kind very distinct from the common office of the other apostles, as the office of a king from the office of a subject." (*Sup. p.* 51.) Dr. Barrow is inaccurate in his statement of the relations between S. Peter and the Twelve. To this day it is no article of Faith in the Roman Church, nor is it the opinion of any section of Roman Catholics, that the Pope is the Sovereign of the Bishops, in the *same sense* as the king is the sovereign of a people. The whole Episcopate, inclusive of the Pope, form together one High-priesthood, the difference consisting, not in superiority of Order, but in Jurisdiction.

The following passages from writings of celebrated Popes explain the position of S. Peter and his successors in the apostolical and episcopal college :—

Pope S. Leo says, " The right of this power (the keys) passed also indeed to the other Apostles, and what was ordained by this decree has passed unto all the Princes of the Church, but not in vain is that intrusted to one which may be intimated to all." (*T.* i. *Serm.* iv. *in Anniver. Assumpt. c.* i.-iv. *col.* 16-19.) " But the Lord willed the sacrament of this office (apostolic trumpet, *i.e.* evangelization of the world) to pertain to all the Apostles in such manner, as that He placed it principally in the blessed Peter, the Chief of all the Apostles, and wishes His gifts to flow unto the whole body from him (Peter) as from a Head ; that whoso should dare withdraw from the solidity of Peter, might know himself to be an alien from the divine mystery." (*Ib. Ep. ad Epis. per Provinc. Vienn. constitutos, in caussa Hil. Arelat.* (*Epis. c.* i. *p.* 633.)

Pope S. Gelasius, " There were assuredly twelve Apostles, endowed with equal merits and equal dignity; and whereas all shone equally with spiritual light, yet was it Christ's will that one amongst them should be the Ruler or Prince." (*Galland. T.* x. *p.* 677.)

And again, Pope S. Celestine, in his letter to the Council of Ephesus, " This charge of teaching has descended in common to all bishops. We are all engaged to it by an hereditary right; all we who having come in their (Apostles') stead, preach the Name of our Lord to all the countries of the world, according to what was said to them, 'Go ye and teach all nations.'" (*Labbé, Concil. t.* ii. *col.* 88.)

S. Celestine does not, indeed, assert in this epistle S. Peter's Supremacy, but who can doubt that he held it, when by virtue of his position as successor of S. Peter, he deposed Nestorius from the see of Constantinople by his own sole authority, S. Cyril of Alexandria, acting by commission from him, the Œcumenical Council of Ephesus confirming without reserve all he had done in this case? All the Apostles were equal as to priestly honour and dignity, yet S. Peter was the Ruler, and the Prince. Upon this point the Fathers are very explicit, for they assert that S. Peter was " preferred to all the Apostles," that he was First in Authority, " in whom was the control over the brethren." These are terms which imply not a mere Primacy of order or worth, but a Primacy of Rule, Government, and Authority. Therefore, though the Apostles were not subjects of S. Peter in the sense that subjects are to their lawful king, yet they were under his rule and government, and in order to exercise lawfully their mission they must perforce be in his communion.

Dr. Barrow makes a great point in the fact that S. Peter was not called " Arch-apostle, Arch-pastor, High-priest, Sovereign Pontiff," * &c. It is doubtful whether the *first* order in the ministry was known exclusively by the title of Bishop in the first age; so the absence of a mere title proves nothing.

The title of Archbishop or Metropolitan, though very ancient, does not appear to have been in use in the days of the Apostles. But after all it is not the title which determines a man's authority, but the functions he performs. Did S. Peter assume the Leadership, or did he not? Did he not by his own sole authority (I mean apart from the Apostles) expand the Kingdom so as to admit the Gentiles? Did he not determine the question about circumcision at the first Council of Jerusalem? And did not S. Paul visit him, seeing none of the other Apostles, save James, the Lord's brother? If these queries, or any one of them, can be answered in the affirmative (no other Apostle exercising similar functions), then it must be conceded that S. Peter had a defined position. distinct from the other Apostles, and that consisted in his being the Head and Chief.

Dr. Barrow adds, " There was indeed no office above that of an apostle known to the apostles or to the primitive church" (*Sup. p.* 52). This is quite true. The Apostles were a confederate body, subject to one Head and Leader, who possessed an authority at least co-ordinate with them, so that if S. Peter could not exercise supreme authority without

---

* Tertullian (A.D. 195-218), after he became a heretic, ironically describes the Pope, as "The Supreme Pontiff." *De Pudic. n.* 1.

their consent (which, however, he did in the case of the Gentiles), they at any rate could not without his concurrence. This must be evident if the Fathers are correct that S. Peter was invested with the Prerogative of Government.

III.

COUNTER ARGUMENTS AGAINST THE SUPREMACY OF S. PETER.

Dr. Barrow affirms that our Lord "at several times declared against this kind of Primacy, instituting equality among His apostles, prohibiting them to affect, to seek, to assume, or admit a superiority of power one above another." (*Sup. p.* 52). This is a sweeping assertion, but what are the proofs he adduces? Dr. Barrow, in the first place, quotes a portion of the famous passage, "And there was also a strife among them, which of them should be accounted the greatest; and He said unto them, The kings of the Gentiles exercise lordship over them; and they that exercise authority upon them, are called benefactors. But ye shall not be so: but he that is greatest among you, let him be as the younger; and he that is chief as He that doth serve. For whether is greater, he that sitteth at meat, or he that serveth? is not he that sitteth at meat? but I am among you as he that serveth." (S. Luke, xxii. 24–27.) Why Dr. Barrow should have omitted the concluding verse of this extract, is inexplicable, for it has, surely, much to do in determining our Lord's meaning. The object of our Lord was (1) to declare, that the Kingdom of God was not to be a temporal or secular one, in the ordinary sense of the word; (2) to reprove ambition and lust of dominion and power; and (3) to inculcate humility. The error Dr. Barrow has fallen into, is, in assuming that the words, "he that is greatest among you, let him be as the younger; and he that is chief, as he that doth serve," precluded the appointment of one of them as their chief. Had he quoted the last verse, "For whether is greater, he that sitteth at meat, or he that serveth? is not he that sitteth at meat? but I am among you, as He that serveth:" he would have seen the point of our Lord's reproof, not that there was to be no Head, but that he that aspired to be the Chief should be as the younger, and "as he that doth serve;" and then He points to Himself as their model of humility, "but I am among you, as He that serveth." This last clause, which the Doctor omitted, gives the key to our Lord's meaning, viz., that ambition shall be punished by degradation. Doctor Barrow asserts that the Lord checked this ambitious spirit in the Apostles, "not by telling them, that He already had decided the case in appointing them a superior, but rather by assuring them, that He did intend none such to be; that he would have no monarchy, no exercise of any dominion or authority of one among them over the rest." (*Sup. p.* 53.) Did He? Let us see: immediately after Christ had administered this reproof, He constituted His kingdom, appointing His Apostles as kings to rule over it, and then, turning to S. Peter, He said, "Simon, Simon, behold! Satan hath desired to have you, that he may sift you as wheat; but I have prayed for thee, that thy faith fail not, and when thou art converted, Strengthen (or confirm, or make fixed) thy brethren." Was not S. Peter, by these words, appointed to a position of Superiority to the other Apostles? If not, how could he become their prop, their support, and their confirmer; in a word, their centre of unity? But Dr. Barrow ignores the force of this passage, and evidently considers it of no importance in this inquiry: the early Fathers, however, thought otherwise. S. Ambrose, quoting it, and comparing with it the words, "Thou art Peter," says, "How could He not confirm his faith, unto whom, of His own authority, He gave the kingdom, and whom He styles the Rock, He pointed out the Foundation of the Church." (*See T.* ii. *l.* iv. *De Fide c.* v. *n.* 56, *p.* 531.) S. Cyril, Patriarch of Alexandria, considers that when Christ said, "When thou art converted confirm thy brethren," that S. Peter was henceforth to be "the Foundation and Teacher of all who should come to Christ by Faith." (*See Mai, Nov. Bibliot. Pat. T.* ii. *pp.* 419, 420.) S. Leo, likewise referring to the same passage, informs us that "special care is taken by the Lord, and for the faith of Peter in particular does He pray, as though the condition of the rest would be more secure, provided the mind of Peter was not subdued. In Peter, therefore, is the strength of all defended, and the aid of divine grace is so disposed as that the firmness which is bestowed on Peter, may be conferred by Peter on the Apostles." (*See T.* i. *Serm.* iv. *in Anniver. Assumpt. c.* i.-iv. *col.* 16-19). It is impossible, then, honestly to ignore the literal interpretation of the passage in question, for it signifies what it clearly means, viz. that S. Peter was directed by his Lord to confirm or strengthen with the enduring firmness of the Rock (which he had now become by Christ's appointment) the faith of his brethren of the Apostolic College.

2. The learned Doctor further says, "Was St. Peter a rock, on which the Church was to be founded? Be it so: but no less were they all: for the wall of Jerusalem, which *came down from heaven,* had *twelve foundations, on which were inscribed the names of the twelve apostles of the Lamb;* and *we,* saith S. Paul, *do all build upon the foundation of the prophets and apostles, Christ Himself being the chief corner-stone;* whence *equally,* saith S. Jerome, *the strength of the Church is settled upon them."* (*Sup.* 59, 60.) Now had Dr. Barrow thought for one moment, he would have seen that although it is true that all the Apostles were foundation stones of the city wall, yet the First Stone was pre-eminent, and not only pre-eminent, but predominant. It was a Jasper stone, the same stone which is the symbol of the Lamb, and the same stone which composed the material of the city wall: so that while it is quite true that all the Apostles were rocks and stones, yet S. Peter's Rock is THE ROCK, on which the Church is built; and S. Peter's Stone—the Jasper— the material of the wall. The passage taken from S. Jerome is inaccurately quoted, it is this: "The strength of the Church is settled equally upon them (the Apostles); yet for this reason ONE is chosen out of the Twelve, that a Head being appointed, the occasion of schism might

be removed." (*See Rev.* xxi. 11–20, *and S. Jerom. t.* iv. *Adv. Jovin. Pt.* ii. *Col.* 170.)

3. Dr. Barrow next demands, " Had St. Peter a power given him of binding and loosing effectually? so had they, immediately granted by our Saviour, in as full manner, and couched in the same terms: *If thou shalt bind,*" &c. (*Sup. p.* 60.) This is but partially true. Though all had the power of binding and loosing, yet the Keys,— the symbol of supreme jurisdiction,— were given to S. Peter *alone.* The other Apostles had the use of them, in union with S. Peter ; but not otherwise. When Christ addressed the Twelve, saying, " Whatsoever ye shall bind on earth, shall be bound in heaven," &c. (S. Matt. xviii. 18), S. Peter asked him, " How oft shall my brother sin against me, and I forgive him ? till seven times ?" to which our Lord answered, " I say not unto thee until seven times, but until seventy times seven." (*Ib.* xviii. 21, 22.) The Primacy of Jurisdiction, in the use of the keys, is here apparent, so that while all had the use of them, yet S. Peter had them principally. On this point, Origen says, " But as it was fit—even though something in common was spoken of Peter, and of those who should thrice admonish the brethren,—that Peter should have something peculiar above those who should thrice admonish ; this was previously ordained separately respecting Peter : thus, *I will give to thee the keys of the kingdom of heaven,* before (it was said) *and whatsoever you shall bind on earth,* and what follows : and truly, if we sedulously attend to the evangelical writings, even in them we may discover,—with regard even to those things which seem to be common to Peter and to those who have thrice admonished their brethren,—much difference and pre-eminence in the words spoken to Peter, beyond those spoken to in the second place." (*T.* iii. *in Matt. Tom.* xiii. *n.* 31, p. 613-4.)

4. Dr. Barrow gets rid of the famous passage, " Feed My sheep," by referring to Eph. iv. 11, and Acts, xx. 28, to show that all the Apostles had an equal share in the pastoral charge of the flock. He quotes also the first commission to the Apostles, to evangelize the world, and concludes in the words of S. Chrysostom, they *were all in common intrusted with the whole world, and had the care of all nations* (*Sup. p.* 60, 61); and yet in another place this Father thus comments on the words, " And in those days, Peter rising up in the midst of the disciples :" " Both as being ardent, and as having had intrusted to him by Christ the flock ; as the First of the Choir, he always is the First to begin the discourse. . . . . justly he has the First authority in the matter, as having had all intrusted to him." (*T.* ix. *Hom.* iii. *in Act. App. n.* 3, *p.* 26.)

IV.

APOSTOLIC CUSTOM.

Our author, respecting the practice of the Apostles, asserts that " in the Apostolic history, the proper place of exercising his power . . . no footstep thereof doth appear." And he adds, " We cannot there discern whether St.

Peter did assume any extraordinary authority, or that any deference by his brethren was rendered to him, as to their governor or judge" (*Sup. p.* 63). One would have thought that if a member of an association on all occasions, when present, assumed the functions of a president, or a director, or a moderator; if he always when present, acted, or spoke in the name of, and on behalf of the society he belonged to; and if it was the case, that no other member, when this person was present, ever took upon himself this position, reasonable people would without any hesitation conclude that he had some right or authority,—either inherent in himself or by delegation from a superior power, or by the election of his brethren— to presume so to act. Now two startling facts are apparent to any careful student of Scripture, especially of the Acts of the Apostles: (1) That S. Peter on every occasion, when present, did assume and exercise the right of leading, directing, and governing the body over which he undoubtedly seems to have been the recognised Head and Chief; and (2) That there is no evidence whatever, direct or indirect, that S. Peter was ever elected by his brother Apostles to this position; but there is very strong testimony, both direct and indirect, in S. Matthew, that our blessed Lord did choose him to be His Representative and the Ruler of the Church. Let us take what examples there are which are given us in Holy Writ.

1. The first act of the Apostolic College, after the Ascension of Christ, was to fill up the vacancy caused by the treason and death of Judas Iscariot. " In those days," says the inspired historian, "Peter stood up in the midst of the disciples, and said. . . . Men and brethren, this Scripture must needs have been fulfilled, which the Holy Ghost by the mouth of David spake before concerning Judas, which was guide to them that took Jesus. For he was numbered with us, and had obtained part of this ministry." Then describing the death of Judas, and quoting the 59th Psalm, continues: " Wherefore of these men which have companied with us all the time that the Lord Jesus went in and out amongst us, beginning from the baptism of John unto that same day that He was taken up from us, must one be ordained to be a witness with us of His resurrection." (Acts, i. 21, 22.) The assembled disciples then proceeded to elect a successor to Judas Iscariot. S. Peter's action here was that of a Ruler or Governor, or as one who had received authority to see that the offices of the Church were duly filled up. Dr. Barrow, ignoring the tone and matter of S. Peter's address, that one "must be ordained," says that " he did indeed suggest the matter, and lay the case before them; he first declared his sense, but the whole company did choose two, and referred the determination of one to lot, or to God's arbitration." (*Sup. p.* 64.) This language seems to me a thorough misconception of the case. In reading over the address of S. Peter, it means far more than to "suggest the matter," much more than the declaration of "his sense." The whole form and matter of the address is that of one who had authority, and its tone is that of command, couched in the language of love and courtesy. This will appear evident if we examine carefully the terms of his address, which may be thus summarised :—(1) The announcement of the vacancy; (2) The statement of the necessity of a successor being appointed; and

(3) The decree concerning the qualification of the candidate, viz. one who had companioned with Christ and the Apostles from the commencement of the Lord's ministry till the Ascension. And it should be noted, not-withstanding Dr. Barrow's gloss, that there is not a particle of evidence producible that S. Peter ever consulted the other Apostles. S. Chrysostom says he so acted "as having had intrusted to him by Christ the flock . . . as having had all intrusted to him." The fact that the appointment was made by election, proves nothing against the position of the Apostle, for in every part of the Church from the earliest period, Bishops have been elected, subject to the confirmation of the Metropolitan, either by all the clergy and laity of the diocese, or by the Chapter of the Cathedral ; and in this matter of the election of S. Matthias, there is nothing to show that his election had not been approved of by S. Peter.

2. Dr. Barrow adduces the narrative of the institution of the Diaconate and the election of Deacons. He says the "*twelve did call the mul-titude of disciples,* and directed them *to elect* the persons ; and the proposal being *acceptable* to them, it was done accordingly ; *they chose Stephen, &c.,* whom *they set before the Apostles, and when they had prayed, they laid their hands upon them.*" (*Sup. p.* 64). There is nothing here which in any way excludes the action of S. Peter. Indeed, when on every other occasion the Twelve assembled we find S. Peter taking the lead as the Director of the business in hand, it is simply absurd to object that, because in this *single* instance his name is not separately mentioned, he did not perform his accustomed duties as the Head of the Apostolic Body.

3. The next incident Dr. Barrow appeals to as justifying his argument, is that of the first Synod of Jerusalem. (Acts, xv.) He says, "In that important transaction about the observance of Mosaical institutions, *a great stir and debate being started,* which St. Paul and St. Barnabas by disputation could not appease, what course was then taken ? Did they appeal to St. Peter as to the supreme dictator and judge of con-troversies ? Not so ; but they *sent to the Apostles and elders at Jerusalem* to inquire about the question. . . . In this assembly, *after much debate* passed, and that many had fully uttered their sense, St. Peter *rose up,* with apostolical gravity, declaring what his reason and experience did suggest, conducing to a resolution of the point ; whereto his words might indeed be much available, grounded, not only upon common reason, but upon special revelation concerning the case ; whereupon St. James, obeying that revelation, and backing it with reason drawn from Scripture, with much authority pronounceth his judgment : *Therefore,* saith he, *I judge* (that is, saith St. Chrysostom, *I* authoritatively) say, *that we trouble not them, &c.* And the result was, that according to the proposal of St. James it was by general consent determined to send a decretal letter unto the Gentile Christians, containing a canon, or advice directive of the practice in this case. *It then* seemed *good to* (or was decreed by) *the Apostles and elders, with the whole Church to send* — and the letter ran thus :—'*The Apostles, and elders, and brethren, to the brethren of the Gentiles.*' Now in all this action . . . . where can the sharpest sight

descry any mark of distinction or pre-eminence which St. Peter had in respect to the other Apostles? Did St. Peter in anywise behave himself like his pretended successors upon that occasion? What authority did he claim or use before that assembly, or in it, or after it? Did he summon or convocate it? No; they met upon common agreement. Did he preside there? No; but rather St. James, *to whom* (saith St. Chrysostom) as *Bishop of Jerusalem*, the government was committed.... Did he more than use his freedom of speech becoming an apostle, in arguing the case and passing his vote? No; for in so exact a relation nothing more doth appear. Did he form the definitions, or pronounce the decree resulting? No; St. James rather did that; for (as an ancient author saith) *Peter did make an oration, but St. James did make the law.* Was, beside his suffrage in the debate, any singular approbation required from him, or did he by any bull confirm the decrees? No such matter; that was devices of ambition, creeping on and growing up to the pitch where they are now. In short, doth any thing correspondent to papal pretences appear assumed by St. Peter, or deferred to him?" (*Sup. pp.* 64–66.) There is nothing in the account of the first synod of Jerusalem, which militates in any way against S. Peter's position as Head of the Apostolic College. Dr. Barrow treats S. Peter's action in this council almost with contempt, as if he had but little to do in the determination of the great question to be decided. He says, S. Peter declared " what his reason and experience did suggest, conducing to a resolution of the point." Now if we look carefully at the speech which he delivered, we find two things, (1) a narrative how God had revealed to him the points about the matter; and (2) a reproof directed against those who enforced Judaism upon the Gentiles. " Now, therefore, why tempt ye God, to put a yoke upon the neck of the disciples, which neither our fathers nor we were able to bear?" (Acts, xv. 10.) His address is not suggestive, as Dr. Barrow seems to believe; but authoritative and conclusive. This is clear from what follows; for after S. Paul and S. Barnabas had spoken, recounting "what miracles and wonders had been wrought among the Gentiles by them," S. James rose up and delivered his decree, based on the judgment of S. Peter. " Simeon hath declared how God at the first did visit the Gentiles, to take out of them a people for His Name;" and after showing how this was agreeable to prophecy, adds, " Wherefore my sentence or decree is, that we trouble not them, which from among the Gentiles are turned to God." I confess I cannot conceive a stronger proof of S. Peter's position in the council than this which is recorded. A disagreement arises, a council assembles to consider it, and after much disputing, S. Peter addresses the Synod, and, in point of fact, settles it, by delivering the oracle of God on the subject, which the whole assembled body immediately accept, and promulge in the form of the decree addressed to the Gentile Church. " The result " then was not " that according to the proposal of S. James," merely, but according to the judgment of S. Peter, accepted by S. James and the whole Church. This seems to me the true interpretation to be put upon this transaction. Clearly S. James did not by his own single authority determine this question, he says, *Wherefore, my sentence* is ; and that sentence, or decree, was without doubt founded upon what fell from S. Peter.

With respect to the formal manner of celebrating this council, there is nothing to show that S. Peter did not "summon or convocate it," or that he did not "preside there ;" nor is there any authority for supposing that S. James did so; nor is there anything said about confirming the decrees: but one thing is evident, viz., that S. Peter must have assented to them, inasmuch as they were founded upon that judgment, or whatever it is called, which he delivered. I conclude this part of the subject with two extracts from the Homilies of S. Chrysostom, whom Dr. Barrow so often quotes against S. Peter : "But observe how Peter does everything with the common consent ; nothing imperiously." *Hom.* iii. in Acts, *Lib. Fath. p.* 37. "Like the commander of an army, he (Peter) went about, inspecting the ranks, what part was compact, what in good order, what needed his presence. See how on all occasions he goes about as foremost. When an Apostle was to be chosen, he was the foremost : when the Jews were to be told, that they were *not drunken*, when the lame man was to be healed, when harangues are to be made, he is before the rest. When the rulers were to be spoken to, he was the man ; when Ananias, he : . . . . And look ; when there was danger, he was the man, and when good management (was needed) ; but where all is calm, then they act all in common, and he demands no greater honour (than the others)." (*Hom.* xxi. in Acts, *ib. p.* 300.) Can any one suppose for one moment, that S. Chrysostom believed, that S. Peter was merely suggesting what was to be done in this council, or that he was merely "arguing the case and passing his vote?" There can be no doubt he acted as the Head, and the Chief of the Apostolic body. He was the man that quashed the disputation, he informed the council of the will of God, and the council obeyed, and promulged the decree, accordingly.*

4. Dr. Barrow thinks he has made a good point against S. Peter's position, when "they of the circumcision contended with him," with respect to his receiving the Gentile Cornelius into the Church ; and he infers from this that they had no notion of "his supreme unaccountable authority (not to say of that infallibility, with which the canonists and Jesuits have invested him)." (*Sup. p.* 66.) If this argument proves anything, it tells against S. Peter, as an inspired Apostle. The circumcision party seems to have been a very troublesome one, and withal impatient of authority. It was this party, who "taught" in defiance of apostolic authority, "saying, Except ye be circumcised after the manner of Moses, ye cannot be saved." (Acts, xv. 1.) S. Paul and S. Barnabas resisted them, and "had no small discussion and disputation with them," but all to no purpose, they would not submit to their authority, although they were men full of the Holy Ghost ; and nothing would satisfy them, until the matter had been brought before the Apostles and elders at Jerusalem. The fact then of this insubordinate party opposing S. Peter witnesses

---

* With respect to the passage from S. Chrysostom, quoted by Dr. Barrow, to the effect that S. James presided, see "Comment," *supra, p.* 44.

nothing against his Supremacy; and the mere circumstance of this Apostle condescending to them, "gently satisfying them with reason," really proves nothing.

Dr. Barrow adds, "Further, so far was S. Peter from assuming command over his brethren that he was upon all occasions ready to obey their orders, as we may see by this passage, when, upon the conversion of divers persons in Samaria, it is said that *the Apostle hearing it, did send to them Peter and John, who going down, prayed for them, that they might receive the Holy Ghost.* The Apostles sent him; that, had he been their sovereign, would have been somewhat unseemly and presumptuous, for subjects are not wont to send their princes, or soldiers their captain; to be sent being a mark of inferiority, as our Lord himself did teach: *a servant,* said He, *is not greater than his lord, nor he that is sent greater than he that sent him. (Sup. p. 67).* If Dr. Barrow's argument can be sustained, then S. Paul and S. Barnabas were inferior to the Church of Antioch, and our Lord Himself to the Apostles. We will discuss these two points separately. The Church of Antioch was afflicted by the party of the circumcision alluded to above, and S. Paul and S. Barnabas not being regarded by their party as of sufficient authority to settle the questions they raised (notwithstanding they were inspired men) "determined that Paul and Barnabas, and certain others of them, should go up to Jerusalem unto the Apostles and Elders about this question." (Acts, xv. 2.) The Apostle of the Gentiles, together with his co-apostle, according to Dr. Barrow's method of argument, was inferior to the authorities of the Church of Antioch, because they sent him up to Jerusalem to confer with the Apostles respecting this point! Again, Dr. Barrow has quoted our Lord's words, "A servant is not greater than his lord;" but this passage, together with another similar one, tells forcibly against his argument. Two incidents occurred in the upper chamber, where Christ and His disciples were eating the Passover. The one incident which Dr. Barrow has referred to was the washing of the disciples' feet, which was followed by the words of our Lord, "You call Me Master and Lord; and ye say well, for so I am. If I thus, your Lord and Master, have washed your feet, you also ought to wash one another's feet. For I have given you an example, that you should do as I have done to you. Verily, verily, I say unto you, The servant is not greater than his lord; neither he that is sent greater than He that sent him." Christ was here teaching His Apostles humility, and the duty of serving others, and He points to Himself as their model of humility.

In order to have ascertained the true meaning of our Lord, Dr. Barrow should have referred to another passage similar in import, but with a most important addition, " For whether is greater, he that sitteth at meat, or he that serveth? is not he that sitteth at meat? but I am among you as he that serveth." (S. Luke, xxii. 27.) Now if Dr. Barrow's argument is really cogent, then it would follow that Christ was inferior to His own Apostles, because he said, " I am among you as he that serveth," for he had just said that he that sitteth at meat is greater than he that serveth. During the last Passover which our Lord kept He acted the part of a servant, nay, as a menial, for he had washed the disciples' feet ; so low had He condescended that it was not until He had threatened S. Peter with the loss of his high position that he yielded to His humility. This *argumentum ad absurdum* shows how untenable is the Doctor's position. As our Lord had served the Apostles, so did S. Peter serve his brethren, so also did S. Paul and S. Barnabas serve the Church of Antioch, but in so doing they were not acting the part of inferiors any more than their Master, when He said, " I am among you as one that serveth."

5. Upon the words, " I am of Paul ; and I of Apollos ; and I of Cephas ; and I of Christ," Dr. Barrow argues, " Now supposing the case had been clear and certain (and if it were not so then, how can it be so now ?) that St. Peter was sovereign of the Apostles, is it not wonderful that any Christian should prefer any apostle or any preacher before him ? as if it were now clear and generally acknowledged that the Pope is truly what he pretendeth to be, would anybody stand in competition with him, would any glory in a relation to any other minister before him ? " (*Sup. p.* 69.) It is evident that Dr. Barrow has mistaken the drift of the passage in question ; so far from its witnessing against S. Peter, it tends to establish his position as the Chief Apostle. As S. Chrysostom's remarks on this text are extremely apposite, they shall be employed as an answer in refutation of Dr. Barrow's absurd argument. " ' I say *contentions*,' saith he (*i. e.* Paul), ' I mean not about private matters, but of the more grievous sort.' *That every one of you saith ;* for the corruption pervaded not a part, but the whole of the Church. And yet they were not speaking about himself (Paul), nor about Peter, nor about Apollos ; but he signifies that if these were not to be leaned on, much less others. For that they had not spoken about them, he saith further on : *And these things I have transferred in a figure unto myself and Apollos, that you may learn in us not to think above what is written.* For if it were not right for them to call themselves by the name of Paul, and of Apollos, and of Cephas, much less of any other. If under the Teacher and the First of the Apostles, and one that had instructed so much people, it were not right to enrol themselves, much less under those who were nothing." (*Hom.* iii. *in* I *Cor. c.* i. *v.* 12. Observe how fundamentally the great S. Chrysostom,—one of the most illustrious Doctors of the Church—and Dr. Barrow differ in their interpretation. The latter is of opinion that the preference of other Apostles to S. Peter contributes to prove that S. Peter had no superiority, whereas the former maintains that S. Paul strengthens his reproof by his graduated method of argument. S. Chrysostom's comment may be thus paraphrased, " It is not lawful for you, Corinthians, to call yourselves after the name of any man—not from Paul, not from Apollos, no, not even may you enrol yourselves under the name of Peter, "the Teacher and the First of the Apostles," for in so doing you divide, as far as you can, the Church." Indeed, S. Chrysostom gives his reason for this method of argument, for he says, " He (Paul) hath arranged his statement in the way of climax." (*Ib.*) S. Paul, writing his own Epistle, in the spirit of humility (as is natural to holy men) puts his own name lowest in order, then Apollos,

and then highest of all S. Peter, the Chief Apostle—showing that not even the name of Peter should be used as the designation of any sect or party in the Church.

But let us suppose that S. Chrysostom's comment on the words, " I am of Paul, and I of Apollos, and I of Cephas," is untenable, still there is nothing in them which in any way affects S. Peter's place in the Apostleship. Dr. Barrow asks triumphantly, assuming S. Peter "was Sovereign of the Apostles," " Is it not wonderful that any Christian should prefer any apostle, or any preacher before him?" But, surely, Apollos was inferior in ecclesiastical rank, and in jurisdiction to both S. Peter and S. Paul, and yet notwithstanding, some of the Corinthians seem to have preferred him to these great Apostles, "is it not wonderful (then) that any Christian should prefer a "preacher" (to use Dr. Barrow's expression) " to an apostle?" It would, therefore, follow from the Doctor's mode of argument, that both S. Peter and S. Paul were not superior to Apollos, because he was by some preferred to them! This alone demonstrates the utter absurdity of Dr. Barrow's argument, for in his endeavours to upset the Chieftainship, he knocks down the Apostleship! It may be fairly concluded, then, that the passage under discussion does not witness against the position of S. Peter as the Head of the Apostles; if anything, it supports it. Of the two interpretations—the ancient and the modern—S. Chrysostom's is natural, and in harmony with other parts of Scripture, and in accordance with Catholic Tradition, whereas Dr. Barrow's is unnatural, unscriptural, contrary to the Tradition of the Church, and forced.

It is to be noted that the learned Doctor refers to S. Clement, and puts himself under the protection of S. Augustine. The former merely reminds the Corinthians of their schism in the time of the Apostles, without entering into any details, so why the Doctor should have quoted him, is not apparent? The latter Father—S. Augustine—Dr. Barrow must have known, would have rejected his interpretation, for he has over and over again asserted, in language too plain to be misunderstood, that S. Peter held the " Primacy of the Apostles." and the " Princedom of the Apostolate."

6. S. Paul's visit to S. Peter, Dr. Barrow considers as one only " of respect and love; " or "to confer with him for mutual edification and comfort; or at most to obtain approbation from him and the other apostles, which might satisfy some doubters, but not to receive his commands or authoritative instructions from him; it being, as we shall afterwards see, the design of St. Paul's discourse to disavow any such dependence on any man whatever." (*Sup. pp.* 70, 71.)

In the text itself, no reason is given for the Apostle going up to Jerusalem to see S. Peter, nor is there any account of what passed between them, so it is impossible to form any decided opinion one way or the other on this incident. The reasons advanced by Dr. Barrow may be tenable, but it is doubtful whether they would naturally occur to any one who was not prejudiced against S. Peter's claim. Those who believe that S. Peter was the Head of the apostolic body, see at once the object of S. Paul's visit; those who hold the contrary opinion that S. Peter was no greater than any other Apostle, naturally believe that it was, as Dr. Barrow concludes, one merely of "respect and love." But then arises an important question, if the object of the visit was only to show "respect and love," and to "confer for mutual edification and comfort," how comes it that the other Apostles were excluded from all share of that "love and respect," which S. Paul was anxious to show? Dr. Barrow seems to have perceived that such a question might be asked, and very conveniently he adds the words, "at most to obtain approbation from him (S. Peter) and the other Apostles." Here is an inaccuracy. S. Paul does not say that he saw "the other Apostles," but on the contrary, "other of the Apostles saw I none, save James, the Lord's brother." Therefore it was not the object of the Apostle to pay "respect and love" to ten of the Apostles, nor to "confer" with them, "for mutual edification and comfort," but to visit only one of them, even S. Peter. This was *the* object of his visit. He indeed saw S. James. Why? because he was "the Lord's brother," and the Bishop of Jerusalem; and not to have visited him would have been an act of disrespect, but his *object* was to "see Peter." "Then, after three years, I went up to Jerusalem to see Peter;" (Gal. i. 18), these are the words of the text. Dr. Barrow quotes S. Chrysostom, to the effect, that this visit to S. Peter was really nothing more than one of "respect and love :" let us, however, examine the extract he has favoured us with. " *What can be more humble than this soul? After so many and so great exploits, having no need at all of Peter, or of his discourse, but being in dignity equal to him (for I will now say no more), he yet doth go up to him, as to one greater and ancienter; and a sight alone of Peter is the cause of his journey thither;* and *he went*, saith he again, *not to learn anything of him, nor to receive any correction from him, but this only that he might see him, and honour him with his presence.*" But why did not Dr. Barrow continue the quotation? For had he done so, he would have ascertained S. Chrysostom's opinion more accurately. The following sentence is in immediate sequence to that which he has given us. " He (Paul) said not ἰδὼν, that is to see Peter (only), but ἱστορῆσαι, that is to behold and observe him, as men are accustomed to speak when observing the great and splendid cities they visit. Much more, then, did he (Paul) deem it worth the toil of (going up to Jerusalem) if only he might see this man (Peter)." (*T.* x. *ad Gal. c.* i. *v.* 18, *p.* 631, edit. Migne.) Surely this sentence, which the learned Doctor conveniently omitted, implies far more than that S. Paul visited S. Peter out of mere " respect and love." A great and splendid city in the age of S. Chrysostom meant something more than a similar description of such cities as, for instance, Liverpool, or Manchester, or Leeds. "A great and splendid city" at that period meant such cities as Rome, Constantinople, Antioch, Alexandria, Carthage, and perhaps York, &c., each of which was a capital or a metropolis of a chief or subordinate government. Let us now transpose S. Chrysostom's simile from a city to an emperor or governor. S. Paul, soon after his conversion, heard of one who was regarded by Christians as occupying a very peculiar position in the Church ; that he was named by the Lord a

G

Rock; that upon that Rock Christ built His Church; that to him He gave the keys of heaven; that against the Church so built upon him the gates of hell should not prevail; that He commissioned him to confirm or strengthen the brethren, and to feed the sheep and lambs of the flock. Well, S. Paul desires to behold this great man, who is the Head, the Chief, the Supreme Pastor of the Universal Church; he therefore resolves to go up and "observe him," as men travel to the capital to "observe" the emperor, that they may feast their eyes on him, who is the symbol and personification of imperial power, grandeur, and splendour. According to S. Chrysostom, such a man was S. Peter, whom S. Paul "went up to Jerusalem to see," only far greater than an emperor, and whose power by divine delegation was far superior to that of any earthly potentate. But in order that there may be no mistake as to S. Chrysostom's opinion touching this visit, let us turn to another passage taken from one of his homilies on S. John's Gospel, which Dr. Barrow ought to have quoted: "Jesus saith to Simon Peter, *Simon, son of Jonas, lovest thou Me more than these? &c.* And why, then, passing by the rest, does He discourse with Peter concerning these things? He was the Chosen One of the Apostles, and the Mouth of the disciples, and the Head of the choir. For this cause, mark these words, *"for this cause* also did Paul come upon an occasion to see him before the rest. And withal showing him, that thenceforward he must be confident, as having done away with his denial, He (Christ) places in his hands the Government ($\pi\rho\omega\sigma\tau\alpha\sigma\iota\alpha\nu$*) over the brethren." (*T.* viii. *Hom.* lxxxviii. *in Joan. n.* 1, *p.* 525.) What then is the truth of this matter? Clearly this, that all the Apostles were equal in dignity, all were constituted Apostles by our Lord, but one was chosen to be the Head, in order, as S. Jerome informs us, "that the occasion of schism might be removed;" and hence, S. Paul's visit was intended, at least, to honour his Chief, his Superior, and his Prince.

7. "St. Paul doth often purposely assert to himself an independent and absolute power, inferior or subordinate to none other, insisting thereon for the enforcement or necessary defence of his doctrine and practice . . . . As for his call and commission to the apostolical office, he maintaineth (as he meant designedly to exclude those pretences, that other Apostles were only called *in partem solicitudinis* with St. Peter), that he was *an apostle, not from men, nor by man, but by Jesus Christ, and God the Father;* that is, that he derived not his office immediately or mediately from men, or by the ministry of any man, but immediately had received the grant and charge thereof from our Lord; as indeed the history plainly showeth, in which our Lord telleth him, that he did *constitute Him an officer, and a chosen instrument to Him, to bear His name to the Gentiles.*" (*Sup.* p. 73.) But what does Dr. Barrow infer from this? All the Apostles were equally Apostles, "not of men, nor by man, but by Jesus Christ, and God the Father." Every one of them, no less

---

* In "The Library of the Fathers," the Editors translate this word, "Chief authority among the brethren." (See *Hom. S. Chrysos. in S. John, p.* 790.) But it means more than this, viz. *to have authority and power to command others.* According to this Father, S. Peter was not merely the "chief authority among," but he had the "government over," the brethren.

than S. Paul, had been called and constituted an Apostle by Him ; and yet human instrumentality was employed by our Lord after His withdrawal from this earthly scene. It was by election by men, guided by the Holy Ghost, that S. Matthias was chosen in the room of Judas Iscariot ; and in the case of S. Paul himself, after his call, he had to submit to baptism by a human minister ; and when the time had arrived for him to assume his apostleship, the Holy Ghost said to certain *men*, who were "prophets and teachers," "Separate Me, Barnabas and Saul, for the work whereunto I have called them. And when they had fasted and prayed, and laid their hands on them, they sent them away." (Acts, xiii. 2, 3.) So that whatever S. Paul might have meant by the assertion that his office had been derived from heaven, and not from man, he could not have intended to deny, that he had had to submit to baptism, and the imposition of hands, by *human* ministers, before he could have obeyed the call of Jesus, and before he could have promulged that revelation, which he had received direct from the court of Heaven. Bearing this in mind, that he was no more than an Apostle, that all the other Apostles had equally with him received their revelation direct from the Lord Jesus, and remembering also that two at least, if not all, had received their apostolic power by the ministration of men, it does not seem difficult to conclude, that if S. Paul did not intend by his language to ignore his own obligations to Ananias of Damascus, and the prophets and teachers at Antioch, no more did he intend to ignore the position of S. Peter in the Apostolic College, who had been constituted by Christ as the Supreme Prince of His Kingdom, and the Supreme Pastor of His Church. Dr. Barrow then had no authority for asserting that S. Paul "meant designedly to exclude those pretences that other Apostles were only called *in partem solicitudinis* with St. Peter." He does not touch the question of canonical (if I may use such a word here) relationship of the Apostles to each other, or to their Chief ; he simply asserts his position as equal in dignity and authority with the other Apostles,—a position which is really not disputed.

It is true that very little is said about S. Peter in any of S. Paul's Epistles, but what little is said, is with respect for him and his office. The visit to S. Peter, let Dr. Barrow assert what he pleases, was one intended to do honour to his Chief, at least so thought S. Chrysostom. Then, again, it is to be remarked, that sometimes in speaking of the Twelve, he distinguishes their Chief by name. "Have we not power to lead about a sister, a wife, as well as other Apostles, and as the brethren of the Lord, and Cephas ?" (1 Cor. ix. 5.) If S. Peter had no greater jurisdiction or authority than any other of the Apostles, why does S. Paul separate his name from them, as if he was their Superior ? The evident meaning of this seems to be, that S. Paul claimed to have certain privileges as other Apostles had, as the brethren of the Lord, and *even* as S. Peter had. The favourite author of Dr. Barrow, S. Chrysostom, has a commentary on this text : "Observe his (S. Paul's) skilfulness. The Leader of the Choir stands last in his arrangement : since that is the time for laying down the strongest of all one's topics. Nor was it so wonderful for one to be able to point out examples of this conduct in the rest, as in the Foremost champion, and in him (S. Peter) who was intrusted with the keys of heaven." (*Hom.* xxi. *in* 1 *Cor.* ix. 5, *Lib. of Fath. p.* 280.)   What little then is said about S. Peter in S. Paul's Epistles, is with respect, recognising implicitly, at least, his exalted position as the Head of the apostolic body.

8. Dr. Barrow makes much of the passage in the Galatians, "I withstood him to the face, because he was to be blamed." (Gal. ii. 11.) He thus argues, "which behaviour of St. Paul doth not well consist with the *supposition, that St. Peter was his superior in office* (quoting S. Jerome); if that had been, Porphyrius with good colour of reason might have objected procacity to St. Paul in taxing his betters; for he then indeed had showed us no commendable pattern of demeanour towards our governors, in so boldly opposing St. Peter, in so openly censuring him, in so smartly confuting him." (*Sup. p.* 76.)   Dr. Barrow is somewhat satirical in his argument, and thinks he has planted a mortal blow against the notion of S. Peter's Supremacy.   Why should not S. Paul rebuke S. Peter, his Superior, if he erred, not in faith, but in conduct?   Do the princes and great men of a kingdom never rebuke their Sovereign, if he, by his conduct and policy, endanger the peace of the realm, or the rights and liberties of his people?   And does the administration of such a rebuke or remonstrance amount to a denial of his kingly office ?   S. Ambrose more than once severely censured the Emperor's conduct, and on one occasion imposed upon Theodosius a public penance for a great crime; did he thereby deny his imperial rights and prerogatives?   Certainly not; no more did the rebuke, which S. Paul, who was not a subject of S. Peter, in the ordinary sense of the term, imply any denial on his part of that superiority which S. Peter — according to the Scriptures, "as interpreted by the Catholic Fathers and ancient Bishops"—undoubtedly possessed?   Dr. Barrow quotes S. Cyprian, and appeals to S. Chrysostom to support his views, that this rebuke was administered "upon supposition that St. Peter and St. Paul were equals, or (as S. Cyprian calleth them) colleagues and brethren, in rank co-ordinate." (*Sup. p.* 78.)   Here, again, is a *suppressio veri;* no doubt the Apostles were co-equal and co-ordinate, but did they deny that S. Peter was their Chief, their Head, and their Prince?   S. Cyprian says, "The Lord said to Peter, *I say unto thee, that thou art Peter,*" &c., upon that one (Peter) He builds His Church, and to him assigns His sheep to be fed.   And although to all the Apostles after His resurrection, he gives an equal power, and says, *As My Father sent Me, even so send I you, &c.;* yet, in order to manifest unity, He has, by His own authority, so placed the origin of that same unity, as that it begins from one.   Certainly, the other Apostles also were what Peter was, endowed with an equal fellowship both of honour and power, but the commencement proceeds from unity. . . . . He who strives against and resists the Church, he who abandons the Chair of Peter, upon whom the Church was founded, does he feel con-

fident that he is in the Church?"* (*De Unitate, p.* 195.) Again, "God is one, and Christ one, and the Chair one, founded by the Lord's Word, upon a Rock." (*Ep.* xl. *ad Pleb.*) " Peter also, to whom the Lord commends His sheep to be fed and guarded, on whom He laid and founded the Church." (*De Habitu Virg. p.* 176.) In the face of these testimonies, how can it be asserted with any truth that in S. Cyprian's opinion S. Peter did not hold a position superior in jurisdiction to the other Apostles?

Dr. Barrow further says that "he (S. Cyprian) doth, indeed plainly enough in the forecited words, signify that in his judgment St. Peter had done *insolently and arrogantly* if he assumed any *obedience* from St. Paul." (*Sup. p.* 78.) It is really sickening to witness Dr. Barrow's mode of perverting and misquoting the Fathers. This is what S. Cyprian really says, " For not even did Peter, whom the Lord had chosen the First, and upon whom He built His Church, when Paul afterwards disputed with him respecting circumcision, claim anything to himself insolently, or assume anything arrogantly,† so as to say, that he held the Primacy (*primatum,* chief government), and that obedience ought rather to be paid to him by those who were novices, and had come after him . . . giving, to wit, to us an example of unanimity and patience, &c." (*Ep.* lxxi. *ad Quintum, p.* 127.) Can there be a doubt of S. Cyprian's belief that S. Peter held the Primacy, though on this occasion he yielded to S. Paul's remonstrance, because he knew that he was right? So far from this extract witnessing against S. Peter's position, it confirms it ; for if the Primacy had been an innovation of a later age, how could S. Cyprian have even alluded to an office which, according to Dr. Barrow, did not at that time exist?

The Doctor appeals also to S. Augustine, and asserts that he " also doth in several places of his writings make the like application of this passage" (*Ib.*) ; and yet this great Father witnesses that S. Peter had " the Primacy (*primatum*) of the Apostleship," that he figured and personated the Church, "because he held the Princedom (*principatum*) of the Apostolate." (*T.* iii. *n.* 5, *col.* 599, and v. *col.* 291.) This is sufficient to show how utterly unscrupulous Dr. Barrow is in his manipulation of the Fathers for the objects he has in view.

S. Paul's reproof of S. Peter does not in any way touch the question of his Supremacy ; and Dr. Barrow's argument on this subject is pointless.

I have now I think answered all the principal arguments advanced by Dr. Barrow against S. Peter's Supremacy, so far as the practice of the Apostles is concerned, and what do they amount to? Absolutely to nothing ; and I think I have shown in most of the several cases, as, the appointment of S. Matthias to the apostleship, and the judgment of the Council of Jerusalem, that S. Peter really held and exercised an authority which none of the other Apostles aspired to ; and as regards

---

* See remarks on this passage in Comment, *supra, p.* 24.

† See Comment, *supra, p.* 24.

other matters, such as the "visit" to S. Peter, and the reproof of the Apostle by S. Paul, really nothing can be proved against the lawfulness of the office he occupied.

9. But there are other points in apostolic practice which the Doctor has altogether omitted to notice, which I will now touch upon.

(1.) The position occupied by S. Peter on the day of Pentecost ought not to have been passed over. When the Jews ridiculed the Apostles, mocking them, saying, "These men are full of new wine," it was S. Peter, who, "standing up with the eleven," after rebuking them, delivered that remarkable sermon, which resulted in the conversion of many to the faith of Christ. It was to S. Peter principally that these converts looked for assistance, for they "said unto Peter, and the rest of the Apostles, Men and brethren, what shall we do?" (Acts, ii. 37.) Now on the hypothesis that there was no Chief of the Apostles, that no one Apostle had been set over the rest, by what authority did S. Peter venture in the name and in behalf of his brethren, to address the people, rebuking them, and expounding authoritatively the ancient prophecies? Why did not S. James, the Bishop of Jerusalem, assume this position; in the absence of a Supreme Head, he would have been the proper person to have been the mouthpiece of the Apostles. The fact then of S. Peter assuming this office at the moment of the out-pouring of the Holy Ghost, and in the presence of the brethren, is conclusive evidence of the Primacy of S. Peter's power,—a primacy derived from the commission he had received, viz., to hold and use the keys, and to feed the sheep and lambs of the Church.

(2.) The opening of the Kingdom of heaven to the Gentiles, by S. Peter alone, without the previous concurrence of his brother Apostles, and thereby changing the whole character of the Church, from an exclusive communion to a universal body, was, in the extremest sense, an act of supreme authority. No doubt he was commanded by God to do as he did, but then why did God choose him to make known His will respecting the heathen? And why did He inspire him to admit without the knowledge and consent of his brethren, Cornelius, and the Gentiles? The answer is obvious, because he held the keys, and he was commanded to use them in their favour.

In the apostolical history, then, there may be, to use the Doctor's language, discerned several important "footsteps," which show conclusively S. Peter's Supremacy. First, the direction that a new Apostle should be ordained in the place of Judas Iscariot; Secondly, the address of S. Peter to the mocking Jews as the mouthpiece of the Church, and that too in the presence of S. James, the Bishop of Jerusalem; Thirdly, the opening of the Kingdom of heaven to the Gentiles by S. Peter alone, independently of his brethren; Fourthly, the judgment of S. Peter, on the circumcision case, at the Council of Jerusalem, followed by S. James, whose decree was founded on the judgment of S. Peter; and Lastly, the visit of S. Paul to S. Peter, after his conversion, in recognition, according to S. Chrysostom, of his Headship. The instances, advanced by Dr. Barrow to disprove S. Peter's Supremacy, are *nihil ad rem*. The fact of the institution of the order of Deacons by the

Twelve proves nothing against S. Peter, for he was a consenting party; and the rebuke of S. Peter by S. Paul is no greater argument against his right to rule, than a similar remonstrance administered by the Prime Minister, or any peer of England to the Queen, would prove that she was not Sovereign. Dr. Barrow has failed to assail in any one point of practice S. Peter's undoubted Supremacy.

V.

COUNTER ALLEGATIONS.

I will now consider Dr. Barrow's assertion, that some of the other Apostles might be proved to have been supreme Heads of the Church. It is alleged that "upon the same grounds, on which a Supremacy of power is claimed for S. Peter, other apostles might also challenge a superiority therein over their brethren." (*Sup. p.* 81.) Dr. Barrow instances S. James and S. John, "who upon the same probabilities had (after S. Peter) a preference to the other apostles." (*Ib. p.* 82.) Now one or two questions occur to me. Did our Lord ever say to S. James or to S. John, "I will give thee the keys?" or did he ever say, "Strengthen or confirm thy brethren?" or, "Feed my sheep and lambs?" Did either S. James or S. John preside at the first assembly at Jerusalem, on the occasion of the election of S. Matthias? Did they, or either of them, ever address the people in the name and in behalf of the eleven? Had they, or either of them, any share in the admission of the Gentiles into the Church? When the Council of Jerusalem met, did they, or either of them, determine the controversy, except as in union and in agreement with S. Peter, who had previously determined the point in question? If Dr. Barrow could show a single instance of these, or any other of the Apostles, taking the lead, and speaking in their behalf, then something might be said in their favour. Not even did S. Paul ever speak in the name of his brethren. Dr. Barrow alludes to the surnaming of these Apostles as Boanerges, "signifying the efficacy of their endeavour in their Master's service." Nobody disputes the privileges and powers of these Apostles as Sons of Thunder; but why, then, dispute the meaning of Peter, the Rock,—Peter, the Foundation,—Peter, the Representative of the Church? Why dispute the "efficacy of his endeavour in his Master's service," to use the keys in their fulness of jurisdiction and power, and as a Rock to support the brethren, and to protect and sustain the sheep of the Church? If Boanerges is to be considered, much more *Petrus.* True, S. John was "*the disciple whom Jesus loved,*" but is there any evidence whatever that our Lord ever gave him a commission distinct from the other Apostles? In the first chapter of the Acts, we find the Apostles S. Peter and S. John associated, but the latter always following the lead of S. Peter. And besides, though he was the one "Jesus loved," it does not follow that he was for that reason the fittest, in the mind of his Master, for the Headship of the Church. S. James was no doubt our Lord's kinsman after the flesh, but that does not constitute any claim to occupy the Chief Place. It formed no part of the Lord's practice to benefit His earthly relatives and friends, merely because they were connected with Him by ties of consanguinity or personal affection. He selected twelve men, whom He knew were adapted for the work He had designed for them to perform. Of that number, after a severe trial of faith and love, he selected one for the Chief Place, and he who first believed, who first confessed Him, and who declared his love, even beyond the others, obtained the principal throne in the Kingdom of Grace.

VI.

ADMISSIONS.

But the learned Doctor admits the whole question when he informs his readers that the Fathers style S. Peter "ἔξαρχον (the prince); κορυφαῖον (the ringleader); κεφαλὴν (the head); πρόεδρον (the president); ἀρχηγὸν (the captain); προήγορον (the prolocutor); πρωτοστάτην (the foreman); πρόστατην (the warden); ἔκκριτον τῶν ἀπόστολων (the choice or egregious Apostle) ; *majorem* (the greater, or grandee among them) ; *primum* (the first, or prime Apostle)." (*Sup. p.* 104.)

Dr. Barrow, however, endeavours to get rid of the force of these titles, by asserting that they are "hyperbolical flash or flourish," which occurs in the writings of the Fathers, "it being well known that they in their encomiastic speeches, as orators are wont, following the bent and gaiety of fancy, will sometimes overlash." (*Ib.*)

No doubt poetical authors are given to flights of imagination; but then if they are men of sense they start from some substantial foundation. When any poet addresses a high-flown panegyric to a Sovereign, especially if she be a lady, bestowing upon her all manner of exalted titles, and expatiating extravagantly on her virtues and her beauty, her glory as a Queen, the magnificence and splendour of her court; are we to conclude that all this is nothing more than "hyperbolical flash or flourish," that is, that there is no truth whatever underlying all this extravagance? And are we bound, consequently, to believe that after all she is in no sense a Sovereign, and that her splendid court, so graphically described, is only an imaginary assembly of aërial worthies from some fairy land? If so, then the sweet music of the muse is nothing better than frivolous nonsense. No believer in that article of the Creed, "I believe in one holy, Catholic, and Apostolic Church," can with any feelings of loyalty to Christ and His saints, believe that the Fathers of old were no better than crack-brained enthusiasts, who exercised their imaginative faculties without the governing principle of a sober and discriminating reason. And if Dr. Barrow is right, that all these varied modes of expressing the nature of that office S. Peter filled be nothing better than "hyperbolical flash or flourish," then, indeed, the literature of the Church is little better than rubbish. I assert, if the Fathers declare that S. Peter was the " Prince," " the Head," or the " Captain," &c., then we are bound to believe they meant what they said, and I therefore claim Dr. Barrow as a witness-in-chief against himself to this fact which he acknowledges, though he endeavours, on the principle, I suppose, that the end justifies the means, to elude the force of the evidence, by the baseless assumption that they were merely giving rein to their " gaiety and fancy," and did consequently " overlash." It is really pitiable to see how a man of talent, like this Doctor, can so overreach himself in his vain and futile efforts to demolish that Rock which Christ planted in the midst of the earth, and which He defied all hell to destroy.

There is one point more to be touched upon ; Dr. Barrow says, " We may observe that such turgid eulogies of St. Peter are not found in the more ancient Fathers ; for Clemens Romanus, Irenæus, Clemens Alexandrinus, Tertullian, Origen, Cyprian, Firmilian,—when they mention St. Peter, do speak more temperately and simply, according to the current notions and traditions of the Church in those times : using, indeed, fair terms of respect, but not such high strains of courtship about him." (*Sup. p.* 105). Possibly, but what then ? Did Dr. Barrow mean to say that none of the early Fathers believed in S. Peter's high position as " the Head," " the Prince," and " the Captain ?" It has been shown above that they did ; and for further proof, the reader is referred to pp. 17–25 of this work, where he will find ample testimony as to this point.

VII.

CONCLUSION.

In conclusion, after carefully examining Dr. Barrow's argument against the Supremacy of S. Peter, I am confirmed in my opinion that that doctrine so clearly enunciated by the Fathers, is unassailable. The counter evidence presented by the Doctor in his treatise will not bear investigation. Dr. Barrow lays great stress on S. Paul's exalted position in the Church, quoting the words of S. Gregory I., that he " was made Head of the nations, because he obtained the Principate of the whole Church." (*Sup. p.* 109.) But all the Apostles were Principates of the whole Church, for their jurisdiction was universal, though subject to one, of whom it was said that he held " the Princedom of the Apostolate ;" that is, as S. Avitus says, " the Prince of the Princes," and for this purpose, as S. Jerome witnesses, " that the occasion of schism might be removed." But S. Gregory does not forget S. Peter, for he says, in allusion to S. Paul's rebuke, " And yet in the matter of circumcision (he) boldly rebuked the notion of one (Peter) by great inequality his Superior." (*Mor. Pt.* ii. *l.* x. *n.* 9.) Many of the passages from the Fathers are disgracefully garbled, and some, by supplying the context or the clause immediately following the quotations (which the learned Doctor conveniently omits), essentially modify, if they do not always absolutely contradict, the position he labours to establish. And

as regards the vast amount of evidence in favour of the Supremacy of
S. Peter, he is discreetly silent, contenting himself with an allusion to
the assignment of certain "titles" expressive of S. Peter's office, which
he describes as "hyperbolical flash or flourish." His attempt to show
that other Apostles were sometimes similarly titled is *nihil ad rem*, for
to render such evidence effective, he should have shown (which he has
not attempted to do), that each of them exercised those functions of
government and administration, which were peculiar to the office, the
Fathers assert, S. Peter filled. In his eagerness to prove the absolute
equality of the eleven to S. Peter, Dr. Barrow has unaccountably
overlooked the other side of the case, viz., that S. Peter was in His
position, as the appointed Rock and Foundation of the Church, as
the Origin and Centre of unity, as the Prince of the Apostles, and the
Chief Pastor of the universal Church, co-equal and co-ordinate with the
college of the Apostles ; and further, that while S. Peter could act independently of his brethren, there is no evidence to show that the
Apostles, on the other hand, could have performed their functions, except
as in union with him. Indeed, this is implied by the very fact that he
was esteemed by the Fathers as the Head and Prince. Such seems to
be the clear evidence of Scripture and of primitive antiquity.

THE PAPAL SUPREMACY.

SECOND INQUIRY.

PAPAL SUPREMACY.

INTRODUCTORY OBSERVATIONS.

UNDER " the First Inquiry" two positions, have, it is maintained,
been established : (1) That Christ our Lord did deliver to S. Peter
a commission distinct in kind from that of the other Apostles, which
empowered him to rule and govern the Kingdom and Church He had
founded, as its Supreme Head and Chief Pastor ; and (2) That S. Peter
after the ascension, with the tacit approval of his brethren, exercised
this office of Supreme Head and Chief Pastor. If the language of
Holy Scripture is to be understood in a natural sense, *i.e.*, according
to its plain grammatical construction, and if the unanimous testimony
of the early Fathers is to be relied upon, then this position of the
Prince of the Apostles is absolutely unassailable. Dr. Barrow, perceiving the vital point of the controversy, has laboured with all his
might, with what success has been seen, to overthrow the arguments
advanced in behalf of S. Peter's claim ; for he well knew that if S. Peter
really possessed an independent commission to rule and govern the
Apostolic College and the Catholic Church, the main point in the
controversy has been irrefragably established, viz., that Christ did institute a supreme executive authority, which He delivered *exclusively*
to S. Peter. But it was shown how baseless were the learned Doctor's
arguments, and it was further proved that they were supported by a
system of misquotations from Scripture and the Fathers, most of
which when the immediate context, or succeeding clause or sentence
was supplied, meant the exact opposite he intended. In point of fact,
he proved conclusively S. Peter's Supreme Apostleship.

Unless, then, Scripture and the Fathers are to be interpreted in
a sense contrary to the ordinary rules of construction, I have a right
to assume, especially after the solid proofs advanced under the

"First Inquiry," that S. Peter was appointed by our Lord to the office of Supreme Head and Pastor of the universal Church, in which capacity he ruled and governed the Church; exercised the power of the keys, *i.e.*, the Supreme Jurisdiction; and performed the function of Chief Pastor over all, the Apostles included.

Starting then from this premiss, I venture to assert, that a succession to S. Peter's Chair, together with all the prerogatives appertaining to it, is a necessity—that is, if it be granted that the Polity which Christ instituted was intended to endure till the close of the Christian dispensation.

I.

MONARCHY, THE GOVERNMENTAL LAW OF GOD IN THE UNIVERSE.

It cannot be supposed that any work undertaken by Almighty God can be defective, or be otherwise than "very good;" nor can it ever cease in its operations, until the time fore-ordained has been fully accomplished. Let us pause and consider this point somewhat in detail. Almighty God, from the moment He began to create the heavens and the earth, conducted His great work according to method, and when He had completed it, established a fixed unalterable law, by which the whole universe would be continually governed and sustained. Let us raise our eyes to the heavens above, and contemplate there the beauty and the grandeur of those celestial orbs, which night after night illuminate the spacious universe of God. See how Law reigns supreme in all its glory and excellence. Reflect how it is by a Law as unchangeable as God Himself, that each planet revolves on its own axis with a rapidity we can scarce measure; that each runs its ceaseless course along its appointed orbit round its central sun; that millions of solar systems, including our own, with their suns, and planets, and satellites, are for ever revolving round some grand Central Luminary, which under'God propels, and regulates, and illuminates the mighty orrery of the vast and stupendous universe. It is indeed a subject worthy of contemplation that Law reigns predominant within the entire circumference of occupied space.

Let us now descend to our own earth. There was a time when this planet was a shapeless and formless mass, when darkness covered the earth, and when it was void. I pass over the causes of that chaotic condition, as beside the purpose of this inquiry. When God resolved upon its reconstruction, what did He do? He first restored this world, and then established once and for all His Law, for the government, perpetuation, and conservation of all that He had made. The great fundamental Law which He instituted was, that each department should contain the germ or "the yielding seed after its kind," by which provision the animal, the vegetable, and mineral kingdoms, are for ever maintained in all their integrity. Nothing illustrates this great principle of Law more than the contemplation of the smallest insect that lives,—a creature which cannot be discerned by the naked eye of man. Observe how complete is every department of its invisible (to us) organization, how every member performs its function with the same order and precision, as that of the largest of the animal creation. In nature then, from the heavens to this lower earth, from the glorious manifestation of God's power in the immensity of the firmament, down to the minutest particle of living matter, Law reigns supreme, as perfect as on the day it was created by the Almighty Legislator, needing no amendment, unalterable, and eternal in its duration for its specified period or dispensation.

But further, Law reigns not only throughout the universe and in nature, but in God's government of His universal Realm. Little is said in Scripture respecting the mode by which God carries on, as it were, His universal government of heaven and earth, but there are indications by which we may ascertain with sufficient accuracy the fundamental principles of His executive Law. There can be no doubt that the system which He has ordained, is that which is called hierarchical. The angelic hosts, whose employment is to execute the will of God all over the wide world, are divided into several orders and ranks, each of which has its place in the great economy of God's universal government. We know nothing of their employments in the myriads of orbs that float in the heavens; but we may, however, learn much from analogy derived from what has occurred in our own world. Any one who is conversant with the Bible knows that in the affairs of men and nations, angel hosts have had much to do. Even in the strifes of nations, especially when God's peculiar people were especially concerned, they have taken an active part. The angelic guard that protected the Israelites from Pharaoh (*Exod.* xiv.) ; the slaughter of the enemies of Hezekiah by the Angel of the Lord (2 *Kings*, xix. 35) ; and the action of the luminous Being that Daniel saw in an attitude of opposition to Persia, which seems to have "withstood" him, until he was assisted by Michael (*Dan.* x. 13) ; show with clearness, the method God has prescribed for the execution of

His will all over the world; and judging from analogy, in every part of the inhabited heavens, viz., by His angelic army, which daily and hourly wait in adoring posture at the threshold of His great presence-chamber. What a picture does Micaiah paint of this great court of the Lord of All! "I saw the Lord sitting on His throne, and all the host of heaven standing by Him, on His right hand and on His left. And the Lord said, Who shall persuade Ahab, that he may go up and fall at Ramoth-gilead? And one said on this manner, and another said on that manner. And there came forth a spirit, and stood before the Lord, and said, I will persuade him. And the Lord said unto him, Wherewith? And he said, I will go forth, and I will be a lying spirit in the mouth of all his prophets. And he said, Thou shalt persuade him, and prevail also: go forth, and do so." (1 *Kings*, xxii. 19-22.) This graphic account gives one an insight into the court of Heaven, where God is sitting on His throne, and governing all things, as it were, with the aid and assistance of His celestial council. God in council, His creatures being His counsellors, is an idea far transcending our earthly comprehension, and there let us leave it, for explanation is impossible; but this much we see, viz., that the angelic hosts are the counsellors, apparently, of God, and the instruments for executing His divine will.

We arrive now at the important part of the subject under discussion. What is the primordial principle of God's Governmental Law? The true answer, it is submitted, is MONARCHY; or, if I may be permitted to coin a new word, CENTRALISM. The monarchical or central principle is the norm of God's governmental system. He Himself is the Monarch of monarchs. In the heavens above, the sun rules its own system, the planets receiving their light from that great luminary, and all revolving round it as their common centre. In the order of nature, each animate and inanimate system is governed either by its own head, its own root, or its own germ, from which it is developed and sustained for its allotted term of life or existence. In the angelic hosts, we have glimpses given us of this principle of monarchy, " But the prince of the kingdom of Persia withstood me (the great angel whom Daniel saw) one and twenty days : but lo, Michael, one (or rather ' The First,'—see *marginal reference*) of the chief princes, came to help me." (*Dan.* x. 13). S. Jude describes Michael as " the archangel" (*S. Jude*, 9), and S. Paul evidently alluded to the same great " archangel" (1 *Thess.* iv. 16); for he it is who seems to be the agent employed (so to speak) on that great day when those " that sleep in the dust of the earth shall awake, some to everlasting life, and some to shame and everlasting contempt." (*Dan.* xii. 1, 2.) Again, " And there was war in heaven ; Michael and his Angels fought against the dragon, and the dragon fought and his angels." (*Rev.* xii. 7.) What a beautiful picture does this give us of the hierarchical system, which God has established in the heavens for the purpose of working out His will in every part of the wide universe : and of what does that system consist? A chief with his subject angels. "Michael and his angels," *i.e.*, the Angelic Hosts under their leader and head. Here we see the monarchical system as a fixed Law in the divine constitution of the universal Realm of Almighty God. But S. Michael was not only the chief of an order in the angelic hierarchy, he was and is the Chief of the Princes, "the First of the Chief Princes," *i.e.*, of those who, like Gabriel, "stand in the presence of God," and who go forth, whenever sent, to execute the commands of the Lord.

The following curious passage in the "Recognitions of Clement"* fully supports this idea of "Monarchy" and "Centralism" as the Governmental Law of God : "Then Peter began to instruct me in this manner : ' When God had made the world, as Lord of the universe, He appointed Chiefs over the several creatures, over the trees even, and the mountains, and the fountains, and the rivers, and all things which He had made, as we have told you; for it were too long to mention them one by one. He sets, therefore, an angel as chief over the angels, a spirit over the spirits, a star over the stars, a demon over the demons, a bird over the birds, a beast over the beasts, a serpent over the serpents, a fish over the fishes, a Man over men, who is Christ Jesus. But He is called *Christ* by a certain excellent rite of religion : for as there are certain names common to kings, as Arsaces among the Persians, Cæsar among the Romans, Pharaoh among the Egyptians, so among the Jews a king is called *Christ.'*" (*Recog. l.* 1, *c.* xlv.)

We have now arrived at two conclusions, (1) That Almighty God governs by means of a fixed Law, which was perfect from the first, needing no amendment, and which remains in full force and operation as long as the term fore-ordained shall last ; and (2) that the fundamental principle of that Law is what I call, for want of a better word, MONARCHY—that is, that under God all things proceed respectively from one, are propagated from one, governed by one, and maintained in unity, integrity, and vigour by one. In a word, the monarchical or the central principle is the basis on which the universal Governmental Law of God, both in the natural and the celestial systems, is founded and sustained.

* This work, though attributed to S. Clement, was not written till the third century, and it is doubtful who was the real author of it. It is described by some as a sort of religious romance. It is quoted in the text, because it witnesses to the fact, that the idea of monarchy or centralism in animate and inanimate creation, was an accepted principle in that early age.

H

II.

MONARCHY, THE GOVERNMENTAL LAW OF GOD IN HIS KINGDOM ON EARTH.

Now if the sentiments expressed above are sound, we shall have a right to assume that this universal law would be applied by Almighty God to His political and ecclesiastical government upon earth, in which we now are more especially interested. I say we have a right to assume this, because the mind of God is, like Himself, universal; it is one, and unchangeable. " He is the same yesterday, to-day, and for ever." Duality of thought and principle, on any one point, is impossible with God, for on each He once for all conceives, once for all wills, and once for all executes, and it being necessarily " very good," what He wills is so perfect, that it is incapable of improvement. If then the monarchical or central principle is the fundamental Law of God in His administration of the universe, and of the many-ordered Hierarchy that stand right and left of the great white throne, it follows as an evident consequence that its application must be universal and eternal—that is, that whatsoever God creates, whether in unoccupied space beyond the sidereal system, or on this lower earth, wherein we dwell, the same principle will prevail, for being a Law once enacted by God, it can be neither repealed nor modified.

Let us now proceed to inquire whether this monarchical or central principle has been established in the hierarchical system God has introduced into this world?

1. After the creation, God addressed these words to Adam, " Be fruitful, and multiply, and replenish the earth, and subdue it : and have dominion over the fish of the sea, and over the fowl of the air, and over every living thing that moveth upon the earth." (*Gen.* i. 28.) And then in order to show how God had made Adam lord of the whole earth, He caused all the animals He had created to be brought before him to be named, " and whatsoever Adam called every living creature, that was the name thereof." (*Ib.* ii. 19.) His dominion included all his children that should be born of him, and his children's children, for the commission he received was to " replenish the earth," with his seed, and to " subdue it," that is, to reduce all to subjection to himself. The monarchical principle was thus introduced into the world by God Himself in the person of Adam. By his rebellion he forfeited his high trust, but we shall see

how God provided a remedy, and in so doing carefully maintained in all its integrity the same unalterable Law.

2. By the Fall, the world was reduced to a moral chaos, every one did right in his own eyes, and the imaginations of men were evil continually, so much so that God determined to destroy the world He had made. Subsequently He commenced the great work of moral re-creation, by the call of Abraham, who was destined to be the foundation of that great Polity which was at the proper time to be inaugurated, from whom was to proceed a people,—a peculiar people —and a nation of kings and priests ; from whom too was to arise the Messiah,—the Second Adam,—the Redeemer and restorer of fallen humanity. About the fifth century after the call of Abraham, this great Polity was introduced into the world, in the midst of thunder, lightnings, and earthquakes, " the voice of the trumpet exceeding loud." Upon this great occasion, God delivered to His people the Law, full, complete, and as perfect for its purpose, as that Law which He had ordained for the government and maintenance of the heavens, and the earth, and of all things therein. That this was so, is manifest, from the circumstance that the authorities of the kingdom of Israel had no power to alter "one jot or one tittle of the Law." The Law —political, ecclesiastical, and ceremonial —continued in full vigour and operation until the consummation of the Mosaic dispensation.

Now what was the essential principle of the Law of Moses so far as regards the executive and governmental department of this ecclesiastico-civil state? As with the Hierarchies of heaven, so it was on earth in the Kingdom God had established ; it consisted of the monarchical or central system, *i. e.* government and jurisdiction, flowing from and centering in one person. Any one who reads the Pentateuch cannot fail to perceive that Moses was the Vice-gerent of Almighty God, and as such he was the Governor, the Ruler, the Prince, and the supreme Judge over all the people. This supremacy was enforced by Almighty God on every occasion when the people rebelled against his authority. Witness the case of Korah, Dathan, and Abiram, and their miserable followers. But the exalted position of Moses was still more manifested when the magnitude of his work led him to seek from God assistants in his government. How did God respond to this? "And the Lord said unto Moses, Gather unto me seventy men of the elders of Israel, whom thou knowest to be the elders of the people, and officers over them ; and bring them unto the tabernacle of the congregation, that they may stand there with thee. And I will come down and talk with thee there ; and I will take of the spirit which is upon thee, and will put it upon them ; and they shall bear the burden of the people with thee, that thou bear it not thyself alone." (*Numb.* xi. 16, 17.) I know not any proof more incontestable than this, that God had appointed Moses as His Vicar in the government of Israel; and when the work became so great that he could no longer administer it without assistance, God appointed seventy of the elders of the people to be his associates in the government; and in order to manifest unity, and to maintain the supremacy of His Vicar, He, instead of pouring upon them His Spirit *immediately* from Himself, He took of the spirit of Moses, and put it upon them, "and when the spirit rested upon them they prophesied." We see then how the universal principle of monarchy was introduced by God into the Kingdom He had constituted. It was the same in the Priesthood, which consisted of a High Priest, who had authority over the priests of the Tabernacle ; but the jurisdiction of the whole Kingdom was, under the Law, reserved to the Head of the State.

It will perhaps be asserted, that this monarchical system died with Moses, but fortunately Holy Scripture itself refutes this idea. To Moses succeeded Joshua, who " was full of the spirit of wisdom ; for Moses had laid his hands upon him : and the children of Israel hearkened unto him, and did as the Lord commanded Moses." (*Deut.* xxxiv. 9.) From the death of Joshua to Saul there was an interim of nearly 400 years, during which we find the monarchical principle in full force. About fifteen Judges* ruled and judged Israel, after intervals of interregnum and anarchy, in the course of those four centuries. To them the people looked for judgment and protection, and God Himself recognised their authority in a variety of ways.

It had been contemplated from the very beginning, and indeed it was part of the original scheme of Almighty God, to establish a dynastic monarchy in the kingdom of Israel ; and this was a further proof of the universality and perpetuity of that principle of government which had from all eternity been maintained by the Most High. " When thou art come unto the land which the Lord thy God giveth thee, and shalt possess it, and shalt dwell therein, and shalt say, I will set a king over me, like as all the nations that are about me ;

---

* It is held by some that the term "Judges," used in the English Bible, does not accurately represent the original Hebrew word *shophetim*, which is said to signify " Rulers of the people." See Kitto's *Cyclopædia of Biblical Literature*, Article *Judges*. Calmet observes, "The authority of Judges was not inferior to that of Kings : it extended to peace and war : they decided causes with absolute authority ; but had no power to make new laws, or to impose new burdens on the people." See Calmet's *Dict. of Bible*, Article *Judges*.

thou shalt in any wise set him king over thee, whom the Lord thy God shall choose : one from among thy brethren shalt thou set king over thee." (*Deut.* xvii. 14.) We know how some three centuries hence Saul was nominated by God as king, and on his forfeiture, David and his heirs for ever.

The monarchical system thus prevailed from the very commencement of the divine Polity of Israel, and continued till its dissolution ; and we know, too, that the office of the High Priest never failed till the close of the dispensation.

3. We have come now to the commencement of that period of the world's history when our Lord made His appearance on earth as the God-Man, who was the anti-type of Moses, the lineal heir of David, the legitimate King of Israel, and the successor of Aaron, inasmuch as He was the Lord of Aaron, and united in Himself the office of Priest and Victim. In a word, the Kingly and Priestly dignity merged into Him as the Son of God and the Son of Man.

The mission of our blessed Lord was threefold : (1) to reconstruct fallen humanity ; (2) to create a new Polity, for the union into one nation of all His people ; and (3) to make an atonement for the sins of the whole world, thereby reconciling fallen man with God.

Assuming that the monarchical or central system is that which was originally constituted by God, and that it has ever been in full operation, both in heaven and on earth, to the exclusion of all other systems, we have a right to suppose that Christ would perpetuate the same principle in the Polity He was about to institute. I say we have a right to suppose so, because the mind of God (and Christ was and is God) is unchangeable, being the same " yesterday, to-day, and for ever." If then the monarchical or central system is that which God originally ordained for the government of all things animate and inanimate ; if this system prevails among the Hierarchies of the court of heaven ; if it is true that the starry hosts obey their common centres, and if all centres are governed, as has been said, by one grand Central Luminary situated somewhere in the midst of space ; and if it is further true that this monarchical or central system was introduced on this earth, and continued in its integrity up to the period of the First Advent, then by virtue of God's immutability this system must have been introduced into the Polity He constituted before His departure from this planet, and which He intended to continue till the end of the world. It is an impossibility it could be otherwise, for else He would be changeable in mind, and diverse in His mode of action. I repeat, then, we have a right to suppose from the precedents of all former ages, that in the constitution of His new Kingdom He would establish therein the monarchical or central principle of government.

The Gospel informs us that He did so. As Moses had been appointed the Vicar of God for founding, establishing, and building up His kingdom, and for governing the chosen people under the former Dispensation, so did Christ constitute S. Peter as His second self (as S. Augustine says) for a like purpose in the new Kingdom He had called into existence; and, further, as God selected the elders of the children of Israel to become associates with Moses in the government of Israel, so did Christ select in His lifetime eleven Apostles to share with S. Peter in the great work of ruling the new Israel. Under the " First Inquiry," it was abundantly proved from Scripture, and by the testimony of .the Fathers, that S. Peter was appointed to be the Rock and Foundation of the Church, to be the Head and Governor of the Body, and the Supreme Pastor of the universal Flock. It is impossible then for any one to deny, with any truth, that the monarchical or central system was established by Christ in His Kingdom and Church, by which it was to be governed and sustained for ever. Nothing can be more clear than the Gospel account of S. Peter's monarchical position, for He, as has been proved, received a commission from God, distinct and separate from the other Apostles, whereas they received nothing without him. Indeed it is remarkable that in the several commissions that were given to the Apostles in common, concerning government and jurisdiction, either a saving clause in S. Peter's favour is to be found, or some inference given showing the distinction between him and his Apostolic brethren. For example, when Christ, addressing the twelve, said, " Whatsoever ye shall bind on earth shall be bound in heaven : and whatsoever ye shall loose on earth shall be loosed in heaven," S. Peter immediately asks his Lord for instructions, saying, " Lord, how oft shall my brother sin against me, and I forgive him? till seven times?" Then Christ answered, " I say not unto thee, Until seven times, but Until seventy times seven." (S. Matt. xviii. 18, 21, 22.) It is impossible to compare the promise that our Lord made to all the Apostles generally, with what passed between Christ and S. Peter, without perceiving that the peculiar position of the Chief Apostle was not overlooked.*
And the same thing is to be observed when after the Resurrection Christ actually conferred the power of remitting and retaining sins upon all the Apostles, He reserved for S. Peter the Supreme Pastorate of the whole Church. (S. John, xxi. 15-17.) Again, when He constituted His kingdom, and appointed all the Apostles as

* See Origen's remarks on this passage under the First Inquiry, p. 20,

His Viceroys, He at the same time pointed out S. Peter as the one to whom they were to look for strength and support in all that concerned the Faith. (*S. Luke*, xxii. 32.)

The great principle, then, of monarchy was established by Jesus Christ in His new Kingdom; and the one chosen to rule, confirm, and shepherdise the flock, was S. Peter, and S. Peter alone, to the exclusion of all the Apostles, save as in union with him.

4. The next point to be discussed is, Did Christ intend this monarchy to continue after S. Peter's death?

Now we have already seen that the monarchical or central principle is universal and everlasting. We have seen how this principle prevails in the heavens and on the earth, in the Angelic Hosts that surround the court of the Most High ; we have perceived how God thus recognised this principle when He created Adam, and gave him dominion over all things, how He introduced it into the Polity of the elder dispensation, and also into that Kingdom which Jesus Christ created before His departure to the realms above. If all this is true (and it cannot be disputed), how could the monarchical or central principle cease on the death of S. Peter ? If the Lord really did constitute S. Peter as the Head and the Supreme Pastor of the Church, the Source of jurisdiction (for he had the keys), and the Centre of unity, how could those offices become extinct on the decease of the Chief Apostle ? It is impossible, and for this reason, because, as has been said, the mind of God is unchangeable, and consequently having once for all willed that all things should be sustained by Unities, it follows that His Kingdom which He had constituted should for ever be governed and maintained by ONE who should be His Representative and Vicar. In a word, what S. Michael was to the angelic Hierarchies, what Moses, Joshua, the Judges, and the Kings were to Israel, that S. Peter and his successors were to be to the universal Kingdom of grace.

The Second Inquiry, to which this is an introduction, will furnish the proofs for the Supremacy of the Successors of S. Peter to his Chair in the Holy Roman Church. Holy Scripture will be consulted, so far as it can help our inquiry, and afterwards the Tradition of the Universal Church of the first five centuries. This evidence it is proposed to divide into three sections, shewing first the testimony of individual Fathers; secondly, the witness of plenary councils, which for the most part assume the fact of the Supremacy of the Roman Pontiffs; and thirdly, the acts and proceedings of Popes, by which it will be seen that from the very commencement of the Christian Church they have exercised the office of Chief Pastor in every part of the Christian world.

I would, however, maintain that evidence on this subject is in point of fact unnecessary; it would not really signify if every folio of Fathers and Councils had been lost, as many have perished in the days of persecution. What we have to do is to ascertain the fundamental Law of God in His governmental and executive department. If monarchy or centralism should be found to be a universal principle in all creation, in the realms above, in the various worlds which roll their course in boundless space, in the three kingdoms of our earth, animate and inanimate; and further, if God introduced this identically same principle in the Mosaic Polity, then by virtue of His consistency and immutability He could not have constituted the Catholic Church otherwise than as a monarchy, and having so done, as has been proved, it follows as a certain consequence ,that the monarchical principle must continue in full vigour and integrity until the Sovereign Lord of all shall return to resume in His own Person the monarchy He had delegated to S. Peter, and to the Roman Pontiffs, the successors to his Cathedra and prerogatives.

SECOND INQUIRY.

II. WHETHER THE BISHOPS OF ROME ARE THE SUCCESSORS OF S. PETER IN HIS OFFICE AS HEAD OF THE BROTHERHOOD, AND AS THE CHIEF PASTOR OF THE CATHOLIC CHURCH; AND, FURTHER, WHETHER THEY, THE SAID BISHOPS OF ROME, HAVE BEEN RECOGNISED AS SUCH FROM PRIMITIVE TIMES.

PART I. HOLY SCRIPTURE.

" . . . . And the Stone that smote the image became a great mountain, and filled the whole earth. . . . . And in the days of these kings shall the God of heaven set up a kingdom, which shall never be destroyed : and the kingdom shall not be left to other people, but it shall break in pieces and consume all these kingdoms, and it shall stand for ever." (*Dan.* ii. 35, 44.)

" And I say unto thee, That thou art Peter (a Rock), and upon this Rock I will build My Church ; and the gates of hell shall not prevail against it." (*S. Matt.* xvi. 18.)

" And I will pray the Father, and He will give you another Comforter (or Paraclete), that He may abide with you for ever (εἰς τὸν αἰῶνα) ; even the Spirit of Truth." (*S. John*, xiv. 16, 17.)

" All power is given unto Me in heaven and on earth. Go ye, therefore, and teach all nations. . . . . . And, lo, I am with you alway, even unto the end of the world (or, all the days till the close of the age or dispensation, πάσας τὰς ἡμέρας ἕως τῆς συντελείας τοῦ αἰῶνος). Amen." (*S. Matt.* xxviii. 18, 20.)

" The Church that is at Babylon elected together with you, saluteth you." (1 *S. Peter*, v. 13.)

OBSERVATIONS.

It is impossible to read these passages without perceiving that the Kingdom which our Lord had created, together with the governing Apostolic College, was intended to be an institution of perpetual duration.

1. The Prophecy is very distinct in this respect in its utterance ; the Kingdom which grew out of the Stone (*i. e.* Christ, the True Stone, and Peter, the Secondary Stone) and became a great universal spiritual empire, is declared to be impregnable and everlasting, for it is said it " shall not be destroyed ;" it " shall not," like other nations, be subdued

and "left to other people;" but, on the contrary, it "shall break in pieces, and consume all these kingdoms (*i. e.* the kingdoms included in the prophecy), and it shall stand for ever." No language can possibly be stronger or more explicit, "It shall never be destroyed;" "it shall stand for ever." The only point is when does this prophecy *begin* to be fulfilled —at the first coming of Christ, or subsequently, after His second advent? The answer to this question may be perceived in the Prophecy itself, as interpreted by the light of history. According to the Prophecy, up to the moment of the descent of the Stone, the Roman Empire, together with the incorporated kingdoms of Babylon, Medo-Persia, and Macedonia, was standing erect in its integrity, and in all its grandeur, power, and pride. After the descent of the Stone, it gradually disappears, and in the place of it there is established a great Universal Empire, expressly called "the Kingdom of God"—a Kingdom which "shall never be destroyed," and which "shall stand for ever."

Now to determine these points—whether the Prophecy has been in some measure at least fulfilled, we must ask ourselves this question, Is the Roman Empire (the legs of the Image and the fourth Beast) at this moment existing in its full proportion, power, and greatness (for such is the condition at the moment it is struck)? If it is, then the Stone has not yet come, and the Kingdom has not been erected. But, on the other hand, if the Roman Empire has fallen, then it is manifest that the Stone has smitten it; and the prediction concerning this Universal Empire which grows out of this Stone has begun to be fulfilled, is still in the course of fulfilment, and will be finally accomplished in the reign of glory.

Let us now examine a few historical facts. (1.) Our Lord constituted His Kingdom and Church upon S. Peter, whom He called a Stone, and afterwards transformed him, metaphorically, into a Rock. (2.) Upon the eve of His Passion He delivered the Kingdom to S. Peter and the other Apostles, charging the former as soon as he was converted to confirm the brethren, and just before His Ascension, to shepherdise the universal flock. (3.) S. Peter, the Stone and Rock, came to Rome, and there, in conjunction with S. Paul, the great Apostle of the Uncircumcision (*i. e.* the Gentiles), founded and constituted the Holy Roman Church, which they made, as S. Irenæus says, a superior Principality, and in that Church S. Peter established his Cathedra. (4.) After this the decline of the Roman Empire commenced; (5.) The capital was by Constantine translated from Rome to Byzantium, and (6.) subsequently, Rome became the property of the Church, and is at this moment the metropolis and centre of Christendom.

Observe how the prophecy has long ago begun to be fulfilled, for the Stone—Christ—has founded His Kingdom; He sent His Chief Apostle Peter—also the Stone—to smite the Roman Beast, and lo! it has fallen, and its place and Capital become the spoil of the conqueror.

Those who assert that this prophecy of the Stone and the Kingdom of Christ is still future, rely much upon the language of some of the early Fathers. But it is doubtful whether the testimony of the Fathers with respect to unfulfilled prophecy can be relied upon as infallible. Christ gave no commission to His Church to interpret beforehand the language of prophecy, except only certain Apostles and others whom the Holy Ghost specially named, as for example, S. John, who in point of fact expounded, expanded, and continued the predictions of Daniel. Now there are several reasons why we who live in this period of the world cannot depend with certainty upon the opinions of the Fathers respecting unfulfilled prophecy. In the first place, the tradition of the anti-Nicene age is not very clear, for many commentaries then existing were lost, and moreover, it does not appear to have been very free from corruption; certain it is that the later primitive Fathers of the fourth, fifth, and sixth centuries differed from their predecessors of the three first ages; they certainly did not regard the expositions of S. Irenæus, Tertullian, &c. as on all points conclusive and binding upon them. Secondly, for the interpretation of some of the prophecies they had not, of course, the advantage of historical evidence for proving the correctness of their speculations, and consequently it was more than probable that they would err in many particulars. They certainly were in error when they supposed that the Second Advent was close at hand; on this point even the Apostles were mistaken; so that, except on doctrines of faith and morals, the exposition of the Fathers on prophecy, though of course extremely valuable, cannot be accepted as infallibly true. Prophecy is like the "lamp of fire" which Abraham saw passing through the "horror of great darkness" of futurity, emitting to centuries beyond, its mysterious rays, indicating here and there some historic feature, or some scene in the great drama of the world of the future not yet performed. The shadowy forms of future events are more or less distinct, but the details by which alone the prediction and fulfilment can be harmonised are generally wanting. The early Fathers, then, who lived at the time when the prophecy of the "Stone" and the "Mountain" were but *beginning* to be fulfilled, were not altogether qualified to discuss the whole scope of the predictions of Daniel and S. John. They knew that Rome was the fourth Beast, and that upon the final fall of the Roman Empire Antichrist was to arise, to be followed quickly by the Second Advent, the last judgment and the triumph of the Church; but it never could have entered their minds to suppose, without a revelation, that Pagan Rome was destined to fall before the destruction of the empire subject to it; that the Tarpeian Rock was to become the Rock of Peter; that its place was to be given to the Kingdom and Church of Christ, of which Rome was be the metropolis, and the Chief Pastor of the flock its Sovereign Lord. We who live in the nineteenth century, having behind us the long vista of past events, may see many things by the light of historical facts, which, short of a special revelation, they never could even have imagined. If then the Fathers, or some of them, assert that the Stone will not descend till the end of the world upon the Image and the fourth Beast, may they not be partially, or even entirely, mistaken? May it not be open to us, in this age of the world, to affirm, in accordance with fact, that Rome having fallen, the Stone is proved to have come, and that the Kingdom of God has been set up, never to be destroyed. The Stone will doubtless come a second time, to complete the work, for the destruction of the remnants of the Babylo-Roman Empire, which will be represented finally by Antichrist, but that does not affect the fact that it has already annihilated imperial Rome.

And, after all, is not the existence of Rome at this moment as the glorious Capital of the Universal Empire of Christ under the Pope-King, the successor of the Stone—Peter—the sign to us that the prophecy has been at least partially fulfilled, the Stone having come and grown into that great mountain which filleth the whole earth, whose summit is now piercing the heavens?

This great visible and material, yet spiritual, Empire of Christ, the centre of which is Rome, is, according to the terms of the prophecy, one that is everlasting, for "it shall never be destroyed;" it "shall not be left for other people," but it "shall stand for ever," in its unity, its strength, and its glory, for it is founded upon the massive and adamantine Rock.

2. When Christ founded His Church on S. Peter, He said that "the gates of hell shall not prevail against it." It cannot be doubted that He who said these words regarded the Rock, and the Church built upon it, *i. e.* upon S. Peter, as a perpetual institution. Had the Rock and the Church disappeared from the earth on the decease of S. Peter and the Apostles, then the gates of hell would have prevailed, *i. e.* would have prevailed to destroy our Lord's work on earth ; for this Rock was a visible symbol of the power, the strength, the indivisibility, and the everlasting endurance of the Church as a visible organisation ; and further, it was a guarantee, pronounced in terms most absolute, that it would have a never-ending life. The devil could have had no greater triumph than that this Rock and Church should only have had a mere temporary existence on earth.

3. The promise that the Holy Ghost should abide with the Apostles for ever, and that Christ Himself should be present all the days till the consummation, demonstratively proves that the Apostolate was never to die. This promise was made to the Apostles alone ; to no one else did our Lord address Himself. The Apostles are now all dead, the dispensation is not yet closed, for this cannot be until the Second Advent. It was then to the office of the Apostleship that this promise was made. This is a proof which cannot be gainsayed, that the Apostolate as a corporate body, was endowed with an inextinguishable life. Indeed, after the Ascension we learn how this corporate life was to be perpetually sustained, viz. by the succession to the several thrones as they became vacant. When Judas Iscariot fell, his place was filled up by the election of S. Matthias, who was numbered with the eleven Apostles ; and so it has continued to this day, as Apostolic Prelates deceased, others were appointed to their chairs, and thus the Apostolate never ceases to live. As we say, the king never dies, so in the Church the Apostolate enjoys an everlasting life on earth.

4. This brings us now to a very important point of our inquiry. If the Apostolic succession be a verity, then it must be maintained in its full integrity. It has been proved under the "First Inquiry" that Christ did constitute one of the Apostles as the Head of the Brotherhood, and the Chief Pastor of His universal Flock ; it follows as a necessary con-

sequence that if there be an Apostolic succession at all, there must be a succession to the office of the Head and Chief. This is a self-evident verity. Grant the premiss that Christ formed a divine Polity, consisting of an earthly Head and Body, which should " never be destroyed," and which should " stand for ever," then a perpetual succession to the office of the Head, no less than to the Body itself, is proved to be a law of perpetual obligation. It is impossible to avoid this conclusion, if S. Peter was really constituted the Rock of the Church, the Custodian of the keys, the Confirmer of the Brethren, and the Shepherd of the entire Flock. That he was so constituted has been, as just stated, abundantly proved under the " First Inquiry," and no testimony can be more unanimous than that of the holy Fathers on this point from the earliest period of ecclesiastical history.

The Apostolical succession, then, necessarily involves a succession to the chief office, no less than to the several members of the Apostolic College—an office which Christ Himself established for the purpose, as S. Jerome and others say, of removing the occasion of schism.

5. If this be so, how is it that nothing is said about S. Peter's succession in the Holy Scriptures? S. Peter was martyred at Rome in A.D. 67, and the Gospel and Epistle of S. John together with the Apocalypse, are said to have been written some twenty years afterwards, how is it that nothing is to be found in those books of the successors of S. Peter as the Head and Chief of the Church? The simple answer to this is that the scope of the Apostle's writings did not include any account of Church government. The Gospel of the fourth Evangelist was written for the main purpose of providing the Church with an inspired testimony of the Divinity of our Lord, and of supplementing the other Gospels. His three Epistles were intended to promote faith and charity, and to warn all against idolatry, and especially against the Antichrist. The Apocalypse is taken up with those mystical prophecies relating to the chief events affecting the Church in future ages. There was, therefore, no special reason why this Apostle should touch upon the government of the Church. Indeed the Apostles are remarkably silent on this point, even as regards their own inspired authority. S. Paul, it is true, here and there threatens to excommunicate heretical and evil persons, but on questions of ecclesiastical government he is silent. And so also is S. James and S. Jude. All the faithful were fully acquainted as to this point, so there was no necessity to allude to it. The Church was an inspired body, under the government of a living system, of which all were cognizant, so that it was unnecessary to advert to such questions. It is assumed that the New Testament is exhaustive as regards doctrine and discipline, but there is no proof of this to be found anywhere in the Scriptures.* It was written

---

* The writing of the Gospel of S. John implies that the previous Gospels of S. Matthew, S. Mark, and S. Luke, were not as a whole complete. This Gospel by S. John was written about A.D. 90, evidently for the purpose of supplementing the three previous Gospels. At the end of his Gospel he says, "And there are also many other things which Jesus did, the which, if they should be written every one, I suppose that even the world itself could not contain the books that should be

for the Faithful, and almost every book assumes on their part a previous knowledge of truth.   The object of the Apostles in their writings was to build up on a foundation already laid, to exhort the good to persevere, to support such as were weak, and to warn the wicked of evil to come if they did not repent.

6. There is one more point to be considered, viz., whether there is any evidence in Scripture that S. Peter was ever at Rome?   The following is the only passage that throws any light on this question : " The Church which is at Babylon . . . . . saluteth you." (1 Pet. v. 13.)   There is little doubt that Babylon here meant Rome.*   Horne says, " From a

written." (S. John, xxi. 25.)   In the Acts of the Apostles, we are informed that Jesus, after His resurrection, " showed himself alive after His Passion . . . . being seen of them forty days, and speaking of the things pertaining to the Kingdom of God." (Acts, i. 3.)   Doubtless He spoke of the doctrine and the discipline the Apostles were to teach and to enforce, and probably something was said respecting Church government.   But so far as we know, very little, if any, of what was said during these forty days, was committed to writing by the Apostles.   It was stored in the treasury of the Church's tradition, and delivered to the safe keeping of the Apostolic Sees.

Then, again, St. Paul alludes to a " form of sound words," to a "form of doctrine," to something that was "committed to (S. Timothy's) trust," and to certain "traditions and ordinances," which do not appear to have been written by the Apostles in their inspired Books.   It is impossible then to assert that the New Testament is exhaustive, either as regards doctrine or discipline.   This is a Protestant idea, which has no other foundation than the opinions of their leading divines.   For obtaining a true knowledge of truth we must go to the Church, to the *existing* Church, which S. Paul says is "the Pillar and ground of the Truth," and therefore it is an infallible authority on all matters concerning the Church.

* It by no means follows, it is submitted, because the Babylon in S. Peter's Epistle signified Rome, that the Babylon in the Apocalypse is also Rome, and this for the following reasons :—

1. It is evident that Babylon is the name proper of the capital of the ancient Chaldaic empire, and subsequently the mystical designation of the seat of empire in its Roman development, and also hereafter of that great city which will be subject to the Antichrist.

Nebuchadnezzar saw in its full stature, under the form of a human figure, the several empires that would intervene between himself and the coming of Christ, and, again, the fortunes of certain portions of the empire, culminating in the rise, progress, and destruction of its last king.   Daniel also saw the same thing under the type of the four beasts—the lion, the bear, the leopard, and the indescribable monster that denoted the fourth kingdom.   Pagan Rome was mystically the Babylon as long as the fourth empire of the Babylonian Image remained in its full glory and integrity.

2. The following observations will, it is thought, show that Rome of the present and future ages cannot be the Apocalyptic Babylon.   In the first place, the blasphemous power with seven heads and ten horns which S. John saw arise in the distant future, was one distinct from that which was existing in his day, viz. the Roman empire ; it was altogether a new development of the Babylonian mystery.   The key to the whole prophecy would seem to be contained in the following passage, "And there are seven kings ; five are fallen, and one is, and the other is not yet come ; and when he cometh he must continue a short space.   And the

careful examination of the evidence adduced for the literal meaning of the word Babylon, and of the evidence of its figurative or mystical application to Rome, we think that the latter (*i.e.* Rome) was intended, and

beast that was, and is not, even he is the eighth, and is of the seven, and goeth into perdition." (Rev. xvii. 11.) The future Babylon, the Capital of the Antichrist, in S. John's time was "not yet come," therefore Rome, it may be held, cannot be the mystic Babylon of prophecy. This will appear more clear if we consider what may be understood by the seven kings. Many attempts have been made to interpret this passage, but none have been satisfactory, and the reason of this seems to be, because most commentators have assumed that Babylon and Rome are the names of one and the same city. Let us see whether another view may not be worth some consideration ; the seven kings evidently typify those seven powers which are distinguished for their opposition to God and His people. These may be enumerated as follows : Egypt, which persecuted the children of Israel ; Assyria, which made captive the ten tribes, and trod under foot their dominion ; Babylon, which carried off and enslaved the Jews ; the fourth and fifth, Medo-Persia and the Macedonian Empire, which succeeded to Babylon, and more or less continued the oppression, till, under Cyrus, the Jews returned to their native land, and 'rebuilt the Temple ; the sixth, the Roman empire, which destroyed Jerusalem, and dispersed to the four quarters of the world the miserable Jews. The first five had fallen in S. John's time ; the sixth was the power that was "now is ;" the seventh that which was "not yet (then) come." Upon the fall of the seventh the Empire will be divided into ten kingdoms, of which one will be that infidel eighth power, which S. John saw rise out of the sea. Babylon would then appear to be the mystic name of all these powers, for they are all one according to the Apocalypse, "being of the seven, and goeth into perdition ;" Babel was the root, the building of which was the first public act of rebellion against God ; Babylon, under Nebuchadnezzar, was the head of the prophetic image ; Rome was the mistress of Judæa long before the fall of Jerusalem, and was aptly called Babylon ; Constantinople, under the Turkish phase of the Roman empire, continues the persecution of God's people, and is fully entitled to the mystic designation of Babylon. From this it would appear that the Babylon of prophecy signifies that power, which is noted for its rebellion against God, and the persecution of His people. It would seem, then, on these grounds, and also on the fact that in S. John's time, the kingdom of Antichrist had "not (as) yet come," that the infidel power seen by S. John in the long distant future, was distinct from the Rome and the Roman Empire of his period, and consequently it may be concluded that the Apocalyptic Babylon is not the same city as the ancient Capital of the world.

Secondly. And historical evidence seems to confirm the probability of this view. Two remarkable events concerning Rome point to this conclusion. (1) The translation of the seat of government from Old Rome to Byzantium, or Constantinople. By this act alone, it is contended, Rome ceased to be mystic Babylon ; for it ceased to be the head or metropolis of the empire as a whole. Constantinople succeeded to the royalties of Rome (Rome retaining only an honorary precedence) and became the heir to its mystical title of "Babylon." (2) The offering of Rome and its provinces to God by Pepin, and their occupation by the Chief Pastor of the universal fold of Christ as its Sovereign Lord, dissolved for ever all connexion between that ancient capital and the Babylonian empire. It seems then plain that ecclesiastical and modern Rome cannot possibly be mystic Babylon.

3. Again, the prophetic description of the future Babylon is totally at variance

for the following reasons :—1. This opinion is confirmed by the general testimony of antiquity, which . . . . is of no small weight.

Eusebius relates, on the authority of Clement of Alexandria and

with the character and condition of ecclesiastical Rome. The Apocalyptic Babylon is described as a first-rate commercial city, its great men are merchant-princes, who trade with all the world, and all the world is made rich by her merchandise. She trades in "gold, and silver, and precious stones, and (in) pearls, and fine linen, and purple, and silk, and scarlet, and all thyine-wood, and all manner vessels of ivory, and all manner vessels of most precious wood, and (in) brass, and iron, and marble, and cinnamon, and odours, and ointment, and frankincense, and wine, and oil, and fine flour, and wheat, and beasts, and sheep, and horses, and chariots, and slaves, and souls of men." (Rev. xviii. 12, 13.) "Shipmasters," and "sailors," "and as many as trade by sea," crowd her streets, and ships abound in her harbours. Now what resemblance is there between this great Babylon and Rome as it is? Is the holy city at this moment, the emporium of commerce? are its chief men merchant-princes, and its inhabitants, sailors and ship-masters or artizans? and are ships seen navigating the Tiber, or lying at anchor at Civita Vecchia, the ancient Ostia? The two cities differ *in toto* in every particular, there is no resemblance whatever between the Holy City and the future Babylon.

4. Let us now inquire if there are any indications in Scripture where the future mystical Babylon will be situated. Will it be London, popularly called the modern Babylon, Paris, Constantinople, Jerusalem, or Alexandria? The Apocalypse, it is submitted, throws some light on this question. It will be remembered that the ten toes of the Image, and the ten horns of the fourth Beast symbolised ten kings, which shall appear after the final fall of the empire, among which will arise a little horn or kingdom, which will become very great and powerful, and be remarkable for its hatred of God and the saints. This is the predicted Antichrist, and S. John, supplementing the prophecy of Daniel, informs us of the quarter of the world from whence he will appear. He says, "And I stood upon the sand of the sea, and saw a beast rise up out of the sea, having seven heads and ten horns, and upon his heads the name of blasphemy. And the beast which I saw was like unto a leopard, and his feet were as the feet of a bear, and his mouth as the mouth of a lion : and the dragon gave him his power, and his seat, and great authority." (Rev. xiii. 1, 2.) If these symbols are identical with those in the book of Daniel, then there can be little doubt that the kingdom of Antichrist will be composed of that portion of the old Babylo-Roman empire, as was typified by the lion, the bear, and the leopard ; even that dominion as was comprised in the Macedonian empire under Alexander the Great. The last mystic Babylon will then necessarily be situated somewhere in this dominion, and in close proximity to the sea or some considerable river. It will probably be Byzantium, *i.e.* Constantinople, for these three reasons (1), because it is the capital of the existing remnant of the old Babylo-Roman empire, in consequence of the translation of the seat of government thither from old Rome ; (2) because it is the most eligible port in Oriental Europe for commerce on a large scale ; and (3) because it is admirably suited to be the seat of government of a great, overbearing, and dominant power.

5. There is one more point which must be touched upon : it is alleged because the Pontiff is Sovereign of Rome, therefore he is officially the Man of Sin, *i.e.* the Antichrist, and the false prophet. This view is justified because it is supposed by controversialists that Rome is the mystic Babylon of prophecy, and, as

Papias Bishop of Jerusalem, that Mark's gospel was written at the request of Peter's hearers in Rome ; and that "Peter makes mention of Mark in his first Epistle, which was written at Rome itself. And that he (Peter) signifies this, calling that city figuratively Babylon, in these words, *The church which is at Babylon, elected jointly with you, saluteth you. And so does Mark my son."* This passage of Eusebius is transcribed by Jerome, who adds positively that "S. Peter mentions this Mark in his first Epistle, figuratively denoting Rome by the name of Babylon ; *the church which is at Babylon,* &c." Œcumenius, Bede, and other Fathers, also understand Rome by Babylon. . . . 2. From the total silence of ecclesiastical history, it is not probable that Peter ever visited Babylon in Chaldæa ; and Babylon in Egypt was too small and insignificant to be the subject of consideration. 3. Silvanus, or Silas the bearer, was the *faithful brother,* or associate, of S. Paul in most of the churches which he had planted. And though he was not at Rome with the apostle when he wrote his last Epistle to Timothy, he might naturally have come thither soon after ; and have been sent by Paul and Peter jointly, to confirm the Churches in Asia Minor, &c., which he had assisted in planting. But

in the Prophecy of the "seven kings," it "goeth into perdition." Having, as it is submitted, shown that ecclesiastical Rome is not the Babylon of the present or the future, it follows, too, that the Pope-King cannot be either the infidel king or false prophet of the Apocalypse.

But there are other reasons why this is impossible. The peculiarity of Antichrist is, that he denies "the Father and the Son." and that "Jesus Christ is come in the flesh," (1 S. John, ii. 23, and iv. 3,.) Another peculiarity is, that the Antichrist blasphemes "God," "His Name, and His tabernacle, and them that dwell in heaven," *i.e.* the Saints and Angels (Rev. xiii. 6) ; and, further, that the false prophet uses his influence to cause the world to worship the image of Antichrist, the blasphemer of God and the saints, and to cause all who decline to do so "to be killed." Now, whatever opinions Anglicans and Protestants may entertain of the Pope and the doctrines of the Catholic Church, one thing they must admit as certain, that none of the Popes have ever denied the Father and the Son, or that Christ has come in the flesh ; or have ever blasphemed God, His tabernacle, and His Saints ; and certainly none of them have ever, as yet, caused the world to worship the image of Cæsar, or any other potentate. The complaint is all the other way, that they have been too dogmatic in matters of faith, that they have honoured the Saints too much, and that they have been too fond of humbling kings to the dust.

It is a fact, which none can gainsay, that the whole history of the Papacy is one standing witness and protest against all impugners of Catholic doctrine, against the false liberalism of the age, and against the arrogance and tyranny of kings.

Enough has been said to demonstrate that it is utterly impossible that ecclesiastical or modern Rome can be the Apocalyptic Babylon.

N.B.—I wish to modify a passage in page 3 of this work, which has been already printed, "This colossal empire first tottered, declined, and then was *utterly annihilated."* This is true of Rome and the West, but, in the East, it would seem that the Roman empire still lingers under the Turkish rule; when it ultimately falls, it will according to the prophecy, be divided into ten kingdoms or states, one of which will be the Antichrist.

Silvanus, Paul, and Peter, had no connection with (literal) Babylon, which lay beyond their district ; and therefore they were not likely, at any time, to build upon another's foundation. The Gospel was preached in Persia and Parthia (*i.e.* where literal Babylon was situated) by the apostle Thaddeus, or Jude, according to Cosmas. . . . 4. The Jews, to whom this Epistle was written, were fond of mystical appellations, especially in their captivities : Edom was a frequent title for their Heathen oppressors ; and as Babylon was the principal scene of their first captivity, it was highly probable that Rome, the principal scene of their second, and which so strongly resembled the former in her "abominations, her idolatries, and persecutions of the saints," should be denominated by the same title. And this argument is corroborated by the similar usage of the Apocalypse, where the mystical application is unquestionable. (Rev. xiv. 8 ; xvi. 19 ; xviii. 2, &c.) It is highly probable, indeed, that John borrowed it from Peter ; or rather that both derived it, *by inspiration*, from the prophecy of Isaiah (xxi. 9). 5. The second Epistle is generally agreed to have been written *shortly* before Peter's death ; but a journey from (literal) Babylon to Rome (where he unquestionably suffered) must have employed a long time, even by the shortest route that could be taken, and Peter must have passed through Pontus, &c., in his way to Rome, and therefore it must have been unnecessary for him to write. Writing from Rome, indeed, the case was different, as he never expected to see them more. (*Horne's " Introd. to Study of the Holy Script."* vol. iv. *pp.* 435, 436. *Lond.* 1839.) Maitland observes, " At this time Rome is first called Babylon by St. Peter, who thus prepares his readers for the coming transfer of Old Testament prophecies in the Apocalypse. This use of the name is so entirely in conformity with the usual style of Rabbinical disguise, that the Apostle's meaning was never doubted till the fifteenth century." (*Apost. School of Prophecy, p.* 106. *Lond.* 1849.) The arguments of these two Anglican divines in favour of the Babylon mentioned in S. Peter's first Epistle being Rome is exhaustive. In the fifteenth century attempts were made to prove that this Babylon did not mean Rome, in order, if possible, to effect the destruction of the Papacy by cutting it off from its fountain-head, S. Peter, the first Pontiff; but the testimony of the Fathers and ecclesiastical history, as will be shown in the proper place, is so clear and unmistakable that there is no room to doubt the fact that S. Peter really was at Rome, and that he did, in conjunction with S. Paul, found and constitute the Roman Church.

Holy Scripture then informs us of the following important facts (1), that the Kingdom and Church which Christ established was to be an everlasting one, which should " never be destroyed," but which should " stand for ever ;" (2) that " the gates of hell should not prevail against it ;" (3) that the Paraclete, " even the Spirit of Truth," should abide in the Apostolate " for ever :" and (4) that Christ would be present all the days of the Christian dispensation with His Apostolate:—these sacred promises taken together demonstratively prove that the divine Kingdom which Christ instituted was designed to have a perpetual existence, even unto the end of the dispensation. This great fundamental truth being established, two conclusions necessarily follow; first, a succession to the

Apostolate in order to maintain its political existence; and, secondly, a succession to the office of the Chief Pastor and Prince for the good government of the body, and that all occasion of schism might be removed. It has been further shown that Holy Scripture witnesses to the fact that S. Peter was at Rome at the time he indited his first epistle, for Babylon, according to the ancients, signified heathen Rome.

The Fathers of the Church will next be consulted for the purpose of ascertaining not only whether S. Peter ever was really at Rome, but whether he established there his Cathedra, and thus made it the chief and ruling Church.

PART II.

CONSENSUS PATRUM.

PRELIMINARY REMARKS ON THE STUDY OF THE PRIMITIVE FATHERS RESPECTING THE SUPREMACY.

There are two points to be established under this head, (1) That S. Peter visited Rome, and erected in that city his Cathedra, or Chair of teaching; and (2) That his Successors, Bishops of Rome, succeeded to his Primacy, together with all the prerogatives included in that term.

1. In order that the reader may thoroughly appreciate the evidence that will be adduced, it is necessary he should bear in mind several important particulars; first, that the Fathers agree with one voice that S. Peter held a position distinct from all the other Apostles; that, while all were equal to him in merit and dignity, and in the power of priesthood, yet he was nevertheless regarded as the Foundation of the Church, the Source of Unity, the Head of the Brotherhood, and the Chief Pastor of all the Faithful. If the reader doubts this, let him again peruse the evidence as contained under the "First Inquiry," and he will see that this position of the First Apostle is abundantly proved. Secondly, that, according to the written Word of God, monarchy or centralism is God's universal Law in all that concerns government, and therefore it was an impossibility, so to speak, for Him to constitute His Kingdom and Church in any other form than as a monarchy, *i. e.* establishing it upon one person in the first instance, whom He appointed His Vicegerent, committing to him the government of the Brotherhood and the supreme pastoral care of the entire flock. This, we have seen, has been done in the person of S. Peter, who was a Rock from the Rock, a Sovereign deputed by the Sovereign of all, and a Shepherd, the deputy of the True Shepherd and Bishop of our souls. Thirdly, that, if S. Peter really was made the Vicar of Christ, and in accordance with that universal Law of monarchy and centralism, it must be conceded that whatever See S. Peter finally selected as his own, wherein he erected upon an immovable foundation his Cathedra, that there, and there alone, and for ever, would be the seat of government of Christ's universal Kingdom and Church, and that consequently this Cathedra would necessarily become the original source of all authority, and power, and jurisdiction to the whole Church, even as the throne of an earthly kingdom is the source of jurisdiction and honour to every one subject to it.

The reader, then, in studying the evidence for the Supremacy of Rome, is bound to take these primary questions into consideration, and apply them for the interpretation of passages from the Fathers, which will be adduced—both implicit and explicit—bearing upon this subject. It is therefore essential to remember that the Patristic evidence under the "Second Inquiry" rests upon that contained under the "First Inquiry"—the one is the base of the other, the former being the "crown of the edifice." For if there be a Rock or Foundation on earth, and that Rock or Foundation be S. Peter, then there must be a superstructure; and, conversely, if there be a superstructure, there must necessarily be a base on which it stands.

In order, then, to appreciate the evidence for the Supremacy, it is necessary to bear these points in mind. What we have to do is to endeavour fully to comprehend the true position of S. Peter—who he was, and what our Lord made him—and, then, the nature of the Papal Supremacy, and of what prerogatives it consisted. The two—S. Peter and the Successors to his Chair—are inseparable; what one was in all that concerned government and jurisdiction, the other was, is, and ever will be.

If our Lord had made no distinction between S. Peter and his brother Apostles, then the Papal Supremacy is a blasphemous usurpation : if He did, then the Successors to his Chair must be endowed with the same governmental authority. I assert this, because it is impossible to conceive that God could have formed a Church polity, consisting of an earthly Head and Body, intended to last till the close of the Christian dispensation, and permit the principal and governing member thereof to become extinct on the death of the Prince of the Apostles and the Shepherd of the flock. If then Christ ever did appoint an earthly Head to His Body the Church, there must unquestionably be an earthly Head now ; and that Head must necessarily be the Prelate for the time being of that See, who has always been recognised as such from the very commencement of Christianity. I am conscious of much repetition of this argument, but it is unavoidable, for it is a matter of observation that those who study the Fathers with reference to the Papacy, are apt to forget that they—the Fathers—have spoken very strongly in favour of S. Peter's position, which in point of fact is the foundation of the whole governmental and executive Law of the universal Church.

2. I pass on now to another important point in reference to this subject. Much stress is laid by controversialists upon the alleged paucity of evidence respecting the Roman Supremacy, and hence it is that Anglicans and Protestants assume that by reason of this there is no sufficient proof existing for this Supreme Authority.

This argument appears to me utterly fallacious : if pressed, it would be equally fatal against the Episcopate. Protestants are consistent, for they reject both Papacy and Episcopacy ; Anglicans are inconsistent, because they accept the latter on scanty evidence, and reject the former on the same grounds. True, S. Ignatius and S. Cyprian strongly enforce the rights of Bishops, but it is equally true that Ignatius addressed the Church of Rome as the presiding Church, that S. Irenæus and S. Cyprian described it as the Principal or Chief Church, the latter adding, "Where is the Chair of Peter, from which (*i. e.* from the Chair AND the Principal Church) the unity of the Priesthood took its rise." Is it consistent, then, for Anglicans to lay great stress on the testimony of those illustrious saints on behalf of Episcopacy, and reject or ignore the equally plain language of these and other Fathers with respect to the exalted position of the Roman Church?

Again, it is not customary for the Fathers to dilate on subjects in which no fundamental difference of opinion exists. In the New Testament the Apostles say very little about themselves, and the constitution of the Church. The Gospel contains the several commissions of our Lord to S. Peter and to the Apostles, but in the Acts and the Epistles we find no explanation of their scope and meaning. S. Peter's position as Head and Leader is assumed; it is impossible to read the Acts of the Apostles without observing that S. Peter took this office on himself, as a matter of course, and that his brother Apostles not only did not protest, but by their silence on the subject, and their co-operation and agreement with him, fully admitted his right. So in like manner with respect to the commissions to the Apostles generally, they allude to them here and there, but they enter into no details.

If the Apostles were for the most part silent concerning their own office, and that of their Chief, it is not unreasonable to believe that the ante-Nicene Fathers should, upon the whole, observe a similar reticence respecting the relation that subsisted between themselves and the Supreme Pontiff. During the first three centuries there were disputes about points of faith, but none (except perhaps by the Montanists) as regards the Popedom, so there was no occasion to say much about it. That the supreme authority of the Pope was tacitly assumed and admitted, is evident from the conduct of S. Polycarp, who visited the Roman See for the settlement of the Paschal question; from the language of S. Irenæus and Polycrates, who, while protesting against the severity of Pope S. Victor, said nothing in opposition to his right of supervision over the Church; from the writings and conduct of S. Cyprian; and even in the case of Apiarius, on which so much stress is laid by Anglicans, and which will be considered in a subsequent part of this work. The circumstance, then, that little is said about the Papal Supremacy, tells no more against the supreme authority of the Holy See than a similar reserve on the part of Bishops does against the Episcopate, and Apostles against the Apostolate.

But, further, there are other reasons which will account for the alleged paucity of evidence, and for the apparent quiescence (*i. e.* so far as we know) of the Papacy during the first three centuries. First, the loss of much of the literature of the early Primitive Church: for aught we know, much valuable evidence has by consequence perished. If we may rely upon Eusebius, the first Historian of the Church, this was so; and he mentions several writers whose works have been lost, wherein information on this subject might possibly have been obtained. Secondly, we must recall to our recollection the ten persecutions that decimated the Church, with scarce intermission, during those three long bloody centuries. During that period the intercourse between Popes and Bishops was necessarily, in a large measure at least, suspended. The Church in those ages was, more or less, in an abnormal state — many of the Bishops were in hiding, the Priests were in many instances severed from the people, and their flocks were scattered like sheep in the howling wilderness, torn to pieces and devoured by wolves and wild beasts. No better illustration can be given of this terrible period than the fact that out of some thirty Popes who reigned from S. Peter to the Council of Nicæa, full twenty-five were martyred, and the rest were Confessors. This alone explains the alleged inaction of the Popes, for it was an impossibility for them, except at rare intervals, to exercise their universal Pastorate beyond the provinces immediately contiguous to Rome.

Considering all things, it is wonderful that we have any evidence at all during those terrible ages, either of the fact of the Supremacy or of the action of the Papacy. But what evidence we do possess, as will be seen presently, is extremely weighty.

3. There is, however, another question which is ignored by Anglicans and Protestants, and which they do not attempt to explain in any fair and satisfactory manner, viz. that no sooner is the pressure of the Pagan government removed from the Church than we find the Popes exercising their supreme authority all over the world, in the East no less than in the West, advising, admonishing, censuring, and punishing all who rebelled against the Faith and the Holy See; convoking, conjointly with the Emperors, Œcumenical Councils, approving or disapproving the decisions of the Fathers, confirming or annulling them as they judged expedient. We find them also deposing, by their own single authority, heretical Bishops, inclusive of the heretical Patriarchs of such great Sees as Alexandria, Antioch, and Constantinople. Anglicans allege this was the result of ambition on the part of successive Popes, effected under favourable circumstances. But there are overwhelming difficulties against this argument; first, the Popes who did exercise this tremendous power were well known as men not merely of exemplary lives, but remarkable for great sanctity, and for humility which is the stepping-stone to sanctity; no thoughts of ambition could have had place in their minds. It is evident that the Supreme Jurisdiction they claimed and exercised was one which they had received from their predecessors, who in their turn had obtained it from S. Peter, the Prince of the Apostles, in whose Cathedra they sat. And not only did the Popes claim and exercise this power, but we find that Emperors and Fathers conceded it to them as their undoubted right; even the Œcumenical Councils admitted it in the most ample manner. How, then, are we to account for this phenomenon? Are we to suppose that Fathers, Œcumenical Councils, and Popes, all conspired to effect an innovation in the governmental system of the universal Church, of so grave a nature as to amount to a thorough revolution, overthrowing the form of government Christ had established, and the ecclesiastical constitution He had instituted, and in its place setting up an irresponsible and despotic Ruler, whom they regarded, not merely as the Head of the Church, but as the living Vicar and Repre-

sentative of our Lord and God, endowed with all His prerogatives and powers? Are we then to conclude that Popes, Councils, and Fathers, consented to such an innovation as this—that is, if it was an innovation? It is simply an impossibility. How, then, are we to account for the exhibition of Papal power and authority in the fourth century? The true answer to be given is, that when the persecutions ceased, it resumed its rightful position, and Fathers and Councils admitted it without question, because they knew it was founded on a divine institution (1) in the person of S. Peter ; and (2) after him in the Successors to his Chair till the end of time. In the presence, then, of the overwhelming testimony of the post-Nicene age, the allusions of the early Fathers to the authority of the Holy See become intelligible ; the shadows of truth thrown out here and there, grow into substance, implicitness of language is rendered explicit.

In approaching, then, the study of the evidence for the Papal Supremacy, it is necessary to take into consideration (1) the exalted position of the Apostle S. Peter, as declared in the Scriptures and maintained by the Fathers ; (2) The great fundamental principle of Law ordained by God for the government of the world and of religion, viz. monarchy and centralism ; and (3) If S. Peter really had been appointed the Head and Chief ; and if monarchy or centralism be a fundamental Law of God in matters relating to government, then the See which can be proved always to have exercised this office must necessarily be that primatial See to which all Churches are, by Law divine, subject. And further, if the student of this question be puzzled at the alleged paucity of the evidence to be found in the ante-Nicene age, and of the comparative inaction of the Popes during that period, he should take into consideration the circumstances of the times, the reticence of the Fathers concerning matters not in dispute, the bitter persecutions that ravaged the Church during those times, which necessarily caused for a season the almost entire suspension of all ecclesiastical offices — the Papal no less than the Episcopal—and other circumstances which would of themselves alone account for the little that is said respecting the Supremacy during the first three centuries. And, lastly, he is bound, I think, before dismissing as untenable the early primitive evidence for the Supremacy to account, if he can, for the manifestation of Papal power in the fourth century, with the evident consent of all the Fathers and Councils of that period. If he be possessed of a logical mind, he must perforce conclude, either that the Papal power, so freely employed in the fourth century, was an innovation of that age—an innovation, mark, accepted by the universal Church— or if this hypothesis be regarded as impossible, as assuredly it is, then he will conclude that the tradition of the fourth century in respect to the Roman Supremacy was derived from the three preceding ages, originating in S. Peter, the Chief of the Apostles, who received his vicariate from his Master, the Lord Jesus Christ.

I.—S. PETER AT ROME.

S. CLEMENT.

A.D. 91.

1. "But not to dwell upon ancient examples, let us come to the most recent spiritual heroes. Let us take the noble examples furnished in our generation. Through envy and jealousy the greatest and most righteous pillars (of the Church) have been persecuted and put to death. Let us set before our eyes the illustrious Apostles. Peter, through unrighteous envy, endured not one or two, but numerous labours ; and when he had at length suffered martyrdom, departed to the place of glory due to him. Owing to envy, Paul also obtained the reward of patient endurance, after being seven times thrown into captivity . . . . after preaching both in the East and West . . . suffered martyrdom under the Prefects." *First Epist. to Cor. c.* v.

COMMENT.

S. Clement, Bishop of Rome, in his epistle to the Corinthians, evidently alludes to S. Peter and S. Paul as having been at Rome, and as having there suffered. He does not enter into particulars ; he speaks of events well known to all, and points to the Apostles, &c. as examples to all the faithful. " Not to dwell upon ancient examples, let us come to the most recent spiritual heroes. Let us take the noble examples fur- nished in our generation ;" and then he refers to S. Peter, and to S. Paul who suffered martyrdom under the Prefects. He does not say who were the Prefects, or in what country they served ; but he speaks of " the Prefects" as evidently the Prefects of Rome, under whom he suf- fered. This is, however, a matter other Fathers will explain, which will appear as we progress further in this work.

S. IGNATIUS.

A.D. 107.

2. "Entreat Christ for me, that by these instruments I may be found a sacrifice. I do not, as Peter and Paul, issue commandments unto you. They were Apostles ; I am but a condemned man." *Ep. ad Rom. c.* iv.

COMMENT.

It is impossible not to see by the manner S. Ignatius names S. Peter and S. Paul in this epistle that he was alluding to them as specially connected with the Roman Church. The great anxiety of his soul was to be martyred, and he entreats the Roman Christians " not to show an unreasonable good-will towards him," that is, to take no steps to hinder the realisation of his great desire. He says, I do not command you, as did the Apostle S. Peter and Paul, who founded and established your glorious Church, but I entreat you to allow me to have my own way. It is impossible to entertain any reasonable doubt that S. Ignatius alluded to those Apostles as the Fathers and founders of the Roman Church. S. Peter had, according to this Father, visited Rome.

S. CLEMENT AND S. PAPIAS.

A.D. 91–118.

3. " This account (*i. e.* the writing of the Gospel of S. Mark) is given by Clement in the sixth book of his Institutions, whose testimony is corroborated also by Papias, Bishop of Hierapolis. But Peter makes mention of Mark in the first Epistle, which he is also said to have composed at the same city of Rome, and that he shows this fact by calling the city by an unusual trope, Babylon ; thus, ' The Church at Babylon, elected together with you, saluteth you, as also my son Marcus.'" *Apud Eus. H. E. l.* ii. *c.* 15.

COMMENT.

The value of this extract is that it explains the meaning of " Babylon," at the end of S. Peter's First Epistle (v. 13), which S. Papias explained to the Romans. S. Peter was, therefore, at Rome. S. Papias was Bishop of Hierapolis, and was a disciple of S. Polycarp, if not of S. John himself.

S. DIONYSIUS AND CAIUS.

A.D. CIR. 168–202.

4. " But I can show the trophies of the Apostles. For if you will go to the Vatican, or to the Ostian road, you will find the trophies of those who have laid the foundation of this Church. And that both suffered martyrdom about the same time, Dionysius, Bishop of Corinth, bears the following testimony, in his discourse addressed to the Romans. ' Thus, likewise, you by means of this admonition, have mingled the flourishing seed that had been planted by Peter and Paul at Rome and Corinth. For both of these having planted us at Corinth, likewise instructed us ; and having in like manner taught in Italy, they suffered martyrdom about the same time.'" *Apud Eus. l.* ii. *c.* 25.

COMMENT.

Caius, an ecclesiastic, in his dispute with Proclus, the leader of the Phrygian sect, points to the trophies of the Apostles, which any one might find at the Vatican, and in the Ostian Road, where, in the former, was buried S. Peter, and in the latter, S. Paul. He then quotes S. Dionysius of Corinth, who flourished A.D. 168, and testified that the Apostles Peter and Paul founded the Church in Rome and in Corinth, and were martyred there.

S. IRENÆUS.

A.D. 178.

5. " Matthew also issued a written gospel among the Hebrews in their own dialect, while Peter and Paul were preaching at Rome, and laying the foundations of the Church." *Adv. Hæres. l.* iii. *c.* 1, *n.* 1, *p.* 174.

6. " . . . . The very great, the very ancient, and universally known Church, founded and constituted at Rome by the two most glorious Apostles, Peter and Paul." *Ib. l.* iii. *c.* 3, *n.* 2, *p.* 175.

COMMENT.

The witness of S. Irenæus is very explicit. He says distinctly that S. Peter and S. Paul preached in Rome, and laid the foundations of the Church, which Church they there "founded and constituted." S. Irenæus was a disciple of S. Polycarp, who had been ordained Bishop of Smyrna by the Apostle S. John, and therefore he could not be ignorant of the fact that S. Peter had been at Rome, and had there, in concert with S. Paul, founded and constituted the Roman Church.

TERTULLIAN.

A.D. 195.

7. " . . . . Let us see what . . . the Romans close at hand trumpet forth, to whom both Peter and Paul left the Gospel, sealed with their blood." *T.* ii. *Adv. Marcion. l.* iv. *n.* 5, *p.* 366. *Migne.*

8. " . . . . As that of the Romans does that Clement who was in like manner ordained by Peter." *Ib. De Prescript. Hæret. n.* 32, p. 46. *Migne.*

9. " But if thou art near to Italy, thou hast Rome . . . . where Peter had a like Passion with the Lord, where Paul is crowned with an end like the Baptist, &c." *Ib. n.* 36, *p.* 49. *Migne.*

COMMENT.

Tertullian, a contemporary with S. Irenæus, bears the same explicit witness to the fact that the Apostle S. Peter had visited Rome, that he ordained S. Clement as Bishop of the Holy City, and that he there suffered martyrdom.

S. CYPRIAN.

A.D. 246.

10. " Cornelius was made Bishop (of Rome) .... at a time .... when the place of Fabian (Bishop of Rome), that is when the Place of Peter (*locus Petri*) and the grade of the Sacerdotal chair was vacant." *Ep.* lii. *ad Anton. p.* 68.

11. " .... They dare to sail and to carry letters .... to the Chair of Peter, and to the Chief Church, &c." *Ep.* lv. *ad Cornel. p.* 86.

COMMENT.

S. Cyprian, in agreement with his predecessors, carries on the tradition, and affirms that Rome is the " Place of Peter," where "the Chair of Peter" is located. It is evident S. Cyprian believed that S. Peter had been at Rome, and had there founded' the Roman Church.

EUSEBIUS.

A.D. 325.

12. " This, however, did not continue long (*i. e.* the success of Simon Magus) for immediately under the reign of Claudius, by the benign and gracious providence of God, Peter, that powerful and great Apostle, who by his courage took the lead of all the rest, was conducted to Rome against this pest of mankind. He, like a noble commander of God, fortified with divine armour, bore the precious merchandise of the revealed light from the East to those in the West, announcing the Light itself, and salutary doctrine of the soul, the proclamation of the Kingdom of God." *Eus. H. E. l.* ii. *c.* 14.

13. " The divine word having thus been established among the Romans, the power of Simon (Magus) was soon extinguished and destroyed together with the man. So greatly, however, did the splen- dour of piety enlighten the minds of Peter's hearers, that it was not sufficient to hear but once, nor to receive the unwritten doctrine of the Gospel of God, but they persevered in every variety of entreaties, to solicit Mark as the companion of Peter, and whose Gospel we have, that he should leave them a monument of the doctrine thus orally communicated in writing." *Ib. c.* 15.

14. "Thus Nero publicly announcing himself as the chief enemy of God, was led on in his fury to slaughter the Apostles. Paul is, therefore, said to have been beheaded at Rome, and Peter to have been crucified under him. And this account is confirmed by the fact that the names of Peter and Paul still remain in the cemeteries of that city even to this day." *Ib. c.* 25.

COMMENT.

Eusebius, the first ecclesiastical historian, informs us from the records of the Church and of the State, to which he had access, that S. Peter arrived at Rome in the reign of Claudius, A.D. 44, and came there in the first instance in his capacity as the Leader of the Apostles and Commander of the Faithful, to overthrow Simon Magus, the most powerful magician of that age. He also in Rome "proclaimed the Kingdom of God." Hence S. Peter was originally the sole founder of the Roman Church. Eusebius gives us a most important proof of the fact of S. Peter and S. Paul having been at Rome, viz. that in his day their names still remained in the cemeteries of that city. This is conclusive evidence of S. Peter having been at Rome.

S. OPTATUS OF MILEVIS.

A.D. 368.

15. ". . . Thou canst not then deny that thou knowest that in the city of Rome, on Peter the first was the episcopal Chair conferred, wherein might sit of all the Apostles the Head, Peter." *De Schism. Donat.* lii. *n.* 2, *p.* 471.

16. " Peter, therefore, first filled that individual Chair . . . . to him succeeded Linus; to Linus succeeded Clement; &c." *Ib. n.* 3, 4.

COMMENT.

This Father, in concert with all others, believed that S. Peter was at Rome, and that he established his Cathedra in the imperial city.

S. JEROME.

A.D. 385.

17. " Envy avaunt ; away with the pride of the topmost dignity of Rome ; I speak with the Successor of the Fisherman, and the disciple of the Cross. Following no chief but Christ, I am joined in communion with your Holiness, that is, with the Chair of Peter." *T.* iv. *Ep.* xiv. *Ad Damas. Papam, col.* 19, 20.

COMMENT.

S. Jerome, too, held that the Cathedra of Peter was located in Rome, and that Pope Damasus was his Successor in that Chair.

S. EPIPHANIUS.

A.D. 385.

18. " For, in Rome Peter and Paul were the first both Apostles and Bishops; then came Linus, then Cletus, then Clement, the contemporary of Peter and Paul, of whom Paul makes mention in his Epistle

to the Romans . . . . whether it was that while the Apostles were still living, he received the imposition of hands as a Bishop from Peter, and having declined that office he remained unengaged . . . . or whether after the succession of the Apostles, he was appointed by Bishop Cletus, we do not clearly know . . . . However, the succession of the Bishops in Rome was in the following order: Peter and Paul, and Cletus, Clement, &c." *T.* ii. *Adv. Hæres. n.* 6, *p.* 107,

COMMENT.

S. Epiphanius informs us that in Rome S. Peter and S. Paul "were the first both Apostles and Bishops;" that is, that they exercised at the same time both Apostolic and Episcopal functions. S. Peter was, therefore, at Rome, and was its first Bishop.

S. CHRYSOSTOM.

A.D. 387.

19. " . . . . For, it was befitting that that city (Antioch) which, before the rest of the world, was crowned with the Christian name, should receive as Shepherd the First of the Apostles. But after having had him as our Teacher, we did not retain him, but surrendered him to regal Rome." *T.* iii. *Hom.* ii. *In Inscr. Act. n.* 6, *p.* 70.

COMMENT.

This great Oriental Father has no doubt whatever of the fact that S. Peter translated his Cathedra from Antioch to Rome. As he was a Priest of the great Church of Antioch, he was necessarily well acquainted with the Tradition of the Church, and that Tradition was that S. Peter first settled in the golden city; but says S. Chrysostom, "we did not retain him, but surrendered him to regal Rome."

S. AUGUSTINE.

A.D. 400.

20. " Nay, if all throughout the world were such as you most idly slander them, what has the Chair of the Roman Church, in which Peter sat, and in which Anastasius now sits, done to thee?" *T.* ix. *l.* ii. *Contr. Litt. Petil. n.* 118, *p.* 300. *Migne.*

COMMENT.

No one can doubt, when S. Augustine asked Petilianus, " What has the Chair of the Roman Church, in which Peter sat, and in which Anastasius (the then Pope) now sits, done to thee?" that he held with all others, his contemporaries and predecessors, that S. Peter came to Rome, and erected in that city his Cathedra.

SUMMARY OF EVIDENCE.

It must be manifest to every reasonable mind, after examining the evidence which has been adduced, that S. Peter visited Rome in the reign of the Emperor Claudius, and that he there established his Cathedra. His reign as Bishop of Rome seems to have been, according to Eusebius, about twenty-five years, at the end of which period he suffered martyrdom.

From the time of S. Clement all the Fathers who have alluded to the subject, witness to the fact of S. Peter having visited Rome, and having there, together with S. Paul, founded the Holy Roman Church, establishing therein his Cathedra. S. Ignatius, A.D. 107, in his epistle to the Roman Church, evidently believed that S. Peter and S. Paul were its first Apostles and Bishops. S. Papias, Bishop of Hierapolis (A.D. 118), held that Babylon, from which place S. Peter indited his first Catholic Epistle, was Rome. Dionysius, Bishop of Corinth (A.D. 168), addressing the Romans, refers to S. Peter and S. Paul as the founders of the Church, both in Rome and Corinth; and Caius (A.D. 202) points to the " trophies of the Apostles" as existing in Rome in his day. S. Irenæus, the early disciple of S. Polycarp, who had been ordained Bishop by S. John the Apostle, speaks of " Peter and Paul" " preaching at Rome, and laying the foundations of the Church." Tertullian, too, witnesses that " both Peter and Paul left the Gospel" at Rome, which "they sealed with their blood." S. Cyprian, also, the greatest of the ante-Nicene Fathers, describes Rome as the " Place of Peter," where the " Cathedra of Peter" is located. Eusebius, the first Ecclesiastical Historian, not only testifies that S. Peter had been at Rome, and had there with S. Paul been martyred ; but he declares the important fact, that in his day the names of S. Peter and S. Paul still remained in the cemeteries of that city. The other Fathers which follow—S. Optatus of Milevis, S. Jerome, S. Epiphanius, the great S. Chrysostom, and that profound theologian S. Augustine, unanimously bear witness that S. Peter not only visited Rome, but that he planted there his Cathedra.

As we advance in this work we shall see that the Popes, both before and after the Council of Nicæa, and all the Councils which have ever touched upon this point, assert with one voice the indisputable fact that S. Peter came to Rome, that he was Bishop of Rome, that he established in that imperial city his Chair, and committed to his Successors to that Chair his Prerogatives as Vicar of Christ, as the Head of the Brotherhood, and as the Supreme Pastor of the universal Flock.

II. THE PAPAL SUPREMACY.

1. TESTIMONY OF FATHERS AND DOCTORS.

S. IGNATIUS.

A.D. 107.

21. "Ignatius . . . . to the Church which hath found mercy in the Majesty of the Father Most High, and of Jesus Christ His only Son, beloved and enlightened in the Will of Him who willeth all things, which are in accordance with the love of Jesus Christ, our God, and which (Church) presides (προκάθηται) in place of the Romans, all-godly, all-gracious, all-blessed, all-praised, all-prospering, all-hallowed, and pre-siding (προκαθημένη) over the Love (τῆς ἀγάπης) with the Name of Christ, with the Name of the Father (χριστώνυμος, πατρώνυμος)." Ep. ad Rom. Proœm.)

COMMENT.

The testimony of this Father to the position and character of the Roman Church is especially valuable, as he was a disciple of S. John the Apostle, and was martyred within six years after his death. The following points are worthy of notice : (1.) The Church of Rome is described as "beloved and enlight-ened in the Will of Him who willeth all things, which are according to the love of Jesus Christ our God." (2.) As "all-godly, all-gracious, all-blessed, all-praised, all-prospering, all-hallowed." (3.) As presiding "in the place of the Romans," "presiding over the Love, with the Name of Christ, with the Name of the Father." It was remarked in the comment on this passage under the " First Inquiry" (see pp. 17, 18), that this description of the Roman Church, as contained in the Proœm to the Epistle to that Church, differs essentially from those prefixed to Epistles ad-dressed to the other Churches. The difference is so marked that it must have been intended, and it consists in this, that while all the other Churches addressed are renowned for their gifts and privileges, the Roman Church is distinguished for its high prerogatives and virtue, which may be thus summed up in Presidency, Perfection, and Power.

1. The verb προκάθημαι, translated "presiding over," signifies literally to sit before, or in front ; if used in reference to a city, it means to preside or rule over it. When then S. Ignatius speaks

of the Church " presiding over," or ruling "in the place of the Romans," and
"over the Love," he alludes to the
Church, which was endowed with a
higher principality than that of any
other Church—in a word, the Church
which is the Chief or presiding Church.
That S. Ignatius uses the word προκάθημαι in the sense of a ruling or governing presidency, is clear from his
use of the same verb in some of his
other writings ; for instance, "I exhort
you to study to do all things with a
divine harmony, while your Bishop
presides in the place of God (προ-
καθημίνου τοῦ ἐπισκόπου εἰς τόπον Θεοῦ), and
your presbytery in the place of the assembly of the Apostles, along with your
deacons . . . . Be ye united with your
Bishop, and those who preside over
you (ἱνώθητε τῷ ἐπισκόπω, καὶ τοῖς προ-
καθημίνοις)." (Ep. Mag. c. vi.) It is
clear that S. Ignatius employs the verb
"presiding over" in the sense of one
ruling in the place of God, in a word,
as His Vicar. That he so employs this
word is further evident from his incul-
cating the duty of subjection to the
Bishop and the Presbytery, to the end
that unity may be maintained. "Deacons to the Presbyters, as to High
Priests ; the Presbyters and Deacons, and the rest of the Clergy, together with all the people, and the
soldiers, and the governors, and Cæsar
(himself) to the Bishop ; the Bishop to
Christ, even as Christ to the Father.
And this unity is preserved throughout." (Ep. ad Philad. c. iv.) This
perfect unity is compared to the strings
of a harp, "for," saith he, "your justly-
renowned presbytery, worthy of God,
is fitted as exactly to the Bishop as the
strings are to the harp." (Ep. ad
Ephes. c. iv.) When addressing ordinary Churches, he does not, in
speaking of the Bishop, distinguish the
several grades in the Episcopate, because every Bishop is to the diocese the
Vicar and representative of Christ ; to
the diocese he is, immediately under
Christ (being lawfully appointed), the

centre of unity, and the source of Jurisdiction. But in his Epistle to the
Roman Church, he there recognises
its exalted position, as " presiding or
ruling in the place of the Romans," and
as "presiding or ruling over the Love :"
using on behalf of the Roman Church
precisely the same term as he does in
respect to the Bishop, to whom all the
clergy and laity of a diocese are subject.
As, then, all those in the diocese are
under the Bishop, so all, inclusive of
Bishops, are subject to the See of Rome.
S. Ignatius says the Roman Church
" presides over the Love (τῆς ἀγάπης)."
What is the meaning of this word ?
From the context, from what follows,
and from the use of the term in this
same Epistle, and in that to the Smyrnæans, it would seem that it referred
to Christ, the Sacraments, and the
Church. In the Epistle of this Father
to the Romans, he says, "My Love
has been crucified" (c. vii.) Some
think this refers to carnal desires, but
more probably to Christ, for whom he
desired martyrdom. This seems so,
because after speaking of the "water
that liveth and speaketh," which is
" within (him)," he expresses his
earnest wish to receive "the Bread of
God," and to " drink of God, namely,
His Blood, which is incorruptible Love
and eternal life." (Ib.) To the Smyrnæans he wrote, " It is not lawful, without the Bishop, either to baptize or to
celebrate a Love-feast ; but whatsoever
he shall approve of, that is well pleasing
to God, so that every thing that is done
may be secure and valid" (c. viii.) The
" Love-feast" here cannot be understood by what was ordinarily meant by
" love-feasts," following, as it does, immediately after Baptism, and the necessity of the Bishop's license or faculty
for celebrating the Sacrament of Baptism
and this "Love-feast," in order that what
is "done may be secure and valid," shows
clearly enough that S. Ignatius meant
here the " Blessed Eucharist." The
word (Love), too, is used in Scripture
in several senses ; (1) in reference to

K

Christ the Bridegroom; and (2) to the Church as the Spouse of Christ. Love in its highest, purest sense, taken in connexion with ourselves as human beings, has reference to that love which exists in the holy marriage estate. So holy and so pure is this love that S. Paul compares it to the love Christ entertains for His Church, which is His Bride. "This is a great mystery (a Sacrament)," he says, "but I speak concerning Christ and the Church." (Eph. v. 32.) It is then abundantly clear that when S. Ignatius used these words, "presiding and ruling over the Love," he meant to express the Presidency, *i. e.* the ruling Presidency over the Sacraments, and over the whole Church of God. Döllinger thus interprets S. Ignatius' meaning, "who, in the superscription of his letter to the Romans, gives the Supremacy to their Church, naming it the *Directress of the testament of Love*, that is, of all Christianity." *Hist. of the Church*, translated by Cox, *vol.* i. *p.* 255, Lond. 1840.

2. The next point is the Perfection of the Roman Church, for it is described (1) as "beloved and enlightened in the Will of Him;" (2) as "all-Godly, all-gracious, all-blessed, all-praised, all-prospering, all-hallowed." It is impossible to read these words without concluding that S. Ignatius believed that the Roman Church was endowed with the gift of perfection. For, first, it is so illuminated that it possesses the full knowledge of the divine Will, and hence, in the second place, it is "all-Godly," that is, full of sanctity; "all-gracious," abounding with the grace of God; "all-praised," worthy of all glory and honour; "all-prospering," *i. e.* overflowing with merits; "all-hallowed," in that it is sanctified for the great function it has to perform in relation to its presiding over the Love. No language can be more exhaustive than that which is employed by this Father, and it is impossible to help seeing that he believed that the Church of Rome was the

sacred depository of all Sanctity and Faith, and hence its dominion over all the Faithful—the sons and daughters of the marriage of Christ and His Church, by which they are "members of His Body, of His Flesh, and of His Bones."

3. The Roman Church presides with power, for she does so " with the Name of Christ, with the Name of the Father." The Name of Jesus is the Name of Power, at the hearing of which Satan trembles, by the invocation of which the Church becomes armed with all the might of heaven. Christ is called the Rock — the Rock of Ages—a Name symbolic of indivisible unity, of massive strength, of immovable durability, and irresistible power. This Name he gave to Peter. "Thou art Peter" (a Rock), and upon this Rock He founded and built His Church, against which the gates of hell should not prevail. It is a historical fact, as has been proved, that the Rock—which Christ created out of Himself, the True Rock, even Peter, came in person to Rome, and there founded and constituted, together with S. Paul, the Apostle of the Uncircumcision, the Holy Roman Church, establishing in it his Cathedra, and transmitting to it (*i. e.* to his Successors to that Chair) the Name of Christ, which he had received, in order that they might, with the full authority of the Name of Jesus, and with the tenacious and immovable power and strength of the enduring Rock, " preside" during the absence of the Lord, "over (His) Love" — the Church Universal, performing the part of the Good Shepherd.

Such are the great truths contained in this most remarkable Proœm to the Epistle of this Father to the Romans, which letter, with the testimony of S. Irenæus, will prove demonstratively the great doctrine of the Roman Supremacy over the whole Catholic Church.

Many attempts have been made to create difficulties touching the authenticity of the Epistles of S. Ignatius, including that to the Romans, but in vain. Indeed all excuse for doubt was set at rest on the discovery in 1838, 1839, and 1842, of some of the Syriac MSS. of this Father, (and among them the Epistle to the Romans,) supposed to belong to the sixth, the seventh, or eighth century. The Proœm in the Syriac version of this Epistle is much shorter than the standard one, but it contains all that is needed for this inquiry; it is as follows : " Ignatius . . . to the Church which has received grace through the greatness of the Father Most High ; to her who presideth in the place of the region of the Romans, who is worthy of God, and worthy of life, and happiness, and praise, and remembrance, and is worthy of prosperity, and presideth in (or over) Love, and is perfected in the law of Christ unblamable."

Here we discern the same great truths as were drawn from the standard version, Presidency and Perfection ; for the Church of Rome is said to " preside," and to be "worthy of God," " worthy of life, and happiness, and praise, and remembrance, and is worthy of prosperity." And it possesses Power, inasmuch as " it is perfected in the law of Christ unblamable."

S. IRENÆUS.

A.D. 178.

22. " But as it would be a very long task to enumerate in such a volume as this the successions of all the Churches, we do put to confusion all those who, in whatever manner, whether by an evil self-pleasing, by vain-glory, or by blindness, and perverse opinion, assemble in unauthorised meetings ; (we do this, I say), by indicating that tradition, derived from the Apostles, of the very great, the very ancient, and universally known Church founded and constituted at Rome by the two most glorious Apostles, Peter and Paul ; as also (by pointing out) the faith preached to men, which comes down to our time by means of the successions of the Bishops. For it is a matter of necessity that every Church should agree (or, assemble) with this (the Roman) Church, on account of its preeminent authority (or, its more powerful or superior principality : *Ad hanc enim ecclesiam propter potentiorem* (or, *potiorem*) *principalitatem necesse est omnem convenire ecclesiam*), that is, the faithful everywhere, inasmuch as the Apostolical tradition has been preserved continuously by those who exist everywhere." *Adv. Hæres. l.* iii. *c.* 3, *n.* 2, *pp.* 175, 176.

COMMENT.

The testimony of S. Irenæus is especially valuable, for it gives us an insight into the constitution of the Catholic Church, as it was understood, in very early times, within little more than half a century after the death of the last surviving Apostle. The following is what S. Irenæus asserts, put into modern language :—

1. He holds that when heresy and schism prevail, recourse should be had to the Apostolical Churches, where the succession has been preserved, on the ground that they have retained the Apostolic Tradition. He, however, says, that " as it would be an endless task to enumerate the successions of all the Churches," it would be sufficient to refer to one particular Church, by which the lawfulness of those schismatic assemblies may be tested. The Church he selects as all-sufficient for this purpose is the Holy Roman Church. The point to be considered here is, why did he se-

lect the Roman Church in preference to any other church ? S. Irenæus himself furnishes the answer : (1) Because it was "founded and constituted by the two most glorious Apostles Peter and Paul ;" (2) Because "it is a matter of necessity that every Church should agree, or assemble, with this Church." And he proceeds to state why this is necessary, viz. (3) Because "of its pre-eminent authority" (or more literally, according to the Latin translation) "of its more powerful principality." It will be recollected that Christ divided His Kingdom into Twelve Principalities, answering to the Twelve Tribes of Israel, one of which was the principal or chief one. Before the Incarnation Judah possessed this privilege, and afterwards, in the Spiritual Israel S. Peter, by express appointment of Christ. S. Peter came to Rome, and in concert with S. Paul, the Apostle of the Uncircumcision, founded and constituted the Holy Roman Church, and made it a superior or more powerful Principality. It has been maintained by some that the greatness of. the Roman Church was derived from the fact of its having been established in the Imperial city. But there are several fatal objections to this opinion, first, because the city at that time was a Pagan one, governed not only by a Pagan Emperor, but its religion was essentially Pagan, and although the number of the Faithful were numerous, yet they bore no such proportion to the population as could justify the notion that the glory of the Church in Rome at that time was in consequence of the rank of that great city. The Bishops of Rome, before the conversion of the Empire, possessed no privileges whatever of a civil or political character; on the contrary, they were regarded as rebels to the Emperor, and enemies to society, and they were hunted down like wild beasts; the streets and theatres of Rome being plentifully watered with their blood. It cannot be said that a Church which for many a long year had to hide in the dark catacombs under Rome, could have enjoyed any principality of a civil status, or by reason of the grandeur of the city. But let us examine more carefully the text. S. Irenæus does not say that the pre-eminence of the Roman Church was due to the fact that it was the Church of the Imperial city, but that it was itself a more powerful Principality, ad hanc Ecclesiam, to this Church by reason of "its more powerful Principality," that is, that in relation to all other Churches throughout the world it was superior in dignity and power, not because of its connexion with Imperial Rome, but because, as the context infers, of its foundation by S. Peter, who was the Chief of all the Apostles, and by S. Paul in union with him, who was the Chief Apostle of the Uncircumcision.

The original Greek of this work of S. Irenæus has been much corrupted, and in many parts lost ; it is supposed that the original for *principalitatem* was either πρωτεῖον* or ἀρχήν ; let us examine the exact meaning of each of these words. Πρωτεῖον literally signifies the chief rank, or the first place, *i.e.* the Primacy. The definition of Primacy must depend upon the meaning of the whole passage in which the word occurs. If it has reference to mere gradations of rank,—as for instance in the peerage, it signifies no more than Primacy of honour and courtesy, as we say, So and so is the premier duke, or the premier earl ; but if used in relation to the king, or governing authority, then it means, primacy in jurisdiction, authority and power. There is a passage in the New Testament which fixes this rendering of the word, when employed in reference to a Sovereign Head. "And He (*i.e.* Christ) is the Head of the Body, the Church : who is the beginning, the first-born from the

---

* It is worthy of remark that in *l.* iv. *c.* 38, *n.* 3, *p.* 284, the Greek for principatlitatem is πρωτεῖον.

dead ; that in all things He might have the pre-eminence (ἵνα γίνηται ἐν πᾶσιν αὐτὸς πρωτεύων.") Col. i. 18. There can be no question then that in this passage, the word πρωτεύων signifies a Primacy of Supremacy, that is, that Christ, who is the Head of the Body, the Church, is Supreme in all things.

To interpret S. Irenæus' meaning of the words "superior pre-eminence or principality (πρωτεῖον,") we must ascertain the object he had in view in writing this passage, and the expressions he uses in describing the relation of other Churches to the Roman Church. He points to the Roman Church as *the* one, as containing the fulness of Divine Tradition : he affirms that it had been "founded and constituted by the two most glorious Apostles, Peter and Paul ;" and further, he gives the reason why reference should be made to this Church, " For to this Church," he says, " on account of its superior pre-eminence (or, more powerful principality), it is necessary, that every Church . . . . agree (or resort to, or assemble with"). Why "necessary" (*necesse est*) because of " its superior pre-eminence (or more powerful principality"). If this "pre-eminence" had been one merely of courtesy or of honour, as is alleged, then it would not have been "*necessary*," —or rather *absolutely* necessary, as the word *necesse* ought to be rendered'— for every Church, that is, the Faithful on all sides, to "agree with, or resort." The word *necesse est* (absolutely necessary) fixes the interpretation of " pre-eminence" in this passage, as signifying a Supremacy of authority, to whom the Church or "the Faithful on every side," were obliged to "agree, or assemble with."

But a further reason is given for this "superior pre-eminence," viz. the Tradition which is from the Apostles, even " the two most glorious Apostles, Peter and Paul," from whom was derived "that faith announced to all men, which through the succession of Bishops has come done to us," by which " we put to

confusion all those, who, in whatever manner, whether by an evil self-pleasing, or by vain-glory, or by blindness and perverse opinion, assembled in unauthorised meetings," *i.e.* schismatically. "For to this Church, on account of its superior pre-eminence, it is absolutely necessary, every Church, that is, the Faithful on all sides, should agree," that is, assemble with, in agreement, for such is the true rendering of the word, *convenire*. The Roman Church then, by reason of its foundation, its tradition, and its superior pre-eminence, or more powerful principality, possesses the prerogatives of the Primacy, not of honour or rank merely (in the modern meaning of the word), but of power and authority, for if it " is absolutely necessary" that every Church should agree, or assemble with this Church, it follows that she must be Supreme. The drift, then, of the whole passage, determines the meaning of the word πρωτεῖον (pre-eminence). As then, our Lord, the Head, was pre-eminent (πρωτεύων) over all things, as stated in the Epistle to the Col. (i. 18), so is the Roman Church pre-eminent (πρωτεῖον) over all Churches, *i.e.*, she is their Supreme Mistress.

If the word ἀρχή is the one employed in the original of S. Irenæus' work, then there can be no doubt what he meant by it. When used in reference to kingdoms and polities, it signifies a spiritual or temporal dominion or sovereignty.

The word ἀρχή in various forms is used by the inspired writers in this sense, as for example, ἀρχαί, Rom. viii. 38 ; ἀρχή, I Cor. xv. 24 ; ἀρχῆς, Eph. i. 21 ; ἀρχαῖς, iii. 10 ; ἀρχάς, vi. 12 ; ἀρχάς, Col. i. 16 ; ἀρχῆς, ii. 10-15 ; ἀρχαῖς, Titus, iii. 1. Our Lord employs this same word, when speaking of magistrates, or rulers, as in S. Luke, xii. 11 ; xx. 20. Liddell thus interprets this word, when it relates to kingdoms, &c., " *The first place or power, sovereignty, dominion,* first in Pind., Διὸς ἀρχή, Θιῶν ἀρχαί, &c., also gen. rei, ἀρχὴ τῶν νιῶν, τῆς θαλάσσης, τῆς 'Ασίας, *power over* them, *Thuc.* 3. 90, &c. . . . . . 2, *A sove-*

reignty, empire, realm, as Κύρου, Πιρδίκκου ἀρχή, *i.e.,* Persia, Macedonia, [*i.e.* the Persian empire or realm of Cyrus], *Hdt.* I. 91 ; *Thuc.* I. 128, &c. 3. In Att. Prose, *a magistracy, office* in the government, ἀρχὴν ἀρχιιν, λαμβάνιιν, to hold *an office, Hdt.* 3. 80 ; 4. 147 . . . 4, in plur., αἱ ἀρχαί (as we say) *the authorities, magistrates* of the country, *Thuc.* 5. 47, of *Decr. ap. Andoc.* 11. 29 ; also ἡ ἀρχή collectively, "*the government,*" *Dem.* 1145. 26, &c. (*Gr. Lex. Liddell and Scott, see p.* 189, *Oxf.* 1864.) Some of the Fathers too, such as S. Chrysostom (*T.* ix. *Hom. in Ep. ad Rom.*) uses the same word ἀρχή to express the Roman Empire.

The Latin rendering of the word, whichever it was (*i.e.* πρωτιῖον or ἀρχήν) is, *principalitatem,* which denotes principality, dominion, or sovereignty ; and inasmuch as the Latin translation is very ancient, this term *principalitatem* may be fairly taken as interpretative of the original, especially, too, as both the context and the clause immediately following require some such word to explain what this Father so evidently intended.

It may seem pedantic to enter into these particulars, for every scholar is fully aware of the exact signification of these words when applied to kingdoms, polities, and their rulers ; but as it seems to be a point with Anglican and Protestant controversialists, not to give the full meaning of these terms, when the Church of Rome is in question, it is necessary to remind them, that whenever either of them is employed to describe the Roman ecclesiastical principality or dominion, the intention, as S. Irenæus so clearly infers, is to assert that that pre-eminence or principality of the Roman Church, was one which consisted of its being the Chief among all other ecclesiastical principalities, dominions, and powers, to which Supreme Authority all are subject.

In conclusion, I would observe that the testimonies of these two Apostolic fathers,—S. Ignatius of the East, and S. Irenæus of the West — the one a disciple of S. Peter, and the other of S. Polycarp (who was a spiritual son of S. John the Apostle), are conclusive, viz., that the Roman Church was regarded as the presiding Church, "presiding over the Love," *i.e.* the Church, "with the Name of Christ," and "with the Name of the Father;" and that that Church, by reason of its foundation, of its tradition, and, above all, on account of its Superior Pre-eminence, or more powerful principality, was the Head and Mistress of all Churches, for it is said, it was "absolutely necessary," that "all Churches should agree or assemble" with her,—the Roman Church. Thus these Fathers taken together, prove demonstratively the Roman Supremacy.

TERTULLIAN.

A.D 195.

24. "Come now, thou that wilt exercise thy curiosity to better purpose in the business of thy salvation, run over the Apostolic Churches, in which the very chairs of the Apostles, to this very day, preside over their own places, in which their own authentic writings are read, echoing the voice, and making the face of each present. Is Achaia near to thee? Thou hast Corinth. If thou art not far from Macedonia, thou hast Philippi, thou hast the Thessalonians. If thou canst travel into Asia, thou hast Ephesus. But if thou art near to Italy, thou hast Rome, whence we also have an authority at hand. That Church how happy ! on which the Apostles poured out

all their doctrine with their blood ; where Peter had a like passion with the Lord ; where Paul is honoured with an end like the Baptist's; where the Apostle John was plunged into boiling oil, and suffered nothing, and was afterwards banished to an island ; let us see what she hath learned, what taught, what fellowship she hath with the Church of Africa likewise." *T*. ii. *De Præscript. Hæres. n.* 36, *p.* 49. *Migne.*

TERTULLIAN, WHEN A HERETIC.

25. " I hear that an edict has been issued, and that a peremptory one. The Supreme Pontiff, forsooth, the Bishop of Bishops (*Pontifex maximus, quod est, episcopus episcoporum*), says, ' I give absolution even for the sins of adultery and fornication to those who have done due penance. This is read in the Church, in the Church is this proclaimed, and she a virgin !'" *T*. ii. *De Pudicit. c.* 1, *p.* 981. *Migne.*

26. "Tell me, thou most benign interpreter of God. . . . ." *Ib.*

27. " And thou, O good Shepherd and most blessed Pope, preachest penitence to adulterers, &c." *c.* 13, *p.* 1003.

28. " . . . . Let me behold then now, may it please your Apostleship, some prophetical signs, and I will acknowledge your divine right, and you may assert your claim to the power of forgiving such sins. But if it is only the functions of discipline that you possess, and if it is not by sovereignty, but only in your ministerial capacity, that you preside, who or what are you to pardon, you, who neither showing yourself a prophet nor an Apostle, lack the virtue out of which pardon proceeds? But do you say the Church has the power of forgiving sins? This is mine rather both to assert and to administer, for I have the Paraclete Himself saying in the new prophets, ' The Church can forgive, but I will not, lest other should sin.' The spirit of truth (*i.e.* Montanus) can pardon fornications ; but he will not, as it would be for the evil of many. Now, in your own opinion, pray whence do you usurp this right of the Church ? (*i.e.* of Montanus, &c.) If because the Lord said to Peter, *On this Rock I will build My Church, and to thee I have given the keys of the kingdom of heaven ;* or, *Whatsoever thou shalt bind or loose on earth shall be bound or loosed in heaven ;* if on this it is you presume that the power of binding and loosing has descended to you, that is, to the whole Church which is related to Peter ; who are you to overturn and change the manifest intention of our Lord to confer this privilege upon S. Peter personally? . . . Why then do you claim it for the Church ?—and your Church indeed ; you carnal man ! In accordance with this personal privilege of Peter, that power suits an Apostle, or a Prophet, and the Spiritual. For the very .Church is properly and principally the Spirit Himself. The Church is the Spirit through a Spiritual man, not a number of Bishops ; the Church which the Lord has placed in three " (*i.e.* in Montanus, Prisca, and Maximilian.) *Ib. c.* 21, *p.* 1023-6.

Tertullian follows S. Irenæus in his method of treating heretics, first refuting them, and then appealing to the Tradition of the several Apostolical Churches. When pointing to Rome, his language becomes more marked and peculiar. "That Church" (the Roman), exclaims Tertullian, "how happy! on which the Apostles poured out all their doctrine with their blood; where Peter had a like passion with the Lord; where Paul is honoured with an end like the Baptist's; where the Apostle John was plunged into boiling oil, and suffered nothing." Yes, how happy! that Church in the foundation of which the Prince of the Apostles—the chosen deputy of Christ—the great Apostle of the Gentiles, and the beloved Apostle, the sacred Seer under the new Law, conjoined in that great work, of establishing therein, in all the fulness of truth and authority, that sacred depository of faith; whereby the whole Church might be kept in the truth, and maintained in unity and concord, the faithful commended, and heretics and schismatics condemned.

There can be no doubt that Tertullian believed that the Church of Rome was founded by S. Peter and S. Paul, that in that Church they poured out all their doctrine, S. John co-operating with them. It is clear from the language he adopts when speaking of the Church of Rome, that he regarded it as a pre-eminent authority, inasmuch as it had these Apostles as its founder and source of doctrine. With respect to S. Peter, Tertullian had affirmed, that nothing was hidden from him, that he "was called the Rock whence the Church was to be built," and that he had "obtained the *keys of the kingdom*

of heaven, and the power of loosing and of binding in heaven and on earth." (*De Præscript. n.* 22.) So when S. Peter came to Rome, he established there the Rock of which he was the visible representative, bringing with him the keys: hence it was, as S. Ignatius said, that the Roman Church "presided over the Love, with the Name of Christ, (and) with the Name of the Father:" and, as S. Irenæus declared "a more powerful Principality," with which "it is a matter of absolute necessity that every Church should agree." Well indeed might Tertullian exclaim, "Thou Church, how happy!" for it had for its ancestor the Chief of the Apostles, the Vicar of Jesus Christ.

This testimony of Tertullian is extremely valuable, as it illustrates what was said above (p. 118), viz., that the early Fathers, unless there was some necessity, seldom entered into particulars respecting the regime or discipline of the Church. Tertullian the Catholic does no more than *touch* upon the status of the Roman Church; but as a heretic, he addresses himself more explicitly, and in his insane wrath against the Pope gives, involuntarily, no doubt, clear testimony as to the nature of that position in the Church which the Pope filled. Speaking ironically and profanely, he commits himself to the following explicit statements. That the Pope was regarded (1) as "the Supreme Pontiff,* the Bishop of Bishops;"* (2) as "the Interpreter of God;" (3) as "the good Shepherd and most blessed Pope;" (4) as holding and dispensing the jurisdiction symbolised by the keys; (5) as "Presiding Bishop," in which capacity he presumed to forgive sins.

---

* These titles subsequently became common to all Bishops, but the point of Tertullian's attack of the Pope is, that he claims to be the Chief Pontiff of the whole Church, to be the representative of S. Peter, to whom were granted personally the keys, and to be the Shepherd of the flock. His quarrel was, that the Pope usurped a power which belonged, as he maintained, to Montanus.

Tertullian further abuses the Pope for claiming that power for himself, by virtue of his spiritual descent from S. Peter, to whom our Lord said, "*On this Rock I will build My Church, &c;*" and for the Church which is related to this Apostle.

Now on what grounds did Tertullian reject the authority of the Supreme Pontiff? Was it because he was of opinion that so exalted an office could not be held by a man? Certainly not. His opinion was, that S. Peter possessed these high prerogatives *personally* only, and that consequently they were not transmissible, but lapsed to the Divine donor, to be again committed to special persons judged by the Holy Spirit as suitable for the purpose. "The Church," says he, "is the Spirit,

through a spiritual man," as for instance, Montanus and himself. Catholics hold that the Church of Christ was placed under the care of Peter and his Successors ; Tertullian, first in Peter, and subsequently, in Montanus.

The testimony of Tertullian as respects the regime and discipline of the Church in her executive government, is perfectly clear and conclusive, viz., that the Pope was regarded in the second century as the Head and Chief of the Catholic Church, as the Supreme Pastor of the universal fold, and the dispenser of the supreme jurisdiction as symbolised by the keys. How forcibly does Tertullian, the heretic, in his mad opposition to the Pope, explain and illustrate the language of S. Ignatius and S. Irenæus on the Roman Supremacy !

S. CYPRIAN.

A.D. 246.

29. " To the seven children there is evidently conjoined their mother, the origin and root (*origo et radix*), which afterwards bare seven churches, herself having been founded first and alone, by the grace of the Lord, upon Peter. (*Ipsa prima et una super Petrum Domini voce fundata*)." *De Exhort. Martyr. p.* 270.

30. " God is one, and Christ is one, and the Church (is) one, and the Chair (is) one, founded, by the Lord's word, upon a Rock (*et una ecclesia, et cathedra una super petram Domini voce fundata*). Another altar and a new priesthood, besides the one altar and the one priesthood cannot be set up." *Ep.* xl. *ad Pleb., p.* 53.

31. " Certain persons however sometimes disturb men's minds by their reports, representing some

things otherwise than the truth is. For we, furnishing all who sail hence (*i. e.* to Rome) with a rule, lest in their voyage they any way offend, know well that we have exhorted them to acknowledge and hold to the Root and Womb of the Catholic Church." *Ep.* xlviii. *ad Corn. p.* 59.

32. " Cornelius was made Bishop (of Rome) by the judgment of God and His Christ, by the testimony of almost all the clergy, by the suffrage of the people who were present at a time when no one had been made (Bishop) before him ; when the Place of Peter, and the Rank of the Apostolic Chair, was vacant (*cum Fabiani locus, id est, cum locus Petri et gradus Cathedræ sacerdotalis vacaret*)." *Ep.* lii. *ad Antoni. p.* 68.

33. " Moreover, after all this, a

pseudo-bishop having been set up for themselves by heretics, they dare to sail, and to carry letters from some schismatics and profane persons, to the Chair of Peter, and to the Principal Church (or, Chief Church, *ecclesiam principalem*), whence the unity of the priesthood took its rise ; nor do they consider that the Romans are those whose faith was praised in the preaching of the Apostle, to whom faithlessness can have no access (*ad quos perfidia habere non possit accessum*). . . . . For since it has been decreed by all of us, and it is alike equitable and just, that the cause of each individual be heard there where the crime was committed.; and a portion of the flock has been assigned to the several Shepherds which each is to rule and govern, having hereafter to render an account of his conduct to the Lord; it therefore behoves those over whom we preside not to run from place to place, nor, by their crafty and deceitful temerity, to bring into collision the cohering concord of the Bishops ; but there to plead their cause, where they can hear both accusers and witnesses of their crime ; unless, perhaps, to a few desperate and abandoned men, the authority of the Bishops appointed in Africa seems inferior,—Bishops who have already passed judgment upon them." *Ep.* lv. *ad. Cornel. p.* 86.

34. " Wherefore it behoves you to write a very full letter to our fellow-bishops established in Gaul, that they no longer suffer the froward and proud Marcianus, an enemy both to the mercy of God and the salvation of the brethren, to insult even our college, because he seemeth as yet not to be excommunicated by us, who this long while boasts and publishes, that, siding with Nova-tian and following his frowardness, he has separated himself from our communion . . . . How idle were it, dearest brother, when Novatian has been lately repulsed and cast back and excommunicated by the Priests of God throughout the world, were we now to suffer his flatterers still to mock us, and to judge respecting the majesty and dignity of the Church. Let letters be addressed from thee to the province and to the people dwelling at Arles, whereby Marcianus being excommunicated, another may be substituted in his room, and the flock of Christ, which to this day is overlooked, scattered by him and wounded, be again collected together. . . . . Signify plainly to us, who has been substituted in Arles in the room of Marcianus, that we may know to whom we should direct our brethren, and to whom write." *Ep.* lxvii. *ad Step.*, *p.* 115, 117.

35. " . . . . And since there are many other and heinous sins in which Basilides and Martialis are held implicated ; in vain do such attempt to usurp the Episcopate, it being evident that men of that mind can neither preside over the Church of Christ, nor ought to offer sacrifices to God ; especially since our colleague Cornelius (the Pope), a peaceable and righteous Priest, and by the favour of the Lord honoured also with martyrdom, long since decreed, in conjunction with us and with all the Bishops constituted throughout the whole world, that such men might indeed be admitted to do penance, but must be kept back from the Orders of the Clergy and the honour of the Priesthood." *Ep.* LXVIII. *ad Clerum et Pleb. in Hisp. p.* 119, 120.

36. " In order to the settling certain matters, and regulating them

by the aid of our common counsel, we deemed it necessary, dearest brother, to assemble and hold a a council, whereat many Prelates were gathered together. In which council many things were propounded and transacted. But whereon chiefly we thought it right to write to thee, to confer with thy gravity and wisdom, is that which most concerneth the Episcopal authority, and the unity as well as the dignity of the Catholic Church descending from the ordinance of the Divine appointment, &c. . . . These things, dearest brother, by reason of our mutual respect and single-hearted affection, we have brought to thy knowledge, believing that what is alike religious and true will, according to the truth of thy religion and faith, be approved by thee also. But we know that some will not lay aside what they have once imbibed, nor easily change their resolves, by keeping the bond of peace and concord with their colleagues, retain certain practices of their own which have been once adopted among them. In this matter we neither do violence to any, nor lay down a law, since each Prelate hath, in the government of the Church, his own choice and free-will, hereafter to give account of his conduct to the Lord." *Ep.* lxxii. *ad Steph. pp.* 128, 129.

37. " Wherefore since the Church alone has the living water and the power of baptizing and cleansing men, whoso says that one can be baptized and sanctified by Novatian (the Antipope), must first show and prove that Novatian is in the Church, or presides over the Church. For the Church is one, and being one, cannot be both within and without. For if she is with Novatian she cannot be

with Cornelius (the Pope). But if she was with Cornelius, who succeeded the Bishop Fabian as by lawful ordination . . . . Novatian is not in the Church ; nor can he be reckoned as a Bishop, who, succeeding to no one, and despising the evangelical and apostolic tradition, has sprung from himself. For he who has not been ordained in the Church can neither have nor hold to the Church in any way . . . . And, therefore, the Lord, intimating to us that unity cometh from divine authority, lays it down, saying, *I and My Father are one.* To which unity reducing His Church, he says again, " *And there shall be one flock* (*grex*) *and one Shepherd.*" But if the flock is one, how can he (Novatian) be numbered among the flock who is not in the number of the flock ? or how can he be esteemed a pastor who—while the true Shepherd (*i. e.* Cornelius) remains, would preside over the Church of God by successive ordination—succeeding to no one, and beginning from himself, becomes a stranger and a profane person, an enemy to the Lord's peace and to the divine unity, not dwelling in the house of God, that is the Church of God ? . . . For even Korah, Dathan, and Abiram, knew the same God as did the priest Aaron, and Moses. Living under the same law and religion, they invoked the one and true God, who was to be invoked and worshipped ; yet because they transgressed the ministry of their office, in opposition to Aaron the priest, who had received the legitimate priesthood by the condescension of God and the ordination of the Lord, and claimed to themselves the power of sacrificing, divinely stricken, they immediately suffered punishment for their unlawful endeavours ; and sacrifices offered irreligiously and lawlessly, contrary to the right of Divine appointment, could not be accepted, nor profit them . . . . and yet those men had not made a schism, nor had gone abroad (though) in opposition to God's priests, rebelled shamelessly and with hostility ; but this, these men (the Novatians), are now doing who divide the Church, and, as rebels against the peace and unity of the Church, attempt to set up a Chair (or Cathedra) for themselves, and to assume the Primacy, and to claim the right of baptizing and of offering." *Ep.* lxxvi. *ad Magnum*, *p.* 154.

COMMENT.

The witness of S. Cyprian on the subject of this Work is extremely valuable, the more so because he held very high notions respecting the dignity, equality, and independence (these words being rightly and canonically understood) of the universal Episcopate. S. Cyprian went so far as to say that a Bishop was responsible to no one, and that no one could judge him except the Lord. This opinion, it is obvious, if pressed too far, would not only tend to upset the Papacy, but would be detrimental to all discipline whatever, and extinguish the authority even of Provincial and General Councils. S. Cyprian in several of his Epistles had occasion to speak of the position of the Holy See and its Pontiff, and we shall perceive that he was not behind hand in recognising its Supreme authority. Before his time the external unity of the Church had not been broken, that is to say, that, although heresies had abounded, yet there had not been as yet any Bishop against Bishop, or altar against altar.

The election of Novatian by a section of the Roman clergy and people, after the vacancy of the Holy See, caused by the death of Flavian, had been filled up, was the first formal act of schism, and Novatian became in consequence the first anti-Pope. S. Cyprian exercised all the influence he possessed, in concert with the reigning Pope, to destroy this schism, as may be seen in his addresses to the Pope and other Prelates. The occasion of that schism gave S. Cyprian many opportunities for alluding to the origin, the dignity, and the authority of the Roman Church, which we now proceed to consider.

1. The first point which calls for notice is the expression, "the Place of Peter." S. Cyprian evidently used these words in two senses, (1) "the Place of Peter" in the Apostolic Hierarchy, and (2) "the Place" where he established his Cathedra.

(1.) Under the "First Inquiry" it was shown that in S. Cyprian's opinion S. Peter was not only "chosen the First," but that the Lord Jesus Christ "laid and founded," and "built His Church" "first and alone upon Peter;" that he made him "an Original and Principle of Unity;" that He delivered to him the keys, "that that should be loosed in heaven which he should have loosed on earth;" and further, He commended His Sheep to be by him "fed and guarded." S. Peter, therefore, became the Representative of Christ, and also the Representative of the Church, "for he spoke for all, and replied with the voice of the Church." S. Peter was then the Foundation, the Source, and the Principle of Unity, the Head and Governor of the Church, and the Shepherd of the entire Flock. Such was "the Place of Peter" in the Apostolic Hierarchy, and in the whole Church.

But in order thoroughly to understand what "the Place of Peter" means, we must investigate S. Cyprian's expression, "Origin and Principle of unity." The following will explain this: "To the seven children there is evidently conjoined their mother, the Origin and Root, which afterwards bare seven Churches, herself (*i. e.* the Root and Mother Church) having been founded first and alone, by the voice of the Lord, upon Peter." The Church, thus founded on Peter, "first and alone," is the Mother Church, from which all other Churches, as from an Original, spring; so truly so that unless they are derived originally from Peter, they are no true Churches at all. Again, not only is the Church built upon Peter as upon an Original, it is also the "Root," and the " Principle of Unity," that is the law by which the unity of the Church is maintained ; for the Root is not only the Source of life to the tree, it is also its sustainer, severance from which is nothing less than death. Hence S. Cyprian says, that "to the seven children (*i. e.* Churches) is evidently conjoined their Mother," *i. e.* the Mother Church built on, and proceeding from S. Peter—for she not only bare them, but nourished them at her breast. Hence, also, S. Cyprian taught that the Church is one, "and was by the voice of the Lord founded upon one (Peter), who also received the keys thereof." She it is (viz. the Church founded on Peter) "that alone holds and possesses the whole power of her Spouse and Lord :" that is, the Church which originates in Peter,— which is in union with Peter, and which is conjoined to him, as the child to the mother, and the tree to the root, and governed by this Principle or Law of unity,—is alone, to the exclusion of all others, that one indivisible Church, which alone "holds and possesses the whole power" of Jesus Christ, as the King of kings, and the High Priest over the one household of God, both in heaven and earth. And this unity founded on, and maintained by Peter— as the Origin, Root, and Principle of unity—is powerfully described by S. Cyprian in these words : "God is one, and Christ is one, the Church is one,

and the Chair one, founded by the Lord's voice upon a Rock" (*i.e.* Peter, — for the Mother Church was built on Peter). Another altar and a new priest-hood, besides the one altar and the one priesthood (*i.e.* that which originated in Peter), cannot be set up. At the risk of repetition of much that has been already said on this subject un-der the " First Inquiry," it has been deemed important to explain as fully as possible what was meant by the " Place of Peter" in the Church of Christ as originally established by our Lord. We observe, then, these in-controvertible facts, viz. that the Church was founded upon one ; that the Church so founded upon one was the Origi-nal, the Root, and the Mother of all Churches : that this one Church was in S. Peter alone, and consequently he be-came the recipient of all the Royalties and Prerogatives of Christ his Master ; and the Church so founded upon him "first and alone " became the Mother Church of all Churches.

(2.) This "Place of Peter," S. Cyprian explicitly informs us, the Bishop of Rome occupied. "Cornelius was made Bishop (of Rome) . . . at a time when no one had been made (Bishop) before him; when the Place of Peter, and the grade of the Apostolic Chair, or Cathedra, was vacant." This means, of course, the " Place of Peter" at Rome ; and the " grade of the Apostolic Chair" signifies the pre-eminent authority of the Apostle, as the Supreme Head and Pastor, the Vicar of Christ, and the Representative of the whole Catholic Church. There can be no doubt that the words, "grade of the Apostolic Chair," refer to the " Place of Peter ;" and the " Place of Peter," first, to the city of Rome, where he established his Cathedra, and secondly, to the position he himself (Peter) filled, and still fills in the person of his Succes-sors, for the time being, in the Hier-archy of the Catholic Church. As S. Peter was the Origin, the Source, and Principle or Law of Unity, as he alone was the Key-bearer, and the Shepherd of the entire Flock, so were all his Successors to his Cathedra, each in his generation the Origin, the Source, the Principle or Law of Unity, and also the Key-bearer and Pastor of the Universal Flock. But more than this. S. Cyprian held that the Church specially built upon Peter was "the Root and Matrix of the Church," to which "the Seven Churches," *i. e.* the whole Church, "were conjoined," as to its root or mother; that is to say, that as no branch can possibly be part of the Tree unless it be "conjoined" to its root, so no Church can be a Church unless it is "conjoined" to its Mother, which S. Cyprian affirms was that Church which was founded "first and alone" by the voice of the Lord upon Peter. The Roman Church, with its Pontiff, succeeded to the dignity and prerogatives of "the Place of Peter"—the offices of the Root, Mother, and Matrix, were continued in that Church, which by virtue of the Cathedra of Peter there established, became for ever the Mother and Mistress of all Churches. As in the case of S. Peter and the Church built on him, personally, so it was with his Successors to his "Place;" and the Roman Church, and all Churches throughout the world which are "conjoined" to her, are true Churches; and all such as are not so "conjoined" are no true Churches, no more than a Branch is part of a Tree, when severed from its parent Root.

2. That this is S. Cyprian's doctrine is clear from what he wrote to Pope Stephen. He complains to him that certain heretics with letters from schismatics and profane persons, dared to sail, and to carry these letters "to the Cathedra of Peter, and to the Principal or Chief Church, whence the unity of the Priesthood took its rise." We see here how the "Place of Peter" appears in the "Cathedra of Peter," thus occupied by his Successor S. Stephen; the Church in immediate connexion with which, being by virtue of the presence of that Cathedra, the "Principal or the Chief Church," from which "the unity of the Priesthood took its rise." Here is demonstrated the "Source," the "Origin," and "Principle of Unity," for it was from that Cathedra and that Chief Church "that the unity of the Priesthood took its rise." And further it is shown how that Cathedra and Church is the Root and Matrix of the whole Church, for S. Cyprian in another place says, "For we, furnishing all who sail hence (*i. e.* to Rome) with a rule, lest in their voyage they any way offend, know well that we have exhorted them to acknowledge and hold to the Root and Matrix of the Catholic Church;" that is, the Roman Church, for the place they were sailing to was Rome, and this epistle of S. Cyprian was addressed to the Pope. Again, S. Cyprian describes the Church of Rome as the Principal or Chief Church (*ecclesiam principalem*). There can be no doubt that this word Chief Church signifies the ruling and governing Church, and this for the following reasons : because (1) of "the Place of Peter;" (2) of the "Cathedra of Peter," which stands in the midst of the Roman Church, and which is occupied by its Pontiff; (3) because the unity of the Priesthood took its rise in that "Place," in that "Cathedra," and in that Church; and (4) because the Roman Church is the Root and Matrix from which the whole Catholic Church proceeded : hence the irresistible conclusion that the Church of Rome, with its Cathedra, occupying the "Place of Peter," is the Principal or Chief, or ruling Church, union with which is indispensable to the catholicity of all churches, separation from which is ecclesiastical dissolution.

That this is a correct view of S. Cyprian's doctrine of the Roman Supremacy, is evident from what he has further said respecting the Novatian schism.

In a letter which S. Cyprian addressed to Magnus, his son in Christ, he first of all establishes the fact that the Church is one, and cannot be divided, and consequently she "cannot" be both "within" and "without"—that is to say, the true Church remains one and indivisible, notwithstanding schisms, for they who make the schism are "without" the Church's communion. Hence he asserts that "if she is with Novatian (the antipope) she could not be with Cornelius (the true Pope); but if she were with Cornelius, who succeeded the Bishop Fabian by lawful ordination . . . (this) Novatian is not in the Church," "and," he continues, "if the Flock is one, how can he (Novatian) be numbered among the Flock, who is not in the number of the Flock? or how can he be esteemed a Pastor, while the true Shepherd (*i. e.* the Roman Bishop Cornelius) remains and presides over the Church of God by successive ordination?" Then, further on, S. Cyprian compares the Novatian schism to the rebellion of Korah, Dathan, and Abiram against "Aaron, the priest, who had received the legitimate priesthood by the condescension of God." "And yet these men had not made any schism, nor had gone abroad, (though) in opposition to God's priests they had rebelled shamefully and with hostility. But this, these men,—*i.e.* the Novatians—now do, who rending the Church, and rebelling against the peace and unity of Christ, attempt to set up a Chair or Cathedra for themselves, and to assume the Primacy." Now there are three points herein to be noted, (1) the indivisible unity of the Church, so that if Novatian was Pope, Cornelius (the true Pope) was not even in the Church, and *vice versa ;* (2) the Flock being one, has but one Shepherd,—*i.e.* according to S. Cyprian, Cornelius,—who "presided over (not the Roman Church merely, but) the Church of God ;" and (3) the Novatians, endeavouring to establish a Chair or Cathedra, and to assume the Primacy. This Primacy which they claimed, was the Primacy of the Roman Church, whose

Bishop, S. Cyprian said, "presides over the Church of God," that is, over that one universal Flock, which cannot be divided. Can there be the remotest doubt that in S. Cyprian's opinion the Roman Bishop held the Primacy? He even puts him in antithesis to the High Priest Aaron, against whom Korah, Dathan, and Abiram rebelled, showing thereby that the Chief Priest of the Church under the Law, and the Chief Priest under the Gospel, both held under their several economies a somewhat similar position.

(3) But did S. Cyprian believe that the Primacy of the Pope was one of honour, or of authority and power? The following incident will prove which it was. His letter to Pope S. Stephen, urging him to take measures for effecting the deposition of Marcianus, Bishop of Arles in Gaul, is conclusive on this point. "Wherefore," says S. Cyprian, "it behoves you (Pope S. Stephen) to write a very full letter to our fellow-Bishops established in Gaul, that they no longer suffer the froward and proud Marcianus . . . . to insult our College. . . . Let letters be addressed by thee to the Province, and to the people of Arles, whereby Marcianus being excommunicated, another may be substituted in his room . . . . signify plainly to us who has been substituted at Arles for Marcianus, that we may know to whom we should direct our brethren, and to whom to write." Here we observe S. Cyprian asking the Pope, (1) to address a very "full letter" to the Bishops of Gaul, *i. e.* France ; (2) to exhort them not to suffer Marcianus any longer to insult the Episcopate ; (3) to address also the Province and people of Arles to substitute another Bishop in the room of the excommunicated Marcianus ; and (4) after the election to inform the African Bishops, with whom they are in future to hold communion in the See of Arles. Now if the Pope was nothing more than a Bishop, or a Metropolitan, or the Pa-

triarch of the Suburbicarian provinces,* or if he had merely a Primacy of honour, it is clear he had no right to address such a letter of authority to the Gallican Bishops, urging them to proceed to extremities with the schismatic Prelate of Arles. Upon the hypothesis that all Bishops are equal, and that no Bishop is responsible to any earthly Chief, but to Christ alone, it is manifest that S. Cyprian was urging the Pope to do what he had no right to do, viz. to in-

---

* It has been the policy of Anglican and Protestant commentators to maintain that the Patriarchate of Rome only included the ten Suburbicarian Provinces " which were immediately subjected to the civil disposition and jurisdiction of the *vicarius urbis.*" Bingham, who entertains this opinion, remarks, " Some think that the Bishop of Rome was only a Metropolitan when this canon was made, as Launoy, Bishop Beveridge, Bishop Stillingfleet, Dr. Cave ; according to whose sentiments it must follow that the Suburbicarian Churches were the district, or subject of his Metropolitan power. Brerewood and Spalatensis, after S. Jerome, think he was properly a patriarch ; and I have showed elsewhere also that there are some reasons to countenance their opinion ; but then the limits of this patriarchal power were still the same (according as it was at Alexandria) and the ten provinces of the Roman diocese were the legal bounds of his jurisdiction. And so Du Pin amongst the Romanists makes no scruple ingenuously to confess ; exempting Germany, Spain, France, Britain, Africa, Illyricum, and seven of the Italic provinces, from any subjection to the Roman Patriarch in those first and primitive ages." *Bing. Antiq. Bk.* ix. *c.* 1, *sect.* 10. We will admit, for the sake of argument, that it is true that the Patriarchate *proper* of Rome only included what were called the Suburbicarian Provinces, and that all other provinces beyond these were not subject to him in his *capacity* as Patriarch. We know that certain Bishops hold several offices in the Ecclesiastical Hierarchy. A Metropolitan is both a Primate —having jurisdiction over a Province consisting of any number of Bishops—and at the same time what we now understand by the term Diocesan Bishop. A Patriarch is both a Diocesan Bishop and a Metropolitan, as well as a Primate. What is there to prevent us from accepting the truth, that the Prelate of the Holy See is (1) a Diocesan Bishop ; (2) a Metropolitan ; (3) a Primate, (4) a Patriarch, and (5) a Pope, *i.e.* Supreme Chief over all Patriarchs, Primates, Metropolitans, and Bishops of the Universal Church. Assuming then that Bingham is correct, viz. that the Patriarchate of Rome included only the ten Suburbicarian Provinces, in what capacity did S. Cyprian address Pope S. Stephen, urging him to write a very "full letter" to the Bishops of Gaul or France, exhorting them in fact to do their duty in reference to Marcianus ; and also another letter to the province and *people* of Arles, to substitute another Bishop in his room ; and then after the election to inform him (S. Cyprian) and the Bishops of Africa, with whom he and they were to communicate? If France was not within the Patriarchate of Rome, and if its Bishop had no jurisdiction as Patriarch simply, it is clear to demonstration that S. Cyprian was invoking an authority of a far higher grade or degree than that of a Patriarch. In a word, he was setting in motion, for the deliverance of the Church from schism, the power of the Papal Chair of S. Peter, to which all episcopal chairs throughout the world are subject. Assuming that Anglican and Protestant controversialists are correct that the Patriarchate proper of Rome is limited to the Suburbicarian Provinces, the action of the Pope in France can only be justified on one ground, viz. that he was, besides Patriarch, the Chief Shepherd of the Universal Church, whose authority is conterminous with the whole world.

terfere in the ecclesiastical affairs of a distant province, where he had no jurisdiction. And further, if it was true that all ecclesiastical matters should be settled in each Province, without any interference of any foreign Bishop, no matter how high or exalted his rank in the Episcopal Hierarchy, then it was an act of gross disrespect to the Bishops of Gaul for S. Cyprian to petition the Bishop of Rome to address them a " very full letter," evidently of remonstrance ; and not only the Bishops, *but the people* likewise, urging them to expel Marcianus, and to substitute another in his room. The Bishops of Gaul were perfectly competent to do what was proper, without the action of the Pope, *i. e.* if he had no jurisdiction over them.

But it is manifest from this letter of S. Cyprian that he believed the Pope was invested with an authority which he himself did not possess as Bishop of Carthage and Primate of Africa. He believed that the Pope, as the one Shepherd of the one Flock, presided over the Church of God. He believed this, because he succeeded to the " Place of Peter," to the "Cathedra of Peter," and being by consequence the Prelate of the "Principal or Chief Church," he had plenary jurisdiction and authority over the whole Catholic Church. It is impossible to doubt the nature of S. Cyprian's doctrine. Anglicans have endeavoured to explain away all these testimonies, but, as we shall see further on in this work, without any success.

In conclusion, S. Cyprian, the most illustrious Father of the ante-Nicene age, taught that the " Place of Peter" in the Apostolic College and in the Church, consisted of his being the Foundation, the Source and the Principle of unity, the key-bearer having power to open and shut heaven at his pleasure, the one to whom the Lord committed the feeding and guardianship of the entire Flock ; in a word, that S. Peter was the Source and Centre of unity, and the Chief Pastor of the universal Church. S. Cyprian further taught that the sevenfold Church was conjoined to its Root and Mother, herself being founded upon S. Peter, so that union with S. Peter was essential to Catholic unity, severance from which is destruction. To this " Place of Peter" the Bishop of Rome succeeded, occupying the "Cathedra of Peter," and thereby elevating the Roman Church to the grade and dignity of the Presiding and Ruling Church. Hence he says that Cornelius, as the one Shepherd of the one Flock, "presides over the Church of God." Hence he asserts that the Roman Church is the Root and Matrix, *i. e.* the original Church built on Peter, from which "the unity of the Priesthood took its rise." And because the Church of Rome occupied this high position, S. Cyprian called upon the Pope to address the Bishops of Gaul and the people of Arles, a country distant from Rome, and far beyond the confines of his province and patriarchate, according to Anglicans, to expel a schismatic Bishop, and to elect a successor. No testimony for the Papal authority can be stronger than this. If S. Cyprian did not mean this, then his language is utterly unintelligible.

S. FIRMILIAN.

A.D. 257.

38. " . . . . And here in this matter I am justly indignant at this so open and manifest folly of Stephen, that he who so prides himself on the Place of his Episcopate, and contends that he holds the

L

succession of Peter, upon whom the foundations of the Church were laid, introduces many other rocks, and sets up the new buildings of many Churches, while by his authority he maintains that there is baptism amongst them . . . Stephen, who proclaims that he occupies by succession the Chair of Peter, is moved by no kind of zeal against heretics." *Inter Ep. S. Cyp. Ep.* lxxv. *p.* 148.

COMMENT.

Firmilian, in his epistle to S. Cyprian, says that Pope S. Stephen "prides himself on the Place of his Episcopate, and contends that he holds the succession of Peter, upon whom the foundations of the Church were laid ;" and also that he "occupies by succession the Chair or Cathedra of Peter." Now the point to be noted is this, he complained of S. Stephen's laxity in that he was "moved by no kind of zeal against the heretics,"— that is the burden of his complaint. He does not, either directly or indirectly, deny S. Stephen's assertion and claim, which he would have done, especially as an Oriental Bishop, if it had not been founded upon a divine law, handed down from the days of the Apostles. The fact that Firmilian makes no objection whatever to the Pope's claim is a witness of its legitimacy ; there is no escape from this conclusion.

S. HILARY OF POICTIERS.

A.D. 356.

39. "And you (Julius) most dearly beloved brother, though absent from us in the body, were present in mind concordant, and will ; and your plea of absence was honourable and required ; lest, that is, either schismatical wolves might steal and plunder stealthily, or heretical dogs, smitten with rabid frenzy, might madly bark ; or doubtless that serpent the devil, scatter the venom of his blasphemies. For this will be seen to be best, and by far the most befitting thing, if to the Head, that is to the See of the Apostle Peter, the priests (Bishops) of the Lord report from every one of the provinces (. . . *si ad Caput, id est ad Petri Apostoli sedem, de singulis quibusque provinciis Domini referant sacerdotes.*)" *Fragm.* ii. *ex opere Historico* (*ex Epist. Sardic. Concil. ad Julium*), *n.* 9, *p.* 629.

COMMENT.

The age in which S. Hilary lived was distinguished for the greatest trial the Catholic Church ever had to endure. The Arian heresy had, indeed, been condemned by the great Council of Nicæa, but it took many years to root it out of the Church. S. Athanasius was by turns supported and condemned by the Emperor, and at last by his authority ejected from his See. At this time two Arian and semi-Arian Councils were held, which condemned the Catholics and supported the heretics. From the first quarter of the fourth century to the close of the seventh century the Church was employed in repelling, condemning, and rooting out heresies, and punishing schismatics. If the Papacy was a real Divine Power, we should naturally expect that this state of things would force it into vehement action ; that the orthodox would appeal to it for protection, and urge the Sovereign Pontiffs to exercise their coercive jurisdiction to the utmost extent of their power. Up to this period there had not been many opportunities for invoking this supreme authority, but now, as we shall see, there were many occasions for its beneficial exercise.

S. Hilary, referring to the state of things alluded to above, says it is "by far the most befitting thing, if to the Head (caput), that is to the See of the Apostle Peter, the Priests of the Lord report from every one of the provinces." Here is a distinct acknowledgment that the Apostolic See is the Head, and by virtue of the Cathedra of Peter at Rome; and it is more than inferred that S. Julius, the then occupant of that Cathedra, was not only the Successor of the Apostle Peter, but that S. Peter presided by him in his own See. In order that the force of this expression may be fully understood, let us recall to our recollection what this Father had committed himself to when commenting upon the office S. Peter filled in the Apostolic College. It will be remembered that he had described him as the "Prince of the Apostolate," "the Foundation of the Church, and the Rock worthy of the building up that (Church) which was to scatter the infernal laws and the gates of hell, and all the bars of death;" and he further described him as the "Door-keeper of the heavenly Kingdom, and in his judgment on earth a Judge of heaven," "to whose disposal are delivered the keys of the entrance into eternity, whose judgment on earth is an authority prejudged in heaven, so that the things that are either loosed or bound on earth, acquire in heaven too a like state of settlement." (See sup. pp. 27, 28.) Such, in S. Hilary's opinion, was the position of S. Peter in respect to the whole Church. According to this Father,

the Pope, i. e. the "See of the Apostle Peter," which he in succession filled, occupies a similar office. "To the Head (the Pope), that is to the See of the Apostle Peter, the Priests (Bishops) of the Lord (should) report from every one of the provinces;" why? Because of the Prerogative of Supremacy which is vested in the "See of the Apostle Peter," by the authority of which supreme judgment is pronounced, which judgment "acquires in heaven a like state of settlement." Comparing S. Hilary's comment on S. Peter with that on the Succession to his Cathedra, we necessarily draw the following conclusion : (1) That as S. Peter was the "Prince of the Apostolate," so the Pope is the "Prince of the Episcopate;" (2) That as S. Peter was the "Door-keeper of the heavenly Kingdom," so is the Pope; (3) That as the "keys of the entrance into eternity" were "at the disposal" of S. Peter, so are they at the disposal of the Successors to his Chair; and (4) That as S. Peter's "judgment on earth" acquired a "like state of settlement" in heaven, so does the judgment of his Successor to his Cathedra acquire a similar "state of settlement in heaven." Nothing can be clearer than S. Hilary's evidence; he believed that the Cathedra or See of Peter was an ever-standing authority in the Church, to which, as to the Head, the Bishops of all the Provinces of the Universal Church were bound to refer. S. Hilary rightly shows the distinction between the power of the Popes and the See, for it is not to him as a mere Bishop that the Churches are bound to "refer," but to the See of Peter, that is to the Pope sitting and pronouncing ex-cathedra, in which capacity the decisions of the Pope are binding upon all.

S. OPTATUS OF MILEVIS.

A.D. 368.

40. "... We have, therefore, proved that to be the Catholic Church, which is spread over the whole earth. We have now to commemorate its adornments, and to see where are the five marks, which by you are propounded as six ; amongst which (marks) the Chair is the first, where unless a Bishop sit, the second gift, which is the angel (*i.e.* Bishop ?), cannot be added ; and we have to see who first filled the Chair, and where (he filled it). . . . Thou canst not then deny that thou knowest how in the city of Rome, on Peter, first was the episcopal chair conferred, wherein might sit of all the Apostles the Head (*caput*), Peter ; . . . so that in that one Chair, unity might be preserved by all ; nor did the other Apostles, each contend for a distinct Chair for himself ; and that whoso should set ·up another chair against the Single Chair, might at once be a schismatic and a sinner. Peter, therefore, first filled that individual Chair, which is the first of the marks (of the Church) ; to him succeeded Linus ; to Linus, Clement ; to Clement . . . . to Damasus, Siricius, who is now our colleague, with whom the whole world, by the mutual exchange of circular letters, is concordant with us in one fellowship of communion. . . . But you say that you have a certain chair in the city of Rome. This is a branch of your error, shooting forth from falsehood, not from the root of truth. In fact, if Macrobius be asked what chair he fills in that city, can he answer, 'Peter's Chair ?' which I do not know that he even knows by sight, and unto whose memorial, like a schismatic, he has not approached. ·

"... Whence, then, is it that you strive to usurp unto yourselves the keys of the Kingdom of heaven, you who sacrilegiously fight against the Chair of Peter (*qui contra cathedram Petri . . . . . sacrilegio militatis*), by your presumption and audacity. . . . . Since then it is manifest, and clearer than the light, that we are in connexion with so many countless nations, and that so many provinces are in connexion with us, you now see that you, who are but a portion of our country, are by your errors separated from the Church, and in vain claim for yourselves the designation of the Church with its marks, which are rather with us than with you ; marks which it is evident are so connected together and indivisible, that it is felt that one cannot be separated from the other. For they are, indeed, reckoned by (distinct) names, but they are united in the body (the Church) by a single act of the understanding, as are the fingers in the hand, which we see are kept distinct by the divisions between them. Whence he that holds one, must needs hold all, as each cannot be separated from the rest. Add to this, that we are in possession not of one (of these marks), but we have them as properly ours. Of the aforesaid marks, then, the Chair is, as we have said, the first, which we have proved is ours through Peter, and this first mark carries with it the angel (or jurisdiction)." *De Schism. l.* ii. *n.* 1-6, *p.* 470-2.

This Father is, perhaps, the first who defines with some precision the nature and limits of Catholic communion. He alludes to the five marks or notes by which the Church is known. The first mark is the Chair or Cathedra in which is seated the Bishop. To distinguish the schismatic from the orthodox Bishop, he says, we must ascertain "who first filled the Chair, and where he filled it." But this is not sufficient, for even the Bishop of an original See might be a heretic, and, consequently, excommunicated; a further test is evidently required. This S. Optatus supplies; he says, "Thou canst not deny . . . that in the city of Rome on Peter first was the episcopal Chair (or Cathedra) conferred, wherein might sit of all the Apostles the Head (Peter); that in that One Chair unity might be preserved by all." And explaining how this unity is maintained, he adds, "None of the other Apostles ever contended for a distinct Chair for himself, that is, that although all had their Chairs yet they were united and subject to the One Chair of Peter." And, further, in order to show what constitutes formal schism, he affirms that "whoso should set up another Chair against that single Chair, might at once be (known) as a schismatic and a sinner." This Father then proceeds to show that the Cathedra of Rome is the Cathedra of Peter, wherein sit all his Successors to the Holy See. "Peter therefore first filled that individual Chair (or Cathedra), which is the first of the marks; to him succeeded Linus, to Linus Clement, to Clement," and then so on, down to "Siricius," the reigning Pope in S. Optatus' time. The Roman Chair, then, *i.e.* S. Peter's Chair, is the first mark of the Church. From this, then, we learn what is the Law of Unity and what constitutes schism. If the Roman Cathedra of Peter be the first mark of the Church, then all other Chairs must necessarily be subject to it; and all who refuse to be subject to it are unquestionably schismatical. It follows, then, that the Catholic Church is that communion which is conjoined to the Head, who sits in the Cathedra of Peter at Rome; and that community which declines to be subject to that Cathedra is no part of the Church, it is "without," it is alien, it is schismatical, and by consequence in a state of open rebellion against Christ and his Vicar. How completely in harmony this doctrine is with that of S. Cyprian, who held that the "Chair (was) one, founded upon a Rock,"—as much one as "God is one, and Christ is one, and the Church one." These two Fathers, then, agree that the Chair—*i. e.* the one single Chair of Peter, even that Chair which was established in Rome, to which all other Chairs are subject,—is the chief mark or note by which the true Catholic Church is discerned, and by which schism is detected and condemned.

S. BASIL.

(A.D. 370.)

41. "We have looked forward to the visit (ἐπίσκεψιν) of your kindliness (Pope Damasus) as the only solution of these things (viz. the state of religion, and of heresy in the East); and your marvellous love, as exhibited in times past, has always consoled us: and we have had our minds strengthened for a while, by the delightful rumour that we were to have a visit from you (τινός ἐπισκέψεως παρ' ὑμῶν).

But as this hope has failed us, unable to endure any longer, we have come to this step, to appeal to you by letter to move you to help us, and to send persons who agree with us in sentiment, who may reconcile those who are at variance ; restore to mutual love the Churches of God ; or, at all events, make those who are the causes of this disunion more clearly known to you : that thus it may be to you also henceforward plain, with whom you ought to communicate. And, after all, we ask nothing new; but a thing usual with the other blessed and God-loving men of old, and especially with you. For we know,—our knowledge being derived from an uninterrupted remembrance (of the fact), from inquiries from our fathers, and from records which are even now preserved amongst us—as that Dionysius (A. D. 259), that most blessed Bishop, who was eminent amongst you for orthodoxy, and other virtues, visited by his letters our Church of Cæsarea, and comforted by them our fathers, and sent persons to redeem our brethren from slavery. But things are now with us in a more difficult and sad position, and need great care. For, we grieve not over the overthrow of earthly buildings, but over the downfall of churches ; nor do we behold bodily slavery, but the slavery of souls daily effected by those who are battling for heresy. So that unless you be moved to aid us at once, you will not, in a short time, find any one to stretch out your hand to, as all will have passed under the sway of heresy." *T.* iii. *Ep.* lxx. *Ad Damas. p.* 164.

42. " One of those that cause us the greatest trouble is Eustathius, of Sebaste . . . who having been deprived of his bishopric, for the same cause that he had been previously deposed at Militina (for Arianism), devised, as a way of being restored, a journey unto you. And what it was that was proposed to him by the most blessed Bishop Liberius (of Rome), and what it was that he assented to, we know not, except that he brought back a letter that restored him, which when he had shown to the synod of Tyana, he recovered his see. Since, then, from you has arisen his power to injure the Churches, and he has used the confidence given him by you to the subversion of many, from you must come also the correction, and must be communicated to the Churches by letter, on what account he was received, and how that since he has now changed, he has destroyed the effect of the favour thus granted to him by the Fathers." *T.* iii. *Ep.* cclxiii. *Occident. p.* 587–8.

COMMENT.

This great Oriental Prelate and Doctor regarded St. Peter as the Apostle "who was preferred before all the disciples ;" to whom were "intrusted the keys of the Kingdom of heaven ;" and who, on "account of the pre-eminence of his faith received upon himself the building of the Church." To the Successor of this Apostle in his Cathedra, does S. Basil appeal for assistance for the rescue of the Church of Cæsarea and the brethren from the slavery of heresy.

In his letter to Pope Damasus he says, " We have looked forward to the visit of your kindliness." This word "visit " he expressed by ἰπίσκιψιν, which signifies supervision by a " ruler " or "general," or by one who has authority to "visit." That this is the evident meaning of "visit" is clear from what S. Basil further adds, viz. that S. Dionysius "visited by his letters our Church of Cæsarea." S. Basil recognised the authority of the Pope, as visitor of his diocese of Cæsarea, and consequently he believed that his jurisdiction extended to the easternmost part of the world, *i.e.* that his jurisdiction was universal.

Acknowledging, then, as he does, the Papal supremacy, S. Basil first appeals to Pope S. Damasus, for "help" in the straits he and the Oriental Church were in; and "to send persons who agree with us in sentiment," *i.e.* who are orthodox, "who may reconcile those who are at variance;" and "restore to mutual love the Churches of God." In a word, he asked the Pope to send legates to restore peace to the afflicted Churches. S. Basil apologises, as it seems, for thus troubling the Pope, for he says, "We ask nothing new; but a thing usual with the other blessed and God-loving men of old, and especially with you;" that is, that Bishops seek the aid of other Bishops under great emergencies, but especially of that Bishop who holds the first place, and who has authority to "visit" either in person, or by his legates, or by his letters.

And now follows a very remarkable piece of evidence which throws much light on the ante-Nicene doctrine of Papal supremacy. It seems that when heresy enslaved the Church of Cæsarea in the time of S. Basil's predecessors, S. Dionysius of Rome "visited by his letters our Church of Cæsarea, and comforted by turns our fathers, and sent persons to redeem our brethren from slavery." Hence we see the action of the Church of Rome in the ante-Nicene age, in a Church situated in the far east, which was aided by the Roman Pontiff.

But S. Basil gives us a very important statement, which shows that the Pope's authority, even before his time, was regarded as superior even to a council. Eustathius of Sebaste had been deposed for heresy, and he appealed to the Pope, and was restored by his authority; S. Basil says, "What it was that was proposed to him by the most blessed Bishop Liberius, and what it was that he assented to, we know not, except that he brought back a letter that restored him, which when he had shown to the synod of Tyana, he recovered his See." This Bishop seems to have imposed on the Pope, and that injury was done in consequence of his restitution, is clear from S. Basil, who adds, "Since from you has arisen the power to injure the Churches, . . . from you must come also the correction."

It is impossible not to perceive that S. Basil regarded the Pope as Supreme Bishop; as one who possessed the prerogative of visitation of the whole Church, and whose authority extended even so far as to supersede the decision of a Synod with respect to the conduct of Bishops. Had he no such power, S. Basil would not have been content with a mere complaint of its misuse in a particular instance; he would have loudly protested, as in duty bound, against the arrogancy of the Pope in assuming a right which did not canonically belong to him; and doubtless, too, the synod of Tyana would not have submitted to be over-ruled in a judgment at which they had probably arrived after much care and consideration.

S. AMBROSE.

(A.D. 385.)

43. "He called the Bishop to him, and not accounting any grace true which was not of the true faith, he inquired of him whether he agreed (or, assembled) with the Catholic Bishops, that is, with the Roman Church (*percontatusque ex eo est utrumnam cum episcopis catholicis, hoc est, cum Romana Ecclesia conveniret*)." *T.* ii. *l.* I. *De Excessu Fratris, n.* 47, *p.* 1126.

44. "Thou, O Lord, didst say to Peter, when he excused himself from Thy washing his feet, *If I wash thee not,* &c., what fellowship, then, can these men (Novatians) have with Thee ; men who received not the keys of the Kingdom, and who deny that they ought to forgive sins ? Which is, indeed, rightly acknowledged on their part ; for they have not Peter's inheritance who have not Peter's Chair (*non habent Petri hereditatem, qui Petri sedem non habent*)." *Ib. De Pœnit. l.* I. *c.* vii. *n.* 32, 33, *p.* 399.

45. "Yet was your clemency (the Emperor) to be petitioned, not to suffer the Head of the Roman world—the Roman Church—to be thrown into confusion ; for thence flow unto all the rights of venerable communion." *Ib. Ep.* xi. *Concil. Aquil. Impp. Gratian. Valentin. et Theodos. n.* 4, *p.* 811.

COMMENT.

The evidence taken from S. Ambrose's works, touching the Supremacy, is extremely valuable, and is of itself sufficient to prove the whole question under discussion.

1. He first lays down the fundamental principle that no "grace" is "true," that is, no "grace" is really genuine, unless it be of the "true Faith." By "the true Faith" he means, of course, the Catholic Faith. According to S. Ambrose, no heretic, no schismatic, no person not in communion with the Catholic Church, no matter how good and virtuous he may be, can possibly possess any genuine "grace," *i.e.* that grace which is the peculiar offspring of the Holy Ghost through the Catholic Church.

2. This principle being laid down, S. Ambrose next shows how the orthodoxy of a Bishop may be tested. He says, "he called the (heretical) Bishop to him, and asked him ' whether he agreed or assembled with '—or rather whether he communicated—with the Catholic Bishops," for unless he was in their communion, he could not claim to be an orthodox or Catholic Bishop. But it was further necessary that it should be clearly understood what was meant by the term "Catholic Bishops." We know how in these days some Bishops of the Reformed Church, and all the Bishops of the East, assert that they are Bishops of the Catholic and Apostolic Church : it is therefore essential we should comprehend what is understood by "Catholic Bishops." S. Ambrose explains this unequivocally by adding the qualifying words, "the Roman Church." To be a "Catholic Bishop," then, he must of necessity be in communion with " the Roman Church," otherwise he is no Catholic Bishop at all, but a heretic and a schismatic. The Roman Catholic Church is, according to this great Father, the *alone* Catholic Church, being composed of the local Roman Church, and all the Churches throughout the world in communion with her.

3. That this is the doctrine of S.

Ambrose is clear from two or three of his statements. Alluding to the Novatian schismatics, he asks, "What fellowship, then, can these men," and we may add all schismatics and heretics, "have with Thee ; men who receive not the keys of the Kingdom?" They have no fellowship with Christ, that is, no sacramental communion with Him ; for they have "not the keys of the Kingdom." Without the keys there can be no entrance, and if there can be no entrance into the Kingdom of heaven, there can be no salvation ; therefore heretics and schismatics cannot be saved, that is to say, through the ministration of the Church ; for not believing in the covenant of grace they cannot be saved by those means which Christ has provided, and according to the terms of the covenant He has prescribed. But how is it that schismatic Bishops have not the keys? Because they have no jurisdiction, and S. Ambrose gives the reason, "for they have not Peter's inheritance who have not Peter's See :" that is, they do not inherit the jurisdiction of S. Peter, unless they are attached to, or rather in communion with, the See of Peter ; that is the Roman Church, as this Father has above inferred, when he described "the Catholic Bishops" as synonymous with "the Roman Church." The jurisdiction of the keys, the power of opening and shutting heaven, the right of entrance into the Kingdom of heaven, ceases to any Bishop or Priest who is cut off from the communion of the See of Peter, and consequently all confessions and absolutions pronounced by confessors, out of the Roman Catholic pale, are invalid : and further, that salvation cannot be obtained by persons out of the Roman Catholic Church, except by a *special* act of God's mercy, who alone knows the hearts of men. But what hope can any man have if he knows the truth and remains out of the communion of the alone Catholic Church ? that is, the Roman Church, which is the See of Peter ; "for they have not Peter's inheritance who have not Peter's See :" or, in other words, who are not in communion with the Chair or See of the Roman Church.

4. That this is the indisputable doctrine of S. Ambrose is rendered much more evident in his epistle, which obtained the sanction of the council of Aquileia, to the Emperor ; he tells them "not to suffer the Head of the Roman world—the Roman Church—to be thrown into confusion." Three points are here mentioned, " the Head," "the Roman World," "the Roman Church." The " Roman Church " is identical with "the Roman World," *i.e.* the Roman Empire, and that empire comprising within its limits the whole civilised world. Over the Roman Church was, according to S. Ambrose, a Head, that is, of course, the Pope, who occupied the See of Peter : to him were subject the four Patriarchs, who governed the eastern portion of the empire : to him were subject every Archbishop, Primate, and Metropolitan of the western part ; in a word, the Sovereign Pontiff was the Head of every Bishop in the Empire, that is, of every Bishop of the Universal Church. Here we have an unmistakable assertion by S. Ambrose that the Pope was the Head Bishop of the World, the presiding Bishop, to persecute whom was "to throw the whole Roman world, —the Roman Church—into confusion."

But why should the persecution of the Bishop of Rome have this effect ? If he was only the first Bishop, if he held the primacy of honour and rank merely, if he was nothing more than a *Primus inter pares* (first among his equals), how could any calamity befalling him individually, or his Chair particularly, throw the " Roman World—the Roman Church—into confusion?" for if all Bishops were equal, and all had their jurisdiction direct from Christ, it would not have signified, ecclesiastically and canonically speaking, whether the Bishop of Rome were deposed, and his Chair or See abolished ? S. Ambrose, however, gives the reason why this would throw "the Roman world—the Roman Church,"—(that is, the whole Catholic Church)—"into confusion;" and it is this, "for thence flow unto all the rights of venerable communion." From this it is manifest that by the term Head, S. Ambrose means a Sovereign Pontiff over the whole Church, one who is the source of all ecclesiastical authority and jurisdiction, one from whom the right of communion proceeds. So much so that whenever the Pope is persecuted, or made captive, the whole Church is thrown into confusion; the regular course of jurisdiction becomes interrupted, and canonical communion liable to be suspended.

The witness of this great Father and Doctor is plain (1), That no grace is genuine unless it be of the true faith; (2) That orthodoxy consists of communion with the Catholic Bishops; (3) That by Catholic Bishops is meant Bishops in communion with the Roman Church; (4) That schismatics have not the keys of the Kingdom of heaven, because they have no inheritance from the apostle S. Peter, on account of their not being in union with the See of Peter; and, finally, this Father informs us that the Head of the Roman Church, is the Source of communion to all, that is, that to be in Catholic communion we must be united to this Head. Here we perceive how his doctrine is the same as that of S. Cyprian, S. Optatus, S. Irenæus, and S. Ignatius. The stream of the apostolic tradition touching the Supremacy of the Holy See, which originated in the words of our Lord to S. Peter, and testified first by the Apostolic Father S. Ignatius, flows on, receiving more and more consistency till the whole world will, in time, receive the truth, viz. that the Catholic and Apostolic Church is that Church, and that Church alone, which adheres to the Chair of the apostolic Roman See, the Mother and Mistress of all Churches.

S. JEROME.

A.D. 385.

46. " . . . Therefore have I thought that I ought to consult the Chair of Peter, and the *faith* that *was commended* by the mouth of the Apostle, seeking now the food of my soul from that place where, in other days, I received the robe of Christ. . . . Wherefore, although your greatness deters me, yet does your mildness invite me. From a priest a victim asks safety; from a shepherd a sheep asks protection. Envy avaunt; away with the pride of the topmost dignity of Rome: I speak with the Fisherman's (Peter's) Successor, and the disciple of the cross. Following no chief but Christ, I am joined in communion with your Holiness, that is, with the Chair of Peter. Upon that Rock I know that the Church is built. Whosoever eats the Lamb out of this house is profane. If any be not in the ark of Noah, he will perish whilst the deluge prevaileth. And as, for my sins, I have wandered to that desert, which bounds Syria, and I cannot at all times, with such a distance between us, ask for the holy of the Lord at the hands of your Holiness; therefore, do I here follow your colleagues, the Egyptian confessors, as my little skiff lies concealed behind those deeply laden vessels. I know not Vitalis; I repudiate Meletius;

I am a stranger to Paulinus. Whosoever *gathereth not with* thee, *scattereth;* that is, whosoever is not of Christ, is of Antichrist. (*Facessat invidia. . . . Romani culminis recedat ambitio, cum successore piscatoris. . . . loquor. Ego nullum primum, nisi Christum sequens, Beatitudini tuæ, id est Cathedræ Petri, communione consocior. Supra illam petram ædificatam ecclesiam scio. Quicumque extra hanc domum agnum comederit, profanus est. Si quis in arca Noe non fuerit, peribit regnante diluvio. . . . Quicumque tecum non colligit, spargit; hoc est, qui Christi non est, Antichristi est.*") *T.* iv. *Ep.* xiv. *Ad Damas. Papam, Col.* 19, 20.

47. " The Church here is rent into three parts, each of which is eager to drag me to itself. . . . Meanwhile I cry aloud, If any one is united to the Chair of Peter, he is mine (*ego interim clamito, si quis Cathedræ Petri jungitur, meus est.*) Meletius, Vitalis, and Paulinus, all assert that they adhere to thee : I might assent, if only one of them declared this : as it is, either two, or all of them, are liars. Wherefore, I beseech your Holiness, by the cross of the Lord— that, as you follow the Apostles in honour, you may follow them in merit,—you would, by your letter, make known to me with whom I ought to hold communion in

Syria. (*Ut mihi, litteris tuis, apud quem in Syria debeam communicare, significes.*") *Ib. Ep.* xvi. *col.* 22, 23.

48. " For your admonition concerning the canons of the Church, we return you thanks ; but meanwhile, know that we have had no earlier custom (as nothing is dearer to us) than to guard the rights of the Christ, and not to move the landmarks of the fathers, and ever to bear in mind the Roman Faith, commended by the mouth of an Apostle, and of which faith the Church of Alexandria boasts that it is a partaker." *Ib. Ep.* lvii. *ad Theoph. col.* 597.

49. "And because I am afraid you have by report learnt, that in certain places the venomous plants even yet live and put forth shoots, I think, in the pious affection of my love, that I ought to give you this warning, that you hold fast the faith of holy Innocent, who is both the Successor and the son of the aforesaid named man (Anastasius), and of the Apostolic Chair. (*Illud te pio charitatis affectu præmonendam puto, ut sancti Innocentii, qui Apostolicæ Cathedræ, et supradicti viri successor et filius est, teneas fidem;*) nor, however wise and shrewd you may seem to yourself, receive any strange doctrine." *Ib. Ep.* xcvii. *Ad. Demetri. n.* 16, *col.* 793.

COMMENT.

There are some very weighty assertions made by this great Doctor of the Church upon the Roman Supremacy. S. Jerome, it will be remembered, respecting S. Peter and the Twelve, said, " that the strength of the Church was settled equally upon the Twelve, yet it was the will of the Lord that one should be chosen the Head, in order that the

occasion of schism might be removed." He now addresses himself to the Successor of S. Peter—the Head— at Rome, whom he recognises as holding in the Church a similar position. "I speak unto the Successor of the Fisherman (Peter) and the disciple of the cross. Following no chief but Christ, I am joined in communion with your

Holiness (the Pope), that is, with the Chair of Peter. Upon this Rock (Peter) I know that the Church is built. Whosoever eats the Lamb (*i. e.* the Eucharist) out of this house (*i. e.* the Church in union with the Chair of Peter) is profane." Here we observe again how the Cathedra of Peter at Rome is the source of communion, so that all who are not united with that Chair are not of the Catholic Church. This is clearly what S. Jerome means, for he says, "If any be not in the ark of Noah (*i. e.* the Church in union with the Chair of Peter), he will perish when the deluge prevaileth ; and as for my sins, I have wandered in the desert which bounds Syria, and I cannot at all times, with such a distance between us, ask for the help of the Lord at the hands of your Holiness ; therefore," he concludes, "do I now follow your colleagues, the Egyptian confessors, and my little skiff lies concealed behind those deeply laden vessels." S. Jerome, with many others, was harassed by the many heresies and schisms that prevailed, and he looks to Rome for solution and guidance. "I know not Vitalis," says he, emphatically ; "I repudiate Meletius : I am a stranger to Paulinus : whosoever gathereth not with thee, scattereth ; that is, whosoever is not of Christ, is Antichrist." It is unquestionable that S. Jerome regarded the Pope as the one Head of the Church, whom he felt he

was bound to obey and follow, because he was the Successor of the Fisherman, and sat in the "Cathedra of Peter."—This view of S. Jerome is confirmed in another of his Epistles. "The Church here is rent into three parts, each of which is eager to drag me to itself. . . . Meanwhile I cry aloud, If any one is united to the Chair of Peter, he is mine. Meletius, Vitalis, and Paulinus, all assert that they adhere to thee (the Pope) : I might assent, if only one of them declared this : as it is, either two, or all of them, are liars. Wherefore I beseech your Holiness . . . you would, by your letter, make known to me with whom I ought to hold communion in Syria." Again, we perceive how the Cathedra of Peter is the one beacon of the universal Church, the guide of all Shepherds, to whom they look for illumination, direction, and assistance, under all emergencies.

S. Jerome then, like S. Optatus and S. Ambrose, holds (1), That the Cathedra of Peter at Rome is the governing and ruling Church ; (2), That the Church is that body which is in communion with that Chair ; (3), That he who eats the Lamb (*i. e.* the Eucharist) out of that house (*i. e.* the Church in union with that Chair) is profane ; and (4), That in all doubts and difficulties, reference is to be made to the Apostolic See for their settlement.—Such is the teaching of this most illustrious Doctor of the Church.

S. CHRYSOSTOM.

A.D. 387.

50. "Christ, speaking to the Leader of the Apostles, says, *Peter, lovest thou Me?* and upon his affirming that he did, he replies, If thou lovest Me, *feed My Sheep.* . . . Why did Christ shed His Blood? That He might obtain

possession of those very sheep, which he entrusted to Peter, and to his Successors (ἃ (τὰ πρόβατα) τῷ Πέτρῳ καὶ τοῖς μετ' ἐκεῖνον ἐνεχείρισεν.)" *T.* i. *l.* ii. *De Sacerd. n.* i. *p.* 371.

51. "And, as I have named Peter,

I am reminded of another Peter (Flavian, Bishop of Antioch), our common father and teacher, who has both inherited Peter's virtue and his Chair (at Antioch). Yet this is one privilege of this our city (Antioch) that it had at first, as teacher, the Leader of the Apostles. For, it was befitting that this city which, before the rest of the world, was crowned with the Christian name, should receive as Shepherd the First of the Apostles. But after having had him as our Teacher, we did not retain him, but surrendered him to regal Rome. *T*. iii. *Hom*. ii. *In Inscr. Act. n*. 6, *p*. 70.

52. " Now that you have become acquainted with all these things, my honoured and religious Lords, display that vigour and zeal which becomes you, so as to repress so

great a wickedness which has invaded the Churches ... Vouchsafe to write back how that which has been wickedly done by one party, whilst I was absent, and did not decline a trial, has no force, as indeed it has not of its own nature; and that they who have been proved to have acted thus against all law, be subjected to the laws of the Church; and allow us to enjoy uninterruptedly your letters, and love, and all the rest, as we formerly did. . . . Having stated all the above matters, and you having learnt everything more clearly from the religious Lords, my fellow Bishops, bring to this matter for me, I beseech you, that zeal which is required at your hands." *T*. iii. *Ep*. i. *ad Innocent. n.* 4, *p*. 520.

COMMENT.

Of all the Fathers and Doctors, perhaps this great Prelate is the most explicit on the subject of S. Peter's position in the Church. He regards him as " the First," " the Head," " the Leader," and " the Teacher," not of any particular place, but " of the whole world." He describes him as the " unshaken Rock," and the " sure Foundation " of the Church, to whom was committed " the charge of the sheep and lambs of the flock."

S. Chrysostom informs us that not only were the sheep entrusted to S. Peter, but they were " entrusted to Peter and his Successors "— that is, to the Successors to his Chair of Teaching. At first he established his see at Antioch, and then, to use the language of S. Chrysostom, " We," (*i. e.* the Church of Antioch), " did not retain him, but surrendered him to regal Rome :"—that is, when S. Peter translated his Chair to Rome, the capital of the world : for it was meet that the Chief of the Apostles should rule the Church in the chief city of the world.

S. Chrysostom, when Patriarch of Constantinople, gave effect to his belief in the supreme authority of the Roman Church ; for, in the midst of his difficulties and persecutions, in which he was plunged by the violence of the Patriarch of Alexandria and others, he had recourse to the Pope and Church of Rome. He called upon the Church to " display that vigour and zeal " for which it was celebrated, for the purpose of repressing " so great a wickedness which was revealed to Christians." He implores the Pope to write to the effect " that what has been wickedly done by one party," in his absence, and when asking to be tried, " has no force ;" and that they who have acted illegally may " be subjected to the laws of the Church." It is impossible to have a clearer recognition of the Prerogatives of the Roman Church, as the Chief of all Churches, than what is contained in this memorable epistle to the Sovereign Pontiff, and his episcopal counsellors.

S. Chrysostom witnesses to the fact that the sheep were committed first to

S. Peter, and after him to his Successors; and secondly, that S. Peter translated his Cathedra to Rome, and that the Roman Pontiff had jurisdiction over all Bishops, for he himself, one of the greatest and most dignified of the Episcopate, sought his intervention, when in difficulties and suffering from injustice and hardship.

S. AUGUSTINE.

A. D. 400.

53. " The Christian religion is to be held by us, and the communion of that Church, which is Catholic, and is called Catholic, not only by its own members, but also by all its adversaries; for in spite of themselves, even the very heretics, and disciples of schism, when speaking not with their fellows, but with strangers, call the Catholic Church nothing else but the Catholic Church. For they cannot be understood, unless they distinguish her by that name by which she is designated by the whole world." *T.* i. *De Vera Relig. n.* 12, *col.* 561.

54. " That city (Carthage) had a Bishop of no slight authority, who was able not to heed the multitude of enemies conspiring against him, when he saw himself united by letters of communion, both with the Roman Church, in which the Princedom of the Apostolic Chair has always been in force (*Romanæ Ecclesiæ, in qua semper apostolicæ cathedræ viguit principatus*), and with other lands, whence the Gospel came into Africa itself, where he might be ready to plead his own cause, if his adversaries should attempt to alienate those Churches from him." *T.* ii. *Ep.* xliii. *Glorio et aliis Donat. n.* 7, *col.* 69.

55. " For if the order of Bishops succeeding to each other is to be considered, how much more securely, and really beneficially, do we reckon from Peter himself, to whom, bearing a figure of the Church, the Lord says, *Upon this Rock I will build My Church, &c.* For to Peter succeeded Linus; to Linus Clement, &c.; to Damasus Siricius; to Siricius Anastasius." *T.* ii. *Ep.* liii. *Generoso, n.* 1, 2, *col.* 90, 91.

56. " In the Catholic Church . . . the agreement of peoples and of nations keeps me; an authority begun with miracles, nourished with hope, increased with charity, strengthened by antiquity, keeps me; the succession of priests (Bishops) from the Chair itself of Peter, unto whom the Lord, after His resurrection, committed His sheep to be fed, down even to the present Bishop, keeps me; finally, the name itself of the Catholic Church keeps me—a name which, in the midst of so many heresies, this Church alone has, not without cause, so held possession of (or obtained), as that though all heretics would fain have themselves called Catholics, yet, on the inquiry of any stranger, ' Where is the meeting of the Catholic Church held ?' no heretic would dare to point out his

own basilica or house." *T.* viii. *Contr. Ep. Manich. Fundam. n.* 5, *col.* 110.

57. "Who is ignorant that the Princedom of the Apostolate, is to be preferred before every Episcopate?" *T.* ix. *De Bapt. contra Donat. l.* ii. *n.* 2, *col.* 65, Antverp. 1700.

58. "The Eastern heresy endeavoured to unite itself with that of Africa. This is the more evident, because no Eastern Catholic ever communicated by letters with the Bishop of Carthage, except through the Bishop of Rome (*quod ad Carthaginis episcopum Romano prætermisso, nunquam Orientalis Catholica scriberet.*)" *Cont. Crescon. Donat. l.* iii. *n.* 38.

59. "Your letters reached me when I was at Cæsarea, whither I had been brought by an ecclesiastical necessity laid upon us by the venerable Pope Zosimus, the Bishop of the Apostolic See." *Ep.* cxc. *ad Optat. n.* 1.

COMMENT.

It is impossible to doubt that S. Augustine held the doctrine of the Supremacy of the Holy See.

1. In the extract first given from his works, it is evident that he regarded the Catholic Church as something very different from other bodies which have dissented or seceded from the Church ; and he notices the very significant fact, that external religious communities never call themselves or each other by the Catholic name, nor do they ordinarily describe the Catholic Church by any other than the name of "Catholic." "For in spite of themselves," he says, "even the very heretics and disciples of schism, when speaking not with their fellows, but with strangers, call the Catholic Church nothing else but the Catholic Church."

It is certainly to be noted that this remark of S. Augustine is equally applicable to the present day. Neither the Church of England, by her Bishops and Clergy, nor any Protestant sect by its ministers, ever (as a rule) style the Roman communion otherwise than as "the Catholic Church." If a stranger in a town inquire where is "the Catholic Church," he is certain to be directed, not to "the Parish Church," but to "the Catholic Chapel."

The Church of England has never claimed the name "Catholic" exclusively for herself, and she does not, as a rule, describe her children as "Catholics," but almost universally as "*Churchmen.*" The Episcopal Church in Scotland has formally adopted the style of the "*Protestant* Episcopal Church of Scotland ;" and similarly the Anglican communion in the United States.

The Oriental Churches are not known under any other name than as the "Orthodox Greek Church," and the vast number of sects, Episcopal or otherwise, are distinguishable by the name of Armenian, Greek, Coptic, or Nestorian ; and non-episcopal communities by the names of their founders, Luther, Calvin, Wesley, &c. The Holy Roman Church alone enjoys, by universal consent, the exclusive use of the name "Catholic ;" for when men speak of her they, as a general rule, simply call her "the Catholic Church" —a name or style they *never* give to any other religious community without a qualifying prefix, such as Anglican or English, Orthodox or Greek. As a matter of fact, then, the only Church in the world which by universal custom is denominated "the Catholic Church" is that Church which, throughout the world, is in communion with the Chair of S. Peter at Rome.

2. Now the question is, what did S. Augustine understand by "the Catholic Church ?" The evidence adduced

will show what he meant by the term.

The most striking passage in reference to this subject is that wherein he gives his reasons for continuing a Catholic. These may be thus summarised, (1) unity and universality; (2) antiquity; (3) the Chair of Peter; and (4) the Catholic name.

We have already commented on what he has said respecting the "Catholic name." Let us ascertain what he understands by the "Chair of Peter," and that will determine what he means by the term "Catholic Church." What, then, does he mean by "the Chair of Peter?" Does he suppose, as some have done, the existence of separate Chairs in every See—*i. e.* as distinct and independent of the one Chair of the Roman Church? Does he believe that all Bishops, whether in communion with the See of Rome or not, are equally Successors of S. Peter, and that, consequently, all Clergy and Laity adhering to them, are necessarily in communion with the Catholic Church? That is to say, if S. Augustine were now living would he regard Orthodox Greeks and Anglicans as Catholics? No doubt all Bishops are in a sense the Successors of S. Peter, inasmuch as whatever priestly powers they possess by valid ordination, were derived originally from him, on whom our Lord "first and alone" established His Church; but this is not his meaning in this passage. The Chair he alludes to is not by any means an ideal Chair, but a real one, for he says, "The Chair *itself* of Peter," *i. e.* not any episcopal Chair, but one particular Chair, which is located somewhere, and which is the depository of certain tremendous powers, by which the Church is cemented in an indivisible unity, and by which it is known and identified. Two questions arise (1) What are the prerogatives of the "Chair of Peter?" and (2) Where is the place in which it stands? S. Augustine, as was seen under the "First Inquiry," believed that S. Peter was in "the

order of the Apostles First;" that "he bore the figure of the Church;" that he "represented the whole Church;" that he "sustained the Person of the Church;" that he "received the whole world." Hence, according to this Father, he held the "Primacy of the Apostleship," and "the Princedom of the Apostolate," to whom the Lord committed the feeding of the Sheep. In the Chair, then of S. Peter, were vested all the rights, prerogatives, and royalties of the Chief of the Apostles. It was to the existence of this Chair that S. Augustine pointed, as a reason for his continuing in the Catholic Church. Where, then, (2) was that Chair located? His answer is, in the Roman Church, for he says, "The Succession of priests (Bishops) from the Chair itself of Peter, unto whom the Lord committed His sheep to be fed, down to the present Bishop, keeps me." And again, "For if the order of Bishops succeeding to each other is to be considered, how much more securely and really beneficially do we reckon from Peter himself, to whom, being a figure of the Church, the Lord says, *Upon this Church I will build My Church, &c.*;" and then he adds the Roman line of Bishops as his Successors, "For to Peter succeeded Linus; to Linus Clement, &c.; to Damasus Siricius; to Siricius Anastasius," the presiding Bishop of his day. The Chair of S. Peter, to which S. Augustine points as an essential mark or note of the Catholic Church, by which it is known, is acknowledged by him to be the Roman Church: in a word, the Cathedra of Rome is the Cathedra of Peter, and hence, according to this Great Father and Doctor, the See of Rome is the visible symbol of unity in the Catholic Church, by which the Catholic Church is known, and communion with which alone gives one a title to the name of Catholic. Hence then the expression of S. Augustine, "the Succession of Priests (Bishops) from the Chair of Peter *itself* . . . . down to the present Bishop" (that is the Bishop of Rome of the day) "keeps me," *i.e.* I am a Catholic because I am a Roman Catholic. And this doctrine of S. Augustine is rendered still more clear from the following : " That city (Carthage) had a Bishop of no slight authority, who was able not to heed the multitude of enemies conspiring against him, when he saw himself united by letters of communion with the Roman Church, in which the Princedom of the Apostolic Chair has always been in force, and with other lands," &c. It is manifest that Cecilian's independence of his enemies was, according to S. Augustine, in consequence of his being in communion principally with the Roman Church, which possessed "the Princedom of the Apostolic Chair," and which " Princedom" had "always been in force :" and secondly, with the Church throughout the world in communion with Rome. What, then, made Cecilian's position so strong, was his union with the Apostolic See, in which were vested all the prerogatives of the Apostle S. Peter. By the term "Catholic Church," then, S. Augustine understood not any episcopal Church like that of the East, or of England, but that one great community which is one and universal, and which is in visible communion "with the Chair itself of Peter," and which is established in one city alone, viz. the city of Rome.

That S. Augustine really believed in the superior authority of the Roman Chair is evident from his acceptance of a commission from the Pope—which the Pope had no right to appoint, and

S. Augustine to accept, except on the hypothesis of this superiority—to visit on his behalf the Church of Cæsarea in Mauritania, then distracted with the Donatist sect, which the local Catholic Bishop could not subdue, for the purpose of delivering it from heresy and schism, and of restoring peace. In his letter to S. Optatus, he says, he was "brought there by an ecclesiastical necessity, laid upon (him) by the venerable Pope Zosimus, the Bishop of the Apostolic See."

Such, then, is the evidence of this great Father and Doctor of the Church, who held that the Roman Catholic Church throughout the world was the *alone* Catholic Church, to the exclusion of all other religious Communities, and this because he believed (1) That in the Chair of S. Peter was vested " the Princedom of the Apostleship ;" (2) That this Chair is located in Rome, and that the Bishops of the Apostolic See are in their time his representatives, succeeding to all his royalties and prerogatives ; (3) That " the Princedom of the Apostolic Chair has always," *i.e.* from the very beginning, "been in force" in that Church—an expression indicative of superiority of jurisdiction, authority, and power : and (4) That in consequence of this " Princedom of the Apostleship"—vested in the Apostolic See —the Church of Rome is necessarily the Head of the whole Church, union with which is essential to the lawful use of the " Catholic" name, and to all the privileges of Catholic communion.

S. PAULINUS.

A.D. 418.

60. " I appeal to the justice of your Holiness, my Lord Zosimus, venerable Pope. The true faith is never troubled, and this especially in the Apostolic Church, wherein the teachers of a corrupt faith are as easily detected as they are truly

punished . . . . that they may have in them that true faith which the Apostles taught, and which is held by the Roman Church, and by all the teachers of the Catholic faith." *Libell. adv. Cœlest. Zozimo oblatus, n.* 1, *Galland. t.* ix. *p.* 32.

M

S. Paulinus, a deacon of Milan—a city out of the Patriarchate proper of Rome — bears witness to the pre-eminence of the Roman Church, for he distinguishes it from all other Churches: which would be unintelligible, if it was nothing more than a branch of the Catholic Church. As S. Paul, in his allusion to the Apostles, separates S. Peter's name from them as one at least pre-eminent, so does S. Paulinus in like manner with respect to the Catholic Church, naming the Roman Church first, and secondly, " the teachers of the Catholic faith."

BACCHIARIUS.

A.D. 420.

61. " If, for one man's fault, the population of a whole province is to be anathematised, then will be condemned also that most blessed disciple (of Peter), Rome to wit, out of which there have sprung up not one, but two or three, or even more heresies, and yet not one of them has been able either to have possession, or to move the Chair of Peter, that is, the Seat of Faith . . . . Seeing that the institutes of the Apostolic doctrine exhort us, to *produce to all that ask us the reason of the faith and hope that is in us*, we will not delay to place the rule of our faith before your Holiness, who are the builder of that edifice" (*qui artifex es ipsius ædificii.*) *De Fide, n.* 2, *Galland, T.* ix. *pp.* 183, 4.

This learned monk of the fifth century believed most firmly in the Roman Supremacy. According to him, the Roman Church contains the "Chair of Peter ; " and although many heresies have arisen, and the population of a whole province have in consequence been anathematised, yet not one of these heresies has " been able either to have possession or to move the Chair of Peter, that is, the seat of the Faith." This is strong evidence of the indefectibility of the Roman Church, that heresies cannot obtain possession of it ; and that the Chair of Peter is immoveable. Here we are reminded of the word of our Lord : " Upon this Rock I will build my Church, and the gates of hell shall not prevail against it," that is, as the Fathers say, that neither heresies nor vices shall prevail so as to overthrow that Church which is built upon Peter, whose visible symbol is his Chair. But this "Chair of Peter," this Father affirms, is the "Seat or See of Faith," that is, that containing—as S. Ignatius, S. Irenæus, Tertullian and others say—the fulness of apostolical tradition, being " enlightened in the will of him," and being "all-godly, all-gracious, all-blessed, all-praised, all-prosperous, all-hallowed, and having the Presidency in the place of the Romans, and presiding over the Love," it possesses the great privilege of being the Depository of Faith, and, by consequence, the prerogative of being the Teacher of the world. That this was evidently the opinion of this Father, is clear from what he says respecting the Pope, whom he declares is "the Builder of that edifice," that is, the Catholic Faith.

S. CYRIL OF ALEXANDRIA.

A.D. 424.

62. "That these things really are so, let us produce a witness most worthy of faith, a most holy man, and Archbishop of all the habitable world, that Celestine, who is both Father and Patriarch of the mighty city of Rome (ἀρχιεπίσκοπον πάσης τῆς οἰκουμένης, πατέρα τι καὶ πατρι-

ἀρχην Κελέστινον τὸν τῆς μεγαλοπόλεως 'Ρώμης), who himself also exhorted thee by letters, bidding thee desist from that maddest of blasphemies, and thou didst not obey him." *T. v. P.* ii. *Encom. in S. Mariam Deip. p.* 384.

COMMENT.

The testimony of this illustrious Father, the great defender of the faith in the fifth century, is most remarkable. In his letter to Nestorius, he describes Pope S. Celestine (1) as "Archbishop of all the habitable world;" and (2) as "Father and Patriarch of the mighty city of Rome." This is the first time that the several offices of the Bishop of Rome are formally and accurately described: and coming from the great patriarchal See of Alexandria is very conclusive evidence of the real position of the Holy See in the universal Catholic hierarchy. S. Cyril, in this passage, distinguishes the three grades in the Roman Church proper: (1) as Father, or Bishop of the diocese (to use modern language) of Rome; (2) as Patriarch, or Father of Fathers, to its provinces, which, according to Anglican and Protestant controversialists, consist only of the Suburbicarian provinces; and (3) as the Pontifex Maximus, or Chief Pontiff, or "Archbishop of the whole habitable world." By this testimony of the Pope's universal jurisdiction, S. Cyril admitted his own inferiority,—*i.e.*, as to grade, —to the Sovereign Pontiff, and the duty of submitting himself to his authority as his Head and Chief. This he proved indeed when he obeyed the mandate of the Pope to depose Nestorius from his See, in the name and by the authority of the Holy See, if he did not recant his wicked error within a very limited period of grace. But in

order to understand S. Cyril's meaning, let us carefully examine his language, and the terms he employs: "Archbishop of the whole habitable world." The word ἀρχιεπίσκοπος, every one will admit, signifies Chief Bishop, or one who has the rule or authority over all Bishops within the province or Patriarchate subject to him. The code of the universal Church, especially in the East, recognises several episcopal grades, from the diocesan Bishop to the Metropolitan, the Metropolitan to the Exarch, or other superior prelate, and these to the Patriarch of Constantinople. Provisions were made for appeals from the lower to the higher, and from the higher to the chief authority; which, in the East, was the Patriarch of the imperial city of Constantinople. Now, it is to be observed, that each of these jurisdictions, even the largest of them, was limited. The Patriarchate of that great city was the most extensive in the world (I mean Patriarchate, strictly and ecclesiastically so called), for it comprised the whole of the eastern division of the Empire; but to that division it was limited. But, according to S. Cyril, the Roman Bishop was Archbishop or Chief Bishop, not of any part of the empire, but of all the habitable world, *i. e.* of every part of the known world, where there were souls to be saved. While then the jurisdiction of the Patriarchates was limited to certain large ecclesiastical domains, that of the Pope was, according to this great Father, conterminous with the boundaries not only of the Roman empire, but of all kingdoms, states, and dominions, in a word, to use his own phraseology, "the whole habitable world."

But let us seek for the grounds of these opinions of S. Cyril. There can be little doubt, that he believed Pope S. Celestine to have obtained his universal jurisdiction from the Apostle S. Peter. Concerning that Apostle he had taught that he was named Peter, because upon him the Church was to be founded. He also taught that this blessed Apostle had been "set over" the holy disciples, as their "Prince," and "Leader:" he further taught, that S. Peter was the "Teacher of all those who by faith should come" unto Christ. With all other Fathers S. Cyril believed that S. Peter established his Chair in the city of Rome; also that the Bishop of Rome was his Successor to that Chair, and, consequently, he held that the Bishop who occupied that Chair in his day,— S. Celestine—was not only the "Father and Patriarch of the mighty city of Rome," but also "the Archbishop of the whole habitable world," to whom were subject, as Chief Pastor, all Patriarchs, himself included, Exarchs, Archbishops, Metropolitans and Bishops; all priests of whatever rank, and finally every soul who named the name of Christ.

THEODORET.

A.D. 424.

63. "If Paul, that herald of the truth, that trumpet of the Holy Ghost, repaired to the Great Peter to bring from him an explanation to those of Antioch, who were disputing concerning questions of the law; with much greater reason do we, who are so worthless and lowly, hasten to your Apostolic Throne, to receive from you a remedy for the wounds of the Churches. For it pertains to you to hold the Primacy in all things. For your Throne is adorned with many prerogatives (διὰ πάντα γὰρ ὑμῖν τὸ πρωτεύειν ἁρμόττει. Πολλοῖς γὰρ ὁ ὑμέτερος θρόνος κοσμεῖται πλεονεκτήμασι.) Other cities indeed, their vastness, their beauty, the number of their citizens adorn; and some, which have not these recommendations, are illustrated by certain spiritual gifts: but on your city (Rome), the Giver of good things has bestowed a treasury of good things. For she is the greatest, and most illustrious of cities; she rules the world, and overflows with a crowd of citizens. Add to this that she now enjoys a victorious Supremacy, and has given her name to subject nations. But her faith especially adorns her; and the divine Paul, a witness worthy of faith, cries out, that your *faith is spoken of in the whole world.* ... She contains also within herself the tombs of our common fathers and teachers of the truth, Peter and Paul,—tombs which illuminate the souls of the faithful. Their thrice-blessed and divine twin-star rose indeed in the East, and diffused its beams on all sides, but had the setting of its existence, by choice, in the West, and thence even now illumines the world. These have made your Throne most illustrious; this is the culminating point of your blessings. And their God has even now made illustrious their Throne, having established therein your Holiness emitting the

rays of orthodoxy. . . . But we, after having admired your spiritual wisdom, give praise to the grace of the Holy Spirit which spoke through you, and we pray and beseech, and beg and supplicate your Holiness, guard from injury (ἰπαμῦναι) the storm - tossed Churches of God. . . . But I await the sentence (περιμίνω τὴν ψῆφον) of your Apostolic Throne, and I pray and beseech your Holiness to aid me (or guard me from injury), who appeal to your upright and just judgment, and to order me (ἰπαμῦναί μοι τὸ ὀρθὸν ὑμῶν . . . . ἰπικαλουμίνω κριτήριον, καὶ κελεῦσαι) to hasten to you, and to exhibit my teaching, which follows in the footsteps of the Apostles. . . . But do not, I pray you, reject my supplication, nor despise my miserable grey hairs so insulted after so many labours. But, above all things, I beg to learn from you, whether I must needs acquiesce in this unjust deposition, or not ; for I await your sentence.

And should you command me to abide by what has been adjudged, I will do so, and to no one will I give further trouble, but will await the just judgment of our God and Saviour." *T. iv. Ep.* cxiii. *Leoni Papæ, pp.* 1187–1192.

64. " . . . I, therefore, beseech your Holiness to persuade the most holy and blessed Archbishop (Leo) to use his Apostolic Power (τῆ ἀποστολικῆ χρήσασθαι ἐξουσίᾳ), and to order me to hasten to your Council. For that most holy Throne has the Sovereignty over the Churches throughout the universe on many grounds (ἔχει γὰρ ὁ πανάγιος θρόνος ἐκεῖνος τῶν κατὰ τὴν οἰκουμίνην ἐκκλησιῶν τὴν ἡγεμονίαν διὰ πολλά), and for this, above all others, that it has remained free from all taint of heresy, and no one holding sentiments contrary (to the truth) has sat in it, but it has pre- served the Apostolic grace uncorrupted." *Ib. Ep.* cxvi. *Renato p.* 1197.

COMMENT.

Theodoret, another Oriental prelate, is not behindhand in his testimony for the Supremacy of Rome. Comparing the city of Rome with other cities, he says, "Other cities, indeed, their vastness, their beauty, the number of their citizens adorn ; and some which have not this recommendation, are illustrated by certain spiritual gifts : but," continues he, "on your city (of Rome) the Giver of good has bestowed a treasury of good things," not merely in stately grandeur and power, but a "victorious Supremacy," that is, not a Supremacy of physical power, but a Supremacy of faith, her great glory arising from the fact, that she contains within her walls, the "tombs of our common Fathers and Teachers of the truth,— Peter and Paul,— tombs which illuminate the souls of the faithful." The "twin-star," he says, arises in the East, but "had the setting of its existence, by choice, in the West," that is, in Rome, "and thence even now illuminates the world." Such is the glory of Rome in the estimation of this Father, as Mistress, not merely of the political world, but of the world of Faith, that is, the Universal Church. Hence Theodoret had grounds for saying, we "hasten to your Apostolic (Roman) Throne, to receive from you a remedy for the wounds of the Churches : for it pertains to you," the Sovereign Pontiff, and Successor of S. Peter and S. Paul, "to hold the Primacy in all things, for your Throne is adorned with many prerogatives." Such was the opinion of this illustrious Prelate. But as a proof that his words were not mere expressions of courtesy meaning nothing, he formally recognised the Papal Supremacy over himself, for he, in reference to his own difficulties, (as he had been unjustly deposed,) said, "I await the sentence of your Apostolic Throne, and I pray your Holiness to aid me, who appeal to your upright and just judgment," and he beseeches him "to summon him," that he may exhibit his teaching, and prove to him that he "follows in the footsteps of the Apostles ;" and should the Pope confirm the judgment of deposition pronounced upon him, he will abide "by what has been adjudged." It is impossible not to perceive that this Eastern Bishop regarded the Pope as Supreme. But to remove all doubts as to his belief in this matter, it will be sufficient to quote another epistle of his, in which he declares that the "most holy Throne" of Rome, "has the Sovereignty over the Churches throughout the Universe on many grounds," inasmuch as, apart from other reasons—reasons which he has already given—it "has remained free from all taint of heresy," and "has

preserved the Apostolic grace uncorrupted." This last clause has an important bearing, on the subject of this Work, for had the Roman Supremacy been a corruption of primitive discipline, (and no Pope has pushed it further than Pope S. Leo) he could not have asserted, with truth, that "the Apostolic grace" had been preserved "uncorrupted." If the Papal authority had been a usurpation, the corruption would have been of so glaring a nature, that the Roman Church would have ceased to have been regarded by the Catholic episcopate as any thing better than the conventicle of Antichrist. Theodoret, however, held the Roman Supremacy, as it had the "Sovereignty over the Churches," and this because of its origin and perfect freedom from heresy. Theodoret agreed with S. Cyril, the Prelate of the great Oriental See of Alexandria, that the "Successor of S. Peter of Rome was the Archbishop of all the habitable world," as well as "Father and Patriarch" of the holy city.

S. PETER CHRYSOLOGUS.

A. D. 440.

65. "We exhort you, honoured brother (Eutyches), that in all things you obediently attend those things which have been written by the most blessed Pope (Leo) of the city of Rome, because blessed Peter, who lives and presides in his own See, gives, to those who seek, the true faith. For we, in our solicitude for truth and faith, cannot, without the consent of the Bishop of the City of Rome, hear causes of faith." *(In omnibus autem hortamur te . . . . ut his, quæ a beato Papa Romanæ civitatis scripta sunt, obedienter attendas, quoniam beatus Petrus, qui in propria sede vivit et præsidet, præstat quærentibus fidei veritatem. Nos enim pro studio pacis et fidei extra consensum Romanæ civitatis episcopi causas fidei audire non possumus.) Ad Eutych. Ep. Leon. t. i. Ep. xxv. p. 743. Migne.*

COMMENT.

S. Peter Chrysologus affirms — (1) that the "Blessed Peter lives and presides in his own See," (2) that "without the consent of the Bishop of Rome," causes concerning the Faith may not be heard. This Father held that the

Roman Church was supreme over all causes having reference to the Catholic Faith, and this because S. Peter "lives and presides in his own See." This doctrine is in perfect accord with that which had been held and taught by all preceding Fathers who have written on this question.

SOCRATES.

A.D. 419.

66. "Athanasius was scarcely able to reach Italy . . . . at the same time also Paul of Constantinople, and Asclepas of Gaza, and Marcellus of Ancyra, a city of Galatia Minor, and Lucius of Adrianople, who had each, for different causes, been accused and driven from their churches, arrived at the imperial city. They make known their individual cases to Julius, Bishop of Rome, and he, in the exercise of the Prerogative peculiar to the Church of Rome (ὁ δὲ, ἅτι προνομία τῆς ἐν Ρώμη ἐκκλησίας ἐχούσης), armed (strengthened) them with authoritative letters, and sent them back to the East, having restored to each his own see, and severely blaming those who had rashly deposed them. And they having departed from Rome, and confiding in the letters of Bishop Julius, recovered their churches." Then follows the counter-declaration of Arian Bishops, to the effect "that it was not his province to take cognisance of their decisions with reference to the expulsion of Bishops from their Churches," and Julius's reply, which asserts that a "canon of the Church ordains that Churches ought not to make decrees contrary to the decree of the Bishop of Rome." *H. E. l.* ii. *c.* 15, 17.

SOZOMEN.

A.D. 445.

67. "It is a sacerdotal law that the things done contrary to the decree of the Bishop of the Romans be looked upon as null." (Εἶναι γὰρ νόμον ἱερατικὸν, ὡς ἄκυρα ἀποφαίνειν, τὰ παρὰ γνώμην πραττόμενα τοῦ Ῥωμαίων ἐπισκόπου.) *H. E. l.* iii. *c.* 10, *p.* 245.

COMMENT.

This is an account of an appeal of the great S. Athanasius, Paul, Patriarch of Constantinople, and other Bishops, who had been deprived of their Sees by the Arians, to S. Julius, Bishop of Rome. The following most important facts are attested by Socrates : (1) That these Bishops came to Rome for the purpose just mentioned : (2) That the Pope entertained their appeal ; (3) That by virtue of a "Prerogative peculiar to the Church of Rome," he restored each to his See, and sent them back armed with his "authoritative" letters ; and (4) That he severely blamed those who had deprived those Prelates ; and on their disputing his authority, he informed them that according to ecclesiastical law no decisions of the Churches are valid unless sanctioned by the Bishop of Rome." The salient point in the account is the allusion to a " Prerogative peculiar to the Church of Rome," as a right fully acknow-leged by the Universal Church, and especially by the great Athanasius, the illustrious defender of the Faith, who received back his See, by means of the exercise of this Prerogative. The Greek word πρεσνομία, translated " Preroga-tive," signifies a privilege, derived not merely from a canon or statute, but from universal usage, that is, from the Common Law of the Church. And Socrates witnesses to several rights which proceeded from this Papal Pre-rogative, viz. the right to judge epi-scopal causes, and to restore Bishops unjustly deprived, and to assent to or veto (for this is inferred) the decrees of the Churches. These rights were not derived from the Council of Sardica, or indeed from any Council, but from an-cient usage. Sozomen puts it more strongly, "It is a sacerdotal law that the things done contrary to the de-cree of the Bishop of the Romans be looked upon as null." There cannot be a more exhaustive testimony in favour of the Papal Supremacy than that given by those two ecclesiastical historians, which may be thus summed, up; viz. Nothing can be done, no decree, or judgment, or ordinance, can bind the whole Church, without the consent of the reigning Pontiff.

S. VINCENT OF LERINS.

A. D. 445.

68. ". . . . Pope Stephen, Pre-late of the Apostolic See, resisted with the rest of his colleagues in-deed, but still beyond the rest; thinking it, I suppose, becoming that he should excel all the rest as much in devotion for the faith as he surpassed them in authority of place." (*Si reliquos omnes tantum fidei devotione vinceret, quantum loci autoritate superabat.*) *Adv. Hæres. n.* 6. *Migne, t.* 49, *pp.* 445–6.

69. "And for proof that not Greece alone, or the East only, but also the Western and Latin world, were always of the same opinion, there were also read there (at the Council of Ephesus) some letters of S. Felix Martyr, and of S. Julius, Bishop of the City of Rome, ad-dressed to certain individuals. And that not only the Head of the world but also the other parts, might give their testimony to that judgment; from the South they had Cyprian." *Ib. n.* 30. *Ib.* 681.

COMMENT.

The testimony of this Father is espe-cially valuable, and ought to be con-clusive with Anglican Divines and Theo-logians, for, from the Reformation down to this time, they have appealed to his doctrine as justifying their position and state of separation in Christendom. The famous saying, *Quod semper, quod ubique, et quod ab omnibus traditum est,* (whatever has been held always, every-where, by everyone) has been relied upon as their mainstay. But they have overlooked what he asserts with regard to the Roman Church. He affirms that the Pope surpasses his colleagues in the episcopate, "in au-thority of place," and also that he is the "Head of the world." "Au-thority of place," and "the Head of the world," must be taken together in order to ascertain S. Vincent's doctrine. The Head is of course the governing member of the body; and inasmuch as the Head is the governor and ruler of the body, it necessarily surpasses all other members "in authority of place." The hand and the foot are members of the body equally with the Head, but who is there that would assert that either the hand or the foot have power to direct the movements of the body, or control the will and the mind ? At best they are but instruments of, and subject to the will and authority of the Head, for carrying into effect what it wills. S. Vincent believed that the Roman Pontiff filled this position in the Body mystical, the Church; and therefore it was that he, "the Head of the world," surpassed all the Bishops "in authority of place." Anglican theologians have accepted his rule respecting tradition, but they have paid no regard to S. Vincent's allusion to a living authority. The works of the Fathers are invaluable, but they need interpretation. Plenary Councils can be but seldom celebrated; but there is one authority which never dies, *i.e.*, "The Head of the world," who surpasses all bishops "in authority of place"—the Sovereign Pontiff.

VICTOR VITENSIS.

A. D. 490.

70. "If the king wishes to know our faith, which is the one true faith, let him send to his friends, and I too will write to my brethren, that my fellow-bishops may come —men who may be able with me to demonstrate to you our common faith ; and especially the Roman Church, which is the Head of all the Churches (*et præcipue Ecclesia Romana, quæ caput est omnium ecclesiarum.*") *De Persec. Afric. l.* ii. *c.* 18, *p.* 215, *Migne.*

S. AVITUS.

A. D. 494.

71. "We were anxious in mind, and fearful, in the matter of the Church of Rome, as feeling our own position tottered, in that our Head was assailed (*in lacessito vertice*). If the Pope of that city is called into question, not a Bishop merely, but the Episcopacy will now seem to totter." (*si Papa urbis vocatur in dubium, episcopatus jam videbitur, non episcopus vacillare*). *Ep.* xxxi. *Galland. t.* x. *p.* 724.

72. "As you know that it is the law of the Councils that, if any doubt have arisen in matters which regard the state of the Church, we are to have recourse to the Chief Priest of the Roman Church, —like members adhering to (following) our Head,—I have, with the consent of the Bishop of Vienne, sent with anxiety our service of due veneration (*quasi ad caput nostrum, membra sequentia recurramus . . . . debitæ venerationis obsequium*) to the holy Hormisdas, or to whomsoever else may now be Pope." *Ep.* xxxvi. *Galland. t.* x. *p.* 726.

COMMENT.

S. Avitus had expressed his belief that S. Peter was "the Prince of the Princes," that is, while all the Apostles were Kings in the Kingdom of Christ, S. Peter was appointed King over them, to whom they were to look up to as the Rock (as his name signifies), from whom they were to seek confirmation in the faith, and by whom, as the Chief Shepherd, they were to be sustained. Holding S. Peter's arch-principality in the Apostolate, we are prepared for what this Father affirms respecting the Pope. He says, if that one Head—the Church of Rome—be assailed, we feel "that our own position tottered;" "if the Pope of that city is called in question, not a Bishop merely, but the Episcopate (*i.e.* all the Bishops) will now seem to totter." What a picture does this gives us of the real constitution of the Catholic Church in the primitive ages. How thoroughly dependent was every member of the ecclesiastical polity on its living visible Head. As in the case of the human body, if the head be assailed, and struck down, every limb is paralysed, or if not paralysed, moves violently in every direction, without order or method, and the body itself becomes convulsed. Of all the members of the body none is so delicate as the head, none so liable to injury. Hence the anxiety of this Father for the safety of the Pope as the Head and Chief Priest of the sacerdotal order; for, if assailed, their position also immediately "totters," that is, it is liable in consequence to be paralysed. There can be no doubt that heretics had many advantages in the early primitive times, when by reason of the fearful persecutions, the Papal authority was by the force of circumstances more or less inactive. The "Head was as-

sailed," and the members were left to their own resources. During the abeyance of the Papal power, Gnosticism, Arianism, &c., the fruitful mothers of innumerable heresies, were able to take root in the Church: it was not till the Papacy asserted and used the divine power, authority, and jurisdiction, that they were rooted out and the Church restored to orthodoxy and unity. General Councils indeed have made decrees, but they were powerless to execute them without the action of the Sovereign Pontiff. The Church is indebted to a Julius, who restored Athanasius; to a Damasus, to an Innocent, to a Celestine, and to a Leo, for the maintenance of the Faith, the destruction of error, and the restoration of unity to the storm-tossed Churches. And it is to be observed that the Church has never been so united as when the authority of the Sovereign Pontiff was fully respected and obeyed.

S. Avitus then affirmed a most important truth, that the Episcopate totters if "that one Head, the Roman Church, be assailed;" and in this he agrees with S. Ambrose, who in his day admonished the Emperor, "not to suffer the Head of the world—the Roman Church —to be thrown into confusion, for thence flow to all the rights of venerable communion." This Father also counselled that "if any doubt arise in matters which regard the state of the Church," we should have recourse to the Chief Priest of the Roman Church, like members adhering to their Head." This is in accordance with the example of S. Jerome, who sought the counsel of the Pope when the Eastern Church was torn to pieces with heresy and schism.

IT has already been proved that S. Peter came to Rome, and there, with S. Paul, founded and constituted the Holy Roman Church. The evidence adduced in this Section proves demonstratively the Supremacy of the Roman Church and of its Sovereign Pontiff over the whole Catholic Church, by virtue of the institution of the Apostles S. Peter and S. Paul, previous to their martyrdom.

1. We are informed by the Fathers (1) That the Roman Church was "founded and constituted by the two most glorious Apostles Peter and Paul;" (2) That the Sheep were first "entrusted to Peter," and subsequently to his Successors; (3) That the Chair of the Roman Church "is the Chair of Peter," "in which sat the Head of all the Apostles Peter;" (4) That "from the Chair of Peter itself, unto whom the Lord after His Resurrection committed His Sheep to be fed, down even to the present Bishop" of Rome, *i. e.* to Peter and his Successors in the Roman Church, "the feeding of the universal Flock was committed;" (5) That consequently the City and Church of Rome has ever been regarded by Catholics as "the Place of Peter," containing "the Chair of Peter," and known as pre-eminently "the Apostolic See," "the See of Peter," &c.

The Fathers then were not slow to acknowledge the great truth that "Peter lives and presides in his own See;" that is, that each of his Successors to his Chair or Cathedra, exercises his jurisdiction over all the Church. Whatever, then, are the rights and prerogatives of the Roman Church and the Roman Pontiff, these derive their origin solely from the Apostle S. Peter, who received from Christ a three-fold commission, viz. to exercise His Supreme Jurisdiction, as symbolised by the exclusive gift of the keys; to confirm in the Faith his Brethren of the Apostolate, and to Shepherdise the entire Flock.

2. By virtue, then, of Rome and the Roman Church becoming the "Place of Peter," wherein is erected "the Chair of Peter," the Church became necessarily the "Foundation," "the Root," "the Matrix," and tho "Mother" of all the Churches upon earth, from which "the unity of the Priesthood took its rise," and from which "the right of venerable communion flows to all."

Such, then, was the position of the Church of Rome, in consequence of the establishment therein of "the Chair or Cathedra of Peter," wherein sits his Successor for the time being, who represents and executes the commission which S. Peter received exclusively from his Lord and Master.

3. Hence it followed that the Fathers describe the Roman Church (1) As the Presiding Church; " presiding in the region of the Romans," " Presiding over the Love"—*i.e.* the Church—"with the Name of Christ, and with the Name of the Father ;" (2) As the Church possessing a " Superior or more powerful Principality ;" (3) As "the Chief Church ;" (4) As " Head of all the Churches ;" (5) As having "the Sovereignty over all Churches throughout the Universe," whence the " Princedom of the Apostolic Chair has always been in force," whence " the unity of the Priesthood took its rise," and with which Church all other Churches " must agree or assemble with," that is, be in its communion.

4. Hence, also, the Bishop of Rome has been styled (1) " The Presiding Bishop ;" (2) "Supreme Pontiff ;" (3) " The Bishop of Bishops ;" (4) " The Interpreter of God ;" (5) " The Good Shepherd ;" (6) " President over the Church of God ;" (7) " Archbishop of the whole habitable globe," as well as "Father and Patriarch of the mighty City of Rome ;" and (8) Chief and Head of the Church.

5. It is natural to suppose, that if the Church of Rome and the Supreme Pontiff were to occupy so exalted a position as the *Locum tenens* of the blessed Apostle Peter, God would so protect this Church as that it should never fall from the Faith, for if it should, the whole Church would fall likewise—which if the word of Christ is to be relied upon, is an impossibility. Accordingly, the Fathers do not scruple to say (1) That the Church of Rome " is enlightened in the Will of God ;" (2) That the Chair of Peter " is the Seat of Faith ;" (3) That the Pope is the Builder of the Edifice, *i.e.* of Faith ; (4) That the Roman Church " is all-Godly, all-gracious, all-blessed, all-praised, all-prospering, and all-hallowed ;" (5) That " faithlessness has no access ;" and (6) That it is " free from all taint of heresy."

Certain it is, that while every other Apostolic Throne has fallen from the Faith, even to a denial of the divinity and of the human nature of the Lord Jesus Christ, and even to this day refusing to affirm the truth that the Holy Ghost proceeds from the Son—thereby dividing the Substance— the Apostolic See has ever taught the Faith, the whole Faith, and nothing but the Faith, as it was received from the beginning. Not a single one of Rome's Bishops, when teaching *ex Cathedrâ*, has ever propounded a heresy. Liberius may have fallen under pressure ; Honorius may have suffered himself to be deceived (a heretic he certainly was not, if we may interpret his epistles literally) ; other Popes, or private Doctors, may have entertained contradictory opinions on theological questions, but as Sovereign Pontiff, exercising the Supreme Jurisdiction as derived from S. Peter, when teaching the Church, and when defining the Truth received from their predecessors, none have ever departed from the Faith, and every dogma that has been promulgated by Popes, whether it be Transubstantiation or the Immaculate Conception, will be found in harmony with Scripture Revelations and the Tradition of the Holy Catholic Church. " Faithlessness has (never had) any access" to the Holy Roman Church ; that has ever been " free from all taint of heresy."

6. The Prerogatives of the Roman Church and the Sovereign

Pontiff, naturally, follow from the presence of the " Chair of Peter." Upon this point the Fathers speak with great clearness. They assert (1) That "the Princedom of the Apostolic See" has always been in force in the Roman Church, *i. e.* that the Sovereign Pontiffs for the time being, possess in themselves supreme Jurisdiction over the whole Church, and over all persons and causes appertaining to the Church ; (2) That they are Supreme Judges over all causes of Faith, for Bishops "cannot, without the consent of the Bishop of the City of Rome, hear causes of Faith ;" (3) That the Bishop of Rome is Supreme over every Province and Diocese of the universal Church, for " to the Head, that is, to the Apostle Peter," " who lives and presides in his own See," " the Priests (Bishops) of the Lord from every one of the Provinces" should "refer ;" (4) That he is the Visitor, personally, or by his Legates, or by his Letters, of every province and diocese of the universal Church, to which he may address " very full Letters," admonishing and censuring, as the case demands, any Bishop or Bishops he deems expedient ; and (5) That he is Supreme over all Councils—Œcumenical, plenary, and provincial—and that Councils cannot lawfully determine any question of Faith without reference to Rome, nor may any decree of any sort be promulged "contrary to the decree of the Bishop of Rome ;" (6) That it is a Sacerdotal Law that "things done contrary to the decree of the Bishop of Rome is null ;" and (7) That where Bishops have been deposed by plenary or provincial Councils, the Pope can, if he deems there is sufficient cause, restore them by means of his " Letters."

7. The Fathers are very explicit as to what they understand by the Catholic Church ; and their testimony on this point brings out into high relief the exalted position of the Holy Roman See. They understand the " Catholic Church" to be that Body which is in union with the Roman Church. Of the many Chairs or Cathedræ which are scattered all over the Catholic world, one " Chair or Cathedra" is regarded as so pre-eminently exalted, as (so to speak) to throw all other " Chairs" into the shade. " God is One, and Christ is one, and the Church is one, and the Chair is one, founded by the Lord's word upon a Rock," *i. e.* upon Peter, upon whom the Church was "founded first and alone." As then, there is but one Lord and one Church, so is there but one Chair, " in which sat of all the Apostles the Head Peter . . . . that in this one Chair unity might be preserved by all." None of the other Apostles ever contended " for a distinct Chair for himself:" by which we learn the truth, that he who should "set up another Chair against the Single Chair" might be known as "a schismatic and a sinner." Hence the Chair of Peter at Rome is the first mark or note by which the Catholic Church is known. The Catholic Church, then, is that Body which is in union with the Chair of Peter, in which he ever lives and presides in the persons of his Successors ; and that Church or other Community which is not in union with that Chair is heretical and schismatical, "for they have not Peter's inheritance who have not Peter's Chair."

(2.) Again, the Fathers understand by the words " Catholic Bishops" Bishops in communion with the Roman Church. It was that great Doctor, S. Ambrose, who furnished the test whereby we should be able to discern whether a Bishop is a Catholic Bishop. "He (Satyrus) called the Bishop to him . . . . he inquired of him whether he agreed (or assembled) with—(*i. e.* whether he was in communion with)—the Catholic Bishops, that is with the Roman Church." So that, to be a Catholic Bishop, it is essential that he should be in outward, as well as internal communion with the Apostolic See.

(3) Once more, the "rights of venerable communion" flow from the Head of the Roman Church, so that adhesion to the Roman Head is absolutely essential to the lawful use of the Blessed Sacraments of the Church, and for the right exercise of ecclesiastical discipline. This doctrine is supported by the remarkable saying of S. Jerome: "Upon this Rock I know the Church is built. Whosoever eats the Lamb out of this House (*i. e.* Roman Church) is profane." Again, "Whosoever gathereth not with thee (the Pope), that is, whosoever is not of Christ, is of Antichrist;" that is, he that is not in union with the Pope as the Vicar of Christ, "is of Antichrist." The Holy Catholic Church, then, is that Body—and exclusively that Body—which is in living communion with the Sovereign Pontiff; whose episcopal Chairs are in union and in subordination to the "Single Chair," which stands in the Roman Church; and whose rights of venerable communion derive their source and supply from the Head of the Roman Church.

Anglicans and Protestants will, doubtless, assert anew the co-equality of all Bishops; and they will point to the strong statements of S. Ignatius and S. Cyprian, but they must not forget that both these Fathers have given overpowering evidence in favour of the Roman Supremacy. No language can be more explicit than that of S. Ignatius, nor stronger than that of S. Cyprian. They, indeed, laid great stress on the dignity and perfect independence within his own diocese of every individual Bishop; but, notwithstanding, both these Fathers taught distinctly and unequivocally the superiority of the Roman Church. The former asserted it was the Presiding Church—"presiding in the region of the Romans; presiding over the Love." The latter described it as the "Chief Church, whence the unity of the Priesthood (Episcopate) took its rise." And S. Cyprian had occasion to give effect to this his belief, for he it was who urged Pope S. Stephen to take action in Gaul for the expulsion of Marcianus, Bishop of Arles, to which he would have had no right except as the Head and Chief Bishop of the Universal Church.

The evidence of the Fathers of the first five centuries proves that by virtue of S. Peter having planted his Chair in Rome, and having there erected the Roman Church into a Presiding Church, or Principal Church, the Sovereign Pontiffs have ever possessed a superior jurisdiction over the Universal Church, to them has been committed its government, and the charge of feeding the Sheep and Lambs of Christ. This right, be it observed, is derived from no merely ecclesiastical source, but from Christ, through His Vicar, S. Peter.

II.

TESTIMONY OF ŒCUMENICAL AND PLENARY COUNCILS.

COUNCIL OF NICÆA.

FIRST ŒCUMENICAL.

A.D. 325.

1. The Council summoned by the Authority of the Holy See and of the Emperor.

73. "Arius, the divider of the Trinity, arose, and forthwith Constantine always Augustus, and Silvester, of praiseworthy memory, assembled the great and famous Synod at Nicæa." *Sermo. Prosphonet. Concil. ad Constant.* (iv.) *Imp.* vide *Concil. Œcumen.* vi. *Act.* xviii. *Hard. act. Concil. Collect. T.* iii. *col.* 1418.

2. Selection of Bishops.

74. "As soon as the evil of heresy began to reach that pitch which the Arian blasphemy has now attained, three hundred and eighteen of our Fathers were selected by the most holy Bishop of Rome to deliberate on the subject at Nice." *Dam. ad. Epis. Illyric. apud. Theod H. E. l.* ii. *c.* 22.

3. Hosius President of the Council and Legate of the Holy See.

75. "For concerning that truly great and happy old man Osius (Hosius), concerning whose sanctity it is needless to speak, inasmuch as it is well known to all, and to the Fathers themselves who were driven into exile ; for he was not an obscure old man, but of all men the most illustrious ; for did he not in the summer preside (or lead) the Synod (*i. e.* of Nicæa) (πoίας γὰρ οὐ καθηγήσατο συνόδου)." *S. Athan. Oper. T.* i. *Apolog. de fuga sua, n.* 5, *p.* 649, *Migne.*

76. "The most celebrated person of the Spaniards (Hosius) took his seat among the rest. The Prelate of the Imperial city was absent

through age, but his Presbyters were present, and filled his place." *Eus. Vit. Constant. l.* iii. *c.* 7.

77. " Hosius was, I believe, Bishop of Cordova in Spain, as I have before stated ; Vito and Vincentius presbyters of Rome ; Alexander, Bishop of Egypt (Alexandria); Anastathius, of Antiochia Magna ; Macarius, of Jerusalem ; and Harpocration, of Cynopolis, were present. The names of the rest are fully reported in *The Synodicon* of Athanasius, Bishop of Alexandria." *Soc. H. E. l.* i. *c.* 13.

78. " The author (Eusebius) relates that Osius (Hosius), Bishop of Cordova, and Bito (Vito) and Vincentius, priests of the Church of Rome, Legates, were present." *Gelas. Cyzicen. Hist. Concil. Nicæni Admonit. Migne, T.* 85 (*Series gr.*) *col.* 1188.

79. " Osius (Hosius) himself, also celebrated by name and for his great reputation, who obtained the place (ἐπίχων καὶ τὸν τόπον) of Silvester, Bishop of Great Rome, together with the Roman Presbyters

Bito (Vito) and Vincentius, and many others, were present sitting with him (in the Council). *Ib. l.* ii. *c.* v. *col.* 1230.

80. " The holy, great, and universal synod of holy Fathers assembled at Nicæa, through the blessed and holy Osius (Hosius), himself Bishop of Cordova in Spain, holding the place of the Bishop of Rome (ἐπίχοντας καὶ τὸν τόπον τοῦ τῆς 'Ρωμαίων ἐπισκόπου), with the aforesaid Presbyters of the same See (of Rome), gives another interpretation." *Ib. c.* xii. *col.* 1250.

81. " But since mention has been made of the aforesaid Osius (Hosius), it is necessary to intimate to all Catholics that this same honourable man was present among the CCCXVIII. most holy Fathers at Nicæa, in Bithynia ; and that he, with the Presbyters Vincentius and Victor (Vito ?), was appointed by the Apostolic See" (to represent it.) *Leo. T.* ii. *De Ant. Collection. et Collect. Can. Append. ad Opera. Pars* III. *c.* ii. *col.* clxxxvii. *J. and P. Baller. Venet.* 1757.

4. CONFIRMATION OF ANCIENT CUSTOMS.

82. " Let the ancient customs prevail, namely, those in Egypt, and Libya, and Pentapolis ; let the Bishop of Alexandria have power over all these, seeing that the same is customary with the Bishop of Rome (ἐπειδὴ καὶ τῷ ἐκ τῇ 'Ρώμη ἐπισκόπῳ τοῦτο σύνηθές ἐστιν). Likewise, in Antioch and other provinces, let the privileges be secured

to the Churches. Saving to the Metropolis (*i. e.* Constantinople) its proper dignity, let the Bishop of Ælia (Jerusalem) have the next place of precedence ; because custom and ancient tradition has obtained that he should be honoured." *Can.* vi. vii. *Labbé, S. Concil. T.* ii. *col.* 35.

5. THE PASCHAL QUESTION.

83. " We have the gratifying intelligence to communicate to you, conducive to unity of judgment on the subject of the most holy feast

of Easter ; for this point which has been happily settled, through your prayers, so that all the brethren in the East who have heretofore kept this feast when the Jews did (*i. e.* the Passover), will henceforth conform to the Romans and to us, and to all who from the earliest times have observed our period of celebrating Easter." *Synod. Ep. Alexand. Eccles. Soc. H. E. l. i. c.* 9.

6. SYNODICAL EPISTLE TO THE POPE.

84. "Forasmuch as all things concerning the divine mysteries have been enforced to ecclesiastical profit, which pertained to the strength of the Holy Catholic and Apostolic Church, we report them to your Roman See, having translated them from the Greek. Whatever, then, we have ordained in the Council of Nicæa, we pray may be confirmed by the fellowship of your countenance" (*Quidquid autem constituimus in concilio Nicæno, precamur vestri oris consortio confirmetur*). *Labb. T.* ii. *col.* 79.

COMMENT.

There have been many disputes between Anglican and Catholic controversialists respecting the Papal position in the first great Œcumenical Council which assembled at Nicæa. As nothing remains of that Council save the Creed and the Canons, and the Synodical epistles, no *explicit* testimony is to be found, one way or the other. There is, however, some *implicit* evidence to be obtained from the decrees and Synodical Epistles, and some collateral, sufficient at least to prove the superior pre-eminence of the Roman Church.

1. The Sixth Œcumenical Council informs us that the Nicene Council was summoned by the joint authority of the Emperor and the Pope, that is to say, that the Prelates of the Catholic Church were convened by the Pope's command, and that the Emperor consented to the convocation, and provided for the necessary expenses of the Bishops.

2. According to Theodoret, the 318 Fathers assembled at Nicæa "were selected by the most holy Bishop of Rome to deliberate on the Arian heresy," &c. It is true this passage in his history is disputed, but Valesius maintains its genuineness.

3. Eusebius informs us that the Pope appointed certain Presbyters, who "were present at the Council, and filled his place." This expression reminds us of a similar one in S. Cyprian's Epistle to Cornelius, in which he spoke of the Roman See or Cathedra as the "Place of Peter." What, then, was the nature of this "Place" which the Papal Legates filled at Nicæa? Without doubt "the place" of S. Silvester the Pope, the Chief of all the Brotherhood, and the Supreme Pastor of the entire Flock, who himself filled the "Place of Peter" in the city and Church of Rome. The Pope, then, by his representatives, occupied in the Council of Nicæa the primatial "Place of Peter."

It is, however, a matter of dispute whether Hosius, or Osius, presided over the Council as Legate of the Pope. That he did preside in that character is attested by Gelasius Cyzenicus and by Pope S. Leo, who both say that he did; the former stating more than once in his history, that he "obtained his (Pope Silvester's) Place." S. Athanasius also infers the same in his "*Apologia de fuga sua.*" Two reasons suffice, it is submitted, to show that this must have been the case. First, it may be affirmed that if the Papal authority was so far acknowledged that the Council itself was summoned by the Pope, no less than by the Emperor (as the Sixth Œcumenical Council informs us, and the Fathers must have seen the Acts, now unfortunately lost), it seems self-evident that the Pope must have presided, either

N

in person or by deputy. For it is an axiom in the science of government that he who possesses the Prerogative of summoning his whole order to the Council Chamber, must of necessity be entitled to preside over it, and direct and control the proceedings, for none can lawfully summon a whole kingdom (and the Church is an Universal Empire) by its representatives, to a General Council or Parliament, unless he is the recognised Head and Chief. This Prerogative principle we may perceive carried out in miniature in every part of the Church. The Bishop has the power to summon, preside over, direct and control the Diocesan Synod; the Metropolitan similarly the provincial Council; and the Patriarch likewise his General Council, composed of the Metropolitans and Bishops of the several provinces comprising his patriarchate. So in like manner the Pope, inasmuch as he is the Head of the Universal Episcopate, alone possesses and exercises the right of convocating or calling an Œcumenical Council. No doubt the Emperor's authority was needed, and for this simple reason, that the Pope could not lawfully collect a vast number of Bishops from various parts of the earth, to meet in a city within the Emperor's dominions without his permission and assistance. Hence it was, as the Sixth Œcumenical Council asserts, that the Council of Nicæa was assembled by "Constantine, always Augustus, and Silvester of praiseworthy memory." Upon the ground then of the Papal Prerogative of summoning a Universal Council his right of presiding is proved, and therefore Hosius must have occupied the place of President on behalf of the Pope, as his Vicar and Legate. But there is another reason why this must have been the case, and this is found in the circumstance of Hosius subscribing first, followed immediately by the two Roman Priests. On this point Héféle well argues. He writes, " Schröckle says that Osius was the first to sign, on account of his great credit with the Emperor; but this reasoning is very weak; the Bishops did not sign according to the greater or lesser degree of favour they had with Constantine. If this rule had been followed, Eusebius of Cæsarea ought to have been one of the first to sign. It is important to know in what order the signatures of the Council were given. The study of the lists proves that they followed the order by province. The Metropolitan signed first, and after him followed the Suffragans; the Metropolitan of another province then signed, and after him came the signatures of the Suffragan Bishops of his province. As to the enumeration of the provinces themselves no regular plan was adopted; thus the province of Alexandria came in the first line, then that of Thebaid and Lybia; after which Palestine, Phœnicia; and after the latter, only, the See of Antioch. At the head of each list of signatures was always inscribed the name of the ecclesiastical province to which they belonged; but this indication is omitted in the signature of Osius, and in those of the two Roman Priests. They sign the first, and without the designation of the diocese. It may be objected, perhaps, that the Synod being principally composed of Greek Bishops, it was wished to pay the compliment to Western Bishops by letting them sign first, but this hypothesis is inadmissible, for at the end of the list of signatures at the Council are found the names of the representatives of the ecclesiastical provinces of the Latin Church. Since Gaul and Africa were placed at the end, the province of Spain would certainly have been added to them, if Osius had only represented this province at Nicæa, and if he had not possessed a higher dignity which entitled him to a far superior position. The two Roman Priests did not represent a particular Church, but the directorium of the whole Synod; therefore no name of any diocese is placed above their signatures—a fresh proof that in him and his colleagues we must recognise the πρόεδροι of which Eusebius speaks. The analogy of the other Councils permits us to come to the same conclusion, in particular the analogy of the Council of Ephesus, in which Cyril of Alexandria, who performed the functions of Papal Legate, as Osius did at Nicæa, signed the first before all his colleagues." *Héfèle. Hist. Concil. T: i. Introd.* § 5, *pp.* 41, 42.*

There can be no room for doubting that Hosius, or Osius, really did preside at the Council of Nicæa as Legate of the Pope, and that in that character he subscribed the decrees.

4. " Let the ancient customs prevail." If the Roman See was really the " Place of Peter," as S. Cyprian asserted ; if the Roman Church was the " Chief Church, from which the unity of the Priesthood took its rise," as this same Father alleged ; if this great Church was, as S. Irenæus said, " a Superior or more powerful Principality ;" if the Roman Church " Presided over the Love,"—*i. e.* the Church and the Sacraments—as S. Ignatius declared, then whatever was customary in connexion with the exercise of the Prerogative of the Holy See, without doubt they received in these words, " Let the ancient customs prevail "—a synodical recognition and confirmation. If the language of the Fathers above named had been regarded as heretical ; if the assertions of some of these same Fathers, together with Origen and Tertullian, respecting

the exalted dignity and position of S. Peter, had been false ;—if the appeal of the Corinthians to Pope S. Clement, and S. Clement's reply ; the appeal of Marcion, the interference of S. Victor in the affairs of the East, and S. Stephen in those of France, at S. Cyprian's instigation ; and also in the matter of Rebaptism in Africa, in which S. Cyprian was concerned,—were uncanonical and contrary to lawful custom, the great Council of Nicæa would have been careful when confirming the "ancient customs" of the Churches, to add a protest against Roman ambition and arrogance. But the Council on this point is silent, and by its silence recognises and approves the " ancient customs" of the Roman Church, no less than those of all other Churches.

But this canon, in confirming the " ancient customs," expressly points to the Roman Church as the authority for the settlement of what " ancient customs" are lawful. This may be inferred from the following language, " Let the ancient customs prevail, namely, those in Egypt, and Libya, and Pentapolis ; let the Bishop of Alexandria have power over all these, seeing that the same is customary for the Bishop of Rome. † Likewise in Antioch and other provinces, let the privileges be secured to the Churches." It is manifest that the customs of this Church of Rome were regarded by the Council as of sufficient authority for the guidance of

---

* Translated from the French of M. l'Abbé Goschlen, et M. l'Abbé Delarc. Paris, 1869.

† The following remarks upon Rufinus, in connexion with this canon, made by Fleury, are very apposite :—" Rufinus, who lived in the same century as the Council of Nicæa, explains the power which is attributed to the Pope in this canon (6th), by saying that he had the care of the suburbicarian Churches, which signifies some extent of provinces subject to Rome in a particular manner. But whatever this obscure word (suburbicarian) means, it only regards the Bishop of Rome as the Patriarch of the West, without prejudice of his position as Chief of the Universal Church, so well established in the preceding centuries. However, it is thought that the attempts of the Meletians against the jurisdiction of the Bishop of Alexandria were the occasion of this canon." *Fleury, H. E. l.* xi. *c.* xx. *p.* 148, 9. *Paris,* 1693.

other Churches. This is a recognition at least of the Pre-eminence of the Roman Church.

The canons may be regarded as a full confirmation of the rights and liberties of all Churches, inclusive of Rome, so that whatever Prerogatives the Church of Rome enjoyed from the beginning —and these have been to a great extent described by the preceding Fathers —were fully recognised by this Council.

5. Another point is to be noted. The important question of the proper time for observing Easter had long been in dispute. There were two traditions, one from S. Peter, which observed the Paschal solemnity on the Sunday, and the other from S. John, which celebrated it on the actual anniversary of our Lord's Resurrection. Various attempts had been made to establish uniformity of practice, but without effect. S. Polycarp travelled all the way from Smyrna to Rome to induce the Pope to conform to S. John's rule, and S. Victor, some forty years after, endeavoured to compel the East to submit to the tradition of S. Peter. It was reserved for the Council of Nicæa, if not to effect this object, at least to confirm the Roman custom ; "for that point also," so says the Synodical epistle, "has been happily settled through your prayers, so that all the brethren in the East, who have heretofore kept this festival when the Jews did, will henceforth conform to the Romans and to us, and to all who from the earliest times have observed our period of celebrating Easter." The question arises, Why the Roman custom,

more than that of the East? The only answer is, that in conflicting traditions of discipline the. Roman custom is that which should prevail ; and this, without doubt, because of the Supremacy of S. Peter, and of his Successors, who occupy his "Place." This is another implicit proof in favour of the superior authority of the Roman Church.

From what remains of the proceedings of the Council of Nicæa as collected from early ecclesiastical historians, and such decrees as have been preserved, we learn (1) That the Council was summoned by the joint authority of the Emperor and Pope S. Silvester ; (2) That the 318 Bishops who sat in the Council were selected by the Pope ; (3) That he appointed Legates to represent him, "who were present and filled his place ;" and (4) That the customs of the Churches were to prevail, and that when custom was diverse and conflicting, the practice of the Roman Church must be followed. From what little has come down to us concerning this Council, it is reasonable to conclude that the acts, had they been preserved, would have contained much valuable evidence for the Supremacy of the Holy See ; but sufficient has been adduced to prove the high Pre-eminence of that Church and its Bishop, whose legates, though two of them were Presbyters, took precedence of all the Patriarchs and Bishops, their subscription to the decrees having been affixed first in order, because of the Place of S. Silvester, which they by delegation filled.

COUNCIL OF SARDICA.

A.D. 347.

APPEALS TO THE POPE.

85. " If judgment be passed upon any Bishop, and he thinks he has sufficient grounds for referring the matter to another judgment ; let us honour the memorial (*memoriam*) of the holy Apostle Peter, by providing that the parties who entertained the case shall write to Julius, Bishop of Rome, and if he judges that a trial be renewed, let

it be renewed." *Can.* III. *Labb. Concil. T.* ii. *col.* 659.

86. " To this let it be added, that when a Bishop has been deposed by the neighbouring Bishops, no Bishop shall after such appeal be substituted in the Chair until the case has been determined by the judgment of the Bishop of Rome." *Can.* iv. *Ib.*

87. " If a Bishop shall have been accused, and sentence passed by the Bishops of his own district assembled in Council, and they shall have deposed him from his See (grade) ; if the said Bishop shall appeal to the Bishop of the Roman Church, and request a hearing, if it seems to him right that the judgment should be renewed, he may deign to write to the Bishops of the neighbouring provinces, requiring them diligently to re-examine the whole case, and decide according to the truth. But if he who asked his case to be reheard shall move by his entreaty the Bishop of Rome to send his Presbyters *de latere suo*, it shall be in the power of the (said) Bishop to exercise his own discretion ; and if he shall judge that they (the Legates) shall be sent, invested with his authority, let it be so as he shall determine. But if, on the other hand, he is of opinion that the Bishops (of the province or neighbourhood), are not sufficient to terminate the matter, let him act as he shall determine according to his own most wise judgment." *Can.* vii. *Ib. col.* 646.

2. SYNOD. EPISTLE TO THE POPE.

88. " For this seems to be the best and most suitable, if the Priests of the Lord in every province refer to the Head, that is to the Apostolic See of Peter" (*si ad caput, id est, ad Petri Apostoli sedem*). *Ib. col.* 690.

COMMENT.

This Council was summoned by order of the Emperors, and it assembled in May A. D. 347. There were upwards of 300 Bishops present—some from Spain, Gaul (France), Italy, Africa, Macedonia, Palestine, Cappadocia, Pontus, Cilicia, the Thebaid, Syria, Thrace, Mesopotamia, &c. Among these, or perhaps in addition, there were about eighty of the Eusebian party, who were semi-Arians, whose object was the condemnation of the great S. Athanasius.

The testimony of this plenary council to the Supremacy of the Chair of S. Peter is very full and complete. Great abuses arising from frequent translations of Bishops, Bishop Hosius proposed certain reforms, which were drawn up in the shape of canons of discipline, in which provisions were made for the protection of Bishops unjustly condemned.

1. The first thought that naturally occurred to the Fathers was " the Chair of S. Peter :" " Let us honour the memorial of the holy Apostle Peter." The Fathers of the Church had ever regarded S. Peter as the Prince of the Apostles, the Head of the Brotherhood, and the Chief Pastor of the Flock, and therefore say they, " Let us honour the memorial," that is the Chair, the symbol of authority, or the shrine of the " holy Apostle Peter."*

---

* The word " *memoriam*" signifies more than " memory," or the act of calling to mind a past event, or a person long deceased. It expresses the symbol

2. Their second thought was his Successor, Julius. "Let us honour the memorial of the holy Apostle Peter, by providing that the parties who entertained the case shall write to Julius, Bishop of Rome." Here they couple the names of S. Peter and his Successor, S. Julius, who occupied his Cathedra, exercising his authority and jurisdiction. To him, then, the parties who entertained the case were to write, *i. e.* to report to the Pope. Their report was to be made, not to the Pope as a mere Metropolitan or Patriarch, but to him who, as the Successor of S. Peter, occupied his "Place." That this was so is evident from two circumstances, (1) The connexion between "the holy Apostle Peter" and "Julius," his Successor to his Cathedra, which the Council fully recognised; and (2) The fact that this was the declaration of not Latin Bishops only, but also of such Catholic orientals as were then present, inclusive of the illustrious S. Athanasius.

3. After this follow certain canons of discipline relating to appeals. The Council provides, (1) That after an appeal has been lodged, the Bishop of Rome may, "if he judge" expedient, order a new trial : (2) That pending the appeal, no new Bishop should be substituted in the room of the appellant ; (3) That if a new trial be ordered, the Pope "may deign to write to the Bishops of the neighbouring provinces, requiring them to re-examine the whole case, and decide according

to the truth ;" and, finally, that if the applicant shall desire it, the Pope may "send his Presbyters" (*de latere suo*), invested with his authority; and the case to be decided "as he shall determine." In these three canons the following principles are conceded : (1) The right to hear appeals, either by neighbouring Bishops, *i. e.* of provinces contiguous to that concerned, or by Presbyters whom he may appoint as his Legates, who were to hear the cause on the part, and in the name of the Pope, and "by his authority" determine the same. The words, however, "as he (the Pope) shall determine," may signify more than this ; they may include a further reference to himself ; that is, that the Legates should report the case to the Pope, and that then he would himself finally determine the cause.

4. After passing these canons, the Fathers address the Holy Father in a Synodical Epistle, in which they say, "It seemed to be best and most suitable" that "the Priests (Bishops) of the Lord in every Province," should refer "to the Head, that is the Apostolic See." Here we have a distinct recognition by the 300 Bishops, who were present at this Council, of the Supremacy of the Pope, in his capacity as Successor to S. Peter in his Cathedra.

It has been held that these concessions, as these canons are held to be by some, were personal to Pope S. Julius, and not in recognition of the

---

by which we are reminded of such event or person. In the highest mysteries of the Church, the Sacred Elements, when offered and consecrated, are the memorials of the Great Sacrifice on the Cross, for they represent and typify, and even more than this, for they are the very things which they signify by which the Church carries on and continues the great Sacrifice (after an unbloody manner) till the end of time. Then, again, the Shrine of a Saint in any Church or place is the memorial or representation of the Saint; so also is a tomb or sepulchre in a cemetery the memorial of a departed one. So also in literature, Chronicles and Records are the memorials of history. There is then no violence done in translating the word *memoriam*, as signifying not merely a calling to recollection the great Apostle S. Peter, but his memorial, his symbolical representative, that is his Cathedra and his See, "whence," as S. Cyprian says, "the Unity of the Priesthood took its rise."

Supremacy of the Holy See. If in every instance the name of the Pope had been employed instead of that of his See and his official title, this objection might possibly have been tenable, but at best it would be an exceedingly weak and inconclusive one. But the name only occurs once in the above canon; and there in such intimate connexion with S. Peter, as to show that they were recognising his position, not on account of his personal holiness or capability, but because he occupied the " Place of Peter." In other canons his name does not appear, but his official title, as " until the case has been determined by the judgment of the Bishop of Rome," *i. e.* the Bishop for the time being. Then again the canons allude to his appointing Legates to re-hear and determine a cause on his behalf, which they were to do by " his Authority." Here is a recognition of some special " Authority" in the See of Rome, or, as Socrates expresses it, of " a Prerogative peculiar to the Church of Rome"—something which was not inherent in other Sees. What was that " Authority?" It was the " Authority" of S. Peter exercised by the Bishop for the time being of the Apostolic See; it is " best and most suitable," wrote the Fathers to the Pope, " that the Priests (Bishops) of the Lord in *every* province"— *i.e.* in every part of the Church, East no less than West—should "refer to the Head, that is, to the Apostolic See of Peter." These concessions, then, were not to S. Julius *personally, i. e.* as apart from the See, but to " the Apostolic See," of which he was the then Incumbent.

Nor were these concessions in the strict sense of the term. From the very commencement the Popes have always enjoyed the Prerogative or right of visiting personally, or by deputy, or by letters, every province and diocese of the Universal Church. This visitorial power was exercised by S. Clement, to whom the Church of Corinth appealed against the seditious ; by S. Victor, who threatened the Orientals with excommunication if they did not conform to the Roman method of keeping Easter, which severity, indeed, was protested against, not the right assumed by the Pope ; and by S. Stephen, in the case of the re-baptism of heretics. This visitorial power was set in motion by S. Cyprian himself, when he urged the Pope to coerce the Bishops of Gaul to expel Marcian from the see of Arles. The canons of Sardica contained no new principle of ecclesiastical government ; at best they were but a new application of the ancient common law of the Church, which was judged more conducive to the better enforcement of discipline. Whether this Council is Œcumenical or not does not affect the question under discussion ; which consists rather in the testimony of Catholic Bishops of every province in the West, and of a few in the East, inclusive of S. Athanasius, to the Papal Supremacy, as derived from the "holy Apostle Peter," and " the Apostolic See of Peter," declared to be the " Head" of the Church, and to which " the Priests of the Lord in every province (should) refer."

COUNCIL OF AQUILEIA.

A.D. 381.

89. " . . . Yet your Clemency (the Emperor) should be petitioned not to suffer the Head of the Roman world—the Roman Church—to be thrown into confusion, for thence flow unto all the rights of venerable communion" *(tamen totius orbis Romani caput Romanam ecclesiam . . . . inde enim in omnes venerandæ communionis jura demanant). Synod. Ep. ad Impp. Labb. S. Concil. T. ii. p. 1185.*

COMMENT.

This was a General Council of the West, which assembled to condemn the Arians and other heretical sects which had their origin in them. Among them was Ursinus, the Antipope, who sought the overthrow of the legitimate Pope. S. Ambrose, who had the chief management of this Council, proposed a synodical letter to the Emperor Gratian, which was approved by the Council, in which the Emperor is entreated " not to hear him any more, and firmly to withstand all his importunities, not only because he had favoured the heretics, but because he endeavoured to disturb the Roman Church, which was the Head of the whole Empire, and from which the right of venerable communion extends to all the other Churches." *See Fleury (Newman's tran.) H. E. Bk.* viii. *c.* xvi.

Now, it should be observed, that at the time of S. Ambrose the boundaries of the Roman Empire and the Catholic Church were conterminous. The whole Empire was Christian, and though the Church may have overflowed at that time in a partial degree the limits of the Empire, yet not to any such extent as to justify the notion that the dominion of the Church at this time in any great degree exceeded territorially that of the Empire in its ancient integrity. When then this Western Council affirmed the fact that the Roman Church was the Head of the Roman Empire, as Fleury has it, they meant that the Roman Church and her Pontiff was the Head of the Universal Church, from whom, as from a fountain, " the rights of venerable communion " " flow unto all ;" or according to Fleury, " extend to all the other Churches." This is, indeed, a most remarkable testimony in favour of the universal jurisdiction of the Sovereign Pontiff and of the Roman Church. For observe what it includes, viz. the Patriarchates of Constantinople, Antioch, Alexandria, Jerusalem, and all other sees situated within the Roman Empire, East and West. We see now what the word *caput* (or Head) signifies : not merely as a title of honour or courtesy, but one which implied supreme jurisdiction and authority. For if it did not mean this, how could an Antipope, successfully seizing the Apostolic See, and occupying it in place of the canonical Pope, have the effect of throwing into confusion the whole Church, and of interrupting (for this is necessarily implied) the stream of venerable communion ? It cannot be doubted that this is a most remarkable testimony in behalf of the Roman Supremacy, and coming from so great a Bishop as S. Ambrose, and from the representatives of the provinces of Gaul, Africa, and other parts of the West, it furnishes an overwhelming proof, as to what was held touching the fundamental principle of ecclesiastical government and communion.

COUNCIL OF CONSTANTINOPLE.

SECOND ŒCUMENICAL COUNCIL.

A.D. 381.

1. NECTARIUS.

90. [The Pope was not present at this Council, nor did he send representatives. The following account is given in Fleury's Ecclesiastical History of the election of Nectarius to the See of Constantinople:] "The Emperor recommended it to the Bishops to consider very carefully who was the most worthy, and they were divided about the choice. There was at that time at Constantinople an old man named Nectarius, who was very venerable for his dignity, his age, and graceful appearance. . . . . His virtues, particularly his gentleness, procured him the admiration of everybody, but he was not yet baptized. Being ready to set out in order to return to his own country, he went to visit Diodorus, Bishop of Tarsus, to know if he had any business to be done at home, and to take his letters. Diodorus was then considering with himself upon the choice of the Bishop of Constantinople. When he considered Nectarius' white hair, his majestic countenance, and the gentleness of his disposition, it made him think him worthy to fill that place, and he stopped at that thought. He then consulted the Bishop of Antioch. The Emperor desired the Bishops to write down the names of such as they thought worthy of the See, reserving to himself whom he would choose. He made choice of Nectarius. Everybody was surprised . . . . and when they were informed that he was not so much as baptized, they were the more surprised at the Emperor's choice. . . . . At length they (the Bishops) yielded to the Prince's will, and the inclination of the people, who likewise desired Nectarius. He was baptized, and while he still wore the habit of a neophyte, he was declared Bishop of Constantinople, with the general consent of the whole Council. . . . . Theodosius sent deputies from his court with certain Bishops, to desire a formal letter from the Pope in confirmation of their choice of Nectarius." *Fleury, H. E. B.* xviii. *c.* 5. *Trans. by Newman.*

2. CASE OF MACEDONIUS.

91. "The Emperor and the Catholic Bishops represented to them that they had sent a deputation to Pope Liberius, under the direction of Eustathius, Bishop of Sebaste ; and that for some time they had voluntarily communicated with the Catholics, without making any distinction ; that they therefore did not do well in overthrowing the faith which they had opposed, and leaving the good part which they had chosen." *Ib. c.* 6.

3. THE PRIMACY.

92. " That the Bishop of Constantinople have the dignity of honour (πϱεσβεία τῆς τιμῆς) next after the Bishop of Rome, for Constantinople is New Rome." *Canon* iii. *Labbé*, *T.* ii. *p.* 1125.

COMMENT.

The Pope was not present at this great Council, neither did he send any Legates ; it became Œcumenical on its being accepted by the West, and confirmed by the Pope.

There are two points worthy of consideration, viz. the case of Nectarius and the Primacy ; this latter I propose to reserve for the comment on the Council of Chalcedon.

The case of Nectarius, if we could be quite sure of its being genuine, is conclusive as far as it goes. It is not to be found in the acts of the Council, and it is well known that some of them have been lost. The only authority known is the account given of it by S. Boniface in his Epistle to Macedonius, about the year 422, that is, about forty years after the celebration of this Council—a period sufficiently short for S. Boniface to have been corrected, if he had made a mistake. The strong probability is that the account is perfectly correct. At all events, having the word of so holy a Pope as S. Boniface, we shall assume it is so, and submit the evidence for what it is worth.

The See of Constantinople became vacant on the resignation of S. Gregory of Nazianzum, its Patriarch, who was after the death of Meletius of Antioch its President. It was necessary that a new appointment should be made as soon as convenient. The Emperor directed the Bishops to write down the names of such persons as they deemed worthy. They did so, and the Emperor selected Nectarius, an aged man, who had not been as yet baptized, though a believer in Christ. The choice of Theodosius was at first opposed by the Prelates, but subsequently they yielded to his wishes. Having agreed upon a fit person, the next step was his ordination, consecration, and installation. Did the Bishops immediately proceed to perform these functions ? Apparently not. Why ? Because something else had to be done before Nectarius could be canonically consecrated and installed. What was that ? The confirmation of the Pope. "Theodosius," it is said, "sent deputies from his court with certain Bishops to desire a formal letter from the Pope in confirmation of their choice of Nectarius." Now if the Pope had occupied no higher office than that of any other great Bishop, if he had not been superior to even the Council itself, it was inconceivable and unnecessary to have sent a deputation all the way to Rome to ask for the Papal confirmation of the Bishop nominate and elect. According to the code of the Universal Church then in force, every

Bishop was constituted by his colleagues of the Province in which his see was situated, subject to the assent of the Metropolitan. The Metropolitan had to be confirmed by the Patriarchs. In that case the *immediate* action of the Apostolic See was not necessary. All that was needful was that the new Bishop on taking possession of his See should forward to the Pope, and to the Patriarch and other Bishops, his confession of faith. But who had authority to confirm a new Patriarch? It is evident from their conduct that this plenary Council had no such authority ; from whence, then was Nectarius to derive his jurisdiction? The synodical epistle of the Council of Aquileia fitly answers this question. It will be remembered that when there was a danger of Gratian supporting the Anti-pope Ursinus, S. Ambrose and this council in their synodical epistle to him, petitioned him not "to suffer the Head of the Roman world—the Roman Church—to be thrown into confusion : for," they added, "thence flow unto all the rights of venerable communion." Theodosius then and the Bishops, as good Catholics, approached by deputation the throne of the Apostolic See, to ask for " a formal letter from the Pope in confirmation of the choice of Nectarius."

It is objected, however, that this application was not in recognition of the Papal Prerogative, but to obtain the consent of the great Bishop of Rome, in order that no difficulties might afterwards arise. But on the hypothesis that the Pope was no more than an equal to the other Patriarchs, though first in honour, it was utterly unnecessary to ask his consent to their election. The Fathers assembled at Constantinople, in the very place where the vacancy occurred, were fully competent to supply all that was required (if this hypothesis be granted) their power was superior to the Pope, whose decrees would have been binding upon him. The question raised refutes itself.

Assuming, then, that this account of the deputation to Rome is genuine, it is conclusive evidence of the Papal Supremacy over all the Sees in Christendom. But even if it were proved to be spurious, this would not touch the question ; for the Council of Aquileia, just quoted, informs us of the earthly source of all communion ; and that of Sardica, of the Prerogative of the Pope as ultimate Judge in all controversies relating to the Episcopate.

COUNCIL OF CARTHAGE.

A.D. 410.

93. " We have considered that what has been done by us was to be made known to your holy charity, that to the decrees made by our lowliness might be added the Authority of the Apostolic See" (*etiam Apostolicæ sedis adhibeatur auctoritas*). Galland, *t.* viii. *ep.* xxvi. *p.* 590, 1.

COMMENT.

It is impossible to deny that the assent of the Apostolic See is necessary to give ecclesiastical validity to the decrees of plenary councils. The Synodical Epistle of the Council of Carthage, the decrees of which were prepared by S. Augustine, witnesses to the form that conciliar decrees ordinarily took effect ; (1), By the judgment of the Bishops in Council, and (2), By the additional " Authority of the Apostolic See." This demonstrates the necessity, for what are sometimes called " National Councils," obtaining the Papal confirmation before they are promulgated. It is this confirmation that gives them binding authority.' This point will be touched upon again in the Comment on the Œcumenical Council of Chalcedon.

COUNCIL OF MILEVIS.

A.D. 416.

94. "As the Lord, by the chief gift of His grace, hath placed you in the Apostolic See, and hath furnished our times with such a Chief .... we pray that you will deign to extend your pastoral diligence to the great dangers of us poor weak members of Christ. . . . . We think that . . . . they who hold such perverse sentiments will more readily yield to the Authority of your Holiness, which is derived from the clear light of the Scriptures" (*de claro Scripturarum lumine deprompta*). *Labb. S. Concil. t.* iii. *col.* 388, 9.

COMMENT.

The African Bishops who assembled in Milevis regarded the Roman as "the Apostolic See," *i. e.* the See of the Apostle Peter ; and they recognised the Roman Bishop as "Chief," *i. e.* as Chief of the Episcopate. They ask him to commiserate their weak condition ; and they add that "they who hold such perverse sentiments will more readily yield t he Auth ority of your Holiness ;" which they say "is derived from the clear light of the Holy Scriptures." This expression shows that the Fathers were in this epistle regarding the Pope in h s character, not as Patriarch, as some think' but as the Supreme Pastor : for the foermr r office is strictly an ecclesiastical one, whereas the latter is Scriptural. The Scriptures they referred to are evidently 'the following :— "Thou art Peter," "To thee will I give the keys of the kingdom of heaven." "Whatsoever thou shalt bind on earth shall be bound in heaven ; and whatsoever thou shalt loose on earth shall be loosed in heaven."

"Confirm thy brethren." "Feed My sheep." "Feed My lambs." They unquestionably referred to all or some of these passages ; for there are none else they could have referred to ; and by so doing they point to the origin of that "Authority," they request the Pope to exercise, which they say is derived from the "clear light of the Scriptures;" that is, that the language of Scripture is so plain that to doubt his "Authority" is impossible. From this it follows that they believed the Pope filled the "Place of Peter," and was his Successor in the government of the Universal Church, and also was in possession of its supreme jurisdiction, as symbolised by the keys.

This testimony is so far valuable, as it materially assists us in the right understanding of the proceedings of another Council in Africa, which questioned the Pope's right to restore Apiarius, who had been condemned for gross immoral conduct.

COUNCIL OF EPHESUS.

THE THIRD ŒCUMENICAL.

A.D. 431.

1. EPISTLE OF POPE S. CELESTINE TO S. CYRIL, PATRIARCH OF
ALEXANDRIA.

95. " Wherefore, having added to you the authority of our Throne, and using with power our Authority of place (*συναφθείσης σοι τοίνυν τῆς αὐθεντίας τοῦ ἡμετέρου θρονου, καὶ τῇ ἡ ἡμιτέρα τοῦ τόπου διαδοχῇ ἐπ' ἐξουσία χρησάμενος*) you will exact with rigorous firmness this definite sentence, that either within ten days, counting from the day of this admonition, he shall anathematise, by a confession under his own hand, this wicked assertion of his, and shall give assurance that he will hold, concerning the generation of the Christ and our God, the same faith as the Church of the Romans, and of your Holiness, and the religion the world holds ; or if he will not do this, your Holiness, having at once provided for this Church (Constantinople), will let him know that he is in every way removed from our Body."— *Ep. ad Cyril. in Concil. Ephes. Labbé, t.* iii. *col.* 898, 9.

2. CONDEMNATION OF NESTORIUS FOR CONTUMACY.

96. " Nestorius himself... refused to obey the citation and to receive the Bishops who were sent to him on our part .... and having convicted him .... of holding and teaching impious doctrine, being compelled by the necessity of the canons, and by the Letters of our most holy Father and Colleague, Celestine, Bishop of the Roman Church ; after having shed many tears, we are agreed upon this unhappy sentence. Our Lord Jesus Christ, whom he hath blasphemed, has declared by this holy Council that he is deprived of the episcopal dignity, and excluded from all ecclesiastical assemblies."— *Ib. col.* 1078.

3. Arrival of the Papal Legates with the Letters of the Pope.

97. " Subsequently the Legates of the Apostolic See arrived, bringing with them the Letters of Pope S. Celestine, which were read to the Council. After which the Legate Philip said : ' We acknowledge our thanks to the holy and venerable Synod, that the Letter of our holy and blessed Pope having been read to you, you have united your holy members by your holy voices and acclamations to that holy Head ; for your blessedness is not ignorant that the blessed Peter the Apostle was the Head of all the Faith (*ὅτι ἡ κεφαλὴ ὅλης τῆς πίστεως*), as also of the Apostles.' "—*Ib. act.* ii. *col.* 1147–50.

98. "Projectus, the Legate, said : ' Remark the form of the Letter of our venerable Father Celestine : he does not pretend to instruct you, as if you were ignorant, but aims at putting you in remembrance of what you know already, wishing you to execute that on which he has long ago adjudicated.' "—*Ib. col.* 1147.

99. "Firmus, Bishop of Cappadocia, said : ' The holy Apostolic See of Celestine has decided this affair, and has pronounced sentence on it before in the Letter addressed to Cyril of Alexandria . . . . In accordance with which sentence, and in furtherance thereof, we have pronounced a canonical judgment against Nestorius, the term which was granted him for recantation being over-past, and we having waited long beyond the day fixed by the Emperor.' "— *Ib. Labbé, t.* iii. *act.* ii. *col.* 1147.

4. Deposition of Nestorius.

100. "When the acts of the Council had been read, Priest Philip, Legate, said : ' No one doubts but that Peter, the Exarch and Head of the Apostles (*ὁ ἔξαρχος καὶ κεφαλὴ τῶν ἀποστόλων*), Pillar of the faith and Foundation of the Catholic Church, received from our Lord Jesus Christ the keys of His Kingdom, and power to bind and loose sins, and that even to the present time he lives, and exercises these judicial powers in his Successors. Our holy Pope, Bishop Celestine, who at this time holds his Place (*ὁ διάδοχος καὶ τοποτηρητής*), has sent us to represent him in this holy Council, which our most Christian Emperors have convened in order to preserve intact the Catholic Faith, which has descended to them from their ancestors.' [He then sums up the proceedings against Nestorius, and adds]: ' The sentence pronounced against him remains firm, agreeable to the judgment of all the Churches [East and West]. Let Nestorius therefore know that he is cut off from the communion of the priesthood of the Catholic Church.' "— *Ib. col.* 1154, 55.

101. " Bishop Arcadius, Legate, next delivered judgment : ' . . . . According to the tradition of the Apostles and the Catholic Church, and in accordance also with the decision of the most holy Pope Celestine, who sent us to execute his part of this business, and pur-

suant to the décrees of the holy Council, let Nestorius know that he is deprived of the episcopal dignity, excluded from the whole Church, and from the communion of all Bishops.'"—*Ib. col.* 1155-8.

102. " Bishop Projectus, also Legate : ' I too, by my authority as Legate of the Apostolic See, being joined by my brother to execute this sentence, declare that Nestorius, enemy of the truth and corrupter of the faith, is deprived of the episcopal dignity, and of the commu-

nion of all orthodox Bishops.'"—*Ib.* 1158.

103. " S. Cyril : —' Since, then, we, beloved of God, have executed the sentence of the most holy Bishop Celestine, of the holy Synod congregated in the metropolitan city of Ephesus, against the heretic Nestorius, let the acts of what passed yesterday and to-day be joined to the preceding, that they may signify their consent by subscription.'"— *Ib.* 1158.

5. SYNODICAL EPISTLES.

104. The following was sent to the Emperor : " God, favouring your zeal, has stirred up that of the Bishops of the West to avenge the injury done to Jesus Christ ; for, although the length of the journey is such that they could not all come to us, yet they assembled in a synod of their own, Celestine, the holy Bishop of Rome, himself presiding. They approved our opinions concerning the faith, and cut off from the priesthood those who differ from us. Celestine had already declared the same before the meeting of the Council, by his Letter to the most holy Bishop Cyril, whom he also appointed to act in his stead. He has now again confirmed it by Letters sent to the Council of Ephesus by the Bishops Arcadius and Projectus, and the Priest Philip, his vicars. On their arrival they made known

to us the opinion of the whole Council of the West, and have also witnessed, in writing, that they perfectly agree with us in regard to the faith. We therefore inform your Majesty of this, that you may be assured that the sentence we have now pronounced is the common judgment of the whole world. . . . ." — *Ib. col.* 1159.

105. In the synodical letter addressed to Pope Celestine is the following : " After the acts relating to the deposition of the impious Pelagians, &c., and their adherents, had been read in the Council, we ordered that the sentence which your Holiness pronounced against them should remain firm, and we are all unanimous in looking upon them as deposed. For your fuller information we send you the acts and subscriptions of the Council."—*Ib. col.* 1329-1338.

COMMENT.

This is the first Œcumenical Council of which we have an accurate and full account. All that we have of the Council of Nicæa — the first Œcumenical—are the Symbol of Faith, the

Canons, the Synodical Epistles. Of the attitude the Legates assumed, their speeches, and their proceedings, we are left for the most part in ignorance, in consequence of the loss of the original documents. At the second Œcumenical Council the Legates were not present, this Council having subsequently become General, on its acceptance by the West, and its confirmation by the Pope. For the first time, then, we have a full account of the manner and form of an Œcumenical Council, and of the relation that subsists between it and the Sovereign Pontiff.

Upon the arrival of the Legates—two Bishops and a Priest—they delivered the Letters of the Pope, which were read to the Council; they then addressed the Council, describing the assembled Prelates as "holy members," united "by their voices and acclamations to that holy Head;" for they add, "Your blessedness is not ignorant that the blessed Peter the Apostle was the Head of all the Faith, as also of the Apostles." This was a formal announcement that S. Peter, the founder of the Roman Church, was "the Head of the Faith and of the Apostles;" and this, it will be remembered, is in accordance with one of the commissions our Lord delivered to the Apostle, "Confirm, or strengthen, thy Brethren:" that is, he was to execute the office of confirming with the strength of the Rock the Faith of the Apostolate, to whom each Apostle was to look up to as his Head. The Legates at another time advance a step further in their pronouncement : " No one doubts but that Peter, the Exarch and Head of the Apostles, Pillar of the Faith, and Foundation of the Catholic Church, received from our Lord Jesus Christ the keys of His Kingdom, and power to bind and loose sins, and that even to the present time he (Peter) lives and exercises these judicial powers in his Successors." The several commissions which our Lord delivered to S. Peter, inclusive of the Supreme Jurisdiction, as symbolised by the keys, were transmitted to his Successors;—not to his Successors generally, but to the Bishops of Rome, for they assert that Bishop Celestine of Rome "at this time holds his Place." This is in accord-

ance with the doctrine of S. Cyprian, who asserted that Rome was "the Place of Peter," where is "the Cathedra of Peter, and the Principal Church, whence the unity of the Priesthood took its rise," which "Place" Cornelius then occupied, and at the period of the Council, the "holy Pope, Bishop Celestine." The judicial power, then, of S. Peter descended to his Successors, the Bishops of Rome, which power the Pope had exercised against the heretic Nestorius, the Council being assembled to confirm what had been done. As Peter, then, was the Head of the whole Faith, and of the Apostles, so also are his Successors, each in his turn, Head of the Faith and of the Episcopate.

The Legates, occupying this ground in behalf of their master the Pope, and occupying his place as the Successor of S. Peter, after summing up the evidence, pronounce sentence in his name : "The sentence pronounced against him (Nestorius) remains firm, agreeable to the judgment of all the Churches. Let Nestorius know that he is cut off from the communion of the Priesthood of the Catholic Church." The second Legate likewise pronounced, "According to the tradition of the Apostles and the Catholic Church; in accordance also to the decision of the most holy Pope Celestine, who sent us to execute his part of this business, and in pursuance of the decrees of the Holy Council, let Nestorius know that he is deprived of the episcopal dignity, excluded from the whole Church, and from the communion of all Bishops." And another Legate also pronounced : " I too, by my authority as Legate of the Apostolic See, being joined with my brothers to execute this sentence, declare that Nestorius, enemy of the truth and corrupter of the Faith, is deprived of the episcopal dignity, and of the communion of all Catholic Bishops." S. Cyril also, who had been appointed by the Pope to preside and to act "in his (the Pope's) stead, and for the Council, announces the sentence passed upon Nestorius by the Pope, and the approval by the Legates of "the judgment passed by the holy Council upon the heretic Nestorius," directs that the acts be prepared for subscription by the Fathers.

The position of the Pope in the Council was as the Successor of the Apostle S. Peter, the Head of the Faith, and the Exarch and Chief of all the Apostles, who alone possessed the prerogative of the Supreme Jurisdiction, which he exercised against Nestorius, both before the celebration of this Council and in the presence of the assembled Prelates of the world.

The attitude the Pope assumed was that of Supreme Judge, whose judgment the whole Episcopate in Council assembled were bound not merely to defer, but to submit to, and accept, as the voice of the Apostle Peter. Now if this assumption of Supreme Authority was founded on no warranty of either Scripture or Tradition, would the Fathers, of whom the greater part were Orientals, and extremely jealous of their rights, have quietly, and without protest of any kind, submitted to it? To estimate this properly, we must realise what an awful crime it would be for any man claiming to be the Head of the Faith, the Head of the Church, and to be the Supreme Judge in all matters concerning the Faith, if such claim had no other foundation than pride of place and of power. Such an assumption, if unfounded, was not only arrogant and presumptuous to the greatest degree ; it was heretical, wicked, profane, and blasphemous. If the position assumed by the Legates on behalf of their master the Pope had been an innovation, we should naturally have expected at least a remonstrance, or a protest, if not an anathema, followed by instant deposition.

But the assembled Fathers accept the position assumed by the Pope without a murmur of dissent. Firmus, Bishop of Cappadocia, a See in Asia

Minor, said, "The Apostolic See of Celestine has decided this affair (of Nestorius), and has pronounced sentence upon it before, in the Letter addressed to Cyril of Alexandria . . . . in accordance with which sentence, and in furtherance thereof, we have pronounced a canonical judgment against Nestorius, the term which was granted him (*i. e.* the ten days allowed by the Pope) for recantation being over past; and we having waited long beyond the day fixed by the Emperor." Here is a distinct recognition of the Papal position of Supreme Judge over the Patriarch of the (then) Second See of the world, the chief seat of authority in the East, and of the Imperial City. The other Bishops follow suit, and not a word is to be found of remonstrance or protest against the action of the Pope in having by his own sole authority deposed Nestorius, or against the lofty attitude the Legates assumed before the Council, to whom they declared, (1) That the blessed Peter was "the Head of the Faith," "the Exarch and Head of the Apostles, the Pillar of the Faith, and Foundation of the Catholic Church," "who received from our Lord Jesus Christ the keys of His Kingdom, and power to bind and loose sins :" (2) That S. Peter "lives and exercises these judicial powers in his Successors :" and (3) That "our holy Pope Bishop Celestine" (of Rome) "at this time holds his Place," that is, "his Place of Head of the Faith," and "the Exarch and Head" of the whole Church, and consequently the office of that Supreme "Judicial power," which S. Peter received from Christ, and which he exercises by his Successors, and, in the present instance, in the person of S. Celestine, Bishop of the Apostolic See.

S. Cyril, the President of this great Council, and the Patriarch of the second Apostolic See, fully admitted all the pretensions of the Pope, when he accepted his commission to execute his sentence upon Nestorius, and to preside "in his stead" over this Council ;

and also when he described S. Celestine as "Archbishop of all the habitable world," as well as " Father and Patriarch of the mighty city of Rome."

The Council of Ephesus then, together with its President, accepted the Papal Supremacy in its fulness.

COUNCIL OF CHALCEDON.

FOURTH ŒCUMENICAL.

A.D. 451.

1. Expulsion of Dioscorus, Patriarch of Alexandria, by Command of the Pope's Legates, from his place in the Council.

106. " Bishop Paschasinus, Vicar of the Apostolic See, stood up with his colleagues and said, ... 'We have orders from the blessed Bishop of Rome, who is the Head of all the Churches, that Dioscorus should not sit in the Council ; therefore, so please your greatness, let him go down, or we must depart.'. . . . The Magistrates and senators said, 'What is the specific charge against the most reverend Bishop Dioscorus?' Lucentius, the (other) Vicar of the Apostolic See, replied, ' He (Dioscorus) must assign a reason for the sentence he passed ; for he has presumed to exercise the office of Judge, which does not belong to him, and to hold a council without the authority of the Holy See—a thing which is never lawful, and cannot be made lawful' (*quod nunquam licuit, numquam factum est*). Paschasinus said, 'We cannot act contrary to the orders of our most blessed Pope, or to the canons of the Church, or to the institutions of the Fathers.' Upon this Dioscorus, by order of the Magistrates, left his place, and took his seat in the midst of the assembly." *Labbé, S. Concil. T.* iv. *col.* 863–6.

2. Admission of Theodoret to the Council.

107. " Constantinus, the most devoted secretary to the Sacred Consistory, commenced reading the letter from (the Emperor) Theodosius the Younger, to Dioscorus, who summoned the (Arian) Council of Ephesus. As it expressly forbade Theodoret to be present there, the Magistrates said, 'Let the most reverend Bishop Theodoret enter that he too may take part in the Council, since the most holy Archbishop Leo has restored him to the episcopal office, and the most pious Emperor has ordered that he should assist at the holy Council.' . . . Theodoret came forward, and said, ' I have presented a petition to the Emperor in which I set forth the cruelties I have endured ; I beg that it may be examined.' The Magistrates said, ' The Bishop Theodoret, having recovered his rank from the Archbishop of Rome, has now entered as a prosecutor ; wherefore to avoid confusion let us finish what we have begun.'" *Ib. col.* 873–4.

3. THE EUTYCHIAN HERESY.

108. "Cecropius, Bishop of Sebastopolis, said, 'The affairs of Eutyches sprang into sudden importance ; the Archbishop of Rome gave a decision about it, and we follow him; we have all subscribed to his Letter.' The Bishops cried out, ' That say we all ; the exposition that has been given is sufficient, it is not lawful that another should be made.' " *Ib.* 1207.

109. ". . . . When the reading was done (*i.e.* of S. Leo's Letter), the Bishop exclaimed, 'This is the faith of the Apostles : We all be-

lieve this, the orthodox believe this, anathema to him who believes not thus. Peter has thus spoken by Leo ; the Apostles taught this, Leo's doctrine is pious and true ; Cyril taught this ; let the memory of Cyril be eternal. Leo and Cyril teach the same. Anathema to him who does not believe. This is the true Faith . . . . . This is the Faith of the Fathers Why was not this done at (the heretical council of) Ephesus? This is what Dioscorus concealed.' " *Ib. col.* 1235.

4. TRIAL AND CONDEMNATION OF DIOSCORUS.

110. [Then the three Legates], "Paschasinus, Lucentius, and Boniface, holding the Place of the blessed Leo, the Bishop of old Rome, pronounced the sentence in these terms : 'The outrage committed against the Canons by Dioscorus, late Bishop of Alexandria, has been plainly proved by the evidence adduced both in the former session and in this. He received to his communion Eutyches, who was condemned by his own Bishop. He persisted in maintaining that what he did at Ephesus was well done, though he ought to mourn for it, and ask pardon, as the others have done. He would not permit the Letter of Pope Leo to Flavianus,

of sacred memory, to be read, he even excommunicated the most blessed and holy Archbishop Leo of great Rome. Several complaints have been presented against him to the Council. He has been three times cited, and refuses to pay obedience. Wherefore, the most holy Archbishop of Rome, Leo, by us and this present Council, thrice blessed, and with the Apostle S. Peter, who is the Rock and Foundation of the Catholic Church and of the orthodox faith, deprives him of the episcopal dignity and every sacerdotal ministry. The Council, therefore, will decree concerning him in conformity with the canons.'" *Ib.* 1303–6.

5. THE PRIMATIAL RANK.

111. " We, following in all things the decisions of the holy Fathers, and acknowledging the canon of the 150 most religious Bishops, do also determine and decree the same thing respecting the privileges (πρεσβείων) of the most holy city of Constantinople, New Rome. For the Fathers with good reason

granted to the See of Old Rome its high privileges (πρεσβεῖα), because it was the reigning city. By the same consideration the 150 most religious Bishops were induced to decree that New Rome, the honoured seat of empire and residence of the Senate, should possess equal privileges (ἴσων . . . πρεσβείων) in ecclesiastical things ; and be second in rank after her (δευτέραν μετ᾽ ἐκείνην ὑπάρχουσαι) ; so that only the Metropolitans of Pontus, Asia, and Thrace, and the Bishop of those dioceses which are among the barbarians, shall be ordained by the See of Constanti-nople, on their receiving a notifi-cation that a canonical election has taken place : but it must be understood that each Metropolitan of these dioceses shall along with his comprovincials ordain the Bis-hops of the provinces according to the canons." *Ib. col.* 1691–4.

6. OBJECTION OF THE LEGATES.

112. "The Legates directed Pas-chasinus (one of them) to address the following remonstrance to the Magistrates : 'Yesterday, after you and ourselves had withdrawn, something, we are told, was trans-acted which we consider opposed to the Canons : we desire it may be read, that all our brethren may see whether it be just or no.' [After some altercation] Aëtius, the Arch-deacon, speaking of the Legates, said, ' If they have received any injunctions, on this head, let them be produced.' Boniface the priest read a paper which contained the following order of Pope Leo : ' Do not suffer the decrees of the Fathers to be infringed or en-croached upon by any rash changes ; preserve in all things the dignity of Our Person, which you repre-sent ; and if any, as may happen, relying on the splendour of their cities, should attempt any usurpa-tion, do you oppose.them with be-coming resolution.' The Magis-trates said, ' Let the Canons be produced by both parties.' [Then followed the reading of the sixth Canon of Nicæa, and the decree of the Council of Constantinople, &c., after which] the Magistrates said, ' It appears from the deposi-tion, first of all, that the Primacy and the Precedency of honour (τὰ πρωτεῖα καὶ τὴν ἐξαίρετον τιμὴν) should be preserved, according to the Canons, for the Archbishop of Old Rome, but that the Archbishop of Constantinople ought to enjoy the same privileges of honour (τῶν αὐτῶν πρεσβείων τῆς τιμῆς) ; and that he has a right to ordain the Metropo-litans of the dioceses of Asia, Pon-tus, &c. These are our views, let the Council state theirs.' The Bishops shouted, 'This is a just proposal ; we all say the same, we all assent to it ; we pray you dis-miss us,' with other similar excla-mations. Lucentius, the Legate, said, ' The Apostolic See ought not to be degraded in our presence ; we therefore desire yesterday's pro-ceedings which relate to the Canons, be rescinded ; otherwise let our opposition be inscribed in the acts that we may know what we ought to report to the Pope, and that he may declare his opinion of the con-tempt of his See and subversion of the Canons.' The Magistrates said, ' The whole Council approves of what is said.'" *Ib. col.* 1731–58.

7. SYNODICAL EPISTLE TO THE POPE.

113. "... Which like to a golden chain coming even unto us by the precept of the Law-giver, thou (Leo) hast kept, being the constituted Interpreter to all of the blessed Peter" (*vocis beati Petri omni-bus constitutus interpres.*) *Ib. col.* 1774, 5.

114. " ... Over whom thou indeed hast presided, as the Head over the members." (*Quibus tu quidem sicut membris caput præeras in his qui tuum tenebant ordinem benevolentiam præferendo.*) *Ib. col.* 1775.

115. " ... Over and above these offences, extending his madness against him (Leo), to whom the Custody of the Vineyard is committed by the Saviour (*cui vineæ custodia a Salvatore commissa est*), that is, against your holy Apostleship, meditating excommunication against thee, who hastenedst to unite the body of the Church." *Ib.* 1775.

116. " ... We have to inform you that there are other things that we have ordained for the establishing of order, and the maintenance of canonical discipline, under the persuasion that our proceedings would have your approval and confirmation as soon as you were made aware of them. We confirmed then the Canon of the 150 Fathers of Constantinople, which ordained that the Bishop of that city should have privileges of honour after your most holy and Apostolic Chair, in the conviction that you dispose of your favours without any invidious feeling towards your brethren, so you would extend your wonted care to the Church of Constantinople, and enlighten it with your Apostolic ray. Deign, therefore, most holy and most blessed Father, to allow our decision. Your Legates, we acknowledge, were averse to this measure, no doubt from a desire of securing to you the honour of advancing, in the first instance, the matter of order, as well as the matter of faith. We acted, however, in accordance with the wishes of the Emperor, the Senate, and the Imperial city. Honour then, we pray you, our judgment, with your decree, that as we have been united to our Head in agreeing upon what was right, so the Head, too (*i.e.* the Pope), may confirm the becoming act of the children. So will our pious princes be pleased, who have ratified as a law whatever your Holiness has determined." (*Rogamus igitur, et tuis decretis nostrum honora judicium; et sicut nos capite in bonis adjicimus consonantiam, sic et summitas tua filiis quod decet adimpleat. Sic enim pii principes complacebunt, qui tamquam legem tuæ sanctitatis judicium firmaverunt.*) *Ib. col.* 1779.

COMMENT.

Strong indeed is the testimony of the Œcumenical Council of Ephesus for the Papal Supremacy, but it is nothing compared to that of the great Synod of Chalcedon, also Œcumenical. The Legates of the Pope assumed precisely the same position in this Council as they did at Ephesus. They maintained before the Council the Superiority of the Pope as the Head of the Episcopate, connecting his authority with that of S. Peter, the origin and source of all his Prerogatives, and who lives and judges through his Successors.

1. The first point to be considered is the expulsion of Dioscorus, Patriarch of Alexandria, from his seat in the Council, by command of the Pope, speaking through his Legates, " We have orders," say the Legates, "from the blessed Bishop of Rome, who is the Head of all the Churches, that Dioscorus should not sit in the Council." This was a peremptory command, addressed to the Emperor's officers, who were present, and to the Council itself—a command which, if not instantly obeyed, would have been followed by their departure from the Council. " Therefore," say

they, "let him go down, or we must depart."

The Magistrates seem to have been taken by surprise, but the Legates exclaimed, "We cannot act contrary to the orders of our most blessed Pope, and the Canons of the Church." The result was, that Dioscorus, the Patriarch of the Second Apostolic Throne, had to vacate his seat in the Council, and to sit "in the midst of the assembly." The Magistrates and Council—of some 600 Fathers, most of whom were Orientals—obeyed the Papal commands, and permitted their Brother Prelate to be deprived of his seat. To give one an idea of this exercise of Supreme power, let us suppose the case of Queen Victoria commanding a Peer to vacate his seat in the House of Lords, or the Emperor Napoleon directing one of the Senate to cease to take part in the deliberations of the national Council. Would either the House of Lords or the French Senate submit to such a stretch of authority without a murmur? But the Pope is a greater person than any Sovereign —greater than the Emperors of old, for he was the recognised Vicar of Jesus Christ; and whatever he commands is instantly to be obeyed under penalty of excommunication, for he, sitting in "the Place of Peter," "alone holds and possesses the whole power" of his Master. So Dioscorus had to submit to the Papal sentence, the Magistrates and the Council acquiescing.

2. But what were the grounds of this despotic action of the Papacy? Because Dioscorus had "assumed the office of Judge, which did not belong to him, and presumed to hold a (plenary) council without the authority of the Holy See: a thing which is never lawful, nor can be made lawful." This was no new claim advanced by the Popes. Socrates the historian admits it as part of the Canon law of the Church; and Pope S. Julius alludes to it in his letter to the Arians, as a Prerogative well known to all as belonging to the Holy See. That it was no new claim is evident from the

silence of the Emperor's Officials and of the Council, and their acquiescence in the sentence of the Pope against Dioscorus, in consequence of his violating this law. So that it is a well-ascertained law, virtually at least confirmed by this great Synod, that no plenary Council can be celebrated in any part of the Universal Church without the sanction of the Pope; and he who presumes thus to intrude upon the Prerogative of the Holy See is liable to be visited by deprivation of his episcopal rights by the sole sentence of the Pope.

3. The restoration of Bishop Theodoret, by the act of the Pope alone, is another testimony of the Supremacy of the Holy See over every diocese. This the Imperial Officials and the Council (for they were a consenting party) recognised, for they said, "Let the most reverend Bishop Theodoret enter, that he too may take part in the Council, since the most holy Archbishop Leo (of Rome) has restored him to the episcopal office." The Pope then may not only deprive by his single Authority, but he can likewise by his own sole act restore a Bishop to his See.

4. The condemnation of Eutyches affords another example of Papal action. Cecropius, Bishop of Sebastopolis—an Eastern diocese—said, "This offence of Eutyches sprang into sudden importance: the Archbishop of Rome gave a decision about it, and we follow him; we have all submitted to his Letter." Why the Pope more than any other Bishop, if he had no higher authority? The Bishops, on hearing this, cried out, "That say we all: the exposition (Leo's) that has been given is sufficient; it is not lawful that another should be made." Why not another, if equally orthodox? The answer to this query is best given by the Bishops, who, when the reading of the celebrated Tome had been completed, exclaimed, "This is the Faith of the Apostles: we all believe this; the orthodox believe this; anathema to him who believes not this. Peter has

thus spoken by Leo; the Apostles taught this; Leo's doctrine is pious and true; Cyril taught this; let the memory of Cyril be eternal. Leo and Cyril teach the same." "Peter has thus spoken by Leo;" S. Peter had himself drawn up the exposition, that is to say, S. Leo declared the doctrine *ex Cathedra*, by which he executed his office of Teacher of the Universal Church. It was unlawful, then, to make another dogmatic exposition, for the one was orthodox and conclusive. But S. Cyril's name is coupled with S. Leo, and this because of the part he took in the last General Council. But he did not act as a simple Bishop, nor merely as the Patriarch of the great Church of Alexandria; he acted as the delegate of the Pope. "In his stead" he excommunicated and deposed Nestorius, and "in his stead" he presided at the Council of Ephesus. It was, then, in his character as Vicar of the Pope that he thus acted, and when he launched his Twelve Anathemas. The Fathers then admitted, without qualification, the position of the Pope, as the Representative of S. Peter, the Teacher of the whole Church. "Peter has thus spoken by Leo," showing that S. Peter still teaches, by his Successors, from his Chair, which is situated in the midst of the Roman Church.

5. The form by which Dioscorus was condemned furnishes another important witness to Supreme Papal Jurisdiction. The Legates commence by recapitulating the offences Dioscorus had been guilty of, (1) The breach of the canon law, in holding a council without the sanction of the Holy See; (2) His receiving into his communion Eutyches; (3) His still maintaining that what he did at (the pseudo-Council of) Ephesus was well done; (4) His refusal to permit the Letter of Pope Leo to Flavian to be read; (5) His presumptuous threat to excommunicate the Pope, &c. . . . . "Wherefore," concludes the Legate, "the most holy Archbishop of Rome, Leo, by us and this present Council thrice blessed, with the Apostle Peter, who is the Rock and Foundation of the Catholic Church and of the orthodox Faith, deprives him of the episcopal dignity, and every sacerdotal ministry. The Council, therefore, will decree concerning him in conformity with the canons." Such was the sentence pronounced in the name of the Pope, and with the authority of the Council — S. Peter pronouncing sentence through his Representative in his See, and the Bishops of the Catholic Church united to him.

6. The next point is the celebrated 28th canon, which is relied upon by Anglicans as justifying their state of separation from Rome; and as a most powerful, and, indeed, invincible argument against the alleged arrogant claims of the Holy See to Supremacy. When Constantinople became the capital of the Empire, the residence of the Emperor, and the place where the Senate assembled, it was natural its Bishop should be elevated to the highest possible rank in the episcopate. The canon of the Second General Council provided "that the Bishop of Constantinople (should) have the dignity of honour (πρεσβεῖα τῆς τιμῆς) next after the Bishop of Rome, for Constantinople is New Rome." The canon of this Council (Chalcedon) thus enacted: "The Fathers, with good reason, granted to the See of ancient Rome its high privileges (τὰ πρεσβεῖα), because it was the reigning city; by the same consideration the 150 Bishops were induced to decide that New Rome, honoured seat of empire, and the residence of the Senate, should possess equal privileges (πρεσβεῖων) in ecclesiastical matters, and be second in rank," &c. It has been assumed that the object of the canon was to place the Church of Constantinople, on all points, upon an exact equality with Rome. Now all that the canon declares with respect to Rome is this, that in consequence of its being the reigning city, the "dignity, or Privilege of honour" (for such is the correct translation of τὰ πρεσβεῖα) should be accorded to the elder Regal Rome. This did not include

that higher office which he held as the Successor of S. Peter ; it was simply the "dignity, or Privilege of honour" due to him as the Bishop of the Imperial City. It should be remembered that from the conversion of the Empire the Pope had, in addition to his office of Patriarch and Pope, a dignity derived from "the honour of the Roman city." Valentinian III. evidently alluded to this in one of his epistles : " Since, therefore, the authority of the sacred synod (Nicæa) has confirmed the Primacy of the Apostolic See, on account of the merit of Peter, the Chief of the corona of Bishops, and of the Dignity of the city' of Rome ; let no one presumptuously dare to attempt anything unlawful in opposition to the Authority of that See." The Primacy of the Pope was of a double nature, (1) on account of his being the Successor of S. Peter ; and (2) because of his being the Bishop of the Imperial City. Now we know as a matter of fact that the Metropolitans of the Church derive their rank from the circumstance of their sees being situated in the chief metropolitan cities of the empire. We are also aware that an elaborate code of ecclesiastical law came into existence in consequence of this metropolitical system of Church government. Provision was made for appeals from Bishops to the Metropolitan, and from the Metropolitan to the Patriarch, who together with his Bishops sitting as assessors, delivered judgment on the conduct of Bishops. When the Emperor desired that Constantinople should be erected into a Patriarchate, he intended it should be similar in all respects to the Patriarchates of Rome, Alexandria, and Antioch. That is to say, as Patriarchs they all should rank equally, Constantinople having the "dignity of honour" next after the Patriarch of Rome, because Constantinople was new Rome. When the Fathers proposed or adopted this Canon, they did not intend to elevate the See of Constantinople to the same level as the Apostolic See ; their idea was not to

set up a rival Chair in the East, which should exclude the Supremacy of the Roman Pontiff ; they meant no more than that the See of New Rome should possess a similar status in *ecclesiastical* matters as that of Old Rome—in a word, they desired that the Patriarchate of Constantinople should be in all respects equal to the Patriarchate of Rome. They had no intention to aspire to the Papacy —an office higher than the Patriarchate. They did not claim for themselves the Prerogatives of S. Peter and of his Successors to his Cathedra ; they claimed no more than equal *ecclesiastical* patriarchal privileges. This is all that the Canon really means.

Anglicans will probably deem this exposition of the 28th canon as forced and unnatural ; yet, as we shall see, it is in accordance with the letter and spirit of the reply of the Magistrates to the objections of the Legates, and of the synodical epistle to the Pope. The Magistrates carefully distinguish between the "Primacy" of Authority and power, and the "dignity, or privilege of honour." Πρωτεῖα, the word translated "Primacy," as proved in the "Comment" on S. Irenæus, signifies Pre-eminence in the sense of the Head, or governing member of the Body. The Magistrates say that the "Primacy," or governing authority, as well as the "Precedency of honour," should be preserved according to the canons for the Archbishop of old Rome ;" but as regards the Chair of Constantinople, they add, "The Archbishop of Constantinople ought to enjoy," not the Primacy of Authority (πρωτεῖα), but "the same dignity or privilege (πρεσβεῖων) of honour." That is, as the Emperor before referred to said, "The Primacy of the Apostolic See, on account of the merit of Peter . . . . . and the Dignity of the city of Rome," *i. e.* as the then Imperial city. The distinction, then, between the Chair of S. Peter and the Chair of Constantinople could not be more exactly drawn than it was by the Magistrates of the Emperor—the Primacy of Authority, and the Precedence of honour to Rome, and a similar dignity of honour to New Rome. In the Synodical Epistle to the Pope, the Fathers are equally careful not to confound the two Primacies. They first declare that the Pope is "the constituted Interpreter to all (*i.e.* the Faithful) of the blessed Peter." Secondly, that "to him (the Pope) is committed by the Saviour the Custody of the Vineyard," *i.e.* the Universal Fold. And they further assert that he presided over the Council "as the Head over the members, *i.e.* the Bishops who formed the Council." This is plain testimony of the Pope being far Superior to any other Bishop of the Church, not excepting even the Patriarch of Constantinople. And when treating upon this Canon, to the effect that they had ordained that the Bishop of Constantinople "should have the privilege of *honour* after (his) most holy and Apostolic Chair," they express their hope that he (the Pope) would extend (his) wonted care to the Church of Constantinople, and (will) enlighten it with (his) Apostolic ray." The Fathers who used this language could not possibly have intended any severance of the old relation between that see and the Apostolic See. They then pray that he would "deign, therefore," *i. e.* condescend, calling him "most holy and blessed Father," "to allow this decision." This is the language of inferiors to superiors, the attitude of supplicants to a Chief. After this they intercede on behalf of that Church, reminding the Pope of "the wishes of the Emperor, the Senate, and the people of the imperial city," and they conclude their prayer thus: "Honour, then, we pray you, our judgment with your decree, that as we have been united to our Head (*i. e.* the Pope) in agreeing upon what is right, so the Head too (*i. e.* the Pope) may confirm the becoming act of the children. So will our pious Princes be blessed who have ratified as a law whatever your Holiness has determined." In the face

of this language can it be for a moment supposed that when the Fathers of Chalcedon (or rather the remnant of them, for the greater part had left), drew up this 28th canon, they intended to provide that the Patriarch of Constantinople should possess Prerogatives similar to those of the Successors of S. Peter in the Apostolic See? If they regarded the Pope as "the constituted Interpreter to all of blessed Peter," "to whom the Custody of the Vineyard was committed by the Saviour," as the "Head" and the "Father," can it be supposed that they meant to erect a second "Interpreter," a second Custodian of the one Vineyard, and to transpose one of the "members" into a second Head, and to promote a child (for they call themselves "children,") into the dignity of a second Common Father of the Universal Church? The whole force of this epistle, the language they employ, is a proof that such was not their intention. Their sole object, as stated above, was "to give to the See of Constantinople—the Imperial City—the "dignity, or privilege of honour," after Rome, that is, the ecclesiastical position of the Second Patriarch of the Universal Church, not the office and dignity, and Prerogative of the Sovereign Pontiff, the Successor of S. Peter in the Cathedra of Rome. Anglicans, in quoting this canon against the Roman Supremacy, never refer the reader to the speech of the Emperor's officials, or to the exposition of it as contained in the Synodical Epistle of the Council ; and for this reason, that it completely contradicts the interpretation they put upon it, by which they have misled the English people, and caused them to continue in their state of schism and rebellion against the Holy See of blessed Peter.

This Œcumenical Council, second to none in importance, which, together with the first three, were regarded by S. Gregory the Great as the Four Gospels, and which are so venerated by England that they are actually included in her Statute Law, witnesses to the following high Prerogatives of the Holy See : (1) That it is Supreme over Bishops, in that t can by its own sole authority depose and restore Bishops, even such exalted Prelates as the Patriarchs ; (2) That its authority over Councils is supreme, in that they must execute its commands and its judgments ; (3) That no plenary Council may be held without its sanction ; (4) That when it teaches *ex Cathedra* it does so with the voice of Peter, who lives and presides over his own See by his Successors ; (5) That when it pronounces judgment, it does so by "the authority of the blessed Peter ;" (6) That the Pope is the " Head," and the Bishops the "members ;" (7) That he is the " Father," and they the "children;" (8) That he "is the constituted Interpreter to all of blessed Peter," and (9) That to him is committed by the Saviour the Custody or care of "the Vineyard," *i.e.* the Universal Church. In a word, the Holy, Great, and Sacred Œcumenical Council of Chalcedon, by its acts and words, accepts the doctrine that the Pope, by virtue of his Succession from S. Peter, is the Head of the Brotherhood, the Father of the Faithful, the Confirmer of the Brethren, the Guardian and Custodian of the Catholic Church, and the Shepherd of the Universal Fold.

BISHOPS OF THE PROVINCE TARRAGONA (SPAIN).
A.D. 465.

117. "Even though no necessity of ecclesiastical discipline had supervened, we might indeed have had recourse to the privilege of your See ; whereby, the keys having been received after the resurrection of the Saviour, the matchless (or individual) preaching of the most blessed Peter had for its object the enlightenment of all men throughout the world ; the Princedom (*principatus*) of whose Vicar, as it is eminent, so it is to be feared and loved by all. Accordingly, we, adoring in you the God whom you serve blamelessly, have recourse to the faith commended by the mouth of the Apostle ; thence seeking for answers, whence nothing by error, nothing by presumption, but all with pontifical (*pontificali*) deliberation is prescribed. These things being so, there is, however, amongst us a false brother, whose presumption, as it can no longer be passed over in silence, so also does the urgency (necessity) of the future judgment compel us to speak. [Then, stating the ground of complaint against Silvanus, they add :] As therefore these acts of presumption which divide unity, which make a schism, ought to be speedily met, we ask of your See that we be instructed, by your Apostolical directions, as to what you would have be observed in this matter. ... It will assuredly be your triumph if in the time of your Apostleship, the Catholic Church hears that the Chair of Peter prevails, if the fresh seeds of the tares be extirpated."—*Labbé, t. v. p.* 56, 57.

COMMENT.

The Bishops of this province in Spain were troubled with an heretical brother, and they appeal to the Pope for the settlement of the case. They begin their epistle by mentioning their right to have recourse, under all necessities, to "that Privilege" of the See of Rome which consists in the Supremacy of jurisdiction, as symbolised by the keys which our Saviour delivered to the See through the blessed Peter. They then mention the peculiar office of the

Pope, as undoubtedly derived from S. Peter, saying, "The Princedom of whose Vicar (*i.e.* the Pope, vicar of Peter), as it is eminent, so it is to be feared and loved by all :" loved by Catholics, but feared by the heterodox. They then conclude their epistle by asking for "Apostolical directions" as to what "should be done in this matter of their false brother."

COUNCIL OF ROME.

A.D. 494.

118. "We have also thought that it ought to be noticed, that although the Catholic Churches, spread over the world, be the one bridal chamber as it were of Christ, yet has the Roman Church been, by certain synodal constitutions, raised above the rest of the Churches ; yea also, by the evangelical voice of the Lord our Saviour, did it attain the Primacy (*voce Domini et Salvatoris nostri primatum obtinuit*), *Thou art Peter, and upon this Rock*, &c. There has been also added the dwelling there of the most blessed Apostle Paul, the vessel of election ; who, not at a different time, as heretics mutter, but at the same time, and on one and the same day, was crowned, together with Peter, by a glorious death in the city of Rome, suffering under Nero ; and together did they consecrate the above-named Roman Church to Christ the Lord, and by their precious and memorable triumph have raised it above all other churches in the whole world. The first See, therefore, of the Apostle Peter is the Roman Church, which has no *spot or wrinkle, or any such thing*."— *Labbé, t. v. col.* 386.

COMMENT.

The following points are to be noticed :—(1) That the Church of God is the one Bridal Chamber, that is, it is one and indivisible ; as Christ is one, so the Church is one. (2) That "the Roman Church, by certain synodal constitutions, has been raised above the rest of the Churches." These constitutions, doubtless of ante-Nicene or Apostolical times, have long ago perished, as many other valuable documents of antiquity. Socrates, in his History, alludes to some such canons. (3) But this Primacy is derived originally from "the Lord our Saviour," evidently alluding to the three-fold commission S. Peter received, to judge, as the keys typify, to confirm the brethren, and to shepherdise the flock. And (4) That S. Peter and S. Paul did "consecrate the above-named Roman Church to Christ the Lord ;" and by their precious and memorable triumph they "have raised it above all the Churches in the whole world." Doubtless it will be objected that this Council was an interested one, and therefore its testimony is not worth much. But the real point is this, that no objections were ever raised, and no protests ever made against these Papal assumptions of Superior power and authority by the Bishops of any part of the Church. East or West. It is impossible to conceive that the Patriarchs, Priests, and Metropolitans of the Universal Church would have been silent, if these assumptions had had no foundation to rest upon ; indeed they would have betrayed their trust if they had not loudly protested against such arrogant claims. Their silence and acquiescence prove that the Roman Council had only spoken the truth.

SUMMARY OF CONCILIAR EVIDENCE.

THE evidence extracted from the plenary Councils, especially those which are Œcumenical, is exhaustive; and he who studies it with any care can arrive at only one conclusion.

1. These Councils testify that S. Peter was the " Head of the Faith," and "the Exarch and Head of the Apostles."

2. They witness to the truth (1) That the Pope "sits in the Place of Peter ;" (2) That he is "the constituted Interpreter to all (*i.e.* the Faithful) of the blessed Peter ;" (3) That "Peter speaks by (him) ;" (4) That to him " is committed by the Saviour the Custody of the Vineyard," that is, the Holy Catholic Church; and (5) That the Roman Church, by virtue of its consecration by S. Peter and S. Paul, "has been raised above the rest of all the Churches."

3. With respect to the Prerogatives of the Pope, as flowing from the commission granted to S. Peter, and through him to his Successors, these Councils admit, without a dissentient voice (1), That the Pope is the Teacher of the Church, "for Peter speaks by" his Successors; (2) That he is Supreme in jurisdiction, for by virtue of his inheriting S. Peter's judicial power, he, by his own sole authority, deposes and restores Bishops inclusive of the Patriarchs (witness the cases of Nestorius and Dioscorus, and that of Theodoret whom he restored) ; (3) That he can depose a Bishop from his sacerdotal ministry ; and (4) That he is the source of the Priesthood, for from him " flows to all the right of universal communion;" so that no Church or Priesthood can lawfully celebrate, administer, or receive sacraments, unless they are in communion with the Holy Roman Church.

4. The Supremacy of the Sovereign Pontiff over all Synods is attested by even Œcumenical Councils. It would seem (1) That is the case of Œcumenical and Plenary Councils, no Council can lawfully be held "without the authority of the Holy See ;" (2) That no canon or ordinance can be made without the sanction of the Apostolic See ; (3) That in the case of Œcumenical Councils, the Pope has the selection of the Bishops who are to take part in them ; (4) That no Bishop can retain his seat, if the Pope objects ; (5) That Bishops restored by the Pope are eligible to a seat in Councils ; (6) That the Pope presides either personally or by his Legates ; (7) That the judgment and decrees of Councils, whether they relate to faith, discipline, or persons, are made, as a rule, pursuant to, and in accordance with, the previous judgment of the Holy

See ; (8) That Councils on the termination of their sessions, apply to the Pope for the confirmation of their decrees ; and (9) That the Pope confirms or annuls them as he deems expedient.   It is very manifest that Catholic Synods, and especially the Œcumenical Councils, accept the doctrine (1) of the Supremacy of S. Peter, " the Rock and Foundation of the Faith," whom they regard as " the Head of the Faith," as " the Exarch and Head of the Apostles ; " and (2) of the Pope who " sits in the Place of Peter," as " his Vicar," by whom S. Peter teaches and judges, and by whom he rules and governs the Universal Church.

Anglicans will no doubt appeal to the Council of Carthage in which S. Cyprian presided, and another African Council, in which a dispute arose respecting the case of Apiarius (which will be hereafter more particularly considered), but what authority can these Councils have against the Œcumenical Councils of Ephesus and Chalcedon, which have accepted every one of the Prerogatives above enumerated ?   The Œcumenical Council of Ephesus confirmed without comment the sentence pronounced by the Pope alone, and, what is more, in submission to his supreme authority ; " Nestorius himself . . . . refused to obey a citation and to receive the Bishops who were sent to him on our part . . . . . and having convicted him . . . . of holding and teaching impious doctrine, being compelled by the necessity of the canons, *and by the Letter of our most holy Father and colleague Celestine*, Bishop of the Roman Church . . . we have agreed upon this unhappy sentence." The Bishops here regarded the Pope in two capacities, first, as their Father, and secondly, as their colleague.   As Father he was their Pope, their Superior, and their Sovereign Pontiff, whose " Letters" they felt bound to carry into effect.   Firmus, the Bishop of Cappadocia, said, " The Holy Apostolic See of Celestine has decided this affair, and has pronounced sentence on it *before* in the letter addressed to Cyril of Alexandria, *and in accordance with which sentence, and in furtherance thereof,* we have pronounced a canonical judgment against Nestorius, *the time which was granted him* (by the Pope) *for recantation being over past,* and we having waited beyond the time fixed by the Emperor."   S. Cyril also, the Patriarch of the second Apostolic See, says, " Since then we have executed the sentence *of the most holy Bishop Celestine*, and of the judgment passed by the Council against the heretic Nestorius."   This Œcumenical Council thus recognised the supreme authority of the Pope in the case of Nestorius. The Œcumenical Council of Chalcedon testifies still more amply in favour of the Papal Supremacy.   It was this Council which declared that the Pope was " the constituted Interpreter to all of the blessed Peter ;" that he was the appointed Guardian of the Vineyard, and that Councils could not be summoned without the sanction of the Holy See.   It was in this Council that the Pope by his Legates, by virtue of his Supremacy, deprived Dioscorus of Alexandria of his seat in the Council ; and by the same authority was Theodoret restored to his Episcopal rights.   Whatever may be the merits of the last African Council alluded to, their authority must yield to that of the Œcumenical Councils, which have admitted to the full the Papal Supremacy.

Some, perhaps, will object that these high pretensions of the Apostolic See were not formally decreed by this Council. Of course not, for it was not customary for the Supreme executive authority to derive its authority from a lower grade in the same order. The Prerogatives of the Queen of England were not derived from the Lords and the people ; they are, as Blackstone says, inherent in herself, *i. e.* her Sovereignty; nor do the rights of the Lords spring from the Commons. It is by no act of Parliament that the Crown of England is supreme, though acts of Parliament have confirmed its Prerogatives. The whole authority of the Crown is assumed. So also as respects the Papacy, it is by no canon that it exists ; it is not derived from the Bishops, nor from any general synod ; it is derived solely from S. Peter, who obtained it from Christ Himself. Canons and Constitutions have, indeed, confirmed the Primacy, but they never presumed to confer it on the Bishop of Rome. Indeed they could not, for he possessed it before any Council was ever convoked.

The Conciliar evidence for the Papacy is conclusive ; and when we consider that the weightiest evidence proceeds from Oriental Bishops—who were always jealous of their rights—it becomes absolutely impregnable.

III.

IMPERIAL TESTIMONY.

AURELIAN.

A.D. 265.

119. " Paul (of Samosata) therefore, having fallen from the Episcopate, and from the true faith, as already said, Domnus succeeded in the administration of the Church of Antioch. But Paul, being unwilling to quit the church (*i. e.* the temporalities), an appeal was made to the Emperor Aurelian, who decided most equitably in the business, ordering the church (*i. e.* the temporalities) to be given up to those whom the Christian Bishops of Italy and Rome should appoint."— *Eus. H. E. l.* vii. *c.* 30.

COMMENT.

Paul of Samosata, .Patriarch of Antioch, had been deposed for heresy; but he declined submission to the sentence, and retained the temporalities of his See. The Emperor was appealed to, and he decided that they were to be given up " to those whom the Christian Bishops of Italy and of Rome should appoint." Supposing the Roman Church was not superior to other Churches, it is not easy to understand why they ("the Bishops of Italy and of Rome") should have been preferred to the orthodox Bishops of the Patriarchate. This decree of the Emperor is an acknowledgment of (1) the superiority of the Italian Church, and (2) of its Chief Pontiff; which Church S. Ignatius had declared "presided in the region of the Romans," and "presiding over the Love," and which S. Irenæus affirmed, when he said that "every Church must agree or assemble with this Church ;" and S. Cyprian, that it was "the Chief Church, whence the unity of the Priesthood took its rise." This testimony is free from all possible suspicion, inasmuch as this Emperor was a heathen, and consequently a thoroughly disinterested witness.

GRATIAN.

A.D. 370.

120. "He (Gratian) immediately manifested the piety with which he was endued, and consecrated the first-fruits of his empire to God. He enacted a law enjoining that the pastors who had been banished should be restored to their flocks, and that the churches should be

given up to those who held com-munion with Damasus, who was the Bishop of Rome, and highly celebrated on account of the sanc-tity of his life ; for he was ready to say and do everything in defence of the Apostolical doctrines. He had succeeded Liberius in the go-vernment of the Church. Gratian sent Sopor, a renowned military chief, to carry the law into exe-cution, to drive away from the Churches, as wild beasts, those who preserved the blasphemies of Arius, and to restore the Churches to the faithful pastors, and to the holy flocks. This law was exe-cuted in all the provinces without opposition. In Antioch, however, which was the metropolis of the East, many disputes arose in con-sequence."—*Theod. H. E. l. v. c.* 2.

COMMENT.

In this epistle of the Emperor Gra-tian we have a distinct recognition of the position of the Pope, as the source of venerable communion to all the Churches (as S. Ambrose and the Council of Aquileia testified), in the East no less than in the West. In restoring the churches to the orthodox pastors, the Emperor, following the precedent set by Aurelian, command-ed that they should be delivered up " to those who held communion with Damasus," Bishop of Rome. The execution of this order was confided to Sopor, " a renowned military chief," who " carried the law into execution . . . in all the provinces," *i. e.* both in East and West. The greater part of the ecclesiastical provinces submitted without opposition, but Antioch re-sisted. This Emperor thus believed in the Papal supremacy, obedience to which he enforced all over the world.

GALLA PLACIDIA.

A. D. 450.

TO HER SON, THEODOSIUS.

121. "While our first care, on en-tering the ancient city, was to render due worship (*cultum*) to the blessed Apostle Peter, the most reverend Bishop Leo, who was himself ador-ing at the altar of the martyr (S. Peter), remained awhile, after he had ended his prayers, and com-plained to me, with tears, about the state of the Catholic faith, calling to witness the Chief of the Apostles, to whom we had just had recourse. He was surrounded by many Bishops, whom, on account of the Princedom or dignity pecu-liar to the Place (Rome, *i. e.* his See), he had assembled from the numerous cities of Italy. . . . . By their favour, then, may your kindliness direct, in opposition to the prevailing confusion, that the true faith of the Catholic religion be preserved immaculate, namely, by seeing that in accordance with the form and definition of the Apostolic See, which we both alike venerate as of surpassing (authority) (ἵνα κατὰ τὸν τύπον καὶ τὸν ὅρον τοῦ ἀποστολικοῦ θρόνου ὃν καὶ ἡμεῖς ὁμοίως ὡς προηγούμενον, προσκυνοῦμεν), Flavian may be se-cured from harm in his see, and

the matter be transferred to the judgment of a Council, and the Apostolic See, in which he who was first worthy to receive the heavenly keys ordained the Princedom (*principatum*) of the Episcopate." *Inter Ep. Leon. T.* i. *Ep.* lvi. *col.* 859–62, *Migne.*

COMMENT.

The Empress Galla describes to us the Court of the Pope, so to speak ; and this throws great light as to how the office of the Pope was regarded by the Church. This princess, while remaining at Rome, went to worship at the shrine of S. Peter. S. Leo, the Pope, was apparently at that time before the altar of the Apostle, adoring his Lord and God. After he had ended his prayer, he "remained awhile," and in conversation with the Empress deplored the state of the Church. "He was surrounded," the Empress says, "by many Bishops," who "had assembled from the numerous cities of Italy." Why was this ? The Empress informs us that this was on account of the Princedom or dignity peculiar to the Place, *i. e.* of his See. This gives us an idea of the Pope's exalted position and dignity as the Successor of the Chief of the Apostles.

The conversation the Pope had with Galla had its effect, for in her letter she admonished her son Theodosius to "direct that the faith of the Catholic religion be preserved immaculate," "in accordance with the form and definition of the Apostolic See, which," she adds, "we both alike venerate, as of surpassing (authority)." No language can be more explicit than this, which signifies in effect that the Roman Pontiff is Supreme in all matters of faith and discipline. Indeed, according to the Empress, a Council is nothing without the co-ordinate authority of the Pope ; for in the case of Flavian, she says, "Let the matter be transferred to the judgment of the Council and the Apostolic See, in which he (S. Peter) who was first worthy to receive the heavenly keys, ordained the Princedom of the Episcopate." No evidence can be more exhaustive than what has fallen from this Empress.

THEODOSIUS AND VALENTINIAN III.

A. D. 450.

122. "Since, therefore, the authority of the sacred Synod (of Nicæa) has made firm the Primacy of the Apostolic See, on account of the merit of Peter, Chief of the Corona of Bishops, and of the dignity of the city of Rome, let no one presumptuously dare to attempt anything unlawful in opposition to the Authority of that See. Then at length will the peace of the churches be maintained, and all will acknowledge their rulers." *Inter Ep. Leon. T.* i. *Ep.* xi. *col.* 637, *Migne.*

VALENTINIAN III.

"When I came to Rome divinely pleasing, I proceeded on the following day to the Basilica of the Apostle Peter, and there, after having worshipped a night and a day, I was requested by the Bishop of Rome, and also by others who were with him, having been assembled from various provinces, to write to your Clemency concerning the Faith. . . . We are bound by the tradition of our ancestors, with all

P

devotion, in our time to defend and maintain inviolate, both the Dignity of particular (or peculiar) reverence to the blessed Apostle Peter, seeing that the most blessed Bishop of Rome, to whom antiquity has at-tributed the Princedom of the Priest-hood over all, may have both place and liberty to judge concerning the Faith and the Priests" (*i.e.* Bishops). *Ib. Ep.* lv. *Valent. ad Theod. Imp. col.* 857-10.

COMMENT.

These Emperors assert that the "Primacy of the Apostolic See" was made firm by the Council of Nicæa. Owing to the loss of the acts of that Council we are unable to ascertain the fact for ourselves, but we may well accept the authority of the Emperors as entirely disinterested. It was, indeed, shown that the words of canon vi. confirming "the ancient customs" involved it, for had this Primacy been from the beginning (as it has been abundantly proved that it was), it was necessarily included in that canon. It is then a matter proved that the Bishop of Rome possessed the Primacy. But now let us inquire what sort of Primacy? Was it a Primacy of honour, of prestige, of rank? and merely because of the dignity of the Imperial city? The Emperors' evidence is directly contrary to such an idea. They say, "It was (1) on account of the merit of Peter, Chief of the Corona of Bishops" (the Episcopate is the Crown of the Priesthood). It was then, because S. Peter had founded the Roman Church, and planted therein his Cathedra or Chair, that it became originally entitled to the Primacy. But the Emperors add (2) " On account of the . . . . dignity of the city of Rome." When the Empire became Christian, it was in the nature of things that the Bishop of Rome, who held the Primacy, by virtue of his succession to the Chair of Peter, should also have a Primacy of dignity and honour, on account of the grandeur of the city of which he was the Bishop." The Emperors thus witness to a double Primacy in the Bishop of Rome, the one as derived from S. Peter, which is divine and Apostolic; and the other, from the Emperor, which was human and political. As shown under the section of Councils, this greatly explains the meaning of the canons of Constantinople and Chalcedon respecting the Second Primacy of the See of Constantinople. But when the Emperors alluded to the Primacy of the Apostolic See, " on account of the merit of Peter, Chief of the Corona of Bishops, and of the Dignity of the city of Rome," did they understand a Primacy of honour or rank only, or of Supremacy and power? The answer is contained in the clauses following : " Let no one presumptuously dare to attempt anything unlawful in opposition to the Authority of that See." The Primacy then was one of " Authority," not that of mere rank or honour, to which every one was to submit. But Valentinian, in a letter to Theodosius, his colleague in the Empire, employs much stronger language ; after referring to the "peculiar reverence" due "to the blessed Apostle Peter," he adds, that to "the most blessed Bishop of Rome" "antiquity has attributed the Princedom of the Priesthood over all"—a position which implies authority and power to rule the whole body of the Kingdom and Church of God.

From the evidence of this Emperor (who had no interest in supporting a usurpation of authority, on the contrary, it was *politically* against his interest as a mere secular Ruler), it is plain to demonstration that the Primacy of Rome from the beginning was one not of courtesy or of dignity, but of Sovereignty and Supremacy over the Universal Household of God.

MARCIAN AND VALENTINIAN III.

A.D. 451.

123. "We deem it right, in the first instance, to address your Holiness, holding as you do the Headship of the Episcopate of the divine Faith (τήν τι σὴν ἁγιωσύνην ἐπισκοπεύουσαν, καὶ ἄρχουσαν τῆς θείας πίστεως), begging and beseeching your Holiness to pray for the strength and stability of our Empire, and that designs and counsels may be so ordered that every error being removed by the Synod (Chalcedon) now to be assembled by your authority (σοῦ αὐθιττοῦντος) the greatest peace may be established among the Bishops of the Catholic faith." *Inter Ep. Leon. Ep.* lxxiii. *T.* i. *col.* 899, *Migne.*

MARCIAN.

124. Writing to the Pope, counselling him about the place where the Fourth Œcumenical Council should meet, the Emperor adds, "Where all the most holy Bishops may assemble, and decree concerning the religion of Christianity and the Catholic Faith, as your Holiness by your own disposition shall define according to the Ecclesiastical Rules." *Ib. Ep.* lxxxvi. *T.* i. *col.* 903–6, *Migne.*

126. "Which (the non-arrival of the Pope's confirmation) has been the cause of much doubt to the minds of some who still pursue after the vanity and perversity of Eutyches, whether your Holiness has sanctioned the decrees of the sacred Synod (Chalcedon). Whereupon your Holiness will see fit to send letters, whereby it may be evident to all the churches and peoples that what has been transacted in the sacred Synod has the sanction of your Holiness." *Inter Ep. Leon. T.* i. *Ep.* cx. *col.* 1019, *Migne.*

COMMENT.

Marcian and Valentinian acknowledge in their joint letter to the Pope that he held "the Headship of the Episcopate of the Divine Faith," and they state that the Council of Chalcedon was soon about "to assemble by his (the Pope's) authority." And Marcian, in another letter to the same Pope on the Council of Chalcedon, expresses his desire that it will execute "what his Holiness," "according to ecclesiastical rule, shall define." And on the conclusion of the Council, finding that the Pope delayed his confirmation of its proceedings, he addresses him another letter, begging him, in fact, to send letters whereby "it may be evident to all the churches and peoples, that what has been done has the sanction of your Holiness."

No Emperor or Sovereign would, if he could help it, acknowledge an *imperium in imperio:* an empire within his empire or kingdom. The whole history of States shows how jealous the civil authority has ever been of any independent power established within their territorial limits. It is difficult to understand how even the catholic Emperors of old could have tolerated a Universal Empire, under the government of an independent Supreme Head, except on one only supposition, viz., that it possessed an authority which even to them was unimpeachable. This authority they evidently believed to be nothing less than divine, and therefore they, as obedient sons of Christ, submitted to it without a murmur.

Now after an examination of their proceedings and their letters, it is plain that they regarded the city of Rome as, in a peculiar sense, ecclesiastical property : inasmuch as it was the Place S. Peter selected for the site of his Cathedra, from which the unity of the Priesthood and the rights of venerable communion should ever after proceed. S. Peter himself, they knew, was the Chief and Head of all the Apostles and Bishops, to whom was due "a peculiar reverence."

Believing then, as the Catholic Emperors undoubtedly did, in the doctrine of the Apostolical Succession, they could not do otherwise than believe in an Apostolical Succession from S. Peter as the Head of the Church. Hence they held that S. Peter "ordained the Princedom of the Episcopate:" hence, too, they described the Pope as having that "Princedom," or "dignity," which is "peculiar" to the See, and as having "the Headship of the Episcopate, and of the Divine Faith." In consequence then of this exalted position, the Emperors of both East and West did all in their power either to exterminate or to honour them. Before the conversion of the Empire, every Pope, save about five (out of thirty-five Pontiffs) was martyred ; no other See was so honoured in this respect as the Primatial one ; it would seem that the Devil, knowing full well that Rome was the supreme seat of divine authority, and that the Church of that city was primarily the subject of our Lord's promise to S. Peter, that "the gates of hell shall not prevail against it," exercised all his malignant energy to effect her destruction. The demoniacal Emperors of Rome strove their utmost to destroy the Presiding Church,—that *imperium in imperio* which they so much dreaded,—but in vain. That they, or some of them, were well aware of the Primatial Authority of that See is evident from the judgment of the heathen Emperor Aurelian (A.D. 265) in the case of Paul of Samosata who was Bishop of Antioch. This Prelate, who had been deposed, nevertheless schismatically retained his Church, and the ecclesiastical authorities had to appeal to the Emperor in order to obtain possession of the temporalities. This Emperor, though a heathen, was a just man, whose mind was governed by the principles of law and equity, and he decided upon depriving Paul of his Church, and handing it over, not to the Bishops of the province or patriarchate, but to "the Christian Bishops of Italy and Rome." Why to the Prelates of "Italy and Rome," and "not of the East?" The only answer that can be given is, that he knew according to the ecclesiastical law, that the Church of Rome (*i.e.* Rome and the circumjacent cities together forming the province) was the "Presiding Church," and the Bishop of Rome the Supreme Pontiff, to whom was committed the government of the Church, and to whom the Patriarchal Churches were especially subject. On no other ground could the Emperor Aurelian have handed over this Church to "Bishops of Italy and Rome."

Since the conversion of the Empire, the Catholic Emperors ever recognised most fully this position, testifying that the Bishop of Rome has the "Princedom of the Episcopate," and "of the Faith," whose judgment, "according to the form and definition of the Apostolic See, is of surpassing" authority, that is, cannot be impugned by any earthly authority. And this they admitted because of the "reverence due to the Apostle Peter," who had ordained the Roman Primacy, to "which antiquity has attributed the Princedom over all."

So real was the belief in the Supremacy of the Pope, that ecclesiastical judgments were left to his cognizance, and when heretical pastors were expelled by the authority of the Emperors from their Sees, the churches were "given up to those who held communion with Damasus, who had succeeded Liberius in the government of the Church:" and when Œcumenical Councils were to be summoned, this was done by the "Authority" of the Pope, who presided over them by his legates, and confirmed their decrees. Such was the position the Emperors of both East and West believed that the Pope occupied in the Universal Church. Before the conversion of the Empire, they honoured the Roman Church by compassing her destruction, and afterwards (at least the Catholics) by venerating her, and, as far as they could, adding to her dignity.

The account Galla gives of the court of the Pope is extremely interesting, and it illustrates how exceedingly exalted was the office he filled, when adoring before the altar of the blessed Peter, she saw him "surrounded by many Bishops," who were in attendance on him, "on account of that Princedom and Dignity" "which were peculiar to his See."

The Catholic Emperors then testify that the Pope, by virtue of his succession from S. Peter, is "the Head of the Episcopate," and "the Head of the Faith," and that his Supremacy extended over the whole Universal Church.

PART III.

PAPAL ACTA, EPISTLES, &c.

PRELIMINARY REMARKS.

Having collected and arranged in chronological order the evidence for the Papacy as contained in the documents of the Catholic Fathers, Councils, and Emperors, it is now proposed to submit, for the consideration of those seeking the truth, some of the proceedings of the Popes commencing from the earliest antiquity.

It is, indeed, much to be regretted that nearly all the epistles of the Popes of the ante-Nicene age have perished, together with many of the writings of the Fathers, and almost all the acts of the councils of that period. The collection known as "Isidore's False Decretals," are admitted to be utterly untrustworthy, but it may be open to doubt whether all of them are forgeries ; but as they have not been pressed into the service of this work, no further allusion to them is necessary. Fortunately there are other sources of information left for us, viz. the Ecclesiastical Historians, who had access to all then extant documents, and were consequently conversant with the chief events of that glorious age. To these historians an appeal has been made for what information they can give us, and it will be found that they are more than sufficient for the purpose.

It is not proposed to add "Comments" to the documents connected with each Pope, for to do so would only be recapitulating what has already been too frequently repeated. Whatever observations may be needed will be found at the end of this Part.

I. POPE S. CLEMENT I.

A.D. 91–107.

TO THE CHURCH OF CORINTH.

The Church of God which sojourns at Rome, to the Church of God sojourning at Corinth, to them that are called. . . . Owing, dear brethren, to the sudden and successive calamitous events which have happened to ourselves, we feel that we have been somewhat tardy in turning our

attention to the points respecting which you consulted us, and especially
to the shameful and detestable sedition, utterly abhorrent to the Church
of God, which a few rash and self-confident persons have kindled to such
a pitch of frenzy, that your venerable and illustrious name, worthy to be
universally loved, has suffered grievous injury. [Then follow praises and
admonitions, &c.] These things, beloved, we write unto you, not merely
to admonish you of your duty, but also to remind ourselves. For we are
struggling in the same arena, and the same conflict is assigned to both
of us. Wherefore let us give up vain and fruitless cares, and approach
to the glorious and venerable rule of our holy calling. Let us attend to
what is good, pleasing, and acceptable in the sight of Him who bought
us. .... Let our whole body, then, be preserved in Christ Jesus ; and
let every one be subject to his neighbour, according to the special gifts
bestowed upon him. .... These things, therefore, being manifest to us,
and since we look into the depths of the divine knowledge, it behoves us
to do all things in order, which the Lord has commanded us to do at
stated times. He has enjoined offerings and services to be performed by
us, and this not thoughtlessly or irregularly, but at the appointed times and
hours. When and by whom He desires these things to be done, He
himself has fixed by His own supreme will, in order that all things,
being piously done according to His good pleasure, may be acceptable
unto Him. Those, therefore, who present their offerings at the appointed
times are accepted and blessed ; for, inasmuch as they follow the laws of
the Lord, they sin not. For his own peculiar services are assigned to
the High-priest (*i. e.* the Bishop), and their one proper place is prescribed
to the Priests, and their one special ministrations devolve on the Levites
(*i. e.* Deacons). The layman is bound by the laws that pertain to laymen.
Let every one of you, brethren, give thanks to God in his own order,
living in all good conscience, with becoming gravity, and not going
beyond the rule of the ministry prescribed to him. . . . . Take up the
Epistle of the blessed Apostle Paul. What did he write to you at the time
when the Gospel first began to be preached? Truly, under the inspiration of the Spirit, he wrote to you concerning himself and Cephas and
Apollos, because even. then partialities had been formed among you.
But that partiality for one before another entailed less guilt upon you,
inasmuch as your partialities were then shown towards Apostles, already
of high reputation, and towards a man whom they had approved.
But now reflect who those were that had persecuted you and lessened
the renown of your far-famed brotherly love. It is disgraceful, beloved—
yea, highly disgraceful, and unworthy of your Christian profession, that
such a thing should be heard of as that the most steadfast and ancient
Church of the Corinthians should be, on account of one or two persons,
engaged in sedition against its presbyters. And this rumour has
reached not only us, but those who are unconnected with us ; so that,
through your infatuation, the Name of the Lord is blasphemed, while
danger is also brought upon yourselves. [Then follow exhortations to
charity.] Ye, therefore, who laid the foundation of this sedition, submit
yourselves to the presbyters, and receive correction so as to repent, bending
the knees of your hearts. Learn to be subject, laying aside the proud

and arrogant self-confidence of your tongue. For it is better for you that you should occupy a humble but honourable place in the flock of Christ, than that, being highly exalted, you should be cast out from the hope of His people. . . . . May God . . . . who chose our Lord Jesus Christ, and us through Him, to be a peculiar people, grant to every soul that calleth upon His glorious and holy Name, faith, fear, peace, patience, long-suffering, self-control, purity, and sobriety, to the well-pleasing of His Name, through our High Priest and Protector Jesus Christ. . . . . Send back speedily to us, in peace and with joy, these our messengers to you,—Claudius Ephebus and Valerius Bito, with Fortunatus ; that they may the sooner announce to us the peace and harmony we so earnestly desire and long for [among you], and that we may the more quickly rejoice over the good order re-established among you." *Epist.* i. *ad Cor. c.* 1, 38, 40, 41, 47, 57, 58, 59.

II. POPE S. ANICETUS.

A.D. 157–8.

Visit of S. Polycarp, Bishop of Smyrna.

"And when the blessed Polycarp went to Rome, in the time of Anicetus, and they had a little difference among themselves likewise respecting other matters, they were immediately reconciled, not disputing much with one another on this head (*i. e.* the Paschal controversy). For neither could Anicetus persuade Polycarp not to observe it, because he had always observed it with John the disciple of our Lord and the rest of the Apostles with whom he associated ; and neither did Polycarp persuade Anicetus to observe it, who said that he was bound to maintain the practice of the presbyters before him. Which things being so, they communed with each other ; and in the church Anicetus yielded to Polycarp, out of respect, no doubt, the office of consecrating ; and they separated from each other in peace, all the Church being at peace ; both those that observed, and those that did not observe, maintaining peace." *Eus. H. E. l.* v. *c.* 24.

III. POPE S. VICTOR.

A.D. 193.

1. The Paschal Controversy.

It having become the opinion of the Church that the Feast of Easter ought to be celebrated on the Lord's day, and not upon the week-day on which the anniversary of the Resurrection might happen to fall, the Pope addressed the Asiatic Churches to that effect ; but the Asiatic

Bishops under Polycrates, Bishop of Ephesus, objected, pleading Apostolic custom; whereupon "Victor, the Bishop of the Church of Rome, forthwith endeavoured to cut off the Churches of all Asia, together with the neighbouring Churches, as heterodox, from the common unity. And he publishes abroad by letters, and proclaims that all the brethren there are excommunicated. But this was not the opinion of all the Bishops. They immediately exhorted him, on the contrary, to contemplate that course that was calculated to promote peace, unity, and love to one another." *Eus. H. E. l.* v. *c.* 24.

2. EXCOMMUNICATION OF THEODOTUS, FATHER OF ARIANISM.

"How, then, could it happen that since the doctrine of the Church has been proclaimed for so many years, that those until the times of Victor preached the Gospel after this manner? And how are they so devoid of shame as to utter these falsehoods against Victor, well knowing that Victor excommunicated that currier Theodotus, the leader and father of this God-denying apostasy, as the first one that asserted that Christ was a mere man?" *Ib.* c. 28.

IV. THE ROMAN CLERGY DURING THE VACANCY* OF THE HOLY SEE.

1. THE ROMAN CLERGY TO THE CARTHAGINIAN CLERGY.

A.D. 250-52.

"We have been informed by Crementius, the sub-deacon, who came to us from you, that the blessed Father Cyprian has for a certain reason withdrawn; in doing which he acted quite rightly, because he is a person of eminence, and because a conflict is impending, which God has allowed in the world, ... since, moreover, it devolves upon us, who appear to be placed on high in the Place of the Shepherd, to keep watch over the flock; if we be found neglectful, it will be said to us, as it was said to our predecessors also, who in such wise negligent, had been placed in charge, that we have not sought for that which was lost, and had not corrected the wanderer, and had not bound up that which was broken, but have taken of their milk and been clothed with their wool; and then also the Lord Himself, fulfilling what had been written in the Law and the Prophets, teaches, saying, 'I am the good Shepherd, who lay down My life for the sheep.' ... To Simon, too, He speaks thus: 'Lovest thou Me?' He answered, 'I do love Thee.' He saith to him, 'Feed My sheep.' We know that this saying arose out of the very circumstance of his withdrawal, and the rest of the disciples did likewise. We are unwilling, therefore, beloved brethren, that you should be found hirelings, but we desire you to be good Shepherds, since you are aware

---

* The Holy See was vacant for two years on account of the persecutions.

that no slight danger threatens you if you do not exhort our brethren to stand steadfast in the faith, so that the brotherhood be not absolutely rooted out, as being of those who rush headlong into idolatry. . . . . And there are other matters which are incumbent on you, which also we have here added, as that, if any who may have fallen into this temptation begin to be taken with sickness, and repent of what they have done, and desire communion, it should in anywise be granted them. Or if you have widows or bedridden people, who are unable to maintain themselves, or those who are in prisons or are excluded from their own dwellings, these ought in all cases to have some to minister to them," &c. *Inter Ep. Cyp. Ep.* ii.

2. S. CYPRIAN TO THE ROMAN CLERGY.

" . . . . Having ascertained, beloved brethren, that what I have done and am doing has been told you in a somewhat garbled and untruthful manner, I have thought it necessary to write this letter to you, wherein I might give an account to you of my doings, my discipline, and my diligence ; for, as the Lord's commands teach, immediately the first burst of the disturbance arose, and the people with violent clamour repeatedly demanded me, I, taking into consideration not so much my own safety as the public peace of the brethren, withdrew for a while, lest by my over-bold presence the tumult which had begun might be still provoked. . . . . And what I did, these thirteen letters, sent forth at various times, declare to you, which I have transmitted to you; in which neither counsel to the clergy nor exhortation to the confessors, nor rebuke, when it was necessary, to the exiles, nor my appeals and persuasions to the whole brotherhood, that they should entreat the mercy of God, was wanting to the full extent that, according to the law of faith and the fear of God, with the Lord's help, my poor abilities could endeavour . . . . But afterwards, when some of the lapsed . . . . broke forth with a daring demand, as though they would endeavour by a violent effort to extort the peace that had been promised them by the martyrs and confessors ; concerning these also I wrote twice to the clergy, and commanded it to be read to them ; that for the mitigation of their violence in any manner for the meantime, if any had received a certificate from the martyrs when departing this life, having made confession, and received the imposition of hands on them for repentance, they should be remitted to the Lord with the peace promised them by the martyrs. Nor in this did I give them a law, or rashly constitute myself the author of the direction ; but as it seemed fit both that honour should be paid to the martyrs, and that the vehemence of those who were anxious to disturb everything should be restrained ; and when, besides, I had read your letter which you lately wrote hither to my clergy by Crementius, the sub-deacon, to the effect that assistance should be given to those who might, after their lapse, be seized with sickness, and might penitently desire communion ; I judged it well to stand by your judgment, lest our proceedings, which ought to be united and to agree in all things, should in any respect be different. The cases of the rest, even although they might have received certificates from the martyrs, I ordered altogether to be put off, and to be reserved till I should be present, that so, when the Lord has given to us peace, and several Bishops shall have begun to assemble in one place, we may be able to arrange and reform everything, having the advantage also of your counsel." *Ib. Ep.* xiv.

3. S. CYPRIAN TO THE ROMAN CLERGY.

"After the letters that I wrote to you, beloved brethren, in which what I had done was explained, and some slight account was given of my discipline and diligence, there came another matter which ought not to be concealed from you any more than the others. For our brother Lucian, who himself also is one of the confessors—earnest indeed in faith and strong in virtue, but little established in the reading of the Lord's Word—has attempted certain things, constituting himself for a time an authority for unskilled people, so that certificates written by his hand were given indiscriminately to many persons in the name of Paulus ; whereas Mappalicus the martyr, cautious and modest, mindful of the law and discipline, wrote no letters contrary to the Gospel, but only moved with domestic affection for his mother, who had fallen, commanded peace to be given to her. . . . . But Lucian, not only while Paulus was still in prison, gave everywhere in his name certificates written with his own hand, but even after the decease of Paulus persisted in doing the same things under his name. . . . In order, in some measure, to put a stop to this practice, I wrote letters to them, which I have sent you under the enclosure of the former letter, in which I did not fail to ask and persuade them that consideration might be had for the law of the Lord and the Gospel." [S. Cyprian then gives an account of the proceedings of Lucian, &c., and then continues :] "I have sent a copy to you of the letters that I wrote to my clergy about these matters, and moreover what Caldonius, my colleague, of his integrity and faithfulness wrote, and what I replied to him. I have sent both to you to read. Copies also of the letters of Celerinus, the good and stout confessor, which he wrote to Lucian the same confessor—also what Lucian replied to him—I have sent to you ; that you may know both my labours in respect of everything and my diligence, and might learn the truth itself, how moderate and cautious is Celerinus the confessor, and how reverent both in his humility and fear for our faith ; while Lucian, as I have said, is less skilful concerning the understanding of the Lord's Word, and by his facility, is mischievous on account of the dislike that he causes for my reverential calling. . . . . But your letter which I received, written to my clergy, came opportunely ; as also did those which the blessed confessors, Moyses and Maximus, Nicostratus, and the rest sent to Saturninus and Aurelius, and the others, in which are contained the full vigour of the Gospel and the strong discipline of the law of the Lord. Your words much assisted me, as I laboured here, and withstood with the whole strength of faith the onset of ill-will, so that my work was shortened from above, and that before the letters which I last sent you reached you, you declared to me that according to the Gospel law your Judgment was strongly and unanimously concurrent with mine." *Ib. Ep.* xxii.

4. THE ROMAN CLERGY TO S. CYPRIAN.

" Although a mind conscious to itself of uprightness, and relying on the vigour of evangelical discipline, and made a true witness to itself in the heavenly decrees, is accustomed to be satisfied with God for its only Judge, and neither to seek the praises nor to dread the charges of any other, yet those are worthy of double praise who, knowing that they owe their conscience to God alone as the Judge, yet desire that their doings should be approved also by their brethren themselves. It is no wonder, brother Cyprian, that you should do this, who, with your usual modesty and inborn industry, have wished that we should be found not so much Judges of, as sharers in, your counsels, so that we might find praise with you in your doings while we approve them ; and might be able to be fellow-heirs with you in your good counsels, because we entirely accord with them. In the same way we are all thought to have laboured in that in which we are all regarded as allied in the same agreement of censure and discipline. . . . . That we are not saying this dishonestly, our former letters have proved, wherein we have declared our opinion to you, with a very plain statement, both against those who had betrayed themselves as unfaithful by the unlawful presentation of wicked certificates, as if they thought that they would escape those ensnaring nets of the devil ; whereas not less than if they had approached to the wicked altars (Pagan), they were held fast by the very fact that they had testified to him ; and against those who had used those certificates when made, although they had not been present when they were made, since they had certainly asserted their presence by ordering that they should be so written. . . . . Far be it from the Roman Church to slacken her vigour with so profane a facility, and to loosen the nerves of her severity by overthrowing the majesty of faith ; so that when the wrecks of your ruined brethren are still not only lying, but are falling around, remedies of a too hasty kind, and certainly not likely to avail, should be afforded for communion ; and by a false mercy, new wounds should be impressed on the old wounds of their transgression ; so that even repentance should be snatched from these wretched beings, but their greater overthrow. . . . . But once more, to return to the point whence our discourse appears to have digressed, you shall find subjoined the sort of letters that we also sent to Sicily ; although upon us is incumbent a greater necessity of delaying this affair, having, since the departure of Fabian (the late Pope), of most noble memory, had no Bishop appointed as yet, on account of the difficulties of affairs and times, who can arrange all things of this kind, and who can take account of those who are lapsed, with authority and wisdom. However, as you also have yourself declared in so important a matter, it is satisfactory to us, that the peace of the Church must first be maintained ; then, that an assembly for counsel being gathered together, with Bishops, presbyters, deacons, and confessors, as well as with the laity who stand fast, we should deal with the case of the lapsed." *Inter Ep. Cyp. Ep.* xxx.

V. POPE S. STEPHEN.

A.D. 253-7.

1. QUESTION OF RE-BAPTISM.

" Cyprian, who was Bishop of the Church of Carthage, was of opinion that they (heretics) should be admitted on no conditions, before they were first purified from their error by baptism. But Stephen, who thought that no innovations should be made contrary to the tradition, that had prevailed from ancient times, was greatly offended at this. Dionysius, therefore, after addressing to him many arguments by letter on this subject . . . . writes as follows : ' Now I wish you to understand, my brother, that all the Churches throughout the East, and further, all that were formerly divided, have been united again. All the Bishops, also, are everywhere in harmony, rejoicing exceedingly at the peace that has been established beyond all expectation. These are Demetrianus of Antioch, Theoctistus of Cæsarea, &c. &c., and all the Churches of Cilicia, Firmilianus, and all Cappadocia ; for I have mentioned only the more distinguished of the Bishops by name, that neither the length of my letter, nor the burden of my words, may offend you. All the provinces of Syria and Arabia, which at different times you supplied with necessaries, and to whom you have now written, Mesopotamia, Pontus, and Bythinia, and, to comprehend all in a word, all are rejoicing everywhere at the unanimity and brotherly love now prevailing, and are glorifying God for the same.' Such are the words of Dionysius. [In a subsequent letter to Pope S. Xystus he thus wrote :] ' He (Stephen) had written before respecting Helenus and Firmilianus, and all those from Cilicia, and Cappadocia, and Galatia, and all the nations adjoining, that he would not have communion with them on this account, because they, said he, rebaptized the heretics. And behold, I pray you, the importance of the matter. For in reality, as I have ascertained, decrees have been passed in the greatest councils of the Bishops, that those who come from the heretics, are first to be instructed, and then are to be washed and purified from the filth of their old and impure leaven. But respecting all these things I have sent letters, entreating them.' After stating other matters, he proceeds : ' But I have also written to our beloved and fellow-presbyters, Dionysius and Philemon, who agreed before with Stephen in sentiment, and wrote to me on these matters. Before, indeed, I wrote briefly, but now more fully.' " *Eus. H. E. l.* vii. *c.* 3, 4, 5.

2. S. CYPRIAN MOVES THE OFFICE OF THE HOLY SEE AGAINST MARCIANUS, BISHOP OF ARLES, IN FRANCE.

" Wherefore it behoves you to write a very full letter to our fellow-Bishops established in Gaul, that they no longer suffer the froward and proud Marcianus . . . . . to insult our college . . . . . Let Letters

be addressed from thee to the province and people of Arles, whereby
Marcianus being excommunicated, another may be substituted in his
room, and the flock of Christ, which to this day is overlooked, scattered
by him and wounded, be again collected together . . . . Signify plainly
to us, who has been substituted in Arles in the room of Marcianus, that
we may know to whom we should direct our brethren, and to whom
write." *S. Cyp. Ep.* lxvii. *ad Step. p.* 115, 117.

VI. POPE S. JULIUS.

A.D. 342.

1. TO THE EUSEBIANS.

"It behoved you, beloved, to come hither (Rome), and not to refuse
(ἴδει ἀπαντῆσαι, καὶ μὴ παραιτήσασθαι), in order that this business may be
terminated ; for reason requires this. . . . . Oh, beloved ! the judgments of
the Church are no longer in accordance with the Gospel, but are (by you,
Arians) to the inflicting of exile and of death. For even though any
transgression had been committed, as you pretend, by these men (*i. e.*
S. Athanasius, Paul of Constantinople, &c.), the judgment ought to have
been in accordance with the ecclesiastical rule, and not thus. It behoved
you to write to all of us, that thus what was just might be decreed by
all. For they who suffered were Bishops, and the Churches that suffered
no common ones, over which the Apostles ruled in person. And why
were we not written to concerning the Church, especially of Alexandria ?
or, are you ignorant that this has been the custom first to write to us,
and thus what is just be decreed from this Place (Rome)? If, therefore,
any such suspicion fell upon the Bishop there (Alexandria), it was befitting to write to this Church (Rome). But now they who acquainted us
not, but did what they themselves chose, proceed to wish us, though
unacquainted with the facts, to become supporters of their views. Not
thus were Paul's ordinances, not thus have the Fathers handed
down to us, this is another form, and a new institution. Bear with
me cheerfully, I beseech you, for what I write is for the common good.
For what we have received from the blessed Apostle Peter, the same do
I make known to you ; and these things I would not have written to
you, deeming them manifest to you all, had not what has been done con-
founded us." *Ep. ad Eusebian. n.* 6, 21. *Galland. T.* v. *p.* 6, 13.

2. HISTORICAL ACCOUNT.

BY SOCRATES.

"Eusebius, however, could by no means remain quiet, but as the
saying is, *left no stone unturned*, in order to effect the purpose he had
in view. He therefore caused a synod to be convened at Antioch, in

Syria, under pretence of dedicating a Church which Constantine, the father of the Augusti, had commenced, and which had been completed by his son Constantius in the tenth year after the foundations were laid : but his real motive was the subversion of the doctrine of consubstantiality. There were present at this synod ninety Bishops from various cities. Nevertheless Maximus, Bishop of Jerusalem, who had succeeded Macarius, declined attending there, for the recollection of the fraudulent means by which he had been induced to subscribe the deposition of Athanasius. Neither was Julius, Bishop of Ancient Rome, there, nor did he indeed send a representative ; although the ecclesiastical rule (or canon) expressly commands that the Churches shall not make any ordinances without the sanction of the Bishop of Rome." *Soc. H. E. l. ii. c. 8.*

" . . . . Eusebius having thus far obtained his object, sent a deputation to Julius, Bishop of Rome, begging that he would himself take cognizance of the charges against Athanasius, and order a judicial investigation to be made in his presence. But Eusebius was prevented from knowing the decree of Julius concerning Athanasius, for he died a short time after the Synod (Antioch) was held . . . . .

. . . . After experiencing considerable difficulties, Athanasius at last reached Italy . . . . At the same time also Paul, Bishop of Constantinople, Asclepas of Gaza, Marcellus of Ancyra, a city of Galatia Minor, and Lucius of Adrianople, who had each from different causes been accused and driven from their churches, arrived at the Imperial city. They made known their individual cases to Julius, Bishop of Rome ; and he, in the exercise of the Prerogative peculiar to the Church of Rome, armed them with authoritative Letters, and sent them back to the East, having restored to each his own See, and severely blaming those who had rashly deposed them. And they having departed from Rome, and confiding in the Letters of Bishop Julius, recovered their Churches. These persons considering themselves treated with indignity by the reproaches of Julius, assemble themselves in (an Arian) Council at Antioch, and dictate a reply to his Letters, as the expression of the unanimous feeling of the whole synod. It was not his province, they said, to take cognizance of their decisions in reference to the expulsion of any Bishops from their Churches, seeing that they had not opposed themselves to him when Novatus was ejected from the Church. Such was the tenor of the Eastern (Arian) Bishops' disclaimers of the right of interference of Julius, Bishop of Rome." *Ib. c. xi. xii. xv.*

" Another accusation was now framed against Athanasius by the Arians, who invented this pretext for it. The father of the Augusti had long before granted an allowance of corn to the Church of the Alexandrians for the relief of the indigent. This they asserted had usually been sold by Athanasius, and the proceeds converted to his own advantage. The Emperor giving credence to this slanderous report, threatened to put Athanasius to death : who becoming alarmed at the intimation of this threat, consulted his safety by flight, and kept himself concealed. When Julius Bishop of Rome was apprised of these fresh

machinations of the Arians against Athanasius, and had also received the
letter of Eusebius, then (just) deceased, he invited the persecuted
Prelate to come to him, having ascertained where he was secreted. The
epistle of the Bishops who had for some time before assembled at
Antioch, just then reached him, together with others from several Bishops
in Egypt, assuring him that the entire charge against Athanasius was a
fabrication. On the receipt of these contradictory communications,
Julius first replied to the Bishops who had written to him from Antioch,
complaining of the acrimonious feeling they had evinced in their letter,
and charging them with a violation of the canons, in neglecting to request
his attendance at the Council, seeing that by ecclesiastical law, no decisions of the Churches are valid unless sanctioned by the Bishop of
Rome : he then censured them with great severity for clandestinely
attempting to pervert the faith." *Ib. c.* 17.

By Sozomen.

"Athanasius, on leaving Alexandria, fled to Rome. Paul, Bishop of
Constantinople, Marcellus, Bishop of Ancyra, and Asclepas, Bishop of
Gaza, repaired thither at the same time. Asclepas, who was strongly
opposed to the Arians, had been accused by them of having thrown
down an altar, and Quintian had been appointed in his stead over the
Church of Gaza. Lucius also, Bishop of Adrianople, who had on
some accusation been deposed from his office, was dwelling at this
period in Rome. The Roman Bishop, on learning the cause of their
condemnation, and on finding that they held the same sentiments as
himself, and adhered to the Nicene doctrines, admitted them to communion ; and as by the dignity of his seat the charge of watching over
the orthodox devolved upon him, he restored them all to their own
Churches. He wrote to the Bishops of the East, and rebuked them for
having judged these Bishops unjustly, and for having disturbed the peace
of the Church by abandoning the Nicene doctrines. He summoned a few
of them to appear before him on an appointed day, in order to account to
him for the sentence they had passed, and threatened to bear with them
no longer, should they introduce any further innovations. Athanasius
and Paul were reinstated in their bishoprics, and they forwarded the
Letter of Julius to the Bishops of the East. The (Arian) Bishops were
highly indignant at this Letter, and they assembled together at Antioch,
and framed a reply to Julius, replete with elegance and the graces of
rhetoric, but couched in a tone of irony and defiance. They confessed in
this epistle that the Church of Rome was entitled to universal honour
(φιλοτιμίαν φέρειν), because it had been founded by the Apostles, and had
enjoyed the rank of a Metropolitan Church from the first preaching of
religion, although those who first propagated a knowledge of Christian
doctrine in this city came from the East . . . . . They called Julius to
account for having admitted Athanasius to communion, and expressed
their indignation against him for having insulted the Synod, and abrogated
their decrees ; and they reprehended his conduct, because they said it

was opposed to justice and to the canons of the Church. After these complaints and protestations, they proceeded to state that they were willing to continue on terms of unity and communion with Julius, provided that he would sanction the deposition of the Bishops whom they had expelled, and the ordination of those whom they had elected in their stead, but that, unless he would accede to those terms, they would have recourse to hostility. They added, that the Bishops who had preceded them in the government of the Eastern Churches had offered no opposition to the deposition of Novatian by the Church of Rome." *Sozomen, H. E. Lib.* iii. *c.* 8.

" The Bishops of Egypt having sent a declaration in writing that these allegations (*i. e.* the charge against S. Athanasius of having sold the wheat that the Emperor had provided for the poor in Alexandria) were false, and Julius having been apprised that Athanasius was far from being in safety in Egypt, sent for him to his own city. He replied at the same time to the letter of the (Arian) Bishops who were convened at Antioch, and accused them of having clandestinely introduced novelties contrary to the decrees of the Council of Nicæa, and of having violated the laws of the Church, by neglecting to invite him to their synod ; for it is a sacerdotal law (νόμος ἱερατικός), which declares that whatever is executed contrary to the decree of the Bishop of Rome is null and void."

3. Marcellus, Bishop of Ancyra, to Pope S. Julius.

"Whereas certain of those who were formerly condemned for not believing rightly, and who were confuted by me at the Council of Nicæa, have dared to write to your Holiness (S. Julius) against me, as though my sentiments were neither orthodox nor ecclesiastical, seeking to transfer to me their own crime, therefore had I deemed it necessary to come to Rome, and admonish thee to summon those who have written against me, that, on their coming, I might convict them on two heads ; that what they have written against me is false, and that they still continue in their former error, and that they have made impious attempts both against the Churches of God, and us who preside over them. But as they have not chosen to appear, though thou hast sent presbyters to them, and I have for a year and three whole months done this, I have deemed it necessary, being about to depart hence, to present to thee, written with mine own hand, in all sincerity, a written profession of my faith " [then follows an account of his faith.] " This faith . . . . I both preach in the House of God, and I have now written to thee, retaining a copy of it for myself ; and I beg of thee to write, in a letter to the Bishops, a counterpart to this, for fear lest some who knew me not perfectly, and who believe what these men have written, be led into error." *Ep. ad Julium, Galland. t.* v. *p.* 16, 17.

VII. POPE S. DAMASUS.

A.D. 370.

1. S. PETER, BISHOP OF ALEXANDRIA.

" . . . . He (S. Athanasius) left as his successor (in the See of Alexandria) Peter, a devout and excellent man. Upon this the Arians, emboldened by their knowledge of the Emperor's religious sentiments, again take courage, and immediately inform him of the circumstance. He was then residing at Antioch, and Euzoïus, who presided over the Arians of that city, eagerly embracing the favourable opportunity thus presented, begs permission to go to Alexandria, for the purpose of putting Lucius the Arian in possession of the Churches there. The Emperor, acceding to this request, Euzoïus proceeds forthwith to Alexandria, attended by the imperial troops, and Magnus, the Emperor's treasurer; they were also the bearers of an imperial mandate to Palladius, the Governor of Egypt, enjoining him to aid them with a military force. Wherefore, having apprehended Peter, they cast him into prison ; and after dispersing the rest of the clergy, they place Lucius in the episcopal chair. . . . Peter, however, has exposed them in the letters he addressed to all the Churches, when he had escaped from prison, and fled to Damasus, Bishop of Rome. . . . . As soon as the Emperor Valens left Antioch, all those who had anywhere been suffering persecution, began again to take courage, and especially the Alexandrians. Peter returned to that city from Rome, with letters from Damasus, the Roman Bishop, in which he confirmed the Homoousian faith, and sanctioned Peter's ordination."—*Soc. H. E. l.* iv. *c.* 20, 21, 22, 37.

2. TO PROSPERUS AND OTHER BISHOPS OF NUMIDIA.

" Although, dearest brethren, the decrees of the Fathers are known to you, yet we cannot wonder at your carefulness as regards the institutes of our forefathers, that you cease not, as the custom ever has been, to refer all those things, which can admit of any doubt, to us, as to the Head, (*caput*) that thence you may derive answers, whence you received the institution and rule (*normam*) of living rightly. Wherefore are we mindful that you also are not forgetful of the canons which command this to be done. Not that you are in any way deficient in the knowledge of the law of the Church, but that, supported by the authority of the Apostolic See, you may not deviate in anything from its regulations. .

. . . It does with reason concern us, who ought to hold the chief government in the Church (the Chief Helm of the Church), if we by our silence favour error " (*summo*, ... *gubernacula*).—*Ep.* v. *Prospero, Numid. et aliis, Labbe, t.* ii. *col.* 876–882.

3. To Valerianus and other Oriental Bishops.

" Now could any disadvantage arise from the number of those who assembled at Rimini, seeing that it is certain, that neither the Roman Bishop, whose opinion ought to have been sought for before that of all others (*cujus ante omnes fuit expetenda sententia*), nor Vincentius, who during so many years persevered in the priestly office without blame, nor others, gave any consent whatever to the decrees of that assembly." —*Ep.* i. *Synod. Orientalibus, Galland, t.* vi. *p.* 321.

3. To the Bishops in the East concerning the Condemnation of Timothy, Disciple of the Heretic Apollinarius.

" Most honoured children, in that your friendliness bestows on the Apostolic Chair the reverence due, you confer the greatest honour upon yourselves. For although especially in this holy Church wherein the holy Apostle sitting taught in what way it beseems us to hold the key which has been put into our hands (*decet nos quodam modo clavum tenere quem regendum suscepimus*), yet do we confess ourselves unequal to the honour ; but therefore do we strive in every way, if it may be that we may be able to attain unto the glory of that blessedness. Know, therefore, that long since we deposed (cut off) the profane Timotheus, the disciple of the heretic Apollinarius, with his impious doctrine . . . . . Why then, do you again require from me the deposition of the same man, who even here by the Judgment of the Apostolic Chair, while Peter, Bishop of Alexandria, was also present, was deposed together with his master Apollinarius ? But if this man, as if he had some hope . . . . gains over certain unstable persons, with him shall also perish whosoever it is that chooses to resist the rule (canon) of the Church."—*Ep.* ix. *Synod. Orient. Ib. p.* 337.   •

VIII. POPE S. SIRICIUS.

A.D. 386.

To Himerius, Bishop of Tarragona in Spain.

" Taking into account my office, it is not for me to choose,—on whom it is incumbent that there should be a zeal for the Christian religion greater than that of all other persons,— to dissemble, and remain silent. I bear the burdens of all who are heavily laden ; yea, rather in me that burden is borne by the blessed Apostle Peter, who we trust, in all things, protects, and has regard to us who are the heirs of his Government (*Hæc portat in nobis beatus Apostolus Petrus, qui nos in omnibus, ut confidimus, administrationis suæ protegit et tuetur hæredes.*)

" Let it suffice that faults have hitherto been committed in this matter ; and now let the above-named rule be observed by all priests

(Bishops) who do not wish to be rent from that solid Apostolic Rock upon which Christ constructed the Universal Church." *Ep.* i. *Ad Himer Tarrac. n.* i. 2. *Galland. t.* vii. *p.* 533, 4.

IX. POPE ANASTASIUS I.

A.D. 399.

To John, Bishop of Jerusalem.

" Far be this from the Catholic discipline of the Roman Church . . . Assuredly care shall not be wanting on my part to guard the faith of the Gospel for my people ; and to visit by Letter, as far as I be able, the members of my body, throughout the divers regions of the earth (*partesque corporis mei, per spatia diversa terrarum*), to prevent any beginning of a profane interpretation from creeping in, which may have for its object to confound devout minds, by spreading its darkness." *Ep.* i. *Ad Joan. Jerosol. n.* 5, *Galland. t.* viii. *p.* 247, 8.

X. POPE S. INNOCENT.

A.D. 410.

1. To Victricius, Bishop of Rouen.

" Though, dearest brother, agreeably to the worth and honour of the priesthood, wherewith you are eminently distinguished, you are acquainted with all the maxims of life and doctrine, contained in the ecclesiastical law, neither is there anything which you have not gathered from your sacred reading . . . . . yet, seeing that you have earnestly requested to be made acquainted with the pattern and authority of the Roman Church (*Ecclesiæ Romanæ normam atque auctoritatem*), I have, from my profound respect for your wish, sent you digested regulations of life, and the approved customs, whereby the people who compose the churches of your country may perceive, by what things and rules the life of Christians, each according to his own profession, ought to be restrained ; and also what discipline is observed in the Church of the city of Rome. It will be for your friendliness diligently to make this known throughout the neighbouring people, and to communicate to our fellow-priests (Bishops), who preside over their respective churches in those countries, this book of rules, as an instructor and a monitor, that they may both be acquainted with our customs, and, by diligent teaching, form, in accordance with the faith, the manners of those who flock unto them. Let us, therefore, begin with the help of the holy Apostle Peter, through whom both the Apostleship and the Episcopate took their rise in Christ" (*per quem et apostolatus et episcopatus in Christo cœpit exordium.*) . . . These, then, are the things which it behoves every Catholic Bishop, having before his eyes the judgment of God, henceforward to observe. . . . . That if any causes, or contentions, arise between clergy of the higher, or even of an inferior order, the dispute be settled agreeably to the Synod of Nicæa, by an assembly of the Bishops of that same province ; and that it be not lawful for any one . . . . . . to leave these priests (Bishops), who by the will of God govern the Church of God, and to have recourse to other provinces. If any greater causes shall have been brought forward (or discussed), let them, after episcopal judgment, be referred to the Apostolic See, as the synod (of Nicæa) resolved,* and a blessed custom requires." *Ep.* ii. *ad Victric. n.* 1, 2, 3, 5, 6, *Galland. t.* viii. *p.* 547.

2. TO THE BISHOPS IN THE SYNOD OF TOLEDO IN SPAIN.

" An exceeding anxiety has often kept me in fear about the dissensions and schisms of the churches in Spain, which report loudly declares are daily spreading and advancing with more rapid strides ; the needful time has now come wherein it is not possible any longer to defer the much-required correction, and wherein a suitable remedy must be provided. For our brother, Hilary, my fellow-Bishop, and Elpidius, presbyter, partly moved by the love of unity, partly influenced, as they ought to be, by the ruinous evils, under which your province labours, have journeyed to the Apostolic See (*ad sedem apostolicam commearunt*) ; and in the very Bosom of faith, have, with sorrow and lamentation, described how peace has been violated within your province." *Ep.* iii. *n.* 1. *Ib. p.* 551.

3. TO RUFUS AND OTHER BISHOPS IN MACEDONIA.

" After having caused your letter to be several times read to me, I noticed a kind of injury was done to the Apostolic See, unto which, as unto the Head of the Churches (*quasi ad caput ecclesiarum*), that statement was sent,—the sentence of that See being still treated as doubtful. The renewed questioning contained in your report compels me, therefore, to repeat in plainer terms, that subjects concerning which I remember having written to you." *Ep.* xvii. *n.* 1. *Ib. p.* 575.

4. TO ALEXANDER, BISHOP OF ANTIOCH.

" Observe, therefore, that this (privilege) has been assigned to this city (Antioch), not so much on account of its magnificence, as because it is known to have been the first see of the First Apostle, where the Christian religion took its name, and has had the honour to have held within it a most celebrated assembly of the Apostles ; a city which

---

* This signifies the written and the unwritten Law, or, in legal language, the Statute and the Common Law. The Council of Sardica enacted the canon of appeal, but it was part of the Common Law of the Church, that all greater causes should be carried to Rome. Custom, legally, is part of the Common Law.

would not yield to the city of Rome, save that Antioch was honoured by him (Peter), but temporarily, whereas this city (Rome) glories in having received him to herself, and that he there consummated (his martyrdom)." *Ep.* xxiv. *n.* 1. *Ib. p.* 584.

5. To Decentius, Bishop of Gubbio.

" . . . . For who knows not, or notices not, that what was delivered to the Roman Church by Peter, the Prince of the Apostles, and is to this day guarded, ought to be observed by all men, and that nothing ought to be superinduced (or, introduced), which has not (that) authority, or which may seem to derive its precedent elsewhere,—clear especially as it is that no one has founded churches throughout the whole of Italy, Gaul, Spain, Africa, and Sicily, and the inter-adjacent islands, except those whom the venerable Apostle Peter, or his Successors, appointed Priests (*i.e.* Bishops). . . . But if they read of no other, for they never can find any other, they ought to follow what is observed by the Roman Church, from which there is no doubt that they derived their origin, lest whilst they court strange assertions, they be seen to set aside the Head (*caput*) of their institutions. It is well known that your friendliness has often been at Rome, been present with us in church, and cognizant of the customs which prevailed both in consecrating the Mysteries, and in the other secret (offices). We should assuredly consider this sufficient for the information, or the reformation of your Church, should it be that your predecessors have in any respect not held with, or held differently from us, had you not thought that we were to be consulted on certain matters. On these we send you replies, not as thinking you in any respect ignorant, but that you may regulate your people with greater authority ; or should any have gone aside from the institutions of the Roman Church, that you may either yourself admonish them, or not delay to point them out to us, that we may know who they are who either introduce novelties, or who think that the custom of any other Church, than that of Rome, is to be followed. *Ep.* xxv. *ad Decent. n.* 1, 3. *Ib. p.* 586.

6. To the Council of Milevis.

" Amongst other cares of the Roman Church, and the occupations of the Apostolic See—whereby we are busied in a faithful and medicinal handling of the consultations by divers parties—our brother and fellow-Bishop, Julius, has unexpectedly pressed on my notice the letter which you have, with a more than ordinary solicitude for the faith, sent me from the Council held at Milevis . . . . Carefully, therefore, as was befitting, do you consult what is the secret wish of this Apostolic dignity (*congrue apostolici consulitis honoris arcana*),—a dignity, I repeat, upon which falls *besides those things that are without, the care of all the Churches,*—as to what opinion is to be held in matters of such moment ; having herein followed the pattern of an ancient rule, which you, equally with myself, know has always been observed by the whole world. But I pass these things by ; for I do not think but that this is manifest to your prudence. Yea, why have you confirmed this by your own act, but that you know that, throughout all the provinces, answers to questions always emanate from the Apostolic Spring. Especially, as often as questions of faith are agitated, I am of opinion that all our brethren and fellow-Bishops ought not to refer but to Peter—that is, to the Author of their name and honour—even as your friendliness has now referred (to ascertain) what may be for the common weal of all the churches throughout the whole world (*quod per omnes provincias de apostolico fonte petentibus responsa semper emanent. Præsertim quoties fidei ratio ventilatur, arbitror omnes fratres et co-episcopos nostros non nisi ad Petrum, id est, sui nominis et honoris auctorem referre debere, velut nunc retulit vestra dilectio, quod per totum mundum possit ecclesiis omnibus in commune prodesse.*) For the authors of these evils must needs be more cautious, in seeing themselves, upon the report of two synods, separated from the communion of the Church, by the Decree of our sentence. . . . . Wherefore, we do by the authority of the Apostolic Power (*Apostolici vigoris auctoritate*), declare Pelagius and Celestius—the inventors, to wit, of novel words, which, as the Apostle has said, are of no edification, but rather are wont to beget most foolish questions,—deprived of the communion of the Church." *Ep.* xxx. *ad Concil. Milev. n.* 1, 2, 6. *Ib. p.* 602-3.

7. To Aurelius, Bishop of Carthage, and others.

" Keeping to the precedents of ancient tradition, and mindful of the discipline of the Church, you have in your examination of the things of God (which it is fitting should be treated of with the utmost care, by priests (Bishops), and especially by a true, and just, and catholic Council), in an undeniable manner, established the firmness of your religion, no less now by consulting (me), than when you previously passed your sentence ; approving, as you have done, by a reference to our Judgment, knowing what is due to the Apostolic See (*scientes quid apostolicæ sedi debeatur*), knowing that all of us, who have been placed in this position, desire to follow that Apostle, from whom the episcopate itself, and the whole authority of this title, has been derived. With him for our model, we both know how to condemn what is evil, and to approve of what is commendable. Yea, even this, that ye guard by your priestly office the institutes of the Fathers,—which you think are not to be trampled on,—they, by a judgment not human, but divine, having decided that whatsoever should be transacted, though in provinces remote and distant from us, they would account that it was not to be completed, until it had come to the knowledge of this See, that so the entire sentence, if justly pronounced, might be confirmed by the Authority of this See, and the rest of the churches thence derive (that they may proceed, like as all waters, from their own parent spring, and the pure stream of an uncorrupted Fountain-Head may flow throughout the divers regions of the whole world) what to order (*non prius ducerent finiendum, nisi ad hujus sedis notitiam perveniret, ut tota hujus auctoritate justa quæ fuerit pronuntiatio firmaretur, indeque sumerent ceteræ ecclesiæ (velut de natali suo fonte aquæ cunctæ procederent, et per diversas totius mundi regiones puri latices incorrupti manarent) quid præcipere)*, whom to cleanse," &c. *Ep.* clxxxi. *Aurelio et cæteris qui in Concil. Carthag. in Ed. Bened. S. Agust. t.* ii. *p.* 949.

8. To Felix, Bishop of Nocera.

"We cannot wonder that your friendliness follows the institutes of those who have gone before you, and refers unto us, as unto the Head and Chief of the Episcopate (*ad nos quasi ad caput atque ad apicem episcopatus referre*), whatsoever can cause any doubt; that by consulting the Apostolic See, to wit, it may, even out of doubtful matters decide on something that is certain, and that ought to be done." *Ep.* xxxvii. *Felici, n.* 1. *Galland. T.* viii. *p.* 608.

XI. POPE S. ZOSIMUS.

A.D. 417.

To Aurelius and others, Bishops in the Council of Carthage.

"Although the tradition of the Fathers has assigned so great an Authority to the Apostolic See, that no one should dare to dispute about a Judgment given by it, and that See, by laws and regulations, has kept to this; and the discipline of the Church, in the laws which it yet follows, still pays to the name of Peter, from whom that See (or discipline) descends, the reverence due,—for canonical antiquity, by universal consent, willed that so great a Power should belong to that Apostle, a Power also derived from the actual promise of Christ our God, that it should be his to loose what was bound, and to bind what was loosed, an equal state of Power being bestowed upon those who, by His will, should be found worthy to inherit his See, for he has charge both of all the Churches, and especially of this One wherein he sat; nor does he allow any storm to shake one particle of the Privilege, or any part of the Sentence of that See to which he has given his name as a foundation firm and not to be weakened by any violence whatever, and which no one can rashly attack but at his peril;—seeing then, that Peter is a Head of such great authority, and that he has confirmed the subsequent decrees (or statutes) of the Fathers; that, by all laws and regulations, both human and divine, the Roman Church is strengthened; and you are not ignorant, you know, dearest brethren, and as priests you are not ignorant, that we rule over his Place, and are in possession also of the Authority of his name (*par potestatis data conditio in eos, qui sedis hereditatem, ipso annuente, meruissent . . . ut tam humanis quam divinis legibus et disciplinis omnibus firmetur Romana Ecclesia, cujus locum nos regere, ipsius quoque potestatem nominis obtinere, non latet vos*), nevertheless, though so great be our Authority that none may refuse (or reconsider) our Sentence (*ut nullus de nostra possit retractare sententia*), we have not done anything, which we have not, of our will referred by letter to your knowledge, conceding this to the Brotherhood." *Ep.* xi. *Ad Africanos, Galland. T.* ix. *pp.* 15, 16.

XII. POPE S. BONIFACE.

A.D. 419.

1. To Rufus, Bishop of Thessalonica.

" The blessed Apostle Peter, as you have faithfully expressed yourself in your letter, looks on you with his own eyes to see how you discharge the office of a supreme ruler. Nor can he fail to be near you, he who was appointed the perpetual Shepherd of the Lord's sheep ; nor can he, in whom we read that the foundation of the Universal Church was laid, help paying regard to any church wheresoever it may be. On you, dearest brother, devolves the entire care of those churches, which you will recognise as having been, by us, entrusted to you as the vicegerent of the Apostolic See." *Ep.* v. *Rufo, Episc. Thessal. Galland. t.* ix. *p.* 50.

2. To the Bishops in Thessaly.

" The institution of the Universal Church took its beginning from the honour bestowed on blessed Peter, in whom its Government and Headship reside (*institutio universalis ecclesiæ de beati Petri sumsit honore principium, in quo regimen ejus et summa consistit*). For from him, as its Source, did ecclesiastical discipline flow over all the churches, when the culture of religion had begun to make progress. The precepts of the Synod of Nicæa bear no other testimony ; insomuch that that Synod did not attempt to make any regulations in his regard, as it saw that nothing could be conferred that was superior to his own dignity (merit) ; it knew, in fine, that everything had been bestowed on him by the Word of the Lord. It is, therefore, certain that this Church is to the churches spread over the whole world, as the Head is to its own members ; from which Church whoso has cut himself off becomes an alien from the Christian religion, whereas he has begun not to be in the same bonds of fellowship (*cum videret nihil supra meritum suum posse conferri, omnia denique huic noverat Domini sermone concessa. Hanc ergo ecclesiis toto orbe diffusis velut caput suorum certum est esse membrorum, a qua se quisquis abscidit, fit Christianæ religionis extorris, cum in eadem non cœperit esse compage*). Now I hear that certain Bishops, the Apostolic right despised, are attempting a novelty which is in direct opposition to the special Injunctions of Christ, seeing that they are trying to separate themselves from communion, or, to speak more correctly, from the communion of the Apostolic See ; seeking aid from men to whom the regulations of the Church have never given their sanction that they should be of superior authority . . . Receive, therefore, from us an admonition and a rebuke, of which we offer one to the Prelates (who side with us), the other to the separatists (quoting 1 Cor. iv. 21). . . . For you know that both are in blessed Peter's Power,—to rebuke, that is, *with meekness* the meek, and the proud with *a rod.* Wherefore, show to the Head the honour due to it (*servate honorem debitum capiti*) ; for we would not have the members at variance with each other, as the strife between them reaches unto us, when our brother and fellow-Bishop, Rufus, is accounted by you a person to be contemned. . . . It is not becoming in the brethren to feel galled at another's power. Assuredly, as the Apostolic See holds the Princedom for this, that it may receive the lawful complaints of all (*ideo tenet sedes Apostolica Principatum, ut querelas omnium licentes acceptet*), if in anything his correction seemed to be excessive, it became you, by sending an embassy, to appeal to us, upon whom you may see the charge of everything devolves (*quos curam omnium rerum manere videatis*) . . . . Let this ᵔnovel presumption cease. Let every one who accounts himself a Bishop, obey our ordinance. Let no one presume to ordain Bishops throughout Illyricum, without our fellow-Bishop Rufus be privy to it." *Ep.* xiv. *Epis. Thess. Ib. p.* 57.

XIII. POPE S. CELESTINE.

A.D. 423.

1. To the Bishop of Illyricum.

" We in a special manner are constrained by our charge, which regards all men, we on whom Christ has, in the Person of the holy Peter the Apostle, when He gave him the keys to open and to shut, imposed as a necessity to be engaged about all men." *Ep.* iii. *Ad Episc. Illyr. Galland. t.* ix. *p.* 292.

2. To S. Cyril, Patriarch of Alexandria.

" Therefore let all those whom he has separated from his communion understand that they continue in ours, and that from this time he himself (Nestorius) cannot continue in communion with us, if he persists in opposing the Apostolic doctrine. Wherefore you shall execute this Judgment with the Authority of our See, acting in our Stead, and having our Power delegated to you ; and that if, in the space of ten days after he has received this admonition, he does not expressly anathematise his impious doctrines, and promise to confess, for the future, that faith which the Roman Church and your Church and all Christendom teach concerning the generation of Jesus Christ our God, your Holiness may forthwith set about to provide for this Church (of Constantinople) under the full assurance that in such a case it is necessary that he should be utterly separated from, our body." *Labbé, Concil. T.* iii. *col.* 898–9.

3. To Nestorius, the Heresiarch.

". . . . Know that if you do not teach concerning Jesus Christ our God, what is held by Rome, Alexandria, and all the Catholic Churches, and which up to your time was held by the holy Church of Constantinople ; and if within ten days after the receipt of this third admonition, you do not unequivocally, and in writing, condemn this impious novelty,—which tends to put asunder what Scripture joins,—you are excluded from the communion of the whole Catholic Church. We have directed this Sentence and all the other writings to be taken by the Deacon Posidonius to the Bishop of Alexandria, that he may act in our Place (τοποτηρῶν) ; and that our decree may be known to you and all our brethren." *Ibid.* 911–14.

4. To the Faithful of Constantinople.

[A letter was addressed by this Pope to the people of Constantinople, exhorting them to constancy, and offering them consolation. He annuls the sentence of excommunication pronounced by Nestorius, from the time he commenced to propagate his errors ; and he informs them that he has commissioned S. Cyril of Alexandria "to act in his Stead" (τὴν ἡμετέραν διαδοχὴν ἀπινειμαμεν), and concludes with a formal statement of the terms of his Sentence. The same in substance is forwarded to the Patriarchs of Antioch and Jerusalem, to Rufus of Thessalonica, and Flavian of Philippi. *Ibid., col.* 914, 923.]

XIV. POPE S. XYSTUS III.

A.D. 434.

To John, Bishop of Antioch.

" You have learned by the result of this present business what it is to agree in sentiment with us. The blessed Apostle Peter, in his Successors, has transmitted what he received (*beatus Petrus in successoribus suis, quod accepit, hoc tradidit*). Who would separate himself from his doctrine, whom the Master Himself declared to be the First amongst the Apostles ?" *Ep.* vi. *Ad Joan. Antioch. n.* 5, *Galland. T.* ix. *p.* 529.

XV. POPE S. LEO THE GREAT.

A.D. 440.

1. To the Metropolitans in Illyricum.

" And whereas our care is extended throughout all the churches,—this being required of us by the Lord, who committed the Primacy (government) of the Apostolic dignity to the most blessed Peter in reward of his faith, establishing the Universal Church on the solidity of him, the

Foundation (*quia per omnes ecclesias cura nostra distenditur, exigente hoc a nobis Domino, qui Apostolicæ dignitatis beatissimo apostolo Petro primatum fidei suæ remuneratione commisit, universalem ecclesiam in fundamenti ipsius soliditate constituens*) ; wherefore, following the example of those whose memory is venerable unto us, we have committed to our brother and fellow-Bishop, Anastasius, to act in our Stead (*vicem nostram commisimus*) . . ." *T.* i. *Ep.* v. *Ad Episcopos Metrop. per Illyricum, c.* 2, *p.* 617.

2. TO THE BISHOPS OF THE PROVINCE OF VIENNE.

" . . . But Hilary, about to disturb this line of conduct which has ever been, by our Fathers, both laudably held to, and beneficially preserved, and about to trouble the state of the churches, and the concord of the priests has departed (from Rome), desiring so to subject you to his own power, as not to suffer himself to be subject to the blessed Apostle Peter (*ut se beato Apostolo Petro non patiatur esse subjectum*), claiming to himself the ordinations of all the churches throughout Gaul, and transferring to his own dignity that which is due to the Metropolitan priests (Bishops) ; by lessening also, with arrogant words, the reverence (due) to the most blessed Peter, to whom, while the power of binding and loosing was given him beyond the others, yet was the care of feeding the sheep more especially assigned. To whom whoso thinks that the Princedom (*principatum*) is to be denied, he can in no wise lessen the dignity of Peter, but, puffed up with the spirit of his own pride, he sinks himself down into hell." *Ib. Ep.* x. *Ad Episcopos per Provinc. Viennens. constitutos, in causa Hilarii Arelat. c.*2, *p.* 635.

3. TO ANASTASIUS, BISHOP OF THESSALONICA.

" For the connexion of our union cannot be firm, unless the bond of charity bind us together into an inseparable solidity . . . . The cohesion of the whole body produces one healthfulness, one beauty ; and this connexion requires indeed the unanimity of the whole body, but demands especially concord amongst the priests (Bishops), whose dignity, though it be common to them all, yet is not their order uniform ; since even amongst the most blessed Apostles, in likeness of honour there was a certain diversity of power ; and whereas the election of them all was equal, nevertheless to One was it given to be Pre-eminent over the rest. (*Quibus cum dignitas sit communis, non est tamen ordo generalis ; quoniam et inter beatissimos Apostolos in similitudine honoris fuit quædam discretio potestatis ; et cum omnium par esset electio, uni tamen datum est, ut ceteris præemineret.*) Out of which pattern also has arisen the distinction amongst the Bishops, and by a mighty regulation has it been provided against, that all claim not all things to themselves, but that there be individuals in individual provinces, whose sentence should, amongst the brethren, be accounted the first ; and again, that certain others, constituted in the greater cities, should take upon them a wider solicitude, through whom the Universal Church might flow together to the One Chair of Peter, and no part be anywhere at variance with its Head" (*per quos ad unam Petri sedem universalis ecclesiæ cura conflueret, et nihil usquam a suo capite dissideret*). *Ib. Ep.* xiv. *Ad Anastasium Thessalon. Episc. c.* xi. *pp.* 691, 692.

4. To Theodoret, Bishop of Cyrus.

"We rejoice in the Lord . . . that what things He had first defined by our ministry, He has confirmed by the irrevocable assent of the whole Brotherhood, that He might show that to have truly emanated from Himself, which having been established by the First of all the Sees, has received the judgment of the whole Christian world, that herein also the members may be in agreement with the Head. And lest the assent of the other sees with that One, which the Lord appointed to preside over the rest, might seem to be flattery, or some other hostile suspicion might creep in, there were at first some found to doubt our Judgments. . . . Finally, the excellence of the sacerdotal office is much more illustrious, when the authority of the chiefs is in such wise derived, as that the liberty of the inferior is accounted in no particular lessened.

"Herein also do we wish to be aided by the solicitude of your watchfulness, that you would, by your own report, inform the Apostolic Chair of what progress is made by the Lord's truth in your districts; in order that we may aid the priests of those countries in whatsoever matters usage may demand." *Ib.* cxx. *Ad Theodoret. Epis. Cyr. c.* vi. *pp.* 1219–1227.

5. To Maximus, Bishop of Antioch.

"It behoves your friendliness to see clearly, with all your soul, over the government of which church the Lord has willed you to preside, and to be mindful of that doctrine, which the most blessed Peter, Chief of all the Apostles, established throughout the whole world indeed, by a uniform teaching, but by a special instruction in the cities of Antioch and of Rome. . . . It behoves you, therefore, to be, with the utmost vigilance careful, lest heretical pravity may claim anything unto itself; since it becomes you, by your sacerdotal authority, to resist such, and frequently, by your reports concerning the progress of the churches, to inform us of what is doing. For it is proper that you be a partner with the Apostolic Chair in this solicitude; and to produce confidence in acting, be conscious of the privileges of the third see, which do not suffer to be limited in anything by the ambition of any individual; for so great is the reverence for the Nicene canons, that I neither have permitted, nor will I permit, the things settled by the Holy Fathers to be violated by any innovation" (*nec permiserim, nec patiar aliqua novitate violari*). *Ep.* cxix. *ad Max. Antioch. c.* 3, *p.* 121.

6. Extracts from Sermons.

"He therefore also rejoices at your affection, and he 'recognises in the partners of his own honour, the observance of the Lord's institution, approving of that well-ordered charity of the whole Church, which, in the see of Peter, acknowledge Peter" (*probans ordinatissimam totius ecclesiæ caritatem, quæ in Petri sede, Petrum suscipit*). *Ib. Sermo* ii. *de Natal. Ordin. suæ, c.* 2, *pp.* 9, 10.

" The solidity of the faith which was commended in the Prince of the Apostles is perpetual ; and as what Peter believed in Christ is permanent, so is what Christ instituted in Peter permanent. . . . In these ways, therefore, my beloved, this day's festival celebrated with *a reasonable service;* that is in the person of my lowliness, he be acknowledged, be honoured, in whom both the solicitude of all pastors, with the care of the sheep entrusted to them, still continues, and whose dignity fails not even in his unworthy heir. Wherefore the Presence so decreed by me, and so honourable, of my venerable brethren and fellow-priests (Bishops) is the more devout and religious, if so be that they refer the affection with which they have vouchsafed to be present at this solemnity, principally to Peter, whom they know not only to be the Prelate of this Chair, but the Primate also of all Bishops. When, therefore, we address our exhortations to the care of your Holinesses, believe that he, in whose Stead we act, is speaking." *Ib. Serm.* iii. *Anniver. Assump. c.* 2–4, *pp.* 11–13.

" For although all pastors soever preside with special solicitude over their own flocks. . . . Yet . . . . neither is there any one's administration which is not a portion of our labour ; so that while recourse is had from every part of the world, to the See of the blessed Apostle Peter, and that love of the Universal Church, which was enjoined on Peter by the Lord, is also required of our administration, we feel that so much the greater burden weighs upon us, as we are indebted for more than all."

. . . He (Peter) ceases not to preside over his own See, and he enjoys a never-ceasing fellowship with the everlasting Priest (Christ). For that solidity which Peter, himself also made a Rock, received from the Rock Christ, has passed onwards to his heirs also, and wheresoever any firmness is exhibited, the constancy of that Pastor is undeniably apparent." *Ib. Serm.* v. *Nat. Ordin. c.* ii. iv. *pp.* 20, 25.

" Yet is this day's festival (S. Peter and S. Paul), besides that reverence which it has deserved from the whole Universe, to be venerated with special and peculiar exultation by this city, that where the departure (death) of the Chief Apostle was made glorious, there be, on the day of their martyrdom, pre-eminent gladness. For thou, O Rome, are the men through whom the Gospel of Christ shone upon thee, and thou who wast the teacher of error hast become the disciple of truth. . . . These are they who advanced thee to this glory, to be a holy nation, a chosen people, a priestly and royal city ; that by the See of the blessed Peter, made the Head of the universe, thou mightest rule more widely by divine religion than by earthly empire. For although, enlarged by many victories, thou hast extended the right of empire by land and sea, yet, what the toil of war has subdued to thee is less than what Christian peace has subjected to thee (*per sacram beati Petri sedem caput orbis effecta, latius præsideres religione divina, quam dominatione terrena . . . . minus tamen est quod tibi bellicus labor subdidit, quam quod pax Christiana subjecit*). . . . For, when the twelve Apostles, having received through the Holy Spirit the gift of speaking in all tongues, had, with the districts of the world distributed amongst them, undertaken to embrace the world with the Gospel, the most blessed Peter, the Prince of the Apostolic order, is assigned to the Capital of the Roman Empire, that the light of truth, which was manifested for the salvation of all nations, might more effectually diffuse itself from that Head throughout the whole body of the world." (*Petrus princeps Apostolici ordinis ad arcem Romani destinatur imperii: ut lux veritatis quæ in omnium gentium revelabatur salutem, efficacius se ab ipso capite per totum mundi corpus effunderet*)." *Ib. Serm.* lxxxiii. *c.* 1-3. *In Natal App. Petri et Pauli, pp.* 321-323.

XVI. POPE S. FELIX III.

A.D. 490.

1. TO THE EMPEROR ZENO.

" Therein also has shone forth your magnanimity, that you desire that the affairs of the Church, even as heaven ordained, be settled by the administration of her Pontiffs; and that you wish that whoever is declared to have been raised to the priestly office, be thence supported, whence, by the will of Christ the full grace of all Pontiffs has been derived. I am also cheered by the purport of your letter, wherein you have not omitted to state that blessed Peter is the Chief of the Apostles, and the Rock of faith, and have judiciously proved that to him were entrusted the keys of the heavenly mysteries. . . . Most venerated Prince, vicar (*vicarius*) such as I am, of blessed Peter, I do not extort these things, as with the authority of Apostolic Power, but I confidently implore them as an anxious Father. . . . For so in me, his vicar, such as I am, does the blessed Peter ask, as Christ Himself asks it in Peter, who suffers not his Church to be rent in pieces. . . . Let the peace of the churches be genuine; let there be a real unity, seeing that the paternal faith, and the communion of blessed Peter, ought to be preferred before any individual whomsoever" (*quoniam cuicumque personæ paterna fides, et beati Petri communio debet præferri*). *Ep.* iv. *Imper. Zenoni, Galland. t.* x. *pp.* 671, 72.

2. TO FLAVIAN, BISHOP OF CONSTANTINOPLE.

" There are many circumstances which cause me to rejoice at the ordination of your friendliness, and which bid me hope, by God's blessing, that the result will be the peace of the Church. . . . Finally, because almost everything which has been done since you first attained to your dignity, manifests both the graciousness of the Sovereign's clemency towards us, and also exhibits signs of your intentions ; matters being, to wit, referred according to rule, to the Apostolic See, by which, by Christ's concession, the dignity of all priests is confirmed. (*Dum scilicet ad Apostolicam sedem regulariter destinatur, per quam, largiente Christo omnium solidatur dignitas sacerdotum*). Because also the letters of your friendliness confesses that blessed Peter was the Chief of the Apostles, and the Rock of faith, as having the keys committed to him, the dispenser of heavenly mystery." *Ep.* v. *ad Flavian. Episc. Constantinop. Ib. pp.* 672, 3.

XVII. POPE S. GELASIUS.

A.D. 492.

I. PETER, BISHOP OF ALEXANDRIA.

" But granting for a while that this man (Peter, Bishop of Alexandria) has repented . . . . yet it never will be taught, never will it be shown, never assuredly will it be proved, that his purgation was lawful, seeing that it was not conducted according to the proper regulations. For no one either could, or ought to expel, or recall the Bishop of the Second See without the consent of the First. Unless it is perhaps to be in this confusion, and troubled state of affairs that neither the existence of a first, nor of a second, nor of a third see ought to be regarded or attended to in accordance with the ancient statutes of our Fathers ; and the Head being removed, as we see, all the members are to be at variance and strife with each other, and that is to be seen amongst us which was written concerning the people of Israel : *In those days there was no king in Israel, every man did which was right in his own eyes (Judges,* xxi. 24). For with what reason and what consistency can other sees be defended, if the ancient and long-existing reverence be not paid to the See of the most blessed Peter, the First See, by which the dignity of all priests (Bishops) has always been strengthened and confirmed (*Si primæ* . . . . *beatissimi Petri sedi antiqua et vetusta reverentia non defertur, per quam omnium sacerdotum dignitas semper est roborata atque firmata*), and to which, by the invincible and special judgment of the 318 Fathers, the highest honour was adjudged,—as being men who bore in mind the Lord's sentence, *Thou art Peter,* &c., and again to the same Peter, *I have prayed for thee that thy faith fail not,* &c., and that sentence, *If thou lovest Me, feed My sheep.* Wherefore, then, is the Lord's discourse so frequently directed to Peter ? Was it that the rest of the holy and blessed Apostles were not clothed with like virtue ? Who dare assert this ? No, but that, by a Head being constituted, the occasion of schism might be removed ; and that the compact bond of the Body of Christ, thus uniformly tending, by the fellowship of a most glorious love, to one Head, might be shown to be one ; and that there might be one Church faithfully believed in, and one house of the one God, and of the one Redeemer, wherein we might be nourished with one Bread and one Chalice . . . There were assuredly twelve Apostles endowed with equal merits and equal dignity ; and whereas they all shone equally with spiritual light, yet was it Christ's will that One amongst them should be The Ruler (prince), and him by an admirable dispensation, did Christ guide to Rome, the queen of nations, that in the principal (or first) city, He might direct that First and Principal (Apostle) Peter. (*Duodecim certe fuere apostoli, paribus meritis parique dignitate suffulti; cumque omnes æqualiter spirituali luce fulgerent, unum tamen principem esse ex illis voluit Christus . . . ut in præcipua urbe vel prima primum et præcipuum dirigeret Petrum.*") And there, as he shone conspicuous for power of doctrine, so also made glorious by the shedding of his blood, does he repose in a place of everlasting rest, granting to the See which he himself blessed, that it be, according to the Lord's promise, never overcome by the gates of hell, and that it be the safest harbour for all who are tempest-tossed. In that harbour (See of Rome) whosoever shall have reposed, shall enjoy a blessed and eternal place of safety, whereas he that shall have despised it, it is for him to see to it what kind of excuses he will plead at the day of judgment." *T.* x. *Galland, p.* 677.

2. To the Emperor Anastasius.

". . . . And if the hearts of the faithful ought to submit to all Bishops generally, who rightly handle holy things, how much the rather is consent to be yielded to the Prelate of that See, whom both the supreme Godhead has called to be Pre-eminent over all priests (Bishops) and the accordant piety of the whole Church has at all times honoured." *Ad Imp. Anastas. Labb. Concil. t.* v. *Col.* 308.

2. To the Bishops of Dardania.

" The First See both confirms every Synod by its own Authority, and is their perpetual Guardian, by reason to wit of its Princedom, which the blessed Apostle Peter having received from the mouth of the Lord, the Church nevertheless seconding—both always has held and retains." *Ad Epis. Dardan. Labb. ib. col.* 326.

4. Decrees of Council of Rome, a.d. 494.

" The holy Roman Catholic and Apostolic Church has been raised above the other churches, not by any synodal decrees, but from the evangelic voice of our Lord and Saviour has it obtained the Primacy, He saying, *Thou art Peter,* &c." *Decret. Concil. Rom. sub Gel. Ib. col.* 386.

POPE ANASTASIUS II.
A.D. 496.
To the Emperor Anastasius.

" Through the ministry of my lowliness . . . may the See o ₚblessed Peter hold the Princedom assigned to it by the Lord our God in the Universal Church (*Sedes beati Petri in universali ecclesia assignatum sibi a Domino Deo teneat principatum*"). *Ep. ad Anast. Aug. Labb. t.* iv. *col.* 1278.

R

OBSERVATIONS.

It seems imposible to suppose that all these holy and devoted Popes, nearly every one of whom in the ante-Nicene age were martyrs, and, subsequently, many, especially under the Arian Emperors, were confessors, could have invented what is called the Papal Supremacy. And yet, if the Papal Supremacy is not of God, what is it but an anti-Christian innovation? There is no allusion by any Father, or Council, to any canon, constitution, or ordinance, as having ever been proposed or adopted for the *creation* of this Power. Canons have been spoken of as once existing which affirmed a principle, as, for instance, it is unlawful to make any constitutions contrary to the decree of the Pope. The Council of Nicæa implicitly included the Primacy in its sixth canon, and other synods have confirmed certain Privileges in favour of the Holy See, but nowhere can we find any statement which, either explicitly or implicitly, asserts that the Papal Authority was created by the Church. Nor can it be discovered that any particular Pope ever invented this office, or for the first time assumed it. S. Julius, S. Innocent, S. Celestine, and S. Leo, may, owing to the peculiar circumstances of their times, when heresies abounded, have stretched their Prerogative and Power to the very fullest extent, but none of these created the office they assumed to fill. Along the whole august line of Popes we find this universal Jurisdiction exercised in various degrees, at one time perhaps imperceptibly, in consequence of the perfectness of the Church's unity and harmony, or more probably because of the terrible persecution that at one age prevailed, and at another with vehemence, accompanied with interdict and excommunication, followed by the deposition or restoration of Prelates of the first magnitude. The well-known saying of S. Gregory is a befitting commentary on what has been just stated, " I know not," says he, " what Bishop is not subject to (the Apostolic See), if any fault be found in Bishops. But where no fault requires it, all are equal according to the estimation of humility."

Another point must not be omitted to be stated, and that is, that not a single Father is to be found who gives the remotest hint of the beginning of this Papal Office. Certain it is that when it was in full force and operation in the fourth and fifth centuries, not a word of protest was heard or expressed against Papal assumption of universal Jurisdiction. So far from there not being any protest, it is admitted to the fullest extent even by Œcumenical Councils. Nor, as has been already shown in the body o this work, is there a word of remonstrance against this Papal authority in the ante-Nicene age; doubtless opposition was raised against certain acts of the Popes, in cases of over-severity, as in the Paschal question ; of episcopal rights, as in the matter of S. Cyprian and the execrable Apiarius ; but none as regards the office itself. Indeed, the Fathers, from the very beginning, assume the existence of this Papal power, and, moreover, they made ample use of it for the quenching of heresies.

The heretics too, schismatics, and bad Bishops and priests, were not slow to seek the assistance of the Papal authority for promoting their own ends, so that the acceptance of the Papal Supremacy, together with the

Superior Jurisdiction annexed to it, was as universal as possible. If, then, neither Popes, nor Councils, nor Fathers, have created this exalted Supreme Power in the Church, whence is it? Is it from God or from man? Is it a divine or an ecclesiastical Institution? For the reasons above given, it cannot be the latter ; it must therefore be the former. Under the "First Inquiry," it was proved demonstratively that S. Peter was appointed to the Chief Government of the Church ; and under the "Second Inquiry," that he came to Rome and established in that city his Cathedra or Chair, and that the Bishops of Rome have regularly succeeded to that Chair, together with all the Prerogatives attached to it, so that the Divine commission which S. Peter had received from Christ, for the government of the whole Church, has passed to his Successors. Popes, Councils, and Fathers, have said, "Peter lives and Presides ;in his own See ;" we all know the constitutional maxim, " The King never dies ;" so may it be said as truly, the " Fisherman never dies," he lives in his Successors, he pronounces judgment by them ; and in and by them he still rules the Universal Church. The Papacy, then, so far from being a human or ecclesiastical Institution, is, on the contrary, intensely Divine ; for its origin can be discovered only, first in S. Peter himself, and then in the Lord Jesus Christ, who created S. Peter as His Vicar on earth, with a commission to hold the keys, to confirm the Faith of the Brethren, and to shepherdise the Universal Fold. How is it possible, then, to have even a reasonable doubt that the Papacy is really and truly a Divine Institution?

It is time now to examine briefly some of the Epistles and other documents immediately connected with the Papacy.

1. The first Papal Epistle is that of S. Clement, who was Bishop of Rome till A.D. 107. It is generally believed to have been written A.D. 97, during the Domitian persecution. So great was the authority of this Epistle that it was read in many churches as Scripture.

Now in examining this Epistle we observe that the Corinthian Church being in trouble, appealed to Pope S. Clement for aid and counsel, "We feel," says the Pope, "we have been somewhat tardy in turning our attention to the points respecting which you consulted us ; and especially to the shameful and detestable sedition, ·utterly abhorrent to the elect of God, which a few rash and self-confident persons have kindled to such a pitch of frenzy, that your venerable and illustrious name, worthy to be loved, has suffered grievous injury." It cannot be doubted, then, that the Corinthians appealed to the Pope concerning certain points which are not stated, and concerning the sedition with which that Church was afflicted. The question raised is this, Why did the Corinthians appeal to Rome in preference to any other See? S. John the Apostle was living then, how was it they did not seek his inspired assistance? True, he himself might have been in exile, but they might have sought him in his exile, as many did S. Paul, when confined to his own hired house at Rome. A voyage to Smyrna or to Patmos was not so arduous an undertaking as a journey to Rome, which was at least twice as distant. And if we suppose that S. John was inaccessible, some observations would naturally have been made in their reference to the Pope and in his reply to them.

The omission to appeal to S. John, the only surviving Apostle of the Lord Jesus, is at least noteworthy.

Again, on the hypothesis that all Bishops are equal in jurisdiction, why did not the Corinthians seek the aid of the Bishops of the neighbouring countries, who would have been equally as competent to aid them as S. Clement was? Perhaps they might have regarded S. Clement as a personal friend, who had been the companion of S. Paul, but the appeal, if we may judge from the Epistle, was not to S. Clement personally, but to the Church of Rome, of which he was the presiding Pontiff. Why then to the Church of Rome more than any other? The answer is obvious. With S. Ignatius they believed that the Church of Rome was the Presiding Church, and therefore they laid their grievances at the feet of the Pope, with a view to obtaining redress. S. Clement addresses them, though humbly and meekly, yet in the tone of a Superior. It is impossible not to perceive that the author of this Epistle believed his Church and himself to be in the possession of full authority to advise and direct all churches—*i. e.* churches far beyond what was afterwards described as the Patriarchate—whenever necessity demanded. This S. Clement and the Roman Church do; reciting the fact of the appeal, the Pope, after giving the Corinthians praise and admonition, gives direction concerning the conduct of the faithful, and respecting the various functions assigned to Bishops, the Priests, and the Deacons. He then addresses himself to the seditious, blaming them for their conduct, and concludes by commanding the Church of Corinth to "send back speedily" the messengers, "that they may sooner announce to us" the restoration of peace and harmony.

It is impossible, in reading this Epistle carefully, not to see that it was written by one who believed himself to possess plenary Authority and Jurisdiction for dealing with the case submitted to him for counsel and redress.

2. The visit of S. Polycarp to Rome for the settlement of the Paschal controversy is certainly a recognition of the exalted office of the Pope. It cannot be supposed that this Saint would have travelled many hundred miles from Smyrna to Rome merely for the purpose of conversing with the Pope on this question, if no result was to follow.

What result did he expect? Nothing less, surely, than a settlement of the controversy. Doubtless he hoped for a settlement in accordance with the tradition he had received from S. John; and in all probability, being ignorant of that derived from S. Peter, he was disappointed at the failure of his self-imposed mission. This termination is, as is well known, held by Anglicans as witnessing against the Roman Supremacy: this view, however, will be considered in another portion of our work. But there remains the fact recorded in history that S. Polycarp, instead of wasting his time in visiting those Patriarchs (as they were afterwards styled) who were nearer to him, and who (on the supposition that all Bishops, without exception, were equal in jurisdiction) might have disposed of this question as any other Prelate, went straight to the fountain-head, to that Church which is said to be the source "whence the Unity of the Priesthood took its rise." This witnesses to the greatness of the Roman Church, to the exalted position of the Pontiff, and t the Jurisdiction of that Church and Pontiff, who, if he had deemed it expedient, would have determined the controversy as he should judge right.

3. This Paschal controversy broke out afresh about forty years after. Many Synods seemed to have been held on this question, convened in pursuance of the Pope's directions. Almost all appear to have agreed that Easter should be celebrated, not as the Jews kept the Passover, but on the Lord's day nearest the vernal equinox ; and Pope S. Victor endeavoured to enforce this decree throughout the Universal Church. He met with resistance from Polycrates and the Bishops of Asia Minor, whom he threatened with excommunication if they did not comply with his commands. Many of the Bishops, both in the East and West, re-monstrated with the Pope, not on account of his assumption of universal authority, but on account of his over-severity. This point will be enlarged upon presently, but what we have now to observe, is the exercise of Authority by Pope S. Victor over provinces and dioceses far beyond his Province and Patriarchate.

4. The Letter of the Roman clergy to the Carthaginian Clergy during the exile of S. Cyprian, is a very strong proof of the doctrine of the Papal Supremacy. It is customary, whenever a vacancy occurs in the Cathedra of a diocese, for the Chapter to assume *pro tempore* the jurisdiction of the vacant Chair.* So in the case of the Roman Church, it would seem to have been the practice in primitive times during the vacancy of the See, for the clergy to assume for the time the functions of the Pope. The Letter they addressed testifies fully to this authority of the Papal office : " Since, moreover, it devolves upon us, who appear to be placed on high, in the Place of the Shepherd, to keep watch over the flock." They then refer to the words of our Lord : " I am the Good Shepherd, who lay down My life for the sheep ;" and then immediately allude to the commission of our Lord to S. Peter, " To Simon, too, He speaks thus, ' Lovest thou Me?' He answered, ' I do love Thee.' He saith to him, ' Feed My sheep.'" The connexion between these words, together with those just before, " I am the Good Shepherd," and the " Place of the Shepherd," which they then *pro tempore* occupied, is obvious. They referred to the Divine office of the Papacy, at that time vacant by reason of the persecutions ; they point to the commission of S. Peter (whose Place Rome was and is), reminding the Carthaginian clergy of its Superior authority. They then proceed to give them such admonitions and counsel as they deemed for their good. S. Cyprian, in his correspondence with the Roman Clergy, enters no protest against their assumption of authority ; on the contrary, in one of his letters he comments approvingly on the directions they had given to his Clergy during his exile. This Letter, it is submitted, is very strong evidence in favour of the Papal Prerogative to visit by Letters distant provinces of the Church.

---

* This is customary to this day in the See of Canterbury.

5. S. Stephen, who succeeded S. Cornelius, assumed the right to determine by his own Authority the controversy about the re-baptism of persons baptized out of the Church, and he, on account of the non-compliance of S. Cyprian, Firmilian, and the Bishops of Cilicia, Cappadocia, Galatia, and of the adjoining provinces, refused to hold communion with them. As this matter has furnished materials for the controversy against the Roman Supremacy, its consideration is reserved for another part of this work ; but, whether S. Stephen was right or wrong, it is unquestionable that he exercised universal Jurisdiction, as his predecessors had done.

6. I have entered somewhat minutely into the acts of the Papacy of the ante-Nicene age, because it is so often alleged that no evidence for the Papal Supremacy is to be found in that period. Indeed it seems to me that there is quite sufficient to show that when occasions arose it was really a living and active power, exercised by the different Pontiffs from time to time, by counselling, by admonishing, by censuring, and by punishing Bishops and others for heresy, schism, or contumacy. We have a distinct reference made to the commission to S. Peter—" to feed the sheep" —by the clergy of Rome, as indicating the source whence they presumed to address the clergy of Carthage. And when we compare the Papal Supremacy, as exercised by the ante-Nicene Popes, with the doctrine of Holy Scripture and the testimony of S. Ignatius, S. Irenæus, Tertullian, Origen, S. Cyprian, Firmilian, S. Peter of Alexandria— all of whom flourished before the great Council of Nicæa was held—it is simply impossible to come to any other conclusion than that this high and exalted office owes its origin, not to man, but to Christ our Lord, and His servant S. Peter, who planted his Chair—that Chair which he received from Him—in the heart of the Imperial city of Rome.

7. It is unnecessary to comment upon the various documents connected with this subject which appeared after the Council of Nicæa, for they all, more or less, speak for themselves; and after perusing them no one can doubt what was the nature of that power of which the Popes claimed to be in possession, and which they exercised with an unsparing hand for the extirpation of the fearful heresies that sprang up like noxious weeds from the fourth to the seventh century. Suffice it to say that these documents, as a whole, assert (1) That S. Peter was the Source and Origin of the Apostolate and the Episcopate, that the Church took her beginning in him, and that from him " ecclesiastical discipline flowed to the Churches :" (2) That the See of Rome is the See of Peter, hence is it frequently described as " the Apostolic See," "the See of Peter," and " the Holy See :" (3) That Rome is " the pattern" or " normal" Church, the "Bosom of Faith," the " Head of the Church," and " the Head of the Universe :" (4) That the Bishop of Rome is the Head, and the Bishops in general the members, of his Body, in whom is the Chief Government, and to whom is committed the charge of the " helm :" (5) That the Prerogatives of the Sovereign Pontiff consist of his being " the Guardian of the Vineyard," and " the Judge of Faith," the right to be first consulted, whose judgment is indisputable : (6) That he has the right to confirm Bishops to their Sees, and power, if need be, to

excommunicate and depose them, to confirm Synods, and to annul the sentences of Bishops ; and (7) That Roman custom must be followed, that nothing may be introduced into the churches without his authority, that no Council may be held without the sanction of the Pope, and that no canon may be made contrary to his decree.

All these claims have been made from time to time, and all these powers have been exercised by the Roman Pontiffs, not in secret, but openly, in their Letters and other missives to Bishops and Councils, so that if these claims had been destitute of any lawful foundation it was competent for the whole Church to have remonstrated with the Popes, to have disclaimed utterly their pretensions, to have declined all submission to them, and, finally, to have repelled them from their communion.   But not a murmur of dissent is heard from any part of the Catholic Church, save in some matters involving the privileges of the Episcopate,—no, not even when the language of the Popes was the most outspoken, and when their actions were the most despotic.   The Universal Church never questioned the Pope's right to excommunicate and depose Nestorius and Dioscorus, Patriarchs, respectively, of Constantinople and Alexandria ; on the contrary, she magnified their office, not scrupling to employ such language as this : " Thou art the constituted Interpreter to all of the voice of the blessed Peter." Thou art the " Custodian of the vineyard."   Thou art the " Head," and we " the members."   Thou art our " Father," and we " the children."   There can be no doubt whatever that the position which the Popes assumed in the fourth and fifth centuries was assumed with the unanimous consent of the Universal Catholic Church, in the East no less than in the West ; and, therefore, the only conclusion to be drawn is this, that the Primitive Church of the first five centuries believed that S. Peter had received a special commission from the Lord to rule the Universal Church ; that S. Peter established his Cathedra in Rome ; that the Roman Pontiffs are his Successors in that Cathedra ; and that as such, they have succeeded to all his Powers and Prerogatives as the Chief of the Brotherhood, the Supreme Pastor of the Flock, the Head and Judge of Faith, and the Guardian of the one Fold of the one Lord.

PART IV.

AUDI ALTERAM PARTEM.

INTRODUCTORY.

One would think, after perusing the vast amount of evidence which has been collected that there could scarcely be any room for an "Audi Alteram Partem." Certainly no evidence in favour of any office, or dignity, or privilege, could be more voluminous, more consistent, and conclusive, than that which has been adduced for the Papacy. The Fathers generally, the Œcumenical and Plenary Councils, and the Catholic Emperors of East and West, with one consentient voice, have accepted, to the full, the doctrine of the Supremacy of the Holy See. How, then, can there be any room for counter evidence of such an extent as would neutralise the multifarious proofs that have been advanced? Doubtless opponents may appeal to the language of a few individual Bishops, and even of a few Councils, protesting against some particular Papal act deemed to be arbitrary or unjust ; but this is not testimony against the Papal position any more than protests of ministers or parliaments are against the office, prerogatives, and rights of the Sovereign of the Realm. If, indeed, it were possible to produce evidence of any great extent such as would directly controvert the plain testimonies of Fathers, Councils, and Emperors in favour of the Roman Supremacy, as derived from S. Peter, then the whole structure of Christianity would necessarily fall : and for this simple reason, that if the Fathers should be found to contradict themselves on a vital point of faith (and if the Papacy be true, it is a vital part of faith) their testimony for Christianity itself would no longer be trustworthy.

But inasmuch as many objections have been raised against the tenability of the Roman position, it is necessary that the most important ones should have a fair consideration.

I.

S. PETER'S PREROGATIVES.

It is alleged by Dr. Barrow and others that the Primacy, of whatever it consisted was personal to S. Peter, that is to say, it did not pass to his Successors. To meet this objection, it will be sufficient to consider three questions, truthful answers to which will determine this point.

First, in granting the commission to S. Peter to exercise the Prerogative of the Supreme Jurisdiction, as symbolised by the keys, which he alone received,—a commission which was addressed solely to himself by our Lord—did Christ, by word or action, limit it to S. Peter personally? It is sufficient to say that there is not a vestige of authority for such a limitation to be found in Holy Scripture; but, on the contrary, such a notion is opposed to the very design which our Lord had in mind when He founded His Church; for the Body corporate which He instituted was destined to continue for ever, that is, till the close of the dispensation, as the following passages plainly testify : " The gates of hell shall not prevail against it." (S. Matt. xvi.) " I will pray the Father, and He shall give you another Comforter, that He may abide with you for ever, even the Spirit of Truth." (S. John, xiv. 16.) " Lo, I am with you alway even until the end of the world," or more literally, "all the days till the consummation." (S. Matt. xxviii. 20.)

It is absurd to suppose that the Body politic, which was intended to continue till the end of time, should, on the death of the Apostles, lose that organization and government with which Christ had supplied it. If then an earthly Head had been provided, it follows, as a necessary consequence, that this Headship must continue no less than the Body. As before observed, if an executive and governmental authority over the Body had been deemed necessary, it can never cease to be necessary till that Body shall be dissolved.

. Secondly, Have the Successors of S. Peter at Rome continuously and from the beginning claimed the Primacy by virtue of that commission which he (Peter) received from Christ? Ecclesiastical history proves that they have, and not only claimed, but constantly exercised it.

Thirdly, Did the Primitive Church object to the claim? The evidence adduced demonstrates that she did not. Why did the Church of Corinth appeal to Rome for assistance in her trouble? Why did S. Polycarp travel all the way to Rome to obtain some decision concerning the period of keeping Easter? How was it that Tertullian, after he fell from the truth, scornfully gave in detail the titles of the Pope, and the characteristics of his Office, as then commonly understood, if no such right existed? On what possible grounds did S. Cyprian set in motion the Pope's authority against the Bishop of Arles, if it is true that the Pope was no more than the Bishop of a diocese, the Metropolitan of a province, or the Patriarch of a patriarchate, of which France, according to Anglican authority, formed no part? Even in the cases of S. Victor, S. Stephen, and S. Zosimus (which I will consider specially farther on), who were violently opposed, no protest has ever been recorded against Papal Prerogatives as derived from S. Peter.

After the conversion of the Empire, and the consequent relief of the Church from the pressure of persecution, we find the claims of the Pope not only enforced, but admitted to the full, by both Bishops and people, including even the Catholic Emperors of East and West.

There is nothing, then, to show that the Prerogatives of S. Peter were personal to himself; Scripture, as has been proved, presumes a succession, and it is clear that the Primitive Church not only did not resist it, but, on the contrary, admitted it. It is evident, then, that the Prerogatives of S. Peter passed to the Successors of his office of Supreme Bishop and Pastor.

II.

S. PETER, BISHOP OF ROME.

It is maintained that, although S. Peter was at Rome, yet he did not sit there as Bishop. It is alleged, too, that the office of Apostle and Bishop could not be held by one and the same person. Dr. Barrow says that "St. Peter's being Bishop of Rome would confound the offices which God made distinct; for *God did appoint first apostles, then prophets, then pastors and teachers;* wherefore St. Peter, after he was an apostle, could not well become a bishop : it would be such an irregularity, as if a bishop should be made a deacon." (*Supp. p.* 119.) There is a fallacy in this argument. It is alleged that one person cannot hold two offices which God had made distinct. But it is well known that S. Peter and S. Paul and the other Apostles did hold and exercise two or more distinct offices. In the first place, S. Peter, S. Paul, and S. John were both Apostles and Prophets, the last-named being pre-eminently the Seer of the New Testament. S. James was both Apostle and also Bishop of Jerusalem. S. Paul, too, was Universal Apostle, and also specially the Apostle of the Uncircumcision. In S. Peter there were three offices—(1), that of the Foundation and the Supremacy ; (2), of the Apostleship generally, and (3), especially of the Circumcision. If he, then, and the other Apostles did hold two or more offices, why should it have the effect of "confounding the offices which God made distinct," for S. Peter to become the local Bishop of Rome, notwithstanding that he was the Chief Pastor of the whole flock? The question, however, is one of fact,—did S. Peter make Rome his See, and did he establish there his Chair or Cathedra? The testimony of all antiquity is conclusive on this point ; and it is admitted by all that the Roman Chair is the "Chair of Peter," and hence Rome has been described as being pre-eminently "the Holy See," "the See of Peter," and "the Apostolic See." That S. Peter was Bishop of Rome seems to be incontestable ; for if he had not been so, what did S. Ignatius mean when he described the Roman Church as the Presiding Church? On what other ground did S. Irenæus assert that the Church of Rome was a "Superior and more Powerful Principality, with which every Church must agree, or assemble," than that it had been "founded and constituted by the two most glorious Apostles Peter and Paul," and that in it was treasured the fulness of Apostolic Tradition? and why did S. Cyprian, too, say that Rome was the "Place of Peter," in which is the "Chair of Peter, and the Principal Church, whence the unity of the Priesthood took its rise?"

It seems, then, plain that S. Peter was Bishop of Rome, and that he established in that Church his Cathedra or Chair.

III.

THE ROMAN PONTIFFS, S. PETER'S SUCCESSORS.

No one who has read ecclesiastical history, even superficially, can have failed to perceive that the Bishops of Rome have ever been regarded as the Successors of S. Peter, and as the occupants, for the time being, of his Chair in the Holy City. This fact is as indisputable as that Queen Victoria is the successor of William the Conqueror and of Alfred the Great. The only point is, did the Prerogatives of S. Peter, as the Head of the Brotherhood, and the Chief Pastor of the flock, pass to those Successors to his Chair? It is alleged, however, that there is an essential difference between an Apostle and a Bishop, and that consequently what might have been the case with the Apostle would have been impossible as respects the Bishop. This distinction is maintained by Barrow: "The apostolical office, as such, was personal and temporary; and therefore, according to its nature and design, not successive or communicable to others in perpetual descendence from them." (*Supp. p.* 112.) Before this objection can be met, let us understand of what the essence of an Apostle consists. As the name infers, he is a person sent on an ambassage to represent an office, and to defend and maintain the interests of the Sovereign Ruler who appointed him. Now the Apostles were sent for the following purposes: (1), To witness the fact of the Resurrection; (2), To carry into effect our Lord's commands respecting the foundation and establishment of His Kingdom and Church; (3), To govern this Kingdom; (4), To preside over the worship of Almighty God, and as priests to offer the unbloody Sacrifice of the altar; (5), To preach the Gospel to all nations; and (6), To provide for the spiritual nourishment of all believing souls: and in order that they might at first perform this work according to Christ's instructions, they were each personally inspired by the Holy Ghost, who remained with them, as it were, after the manner of a Person, not only ruling them by His influence, but by His commands often audibly delivered. Now the only distinction which is apparent between the Apostles of our Lord and their Successors is, that the former were personal witnesses of the Resurrection, and that they held a direct commission to lay the foundations of the Church. In the performance of these two functions, they, of course, could have no Successors, properly speaking; for after the decease of their generation there could be no longer any personal witnesses of the fact of the Resurrection; and the foundations, once laid, could, of course, never be re-laid. S. Paul himself, in these respects, is no Apostle; for he was not a *personal* witness of the Resurrection: what he knew about it was by revelation, not as an eye-witness; nor can it be said that he in any sense founded the Church, for it had been already founded, before his own conversion, on the Twelve Apostles. But these two offices of the Apostolate did not by any means exhaust the Apostleship; for there remained the functions of government, of Priesthood, and of the Pastorate. All these offices were, on the departure of our Lord, in the Apostleship alone. The seventy Elders received from Christ no authority as Priests or Pastors; the utmost extent of their commission was to preach, to visit,

and heal the sick.   In the Apostolate alone centred every office of
Church Government and Priesthood. If, then, the Apostolate died with
the last surviving Apostle, as Dr. Barrow would infer, then we are at
this moment without any authorised Ruler or Priest in religion. And
Dr. Barrow supports this idea by asserting that an Apostle is a func-
tionary who can only be appointed immediately by God in Person. But
happily we know that this is not true ; for S. Matthias, the successor of
Júdas Iscariot, was nominated by the Apostles and the whole Church,
and by them elected under the supervision of the Holy Ghost, "and he
was numbered with the Eleven Apostles." (*Acts*, i. 26.) And in the case
of S. Paul himself, he was indeed called miraculously to the ministry,
but he received his mission by the agency of men.   And we know also
that others, as S. Timothy, S. Titus, S. Silvanus, &c. &c., were
associated with the Apostles in the Government of the Church, and these
were expressly called "Apostles."*   Dr. Barrow, then, is wrong when
he asserts that the Apostolate has no succession, and that to institute
an Apostle it is necessary he should have his call miraculously from
heaven.   The only difference, then, between the Twelve Apostles
and their Successors is, in (1) the personal testimony of the Lord's
Resurrection; (2) the commission to found the Church; and (3) the
gift of personal inspiration to enable them to perform their proper
work ; but in the office of Governor or Ruler over the Household of God,
of Priesthood, and of the Pastorate, if we may rely upon Scripture and
primitive Tradition, they had without doubt Successors, who exhibited
their authority, their power, and their infallibility, not indeed by means
of miraculous or outward manifestations of the Holy Ghost, but by that
personal indwelling which was promised to the Apostolate in the words ;
" I will pray the Father, and He shall give you another Comforter (the
Paraclete), that He may abide with you for ever, even the Spirit of
Truth." And again : " Lo, I am with you all days until the consummation."

Now, if the Apostolate has a succession to the office of Government and
Priesthood, how can it be denied that S. Peter, the Head of the Apostolate, should not have Successors also? Like his brother Apostles, he had
an extraordinary and an ordinary office in his position as Head. He was
(1) the sole Foundation and Origin of the Church, and (2) he was the
Rock on which the Church was to be built. As the Rock and Foundation
can be but once laid, as there cannot be more than one original fount, so
consequently, to these offices S. Peter could have no proper Successor.
But with respect to his Supreme Government—the Supreme Jurisdiction
which he had by virtue of the gift of the keys, the Supremacy in matters

---

* SS. Barnabas, Timothy, Silvanus, Epaphroditus, Titus, and the Brethren,
were called Apostles, ἀπόστολοι, see Acts, xiv. 14, 1 Thess. i. 1, and ii. 6, Phil.
ii. 25, and 2 Cor. viii. 23.   Bingham observes, "The most ancient of these
(titles) is the title of Apostle, which in a large and secondary sense is thought by
many to have been the original name for Bishops, before the name Bishop was
appropriated to their order." *Antiq*. Book II. *c*. ii. *s*. 1.

regarding the faith, and the supremacy as Chief Pastor of the one fold—he necessarily had Successors, and for this reason, because if such an office was deemed necessary by our Lord, when all the Chief Governors were personally inspired, it could not be otherwise than needful in after times, when the Rulers of the Church would no longer be *personally* under similar supervision of the Holy Ghost. It is held, however, that the same argument applies to S. Peter, and that therefore he could have no Successors to his Primacy. But S. Peter received a promise for him-self, which none of the other Apostles singly ever did receive : "The gates of hell shall not prevail against" My Church, as built upon "the Rock ;" so that, that Church, which is built upon Peter alone, possesses the privilege of indefectibility, while Churches proceeding from the other Apostles enjoy no such immunity. As a matter of fact no Bishop of Rome has ever been a heretic. Liberius may have fallen from fear; Honorius may have allowed himself to have been deceived ; but not a single Pope, when declaring the doctrine of the Church, and speaking *ex cathedra*, has ever promulged a heresy. The Bishops of other Apostolic Thrones—as Alexandria, Antioch, Jerusalem—have frequently fallen, at one time denying the Divine, at another the Human, nature of our Lord ; and to this day they all reject the dogma of the Procession of the Holy Ghost from the Father and the Son, thus dividing the Substance.

The Apostle S. Peter obtained a guarantee for the Church built and proceeding from him, that it should never be trampled under the feet of the Devil : and hence the difficulty of a Successor to his Supreme Govern-ment is at once met and disposed of. While the successions of the other Apostles may fail, and their descendants fall into heresy, we have a solemn guarantee from our Lord that the succession in S. Peter's Church shall never fail, and that it shall never fall into heresy. Having now disposed of these difficulties, let us recall to our minds the facts of the case ; for after all it is simply a matter of fact. Now it has already been proved that the Bishops of Rome from the time of S. Peter have claimed and exercised the office of the Head of the Brotherhood and Chief Pastor of the one Flock ; it has also been shown that the Primitive Church admitted the Papal position, and further, that the Catholic Empe-rors submitted to an *imperium in imperio*, which they would never have done if they had not been persuaded that it was founded under the most indefeasible title possible, viz. Right Divine. There can be no doubt that to the exalted office of S. Peter there were Successors, and that all the ordinary functions of Supreme Government, on the decease of S. Peter, passed to all those who in their day personated and repre-sented him.

THE ROMAN ECCLESIASTICAL PRINCEDOM.

Dr. Barrow declares that "the ground of that eminence which the Roman Bishop did obtain in the Church, so as in order to precede other bishops, doth shake this pretence. The Church of Rome was indeed allowed to be *the principal Church*, as St. Cyprian calleth it: but why? Was it preferred by Divine institution? No, surely; Christianity did not make laws of that nature, or constitute differences of places? Was it in regard to the succession of St. Peter? No; that was a slim, upstart device; that did not hold in Antioch, nor in other apostolical churches. But it was for a more substantial reason; the very same on which the dignity and pre-eminency of other churches was founded; that is, the dignity, magnitude, opulency, opportunity of that city in which the bishop of Rome did preside: together with the consequent numerousness, quality, and wealth of his flock; which gave him many great advantages above other his fellow-bishops: It was, saith Rigaltius, called by St. Cyprian the principal Church, *because constituted in the principal city.*" *Supp. p.* 230.

Now it may at once be conceded that the civil dignity of Rome contributed to magnify the grandeur and prestige of the Roman Church, but I deny that the dignity of the Roman Ecclesiastical Principality was derived from the greatness of the Imperial city. Every one who has read the history of any war, knows well enough that it is a main part of the plan of every campaign to seize, as strategetical points, the principal cities of the country invaded; and chiefly its metropolis: and for this end, that if once the army is master of the capital and the chief cities therein, the conquest of the whole country is secured. The conquerors, no doubt, obtain a certain glory from the greatness of the cities they have taken; but who is there that would assert that their greatness was consequent on the prestige of the fallen cities? Who is there that would deny that the author of their dignity and state was the potentate who commanded them to invade and conquer?

The Catholic Church is often called the Church Militant, and this because it is an aggressive power, instituted by the Lord for the specific purpose of subduing the world to His Divine sceptre. To accomplish this end, He has appointed divers officers, such as Bishops, Priests, Deacons, &c., all of whom He has placed under the charge of one Commander-in-chief, viz., S. Peter, and the Successors to his government.

The commission which S. Peter, the Apostles, and all whom they appointed as their associates or successors, received, was to "Go . . . and disciple all nations . . . teaching them to observe all things whatsoever I have commanded you." "He that believeth and is baptized, shall be saved; but he that believeth not shall be damned." (S. Matt. xxviii. 19, 20; and S. Mark, xvi. 16.)

In obedience to this high commission, the Apostles went forth conquering and to conquer. S. James took possession of Jerusalem, S. John the cities of Asia Minor, S. Thomas advanced into India, and S. Paul seized upon the cities of Rome, Corinth, Ephesus, Galatia, Philippi, Colossæ, Thessalonica, and some of the cities of Spain, and probably of Britain and Ireland. With regard to S. Peter, S. Chrysostom commenting on the words, "And it came to pass, as Peter passed throughout all quarters," &c. (Acts, ix. 32), says, "like the Commander of an army, he went about, inspecting the ranks, what part was compact, what in good order, what needed his presence." *In Act. Hom.* xxi. He then visited the churches in Asia, afterwards he travelled to Antioch, and made that city his head-quarters ; and after remaining there for a few years, he advanced on to the Imperial city of Rome, already partially occupied by the spiritual forces of the Lord, and planted therein his Cathedra ; thus making it for ever the capital of Christendom, the source of the Unity of the Priest-hood, the fount of venerable communion to all the Churches : and its court the Chancery of the Universal Church.

Now a very plain question suggests itself, viz., Whether the Princedom of the Roman Church derived its origin from the dignity of the spiritual conquerors of Rome, or from the fact that the city was the metropolis of the world ? Supposing S. Peter had been the secular commander of a great army, and as such had laid siege to Rome, and after he had taken it, had planted his standard on the Capitol, would any man of common sense assert that the dignity of their Commander and his Succes-sors, and the rank and prestige of those who joined his retinue, derived their origin from the grandeur of the city and from the glory of its antece-dents? Certainly not ; and yet, notwithstanding, in order to get rid of most conclusive testimony, that the Roman Church, by virtue of the position of its Founder, and the presence of his Cathedra, is the Principal and Ruling Church, Dr. Barrow attempts to prove that the rank of this Church was a mere accident, the consequence of its being the Church of the Imperial city !

It is time now to descend to particulars, and to examine Dr. Barrow's argument somewhat in detail. 1. He first of all refers to S. Cyprian : " It was," saith Rigaltius, "called by S. Cyprian the principal Church, *because constituted in the principal city.*" Any one who has read the works of S. Cyprian will at once perceive the very questionable manner the above-named controversialist has made use of the name of this most eminent Catholic saint. The unwary and unlearned reader would naturally suppose that S. Cyprian had himself asserted that the Roman Church was the Principal Church, " because constituted in the principal city." But S. Cyprian never said any such thing.

Dr. Barrow, under the protecting authority of Rigaltius, asserts that this was the view of S. Cyprian, that the Roman Church was the Principal Church " because constituted in the principal city." The following is the real passage : " Moreover, after all this, a pseudo-Bishop having been set up for themselves by heretics, they dare to sail, and carry letters from some schismatics and profane persons to the Chair of Peter, and to the Principal Church, whence the unity of the Priesthood (*i. e.* the Episcopate) took its rise ; nor do they consider that the Romans are those whose faith was praised in the preaching of the Apostle, to whom faithlessness can have no access." *Ep.* lv. *ad. Cornel.* Where is there a single expression in the above that can be forced to mean that in S. Cyprian's belief the dignity of the Princedom of the Holy See was derived from the grandeur of the principal city? This idea is not even implied in the text. The rule of construction is utterly opposed to such an interpretation ; and no one but a bigoted partizan could have so interpreted it. Now let the reader ask himself what S. Cyprian understood when he used the words " Principal Church ?" He will observe that immediately before these words are the following : " the Chair of Peter," and immediately after, "whence the unity of the Priesthood took its rise." What, then, was the foundation of the Principality of the Roman Church? Was it the city? or was it "the Chair of Peter?" Assuming for a moment it was the city, did "the unity of the Priesthood take its rise from the Imperial city, or if not the city, from the civico-ecclesiastical Supremacy arising from the fact that this Church was the Church of Imperial Rome?" Will any man who pretends to be a critic maintain that this was S. Cyprian's meaning, that the " Principal Church" was simply a Church which happened to be located in the Imperial city, and that therefore it became the source "whence the unity of the Priesthood took its rise ;" and that "the Chair of Peter " (for this must be included) obtained Supreme authority, because the ground on which it stood was that of the seven-hilled city? The very absurdity of the argument is its best refutation. It is impossible to put any other construction on this passage of S. Cyprian, than that when he used the words " Principal Church" he meant that the Roman Church was the " Principal Church" inasmuch as "the Chair of Peter" was there established, "whence the unity of the Priesthood took its rise." That Dr. Barrow was well aware of the true scope of the passage he has so grossly mutilated, is evident from what he says further on : " S. Cyprian did call the Roman see *the chair of St. Peter, and the principal Church;* yet he disclaimed any authority of the Roman Bishop above his brethren." (*Ib.* 235.) In all sincerity, I ask the most ultra-Protestant, whether such handling of any author can be regarded as honest and straightforward? Certain it is, if the works of S. Cyprian had been those of a secular, and Dr. Barrow a layman, such kind of criticism would have been condemned by every honest man ; and yet the work of this man is regarded by the authorities of the Oxford University Press as a standard one, worthy of the careful study of its alumni ! A more dishonest and disreputable book has never issued from the press of this or of any other country.

But to proceed : in respect of the interpretation he has put upon the words, " Principal Church," he adds the following : " Such a reason of precedence St. Cyprian giveth in another case, ' *Because,* saith he, *Rome for its magnitude ought to precede Carthage.*'" *Supp. p.* 231. To understand S. Cyprian's meaning let us supply the context the learned Doctor has so conveniently suppressed : " It is the same Novatus, who amongst us scattered the first flames of discord and schism, who separated some of the brethren here from their Bishop, who, amid the very persecution, was to ours, as another persecution, in overthrowing the minds of the brethren. He it is who without my permission or knowledge, of his own factiousness and ambition, made Felicissimus his follower, deacon, and . . . . . . sailing to Rome also, to overthrow the Church, he there contrived similar and like plots, rending a portion of the laity from the clergy, cleaving asunder the concord of the Brotherhood, who were closely knit together and mutually loved each other. In short, as Rome from her greatness ought to have precedency of Carthage, there he committed greater and more grievous crimes. He who here made a deacon against the Church, there made a Bishop." *Ep.* xlix. *ad. Cornel.*

Now what is the drift of the passage in S. Cyprian here referred to ? It is simply this, Novatus, the African schismatic, after doing much mischief in the province of Carthage, resolved to go to Rome, where he and his companions, in concert with Novatian, the Anti-Pope, as S. Cyprian says in another epistle, attempted to set up a Chair for themselves, and to assume the Primacy, and to claim the right of baptizing and of offering. (*Ep.* lxxvi. *ad Magnum, p.* 154.) Hence S. Cyprian's observations, "In short, as Rome from her greatness ought to have precedency over Carthage, there he committed greater and more grievous crimes : who here made a deacon against the Church, there made a Bishop." Now, looking fairly at the passage, let the reader ask himself, when S. Cyprian used these words, was he regarding Rome and Carthage in their imperial and secular character, or in their ecclesiastical and spiritual aspect? The context plainly shows that he meant the latter. Novatus sailed to Rome for the avowed purpose of overthrowing the Church, even that "Chief Church whence the unity of the Priesthood took its rise." Hence it is that S. Cyprian's thought, when he penned the passage quoted by Dr. Barrow, was ecclesiastical Rome and ecclesiastical Carthage, and not these cities in their secular and metropolitical character. Who is there that does not know that persons in general converse and write under the influence of the thought naturally uppermost? When politicians speak of Canterbury, London, or York, unless the context fixes a different meaning, they usually refer to them as merely cities of the kingdom. When military men, in time of war, in like manner converse, their thoughts are more upon their positions as strategical points than considered as political municipalities ; so also ecclesiastics, when dilating on ecclesiastical subjects, in their allusions to various cities, describing them simply by name : obviously, their uppermost thought is not the secular, but the ecclesiastical character of such cities. In Dr. Barrow's reference to S. Cyprian, it is clear from the subject-matter of his epistle, sufficiently detailed in the context, that he was not thinking of Imperial Rome, but of Rome, as that Chief Church, which Novatus conspired to overthrow. So far, then, from S. Cyprian supporting Dr. Barrow, his writings witness most mercilessly against him. The reader will not forget all that this Saint has said respecting the position and dignity of S. Peter ; how that on him the Lord "built his Church," on whom "He laid and founded the Church ;" "having founded" it "first and alone" upon him, "for an original and principle of unity ;" "from whom He appointed, and showed that unity should spring," so much so, "that that same unity" begins from one " (Peter) ; to whom Christ delivered the keys, "that that should be loosed in heaven which (Peter) should have loosed on earth," and "to whom the Lord commended His sheep to be fed and guarded." And it will not have slipped the reader's memory that S. Cyprian had declared as plainly as language can express, that "the Chair is one," "for," said he, "God is one, and Christ is one, and the Church is one, and the Chair one, founded by the Lord's Word upon a Rock," which Rock is S. Peter, for he again says, "herself (the Mother Church) having been founded first and alone by the voice of the Lord upon Peter." The reader will further call to mind that S. Cyprian, in consequence of S. Peter having come to Rome, and erected there his Chair—that "one Chair" just alluded to—speaks of Rome as "the Place of Peter," where is the Chair of Peter to which is attached "the rank or grade of the sacerdotal Chair." Will any one, then, in the face of this language, presume to say that the "Principal Church" derived its dignity from Imperial Rome, and not from the "Chair of Peter," from the "Rank or Grade" of him who sat in "the Apostolic Chair," and from Rome, as the conquered city of S. Peter, who made it his "Place," and raised it to a far higher rank, position, and power than it ever had before ; viz., as the Capital and the Metropolis of the Universal Empire of the great King of kings and Lord of lords ?

2. The next authority Dr. Barrow advances is that of S. Irenæus. Thus he quotes and comments upon him : "*To this Church, it is necessary that every Church (that is, the faithful who are all about) should resort, because of its more powerful principality;* what is meant by that *resort*, will be easy to him who considereth how men here are wont to go up to London, drawn thither by interests of trade, law, &c. What he did understand *by more powerful principality*, the words themselves do signify, which exactly do agree to the power and grandeur of the imperial city, but do not well suit to the authority of a church ; especially then when no church did appear to have either principality or puissance. And that sense may clearly be evinced by the context, wherein it doth appear, that S. Irenæus doth not allege the judicial authority of the Roman Church, but its credible testimony, which thereby became more considerable, because Christians commonly had occasions of recourse to it." (*Supp., p.* 231.) In order to perceive S. Irenæus's meaning, let us have before us the whole passage, "But as it would be a very long task to enumerate in such a volume as this the successions of all the Churches, we do put to confusion all those who . . . . assemble in unauthorized meetings ; (we do this, I say) by indicating the tradition derived from the Apostles, of the very great, the very ancient, and universally known Church founded and constituted at Rome by the two most glorious Apostles, Peter and Paul; and also (by pointing out) the faith preached to men, which comes down to our time by means of the succession of the Bishops. For it is a matter of necessity that every Church should agree (or assemble) with this (the Roman) Church on account of its Pre-eminent Authority (or, its more Powerful or Superior Principality) ; that is, the faithful everywhere, inasmuch as the Apostolical tradition has been preserved by those who exist everywhere." Now after forcing the above passage to the utmost, how can it be said that the words, "a more Powerful Principality," "exactly do agree to the power and grandeur of the imperial city ?" On what grounds does Dr. Barrow say, that they "do not well suit to the authority of a church ; especially

then when no church did appear to have either principality or puissance?" But surely Dr. Barrow has got himself here into a net from which he cannot disentangle himself. If the Church in the time of S. Irenæus had no "principality |or puissance" (he using these words according to their political significance), how can these words, "more Powerful Principality," "exactly agree to the power and grandeur of the Imperial city?" It is not to be supposed that Dr. Barrow understood S. Irenæus to be counselling an appeal to pagan Rome, and yet if the Roman Church was not a Principality at all, then the Principality alluded to must be that of the city itself, that is, Pagan Rome.

The truth is, that Dr. Barrow's whole idea of a principality is that of a mere earthly power. The habit of his mind is to regard a Church in no other light than an Established Church, like that of England, whose only principality consists of the grandeur and position accorded to it by the Crown and State. Consequently, he conceives that when the Fathers use the word "Principality," in reference to the Roman Church, they mean the mere political or secular position of that Church, as the established Church of the Imperial city. He does not seem to notice the fact that there are Principalities and Powers which are not of this earth ; that there are some in the heavenly places, composed of the Angelic Hierarchy, and some in the infernal regions, consisting of devils and evil spirits. He seems to have forgotten, so Establishmentarian are his ideas, that Christ our Lord, in total disregard of the Emperor of Rome, founded on earth one great Universal Spiritual Empire, which he divided into Twelve Princedoms, giving to each of the twelve Apostles a Throne, from which they were to judge the twelve portions of the Spiritual Israel. These Principalities owed their existence to no imperial edict ; though on the earth, they were not of the earth ; they formed together the Kingdom of God among men. They may, indeed, resemble, by their power and grandeur, earthly powers, but in truth they are the similitudes of the celestial powers, whom earthly empires and kingdoms strive to copy and emulate. Now Dr. Barrow is quite right when he asserts that in the time of S. Irenæus "no Church did appear to have either principality or puissance," *i.e.* a "principality or puissance" similar to the power and grandeur of the Imperial city. But according to S. Irenæus, the Church of Rome was a Principality, and that a Superior or more Powerful one. If it was not a secular principality, what was it? Assuredly a purely spiritual one, derived from no earthly source whatever. What, then, was its source ? S. Irenæus informs us, viz., "the very great, the very ancient, and universally known Church, founded and constituted at Rome by the two most glorious Apostles Peter and Paul;" and then, after a few words, he adds, "For it is a matter of necessity that every Church should agree (or assemble) with this Church, on account of its Pre-eminent authority (or its more Powerful or superior Principality)." Where, then, is the true source of the greatness of the Principality of the Roman Church ? Is it Imperial Rome? Certainly not. Where then ? In her foundation by S. Peter and S. Paul, the former being the Head of the Brotherhood, the Source of unity and communion ; and the latter the Apostle of the Uncircumcision : who together, united all their authorities, and made the

Roman Church a " more Powerful Principality," by the tradition of which heresies may be refuted, heretics exposed, schismatic assemblies denounced, and the faithful everywhere protected.

3. The learned Doctor next appeals to the Council of Chalcedon : he says, " This is the sole ground upon which the greatest of all ancient synods, that of Chalcedon, did affirm the Papal eminency to be founded ; for, *To the throne*, say they, *of ancient Rome, because that was the royal city, the Fathers reasonably conferred the privileges;* the fountain of papal eminence was in their judgment not any divine institution, not the authority of St. Peter deriving itself to his successors ; but the concession of the Fathers, who were moved to grant it upon account that Rome was the imperial city." (*Supp., p.* 232.) I have already shown, under the Section " Testimony of Councils," the distinction between the dignity of the Pope as the Successor of S. Peter and the privileges granted him by reason of his being the Prelate of the Imperial City. The reader is referred to my observations on this point (see *supra, pp.* 197--202). What I am now more concerned with is the flagrant dishonesty of this appeal to the Council of Chalcedon, the testimony of which, in favour of the Supremacy of the Holy See, by virtue of its having been the See of Peter, is overwhelming and exhaustive. Let the reader re-peruse the extracts taken from the acts of that Council, and then ask himself whether Dr. Barrow is correct when he says, "that the fountain of Papal eminency was, in their judgment not any Divine institution, not the authority of St. Peter deriving itself to his successors, but the concession of the Fathers, who were moved to grant it upon account that Rome was the imperial city?" Why did not Dr. Barrow put before his innocent readers the Synodical Epistle of that Council requesting the Pope to confirm not only the decrees, but this very canon he has referred to? Why did he not at least give them the following extracts from this Synodical Epistle : " Which (*i.e.* the Divine doctrine) like to a golden chain, coming even unto us by the precept of the Lawgiver, thou (Leo) hast preserved, being the constituted Interpreter to all of the voice of the blessed Peter." " Over and above these outrages, he (Dioscorus) extended his madness against him (Leo) to whom the care of the Vineyard has been committed by the Saviour, that is, against your Apostolic Holiness." " . . . . Over whom (*i.e.* the Synod) thou didst Preside, as the Head over the members." " We confirmed, then, the canon of the 150 Fathers of Constantinople, which ordained that the Bishop of that city should have privileges of honour after your most holy and Apostolic Chair, in the conviction that, as you dispose of your favours without any invidious feeling towards your brethren, so you would extend your wonted care to the Church of Constantinople, and enlighten it with your Apostolic ray. Deign, therefore, most holy and blessed Father, to allow our decision. . . . Honour thou, we pray you, our judgment with your Decree, that as we have been united to our Head in agreeing upon what was right, so the Head, too, may confirm the becoming act of the children. So will our pious Princes be pleased, who have ratified as a law whatever your Holiness has determined." See *Labbé. S. Concil. T.* iv. *col.* 1774-79. In face, then, of this Synodical Epistle, what becomes of the force of this

Canon of Chalcedon, so much relied upon as a crushing testimony against Rome? So far from this, that rightly understood, and taken with the Synodical letter asking for its confirmation, it is the strongest possible witness in favour of what is called the most ultramontane idea of Papal Supremacy; and it is the more significant, inasmuch as the authors of this Epistle were not Latin-catholics, but Orientals who were ever jealous of their rights. It is simply marvellous that Dr. Barrow should have ventured to have suppressed so clear a synodical exposition of this famous canon; and it is equally astonishing that English Churchmen should, relying upon his baseless asseverations, still continue brandishing before the Chair of S. Peter a weapon, which, in point of fact, utterly annihilates their schismatical position.

5. Dr. Barrow next refers us to the epistle of the Empress Placidia. "To the same purpose the empress Placidia, in her epistle to Theodosius in behalf of Pope Leo, saith, *It becometh us to preserve to this city* (Rome) *the which is mistress of all lands, a reverence in all things.* This reason had indeed," continues our Doctor, "in it much of equity, of decency, of conveniency ; it was equal that he should have the preference, and more than common respect, who was thence enabled and engaged to do most service to religion. It was decent, that out of conformity to the state, and in respect to the imperial court and senate, the pastor of that place should be graced with repute ; it was convenient, that he who resided in the centre of all business, and had the greatest influence upon affairs, who was the emperor's chief counsellor for direction, and instrument for execution of ecclesiastical affairs, should not be put behind others." (*Supp. p.* 232.) Here, again, I must supply what Dr. Barrow has omitted from his quotation from Placidia. "By their favour, then, may your kindliness direct, in opposition to the prevailing confusion, that the true faith of the Catholic religion be preserved immaculate, namely, by seeing that, in accordance with the Form and Definition of the Apostolic See, which we both (*i.e.* Placidia and her son the Emperor) equally venerate as of surpassing (authority), Flavian may be secured unharmed in his see, and the matter be transferred to the judgment of a council, and of the Apostolic See, in which he (Peter) who was worthy to receive the heavenly keys, ordained the Princedom of the Episcopate. It is fitting, too, that we should pay all due deference to this city which is the mistress of all over which you rule." *Inter Ep. Leo. Ep.* lvi. *T.* 1, *col.* 859–62, *Migne.* According to this Empress, Galla Placidia, it is plain, that the Princedom or Principality of the Roman Church was not due to the dignity of the city of Rome, but to S. Peter, who had "received the heavenly keys," and who established that very Principality which Dr. Barrow has laboured to prove is of secular and imperial origin. So far from Placidia supporting Dr. Barrow, she maintains the authority of the Pope, because he was, by virtue of his succession from S. Peter, the ordained Principate of the whole Episcopate.

Surely this is enough to dispose of Dr. Barrow's strictures against the Roman Principality. The reader must see that his apparent success is owing simply to his having deliberately omitted the context of the several passages upon which he relies for proof that the ecclesiastical status of the

Roman Church, is secular and not religious, is imperial and not spiritual, being derived from him whom Jesus Christ Himself solemnly appointed to be the Head of the Church, giving him, to the exclusion of all the Apostles, except as in union with him the keys of heaven; to whom He assigned the care of his brother Apostles as regards the stability of their faith, and to whom he committed the pastoral charge of the Universal Fold. This office S. Peter, under the inspiration of God, delivered to his Successors to his "Place" and "Chair;" and hence the Roman Church became the Presiding Church, as S. Ignatius said, "presiding over the Love with the Name of Christ, with the Name of the Father;" "a Superior or more Powerful Principality," as S. Irenæus affirmed; the "Place of Peter," where stands in majestic grandeur the venerable "Chair of Peter" to which is attached "the Rank or the Grade of the Sacerdotal Chair," and "the Principal Church, whence the unity of the Priesthood took its rise," as S. Cyprian declared; "whence the right of venerable communion flows to all," said S. Ambrose; and where "the Princedom of the Apostolic Chair has always been in force," as is asserted by S. Augustine. It is impossible for any one to deny that the holy Roman Catholic Church held the Princedom of the Apostolate and Episcopate; and hence she is the Mother and Mistress of all Churches.

V.

POPE S. ANICETUS AND S. POLYCARP.

Anglicans and Protestants allege that the following ecclesiastical events are fatal to the idea of the Roman Supremacy; viz., the conferences between Pope S. Anicetus and S. Polycarp; the opposition of the Asiatic Churches to the proceedings of Pope S. Victor; the attitude S. Cyprian assumed towards the Pope of his day, and the case of Apiarius :—each of these cases shall be considered, commencing with the conference which took place between Pope S. Anicetus and S. Polycarp.

In the early primitive ages there were two traditions observed respecting the proper time for keeping the Easter solemnity,—one from S. Peter, that it should be celebrated upon the Lord's Day next the vernal equinox; and the other from S. John, on the same day on which the Jews' Passover used to be kept. That this disunion on an important matter of discipline caused much disquietude is evident from the circumstance, that S. Polycarp, the disciple of S. John the Apostle, and Bishop of Smyrna, deemed it expedient to travel all the way to Rome with the hope of having the question in dispute determined. A conference took place between this eminent Bishop and Martyr, and the reigning Pope. The following is the account given by Eusebius: " And when the blessed Polycarp went to Rome, in the time of Anicetus, and they had a little difference among themselves likewise respecting other matters, they immediately were reconciled, not disputing much with one another on this head (*i.e.* the Paschal controversy). For neither could Anicetus persuade Polycarp not to observe it, because he had always observed it with John the disciple of our Lord, and the rest of the Apostles, with whom he associated ; and neither did Polycarp persuade Anicetus to observe it, who said that he was bound to maintain the practice of the presbyters before him ; which things being so, they communed with each other ; and in the Church Anicetus yielded to Polycarp, out of respect no doubt, the office of consecrating, and they separated from each other in peace, all the Church being at peace ; both those that observed, and those that did not observe, maintaining peace." *Eus. H. E. l.* v. *c.* 24. Such is the account given by the first ecclesiastical historian of the Church. It is maintained that this conference is fatal to the Roman claim, because, it is alleged, that if S. Polycarp had been aware that the Successor of S. Peter was the Supreme Pontiff, he would have accepted the tradition of S. Peter in preference to that he had received from S. John, and would have petitioned him to settle the controversy by a judicial decree. But this objection stands upon no good foundation, for it is no unusual thing for superiors and inferiors to disagree, even upon points which are of great importance, to dispute and argue with one another, and even to separate without one convincing the other. Such disagreements are not uncommon between a king and his ministers ; while the difference is pending, they argue on equal terms, each striving to convince the other ; and yet who would be so foolish as to assert that such a difference proved, or contributed to prove, that the Royal disputant was not the King ? There is, then, nothing extraordinary, nothing derogatory to the Pontifical office, for these two eminent saints and martyrs, one the Pope, and the other a Bishop, to differ on points not decided, and to argue with one another, it may be, with excitement and warmth. As in the case of the King, so in that of the Pope : differences of opinion, accompanied with discussion, on equal terms, is no proof in any degree against the Papal Supremacy.

But surely, if the Bishop of Rome really was the Supreme Head and Chief Pastor, having the office, too, of Supreme Judge, why did not S. Anicetus decide the controversy, and thus put an end to the dispute ? Many grave reasons might have occurred to the Pope which would make it inexpedient for him at the time to have determined the point in question. To have exercised his Prerogative at that time, would have wounded charity, and possibly have provoked a schism amongst some of the faithful in the East. S. Anicetus doubtless called to mind that S. Polycarp was the son in Christ of S. John, that he and many of his subjects had personally known the Apostle, had loved him with a love second only to their love of Christ, and naturally cherished his memory with an affectionate veneration. To have compelled S. Polycarp and his adherents to have given up the traditions of their master, and to have adopted that of S. Peter, could not have failed to have wounded them to the quick. S. Anicetus thus exercised a most wise discretion in not dealing with the question finally, but in leaving it to be settled by his Successors at some future day. In this difference of opinion, and abstinence of Pontifical action, there is nothing, it is submitted, that witnesses, in any form or degree, against the position of the Pope as the Head and Chief Pastor of the Universal Church.

But there is an important point to consider : viz., why did S. Polycarp travel all the way to Rome to consult the Pope on the question of Easter? The visit was not one of pleasure or recreation ; in his days the disciples of the cross thought little of such luxuries : to have indulged in a voyage of pleasure would have been regarded by them as so much time lost in the service of Christ. It is evident, then, that S. Polycarp went to Rome with the hope of having the Easter controversy settled, which he hoped would have been done in accordance with the tradition he had received from S. John. But why of all the Patriarchs did he select the Bishop of Rome for this conference? Why not the Bishop of Alexandria, or of Antioch, or even of Jerusalem, in preference to the Western Patriarch? For if all Bishops are equal in authority and jurisdiction, what use could it have been to have gone so far as Rome for the settlement of a question, which, on this hypothesis, could only have been settled by a General Council, or by a number of provincial synods? What was the use of the conference, if no action could possibly have been taken? If anything, then, this visit of S. Polycarp to the Roman Pontiff is a testimony that the Pope was regarded, in the second century, as Pre-eminent, at least, in Authority and position : otherwise this great Asiatic Saint never would have taken the trouble of travelling to Rome, thus losing much valuable time in the service of his Lord. In this incident we may fairly conclude there is nothing that can be forced as an argument against the Papal authority: if anything the incident confirms that authority.

VI.

S. VICTOR AND THE ASIATIC CHURCHES.

There was another difference between the Pope and the Asiatic Churches, touching the observance of Easter. Eusebius writes, " There was a considerable discussion raised about this time, in consequence of a difference of opinion respecting the observance of the Paschal season. The churches of all Asia, guided by a remote tradition supposed they ought to keep the fourteenth day of the moon for the festival of the Saviour's passover, on which day the Jews were commanded to kill the Paschal lamb ; but it was incumbent on them, at all times, to make an end of the fast on this day, or whatever day of the week it would happen to fall. But as it was not the custom to celebrate it in this manner in the Churches throughout the rest of the world, who observe the practice that was prescribed from Apostolic tradition until the present time, so that it would not be proper to terminate our fast on any other but the day of the resurrection of our Saviour. Hence there were Synods and Convocations of the Bishops on this question, and they unanimously drew up an ecclesiastical decree, which they communicated to all the churches in all places, that the mystery of our Lord's resurrection should be celebrated on no other day than the Lord's day ; and that on this day alone we should observe the close of the Paschal fasts. There is an epistle extant even now, of those who assembled at the time ; among whom presided Theophilus, Bishop of the Church in Cæsarea, and Narcissus,

Bishop of Jerusalem. There is also another epistle extant on the same question, bearing the name of Victor. An epistle also of the Bishops in Pontus, among whom Palmas, as the most ancient, presided; also of the churches of Gaul, over whom Irenæus presided. Moreover, one from those in Osrhoene, and the cities there. And a particular epistle from Bacchyllus, Bishop of the Corinthians ; and epistles of many others, who, advancing one and the same doctrine, also passed the same vote. And this their unanimous determination was the one already mentioned." (*Eus. H. E. l.* v. *c.* 23.) The Bishops, however, of Asia, with Polycrates at their head, resisted these decrees of the Universal Church. A correspondence ensued between Polycrates and Pope S. Victor, the latter threatening the former with excommunication if he did not submit to the ecclesiastical decrees. Polycrates wrote a long epistle to the Pope, in which he referred to the great lights who had illuminated his Church, who had also observed Easter on the fourteenth day, and he thus concludes, " I therefore, brother, am now sixty-five years in the Lord, and having conferred with the brethren throughout the world, and having studied the whole of the sacred Scriptures, am not at all alarmed at those things with which I am threatened to intimidate me. For they who are greater than I have said, ' We ought to obey God rather than man.' (*Ib. c.* 24.) Again, " I could also mention the Bishops that were present, whom you requested to be summoned by me, and whom I did call. Whose names, did I write them, would present a great number, who, however, seeing my slender body, consented to the epistle, well knowing that I did not bear my gray hairs for nought, but that I did at all times regulate my life in the Lord Jesus." (*Ib.*) Eusebius adds, " Upon this, Victor, the Bishop of the Church of Rome, forthwith endeavoured to cut off the churches of all Asia, together with the neighbouring churches, as heterodox, from the common unity, and he publishes abroad by Letters, and proclaims that all the brethren there are wholly excommunicated. But this was not the opinion of all the Bishops. They immediately exhorted him, on the contrary, to contemplate that course that was calculated to promote peace, unity, and love to one another." Eusebius then continues, " There are also extant the expressions they used, who pressed upon Victor with much severity. Among these, also, was Irenæus, who, in the name of his brethren in Gaul, over whom he presided, wrote an epistle, in which he maintains the duty of celebrating the mystery of the resurrection of our Lord, only on the day of the Lord. He becomingly also admonishes Victor not to cut off whole Churches of God, who observed the tradition of an ancient custom. After many other matters urged upon him, he also adds the following : ' For not only is the dispute respecting the day, but also respecting the manner of fasting. For some think, that they ought to fast only one day, some two, some more days ; some compute their day as consisting of forty hours, night and day ; and this diversity existing among those that observe it, is not a matter that has just sprung up in our times, but long ago among those before us, who perhaps not having ruled with sufficient strictness, established the practice that arose from their simplicity and inexperience.' " (*Ib.*)

Mr. Allies, commenting upon this passage, in the work which he wrote before his conversion to the Catholic Church, asks this question, "Could Polycrates have acknowledged to the Roman See any authority different *in kind* from that of other Bishops, such as the Supremacy? Could he have said distinctly to the power which could cut him off from the Church of God and the covenant of salvation, 'having conferred with my brethren throughout the world, and having studied all Holy Scripture, I am not alarmed at what I am threatened with,' *i.e.* excommunication from Rome." (*Ch. of Eng. Cleared from Schism, 2nd edit. p.* 59.)   Mr. Allies would doubtless acknowledge now that he put the question upon a false issue, or without due regard to all that had before occurred. It must be borne in mind that almost the whole Church, except the Asiatic churches, had decided in favour of the Roman method of keeping Easter; of all the churches, those of Asia were alone in opposition; what, then, was the position of Polycrates and his Bishops in respect to the whole Church? It was without doubt that of disobedience to the will 'of the whole or the greater part of the Universal Church. S. Victor had caused (so we may gather from the letter of Polycrates) Synods to be held in all the provinces on the question of the Paschal solemnity; and after they had concluded their deliberations, the Pope addressed the Asiatic Churches, evidently exhorting them to submit to the unanimous decrees of the Churches; they, speaking through their Metropolitan, decline obedience; S. Victor, as the Supreme Pontiff and guardian of the Canon law, threatened them with excommunication on non-compliance; in reply, Polycrates addressed him an epistle which is disrespectful in tone, in which occurs the passage relied upon as conclusive against Rome, "I am not alarmed at what I am threatened with." This was followed by the Papal excommunication, upon which many Bishops, and S. Irenæus among the number, remonstrated with the Pope upon the severity of his procedure. It is clear that Polycrates and his followers were in the wrong, for they regarded their own rights in preference to the advantage of the Church; they disregarded the ecclesiastical decrees of all the churches, except their own, which were collected by the Pope, and by him promulged. No Bishop could well be in a worse position, short of actual schism. How, then, can such proud words as, "I am not alarmed at what I am threatened with," be other than an affront against the Authority of the Papacy? How can these words contribute even to an argument against the Supremacy? It might just as well be said, that when the Sovereign, after Parliament had decided upon the abrogation of a certain custom held to be injurious to the commonwealth, promulges the new law, it would be open (let us say) to the Lord Lieutenant of Ireland together with all his co-Lieutenants to refuse compliance; and upon being called to account for his conduct, to reply, "I am not alarmed at what I am threatened with." Would such conduct be regarded, by any sensible person, as furnishing a legitimate argument against the civil supremacy of the Sovereign? Such an argument is simply absurd.

There is a point, however, which Mr. Allies has overlooked in his work, *i.e.* that no protest against the Papal assumption of authority was made by Polycrates and his Bishops. Had the Pope exceeded his authority, had he assumed a position he had no right to assume, had he exercised functions beyond his commission, would not Polycrates have called him to account ? Would he not have told him that he had no right to interfere in churches beyond his province or patriarchate ? And while expressing his unconcern relative to the Pope's threat, would he not have expressed his determination to excommunicate him, if he himself should so far forget himself as to trample upon the liberties of his church ? Most certainly he would, if the Pope had really exceeded his authority. But Polycrates did not, and why ? Because, notwithstanding his resistance, he really believed that the Pope was the ruling Bishop ; and this belief is apparent in his epistle, where he says, " The Bishops that were present, whom you (*i.e.* the Pope) requested to be summoned by me, and whom I did call." By these few words much light is thrown upon this point. It was by direction of the Pope that the Asiatic Churches were assembled in Council; so far they obeyed their Chief: after, they resisted him, and the decrees of all the Churches. But they did not go so far as to say, You have no business here ; which they certainly would have said to any other foreign Bishop, who had acted in a similar manner. The opposition of the Church of Asia Minor to the Pope no more witnesses against the Papal Supremacy, than the attitude the Church of England assumed in the sixteenth century tells against Rome.

But, further, it is said that S. Irenæus, and with him the Bishops of Gaul, resisted the Pope. Mr. Allies, before his conversion, remarked, " I suppose that the actions of St. Irenæus towards the Apostolic See of the West are a comment upon his words respecting it; and that when he calls Rome, 'the greatest Church, the most ancient, the most conspicuous, and founded and established by Peter and Paul,' appeals to its tradition not in contrast indeed, but in preference to that of other Churches, and declares that, 'in this Church, every Church, that is the faithful from every side, must meet,' or agree together *propter potiorem principalitatem*, he really means what he says, and what his actions indicate, that the Bishop of Rome was first among his brethren : and he does not mean a totally different thing, which his words are quoted to prove, namely, that the Bishop of Rome stood in the same relation to him and to all the other Bishops of the world as he himself stood in to his own presbyters at Lyons." *pp.* 61, 2.

So far from the conduct towards the Pope of S. Irenæus on the Easter quarrel modifying the terms of the famous passage which Mr. Allies quotes, it is itself a commentary on what actually occurred between that great Father and the Pope ; indeed, it explains very much which needed explanation. S. Irenæus, with other Bishops, remonstrated with Pope S. Victor on the severity of his procedure. He reminds him that the customs of the Church respecting what is now called the Lenten fast, and the .day on which Easter should be kept, were diverse ; that " it is not a matter that has sprung up in our times, but long ago among those before us," who were somewhat lax in their discipline; and he also reminds him that while diversity on these points was the rule, unanimity continued. He also recalls to the memory of the Pope the gentleness of Anicetus, his Predecessor, and the charity and unity that existed between him and S. Polycarp. The evident object of S. Irenæus was to persuade the Pope not to carry into effect his threat of excommunication. It is difficult to perceive how his remonstrance can be regarded as a proof that S. Irenæus did not believe in the Roman Supremacy. S. Paul, we know, " withstood Peter to the face, because he was to be blamed," but, as it was seen in the " First Inquiry," this act did not really touch the question of Supremacy, no more than the remonstrance or the rebuke of any subject would prove that the Sovereign is not the King of his nation. St. Irenæus resisted the Pope in the matter in question, but that circumstance did not prove that he was not the Head of the Church and the Chief Pastor of the people.

But assuming that the Pope was only an ordinary Bishop, or perhaps a Patriarch, how are we to account for S. Irenæus' silence respecting his exercising authority in a province not subject to him? For had the Pope assumed an office which did not belong to him, S. Irenæus would have denounced him as a usurper, and a schismatic; but he does no such thing, and hence the question is repeated, why was he silent when not only a large number of Bishops were on the point of being cast out of the Church, but when the Bishop of Rome was claiming a Power that did not belong to him, and when, by means of such Power, he was endeavouring to trample upon the rights of his brethren of distant lands? There is but one answer to be given, viz., because he knew that the Pope really possessed this high Prerogative, which he believed that he was, on this occasion, misusing. And hence the passage quoted by Mr. Allies materially assists to solve this point, and to explain the silence of S. Irenæus. Explaining the impossibility of consulting all the Apostolic Churches, the Saint points to "the very great, the very ancient, and universally known Church, founded and constituted at Rome by the two most glorious Apostles, Peter and Paul; as also (by pointing out) the faith preached to men, which comes down to our time by means of the successions of the Bishops. For it is a matter of necessity that every Church should agree (or assemble, *i. e.* in communion) with this (the Roman) Church, on account of its Pre-eminent authority (or its more Powerful Principality); that is the faithful everywhere, inasmuch as the Apostolical tradition has been preserved continuously by those who exist everywhere." (*See supra, p.* 131.) S. Irenæus believed that the Roman Church, by virtue of its constitution by S. Peter and S. Paul, was the Principal or Chief Church, with which all other Churches must be in communion. Being, therefore, the Chief or ruling Church, it follows that S. Victor had full right, power, and jurisdiction over the Asiatic dioceses, even to the casting them off from Catholic communion, if he so judged it right to do. S. Irenæus, then, by his silence, recognises the Pope's plenary and universal Authority, but he remonstrates against the expediency and propriety of the step S. Victor was meditating against those contumacious churches,—contumacious not merely against the Pope, but likewise against the Universal Church, which had decreed when Easter should be kept.

It seems then manifest that in the dispute on the Paschal question, and in the defeat sustained by the Pope in enforcing uniformity of observance, there is nothing which could directly or indirectly affect the Papal position. As in the day of S. Anicetus, a portion of the Church was wedded to a particular custom which had been derived from S. John, so in the time of his Successor, S. Victor, the affection of some for the beloved Apostle was so great, that neither the Authority of the Pope, nor the unanimous decrees of the Churches, could avail to induce them to give up their own predilection, and to conform to the will of the Universal Church.

VII.

THE AFRICAN PROTESTS.

S. STEPHEN AND S. CYPRIAN.

There are two cases which are regarded by Anglicans and Protestants as fatal to the Roman claim of Supremacy over the whole Church, viz., the differences between Pope S. Stephen and S. Cyprian with respect to the rebaptism of heretics, and between Pope S. Zosimus and S. Celestine and the Council of Africa (A.D. 418) in the matter of the wicked priest Apiarius.

I propose to devote this section to the case of S. Cyprian.

About fifty years before the time of S. Cyprian, Agrippinus, his predecessor in the see of Carthage, introduced the custom of rebaptizing all persons who had been baptized by heretics. By degrees the custom became common throughout all the provinces in Africa. Some Bishops of the province of Numidia consulted S. Cyprian on this subject, and he contended that baptism administered out of the Church was invalid, and that persons so baptized, upon their submission to the Catholic Church, ought to be rebaptized unconditionally. His opinion seems to have been this, that the Church being one and indivisible, any one, be he priest or layman, on quitting the communion of the Church, lost his character as Priest or Catholic, and that consequently his religious acts became simply null and void. The opinion of S. Cyprian respecting the necessity of rebaptizing all persons baptized by heretics, was affirmed in the Council of Carthage, A.D. 255, and the decision was forwarded to Rome for the approval of the Pope. S. Stephen, the then reigning Pontiff, perceiving the serious error contained in the decree, condemned it, and so incensed was he with S. Cyprian, that he refused to receive his Legates.

Upon the receipt of the Papal reply, S. Cyprian summoned another Council of Carthage, at which eighty-three Bishops were present, when the former decree was re-affirmed.

I propose now to state in detail what passed after this unfortunate rupture with the Holy See ; and in order that I may be the better able to meet the arguments of Anglicans, I have adopted exclusively, as my text-book, [the translated edition of S. Cyprian's Epistles, published in "The Library of the Fathers," wherein are several important notes by the learned editor, which I desire, with all love and respect, to criticise.

I. Such was the result of this unfortunate difference ; but in order fully to comprehend the full extent of this rupture, it will be necessary to give extracts from the letters of S. Cyprian upon this subject, and what subsequently passed in the Council of Carthage.

In an Epistle to Pompeius, S. Cyprian says, "Although in the letters of which I sent you copies, dearest brother, I have fully expressed al which is to be said upon baptizing heretics; yet since you have desired to be informed what answer our brother Stephen returned to my letter, I have sent you a copy of that answer; on reading which, you will more and more discover his error, in that he endeavours to uphold the cause of heretics against Christians and against the Church of God. For among other things, arrogant, or extraneous or self-contradictory, which he wrote without due instruction and caution, he moreover added this, ' If then any shall come to you from any heresy whatsoever let there be no innovations beyond what has been handed down, namely, that hands be laid on such to repentance; since those who are properly heretics do not baptize such as come to them from one another, but only admit them to communion.' He has forbidden one coming from any heresy whatsoever to be baptized in the Church, that is, he has adjudged the baptisms of all heretics to be right and lawful. And whereas the several heresies have several baptisms and divers sins, he, communicating with the baptism of them all, has heaped up the sins of all in one mass into his own bosom. And he has enjoined, ' that there be no innovations beyond what has been handed down;' as though he innovated, who, maintaining unity, claims the one baptism for the one Church, and not he rather, who, forgetful of unity, adopts the deceitful defilements of a profane immersion . . . . But since no heresy whatever, nor indeed, any schism, being without, can have the sanctification of Baptism out of the Church, why has the unyielding obstinacy of our brother Stephen burst out to such a pitch, that he should contend, that sons are born to God even from the baptism of Marcion, of Valentinus also, and Apelles, and of the rest who blaspheme against God the Father? and that he should say that remission of sins is given there in the Name of Jesus Christ, where blasphemies are uttered against the Father and against Christ our Lord God?" *Ep.* lxxiv. (Ben. lxxiv.) *ad Pompeium*, n. 1, 9. Firmilian makes use of some violent expressions in his letter to S. Cyprian: ". . . . However, we may for this thank Stephen; that through his unkindness it hath now happened that we should receive a proof of your faith and wisdom. But though we have received the mercy of this favour through Stephen, yet Stephen has not therefore done what deserves favour and thanks. For neither can Judas, by reason of his perfidy and treachery, wherewith he dealt accursedly against the Saviour, be thought worthy, though he had been the cause of blessings so great, and through him the world and the people of the Gentiles were freed by the Passion of the Lord. But let the acts of Stephen, for the present, be passed over; lest whilst we recall his bold and presuming deeds, we prolong the sadness occasioned by what he has done amiss. . . . But that they who are at Rome do not in all respects observe the things handed down from the beginning, and that they in vain pretend the authority of the Apostles, any one may know even from this, that in celebrating Easter, and in many other divine and sacramental ordinances, we may see that there are certain diversities among them, and that all things are not alike observed by them, which are observed at Jerusalem . . . . This Stephen has now dared to make, breaking the peace with you, what his Predecessors ever maintained with you in mutual affection and respect; moreover, herein defaming the blessed Apostles Peter and Paul, as if they had handed this down; whereas in their Epistles they execrated heretics, and warned us to avoid them . . . . But how great his error, how exceeding his blindness, who says that remission of sins can be given to the synagogues of heretics, and abideth not on the foundation of the one Church, which was once fixed by Christ on a Rock, may be here learnt, that Christ said to Peter alone, *Whatsoever thou shalt bind on earth, &c.,* and again in the Gospel, when Christ breathed upon the Apostles, only saying, *Receive ye the Holy Ghost: whosesoever sins ye remit, &c.* The power then of remitting sins was given to the Apostles, and to the Churches which they, sent by Christ, established, and to the Bishops who succeeded them by vicarious ordination . . . And herein I am justly indignant at such open and manifest folly in Stephen, that he who so boasts of the Seat of his Episcopate, and contends that he holds the succession from Peter, on whom the Foundations of the Church were laid, introduces many other *Rocks* and *buildeth* anew many Churches, in that by his authority he maintains baptism among them. . . . . Stephen, who proclaims that he occupies by succession the Chair of Peter, is roused by no zeal against heretics . . . . And this you of Africa may say in answer to Stephen, that on discovering the truth, you abandoned the error of custom. But we join custom to truth, and to the custom of the Romans we oppose custom, but that of truth; from the beginning holding that which was delivered by Christ and by His Apostles . . . . and is not Stephen ashamed to assert, that remission of sins can be given by those who are themselves set fast in all kinds of sin? . . . . How diligently has Stephen fulfilled these salutary commands and warnings of the Apostle, keeping, in the first place, *lowliness and meekness?* For what can be more *lowly* and *meek* than to have disagreed with so many Bishops throughout the whole world, breaking peace with them severally in various modes of discord, now with the Eastern Churches (as we feel confident you are aware), now with yourselves, who are of the South? From whom he received Episcopal legates, with such *long-suffering and meekness,* that he would not admit them even to the common intercourse of speech; so mindful, moreover, of *love* and charity, that he commanded the whole Brotherhood, that no one admit them to their houses; so that when they come, not only *peace* and communion, but shelter and hospitality, were denied them. This is to *have kept the unity of the Spirit in the bond of peace,* to cast himself off from the unity of charity, and in all things to make himself an alien to the brethren, and with the fury of contumacious discord to rebel against the Sacrament and the Faith . . . . and yet is not Stephen ashamed to give support to such against the Church, and for the upholding of heretics to divide the Brotherhood; nor, farther, to call Cyprian *false Christ,* and *false Apostle,* and *deceitful worker." Firmilian ad Cypr. inter Ep. Cyp. Ep.* lxxv. (*Ben.* lxxv.) *n.* 2, 3, 6, 8, 17, 18, 20, 25, 26, 27.

1. The following is the address of S. Cyprian to the Council of Carthage on the receipt of Pope S. Stephen's epistle in condemnation of the decree or Canon for the re-baptism of heretics: " Ye have heard, most beloved

Colleagues, what Jubaianus, our fellow-Bishop, has written to me, consulting my moderate ability concerning the unlawful and profane baptism of heretics ; and what answer I gave him ; giving a judgment, which we have once and again and often given, that heretics coming to the Church ought to be baptized and sanctified with the Baptism of the Church. Another letter of Jubaianus has likewise been read to you, in which, agreeably to his sincere and religious devotion, in answer to our epistle he not only expressed his assent, but returned thanks also, acknowledging that he had received instruction. It remains that we severally declare our opinion on this same subject, judging no one, nor depriving any one of the right of communion if he differ from us. For no one of us setteth himself up as a Bishop of Bishops, nor by tyrannical terror forceth his Colleagues to a necessity for obeying : inasmuch as every Bishop, in the use of his free liberty and power, has the right of forming his own judgment, and can no more be judged by another than he can himself judge another. But we must all await the judgment of our Lord Jesus Christ, who alone has the power both of setting us in the government of His Church, and of judging of our acts therein." *Concil. Carthag. Lib. of Fathers, pp.* 286–7.

2. I have now set down everything I can find which has been written by S. Cyprian and Firmilian against the Roman Pontiff S. Stephen ; and, no doubt, to a superficial reader and partizan, it is not only very strong, but overwhelming and apparently conclusive against the Supremacy of the Holy See. For, in the first place, did not S. Cyprian and the Council of Carthage re-affirm a decree condemned by the Pope, and did they not assert the principle, that no Bishop is really a Bishop of Bishops ; that no Bishop has any right " by tyrannical terror " to force " his Colleagues to the necessity of obeying " him ; that every Bishop, " in the free use of his liberty and power, has the right of forming his own judgment," and that he " can no more be judged by another man, than he can himself judge another ; " and that " we must all await the judgment of our Lord Jesus Christ, who alone has the power both of setting us in the government of His Church and of judging our acts therein." Such is the position S. Cyprian and the Council of Carthage assumed against Pope S. Stephen. And hence he was not afraid of speaking harshly of the Pope, accusing him of " error," of being " arrogant," and of " unyielding obstinacy." He received, too, a letter from Firmilian, Bishop of Cæsarea in Asia Minor, which is included among his Epistles, in which he, seemingly, compares S. Stephen to Judas Iscariot, censuring him for his " bold and presuming deeds," that he " dared " to break the unity and peace of the Church, and accusing him of " open and manifest folly," of not being " ashamed to assert," " that remission of sin can be given by those who are themselves set fast in all kinds of sins," and " to give support in upholding heretics ;" he then satirically ridicules the Pope ; and finally declares that he has " cut himself from the unity of Charity. To the Anglican and Protestant mind all this is fatal to the claim of the Pope to be the Supreme Head of the Universal Church.

3. Now here I might at once join issue by asserting that no protest or any amount of abuse heaped upon the Pope, on account of any specific act of his, be it erroneous, be it harsh, unjust, or violent, can really touch

the main question, viz., whether he is or is not the Head of the Brotherhood, and the Chief Pastor of the One Fold. It is no uncommon
thing, in political life, for persons to protest against the acts of a King, to
accuse him of injustice and error, and to criticise his conduct with unmer-
ciful and disloyal severity; but is he not, notwithstanding, the King? is he
not the source of all civil jurisdiction, and is not obedience in all things
lawful due to him? Or let us take the case of a family, wherein it
sometimes happens a difference of opinion on some important matter
arises between the Father and his son, during which violent language is
used, which not unfrequently results in estrangement and separation.
Does the Father cease to be a father, or does the attitude which the son
assumes towards his Sire (be he right or be he wrong) amount to a proof
that the Father is no father, and that he occupies no superior position in
the family circle? Or let us take a case more to our purpose : how often
is it that Anglicans quarrel with their Archbishop or Bishop, if either or
both of them should decide some point of doctrine or discipline contrary
to their views? How unmeasured is the language they indulge in against
him ; see how they dispute every word their Prelates give utterance to;
see also how they abuse them and reproach them: and yet not one of
them would deny that the Archbishop of Canterbury is the Primate of all
England, and that the Bishop of the diocese in which they reside is their
legitimate and lawful Diocesan, to whom allegiance is due, if not filial
affection.

We may then conclude that the mere abuse of a King, a Father, or a
Prelate, cannot in any conceivable sense be held as a proof against the
existence or the lawfulness of any such office in a family or kingdom.

Assuming, then, that S. Cyprian and the Church of Africa had violently
opposed the Pope in the matter of re-baptism ; assuming also that the
language that the Holy Father adopted or permitted had been as intemperate and as insulting as possible, still the main question remains un-
touched, viz., whether the Pope was the Head of the Brotherhood and the
Supreme Pastor of the Flock?

Holy men have disputed violently on many points, even S. Paul and
S. Barnabas differed about S. Mark so keenly that they parted asunder,
and it is believed never met again on earth. S. Peter and S. Paul also
had no slight difference about circumcision ; but none of these cases
affect the question under discussion one way or the other. The relation
between superior and inferior, between the head and the members, can
never be determined or unsettled by such incidents as these.

II. In estimating, however, the evidence alleged to prove S. Cyprian's
rejection of the Supremacy of the Pope, several Points must be considered
and carefully weighed.

And, first, let me ask, who was in the wrong in this controversy, the
Pope, or S. Cyprian and his Council? It is admitted by all Catholics and
Anglicans that the Pope was right in his judgment, and S. Cyprian and
his colleagues utterly and hopelessly in the wrong ; nay, more, that
in this question they were in very serious error. There needs but
little proof for this, for the Œcumenical Council of Nicæa, a century later,
decided the controversy in accordance with the judgment of S. Stephen ;

T

and also in the other matter of Easter, about which Firmilian inveighed against the Pope, the Council likewise affirmed the decree of the same Pontiff. After this we have a right to say, *cadit quæstio*,—the whole controversy is at an end, for the admittedly highest authority of the Church, the Pope and the Œcumenical Council, had pronounced a synodical decision which convicted S. Cyprian of error on a question of sacramental doctrine, and Firmilian of error in a matter of discipline. We might, also, with perfect fairness, add here, that S. Cyprian and his Council having erred on one point of doctrine, it is more than probable that they might have fallen into another equally grave and dangerous to the unity of the Church. Let it then be assumed that the language which S. Cyprian used before the Council of Carthage and in his Epistles, was so far as mere construction is concerned, fatal to the pretensions of Rome, it could not now be taken into any account as legitimate evidence, inasmuch as he ceased to be an unexceptionable witness from the moment his orthodoxy on a particular point of faith was impeached. I am, of course, adopting a very extreme view of this case, simply for the purpose of showing, that no matter how strong or how conclusive might be S. Cyprian's testimony against the Supremacy, after he had fallen into error, it became for that reason inadmissible in the court of inquiry before which we are conducting this case.

III. But I deny that the words of S. Cyprian and his Colleagues, and even of Firmilian, directly or indirectly testify against the Roman Supremacy.

1. There is nothing to be found in the language adopted by S. Cyprian, whether at the Council or in his letters, which can possibly amount to even a protest against the Supremacy of the Holy See. No doubt, S. Cyprian says, " For no one of us setteth himself up as a Bishop of Bishops, nor by tyrannical terror forceth his Colleagues to a necessity for obeying ; inasmuch as every Bishop, in the use of his free liberty and power, has the right of forming his own judgment, and can no more be judged by another than he can himself judge another." This, no doubt, is very strong language ; but, as observed in another part of this work, if pressed too far, it would prove too much. For if interpreted as Anglicans would interpret it, it would destroy the whole framework of the Episcopal Hierarchy. If no Bishop is a " Bishop of Bishops," then there can be no Patriarchs, Archbishops, or Primates. S. Cyprian himself was as Primate of Africa, a Bishop of Bishops ; he had certain rights over his colleagues ; he had the right to preside, to veto the acts and the decrees of his Synod, and to judge, in company with his colleagues, any refractory Bishop. If every Bishop has such a " use of his free liberty and power " as to possess " the right of forming his own judgment," and if he can no more be judged by another Bishop "than he himself can judge another," then what right has even a Synod to assume jurisdiction over any Bishop who may be guilty of error or contumacy, seeing that according to S. Cyprian, he is amenable to no one but to "the judgment of our Lord Jesus Christ, who alone has the power of both setting us in the government of His Church, and of judging our acts therein." It is plain, then, that if this is S. Cyprian's real opinion, no Primate, no provincial Synod, not even an Œcumenical

council, has authority to judge any Bishop, that is to say, if it is true that he is amenable to no man, but *solely* to the Lord Jesus Christ. It is simply impossible to suppose that so great, so holy, and so learned a man as S. Cyprian evidently was, could have ever intended to express such views as these ; for what can they amount to, but the assertion of principles subversive of all discipline whatever ?

2. If, then, S. Cyprian did not mean this, what did he intend to affirm when he said, " No one of us setteth himself up as a Bishop of Bishops," &c. ? Did he intend by these words to strike at the Pope ? No doubt he did ; but how and to what extent ? Was it against his office as Supreme Head and Pastor, or against a particular line of conduct, which he deemed to be an invasion of his own rights as Primate of Africa, and of the rights of the Bishops of his Province ? And this brings us face to face with the question of Papal Prerogative, Episcopal rights, and the doctrine of Infallibility. It is a matter of fact, that to this day the exact relations between the Pope and the Bishops of the Universal Church have never been very accurately defined. All Catholics believe as *de fide*, that the Pope is the Successor of S. Peter, that he occupies " the Chair of Peter," that he is the heir of all the Royalties and Prerogatives of S. Peter ; that the Pope is the Teacher of all, the Shepherd of the whole Universal Flock, and the Guardian of the Vine. All Catholics believe that the Bishops of the Universal Church, being in communion with the Pope, are equal to him, in Order, and in Priesthood, and that they share with him in the Government of the Church ; that on the question of Jurisdiction there is a decided difference, inasmuch as he alone holds the keys, and consequently has independent judicial authority, whereas the Bishops can only exercise their functions when in union with him. This has been proved to be both scriptural and patristic doctrine, and therefore I shall not pursue this part of the subject any farther. But while this is true, there has not been as yet any canon or formal decision defining with precision either the limits of Papal Prerogative or the exact relations of the Bishops to the Pope. Indeed we may observe a parallel to this even in this very kingdom.

The imperial hierarchy of England consists of the King, and the Peers, who form together theoretically (*i. e.* according to the old feudal idea) one Order, and of the Commons, representing the people. The King possesses prerogatives which have never been to this hour definitively determined. The Peers, too, have original rights which have never been formally arranged. The King is the source of all Honour, Justice and Law ; the Peers, also, have a sort of original jurisdiction, derived not necessarily from the reigning Sovereign, but of course from a Potentate of perhaps some four or five centuries ago. The Commons likewise have privileges, but these are derived from the King and the Barons. It has often been alleged that the British Constitution was copied in some degree at least from that of the Church ; certain it is, that it aids us in this inquiry so far as it shows that the Pope, the Bishops, and the Priesthood generally, are all in the possession of certain prerogatives, rights, and privileges, which, so far as the two first are concerned, have never been *formally and canonically* expressed in a written code. As in the State, every one knows who is the Supreme

Head in civil matters, so also in the Church every Catholic is fully aware who their Supreme Pastor is, whom they are bound to obey in all things spiritual. Then, again, with respect to the doctrine of Infallibility, it is still an open question among Catholics whether the Pope is or is not infallible ; all agree that an Œcumenical Council, with the Pope at its head, is infallible, and most are of opinion that the Pope alone, when teaching *ex cathedrâ*, and with the expressed intention of teaching the Universal Church, is infallible. But nevertheless it is an open question, and Catholics may hold which of these opinions they please. Now it seems to have been S. Cyprian's opinion that the Episcopate was one Body, one " Brotherhood," and one " College of Prelates," over which the Pope, by virtue of his succession from S. Peter in the See of Rome, was the Presiding Bishop. He believed that in all matters concerning the Government of the Universal Church, each Bishop had a distinct voice, and that no Bishop, not even the Pope himself, had a right to promulge any decree binding upon the Universal Church without the consent of the " College." Any one who will take the trouble of reading his Epistles will see that this idea runs through them all. Bearing, then, this in mind, as well as the fact that no formal definition has ever been made respecting the exact relations between the Holy See and the Bishops of the Universal Church, we may form some idea of the nature of the protest which he delivered before the Council of Carthage respecting the conduct of the Pope. It would seem that in this dispute about the re-baptism of heretics, Pope S. Stephen, without consulting the " College of Prelates," or without obtaining the consent of the Universal " Brotherhood," on receiving the Synodical epistle of the Council of Carthage (which informed him of the decree affirming the necessity of re-baptizing persons who had been baptized out of the Church), condemned it as erroneous, and, as it would appear, severely censured the conduct of S. Cyprian and the African Bishops. Hence the indignation of S. Cyprian, and the impetuosity of his language, when he said, " No one of us setteth hmself up as a Bishop of Bishops," &c. In plain language he denied that the Pope had any right, by his *own single voice*, to condemn the Primate and the Council of Carthage, and to determine the question in dispute without reference to "the College of Prelates," *i. e.* the Universal Episcopate, the consent of which he deemed necessary before being compelled to submit. This seems to me the only rational interpretation that can be put upon S. Cyprian's language before the Council ; indeed it is the only one which will harmonise it with what he has so often affirmed respecting the dignity and position of "the Holy See ;" which has been so fully entered into in the " Comments " on S. Cyprian in the " Second Inquiry."

IV. But let us assume that the language S. Cyprian employed before the Council will admit of no other construction,—*i. e.*, as far as mere words are concerned,—than a direct protest against all Roman authority whatsoever, we are bound, before concluding that this was S. Cyprian's deliberate opinion, to ascertain whether it is in accordance with the other statements he has, from time to time, made on this subject. It is contrary to all rule and to all sound principle of criticism, to press against any man expressions which we know were made by him in the heat of controversy, or when smarting under some supposed grievance. No one can read the inaugural speech of S. Cyprian, before the Council of Carthage, without perceiving that he was under the influence of excited feelings. Indeed his letters, from which quotations have been made, show this clearly, and the intemperate epistle of Firmilian tended greatly to keep up the irritation. The proper course to pursue is to ascertain his real sentiments respecting the Papacy, as contained in various portions of his works.

I have already, in the " Second Inquiry," and in the " Comment " on S. Cyprian, given an exposition of his opinions on the question now under consideration; I do not therefore propose to repeat all the evidence therein adduced, but I would beg the reader, before proceeding, to re-peruse it and the argument founded thereon, and he can scarcely fail to see what were the real sentiments of S. Cyprian on this matter. Suffice it to say, that S. Cyprian believed that the Church was founded, "first and alone," upon S. Peter, who received the keys; "to whom the Lord commended His sheep to be fed and guarded." He believed that Rome was "the Place of Peter," that the "Chair of Peter," to which were attached the Prerogatives of "the Rank or Grade of the Sacerdotal Chair," was located in Rome, and that the Church of Rome was, by consequence, "the Principal or Chief Church whence the Unity of the Priesthood took its rise." Consistently with this view, he believed that the Roman Church was the " Mother," the " Root," and the " Matrix " of the whole Church. I do not propose to repeat evidence, except when necessary for explanation, which has been already presented in detail : but I shall confine myself to certain statements of S. Cyprian, made in the very year he delivered his inaugural speech to the Council of Carthage, in which he gave expression to opinions which have been interpreted by opponents as witness in against the Papacy.

But before proceeding, it is necessary the reader should recall to his recollection the state of things at Rome and in Africa in S. Cyprian's time. A certain priest, by name Novatus, schismatically disturbed the peace of the Church of Carthage, by maintaining that those persons who had lapsed into paganism during the heat of the persecution ought not, even after repentance and penance, to be received to communion. His opinion was condemned, and he was compelled to fly. He went to Rome with several followers, and joined himself to a priest of the name of Novatian, who induced certain of the Roman Clergy and people to elect him as Bishop of Rome ; aspiring to the Popedom, he thus became the first Anti-pope. S. Cyprian exerted all his energies to put down this abominable schism, and with success. He addressed letters to Bishops in almost every quarter of the world in support of Cornelius, the true Bishop, and against Novatian, the Anti-pope. It is in these letters that we find, as is natural, the most valuable evidence concerning the position of the Apostolic See.

In an epistle addressed to Jubaianus upon the subject of the re-baptism of heretics, in the very year in which the Council of Carthage was held, S. Cyprian had occasion to allude to the Roman Church and its Pontiff.

At this time, Novatian, the Anti-pope, possessed a corner of the Holy City, in which he set up a Chair, as a rival to "the Chair of Peter," and, as S. Cyprian said in one of his former letters, "assumed the Primacy."

1. The point S. Cyprian was immediately considering in his letter to Jubaianus, was concerning the Novatians presuming to re-baptize Catholics who had seceded to them. "Nor does that disturb us, dearest brother, which you mention in your letter, that the Novatians re-baptize those whom they withdraw from us ; since what the enemies of the Church do, no way concerneth us, so long as we ourselves uphold the honour of our office and the steadfastness of reason and truth. For Novatian (the Anti-pope), after the manner of apes, which, not being men, yet mimic the things of men, wishes to claim to himself the Authority and truth of the Catholic Church, although himself not in the Church ; nay, further, a rebel and an enemy to the Church. For knowing that there is but one Baptism, this one he claimeth to himself, that so he may say the Church is with him, and may make us to be heretics. But we, who hold the Head and Root of the one Church, know assuredly and are confident, that he, being out of the Church, hath no hallowed office, and that the fountain of Baptism which is one with us, where he too was himself formerly baptized, when he held fast the wisdom and truth of divine unity." *Ep. lxxiii.* (*Ben.* lxxiii) *Ad Jubaian. n.* 2. S. Cyprian then exhorts Jubaianus not to be disturbed, but to be comforted, for "we who hold the Head and Root of the one Church," know well that Novatian "hath no hallowed office." Who or what is this "Head and Root of the one Church," or against what Church was Novatian in opposition? Some, no doubt, would assert Christ our Lord. But there is nothing in the context to show that S. Cyprian referred to our blessed Lord. From the very force of the passage it is clear he was thinking of a visible "Head and Root," which Jubaianus and himself were to hold fast. It was that true Head and Root, which was opposed by a false Head and Root,—that is, Novatian the Anti-pope and his pseudo-chair, which he presumed to set up within the sacred precincts of the Apostolic See ; and that true "Head and Root" was the Roman Church, that "Principal or Chief Church, whence the unity of the Priesthood took its rise." That S. Cyprian really understood "the Head and the Root" to mean the Roman Church is evident from what he has in other epistles said on this point : for instance, in a letter which he addressed to Pope S. Cornelius, he writes, "But since the self-willed and inflexible obstinacy of the adverse party (of Novatian) has not only refused the arms and embraces of her (*i.e.,* the Roman Church), who is their Root and Mother, but has also, with discord, increasing and widening worse and worse, appointed a Bishop for itself, and contrary to the mystery of the Divine appointment and of catholic unity, has set up an adulterous and opposed Head (*i.e.,* Novatian) without the Church," *Ep. xlv.* (*Ben.* xlii.) *Ad Corn. n.* 1. Again, in another epistle to the same blessed Pope, in which S. Cyprian informs him that he was in the habit of "furnishing all who sail hence (*i.e.,* to Rome) with a rule," and that was that "they acknowledge and hold to the Root and Womb of the

Catholic Church," in opposition to those who had set up a false Church under the Anti-pope Novatian. *Ep.* xlviii. (*Ben.* xlv.) *Ad Corn. n.* 2. The Editor of the Oxford translation (to which I am largely indebted) adds a note, "*i. e.*, the Church adhering to the lawful Bishop, which is the Root on which individuals grow, the Mother of their second birth. The passage refers to Cornelius as the lawful Bishop, not specially to the See of Rome." *S. Cyp. Ox. Tr. p.* 105, note *g.* But this subtle distinction is not borne out in the text. S. Cyprian does not say "Root and Matrix" of the particular Roman Church, but of "the Catholic Church," *i. e.*, that one Universal Church throughout the world, which he asserts is "one and cannot be divided." Regarding, then, the Catholic Church as "one,"—*i.e.* one Body, even as God is one, and Christ is one,—it cannot possibly have more than one Mother, one Root, and one Matrix, else it would cease to be one. It is true that the Church is divided into dioceses and provinces, but the Episcopate is nevertheless one "Brother-hood," and one "College," to use S. Cyprian's expression ; and there can be but one original, from which the whole order springs. The Editor seems to think that every Bishop is to his diocese the Mother of the second birth of his subjects ; so that there may be thousands of mothers from whom the faithful derive their second birth, according to the accidence of place. But this is to divide holy Baptism *ad libitum.* It is this false notion that has given rise to the expression so common in the Church of England, "Church of my baptism," which, whatever may be the meaning in the mouth of those who use it, is an heretical ex-pression. There is but one Baptism for the remission of sins, the minister of the Sacrament being any one who uses the prescribed form. The Editor concludes that "the passage (in the text) refers to Cornelius as the lawful Bishop, not specially to the See of Rome." But how can we separate a Bishop from his See? And what was the nature of that See or Cathedra in which S. Cornelius sat ? S. Cyprian tells us it was "the Place of Peter," "the Chair of Peter ;" if Cornelius was Bishop of that "Place," if the "Chair of Peter" was his See, (*sedes*, seat), how, by the most subtle reasoning, can we imagine him as holding some undefinable position as "lawful Bishop," apart from his See? It is the See which gives him authority to act as a Bishop ; apart from the See he is nothing, for he is destitute of all jurisdiction and authority whatsoever, and no subject would own him as his Lord and Father. This ingenious distinction between "the lawful Bishop of Rome," and "the See of Rome," will not bear investigation. It is, however, something gained that the learned Editor admits that the terms "Mother" and "Matrix" apply to the lawful Bishop of Rome, that is, to the Bishop of the Holy See, the See of Peter, and of the Principal and Chief Church.

We have now arrived at this truth, that the Roman Church, which, in the time of S. Cyprian, was afflicted with the presence of an Anti-pope, is the Mother, the Root, and the Matrix of the Catholic Church, of the violation of which, by the intrusion of Novatian and his disciples, S. Cyprian complained, regardless of the "mystery of the divine appoint-ment and of Catholic Unity once determined, saying that an adulterous and opposed Head has been set up (in Rome, but) without the Church."

The "mystery of the divine appointment and of Catholic Unity," undoubtedly refers to the mystery of the Motherhood of the Roman Church, from whence sacerdotal Unity arose, and in which is the centre of Catholic Unity, in opposition to which is set up an adulterous Head (*i.e* Novatian, the Anti-pope) against the true Head (*i. e.* Cornelius, the lawful Bishop of Rome). It is then manifest that S. Cyprian, in his counsel to "hold the Head and Root of the one Church," meant the Holy Catholic Church under the Pontiff.

2. That "The Head" and "Root" referred to the Roman Church, not merely to its "lawful Bishop," but to the "See of Rome," is evident from what S. Cyprian further writes in his letter to Jubaianus, "What then? because Novatian usurps also the honour of the Sacerdotal Chair, ought we to renounce the Chair?" *Ep.* lxxiii. (*Ben.* lxxiii.) *ad Jubaian. n.* 2.

In a former Epistle addressed to his spiritual son, Magnus, S. Cyprian says, "and yet those (Corah, Dathan, and Abiram) had made no schism, ... which these (the Novatians) now do, who, rending the Church, and rebelling against the peace and unity of Christ, attempt to set up a Chair for themselves, and to assume the Primacy." (*Ep.* lxix. (*Ben.* lxvi.) *ad Magnum, n.* 7.) The Editor, however, adds in a note, "*i.e.* Episcopate. Ruf. v. 28," *p.* 226, note *d.* &c. But the two passages explain each other. It would appear that S. Cyprian meant that the "honour of the Sacerdotal Chair," consisted of the "Primacy" of the Roman Church. This S. Cyprian still further explains, when, in a former epistle "to Antonianus, his Brother," he thus writes, concerning the validity of S. Cornelius's election : "Cornelius, moreover, was made Bishop . . . . a a time when the place of Fabian, that is, when the Place of Peter and the Rank of the Sacerdotal Chair, was vacant." *Ep.* lv. (*Ben.* lii) *ad Anton., n.* 6. It is, then, evident that S. Cyprian believed that the office of the "Primacy," "the Rank or Grade." and "the Honour of the Sacerdotal Chair," was inherent in the ee of Rome, and had intimate connection with "the Place of Peter," with "the Chair of Peter," and with "the Principal or Chief Church, whence the Unity of the Priesthood took its rise," which Novatian and his wicked crew attempted to usurp. I confess I cannot see how it is possible to show that S. Cyprian did not hold the doctrine of the Roman Primacy,—not of mere honour and dignity, but of Jurisdiction and Power—at the very time that he, under excitement, and suffering from a sense of wrong as he conceived, uttered those words, "No one of us setteth himself up as Bishop of Bishops," &c. He had described the Roman Church as the "Mother, the Root and Matrix of the Catholic Church," two of these terms signifying, not merely the source of being, but of Authority and Power, for a mother is the mistress of her progeny ; and the Root, not merely the origin of the Tree, but its sustainer. Hence, then, the Primacy was one of Authority and Jurisdiction to which the whole Church was subject, inasmuch as the See of Rome was "the Head and Root of the one Church."

3. The mystery of this Primacy S. Cyprian explains in his same letter to Jubaianus: "Whither shall he come who thirsteth? to heretics,

where is no fountain or river of living water, or to the Church, which is one, and was by the voice of the Lord founded upon one, who also received the keys ? She it is, who alone holds and possesses the whole power of her Spouse and Lord. In her we preside ; for her honour and unity we contend; her grace alike and glory we maintain with faithful devotion . . . . . The faithful, saving, and holy, water of the Church, cannot be corrupted and adulterated ; as the Church herself, also, is uncorrupt and chaste and pure." *Ib. n.* 9.

He holds that the Church "is one ;" elsewhere he asserts that it "is one and cannot be divided" *Ep.* lxxiv. (*Ben.* lxxvi.) *ad Pomp. n.* 6. And in the above passage he further adds, the Church, "also, is uncorrupt, and chaste, and pure :" in a word, he held that the Church is One, indivisible, and infallible. But by what law is its unity maintained ? This we learn from the same Father ; he says that the Church "was by the voice of the Lord founded upon one," *i.e.* upon Peter ; he was the Original, in whom was the Church, "first and alone." In S. Peter was, therefore, originally the Mother Church, which is the " Root and the Matrix of the Catholic Church." From this " Mother Church," from this " Root and Matrix," proceeded forth the Universal Church, expanding itself in every direction, adding circumference to circumference from its one centre, S. Peter ; and so will it continue until it shall embrace the entire earth. " This is the mystery of the Divine appointment and of Catholic unity once delivered," as S. Cyprian said in another epistle : by which it was ordained that the " Unity of the Priesthood should take its rise " from one, even from S. Peter, the Chief of the Apostles. But not only did the Church originate in one, it is also maintained and preserved by one, *i.e.* S. Peter, for he adds, " who also received the keys." These keys are held by one, they cannot be in the custody of more than one ; others may participate in their use, and in the power of which they are the symbol, but they belong to one only, and consequently one only has the independent and unlimited use of them. It is true that S. Cyprian infers that all had the keys, but not in so strict a sense. We know that every chief magistrate of a municipal town has the sword borne before him on state occasions, but every one is aware that there is but one proper sword, which is carried before the Sovereign ; this is the one Sword of State, the other swords are no more than representatives of that one Sword. So also the keys, the keys proper, belong to One, all other keys are but symbols of the power as derived from the true keys, and subject to them. S. Peter " received the keys," and hence S. Cyprian held, that not only was S. Peter the Source, but the Head ; not only did the sacerdotal ministry spring from him, but its unity is maintained by him, who alone possesses those keys. Consequently S. Cyprian held, that " She it is who alone holds and possesses the whole power of her Spouse and Lord ;" that is, the Church founded upon Peter, and governed by him ; and the Catholic Church which proceeded forth from him, and which is even now spreading her borders in every direction. This Church, and this Church alone,—bound to the first Apostle, Peter, by the cords of a fundamental union, which no Samson can break (for it is "one and cannot be divided"),—to the exclusion of all churches and communities which have severed them-

selves from the one ordained author of Unity, "alone holds and possesses the whole power of her Spouse and Lord."

"In her we preside," adds S. Cyprian, that is, in the Universal
Church, which originated in the One,—Peter,—and which is governed by
One, even by the same blessed Apostle, Peter. But S. Peter no
longer lives upon earth, who, then, are his Successors? Anglicans say,
all Bishops are his successors. So they are, but is there no special Successor to this Apostle, by which the unity of the Priesthood may ever issue
forth, and by which all may ever be maintained in consistent unity?
And is there any place to which we may point as the sacred fountain of
Catholic Unity, where the original Mother Church stands in all her
venerable glory; where is imbedded deep in the bowels of the earth,
the sacred Root of the Universal Church; and the original Matrix
which was fruitful in bringing forth children, not "seven" only, but
"seventy times seven," adding perfect numeral to numeral, till the whole
fabric of society shall be included in the one Motherhood of Peter;
where also are deposited those keys, which Christ delivered to Peter
alone, by which the whole family is governed and preserved in unity and
peace? What was S. Cyprian's opinion on this point? Who can doubt
it? In the comment on this Father's testimony I have proved that S.
Cyprian believed that Rome,—the City of Rome,—was the "Place of
Peter," where stands in all its grandeur the sacred "Cathedra of
Peter," to which is attached the Prerogative of the "Rank or Grade,"
and "the honour of the Sacerdotal Chair," which Novatian, the Anti-
pope, usurped, and to which is annexed the "Primacy," which this
man vainly attempted to seize. Hence S. Cyprian described the Roman
Church,—not the mere "lawful Bishop" apart from his "See," but the
Roman Church and its Cathedra,—as the "Head," "the Mother," "the
Root," and "the Matrix of the Catholic Church;" hence also he
described it as "the Principal or Chief Church, from whence the
Unity of the Priesthood took its rise." In this Church, together with
all other Churches in communion with it, the one Episcopate, the one
Brotherhood, the one College of Prelates preside, subject to the Jurisdiction of that one Prelate who is the Successor to the "Place of Peter,"
to "the Chair of Peter," and the "Principal Church." This must be
S. Cyprian's doctrine, for it flows consistently and necessarily from
the principles of unity which he lays down, and from the assertions
which he makes respecting the Church, that it is "one, and cannot be
divided," and that it "is uncorrupt and chaste and pure."

I think that an impartial mind will admit, that, whatever S. Cyprian
may have meant by the speech he delivered before the Council of Carthage, he never could have intended to deny the legitimate authority of
the Pope as Successor to the Prerogatives and the Chair of S. Peter, on
whom, he admits repeatedly, the Church was built; who received the
keys; and to whom the Lord commended His sheep to be fed and
guarded.

VIII.

THE AFRICAN PROTESTS (*continued*).

CASE OF APIARIUS.

The following account of the case of Apiarius is given by Fleury, which, as he belonged to the Gallican party, may be regarded as one fair and unprejudiced, and free from all tendency to favour extreme Papal authority : " Urbanus, Bishop of Sicca in Mauritania Cæsariensis, and a friend of St. Augustine, had excommunicated the Priest Apiarius, as being irregularly ordained, and charged with several infamous crimes, of which he was accused by the inhabitants of Tabraca. Apiarius appealed to Pope Zosimus at Rome, who sent three legates into Africa, Faustinus Bishop of Potentia in Picenum, Philip and Asellus, Priests. When they were arrived at Carthage, the Bishops assembled with Aurelius asked them what the Pope had charged them with ; and not content with a verbal declaration of their commission, they prayed them to cause the instructions which they had brought in writing to be read. They were read accordingly, and were found to contain four articles. The first was on the appeal of Bishops to the Pope ; the second against unnecessary voyages of Bishops to court ; the third on the trial of the causes of Priests and Deacons before the neighbouring Bishops, if their own Bishop had excommunicated them without good reason ; and the fourth spoke of excommunicating the Bishop Urbanus, or even citing him to Rome, if he did not correct what seemed to want correction. These instructions having been read, there was no difficulty on the second article ; because the Bishops of Africa had already made a Canon, in the Council of Carthage, in the year 407, to prevent the Bishops and Priests from going to court on frivolous pretences. But concerning the first Article, which permitted Bishops to appeal to Rome ; and the third, which required that the causes of the clergy should be brought before the neighbouring Bishops ; the Bishops of Africa could not agree to the Pope's claim. And as, to support it, he alleged the Canons of Nicæa, the Bishops of Africa said they could not find those Canons in the copies which they had. Nevertheless, as far as this Council was concerned, they wrote to Pope Zosimus in the year 418, that they would consent to be thus treated provisionally for a short time, till they were better informed of the decrees of Nicæa. The Bishops of Africa were willing that the Clergy should complain of the judgment of their Bishop before the Primate and Council of the province ; but not before the Bishops of the neighbouring provinces. And they did not recognise the Canons of Sardica, brought forward by the Pope under the name of Nicæa, because the Donatists had substituted the false Council of Sardica in the place of the true one. Pope Zosimus died not long after ; that is to say, on the 26th of December of the same year, 418, having held the Holy See one year and nine months. . . . . . .

" The legates, whom Pope Zosimus had sent into Africa upon the affair of Apiarius, were still there, and they were present at a general Council of Africa, which was held at Carthage, in the hall of the Basilica of Faustus, the eighth of the calends of June, after the twelfth consulate of Honorius, and the eighth of Theodosius ; that is, the 25th of May, in the year 419. It is reckoned the Sixth Council of Carthage. Aurelius presided there, with Valentinus, Primate of Numidia ; next was seated Faustinus, Bishop of Potentia, one of the Pope's legates ; then the Bishops deputed from the several provinces of Africa . . . . . . to the number of two hundred and seventeen Bishops ; and after them all were seated the two other legates of the Pope, Philip and Asellus, who were only Priests. The deacons were present, standing. Aurelius began by ordering the canons of the Council of Nicæa to be read ; but the Legate Faustinus interrupted the reading of them, and demanded first to have read the instructions which he and his colleagues had received from Pope Zosimus. These instructions were accordingly read, in which was inserted the canon which allowed a Bishop deposed by the provincial Council to appeal to the Pope, and to demand a revision of his cause before the Bishops of the neighbouring province and a legate of the Pope. This canon was mentioned as being of the Council of Nicæa, though it was in reality the fifth of the Council of Sardica ; and on this account S. Alypius interrupted the reading of it, and said, ' We have already answered on this point by our former letters, and we engage to observe what has been ordained by the Council of Nicæa ; but the obstacle in the present case is, that upon inspecting the Greek copies of the Council of Nicæa, I know not how it is, we do not find those words in them : wherefore we desire you, holy Pope Aurelius, to send to Constantinople, where it is said the original of that Council is preserved ; and also to the venerable Bishops of Alexandria and Antioch, that they may send it to us, together with an attestation of it in their letters, that there may no longer remain any doubt. We must also desire the venerable Bishop of the Roman Church, Boniface, to send also to the said Churches, that copies of the Council of Nicæa may be brought from thence. At present let us cause them to be inserted in these Acts, just as we now have them.'

" The Legate Faustinus protested against any prejudice resulting to the Church of Rome from this remonstrance ; and added, that it would be sufficient for the Pope alone to make that inquiry ; for fear it might seem that some dispute had arisen between the Churches. Aurelius proposed to inform the Pope fully of what had passed, and all the Council agreed to it. At the request of the Bishop Novatus, deputy from Mauritania, there was also read a passage out of the instructions of the Roman Legates, in which was inserted the fourteenth canon of the Council of Sardica, which allows a Priest or Deacon excommunicated by his Bishop, to have recourse to the neighbouring Bishops. S. Augustine said, upon that Article : ' We promise to observe this also, reserving to ourselves the right of obtaining more exact information concerning the Council of Nicæa.' Aurelius asked their opinions, and all agreed to observe all the decrees of the Council of Nicæa. The Legate Faustinus proposed writing to the Pope on the Article, about which S. Augustine had spoken, concerning the clergy below the rank of Bishop, since that, too, was called in question. Then were read the decrees of the Council of Nicæa, according to the copy brought to Africa by Cæcilianus, Bishop of Car-

thage, who had been present at it ; and it was resolved, according to the
proposal of S. Alypius, to send to the Bishops of Antioch, of Alexandria,
and of Constantinople, that so they might admit the authority of the
decrees in question, if they were found in the originals ; or if they were
not, might consider of them in a Council. In the Acts of this Council
were inserted the Creed of Nicæa, and its twenty canons. . . . .

"Afterwards there is another meeting of the same Council, dated the
thirtieth of May, 419, which some reckon the seventh Council of Carthage. As
several Bishops expressed themselves in haste to return to their Churches,
it was resolved to choose commissioners for the affairs that remained, and
twenty-two were named : of which number were S. Augustine, Alypius, and
Possidius. . . . . Then Aurelius broke up the Council, and deferred writing
to Pope Boniface till the next day. The Synodical letter declares that
this affair had occasioned very troublesome altercations, though without
any breach of charity. He then adds : ' The Priest Apiarius, whose
ordination and excommunication had produced so much scandal all over
Africa, having begged pardon for all his faults, has been restored to
communion ; our brother Urbanus, Bishop of Sicca, having first corrected what required correction. But because the peace and quiet of the
Church ought to be provided for, not only for the present, but for the
future, we have ordained that the Priest Apiarius be removed from the
Church of Sicca, without, however, losing the honour of his rank ; and
receive a letter, by virtue of which he may exercise the functions of the
Priesthood, wherever he may be willing and able to do so.'

" They next mention the letter they had written the year before concerning the instructions given by Pope Zosimus to his Legates, and then say,
' We desire that your Holiness will allow us to observe what has been decreed
in the Council of Nicæa, and enforce in your own country what is contained in the instructions of Zosimus ;' that is to say, the two canons of
the Council of Sardica, which they then transcribe. After which they
add : ' If those resolutions be contained in the Council of Nicæa, and
observed with you in Italy, we will mention them no more, and will not
scruple to allow them. But if it be otherwise in the canons of Nicæa, we
believe, with God's mercy, that so long as you preside over the Roman
Church, we shall no longer suffer this annoyance, and that we shall be
treated with the brotherly charity which you so well understand. Wherefore we pray you to write to the Bishops of Antioch, of Alexandria, and
of Constantinople, and to any others, if it so please you, to send us the
canons of Nicæa : for who can doubt of the truth of the copies brought
from those illustrious Churches, if they shall be found to agree together? In the meanwhile we promise to observe the canons quoted in
the instruction concerning the appeals of Bishops to the Bishop of
Rome, and the trial of clergy before the Bishops of their provinces.
Of whatever else has passed in our Council you will be able to inform
yourself from the Acts brought by our brethren, the Bishop Faustinus,
and the Priests Philip and Asellus.' The Pope's Legates, after the
conclusion of this Council, returned home. . . . . It is true, indeed, that
they received the correct copies of the Nicene canons in his (S. Augustine's) time, and sent them to him on the twenty-sixth of November

of the same year, 419; but the Bishops of Africa declared that they would no longer allow any appeals to be made beyond sea, by a synodical letter addressed to Pope Celestine, which must have been written some time after this of S. Augustine, since they do not like him compliment the Pope on his accession to the Pontificate. And, indeed, the war which broke out immediately after the death of Honorius prevented free intercourse between Africa and Rome. But on the restoration of peace, and apparently in 426, the Bishops of Africa received by the hands of the Priest Leo a letter from the Pope St. Celestine, in favour of the Priest Apiarius, whom he had restored to communion, and sent back to Africa, together with Faustinus the Bishop, who had been there before as Legate from Pope Zosimus. On his arrival the Bishops of Africa assembled a Council, in which Aurelius of Carthage, and Valentine, Primate of Numidia, presided. Thirteen more are named, but the name of S. Augustine does not appear among them. This Council, having examined the affair of Apiarius, found him charged with so many crimes that it was impossible for Faustinus to defend him, though he acted the part rather of an advocate than of a judge, and violated all right in the opposition he maintained against the whole Council under pretence of supporting the privileges of the Church of Rome. For he wanted Apiarius to be received to the communion of the Bishops of Africa, because the Pope had restored him to it, believing that he had appealed, though he could not prove even the fact of his appeal. After a debate of three days, Apiarius at last, stung with remorse and moved by God, confessed on a sudden all the crimes of which he had been accused, which were so infamous and incredible as to draw groans from the whole Council; after which he was for ever deprived of all ecclesiastical ministration.

"The Bishops wrote a synodical letter to Pope Celestine, in which they conjure him for the future not to receive to his communion those who have been excommunicated by them; since this was a point ruled by the Nicene Council. 'For,' they added, 'if this be forbidden with respect to the minor clergy or laymen, how much more did the Council intend its observance in respect to Bishops? Those, therefore, who are interdicted from communion in their own provinces ought not to be restored by your Holiness too hastily, and in opposition to the rules; and you ought to reject the Priests and other clergy who are so rash as to have recourse to you. For no ordinance of our fathers has deprived the Church of Africa of this authority, and the decrees of the Nicene Council have subjected the Bishops themselves to their respective Metropolitans.

"They have ordained, with great wisdom and justice, that all matters shall be terminated in the places where they arise; and did not think that the grace of the Holy Ghost would be wanting in any province to bestow on its Bishops the knowledge and strength necessary for their decisions; especially since whoever thinks himself wronged, may appeal to the Council of his province, or even to a general Council, unless it be imagined that God can inspire a single individual with justice, and refuse it to an innumerable multitude of assembled Bishops. And how shall we be able to rely on a sentence passed beyond the sea, since it will not be possible to send thither the necessary witnesses, whether from the weakness of sex, or of advanced age, or any other impediment? For that your Holiness should send any one on your part, we can find ordained by no Council.

"With regard to what you have sent us by our brother Faustinus, as being contained in the Nicene Council, we find nothing of the kind in the more authentic copies of that Council, which we have received from our brother the Bishop of Alexandria and the venerable Atticus of Constantinople, and which we formerly sent to Boniface, your predecessor of happy memory. For the rest, whoever desires you to delegate any of your clergy to execute your orders, we beseech you not to comply, lest it seem that we are introducing the pride of secular dominion into the Church of Christ, which ought to exhibit to all men an example of simplicity and humility. For as to our brother Faustinus, since the wretched Apiarius is cut off from the Church, we depend confidently on your goodness that without violating brotherly charity, Africa shall be no longer forced to endure him.' Such is the letter of the Council of Africa to Pope St. Celestine."—*Fleury, H. E. (Newm. Tr.), Bk.* xxiv. *c.* vi. x. xi. xxxv.

Mr. Allies, before his conversion, considered this case of Apiarius fatal to the Roman Supremacy; and that the action of the Council of Africa, which was never accused of schism, in resisting the Papal demands, justified a similar action of the Church of England in the sixteenth century. "It is precisely the same claim made in both instances, viz. that these two laws should be observed, on which the stability of the Government of the whole Catholic Church rests; as Thomassin remarks—first, that the action of the Bishop in his own Diocese, in matters proper to that Diocese, should not be interfered with; secondly, that the action of the Metropolitan with his suffragans in matters belonging to his Province, should be left equally free." (*Ch. of Eng. cleared from Schism, p.* 144.) But Mr. Allies then forgot a most important distinction, which makes all the difference in the two cases, viz. that the African Church held the doctrine of the Roman Supremacy, and submitted to all its essential Prerogatives, whereas the Church of England rejected it altogether as an usurpation.

Now, after a careful investigation of this matter, it appears to me to resolve itself into a question of Privilege and Discipline. The case is simply this: Apiarius, a wicked Priest, had been excommunicated by his Bishop, not for heresy, but for immoral crimes; he, as every one else did, who believed he had a grievance, appealed to the Pope, and obtained from him restoration to communion, and then he returned to Africa. He was accompanied by a Legate to support him in his cause. Upon their arrival, Aurelius, the Bishop of Carthage, summoned a Council, for the reception of the Pope's Legate. The Legate maintained the right of the Pope to receive appeals from the Provincial Councils, a right which he alleged was founded on the Nicene Canons. The assembled prelates demurred, asserting that no such canons were contained in their copies of the Nicene Code. They proposed that authentic copies should be obtained from the Oriental Patriarchal Sees (for the Council had been held in Asia Minor), and they engaged that if the alleged canons were found to be included, they would cheerfully obey them. And in the meantime they consented to the demand of the Legate. Now it must be borne in mind that this matter was one of pure discipline, and that the Faith was in no way involved. That this was so is evident from the fact that in all that pertained to Faith, in all causes of heresy, and of schism, the African Church was accustomed to refer to Rome. No one can read the Epistles of S. Cyprian, without perceiving that he held that the Apostolic See was the Head of the Faith, on account of the Imperial city being the "Place of Peter," and of the Church of Rome, by virtue of the "Cathedra of Peter," "the Principal or Chief Church." He believed, too, that the Church of Rome was the Spring of sacerdotal unity, that it was the Mother, the Root, and the Matrix of the Universal Church, and that attached to the Chair of that Church was what he describes as the "Grade of the Sacerdotal Chair," *i.e.* the "Primacy." So that he unquestionably held that the Pope, in all matters concerning the Faith, was Supreme. This is proved by the simple fact of his urging Pope S. Stephen to take action against Marcianus of Arles in Gaul. S. Optatus, too, another illustrious African Prelate, held that the Chair of Peter at Rome was the "first mark" of the Catholic Church, and that he who was not united with that Chair, was no Catholic, but a heretic and a schismatic ; and S. Augustine, perhaps the profoundest theologian of his age, asserted that the Princedom of S. Peter, and the Princedom of his Successors in the See of Rome, had always been in force. And then again, the very Bishops, or most of them, who formed this Council which received the Papal Legate, the year before, after condemning Pelagius and Celestius, addressed a Synodical Epistle to the Pope, wherein they request "that the authority of the Apostolic See may be given to the resolutions of our lowliness ;" and in the Synodical Epistle of the Council of Milevis, they say, "As the Lord, by the chief gift of His grace, hath placed you in the Apostolic See, and hath furnished our times with such a Chief . . . . we pray that you will deign to extend your pastoral diligence to the great dangers of us poor weak members of Christ . . . . We think that . . . . they who hold such perverse sentiments will more readily yield to the Authority of your Holiness, which is derived from the clear light of the Holy Scripture." *Labbé*, I. iii., *col.* 388, 9.

It is manifest, then, that the African Bishops believed in the Papal Supremacy as a Divine institution, so that whatever was the nature of the dispute raised in the case of Apiarius, it had no reference whatever to the position of the Pope as the Head and the Chief Pastor of the Universal Church. It was a question purely of privilege and discipline. The African Fathers maintained it was their right guaranteed to them by the canons, that all causes having reference to the discipline of the Church, should be definitively determined in the Province wherein they arise ; and they give very practical reasons for their opinion ; "and how," say they, in their Epistle to the Pope, "shall we be able to rely on a sentence passed beyond the sea, since it will not be possible to send thither the necessary witnesses, whether from the weakness of sex, or of advanced age, or any other impediment ? For that your Holiness should send any one on your part, we can find ordained by no Council."

This single passage alone shows that the whole dispute in the matter of appeals had relation to the privileges of Bishops and to causes of discipline. The African Synod held that in "all lesser causes" (the "greater causes" concerning offences against the Faith, these Bishops had fully, by their proceedings, acknowledged to belong to the Pope), the provincial Synod was supreme, and that no appeal could, according to the Canon Law, be carried to Rome. This seems, then, to be the whole case. But how this can affect the doctrine of the Pope's Supremacy passes my comprehension. The same sort of questions are constantly arising in the political world. Charles I. attempted to levy taxes without authority of Parliament, relying upon his high regal Prerogative. It was resisted by the people, but did that involve his real Supremacy as King? No Englishman would be so foolish as to assert that it did. In our own day the Queen attempted to create an illustrious personage a life peer, and she summoned him by Writ to the House of Lords, but the Peers refused to admit him, on the ground that the Sovereign had invaded the privileges of their order. Would any one, let us say a thousand years hence, after reading the account of this repulse of the Crown in a matter of Prerogative, conclude that in those days the Empire of Great Britain was not monarchical in its form of government? The two cases appear to me exactly parallel. The Legate demanded on behalf of Pope the cession by the African Bishops of the right to hear appeals in causes involving discipline : they refused. The Prime Minister of Queen Victoria attempted to impose upon the House a life peer—a thing unprecedented—the House declined to admit him : how could either of these cases affect the question in dispute? Was the Monarchy reduced to a nullity by the act of the Lords ? No man of sense would assert that it was. Then how can it be gravely assumed that because the African Bishops rejected the Papal claim to hear appeals of lesser causes, that this episcopal act amounted to a testimony against the Supremacy of the Holy See? The whole case of our opponent here breaks down, for, as said above, the question at issue was one simply of Privilege and of Discipline.

But let us assume that the opposition of the African Church went to the extreme length of resisting the Papal Supremacy altogether, as the Church of England did in the sixteenth century, how could this really affect the question at issue between us? True, there was S. Augustine, who took part in this question, and surely his opinion is one that can be relied upon. In answer to this rejoinder, it is sufficient to say, that Africa did not comprise the whole Catholic Church, that neither the Synod of Carthage nor the profound S. Augustine* were infallible, and therefore it was possible they may, as the learned Tertullian of old, and the

---

* It would seem that this great Father took no part in the last debates of the African Council. If so, his name cannot be claimed in support of what was finally determined.

great S. Cyprian, have erred in a matter of vital importance. Be this, however, as it may, it will be conceded by all opponents that the Church of Africa owed allegiance, if not to the Pope, at least to the Universal Church in Council assembled. Now it is well known that Nestorius was deposed by S. Celestine, and Dioscorus by Pope S. Leo; and that the Council of Chalcedon admitted the principle that no Council could be summoned without the sanction of the Holy See, and that in the Synodical address to the Pope they admit to the full all his Prerogatives as the Guardian of the Vineyard, the Head of the Church, and "the Interpreter to all of the blessed Peter:" and it should be further recollected, that according to the testimony of Socrates, "it was a sacerdotal law, that the things done contrary to the decree of the Bishop of the Romans, was regarded as null." *l.* iii. *c.* 10. Let it then be assumed that the Council of Carthage resisted the Pope's Supremacy to the utmost extreme, it stands convicted of a great act of schismatical rebellion against the Holy See, and consequently its witness against the Roman Chair becomes utterly worthless.

But the African Church did not proceed to this extent; all that she resisted was the demands of the Papal Legate that causes relating to discipline should be carried to Rome, and this resistance was grounded on the following considerations : (1) That the provincial Episcopate was fully competent to deal definitively with such causes; (2) That it would be impossible to convey all the witnesses that were needful to Rome, by reason of the weaknesses of sex or age ; and (3) That to do so would be an invasion of the Canon Law.

The Anglican argument against Rome, founded on the precedents of this case, utterly breaks down. So far from the Church of England deriving any support in her schism from this dispute, it entirely condemns her.

IX.

POPE S. GREGORY THE GREAT AND THE TITLE OF "ŒCUMENICAL BISHOP."

Although beyond the period of time to which this Inquiry is limited, this work would scarcely be deemed complete, in design at least, if no reference was made to the controversy that arose between S. Gregory the Great and the Patriarch John the Faster, of Constantinople, relative to the title of "Œcumenical Patriarch," which the latter had assumed. As Anglicans have always regarded the sentiments to which this Pope committed himself as fatal to the doctrine of the Papal Supremacy, it would, therefore, be highly inexpedient to decline any investigation into this question.

The circumstances of this case are simply these. Soon after the translation of the seat of government from Imperial Rome to Byzantium, subsequently called Constantinople, the Emperor and the Church of that city conceived the design of promoting its Episcopal throne (notwithstanding that it was not an Apostolic See), to the dignity of a Patriarchal See next in rank to the Throne of S. Peter in Rome. They succeeded in obtaining a recognition of their claim in the Second Œcumenical Council, held at Constantinople, and also in the Fourth, which was celebrated at Chalcedon, in its last session, when the greater part of the Bishops had returned to their dioceses. This last-named Council offered the title of " Œcumenical Patriarch" to the Pope S. Leo, but he declined to accept it, but subsequently John the Faster assumed it, and ever since the Patriarchs of Constantinople have called themselves by that "proud and profane title."

S. Gregory the Great, who foresaw the terrible evils which lay concealed under this claim (and which time has fully realised), exerted all his authority and power to induce this Prelate to put it aside. S. Gregory's objection may be thus summarised : (1) Because it encroached upon the inherent Prerogatives of the Holy See ; (2) Because it was an ambitious, proud, and profane title ; and (3) Because it virtually, if not effectually, annulled the rights of all Bishops.

The passages in S. Gregory's epistles, relied upon by Anglicans, are thus given by Dr. Barrow. He says, " Thus hath that great Pope taught us to argue, in words expressly condemning some, and consequently all of them, together with the things which they signify : *What* (saith he, writing to the Bishop of Constantinople, who had admitted the title of Universal Bishop or Patriarch), *wilt thou say to Christ, the Head of the Universal Church, in the trial of the last judgment, who by the appellation of* Universal *dost endeavour to subject all His members to thee ? Whom, I pray, dost thou mean to imitate in so perverse a word, but him who, despising the legions of angels constituted in fellowship with him, did endeavour to break forth unto the top of singularity, that he might both be subject to none, and alone be over all ? Who also said, I will ascend into heaven, and will exalt my throne above the stars—for what are thy brethren, all the Bishops of the Universal Church, but the stars of heaven ; to whom while by this haughty word thou desirest to prefer thyself, and trample on their name in comparison to thee, what dost thou say, but, I will climb into heaven ?*—And, again, in another epistle to the Bishops of Alexandria and Antioch, he taxeth the same Patriarch for *assuming to boast so that he attempteth to ascribe all things to himself, and studieth by the elation of pompous speech to subject to himself all the members of Christ, which do cohere to one sole Head, namely, to Christ.* Again, *I confidently say, that whoever doth call himself Universal Bishop, or desireth to be so called, doth in his elation forerun Antichrist, because he pridingly doth set himself before all others." Supp. pp.* 178, 179.

Dr. Barrow then argues : " If those argumentations be sound, or signify anything, what is the pretence of *Universal Sovereignty and pastorship* but a piece of *Luciferian arrogance ?* Who can imagine that even this Pope could approve, could assume, could exercise it ? If he did, was he not monstrously senseless, and above measure impudent, to use such discourses, which so plainly, without altering a word, might be retorted upon him ; which are built upon suppositions, that it is unlawful and wicked to assume superiority over the Church, over all Bishops, over all Christians; the which indeed (seeing never Pope was of greater repute, or did write in any case more solemnly and seriously) have given to the pretences of his Successors so deadly a wound, that no balm of sophistical interpretation can be able to heal it." *Ib. p.* 179. Again, " It was to be sure a visible headship which St. Gregory did so eagerly impugn and exclaim against; for he could not apprehend the Bishop of Constantinople so wild as to affect a jurisdiction over the Church mystical or invisible." *Ib. p.* 180. Once more, " That Pope Gregory I. did not hold himself superior to other Bishops, many sayings of his do infer; for in this he placeth the fault of the Bishop of Constantinople, which he so often and so severely reprehendeth that he did *prefer himself before, and extol himself above, other Bishops.* And would he directly assume that to himself which he chargeth on another, although only following his position by consequence? And when Eulogius, the Bishop of Alexandria, had complimentarily said, *Sicut jussistis, As ye commanded;* he doth thus express his resentment : *That word of* command *I desire you let me not hear; because I know who I am, and who ye are; by place ye are my brethren; in goodness, fathers : I did not, therefore, command ; but what seemed profitable I hinted to you.* That many such instances may not be alleged out of antiquity, the reason is, because the ancient Popes did not understand this power to belong to them, and therefore gave no occasion for Bishops to maintain their honour ; or were more just, prudent, and modest, than to take so much upon them, as their successors did, upon frivolous pretences." *Ib. pp.* 225, 226.

Now, before we can estimate the true value of the passage which Dr. Barrow has put before us, we must ascertain what was the nature of S. Gregory's objection (apart from the profanity of the term, and the pride of place it inferred) to the claims advanced by John the Faster. S. Gregory himself informs us, (1) that all Priests would "be deprived of their due honour by something peculiar being given to one ;" and (2) because " whatever is given to another more than reason requires is so much taken away from yourself ;" for " if your Holiness (Bp. of Alexandria) calls me Universal Pope, you deny that you are yourself what you admit me to be, Universal." These extracts contain the key to S. Gregory's objection to the term " Universal Patriarch." He, together with all his predecessors, and all his Successors in the Chair of Peter, held that the Apostolate was one; that the Bishops were equal to each other in Order and in Priesthood; that every Bishop was, within his diocese, Vicar of Christ, and that he held his See not merely by favour of the Apostolic See, but by the Holy Ghost. That this is the doctrine of the Catholic Church at the present day is evident from the Council of Trent, which affirms that Bishops are the successors of the Apostles, and that they are placed by the Holy Ghost to rule the Church of God. Vide *Sess.* xviii. *c.* iv.

Pope S. Gregory seems to have held that the term " Universal Patriarch" implied that there was but one Bishop and one High Priest in the world, for he said, " If your Holiness call me Universal Pope, you deny that you are yourself what you admit me to be, Universal."

There is but one truly Universal Bishop, and he is the Lord Jesus Christ, for no Pope, or Prelate, is of His order and dignity. They share in His Priesthood, but in *this*, Bishops are not superior, to the priests of the second order of the ministry. He is Universal because none can compete with him in anything. He is as distinct from the Episcopate inclusive of the Pope, as Aaron, the High Priest, was distinct from the priests below him. If then the Pope or any Bishop should call himself Universal Patriarch (according to what S. Gregory understood by the term) he not only reduces the Universal Episcopate to the position of a lower grade or rank ; but he excludes them altogether from his own order or ministry. In a word he puts himself in the position, relatively, of our Lord, and hence S. Gregory says with perfect truth, " I confidently say, that whoever doth call himself Universal Bishop, and desireth to be so called, doth in his elation forerun Antichrist, because he pridingly doth set himself before all others." But while S. Gregory denounced the title of " Universal Patriarch," as profane and Antichristian, did he deny the Superiority and the Universality of his own office, and of the Jurisdiction, which he received from S. Peter, who obtained it from Christ Himself?" No such thing. Dr. Barrow asserts, " That Pope Gregory I. did not hold himself superior to other bishops." Had the learned Doctor given us some more of S. Gregory's "sayings," and given us some account of his practices as the Chief Pastor of the Catholic Church, he himself might have arrived at a different conclusion.

Mr. Allies, before his conversion to the Catholic Church, wrote a very able work, from which I have already quoted, entitled " The Church of England cleared from Schism." He possessed an essentially honest and straightforward mind, and while he exerted his utmost to convince Anglicans that his Church was free from the crime of schism, he never to his knowledge kept back a single passage that witnessed against his own argument. That work has had an overpowering and a diverse influence ; those who desired to be Catholics found in it the proofs of the truth of the Roman Supremacy; and those who wished, for various reasons, to remain where they were, found ample support, not so much from the testimonies adduced, as from the very able manner he conducted, in thoroughly good faith, his argument. But, as I have observed, he was far too honest a man knowingly to keep anything back which told against him. I propose, then, to supply from Mr. Allies' work what Dr. Barrow has omitted, and then we shall see whether S. Gregory did not believe himself to be, a Sovereign Pontiff, " Superior to other Bishops."

" After the letters of my predecessor and my own," wrote S. Gregory, "in the matter of Honoratus the archdeacon, we sent to your Holiness (Nitalis of Salona, in Dalmatia) in despite of the sentence of us both, the above-mentioned Honoratus was deprived of his rank. Had either of the four Patriarchs (*i.e.*, Constantinople, Alexandria, Antioch, and Jerusalem) done this, so great an act of contumacy could not have been passed over without the most grievous scandal. However, as your Brotherhood has since returned to your duty, I take notice neither of the injury done to me nor of that to my predecessor." *S. Greg. Ep. Lib.* 2, 52.* Vide *Allies' Schism, p.* 345.

"As to what he says, that he (a Bishop) is subject to the Apostolical See; I know not what Bishop is not subject to it, if any fault be found in Bishops. But when no fault requires it, all are equal according to the estimation of humility." *Ib. Lib.* 9. 59. *Gieseler*, vide *Allies' Sch.* 36.

In a letter to the Emperor Mauricius, he says, "But since it is not my cause but God's, and since not I only, but the whole Church, is thrown into confusion, since sacred laws, since venerable Synods, since the very commands even of our Lord Jesus Christ, are disturbed by this invention of this haughty and pompous language, let the pious Emperor lance the wound, &c. . . . For to all who know the Gospel it is manifest, that the charge of the whole Church was entrusted by the voice of the Lord to the holy Apostle Peter, chief of all the Apostles. For to him is said, 'Peter, lovest thou Me? Feed My sheep.' To him is said, 'Behold, Satan hath desired to sift you, &c.' To him is said, 'Thou art Peter,' &c. Lo, he hath received the keys of the Kingdom of heaven, the power of binding and loosing is given to him, the care of the whole Church is committed to him, and the Primacy, and yet he is not called Universal Apostle. And that holy man, my fellow-priest John, endeavours to be called Universal Bishop. . . Do I in this matter, most pious Lord, defend only my own cause? Is it a private injury that I pursue? It is the cause of Almighty God, the cause of the Universal Church. Who is he, who in violation of the statutes of the Gospel, in violation of the decrees of Canons, presumes to usurp a new name to himself? Would that he who desires to be called Universal may exist himself without diminution to others ! . . . If then, any one claims to himself that name in that Church, as to the judgment of all good men he has done, the whole Church (which God forbid !) falls from its place, when he who is called Universal falls. But far from your Christian hearts be that blasphemous name, in which the honour of all Priests is taken away, while it is madly arrogated by one to himself! Certainly, to do honour to the blessed Peter, Chief of the Apostles, this was offered to the Roman Pontiff during the venerable Synod of Chalcedon. But no other of them ever consented to use this singular appellation, that all Priests might not be deprived of their due honour by something peculiar being given to one. How is it then, that we seek not the glory of this name, though offered us, yet another presume to claim it, though not offered?" *Lib.* 5, *Ep.* 20. Vide *Allies' Sch., pp.* 356, 7.

In the above passages the following points are noticeable : (1) That the Four Patriarchs, that is, of Constantinople, Alexandria, Antioch, and Jerusalem, are amenable to some authority for their conduct ; (2) That this authority to whom they are subject is "the Apostolical See." "I know not," says S. Gregory, "what Bishop is not subject to it, if any fault be found in Bishops. But when no fault requires it, all are equal according

---

* This and other references are taken, without verification, from Mr. Allies' work.

to the estimation of humility." This is enough, for if every Bishop throughout the world is amenable to the Apostolical See, then the Supremacy of
the Pope is proved: for how could he presume to judge even Patriarchs
unless he were Supreme?

That Pope S. Gregory really believed in the Supremacy of the Holy See
is evident (1) from what he has asserted it to be, and (2) by his practice
as Sovereign Pontiff. The following extract from Father Bottalla's admirable and unanswerable treatise "On the Supreme Authority of the Pope,"
will inform us as to the first point. ". . . It is childish to think that the
objection made by St. Gregory the Great to the use of the title, ' Œcumenical Bishop,' is an unanswerable refutation of the divine supremacy of the
Pope in the Universal Church, when we know that a long line of preceding Pontiffs had publicly and explicitly proclaimed the opposite doctrine. But did S. Gregory the Great in any wise contradict the teaching
of his predecessors? We deny it; and unequivocally maintain that this
great Pope ever spoke in harmony with all the other successors of
S. Peter, both when stating the character of the Papal authority, and when
condemning the term of 'universal bishop.' Unquestionably, St. Gregory
uniformly held the same view as to the authority of the Apostolic See over
he Universal Church. In fact, he called that see 'Head of all the
Churches.'" *Apostolica sedes omnium Ecclesiarum caput est,* (*Epist. l.* xiii.
epist. xlv., capit. ii. *Op. T.* ii., *Edit. Maur. Parisiis, p.* 1254); "Head of
the Faith," *Ep. l.* xiii., epist. lvii. (l.c. *p.* 1244); So that other Churches,
according to his view formed its body and even its members; but the
health of the body, and all its members, depended upon the soundness of
the head. For this reason he frequently and repeatedly inculcated in his
letters, that his Pontifical cares extended over the Universal Church,
since he occupied the Apostolic See which is raised above all the Churches,
Epist. l. iii., epist. xxx. (l.c. *p.* 645); *Epist.* l. v., epist. xiii. (l.c. *p.* 737);
Epist. l. vii., epist. xix. (l.c. *p.* 865), &c.; '*cunctarum ecclesiarum injuncta
sollicitudinis cura constringet;*' that hence no bishop, when rebuked or
corrected by the Supreme Head of the Church, could refuse subjection to
him. Moreover he intimated that the universal authority of the Pope is
derived from the Prerogatives divinely conferred on S. Peter. So that
in some places he speaks of the Apostolic See under the name of S. Peter,
Epist. l. vi., epist. liv., lv., (l.c., *pp.* 831-2). And when Eulogius, the Patriarch of Alexandria, declared his conviction that 'Peter was still living in
his successors in the Roman See,' S. Gregory replied that he had been
extremely delighted with this expression of the Egyptian Patriarch concerning the Chair of St. Peter, the Prince of the Apostles, to the effect that
he still continued to sit therein in the person of his successors. *Epist.* l.
vii., epist. xl. (l.c. *p.* 887, *seq.*), *suavissime mihi sanctitas vestra multa in
Epistolis suis de S. Petri Apostolorum Principis cathedra loquuta est,
dicens, quod ipse in ea nunc usque in suis successoribus sedeat.*) Thus does
S. Gregory speak of the authority of the Apostolic See. His claims are
seen to be neither wider nor more restricted than those of every one of
his predecessors and of his successors down to the present day." *Bottalla,
Sup. Authority of the Pope, pp.* 67-69.

But, after all (2), the best commentary on a man's opinions is his prac-

tice. Was S. Gregory the Great nothing more than the Patriarch of the
West, attending exclusively to the affairs of his diocese, his province, and
that Patriarchate which Bingham and others say consisted of the suburbicarian provinces? Did he take no part, in his position of Sovereign
Pontiff, in the ecclesiastical affairs of England, Gaul, Italy, Spain, Africa,
Alexandria, Constantinople, Antioch, and Jerusalem, and the Churches
subject to the jurisdiction of those Sees? In answer to this queries I cannot do better than quote from Bishop Kenrick's "Primacy." "It cannot
be thought for a moment, that in rejecting the title (Universal Bishop),
S. Gregory disclaimed any superior authority in himself, as successor
of S. Peter, since he affirmed the contrary in the most positive terms,
and exercised, in the most marked manner, the power of a Ruler of the
whole Church . . . . His letters abound with admonitions, injunctions, threats, and decrees, directed to Bishops in every portion of the
Church, all of whom he treated as brethren, whilst they were blameless ;
if they erred, admonishing them as a father ; and punishing them as a
judge when they proved delinquent. When Serenus, Bishop of Marseilles, indignant at the marks of veneration given to a sacred image, broke
it in pieces as an occasion of superstition, and thereby shocked the
feelings of the faithful, Gregory sent a special messenger, and wrote to
admonish him that the excess or abuse should be corrected without
taking sacred images from the Church, in which they served as books for
the unlearned. (*L.* ix., ep. cv., l. xi., ep. xiii.) On complaint being
lodged of excessive levity, amounting almost to connivance, used toward
a licentious priest, by Serenus, Bishop of Marseilles, this prelate was
subject to such punishment as the Bishop of Arles, Vicar of the Holy
See, should inflict. . . . . (*L.* xi., ep. lv.) The proofs of a similar
exercise of power throughout Gaul, Italy, Sicily, and Corsica, are abundant. It was likewise felt in Africa. Gregory enjoined on the Council of
Byzacium, to investigate all the charges made against their primate, and
proceed as justice might require. (*L.* xiii., ep. xxxii.) He directed the
Bishop of Numidia, in conjunction with Victor, the Primate, and other
Bishops, to examine the complaints of the clergy against Paulinus, Bishop
of Tigessis, and proceed according to justice ; and authorised Hilary,
his notary, to be present at the trial. (*Ib.*, ep. xxviii.) His vigilance
extended to Illyricum ; where he commissioned the Bishops of the First
Justiniana, and of Scutari, to inquire into the alleged invasion of the
see by the deposed Bishop Paul, and in case of his conviction, to confine
him in a monastery, and deprive him of the holy communion until death.
(*L.* xii., ep. xxx., xxxi.) The provinces immediately subject to the Patriarchs were not beyond the reach of his authority, although he used it with
the moderation which was inspired by respect for his colleagues. Hearing that simoniacal abuses existed in the Church of Alexandria, he addressed the . Bishop of that city, exhorting him to abolish them without
delay. (*L.* xiii., ep. xii.) He communicated to the Bishop of Jerusalem
the report made to him of simoniacal practices and of strifes, which prevailed in that Church, urging him to remedy those evils." (*L.* xi., ep.
xii.) *Bp. Kenrick's Primacy, pp.* 193, 4. *Lond.* 1849. Certainly, as
observed above, the practice of a man forms the best commentary of his

opinions. If Pope S. Gregory intended, when he disclaimed the title of Universal Bishop, to deny his own Supreme Authority over the whole Church, his actions belie his words. No Pontiff has ever exercised the Supreme Pontificate more universally than this great Pope. It is held, however, that the Supremacy which he possessed differs essentially from that exercised by the present holy Pontiff. In what consists the difference? No doubt in every age of the Church there may be a difference in administration ; at one time the Supreme Pontifical authority may be exercised mediately by Patriarchs, and as Dr. Barrow says, by Metropolitans, and at other times more immediately by Legates, or by personal correspondence. If the Popes of the sixteenth century were accused of usurping the authority of a general Council by cutting off Henry VIII., Cranmer, &c., from their communion, it should not be forgotten, that S. Celestine, by his own single authority, deposed Nestorius from the Patriarchal See of Constantinople, and that Pope S. Leo, in like manner, deposed Dioscorus of Alexandria, and also by his own sole authority restored Theodoret ; their proceedings being approved by the third and fourth Œcumenical Councils. It is just what S. Gregory says, when all the Bishops are without fault, then all are equal in the estimation of humility, but when any are blameworthy then are they subject to the active Jurisdiction of the Supreme Sovereign Pontiff.

So far, then, from S. Gregory's language, in rejecting the title " Œcumenical or Universal Patriarch," witnessing against the Papal Supremacy, it confirms it : for although the Pope is not and never has claimed to be " Universal Bishop " in the sense attributed to that term by S. Gregory, yet it cannot be denied with any semblance of truth that this very Pope believed himself to be, by virtue of the Apostolical Chair of Peter at Rome, the " Head of all the Churches," and " the Head of the Faith," and that in consequence of this belief he exercised his universal Authority in every part of the ecclesiastical world. Even Mr. Allies (before his conversion to the Catholic Church), after labouring in vain against the Rock so firmly established in the ancient Imperial city, is constrained to acknowledge, " And, assuredly, if there was any Pontiff who, like St. Leo, held the most strong and deeply rooted convictions as to the prerogatives of the Roman See, it was St. Gregory. His voluminous correspondence with Bishops, and the most notable persons throughout the world, represents him to us as guarding and superintending the affairs of the whole Church from the watch-tower of St. Peter, the loftiest of all." *Ch. of Eng. Schism, p.* 344.

Mr. Allies, when he wrote these words, was groping in the midst of thick mental darkness after the truth he was searching for. He placed before his readers all the passages he was then aware of, which witnessed both (as he thought) against the Supremacy and for it ; and while Dr. Barrow who, as a rule, only selected those which served his purpose, lived and died (let us hope) in ignorance of the truth, Mr. Allies, who saw the logical force of his own admissions, embraced the truth, and submitted, as every catholic-minded man must, sooner or later, to that " Chair of Peter," and to that " Principal or Chief Church" founded thereon, in which, as S. Augustine says, " the Princedom of the Apostolic Chair has always been in force."

X.

ADMISSIONS.

It has been hitherto shown how utterly groundless are the objections raised against the Supremacy by Anglican controversialists, and especially by Dr. Barrow. It is proposed now to subpœna, as it were, some of these before the tribunal of public ecclesiastical opinion, and compel them to give evidence on the great questions raised respecting the Supremacy of the Holy See. Two representative witnesses shall be selected, our old enemy, Dr. Barrow, who flourished in the middle of the seventeenth century, and Mr. Allies,* whose able work was published some twenty years ago. Both writers wrote exhaustively, especially the latter, on the subject, and therefore these witnesses cannot fail to be unexceptionable.

I. Dr. Barrow thus writes :

1. " The pope's power was much amplified by the importunity of persons condemned or extruded from their places, whether upon just accounts, or wrongfully and by faction ; for they, finding no other more hopeful place of refuge and redress, did often apply to him : for what will not men do, whither will not they go in straits ? Thus did Marcion go to Rome, and sue for admission to communion there. So Fortunatus and Felicissimus in St. Cyprian, being condemned in Afric, did fly to Rome for shelter ; of which absurdity St. Cyprian doth so complain. So likewise Martianus and Basilides, in St. Cyprian, being outed of their sees for having lapsed from the Christian profession, did fly to Stephen for succour, to be restored. So Maximus (the Cynic) went to Rome, to get a confirmation of his election at Constantinople. So Marcellus, being rejected for heterodoxy, went thither to get attestation to his orthodoxy (of which St. Basil complaineth). So Apiarius, being condemned in Afric for his crimes, did appeal to Rome. And on the other side, Athanasius being with great partiality condemned by the synod of Tyre ; Paulus and other bishops being extruded from their sees for orthodoxy ; St. Chrysostom being condemned and expelled by Theophilus and his complices ; Flavianus being deposed by Dioscorus and the Ephesine synod ; Theodoret being condemned by the same,—did cry out for help to Rome. Chelidonius, bishop of Besançon, being deposed by Hilarius of Arles (for crimes) did fly to Pope Leo. Ignatius, patriarch of Constantinople, being extruded from his see by Photius, did complain to the Pope." *Supp., pp.* 263-4.

2. After arguing against the Papal right to confirm Bishops to their sees, Dr. Barrow admits as follows : " To all these evidences of fact our adversaries do oppose some instances of popes meddling in the constitu-

---

* I feel I owe an apology to Mr. Allies for taking such liberties as I have done with his name. His book, however, is on the shelf of many an earnest and catholic-minded Anglican, and notwithstanding his able treatise, written after his own conversion, entitled " The See of S. Peter," it yet exercises a very powerful and fatal influence over their minds. Any attempt, however feeble, to neutralize the effect of that book, cannot but be acceptable to him.

tion of bishops ; as Pope Leo I. saith, that Anatolius did, *by the favour of his assent obtain the bishopric of Constantinople.* The same pope is alleged as having confirmed Maximus of Antioch. The same doth write to the Bishop of Thessalonica (his vicar), that he should *confirm the elections of bishops by his authority.* He also confirmed Donatus, an African bishop ; *We will that Donatus preside over the Lord's flock, upon condition that he remember to send us an account of his faith.* Also Gregory I. doth complain of it, as of an inordinate act, that a bishop of Salonæ was *ordained without his knowledge.* Pope Damasus did confirm the ordination of Peter Alexandrinus ; *The Alexandrians,* saith Sozomen, *did render the Churches to Peter, having returned from Rome, with the letter of Damasus, which confirmed both the Nicene decrees and his ordination;* but what, I pray, doth confirmation here signify, but approbation ? for did he otherwise confirm the Nicene decrees ? did they need other confirmation ?" *Ib. pp.* 330–31.

3. " The popes, indeed, in the fourth century began to practise a fine trick, very serviceable to the enlargement of their power; which was to confer on certain bishops, as occasion served, or for continuance, the title of their vicar or lieutenant : thereby pretending to impart authority to them ; whereby they were enabled for performance of divers things, which otherwise by their own episcopal or metropolitical power they could not perform. By which device they did engage such bishops to such a dependence on them, whereby they did promote the Papal authority in provinces, to the oppression of the ancient rights and liberties of bishops and synods, doing what they pleased, under pretence of this vast power communicated to them ; and for fear of being displaced, or out of affection to their favourer, doing what might serve to advance the Papacy. Thus did Pope Celestine constitute Cyril in his room. Pope Leo appointed Anatolius of Constantinople. Pope Felix Acacius of Constantinople. Pope Hormisdas Epiphanius of Constantinople. Pope Simplicius to Zeno bishop of Seville — *We thought it convenient that you should be held up by the vicariat authority of our see.* So did Siricius and his successors constitute the Bishops of Thessalonica to be their vicars in the diocese of Illyricum, wherein being then a member of the western empire they had caught a special jurisdiction ; to which Pope Leo did refer in those words, which sometimes are impertinently alleged with reference to all Bishops, but concern only Anastasius, bishop of Thessalonica ; *We have intrusted thy charity to be in our stead, so that thou art called into part of the solicitude, not into plenitude of the authority.* So did Pope Zosimus bestow a like pretence of vicarious power over the Bishop of Arles, which city was the seat of the temporal exarch in Gaul. So to the Bishop of Justiniana Prima in Bulgaria (or Dardania Europæa) the like privilege was granted [by procurement of the Emperor Justinian, native of that place].* Afterwards temporary or occasional vicars were appointed (such as Austin in England, Boniface in Germany), who in virtue of that concession did usurp a paramount authority; and, by the exercise thereof did advance the Papal interest ; depressing the authority of metropolitans and provincial synods. *Ib., pp.* 384, 385.

* Addition by Editor of edition of 1836.

Surely these are very large admissions in favour of the Supremacy of the Pope in the primitive ages.

But what has Dr. Barrow to say against his own admissions, for, without doubt, he would not have made them without some object?

Respecting appeals to the Pope, he says, "All princes are proud to heap| honour on the Bishop of their imperial city : it seeming a disgrace to themselves that so near a relation be an inferior to any other ; who is, as it were, their spiritual pastor, who is usually by their special favour advanced. The city itself and the court were restless in assisting him to climb." (*Supp.*, p. 264.) He instances the rise of the Church of Constantinople on account of the royalty of the city; and then he adds, " So, for the honour of their city, the emperors usually did favour the Pope, assisting him in the furtherance of his designs, and extending his privileges by their edicts, at home, and letters to the eastern emperors, recommending their affairs." (*Ib.*) In a word, the Papal Supremacy was based upon the Royal Supremacy !

There is, however, a fatal flaw in his argument, which Dr. Barrow has overlooked, and that is, that some of the appeals to the Pope were made in the ante-Nicene age, when the Emperor, being a heathen, was not much inclined to his " so near a relation,"—when, so far from being disposed to be "restless in assisting him to climb," he was assiduous in his endeavours to exterminate both him and all of his communion : instead of placing him on the right of the throne, he had him dragged through the Forum, to find a bloody grave within the walls of the famous Colosseum at Rome. What object, then, had Marcion, Fortunatus, and Felicissimus, Martianus and Basilides, and Apiarius, and others, both heterodox and orthodox, in view, by flying to the Roman Church for succour, when its Bishop was, so far as mere ecclesiastico-civil power was concerned, as weak and powerless as the meanest and poorest member of the fold of Christ? What power did he possess in that age to coerce S. Cyprian, or any other great Prelate of the Catholic Church? Certain it is, that whatever power the Popes possessed in those days, was not derived from the pagan Emperor of Rome. True, we are told, that the city of Rome being the great capital of the Empire, and the seat of government, the Bishop and Church of Rome partook of its imperial grandeur, and, by the influence obtained from that source, were enabled to enforce their opinions upon the Church Universal. It is by some such exposition as this that the plain statements of S. Ignatius, S. Irenæus, and S. Cyprian,—to the effect that the Church of Rome is the Presiding Church, and the Principal Church,—are explained away. But really how thoroughly childish is this mode of getting rid of the Roman Church as a Superior and a more Powerful Principality. We have in England a See, which, so far as England is concerned, is the Presiding Church; which Church is a more powerful Principality than any other Church in the realm, and which, by consequence, is the " Chief, or Principal Church, whence the Unity of the (Anglo-Catholic) Priesthood took its rise,"—I allude to the Primatial See of Westminster. Can there be found a single Englishman, gifted with common sense, who would assert, in all gravity, that the greatness of the See of Westminster, and the extent of the influence of its Primate for the time being, were in consequence of the splendour and the magnitude of the imperial capital of the British Empire, in which this See happens to be established? Would not any sane man say, that whatever power and influence the See of Westminster possessed, they were derived solely from its source, *i. e.* the Holy See? How is it, then, that we cannot perceive that whatever authority and power the Pope possessed in the Universal Church in the ante-Nicene age, when the Emperor and government of Rome were essentially Pagan in their religion and hostile to them, were derived not from secular Rome, but from the very Chair he occupied? And whose Chair did he occupy? It was the Chair of S. Peter, the Chief of all the Apostles. Hence it was that, both orthodox and heterodox, whenever difficulties arose, rushed off to Rome, with the hope of gaining his ear, and obtaining a decision in their favour. It was to the Successor of S. Peter, and not to the Bishop favoured by the Emperor, that they appealed, whom they knew to have inherited all the Prerogatives of the Apostle, possessing in himself inherently the Supreme Jurisdiction. There is no other way for accounting for these appeals in the ante-Nicene age, and therefore it must be considered that the admission of Dr. Barrow so far favours the doctrine of the Papal Supremacy.

No doubt, after the conversion of the Empire, the Popes received from the Emperor certain privileges, one of which was a coercive jurisdiction, which enabled them to enforce legally the spiritual authority which they derived from S. Peter. The addition of such privileges to their Prerogatives, no doubt, had the effect of increasing the number of appeals, for not only had they the Supreme Jurisdiction of S. Peter, whose Chair they filled, but they had, by special favour of the Catholic Emperors, power to give their decrees the force of law. But this surely helps to prove their original Supreme Authority, for no Emperor would have granted the Popes the privileges they did, unless they were persuaded that they were the Vicars of Christ our Lord.

Dr. Barrow, in his endeavour to explain away the Papal right to confirm Bishops in their sees, advances two arguments, first, the late commencement of the exercise of these rights; and secondly, that other Bishops did the same. A few words on each objection will suffice.

First, that the Papal confirmation "was so few, so late, so lame, so impertinent." *Supp. p.* 331. To this it may be replied that the Church Catholic did not resume its normal condition till the fourth century of the Christian era. During the first 300 years, the whole Church, and especially the Roman Church, was deluged in a sea of blood. Nearly every one of the Popes from S. Peter until the commencement of the fourth century, were martyrs, so there was not much opportunity for exercising, regularly at least, the office of the Primacy. Then, again, many of the works of the early Fathers—almost all, if not all, of the acts and decrees of the early Primitive Church—are lost, so that in point of fact, if there is little evidence in favour of Papal confirmation of Bishops, there is none against it. The presumption is, in the absence of any protest, (and the Churches were not slow to protest, if their privileges were invaded), that these confirmations by the Pope in the fourth century were not innovations. There are, however, some points to be considered which may throw some light on this

point. For instance, appeals to the Pope presume that he has some authority over the sees of the Catholic Church, for no one, be he orthodox or
heretic, would take the trouble of travelling hundreds of miles to Rome if
he did not believe that the Pope possessed the power of adjudicating in
the case, and compelling obedience to his judgment. Then, again, the
judgment of Aurelian the Emperor was conclusive so far, that the Pope and
Italian Bishops had something to say respecting appointment to sees,
even in the East: which implies at least the principle involved in the confirmation of Bishops to their sees. The second objection is this: other
great Bishops confirmed Bishops likewise, and Dr. Barrow instances S.
Athanasius, who "presumed to *ordain in cities which did not belong to
him.*" *Supp. p.* 333. And the learned Doctor mentions other such encroachments on the part of great Prelates in the provinces of others.
All this is very true, but Dr. Barrow has overlooked a most essential
difference in the two cases. Patriarchs and Metropolitans may have
"presumed to ordain in cities which did not belong to them,"—either
through error or from an ambitious motive, or with the view of forcing upon
a chief see a person who was a heretic. The Pope, on the other hand,
ordained and confirmed Bishops, in his capacity as the Successor of the
Chief of the Apostles, as the Supreme Head of the Universal Church, as
the Bishop of the "Principal or Chief Church." He acted, either lawfully
or unlawfully, as the Representative of S. Peter and the Vicar of Christ.
The other Bishops never claimed the power or right to ordain and confirm
Bishops as the Representative of S. Peter and the Vicar of Christ ; but
the Pope did : and this makes the difference in the two cases. Dr. Barrow
has not then succeeded in neutralising his own ample admissions.

With respect to his admission that the Pope, in the fourth century appointed vicars in the various provinces, he says, " Bellarmine doth from
this practice prove the popes' sovereign power; but he might from thence
better have demonstrated their great cunning. It might, from such
extraordinary designation of vicegerents, with far more reason be inferred, that ordinarily Bishops are not his ministers." *Supp. p.* 386.
We are to believe, then, that such Pontiffs as S. Innocent, S. Celestine, S.
Leo the Great, S. Gelasius, S. Anastasius, and subsequently S. Gregory the
Great, who followed their footsteps—Pontiffs than whom none have been
greater, or more holy or more devoted to God,—were actuated by
feelings of "great cunning" in appointing vicars or vice-gerents to
represent them in the various provinces of the Church ! Such an argument as this proves how impossible it is for Dr. Barrow to resist the
assertion of Bellarmine that their practice proved the Popes' Sovereign
power.

But now let us investigate the question of the Pope's Supremacy from
quite another point of view. Let us assume that the Pope had no right
as Bishop of Rome, or Successor of S. Peter, to receive appeals, to
confirm Bishops, and, let us add, to depose them ; to appoint vicars and
vicegerents in many of the provinces ; to admonish, censure, and punish
Bishops, even in the far East; to confirm or annul the decrees of
Councils,—I say, let us assume that the Pope had usurped authority
over the whole Church, that he had reduced the office of Bishops, as is

alleged, to a nullity; how is it, I ask, that the Catholic Church never raised her voice against these usurpations in solemn protest, followed by a withering anathema? The fourth and fifth centuries were the age of Councils; the four first Œcumenical Councils were celebrated during that period, several of them under the patronage of those "cunning" Popes, whom Dr. Barrow especially indicates,—S. Celestine and S. Leo the Great. How was it that the great S. Cyril accepted the Pope's commission to try and depose Nestorius, if within ten days he did not recant his wicked errors? How was it that he, the Patriarch of the second apostolical See, accepted from the Pope the post of President of the Œcumenical Council of Ephesus, with an authority to sit in his Place at the Council? How was it that this great Council submitted to such a Presidency? How was it that the Bishops suffered the Legates, in the name and in behalf of the Pope, as the Successor of S. Peter, "the Exarch and Head of the Apostles," to pronounce the sentence of deposition on Nestorius? How was it that the Papal President was permitted to say, without a word of remonstrance from the Council, "Since then we have executed the sentence of the most holy Bishop Celestine, and have approved of the judgment passed by the holy Council against the heretic Nestorius,"—words which seemed to imply that the Council was little better than the register of the sentence of the Sovereign Pontiff? And, again, in the fourth Œcumenical Council of Chalcedon, how was it that, by the command of the Pope S. Leo as declared by the Legates, Dioscorus, the Patriarch of Alexandria, was forced to quit his seat in the Council? How was it that the following was uttered by the Legates without any challenge, that "no Council could be held without the authority of the Holy See,"—"a thing," the Legates add, "which has never been done (lawfully), and cannot be made lawful?" How was it that Theodoret was admitted to a seat in the Council, simply because Pope S. Leo "had restored him to his episcopal office?" How was it that the Legates, in pronouncing sentence of deposition against Dioscorus were permitted, without remonstrance, to say, "Therefore, the most holy Archbishop of Rome, Leo, by us and this present Council, thrice blessed, and with the Apostle S. Peter, who was the Rock and the Foundation of the Catholic Church and of the Orthodox faith, deprives him of the episcopal dignity and every sacerdotal ministry?" And further, I ask, how came it that this Universal Council exclaimed with one voice, " Peter has thus spoken by Leo?" How was it that in their synodical epistle to Pope S. Leo, the Bishops described him—the Pope—as "the constituted Interpreter to all of the voice of the blessed Peter?" Why did the Fathers say to the Pope, "over whom (*i. e.* the Council) he had presided, as the Head over his members," "to whom the custody of the Vineyard (the Catholic Church) was committed by the Saviour?" Surely there is but one only answer to be given, viz., that the Pope was regarded as the Successor of S. Peter, the Head of the whole Brotherhood, the Supreme Judge, and the Custodian of the Vineyard. That this position of the Pope was accepted by the whole Catholic Church in the Primitive ages, when "doctrine and religion were most pure and uncorrupt," is a fact as well attested by history, as the conquest of England by William the Conqueror, or, as the English so-called Reformmation in the sixteenth century; or, as the great Rebellion that desolated fair Albion for so many years; or, as the Revolution in the seventeenth century. I repeat, it is a fact as patent as that the Act for the deposition of the Irish Church Establishment was passed in this year of grace, 1869.

What becomes then of the "great cunning" of such Popes as the illustrious SS. Celestine and Leo? Are we to believe that the Œcumenical Councils (the great majority of the Bishops being Oriental, and not under the immediate influence of the Pontiffs) were taken in by the "great cunning" of these Popes? Will Dr. Barrow solemnly affirm that the Prelates who sat in those great infallible Councils were deceived by these "cunning" Popes and their Legates? If Dr. Barrow were alive now, he would not presume in this age of criticism to write such execrable trash.

There is another point to be considered before this part of our subject is finally dismissed: it is this, that the position of the Popes, especially SS. Celestine and Leo, was either true or false; and again, its acceptance by the Œcumenical Councils of Ephesus and Chalcedon was either a proper submission to constituted Authority, or a base abandonment of their own office as Bishops of the Catholic Church; and, further, that the language these Councils, especially that of Chalcedon, addressed to the Pope respecting his office, was expressive, either of a truth, founded on the Word of God, or else of a deliberate lie. Our opponents who deny the Papal Supremacy are driven into this dilemma, viz., that the Œcumenical Council, out of abjec tservitude to the Pope, has been guilty of basely betraying the truth on a fundamental point of Church Government, and, by way of flattering the Pope, stooped to utter deliberate falsehoods. If Pope S. Leo was not the "constituted Interpreter to all of the voice of the blessed Peter;" if he was not the Head over the members, i.e., the Episcopate; and if he was not the Custodian of the Vineyard, i.e. the whole Catholic Church, then, without doubt, this Œcumenical Council,—described by S. Gregory the Great as one of the four gospels, and which the Parliament of this Kingdom has included in its Statute-book,—has been guilty of little else than lying blasphemy. Remember the position assumed by Popes SS. Celestine and Leo was one either in accordance with the Law of God, or it was not; and if it was not, then to have assumed it, was a crime of far deeper dye than ever John the Faster was guilty of when he claimed to be Œcumenical or Universal Patriarch. He claimed jurisdiction over the whole of the eastern division of the Catholic Church; SS. Celestine and Leo, and all the Popes before them, and all after them, claimed authority and jurisdiction over the whole Church, East as well as West. If John the Faster was an Antichrist, what must these Popes have been? Some Anglicans perhaps will say they were both Antichrists; and that the Œcumenical Councils of Ephesus and Chalcedon connived in the blackest crime that was ever committed, converting the whole Catholic Church into Anti-christ! Surely this *reductio ad absurdum* disposes of the whole question. Dr. Barrow's admissions, then, come out in bold relief, and they have, as we have seen, the sanction of a greater than Dr. Barrow, the Universal Church of Christ, and, what is noteworthy, of the Church in the primitive ages.

II. The admissions of Mr. Allies, before his conversion, in his work "The Church of England Cleared from Schism," are also very ample.

1. "This precedence or Prerogative of Rome (*i.e.* the Primacy), to whatever extent it reached, was certainly, notwithstanding the famous 28th Canon of Chalcedon, not either claimed or granted, more especially in the West, merely because Rome was the imperial city. It was explicitly claimed by the Bishop of Rome himself, and as freely conceded by others to him, as, in a special sense, successor of S. Peter. From the earliest times that the Church comes before us as an organized body, the germ at least of this pre-eminence is observable. From the very first, the Roman Pontiff seems possessed himself, as from a living tradition which had thoroughly penetrated the local Roman Church, with a consciousness of some peculiar influence he was to exercise on the whole Church. This consciousness does not show itself here and there in the line of Roman Pontiffs, but one and all, whatever their individual characters might be, seem to have imbibed it from the atmosphere which they breathed. St. Victor, St. Stephen, St. Innocent, St. Leo the Great, and St. Gregory, are quite of one mind here. That they were the successors of St. Peter, who himself sat and ruled and spoke in their person, was as strongly felt and as consistently declared, by the Pontiffs who preceded the time of Constantine, and who had continually to pay with their blood the price of that high pre-eminence, as by those who followed the conversion of the empire, when the honour of their post was not accompanied by so much danger. I am speaking now, be it remembered, of the feeling *which possessed them*. The feeling of their brother Bishops concerning them may have been less definite, as was natural ; but, at least, even those who most opposed any arbitrary stretch of authority on their part, as St. Cyprian, fully admitted that they sat in the See of Peter, and ordinarily treated them with the greatest deference. This is written so very legibly upon the records of antiquity, that I am persuaded any one, who is even very slightly acquainted with them, cannot with sincerity dispute it. I cannot think Mr. Newman has the least overstated the fact, but I do not accept his conclusion, &c." *Church of England Cleared from Schism, pp.* 19, 20.

2. "I most fully believe, be it observed, that S. Cyprian acknowledged the Roman Primacy, that he admitted certain high prerogatives to be lodged in the Roman Pontiff, as St. Peter's successor, which did not belong to any other Bishop." *Ib.* 41.

3. "I am fully prepared to admit that the Primacy of the Roman Church, even among the Patriarchs, was a real thing; not a mere title of honour ; but then his very pre-eminence lay in his being called, as First Bishop of the world, to the especial maintenance of the Canons and the Faith ; for them he could do everything, against them nothing." *Ib. p.* 270.

4. "The question then at issue is, whether the Bishop of Rome be the first of the Patriarchs, and first Bishop of the whole world, the head of the Apostolic College, and holding among them the place which Peter held, all which I freely acknowledge as the testimony of antiquity." *Ib.* 275.

5. "The Primacy, being itself of divine institution, might yet have greater or smaller privileges attached to it by the canons of Councils or tacit consent of Bishops, but Primacy and Monarchy are radically different ideas ; so are the Patriarchal and the Papal Systems." *Ib.* 313.

6. Summing up the evidence of seven centuries, Mr. Allies says, "History, then, teaches us that the Primacy of Rome has always existed : and reverence would suggest that what has always been admitted by the Church of Christ, His Bride, was intended and foreordained by Him, with whose voice she speaks. But the same reasons teach us that the powers and privileges exercised by the Primacy may differ, and have, in fact, very largely differed, at various times, and depend on the consent of the Church, and the concession of other Bishops. The notion of universal jurisdiction is not at all involved in the original Primacy ; as St. Peter exercised none over his brother Apostles," &c. *Ib.* 491.

This is enough. Any one who could make these admissions could not fail ere long to perceive, that if the Pope, by virtue of his succession from S. Peter, was really "The Head of the Apostolic College," "holding among them the Place which Peter held ; " and if to this Primacy were attached Prerogatives, "which did not belong to any other Bishop," he must of necessity possess the office of Supremacy over the whole Church. This is necessarily implied, if the Pope has certain high Prerogatives, which belonged to no other Bishop. For if the institution of the Primacy, and the Prerogatives belonging to it, are of Divine ordinance, as Mr. Allies admitted, it follows, as a necessary consequence, that he who holds this Primacy is master of the situation, and, however much a Polycrates or a Cyprian may resist encroachments, they cannot quit his communion without forfeiting Catholicity. Mr. Allies saw that the whole Church was bound up in the Primacy, and the result followed ; viz. his own submission to the Catholic Church.

These witnesses, then, who have made such large admissions of the truth of the Roman Supremacy, have proved the case against the Anglican Church, and against all other communities out of the pale of the Holy Roman Catholic Church, and have also triumphantly shown that the true Church is that which adheres to the Chair of S. Peter at Rome.

XI. SUMMARY.

The principal objections against the Papal Supremacy have now been considered, and, it is submitted, satisfactorily disposed of. Of these, the cases of S. Victor and Polycrates, S. Stephen and S. Cyprian, and the Popes SS. Zosimus and Celestine, and the Council of Carthage in the matter of Apiarius, are chief. But to what do they amount? Absolutely to nothing. Polycrates and S. Cyprian were both in error, on the points of difference between them and the Pope. S. Victor did no more than endeavour to enforce what had been agreed upon by nearly the whole Church. Polycrates and the Bishops of Asia Minor contumaciously resisted him, treating him with disrespect. S. Victor threatened excommunication; the Bishops of East and West remonstrated with him, not on account of any exercise of authority beyond what his Prerogative permitted, but against undue severity. Upon the question of re-baptism of heretics, S. Cyprian's objection was mainly against the Pope deciding a point of doctrine and discipline by his own single authority; that is, without the assent of the College of Bishops. And as to the matter, too, of the Council of Carthage *in re* Apiarius, the whole question really turns upon one of privilege, and of internal discipline. No point of faith whatever was involved in the case. That the Church of Carthage admitted the Papal Supremacy, was shown to be evident from the circumstance that her greatest theologians held it, and made use of it for the benefit of the Church. Tertullian the Montanist, in his fury against the Pope, poured forth in a string of invectives the titles and Prerogatives of the Pope; S. Cyprian asserted principles, the logical sequence of which was nothing less than the Supremacy of the Holy See. S. Optatus, too, had done likewise, and S. Augustine, the profoundest doctor, not of Africa only, but of the Universal Church, had taught the superiority of the Holy See over all others, and he himself received a commission from the Pope Zosimus to visit, in his name, the Church of Cæsarea in Mauritania to extinguish the Donatist schism. The whole Church of Africa, too, acknowledged the Papal authority, in forwarding their acts and decrees to Rome for confirmation.

The witness adduced against the Supremacy by our opponents in the person of the great S.Gregory is, upon examination, *nihil ad rem*. The Pope protested against the proud assumption of John the Faster: he held that the title " Universal Patriarch " was not only one of pride and arrogance, but that it involved the rights and liberties of all Prelates ; for if one is Universal Patriarch or Bishop, it follows that there can be no more than one Patriarch or one Bishop in the world, and that the episcopate generally was of an order distinct from that of the Bishop who calls himself Universal. For the Catholic doctrine on this point is, that all Bishops, inclusive of the Pope, are equal to one another in dignity, order and priesthood, the difference consisting in what S. Cyprian describes as " grade," and in later times, jurisdiction. The jurisdictions of all Bishops vary in extent : the first " grade" is the Metropolitan, the source of jurisdiction to his suffragans ; the second, the Patriarch, who is the source of jurisdiction to the Metropolitans, and through them to all other Bishops of the Patriarchate ; and the third, which is the apex, is the Pope, who is the fountain of all jurisdiction to Patriarchs, Metropolitans, and to all Bishops, either mediately through their Primates, or immediately from himself. The constitution of the Church, then, consists of a number of centres ; the grand centre of all is the " Chair of Peter," which stands upon the immovable Rock in the midst of the Roman Church, from which, as from a fountain, the unity of the whole Priesthood took its rise. That S. Gregory the Great believed this, is evident from his conduct, for he ruled, with authority and power, the Universal Church, both in East and West, admonishing, censuring, and punishing Bishops, in every country, if they in any way transgressed the doctrine or discipline of the Holy Catholic Church.

But let us suppose that all these witnesses were decisive against Rome, what then? How can they militate against the vast amount of Patristic, Conciliar, and Imperial evidence in favour of the Supremacy? Evidence, be it remembered, so varied, and yet so consistent, as to prove how independent is the testimony of each Father, Council, and Emperor. It is impossible to break down this testimony without destroying the whole fabric of the Church,—nay, without annihilating Christianity itself. For if the testimony of the Primitive Church with regard to the Papacy is unreliable, then let the question be put in all seriousness,—On what rest our hopes? It is by the Law and the Testimony we have learnt of the existence of Christ, that He was and is God and Man, that He died for us, rose from the dead, and ascended into heaven, there sitting on the Right Hand of God, unto the end of the world, when He will return to judgment, and save the righteous, giving them everlasting life. It is by the Law and the Testimony that we know these things; it is by the Testimony of the Church we know that the Gospel,—that is, our Law,—is inspired : but what would our position be, if the Testimony upon a fundamental point of our Religion should be proved to be false? for if so, then the whole structure of our religion falls to pieces, and we are, indeed, as sheep in the wilderness without a Pastor to guide us, and without a Priest to stand for us before the altar of God. The whole of Christianity is bound up in the Papacy; if the Papacy is false, then Christianity is a delusion.

It remains only to notice, in conclusion, the admissions of Dr. Barrow and of Mr. Allies before his conversion to the Truth. The former admits the Papal position in the Primitive Church as amply as possible ; he endeavours to account for it on impossible hypotheses, by leading his readers on a wrong scent, and by mystifying them in such a manner as utterly to confuse their minds. But expose his sophistical reasoning before the full blaze of Truth, and, like the mist on the meadow, it dissolves and disappears. Mr. Allies, too, did his best to account for the Papal position in the Primitive ages, but after a while he saw the Truth,—for it was the Truth he sought ; and he found it.

The reader, then, after perusing the evidence adduced for and against the Papacy, can come, it is submitted, to only one conclusion, and that is, that the Church of Christ is one Body, composed of divers orders of ministers and people, subject to one Head, which Christ, our Lord, instituted, viz. S. Peter, the Chief of all the Apostles, and his Successors, the Bishops of Rome, who sit enthroned in his Chair in that city, which was once the mistress of the political world, and is now and ever will be the Mother, the Mistress, the Root, and the Matrix of the Universal Church.

PART V.

RECAPITULATION AND CONCLUSION.

IN the foregoing pages I have submitted to the reader a regular succession of Patristic evidence, from within six years after the death of the
last remaining Apostle till the close of the fifth century, in proof of the
Supremacy of S. Peter and of his Successors to his Government. I began
with Holy Scripture ; I have shown that Prophecy foreshadowed and predicted the fall of the fourth great Universal Empire, *i.e.* the Roman
Empire. It was shown how, at the proper time, a Stone cut out of the
mountain of Zion, without hands, would strike this great colossal empire
at its base ; that it would gradually decline, and finally be destroyed, and
that the Stone which struck it would occupy its place, and from thence
would "grow into a great mountain," filling "the whole earth ;" that it
would consume and break in pieces all the kingdoms of the earth ; that it
would itself never be destroyed, or left to other people, but, on the contrary, would stand for ever, in its strength and might. This was the
prophecy. How has it been fulfilled? for fulfilled in a very large measure
it must have been, because the Roman Empire has long been dissolved,
of which nothing remains, except, perhaps, its Eastern division under the
Turks. In answer to this question, it was proved that Christ was the
true Stone and the true Rock, hewn without hands out of the mountain of
Zion, *i.e.* by His miraculous Conception and Incarnation: who came into
the world not only to redeem man, but to crush the power of the Evil One,
and all the kingdoms which obeyed Satan's will. This was the Stone the
builders refused, which would grind into powder every person and nation
upon whom it should fall. It was further demonstrated that there was
one other Stone, and one other Rock, which Christ our Lord erected, viz.
Simon Bar-jona, whom He named Peter, *i.e.* a Stone or Rock. No
other Apostle bore this name ; it was peculiar to him, and given to him
with a special object. "Thou art Peter (a Rock), and upon this (the)
Rock I will build my Church." This Stone—Peter—it was proved, came
to Rome, and there laid the foundation of the Universal Kingdom and
Church of Christ; this Stone—Peter—placed there, on a foundation of
Rock, his Cathedra or Chair; by this act he—the Stone—created not by
man, but by the God-Man—struck the Roman Empire at its base ; from
that time it began to decline, and within three centuries Rome ceased to
be the capital and seat of Government, and in the eighth century it
passed into the dominion of the Kingdom of Christ, and became the

Metropolis of Christendom,—the Jerusalem of the New Dispensation,—where still reigns the Successor of the Fisherman.

The Stone—Peter—has, too, according to the prediction, grown into a great mountain. It is a great Empire, and it is filling the whole earth, breaking into pieces and consuming, gradually yet surely, all the kingdoms of the earth, reducing them to the obedience of the yoke of Christ. Doubtless the growth of this great Kingdom has received many checks, the blasphemous heresies in the primitive ages, the Eastern schism, and the revolt of the Church of England, with certain portions of the Church abroad, in the sixteenth century, not only retarded her growth, but well-nigh reduced her to the lowest point of vitality, and it may be that she may yet suffer further reverses ; but nevertheless the germinating Stone is still the evangelising principle of the Empire-Church, and in due time it will overcome all obstacles, and will triumph over all enemies and over schismatic Churches, and, in accordance with the Apocalyptic prophecy, will "rule all nations with a rod of iron." Infidels, Sceptics, and Indifferentists point the finger of scorn at the Roman Church, as they did at Christ when hanging on the Cross ;—when heresies and schisms abound, when pseudo-friends forsake what they once fancied they loved, these conclude that the Church has ceased to live. If she was a mere earthly power this would be the case, but in spiritual things weakness is the harbinger of power, impotence the threshold of strength. The Roman Church, though deserted by kings, and states, and people, and deprived of most of her territories, never was more powerful than she is at this very moment ; the kings of the earth tremble before the image of the august Council which the present Pope has had the noble courage to convoke ; even England, notwithstanding her insular pride and arrogance, and notwithstanding her affectation not to "care for these things," feels a tremulous uneasiness on account of the mighty consequences likely to result from this great approaching gathering of the Princes of the Empire of Christ. But out of weakness comes strength, and this Scripture maxim is now on the point of being exhibited in a mode of which Englishmen and others have little idea.

These checks in the growth of the Kingdom of Christ do but exhibit the marvellous power of that Stone,— Peter,— which Christ planted in the heart of the old Empire, which was to grow until it inclosed in its dominion the whole earth. This fulfilment is going on now before our very eyes, and is in itself the inspired commentary on this most wonderful prophecy. Let the reader fix his mental gaze upon Rome, and if he be not blind with unbelief or prejudice, he must see this truth unfolding itself in a way that cannot fail to strike him with amazement and awe, and if he love God, will draw from his inmost heart praise, adoration, and thanksgiving.

We must now recapitulate more particularly the details of this vast question. We must re-consider what was the nature and the properties of this mystical Stone, which destroyed Pagan Rome, and which will, sooner or later, annihilate the kingdoms of Indifferentism, Scepticism, and Infidelity. It was demonstrated that in the formation of the Royal Hierarchy of His Church, Christ did draw a decided line of demarcation between S. Peter—the Stone—and his fellow-Apostles. In my Introduction to " The Second Inquiry," I endeavoured to show that the universal Law of God's Universal Kingdom was Monarchy or Centralism. That God was the One Monarch of monarchs, the One Centre of centres ; that the Angelic Hierarchies of the heavens are each under the government of an Archangel (even the very devils acknowledge their Archangel and Chief —Satan) ; that every system in nature has its focus, its centre, or its germ ; that every individual man and beast recognise, in his or its physical structure, the same principle of Monarchy,—for what is the Head but the ruling member, and the source of the will, which governs the whole body in thought and action ? I showed that this monarchical principle was introduced by God in the creation of Adam, and that in the erection of the Kingdom of Israel this same principle found its place in its constitution. From these premises I deduced that Christ—being the same yesterday, to-day, and for ever—could not have done otherwise than institute the New Kingdom of Grace upon the same immortal principle of Monarchy or Centralism. Hence it was that S. Peter was separated from his brother-Apostles to be the one main Foundation-stone of the Universal Church (of which material the whole city wall was exclusively to be composed), upon which the Church was to be built, and from which, as from a germinating, seed-bearing principle, the boundaries of the Church were to be perpetually expanded, circle by circle, until the whole world should be inclosed within its vast circumference. As Adam and his heirs received the government of the world ; as Abraham received the promise that all the kingdoms of the earth should belong to him ; as Jacob was appointed to be more especially the foundation of the Kingdom of Israel ; as Moses was called to be the Ruler of the chosen people ; as the Judge-Rulers, each in his day, were summoned by God to judge and govern the people ; as Saul, and afterwards David and his successors, were commissioned to rule the Kingdom of God in the former dispensation, so was it proved that S. Peter and his Successors were appointed by Jesus Christ to rule, and govern, and judge the Universal Kingdom which He Himself established upon His Apostle—His Co-Stone, and Co-Rock—S. Peter.

It was, I submit, fully proved, that this idea of monarchy and centralism was contained in the very form of the commission Christ delivered to S. Peter. Let us recapitulate the argument on this point.

The words, " Thou art Peter (a Rock), and upon this (the) Rock I will build my Church," were said to S. Peter alone. They were not addressed to the Apostolic body: the context clearly shows this, for when our Lord asked, "Whom say ye that I am ?" all the Apostles, except S. Peter, were silent, though when Christ a few minutes before had asked them, "Whom do men say that I, the Son of Man, am ?" they replied one and all with alacrity to His question. S. Peter alone answered, saying, "Thou art the Christ, the Son of the living God." He only, of all the Twelve, knew the truth ; for he being worthy to receive it, it was then and there revealed to him, and consequently the Lord addressed him alone. " Blessed art thou, Simon-Barjonà: for flesh and blood hath not revealed it unto thee, but My Father which is in heaven." As S. Peter alone believed, and alone confessed, so he alone received the benediction and the promise that upon him, "first and alone," as S. Cyprian saith, Jesus would build His Church: that against that Church, so built upon this Rock, the gates of hell should not prevail: and that he alone should possess the keys of the Kingdom of Heaven, that whatsoever he should loose on earth, should be loosed in heaven, and whatsoever he should bind on earth, should be bound in heaven. It is true that some of the Fathers say, that what was said to S. Peter was said equally to all the Apostles, who also were Rocks, and who also possessed the keys; but if we examine carefully their opinions on this point, we shall find that they meant the Apostles in union with S. Peter, not as separate from him. S. Peter had in himself everything. The whole Church was in him, and in him alone; as S. Augustine says, he "personated the Church," and was "a figure of the Church," and therefore he possessed, singly and independently of all the others, the supreme use of the keys, which, in point of fact, he alone possessed. The other Apostles never did receive the keys from the Lord. He addressed words to them which gave them a right to share in the use of those keys; as every judge and magistrate participates in the use of the Civil Sword, and even has it carried before him as the emblem of Justice, though every one knows that there is but one true and proper Sword, which forms part of the regalia of the Sovereign. The Apostles, then, and all their Successors, have the use of the keys; but the keys themselves, the symbol of the Supreme Jurisdiction, were delivered to S. Peter alone, and by him committed to the custody of the Successors to his Cathedra. Then, again, the words, "Confirm (or strengthen) thy Brethren," were addressed to S. Peter alone. It is impossible to get rid of the force of these words, for they contain a direct commission to S. Peter to govern the Faith of the Apostolate. Just before these words were uttered, Christ had formally instituted His Kingdom, composed of Twelve Principalities, one of which He determined should be supreme, for immediately afterwards He turned to S. Peter, and said, "Satan has desired to have you, that he may sift you as wheat, but I have prayed for thee, that thy faith fail not; and when thou art converted, strengthen (or rather confirm) thy brethren." No one can assert that what was said to S. Peter on this occasion was said to the others; to suppose so, would be an absurdity. In constituting His divine Kingdom, Christ was providing for its perpetual unity and perfection in the Faith, and so the Apostolate was placed under S. Peter's care. And the further commission, "Feed My sheep," "Feed My lambs," was likewise delivered to S. Peter alone. No doubt, in S. Peter all the Apostles and Bishops received this charge, not, indeed, independently of S. Peter, but in union with him; this was addressed directly to him, and not to the others. And this was evidently the great object our Lord had in view in addressing S. Peter alone, in order that He might impress upon the Church the Law—even His Universal Law of Monarchy and Centralism. Thus all the Apostles and their Successors were to be Shepherds and Priests; yet One was to be the Supreme Ruler, and the Supreme Judge, and that all were to look to him for the Confirmation of the true Faith.

The passage, "The gates of hell shall not prevail against it," must not be summarily disposed of, for much is signified therein. "The gates of hell shall not prevail against it," *i. e.* the Church, founded upon him who was called the Rock, even S. Peter. By no force of reasoning or grammatical construction can it be proved that the Rock here means only Christ. It is true that S. Augustine says that "Christ was the Rock;" but did he mean to assert that S. Peter was not likewise the Rock? By no means. He held, as every Catholic holds, that Christ is the one, true, proper Rock, on which the Church was originally founded. But what was the Church so founded on Christ? It was Peter himself, who alone represented and personated the Church. "For," says S. Augustine, "not without cause among all the Apostles doth Peter sustain the Person of this Church Catholic" ("in whom," as he says elsewhere, "singly" was "formed the Church"); "for unto this Church," *i. e.* the Church of Peter, "were the keys of the Kingdom of Heaven given, when they were given to Peter; and when it is said to him, it is said to all," *i. e.* all in union with him, "Lovest thou Me? Feed My sheep." Hence S. Peter held the "Primacy of the Apostolate," and likewise "the Princedom of the Apostolate;" for he alone sustained the Person of the Church. Christ was then, according to S. Augustine, the Primary Rock, and S. Peter the Secondary Rock, upon whom Christ built His Church, having first founded it in Peter upon Himself. This seems the evident meaning of what S. Augustine says on this point. When our Lord said, "Thou art Peter —a Rock—and upon this (the) Rock I will build my Church," He pointed to S. Peter as the firm Foundation on which He intended to build His Church; against which Church, *i. e.* the Church so founded on Peter, He promised the gates of hell should never prevail. Here, then, is a promise of perpetual indefectibility to the Throne or Cathedra of the blessed Apostle Peter. And certainly it is a most remarkable circumstance— and this alone is the most infallible commentary we can have on this passage—that while every other Apostolic Throne has fallen into deadly heresy, even denying the Lord that bought us, the Apostolic Throne of Peter has never yet departed from the faith, and has never denied the Lord Jesus Christ.

Anglicans and Protestants assert that the Roman Church has "erred not only in living and in manner of ceremonies, but also in matters of faith." But this is only their private opinion; and in things concerning Faith, what is a private opinion—be it individual or corporate—worth? What opinion can worms, whose minds are finite, presume to entertain respecting the Infinite? How can we, who, even in this astonishing age of discovery, are mere babes in science, pretend to judge the subtle questions of Theology, the Queen of all Sciences?· Faith is the subject of revelation, not of opinion; its origin is from the Holy Ghost, and cannot be discerned by means of our mere reason or imagination. These two faculties enable us to understand what is plainly revealed, provided we have a believing heart, but are powerless of themselves only to assist us in the interpretation of Faith. The whole history of the Church shows this. The words, "The Word was God," literally affirm the Godhead of Christ; and "the Word was made Flesh," affirm equally His Manhood; and yet what divisions distracted the early Church on these great truths! In the middle ages, and in modern times, it has been the same; the dicta of our Lord, " This is My Body," " This is My Blood," plainly mean what the words grammatically import, and yet for nearly a thousand years men have speculated as to their true meaning : some taking these words literally, others figuratively, and others again voiding them of all meaning whatever. It is, then, impossible for unsanctified reason or imagination to discover the Truth of God. Therefore mere private opinions on sacred subjects are of no value whatever; and he who sets up his opinions against the Faith is nothing less than a presumptuous heretic. We have been told, however, that the Pope is the greatest Protestant in the world ; that Anglicanism is the *beau idéal* of Catholicity, and Romanism of genuine Protestantism ; because, while the Anglican Church reposes on the Creeds and Councils, the Church of Rome, or rather the Pope, enforces his private opinions on the consciences of the Faithful. But this raises the whole question, viz.' What is the nature of that authority—that infallible authority—which Christ instituted ? What is the true definition of the " Catholic Church ?" Does the Catholic Church consist of all Bishops, whether visibly divided or not into antagonistic Churches or Sects; or of the whole body of Bishops and Faithful throughout the world, united and subject to one Head or Chief? If the latter, then unquestionably the Church of Christ is composed exclusively of the Pope and the Brethren of his communion ; and whatever that Church promulgates as *De Fide*, cannot be a merely authorised opinion, but a solemn Dogma, enunciated by the Holy Ghost speaking through that organism which Christ the Lord instituted. From the evidence adduced from Scripture it is maintained that the Church of Christ was founded, first and alone, upon S. Peter, and afterwards upon S. Peter and the Apostles as one Body, subject to the one Chief—S. Peter. If this be true, then, it is impossible to separate the Apostles from S. Peter, for he who was singly and alone the Church, can never cease to be the Church he once was, though others may be associated with him in his commission—as the seventy Elders were with Moses, under the former dispensation. Against this Church, *i. e.* the Church of Peter, it was promised that the gates of hell should never prevail; and hence we perceive how it is that the Church of Rome—which is the Church of Peter—has never denied the Lord Jesus Christ, and has never departed from that Faith which was delivered to the Apostles : for heresy has never had possession of the Apostolic See of Peter.

3. And now with respect to the evidence of the Fathers, touching the Supremacy of S. Peter. Can there be a serious doubt that the Fathers agree upon this point ? If there be a doubt, let the inquirer again peruse the evidence adduced under the " First Inquiry," and then ask himself very solemnly the question, whether they who taught and wrote as they did could have held any other belief than that S. Peter was the Head of the Brotherhood, the Teacher of the world, and the Supreme Pastor of the Flock, to whom all had been committed, who had received everything, even the whole world, and who had received upon himself the building of the whole Church? It is impossible to ignore the fact that the Fathers on this point are unanimous, that they believed that S. Peter had a

position distinct and separate from all the rest, and while all were equal in Order and Priesthood, yet that all schism might be avoided One— even Peter—was selected to be the Head. It is unnecessary to add more on this point.

4. The whole argument, however, turns upon the point, whether S. Peter ever was at Rome, whether he established his Cathedra in the Imperial city, and whether the Bishops of Rome have succeeded him to that Chair. Dr. Barrow, as it has been shown, has endeavoured to prove that S. Peter never established his Cathedra in Rome ; but the evidence is entirely against him. It has been proved *ex abundanti*, that S. Peter did go to Rome, that he did preach the Gospel in the Imperial city, and that he did erect there that great Spiritual and Supreme Throne which Christ our Lord gave unto him. That great Chair,— the Chair over all other Chairs,— is in Rome to this day : is it a mere symbol of what once was? Is it only a monument of a pre-eminence and an authority long extinct? or is it the emblem of a present living Power, of an existing Supreme Authority, to which all must bow in subjection, under penalty of perdition? If there is any truth in the principles of what the Anglican Church calls a " succession of doctrine from the Apostles' times, and for above 400 years," then there is most decidedly an overwhelming testimony, century by century, from S. John till S. Gregory I., and from S. Gregory I. to Pope Pius IX.

Let me briefly recapitulate the evidence ;—S. Ignatius, who was martyred A.D. 107, six years after the decease of S. John the Apostle, asserted that the Church in Rome, "Presides in the region of the Romans," that it is "enlightened in the will" of God, that it is "all-godly, all-gracious, all-blessed, all-praised, all-prospering, all-hallowed, and Presiding over the Love (*i.e.* the Church and the Sacraments) with the Name of Christ, with the Name of the Father :" S. Irenæus, directing how heresies may be detected, points by preference to the tradition of the Roman Church, and asserts that " it is a matter of absolute necessity that every Church should agree (or assemble) with this (the Roman) Church, on account of its Pre-eminent Authority, or its more Powerful Principality." Tertullian, as an orthodox teacher, dilates on the grandeur of the Roman Church, and, as a heretic, sneers at her and its Pontiff, and in a volley of invectives describes the Pope as the "Pontifex Maximus," "the Interpreter of God :" titles evidently well known and understood in the Primitive Ages. S. Cyprian writes that Rome is the " Place of Peter," where is the " Cathedra of Peter," to which is annexed "the grade, or rank," or the " dignity " of the " Sacerdotal Chair," where is also "the Chief and Principal Church whence the unity of the Priesthood took its rise ;" and that the Roman Church is the "Mother," the "Root," and the "Matrix of the Catholic Church," and that hence she was the foundation of the Church, the Spring and the Centre of Unity. S. Hilary says that it is befitting, that "to the Head, that is, to the See of the Apostle Peter, the Priests (*i.e.* Bishops) of the Lord should report, or refer, from every province." S. Optatus, that the Chair of Peter is the "first of the marks," and that if any one should "contend for a distinct Chair for himself . . . and set up another Chair against the Single Chair, he might at once be convicted as a schismatic and a sinner;" the Council of Sardica, that "the Priests of the Lord in every province should refer to the Head, that is, to the Apostolic See of Peter." S. Ambrose, that "they have not Peter's inheritance who have not Peter's Chair;" and together with the Council of Aquileia, that from the Roman Church "flow unto all the rights of venerable communion." S. Jerome, that "whosoever eats the Lamb (*i.e.* the Eucharist) out of this House, (*i.e.* the Roman Church,) is profane," that union with "the Chair of Peter," is the test of orthodoxy, for "if any one," says he, "is united to the Chair of Peter, he is mine;" that "whosoever gathereth not with thee (the Pope) scattereth, that is, whosoever is not of Christ is Antichrist." S. Chrysostom, that the Sheep were "entrusted to Peter and to his Successors." S. Augustine, that in the Roman Church, "the Princedom of the Apostolic Chair has always been in force," that the Princedom of the Apostolate is to be preferred before every Episcopate." The Council of Milevis, that "the Authority of (the Pope) is derived from the clear light of the Scriptures." Bacchiarius, that the "Chair of Peter" is "the Seat of Faith," and that the Pope is "the Builder of that edifice." S. Cyril of Alexandria, that the Pope is "Archbishop of all the habitable world," as well as "Father and Patriarch of the mighty city of Rome." Theodoret of Cyrus, that "the most holy Throne (of Rome) has the Sovereignty over the Churches throughout the universe." The Œcumenical Council of Ephesus, that Peter was the Head of all the Faith, as also of the Apostles, that "Peter, the Exarch and Head of the Apostles . . . . lives and exercises these judicial powers in his Successors." S. Celestine, his Successor, "at that time (holding) his (Peter's) place." S. Peter Chrysologus, that "blessed Peter lives and Presides in his own See;" and that "we cannot, without the consent of the Bishop of the city of Rome, hear causes of Faith." Socrates, that "Churches ought not to make decrees contrary to the decree of the Bishop of Rome." Sozomen, that "it is a sacerdotal law, that the things done contrary to the decree of the Bishop of the Romans be looked upon as null." The Œcumenical Council of Chalcedon, that "to hold a Council without the Authority of the Holy See, is a thing which has never been done (lawfully) and cannot be made lawful;" that Peter speaks by his Successors; that the Pope is "the constituted Interpreter to all of the voice of the blessed Peter;" that "he is the Head over the members," *i.e.* the Episcopate; that to him "the custody of the Vineyard (*i.e.* the Catholic Church) is committed by the Saviour." S. Vincent of Lerins, that the Pope surpasses his colleagues "in Authority of Place," and that he is "the Head of the world." Victor Vitensis, that "the Roman Church is the Head of all Churches." The Council of Rome, that the Apostles SS. Peter and Paul did "consecrate the Roman Church to Christ the Lord, and by their precious and memorable triumph have raised it above all other Churches in the whole world," and that "the first See, therefore, of the Apostle Peter, is the Roman Church, which has no spot nor wrinkle, nor any such thing." The Catholic (*i.e.* as opposed to Arianism) Emperors of old furnished too their testimony for the Papacy: Aurelian, a heathen, decreed that the Church of Antioch should be "given up to

those whom' the Christian Bishops of Italy and Rome should appoint :"
Gratian, that "the churches (in the East) should be given up to those
who had communion with Damasus, Bishop of Rome :" Galla Placidia,
that "he (Peter) who was first worthy to receive the heavenly keys,
ordained the Princedom of the Episcopate :" Theodosius and Valentinian
III. that "the sacred synod (Nicæa) has made firm the Primacy of the
Apostolic See, on account of the merit of Peter, Chief of the Corona of
Bishops, and of the dignity of the Apostolic See :" Valentinian III., that
he is bound to "maintain inviolate with the dignity of particular (or
peculiar) reverence to the blessed Apostle Peter, seeing that the most
blessed Bishop of Rome, to whom antiquity has attributed the Princedom
of the Priesthood over all ; (that he) may have both place and liberty to
judge concerning the Faith and the Priests," *i. e.* Bishops.   Marcian and
Valentinian III., that the Pope holds "the Headship of the Episcopate
of the Divine Faith," and that Œcumenical Councils were "assembled by
(their) Authority :" Marcian, that "Bishops assemble (in Council) and
decree concerning the religion of Christianity and the Catholic Faith, as
(the Pope) by his own disposition shall define according to the Ecclesiastical Rules." Surely such evidence as this cannot be ignored ; if it
does not mean that the Pope, by virtue of his succession from S. Peter,
and in right of his Chair, is not the Head of the whole Church, the
Chief of the Brotherhood, the Custodian of the Keys, the Guardian
of the Universal Church, the Confirmer of the Brethren, and the Supreme Pastor of the entire Fold,—what does it mean ? Is it all "hyperbolical flash," as Dr. Barrow profanely asserts, and is the testimony of Fathers
and Councils, of every age and clime to be ignored, namely, that to the
Bishop of Rome was committed that Supreme Jurisdiction and authority
which Christ originally delivered to His servant S. Peter? As before
observed, if Dr. Barrow is right, then the whole of Christendom falls to
the ground, for if such testimony as has been adduced in these pages
is worthless, then have we no reliable testimony for any doctrine whatever,
—no, not even for the authenticity and inspiration of the Bible, on which
Protestants place their whole dependence, without any regard to that
interpretation which God intended it to bear. Let the Inquirer therefore take his choice, either to believe the Fathers, Councils, and even
the Emperors of East and West, and accept the Papacy as the system
which God has appointed for the maintenance of Faith and Unity, or
disbelieve them and give up Christianity : for it is come to this, that
Christianity is Roman, or it is nothing—to use Dr. Barrow's style
—"but rubbish." Every effort has been made during these three
centuries of miserable schisms, heresies, and blasphemies, to sap the
foundation of the Roman Supremacy, but in vain. Of all the Churches
throughout the world who name the Name of Christ, she alone exhibits
the marks of real divinity. While all other Churches are tossed about
with every wind of false doctrine, and are divided and subdivided by innumerable divisions, she alone remains one and undivided ; her aged walls
are just as impregnable as ever, her citadel as unassailable as in the
days of the Apostles, and the Cathedra or Chair of S. Peter, which is the

glory of the Roman Church, still stands upon that Rock which Christ Himself laid in the person of His Apostle S. Peter. Great and glorious, indeed, is that grand Apostolic Church of the Romans ; the winds may howl and burst with fury upon that House ; the rain may descend in tremendous and overwhelming torrents, and the floods may come and strive to undermine her sacred foundations, but all in vain, for she is founded upon the Rock, and the gates of hell shall never prevail against that Church.

FINIS.

INDEX.

Abraham, his call, 99 ; God's promises to him, 99, 311

Acacius, bishop of Constantinople, 299

Adam, constituted by God monarch over the earth, 98, 99, 311 ; his high trust forfeited by his disobedience, 99

Advent, the second, 2 *n.*, 107

Ælia, *see* Jerusalem.

African Church, its dissension from Pope S. Stephen in the matter of the re-baptism of heretics, 269 ; and from Popes Zosimus and Celestine in the case of Apiarius, 283

Agrippinus, bishop of Carthage, his views on the re-baptism of heretics, 269

Alexander the Great, 3, 112

Alexandria, confirmation of the powers of its bishops by the Council of Nicæa, 176 ; the dignity of its patriarchs, 293, 294 ; its patriarchs subject to the authority of the Apostolic See, 294

Allies, Mr., a member of the Church of England, afterwards converted to the Catholic faith, 266 ; his comment on the language of Polycrates to Pope Victor, *ib.* ; on the remonstrance of Irenæus with Pope Victor on the severity of his sentence against the Asiatic Churches, 267 ; on the case of Apiarius, 287 ; effect of his work, " The Church of England cleared from Schism," on Catholics and on Protestants, 293 ; on the subjection of the Patriarchs of Constantinople, Alexandria, Antioch, and Jerusalem, to the Apostolic See, 293, 294 ; on Pope Gregory's belief in the supremacy of the Holy See, 294 ; on the prerogatives exercised by the Roman pontiffs, 305, 306

Ambrose, S. (A.D. 385), bishop of Milan, his comment on the words, " Thou art Peter," &c. 37, 38 ; states that where S. Peter is there is the Church, 37 ; that S. Peter destroyed the porches of hell, and opened the heavenly places, *ib.* ; that S. Peter is set over the Church to feed the sheep and to strengthen the brethren, *ib.* ; his comment on the command of Christ to S. Peter, "Launch out into the deep," 8 *n.*, 37 ; says that S. Peter was a Rock from the Rock, 37, 72 ; states that when Christ left the earth He constituted S. Peter the Vicar of His love, 37, 39, 152 ; his comment on the words, " Feed my sheep," *ib.* ; says that they have not Peter's inheritance who have not Peter's Chair, 38 ; on the power of the keys bestowed on S. Peter, *ib.* ; calls S. Paul a vessel of God's election, *ib.* ; says that S. Paul claimed to himself a power of forgiving sins, *ib.* ; calls S. Peter the Foundation of the Church, *ib.* ; declares that S. Peter exercised a primacy, the primacy of confession not of honour, of faith not of rank, *ib.* ; his comment on the words, " The gates of hell," &c., *ib.* ; rebukes and imposes a public penance on the Emperor Theodosius, 84 ; declares that no grace can be true which is not of the true faith, 152 ; states that the test of an orthodox bishop is his agreement with the Catholic bishop, that is, with the Roman Church, *ib.* ; declares that the Novatian schismatics have no fellowship with Christ, *ib.* ; asserts that from the Roman Church, the Head of the Roman world, flow unto all the rights of venerable communion, 182, 184, 262, *et passim ;* is present at the Council of Aquileia, 184 ; writes a synodical letter to the Emperor Gratian, *ib.*

Ananias of Damascus, 83

Anastasius I. Pope S. (A.D. 359), the successor of S. Peter in the cathedra of Rome, 126, 160 ; states that he will, as far as he is able, " visit " by letter the members of his body throughout the divers regions of the earth, 228

Anastasius II. Pope S. (A.D. 496), says that the princedom of the Universal Church was assigned to the see of the blessed Peter, 241

Anastasius, Emperor, 241

Anatolius, bishop of Constantinople, 299

Ancient customs, confirmation of, by the Council of Nicæa, 176, 179

Angels, their employments, 95; their dealings with men, 95, 96; Michael, the prince of, *ib.*; the monarchical principle visible among them, 96

Anglicans, views maintained by them as to the constitution of the Church, xlvii; their desire to substitute the Royal Supremacy in the stead of the Papal, 69; their views of the Pope, and the doctrines of the Catholic Church, 113; their opposition to the Papacy, 117, 262; their opinions as to the co-equality of all bishops, 174; their views respecting the equal privileges of the churches of Rome and Constantinople, 206. *See* Dr. Barrow, Protestants.

Anicetus, Pope S. (A.D. 187, 188), dissension between him and Polycarp respecting the Paschal question, yet they communed with each other, 216; yielded to Polycarp, out of respect, the office of consecrating, *ib.*; exercised a wise discretion in not deciding the Paschal question, 262–264

Ante-Nicene age, action of the Church in the, 151; persecutions to which the Popes were subjected in the, 242

Antichrist, destruction of, 107, 108; S. John's warnings against, 109; the marks of, not to be found in ecclesiastical Rome, 113; the probability of Constantinople being the future capital of his empire, 112, 113; whoever is not of Christ is, 156

Antioch, S. Ignatius bishop of, 17; disciples first called Christians at, *ib.*; S. Paul remonstrates with S. Peter for his conduct at, 22, 24; on the honour put upon it by being the place of residence of S. Peter, 41; the Church of, send S. Paul and S. Barnabas to the Council of Jerusalem, 77, 78; S. Peter translated from the cathedra of, to Rome, 126, 157; was the metropolis of the East, 208; its opposition to the command of the Emperor Gratian, *ib.*; one of the four chief patriarchates, 294

Antioch, synod of, convened by the heretic Eusebius, at which Athanasius

and other bishops were deposed, 167, 223, 224

Apelles, 270

Apiarius, 205; is excommunicated by Bishop Urbanus for immorality, 283; appeals to Pope S. Zosimus, *ib.*; inquiry into his case, *ib.*; is restored to communion by Pope S. Celestine, 286; makes confession of the crimes of which he had been accused, *ib.*; is deprived of all ecclesiastical ministration, *ib.*

Apocalypse, the, when written, 109

Apocalyptic Babylon, 110, 113

Apollinarius, bishop of Laodicea, is deposed on account of his heretical doctrine, 227

Apollos, 79

Apostles, their Divine commission to be priests, kings, judges, and evangelists, 5; S. Peter's pre-eminence over them proved by (1) his being specially called by Christ a Rock, 5; (2) by being commanded to "strengthen the brethren," 6; and (3) to "feed the sheep," *ib.*; (4) by S. Peter being directed to take the stater from the fish's mouth, 7; (5) by Christ's command to S. Peter, "Launch out into the deep," 7, 8; (6) by their acceding to his commands at the appointment of a new Apostle, 8; (7) by his being their mouthpiece at the day of Pentecost, 9; (8) by his being their leader when brought before the Jewish Sanhedrim, *ib.*; (9) by his appointment to go to Cornelius, and so open the kingdom of heaven to the Gentiles, 10; (10) by their acceptance of his judgment at the first Council of Jerusalem, 10, 11; to what extent they may be considered co-equal and co-ordinate in authority, 12; objections to S. Peter's authority over them answered, 12–15; Origen states the keys of heaven were bestowed on them, 20, 21; S. Cyprian holds that they had an equality of honour and power with S. Peter, yet to him was accorded the primacy, 23, 24, 89; the power of forgiving sins granted unto them, 25, 74, 75; to what extent they were co-equal to S. Peter, 69, 70 (*see* SS. Peter, Leo, and Gelasius); the dignity of their office in the primitive Church, 70, 71; their election of an apostle to supply the place of Judas, 74; distinction between them and bishops, 251; Dr. Barrow's statement that as apostles they had no successors, *ib.*; their inspiration and divine commission, 251, 254

z

LONDON:
STRANGEWAYS AND WALDEN, PRINTERS,
Castle St. Leicester Sq.

www.ingramcontent.com/pod-product-compliance
Lightning Source LLC
Chambersburg PA
CBHW051509100726
47898CB00005B/1388